SEVENTH EDITION

BUSINESS DATA COMMUNICATIONS AND NETWORKING

JERRY FITZGERALD
Jerry FitzGerald & Associates

ALAN DENNIS
Indiana University

JOHN WILEY & SONS, INC.

ACQUISITIONS EDITOR	Beth Golub
ASSISTANT EDITOR	Cynthia Snyder
EDITORIAL ASSISTANT	Jennifer Battista
MARKETING MANAGER	Jessica Garcia
SENIOR PRODUCTION EDITOR	Norine M. Pigliucci
SENIOR DESIGNER	Harry Nolan
PRODUCTION MANAGEMENT SERVICES	Hermitage Publishing Services

This book was set in Times Roman by Hermitage Publishing Services and printed and bound by Donnelley Crawfordsville. The cover was printed by Phoenix Color Corporation.

This book is printed on acid-free paper. ∞

Library of Congress Cataloging-in-Publication Data:

FitzGerald, Jerry.
    Business data communications and networking / Jerry FitzGerald, Alan Dennis. — 7th ed.
      p. cm.
    Includes index.
    ISBN 0-471-39100-X (cloth : alk. paper)
    1. Data transmission systems. 2. Computer networks. 3. Office practice—Automation.
    I. Dennis, Alan. II. Title.

TK5105 .F577 2001
004.6—dc21   2001033013

Printed in the United States of America

10 9 8 7 6 5 4 3 2 1

To Eileen and Alec

ABOUT THE AUTHORS

Professor Alan Dennis is professor of information systems in the Kelley School of Business at Indiana University and holds the John T. Chambers Chair in Internet Systems. The Chambers Chair was established to honor John Chambers, president and chief executive officer of Cisco Systems, the worldwide leader of networking technologies for the Internet and the highest-valued company in the world.

Prior to joining Indiana University, Professor Dennis spent 9 years as a professor at the University of Georgia, where he won the Richard B. Russell Award for Excellence in Undergraduate Teaching. Professor Dennis has a bachelor's degree in computer science from Acadia University in Nova Scotia, Canada, and an MBA from Queen's University in Ontario, Canada. His Ph.D. in management of information systems is from the University of Arizona. Prior to entering the Arizona doctoral program, he spent 3 years on the faculty of the Queen's School of Business.

Professor Dennis has extensive experience in the development and application of groupware and Internet technologies and developed a Web-based groupware package called Consensus @nyWARE, now owned by SoftBicycle Corporation. He has won seven awards for theoretical and applied research and has published more than 80 business and research articles, including those in *Management Science, MIS Quarterly, Information Systems Research, Academy of Management Journal, Organizational Behavior and Human Decision Making, Journal of Applied Psychology, Communications of the ACM,* and *IEEE Transactions on Systems, Man, and Cybernetics.* His first book, coauthored with his wife Eileen, was *Getting Started with Microcomputers,* published in 1986. Professor Dennis is also an author (along with Professor Barbara Wixom of the University of Virginia) of *Systems Analysis and Design: An Applied Approach,* also available from Wiley. Professor Dennis is the cochair of the Internet Technologies Track of the Hawaii International Conference on System Sciences. He has served as a consultant to BellSouth, Boeing, IBM, Hughes Missile Systems, the U.S. Department of Defense, and the Australian Army.

Dr. Jerry FitzGerald is the principal in Jerry FitzGerald & Associates, a firm he started in 1977. He has extensive experience in risk analysis, computer security, audit and control of computerized systems, data communications, networks, and systems analysis. He has been active in risk-assessment studies, computer security, audit reviews, designing controls into applications during the new system development process, data communication networks, bank wire transfer systems, and electronic data interchange (EDI) systems. He conducts training seminars on risk analysis, control and security, and data communications networks. Dr. FitzGerald has a Ph.D. in business economics and a master's degree in business economics from the Claremont Graduate School, an MBA from the University of Santa Clara, and a bachelor's degree in industrial engineering from Michigan State University. He is a certified information systems auditor (CISA) and holds a certificate in data processing (CDP). He belongs to the EDP Auditors Association (EDPAA), the Institute of Internal Auditors (IIA), and the Information Systems Security Association (ISSA). Dr. FitzGerald has been a faculty member at several California universities and a consultant at SRI International.

His publications and software include *Business Data Communications: Basic Concepts, Security and Design,* 4th edition, 1993; *Designing Controls into Computerized Systems,* 2nd edition, 1990; RANK-IT: A Risk Assessment Tool for Microcomputers; CONTROL-IT: A Control Spreadsheet Methodology for Microcomputers; *Fundamentals of Systems Analysis: Using Structured Analysis and Design,* 3rd edition, 1987; *Online Auditing Using Microcomputers; Internal Controls for Computerized Systems;* and over 60 articles in various publications.

PREFACE

Over the past few years, many fundamental changes have occurred in data communications and networking that will shape the future for decades to come. Networking applications such as the Internet and World Wide Web have exploded into the business world. High-speed modems providing megabit data rates over regular telephone lines are entering the market. New local area network (LAN) and backbone technologies providing gigabit speeds are now available. Metropolitan area network (MAN) and wide area network (WAN) technologies providing terabit to pedabit speeds are on the horizon. The integration of voice and data communication is moving more rapidly.

Perhaps the most important change has been the recognition of the strategic importance of communications and networking in both the public and private sector. Today, almost all computers are networked. As we look back on the 1990s, we realize that the importance of the computer was surpassed by the importance of networks.

Purpose of This Book

Our goal is to combine the fundamental concepts of data communications and networking with practical applications. Although technologies and applications change rapidly, the fundamental concepts evolve much more slowly; they provide the foundation from which new technologies and applications can be understood, evaluated, and compared.

This book has two intended audiences. First and foremost, it is a university textbook. Each chapter introduces, describes, and then summarizes fundamental concepts and applications. Management Focus boxes highlight key issues and describe how networks are actually being used today. Technical Focus boxes highlight key technical issues and provide additional detail. An ongoing case study at the end of each chapter provides the opportunity to apply these technical and management concepts. Moreover, the text is accompanied by a detailed instructor's Manual that provides additional background information, teaching tips, and sources of material for student exercises, assignments, and exams. Finally, our Web page will continue to update the book.

Second, this book is intended for the professional who works in data communications and networking. The book has many detailed descriptions of the technical aspects of communications, along with illustrations where appropriate. Moreover, managerial, technical, and sales personnel can use this book to gain a better understanding of fundamental concepts and trade-offs not presented in technical books or product summaries.

What's New in this Edition

The seventh edition includes information on numerous new technologies and applications, along with examples. There are two fundamental changes in this edition from the last. First, the fundamental network model that forms the educational foundation of the book has been revised to five layers by splitting the transport and network layers into separate entities. The OSI (Open Systems Interconnection Reference) model is also presented in Chapter 1 to show the differences. Second, a new chapter on the Internet (and Internet 2) has been added to explain the Internet in more detail and to provide an example of a WAN.

The first section, Introduction, now has just one chapter. Chapter 1 provides the background as before, but it now adds the history of the Internet.

The second section, Network Fundamentals, has been reorganized to provide a better flow of concepts and revised to reflect newer technologies. Chapter 2 now includes a discussion of application architectures and uses them to explain the Web and e-mail in much more technical detail so students can better understand how messages flow over networks. The material on e-commerce has been moved to an appendix, as much of this material is now covered in introductory courses. The two separate chapters on the physical layer in the previous edition have been condensed into one chapter, Chapter 3 (although this does make for a longer-than-usual chapter). We have also brought in examples of technologies that use the physical layer concepts (e.g., multiplexing) to increase the relevance of this material to students. Chapter 4, on the data link layer, has seen only minor revisions. Chapter 5 now separates the network layer and transport layer functions and spends more time on the transport layer and on routing.

The third section, Network Technologies, has been reorganized to provide a better flow of concepts, revised to reflect newer technologies, and updated by the addition of a new chapter on the Internet. Chapter 6, on LANs, has been focused on Ethernet (shared, switched, and wireless), with material on Token Ring moved to an appendix. Chapter 7 now includes a discussion of backbone architectures (previously in the network design chapter) so that students better understand the trade-offs among the designs. Chapter 8 also includes a discussion of MAN and WAN architectures (previously in the network design chapter). Chapter 9, the new chapter on the Internet, explains how the Internet works (e.g., network access points, circuits, points of presence), both to explain the Internet and to provide a better understanding of how to design WANs. The Internet access technologies have been moved there from the old WAN chapter, and a new section on Wireless Application Protocol has been included. Chapter 9 also talks about Internet 2.

The fourth section, Network Management, has been reorganized to provide a better flow of concepts and revised to reflect newer technologies. Chapter 10 now covers network security. Because much of it focuses on technologies, we found it easier to teach after the section on technologies rather than waiting until the end of the course. Chapter 11, the network design chapter, has been slimmed down and uses concepts developed earlier in the book. Chapter 12, on network management, has been updated to reflect new technologies.

Acknowledgments

My thanks to the many people who contributed to the preparation of this seventh edition. I am indebted to the staff at John Wiley & Sons for their support, including Beth Lang

Golub, information systems editor; Norine M. Pigliucci, senior production editor; Harry Nolan, senior designer; editorial and production services, Hermitage Publishing Services; and Jessica Garcia, marketing manager.

I would also like to thank the reviewers for their assistance, often under short deadlines:

France Belanger, Virginia Tech
Jay Benson, Anne Arundel Community College
Richard Bower, Rochester Institute of Technology
Deborah Buell, University of Houston—Downtown
Danny Creagan, Bellevue University
Rangadhar Dash, University of Texas at Arlington
Glenn Dietrich, University of Texas at San Antonio
M. Barry Dumas, Baruch College
Rassule Hadidi, University of Illinois at Springfield
Qing Hu, Florida Atlantic University
Boris Jukic, George Mason University
Jean-Pierre Kuilboer, University of Massachusetts—Boston
Terry Landry, Louisiana State University
Richard McMahon, University of Houston—Downtown
Gene Mesher, California State University, Sacramento
Keith Morneau, Northern Virginia Community College
Mihir Parikh, Polytechnic University
Alan Runge, DeVry Institute of Technology, Kansas City
Sharon Tabor, Boise State University
Graham Thorpe, McGill University
Mark Voegele, Pacific Bell Network Integration
Mike Whitman, Kennesaw State University

Alan Dennis
Bloomington, Indiana
http://www.kelley.indiana.edu/ardennis

SUMMARY TABLE OF CONTENTS

CONTENTS

PART 1

INTRODUCTION

CHAPTER 1

INTRODUCTION TO DATA COMMUNICATIONS

THIS CHAPTER introduces the basic concepts of data communications and shows how we have progressed from paper-based systems to modern computer networks. It begins by describing why it is important to study data communications and how the invention of the telephone, the computer, and the Internet has transformed the way we communicate. Next, the basic types and components of a data communication network are discussed. The importance of a network model based on layers and the importance of network standards are examined. The chapter concludes with an overview of three key trends in the future of networking.

OBJECTIVES

- Be aware of the history of communications, information systems, and the Internet
- Be aware of the applications of data communication networks
- Be familiar with the major components of and types of networks
- Understand the role of network layers
- Be familiar with the role of network standards
- Be aware of three key trends in communications and networking

CHAPTER OUTLINE

INTRODUCTION

A Brief History of Communications in North America

A Brief History of Information Systems

A Brief History of the Internet

INTRODUCTION

Over the past few years, it has become clear that world has changed forever. We are now in the Information Age—the second Industrial Revolution, according to John Chambers, CEO (chief executive officer) of Cisco Systems, Inc., one of the world's leading networking technology companies. The first Industrial Revolution revolutionized the way people worked by introducing machines and new organizational forms. New companies and industries emerged and old ones died off.

The second Industrial Revolution is revolutionizing the way people work though networking and data communications. The value of a high-speed data communication network is that it brings people together in way never before possible. In the 1800s, it took several weeks for a message to reach North America by ship from England. By the 1900s, it could be transmitted within the hour. Today, it can be transmitted in seconds. Collapsing the *information lag* to Internet speeds means that people can communicate and access information anywhere in the world regardless of their physical location. In fact, today's problem is that we cannot handle the quantities of information we receive.

Data communications and networking is a truly global area of study, both because the technology enables global communication and because new technologies and applications often emerge from a variety of countries and spread rapidly around the world. The World Wide Web, for example, was born in a Swiss research lab, was nurtured through its first years primarily by European universities, and exploded into mainstream popular culture because of a development at an American research lab.

One of the problems in studying a global phenomenon lies in explaining the different political and regulatory issues that have evolved and currently exist in different parts of the world. Rather than attempt to explain the different paths taken by different countries, we have chosen simplicity instead. Historically, the majority of readers of previous editions of this book have come from North America. Therefore, although we retain a global focus on technology and its business implications, we focus exclusively on North America in describing the political and regulatory issues surrounding communications and networking. We do, however, take care to discuss technological or business issues where fundamental differences exist between North America and the rest of the world (e.g., ISDN (integrated services digital network); see Chapter 8).

A Brief History of Communications in North America

Today we take data communications for granted, but it was pioneers like Samuel Morse, Alexander Graham Bell, and Thomas Edison who developed the basic electrical and electronic systems that ultimately evolved into voice and data communication networks.

In 1837, Samuel Morse exhibited a working telegraph system; today we might consider it the first electronic data communication system. In 1841, a Scot named Alexander Bain used electromagnets to synchronize school clocks. Two years later, he patented a printing telegraph—the predecessor of today's fax machines. In 1874, Alexander Graham Bell developed the concept for the telephone at his father's home in Brantford, Ontario, Canada, but it would take him and his assistant, Tom Watson, another 2 years of work in Boston to develop first telephone capable of transmitting understandable conversation in 1876. Later that year, Bell made the first long-distance call (about 10 miles) from Paris, Ontario, to his father in Brantford.

MANAGEMENT FOCUS *1-1*

CAREER OPPORTUNITIES

It's a great time to be in information technology. The technology-fueled new economy has dramatically increased the demand for skilled information technology (IT) professionals. The U.S. Bureau of Labor estimates that there are currently 80,000 IT jobs that are unfilled. IT employers have responded: Salaries have risen rapidly. Annual starting salaries for our undergraduates at Indiana University range from $40,000 to $50,000. Although all areas of IT have shown rapid growth, the fastest salary growth has been for those with skills in Internet development, networking, and telecommunications. People with a few years of experience in these areas can make $65,000 to $80,000—not counting bonuses.

The demand for networking expertise is growing for two reasons. First, Internet and communication deregulation has significantly changed how businesses operate and has spawned thousands of small start-up companies. Second, a host of new hardware and software innovations have significantly changed the way networking is done.

These trends and the shortage of qualified network experts have also led to the rise in certification. Most large vendors of network technologies, such as Microsoft Corporation, Cisco, and Novell, Inc., provide certification processes (usually a series of courses and formal exams) so that individuals can document their knowledge. Certified network professionals often earn $10,000 to $20,000 more than similarly skilled uncertified professionals—provided they continue to learn and maintain their certification as new technologies emerge.

When the telephone arrived, it was greeted by both skepticism and adoration, but within 5 years, it was clear to all that the world had changed. To meet the demand, Bell started a company in the United States, and his father started a company in Canada. In 1879, the first private manual telephone switchboard (private branch exchange, or PBX) was installed. By 1880, the first pay telephone was in use. The telephone became a way of life, because anyone could call from public telephones. The certificate of incorporation for the American Telephone and Telegraph Company was registered in 1885. By 1889, AT&T had a recognized logo in the shape of the Liberty Bell with the words Long-Distance Telephone written on it.

In 1892, the Canadian government began regulating telephone rates. By 1910, the Interstate Commerce Commission (ICC) had the authority to regulate interstate telephone businesses in the United States. In 1934, this was transferred to the Federal Communications Commission (FCC).

The first transcontinental telephone service and the first transatlantic voice connections were both established in 1915. The telephone system grew so rapidly that by the early 1920s, there were serious concerns that even with the introduction of dial telephones (that eliminated the need for operators to make simple calls) there would not be enough trained operators to work the manual switchboards. Experts predicted that by 1980, every single woman in North America would have to work as a telephone operator if growth in telephone usage continued at the current rate. (At the time, all telephone operators were women.)

The first commercial microwave link for telephone transmission was established in Canada in 1948. In 1951, the first direct long distance dialing without an operator began. The first international satellite telephone call was sent over the *Telstar I* satellite in 1962. By 1965, there was widespread use of commercial international telephone service via satellite. Fax services were introduced in 1962. Touch-tone telephones were first marketed in 1963. Picturefone service, which allows users to see as well as talk with one another, began operating in 1969. The first commercial packet-switched network for computer data was introduced in 1976.

Until 1968, Bell Telephone/AT&T controlled the U.S. telephone system. No telephones or computer equipment other than those made by Bell Telephone could be connected to the phone system and only AT&T could provide telephone services. In 1968, after a series of lawsuits, the Carterfone court decision allowed non-Bell equipment to be connected to the Bell System network. This important milestone permitted independent telephone and modem manufacturers to connect their equipment to the U.S. telephone networks for the first time.

Another key decision in 1970 permitted MCI to provide limited long-distance service in the United States in competition with AT&T. Throughout the 1970s, there were many arguments and court cases over the monopolistic position that AT&T held over U.S. communication services. On January 1, 1984, AT&T was divided in two parts under a consent degree devised by a federal judge. The first part, AT&T, provided long-distance telephone services in competition with other *interexchange carriers* (IXCs) such as MCI and Sprint. The second part, a series of seven *regional Bell operating companies* (RBOCs) or *local exchange carriers* (LECs), provided local telephone services to homes and businesses. AT&T was prohibited from providing local telephone services, and the RBOCs were prohibited from providing long-distance services. Intense competition began in the long-distance market as MCI, Sprint, and a host of other companies began to offer services and dramatically cut prices under the watchful eye of the FCC. Competition was prohibited in the local telephone market, so the RBOCs remained a regulated monopoly under the control of a multitude of state laws. The Canadian long-distance market was opened to competition in 1992.

During 1983 and 1984, traditional radio telephone calls were supplanted by the newer cellular telephone networks. In the 1990s, cellular telephones became commonplace and shrank to pocket size. Demand grew so much that in some cities (e.g., New York and Atlanta), it became difficult to get a dial tone at certain times of the day.

In February 1996, the U.S. Congress enacted the Telecommunications Competition and Deregulation Act of 1996. The act replaced all current laws, FCC regulations, and the 1984 consent degree and subsequent court rulings under which AT&T was broken up. It also overruled all existing state laws and prohibited states from introducing new laws. Practically overnight, the local telephone industry in the U.S. went from a highly regulated and legally restricted monopoly to multiple companies engaged in open competition.

Local service in the United States is now open for competition. The *common carriers* (RBOCs, IXCs, cable TV companies, and other LECs) are permitted to build their own local telephone facilities and offer services to customers. To increase competition, the RBOCs must sell their telephone services to their competitors at wholesale prices, who can then resell them to consumers at retail prices. Most analysts expected the big IXCs (e.g., AT&T) to quickly charge into the local telephone market, but they have been slow to move. Meanwhile, the RBOCs have been aggressively fighting court battles to keep competitors out of their local telephone markets and attempting to merge with each other and with the IXCs, prompting many complaints from Congress and the FCC. At best, the RBOCs can only hope to delay competition, not prevent it, because it is clear that Congress and the FCC want competition.

There has been active competition in the long-distance telephone market for many years, but RBOCs have been prohibited from providing long-distance services. The Telecommunications Act now permits the RBOCs to provide long-distance service outside the regions in which they provide local telephone services. However, they are prohibited from providing long-distance services inside their region until at least one viable competitor exists for local telephone services. Several local telephone companies (e.g., GTE Corporation) have moved aggressively into the long-distance market but have focused exclusively on out-of-region long distance by buying long-distance services from AT&T and other IXCs and reselling them. To date, few RBOCs have moved into the in-region long-distance market because few face real local competition.

Virtually all RBOCs, LECs, and IXCs have aggressively entered the Internet market. Today, there are more than 5,000 Internet service providers (ISPs) who provide dial-in access to the Internet to millions of small business and home users. Most of these are small companies that lease telecommunications circuits from the RBOCs, LECs, and IXCs and use them to provide Internet access to their customers. As the RBOCs, LECs and IXCs move into the Internet market and provide the same services directly to consumers, the smaller ISPs are facing heavy competition.

International competition should also be heightened by an international agreement signed in 1997 by 68 countries to deregulate (or at least lessen regulation in) their telecommunications markets. The countries agreed to permit foreign firms to compete in their internal telephone markets. Major U.S. firms (e.g., AT&T, BellSouth Corporation) now offer telephone service in many of the industrialized and emerging countries in North America, South America, Europe, and Asia. Likewise, overseas telecommunications giants (e.g., British Telecom) are beginning to enter the U.S. market. This should increase competition in the U.S., but the greatest effect is likely to be felt in emerging countries. For example, it costs almost 30 times more to use a telephone in India than it does in the United States.

A Brief History of Information Systems

The natural evolution of information systems in business, government, and home use has forced the widespread use of data communication networks to interconnect various computer systems. However, data communications has not always been considered important.

In the 1950s, computer systems used batch processing, and users carried their punched cards to the computer for processing. By the 1960s, data communication across telephone lines became more common. Users could type their own batches of data for processing using online terminals. Data communications involved the transmission of messages from these terminals to a large central mainframe computer and back to the user.

During the 1970s, online real-time systems were developed that moved the users from batch processing to single transaction-oriented processing. Database management systems replaced the older file systems, and integrated systems were developed in which the entry of an online transaction in one business system (e.g., order entry) might automatically trigger transactions in other business systems (e.g., accounting, purchasing). Computers entered the mainstream of business, and data communications networks became a necessity.

The 1980s witnessed the microcomputer revolution. At first, microcomputers were isolated from the major information systems applications, serving the needs of individual users (e.g., spreadsheets). As more people began to rely on microcomputers for essential applications, the need for networks to exchange data among microcomputers and between microcomputers and central mainframe computers became clear. By the early 1990s, more than 60 percent of all microcomputers in American corporations were networked—connected to other computers.

Today, the microcomputer has evolved from a small, low-power computer into a very powerful, easy-to-use system with a large amount of low-cost software. Today's microcomputers have more raw computing power than a mainframe of the 1980s. Perhaps more surprisingly, corporations today have far more total computing power sitting on desktops in the form of the microcomputers than they have in their large central mainframe computers.

As we begin the new millennium, the most important aspect of computers is *networking*. The Internet is everywhere, and virtually all corporate computers are networked. Most corporations are rapidly building distributed systems in which information system applications are divided among a network of computers. This form of computing, called client–server computing, will dramatically change the way information systems professionals and users interact with computers. The office of the future that interconnects microcomputers, mainframe computers, fax machines, copiers, teleconferencing equipment, and other equipment will put tremendous demands on data communications networks.

These networks already have had a dramatic impact on the way business is conducted. Networking played a key role—among many other factors—in the growth of Wal-Mart Stores, Inc. into one of the largest forces in the North American retail industry. That process has transformed the retailing industry. Wal-Mart has 34 mainframes, 5,000 network file servers, 18,000 microcomputers, 90,000 handheld inventory computers, and 100,000 net-worked cash registers. (As an aside, it is interesting to note that every single microcomputer built by IBM in the United States during the third quarter of 1997 was purchased by Wal-Mart.) At the other end of the spectrum, the lack of a sophisticated data communications network was one of the key factors in the bankruptcy of Macy's in the early 1990s.

In retail sales, a network is critical for managing inventory. Macy's had a traditional 1970s inventory system. At the start of the season, buyers would order products in large lots to get volume discounts. Some products would be very popular and sell out quickly. When the sales clerks did a weekly inventory and noticed the shortage, they would order more. If the items were not available in the warehouse (and very popular products were often not available), it would take 6 to 8 weeks to restock them. Customers would buy from other stores, and Macy's would lose the sales. Other products, also bought in large quanti-ties, would be unpopular and have to be sold at deep discounts.

In contrast, Wal-Mart negotiates volume discounts with suppliers on the basis of total purchases but does not specify particular products. Buyers place initial orders in small quantities. Each time a product is sold, the sale is recorded. Every day or two, the complete list of purchases is transferred over the network (often via a satellite) to the head office, a distribution center, or the supplier. Replacements for the products sold are shipped almost immediately and typically arrive within days. The result is that Wal-Mart seldom has a major problem with overstocking an unwanted product or running out of a popular product (unless, of course, the supplier is unable to produce it fast enough).

A Brief History of the Internet

The *Internet* is one of the most important developments in the history of both information systems and communication systems because it is both an information system and a com-munication system. The Internet was started by the U.S. Department of Defense in the

MANAGEMENT FOCUS *1-2*

NETWORKS IN THE GULF WAR

The lack of a good network can also cost more than money. During Operation Desert Shield/Desert Storm, the U.S. Army, Navy, and Air Force lacked one integrated logistics communications network. Each service had its own series of networks, making communication and cooperation diffi-cult. But communication among the systems was essential. Each day a navy aircraft would fly into Saudi Arabia to exchange diskettes full of logistics information with the army—an expensive form of "wireless" networking.

This lack of an integrated network also created prob-lems transmitting information from the United States into the Persian Gulf. More than 60 percent of the containers of supplies arrived without documentation. They had to be unloaded for someone to see what was in them and then reloaded for shipment to combat units.

The logistics information systems and communication networks experienced such problems that some air force units were unable to quickly order and receive critical spare parts needed to keep planes flying. Officers telephoned the U.S.-based suppliers of these parts and instructed them to send the parts via FedEx.

Fortunately, the war did not start until the United States and its allies were prepared. Had Iraq attacked, things might have turned out differently.

1969 as a network of four computers called ARPANET. Its goal was to link a set of computers operated by several universities doing military research. The original network grew as more computers and more computer *networks* were linked to it. By 1974, there were 62 computers attached. In 1983, the Internet split into two parts, one dedicated solely to military installations (called Milnet) and one dedicated to university research centers (called the Internet) that had just under 1,000 host computers or servers.

In 1985, the Canadian government completed its leg of BITNET to link all Canadian universities from coast to coast and provided connections into the American Internet. (BITNET is a competing network to the Internet developed by the City University of New York and Yale University that uses a different approach.) In 1986, the National Science Foundation in the United States created NSFNET to connect leading U.S. universities. By the end of 1987, there were 10,000 servers on the Internet and 1,000 on BITNET.

Performance began to slow down due to increased network traffic, so in 1987, the National Science Foundation decided to improve performance by building a new high-speed backbone network for NSFNET. It leased high-speed circuits from several IXCs and in 1988 connected 13 regional Internet networks containing 170 LANs (local area networks) and 56,000 servers. The National Research Council of Canada followed in 1989 and replaced BITNET with a high-speed network called CA*net that used the same communication language as the Internet. By the end of 1989, there were almost 200,000 servers on the combined U.S. and Canadian Internet.

Similar initiatives were undertaken by most other countries around world, so that by the early 1990s, most of the individual country networks were linked together into one worldwide network of networks. Each of these individual country networks was distinct (each had its own name, access rules, and fee structures), but all networks used the same standards as the U.S. Internet network so they could easily exchange messages with one another. Gradually, the distinctions among the networks in each of the countries began to disappear, and the U.S. name, the Internet, began to be used to mean the entire worldwide network of networks connected to the U.S. Internet. By the end of 1992, there were more than 1 million servers on the Internet.

Originally, commercial traffic was forbidden on the Internet (and on the other individual country networks), because the key portions of these networks were funded by the various national governments and research organizations. In the early 1990s, commercial networks began connecting into NSFNET, CA*net, and the other government-run networks in each country. New commercial online services began offering access to anyone willing to pay, and a connection into the worldwide Internet became an important marketing issue. The growth in the commercial portion of the Internet was so rapid that it quickly overshadowed university and research use. In 1994, with more than 4 million servers on the Internet (most of which were commercial), the U.S. and Canadian governments stopped funding their few remaining circuits and turned them over to commercial firms. Most other national governments soon followed. The Internet had become commercial.

The Internet has continued to grow at a dramatic pace. No one knows exactly how large the Internet is, but estimates suggest there are 40 million servers and 400 million people on the Internet, both of which are growing rapidly (see cyberatlas.internet.com). In the mid-1990s, most Internet users were young (under 35 years old) and male, but as the Internet matures, its typical user becomes closer to the underlying average in the population as a whole (i.e., older and more evenly split between men and women). In fact, the fastest growing segment of Internet users is retirees.

DATA COMMUNICATIONS NETWORKS

Data communications is the movement of computer information from one point to another by means of electrical or optical transmission systems. Such systems often are called *data communications networks*. This is in contrast to the broader term *telecommunications,* which includes the transmission of voice and video (images and graphics) as well as data and usually implies longer distances. In general, data communications networks collect data from microcomputers and other devices and transmit that data to a central server that is a more powerful microcomputer, minicomputer, or mainframe, or they perform the reverse process, or some combination of the two. Data communications networks facilitate more efficient use of computers and improve the day-to-day control of a business by providing faster information flow. They also provide message transfer services to allow computer users to talk to one another via electronic mail, chat, and video streaming.

TECHNICAL FOCUS

INTERNET DOMAIN NAMES

Internet address names are strictly controlled; otherwise, someone could add a computer to the Internet that had the same address as another computer. Each address name has two parts, the computer name and its domain. The general format of an Internet address is therefore computer.domain. Some computer names have several parts separated by periods, so some addresses have the format computer.computer. computer.domain. For example, the main university Web server at Indiana University (IU) is called www.indiana.edu, whereas the Web server for the Kelley School of Business at IU is www.kelley.indiana.edu.

Since the Internet began in the United States, the American address board was the first to assign domain names to indicate types of organization. Some common U.S. domain names are

EDU	for an educational institution, usually a university
COM	for a commercial business
GOV	for a government department or agency
MIL	for a military unit
ORG	for a nonprofit organization

As networks in other countries were connected to the Internet, they were assigned their own domain names. Some international domain names are

CA	for Canada
AU	for Australia
UK	for the United Kingdom
DE	for Germany

Several new top-level domains were introduced in 2000 that focus on specific types of businesses, such as

AERO	for aerospace companies
MUSEUM	for museums
NAME	for individuals
PRO	for professionals, such as accountants and lawyers

Many international domains structure their addresses in much the same way as the United States does. For example, Australia uses *EDU* to indicate academic institutions, so an address such as xyz.edu.au would indicate an Australian university.

Components of a Network

There are three basic hardware components for a data communications network: a server or host computer (e.g., microcomputer, mainframe), a client (e.g., microcomputer, terminal), and a circuit (e.g., cable, modem) over which messages flow. Both the server and client also need special-purpose network software that enables them to communicate.

The *server* (or *host computer*) stores data or software that can be access by the clients. In client–server computing, several servers may work together over the network with a client computer to support the business application.

The *client* is the input–output hardware device at the user's end of a communication circuit. It typically provides users with access to the network and the data and software on the server.

The *circuit* is the pathway through which the messages travel. It is typically a copper wire, although fiber-optic cable and wireless transmission are becoming more common. There are many devices in the circuit that perform special functions such as hubs, switches, routers, and gateways.

Strictly speaking, a network does not need a server. Some networks are designed to connect a set of similar computers that share their data and software with each other. Such networks are called *peer-to-peer* networks because the computers function as equals, rather than relying on a central server or host computer to store the needed data and software.

Figure 1-1 shows a small network that has four microcomputers (clients) connected by a *hub* and *cables* (circuit). In this network, messages move through the hub to and from the computers. All computers share the same circuit and must take turns sending messages. The *router* is a special device that connects two or more networks. The router enables computers on this network to communicate with computers on other networks (e.g., the Internet).

The network in Figure 1-1 has three servers. Although one server can perform many functions, networks are often designed so that a separate computer is used to provide different services. The *file server* stores data and software that can be used by computers on the network. The *print server,* which is connected to a printer, manages all printing requests from the clients on the network. The *Web server* stores documents and graphics that can be accessed from any Web browser, such as Netscape Navigator or Internet Explorer. The Web server can respond to requests from computers on this network or any computer on the Internet. Servers are usually microcomputers (often more powerful than the other microcomputers on the network) but may be minicomputers or mainframes.

Types of Networks

There are many different ways to categorize networks. One of the most common ways is to look at the geographic scope of the network. Figure 1-2 illustrates four types of networks: LANs, backbone networks (BNs), metropolitan area networks (MANs), and wide area networks (WANs). The distinctions among these are becoming blurry. Some network technologies now used in LANs were originally developed for WANs, whereas some LAN technologies have influenced the development of MAN products. Any rigid classification of technologies is certain to have exceptions.

A *local area network (LAN)* is a group of microcomputers or other workstation devices located in the same general area. A LAN covers a clearly defined small area, such

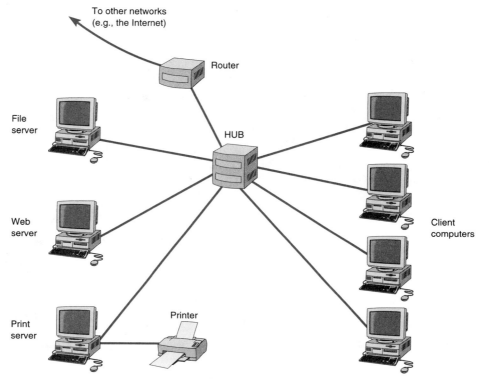

FIGURE 1-1 Example of a local area network (LAN).

one floor or work area, a single building, or a group of buildings. LANs often use shared circuits, where all computers must take turns using the same circuit. The upper left diagram in Figure 1-2 shows a small LAN located in the records building at McClellan Air Force Base in Sacramento. LANs support high-speed data transmission compared with standard telephone circuits, commonly operating at 10 million to 100 million bits per second (10–100 Mbps). LANs are discussed in detail in Chapter 6.

Most LANs are connected to a *backbone network (BN),* a larger, central network connecting several LANs, other BNs, MANs, and WANs. BNs typically span up to several miles and provide very high speed data transmission, commonly to 100 to 1,000 Mbps. The second diagram in Figure 1-2 shows a BN that connects the LANs located in several buildings at McClellan Air Force Base. BNs are discussed in detail in Chapter 7.

A *metropolitan area network (MAN)* connects LANs and BNs located in different areas to each other and to WANs. MANs typically span between 3 and 30 miles. The third diagram in Figure 1-2 shows a MAN connecting the BNs at several military and government complexes in Sacramento. Some organizations develop their own MANs using technologies similar to those of BNs. These networks provide moderately fast transmission rates but can prove costly to install and operate over long distances. Unless an organization has a continuing need to transfer large amounts of data, this type of MAN is usually too

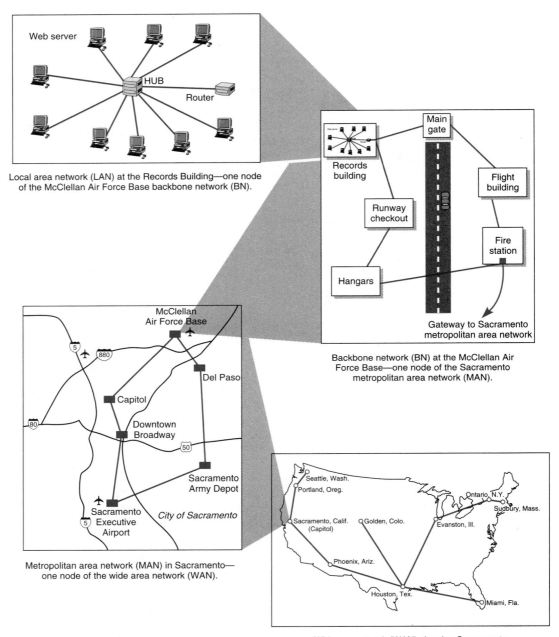

Local area network (LAN) at the Records Building—one node
of the McClellan Air Force Base backbone network (BN).

Backbone network (BN) at the McClellan Air
Force Base—one node of the Sacramento
metropolitan area network (MAN).

Metropolitan area network (MAN) in Sacramento—
one node of the wide area network (WAN).

Wide are network (WAN) showing Sacramento
connected to nine other cities throughout the U.S.

FIGURE 1-2 The hierarchical relationship of a local area network (LAN) to a
backbone network (BN) to a metropolitan area network (MAN) to a wide area
network (WAN).

expensive. More commonly, organizations use public data networks provided by common carriers (e.g., the telephone company) as their MANs. With these MANs, data transmission rates typically range from 64,000 bits per second (64 Kbps) to 100 Mbps, although newer technologies promise data rates of over 10 billion bits per second, or 10 gigabits per second (10 Gbps). MANs are discussed in detail in Chapter 8.

Wide area networks (WANs) connect BNs and MANs (see Figure 1-2). Most organizations do not build their own WANs by laying cable, building microwave towers, or sending up satellites (unless they have unusually heavy data transmission needs or highly specialized requirements, such as those of the Department of Defense). Instead, most organizations lease circuits from IXCs (e.g., AT&T, MCI, Sprint) and use those to transmit their data. WAN circuits provided by IXCs come in all types and sizes but typically span hundreds or thousands of miles and provide data transmission rates from 56 Kbps to 10 Gbps. WANs are also discussed in detail in Chapter 8.

Two other common terms are *intranets* and *extranets*. An intranet is a LAN that uses the same technologies as the Internet (e.g., Web servers, Java, HTML [Hypertext Markup Language]) but is open to only those inside the organization. For example, although some pages on a Web server may be open to the public and accessible by anyone on the Internet, some pages may be on an intranet and therefore hidden from those who connect to the Web server from the Internet at large. Sometimes an intranet is provided by a completely separate Web server hidden from the Internet. The intranet for the Information Systems Department at Indiana University, for example, provides information on faculty expense budgets, class scheduling for future semesters (e.g., room, instructor), and discussion forums.

An extranet is similar to an intranet in that it, too, uses the same technologies as the Internet but instead is provided to invited users outside the organization who access it over the Internet. It can provide access to information services, inventories, and other internal organizational databases that are provided only to customers, suppliers, or those who have paid for access. Typically, users are given passwords to gain access, but more sophisticated technologies such as smart cards or special software may also be required. Many universities provide extranets for Web-based courses so that only those students enrolled in the course can access course materials and discussions.

NETWORK MODELS

There are many ways to describe and analyze data communications networks. All networks provide the same basic functions to transfer a message from sender to receiver, but each network can use different network hardware and software to provide these functions. All of these hardware and software products have to work together to successfully transfer a message.

One way to accomplish this is to break the entire set of communications functions into a series of layers, each of which can be defined separately. In this way, vendors can develop software and hardware to provide the functions of each layer separately. The software or hardware can work in any manner and can be easily updated and improved, as long as the interface between that layer and the ones around it remain unchanged. Each piece of hardware and software can then work together in the overall network.

There are many different ways in which the network layers can be designed. The two most important network models are the Open Systems Interconnection Reference (OSI) model and the Internet model.

Open Systems Interconnection Reference Model

The *Open Systems Interconnection Reference Model* (usually called the *OSI model* for short) helped change the face of network computing. Before the OSI model, most commercial networks used by businesses were built using nonstandardized technologies developed by one vendor (remember that the Internet was in use at the time but was not widespread and certainly was not commercial). During the late 1970s, the International Organization for Standardization (ISO) created the Open System Interconnection Subcommittee, whose task was to develop a framework of standards for computer-to-computer communications. In 1984, this effort produced the OSI model.

The OSI model is the most talked about and most referred to network model. If you choose a career in networking, questions about the OSI model will be on the network certification exams offered by Microsoft, Cisco, Novell, and other vendors of network hardware and software. However, you will probably never use a network based on the OSI model. Simply put, the OSI model never caught on commercially in North America, although some European networks use it, and some network components developed for use in the United States arguably use parts of it. Most networks today use the Internet model, which is discussed in the next section. However, because there are many similarities between the OSI model and the Internet model, and because most people in networking are expected to know the OSI model, we discuss it here. The OSI model has seven layers (see Figure 1-3).

Layer 1: Physical Layer The *physical layer* is concerned primarily with transmitting data bits (zeros or ones) over a communication circuit. This layer defines the rules by which ones and zeros are transmitted, such as voltages of electricity, number of bits sent per second, and the physical format of the cables and connectors used.

Layer 2: Data Link Layer The *data link layer* manages the physical transmission circuit in layer 1 and transforms it into a circuit that is free of transmission errors as far as layers above are concerned. Because layer 1 accepts and transmits only a raw stream of bits without understanding their meaning or structure, the data link layer must create and recognize message boundaries; that is, it must mark where a message starts and where it ends. Another major task of layer 2 is to solve the problems caused by damaged, lost, or duplicate messages so the succeeding layers are shielded from transmission errors. Thus, layer 2 performs error detection, correction, and retransmission. It also decides when a device can transmit so that two computers do not try to transmit at the same time.

Layer 3: Network Layer The *network layer* performs routing. It determines the next computer the message should be sent to so it can follow the best route through the network and finds the full address for that computer if needed.

Layer 4: Transport Layer The *transport layer* deals with end-to-end issues, such as procedures for entering and departing from the network. It establishes, maintains, and

OSI Model	Internet Model	Groups of Layers
7. Application Layer	5. Application Layer	*Application Layer*
6. Presentation Layer		
5. Session Layer		
4. Transport Layer	4. Transport Layer	*Internetwork Layer*
3. Network Layer	3. Network Layer	
2. Data Link Layer	2. Data Link Layer	*Hardware Layer*
1. Physical Layer	1. Physical Layer	

FIGURE 1-3   Network models. OSI = Open Systems Interconnection Reference.

terminates logical connections for the transfer of data between the original sender and the final destination of the message. It is responsible for obtaining the address of the end user (if needed), breaking a large data transmission into smaller packets (if needed), ensuring that all the packets have been received, eliminating duplicate packets, and performing flow control to ensure that no computer is overwhelmed by the number of messages it receives. Although error control is performed by the data link layer, the transport layer can also perform error checking, which is redundant and can be rather wasteful.

Layer 5: Session Layer   The *session layer* is responsible for initiating, maintaining, and terminating each logical session between end users. To understand the session layer, think of your telephone. When you lift the receiver, listen for a dial tone, and dial a number, you begin to create a physical connection that goes through layer 1. When you start speaking with the person at the other end of the telephone circuit, you are engaged in a person-to-person session; the session is the dialogue between the two.

This layer is responsible for managing and structuring all sessions. Session initiation must arrange for all the desired and required services between session participants, such as logging onto circuit equipment, transferring files, using various terminal types, and performing security checks. Session termination provides an orderly way to end the session, as well as a means to abort a session prematurely. It may have some redundancy built in to recover from a broken transport (layer 4) connection in case of failure. The session layer also handles session accounting so the correct party receives the bill.

Layer 6: Presentation Layer   The *presentation layer* formats the data for presentation to the user. Its job is to accommodate different interfaces on different terminals or computers so the application program need not worry about them. It is concerned with displaying, formatting, and editing user inputs and outputs. For example, layer 6 might perform data compression, translation between different data formats, and screen formatting. Any function (except those in layers 1 through 5) that is requested sufficiently often to warrant finding a general solution is placed in the presentation layer, although some of these functions can be performed by separate hardware and software (e.g., encryption).

Layer 7: Application Layer The *application layer* is the end user's access to the network. The primary purpose is to provide a set of utilities for application programs. Each user program determines the set of messages and any action it might take on receipt of a message. Other network-specific applications at this layer include network monitoring and network management.

Internet Model

Although the OSI model is the most talked about network model, the one that dominates current hardware and software is a more simple five-layer Internet model. Unlike the OSI model that was developed by formal committees, the Internet model evolved from the work of thousands of people who developed pieces of the Internet. The OSI model is a formal standard that is documented in one standard, but the Internet model has never been formally defined; it has to be interpreted from a number of standards.[1] The two models have very much in common (see Figure 1-3); simply put, the Internet model collapses the top three OSI layers into one layer. Because it is clear that the Internet has won the "war," we will use the five-layer Internet model for the rest of this book.

Layer 1: The Physical Layer The *physical layer* in the Internet model, as in the OSI Model, is the physical connection between the sender and receiver. Its role is to transfer a series of electrical, radio, or light signals through the circuit. The physical layer includes all the *hardware* devices (e.g., computers, modems, and hubs) and physical *media* (e.g., cables and satellites). The physical layer specifies the type of connection and the electrical signals, radio waves, or light pulses that pass through it. Chapter 3 discusses the physical layer in detail.

Layer 2: The Data Link Layer The *data link layer* is responsible for moving a message from one computer to the next computer in the network path from the sender to the receiver. The data link layer in the Internet model performs the same three functions as the data link layer in the OSI model. First, it controls the physical layer by deciding when to transmit messages over the media. Second, it formats the messages by indicating where they start and end. Third, it detects and corrects any errors that have occurred during transmission. Chapter 4 discusses the data link layer in detail.

Layer 3: The Network Layer The *network layer* is responsible for the end-to-end transfer of messages from the sender to the final destination. The network layer in the Internet model performs the same functions as the network layer in the OSI model. First, it performs routing, in that it selects the next computer to which the message should be sent. Second, it can find the address of that computer if it doesn't already know it. Chapter 5 discusses the network layer in detail.

---

[1] Over the years, our view of the Internet layers has evolved, as has the Internet itself. In the previous edition of this book, we used a four-layer model. It's now clear that most of the Internet community has adopted a five-layer view, so we've moved to it as well. As of this writing, however, Microsoft uses a four-layer view of the Internet for its certification exams.

Layer 4: The Transport Layer   The *transport layer* in the Internet model is very similar to the transport layer in the OSI model. It performs three functions. First, it is responsible for linking the application layer software to the network and establishing end-to-end connections between the sender and receiver when such connection are needed. Second, it provides tools so that addresses used at the application layer (www.indiana.edu) can be translated into the numeric addresses used at the lower layers (e.g., 129.79.78.8). Third, it is responsible for breaking long messages it into several smaller messages to make them easier to transmit. Chapter 5 also discusses the transport layer in detail.

Layer 5: Application Layer   The *application layer* is the application software used by the network user and includes much of what the OSI model contains in the application, presentation, and session layers. It is the user's access to the network. By using the application software, the user defines what messages are sent over the network. Because it is the layer that most people understand best and because starting at the top sometimes helps people understand better, the next chapter, Chapter 2, begins with the application layer. It discusses the architecture of network applications and several types of network application software and the types of messages they generate.

Groups of Layers   The layers in the Internet are often so closely coupled that decisions in one layer impose certain requirements on other layers. The data link layer and the physical layer are closely tied together because the data link layer controls the physical layer in terms of when the physical layer can transmit. Because these two layers are so closely tied together, decisions about the data link layer often drive the decisions about the physical layer. For this reason, some people group the physical and data link layers together and call them the *hardware layers.* Likewise, the transport and network layers are so closely coupled that sometimes these layers are called the *internetwork layers.* See Figure 1-3. When you design a network, you often think about the network design in terms of three groups of layers: the hardware layers (physical and data link), the internetwork layers (network and transport), and the application layer.

Message Transmission Using Layers

Each computer in the network has software that operates at each of the layers and performs the functions required by those layers (or hardware in the case of the physical layer). Each layer in the network uses a formal language, or *protocol,* that is simply a set of rules that define what the layer will do and that provides a clearly defined set of messages that software at the layer needs to understand. For example, the protocol used for Web applications is HTTP (Hypertext Transfer Protocol, which is described in more detail in Chapter 2). In general, all messages sent in a network pass through all layers. Figure 1-4 shows how a message requesting a Web page would be sent on the Internet.

First, the user first creates a message at the application layer using a Web browser by clicking on a link (e.g., get the home page at www.somebody.com). The browser translates the user's message (the click on the Web link) into HTTP. The rules of HTTP define a specific format—called an HTTP request packet—that all Web browsers must use when they request a Web page. For now, you can think of the HTTP request packet as an envelope into which the user's message (*get the Web page*) is placed. In the same way that an envelope

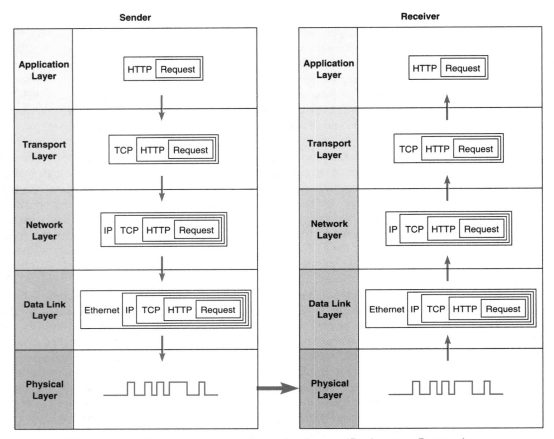

FIGURE 1-4 Message transmission using layers. IP = Internet Protocol; HTTP/Hypertext Transfer Protocol; TCP = Transmission Control Protocol.

placed in the mail needs certain information written in certain places (e.g., return address, destination address), so to does the HTTP packet. The Web browser fills in the necessary information in the HTTP packet, drops the user's request inside the packet, then passes the HTTP packet (containing the Web page request) to the transport layer. The transport layer on the Internet uses a protocol called TCP (Transmission Control Protocol), and it, too, has its own rules and its own packets. TCP is responsible for breaking large files into smaller packets and for opening a connection to the server for the transfer of a large set of packets. In this case, the message is so short that it doesn't need to broken into packets. If the application layer does not know the Internet numeric address for the Web server, then the transport layer can help the application layer translate the text address (i.e., www.somebody. com) into its numeric address. For simplicity, we'll assume that the application layer knows the numeric address. In this case, the transport layer places the HTTP packet inside a TCP packet (which is again much like envelope), fills in the information needed by the TCP packet, and passes the TCP packet (which contains the HTTP packet, which, in turn, contains the message) to the network layer.

The network layer on the Internet uses a protocol called IP (Internet Protocol), which has its rules and packets. IP selects the next stop on the message's route through the network. It places the TCP packet inside an IP packet (and fills in the IP information) and passes the IP packet (which contains the TCP packet, which, in turn, contains the HTTP packet, which, in turn, contains the message) to the data link layer.

If you are connecting to the Internet using a LAN, your data link layer may use a protocol called Ethernet, which also has its own rules and packets. The data link layer formats the message with start and stop markers, adds error checking information, places the IP packet inside an Ethernet packet (fills in the information in the packet), and instructs the physical hardware to transmit the Ethernet packet (which contains the IP packet, which contains the TCP packet, which contains the HTTP packet, which contains the message).

The physical layer in this case is network cable connecting your computer to the rest of the network. The computer will take the Ethernet packet (complete with the IP packet, the TCP packet, the HTTP packet, and the message) and send it as a series of electrical pulses through your cable to the server.

When the server gets the message, this process is performed in reverse. The physical hardware translates the electrical pulses into computer data and passes the message to the data link layer. The data link layer uses the start and stop markers in the Ethernet packet to identify the message. The data link layer checks for errors and, if it discovers one, requests that the message be re-sent. If a message is received without error, the data link layer will then strip off the Ethernet packet and pass the IP packet (which contains the TCP packet, the HTTP packet, and the message) to the network layer. The network layer checks the IP address and, if it is destined for this computer, strips off the IP packet and passes the TCP packet (which contains the HTTP packet and the message) to the transport layer. The transport layer processes the message, strips off the TCP packet, and passes the HTTP packet to the application layer for processing. The application layer (i.e., the Web server) reads the HTTP packet and the message it contains (the request for the Web page) and processes it by generating an HTTP packet containing the Web page you requested. Then the process starts again as the page is sent back to you.

There are three important points in this example. First, there are many different software packages and many different packets that operate at different layers to successfully transfer a message. Networking is in some ways similar to the Russian *Matryoshka,* nested dolls that fit neatly inside each other. The major advantage of using different software and protocols is that it is easy to develop new software, because all one has to do is write software for one level at a time. The developers of Web applications, for example, do not need to write software to perform error checking or routing, because those are performed by the data link and network layers. Developers can simply assume those functions are performed and just focus on the application layer. Likewise, it is simple to change the software at any level (or add new application protocols), as long as the interface between that layer and the ones around it remains unchanged.

Second, it is important to note that for communication to be successful, each layer in one computer must be able to communicate with its matching layer in the other computer. For example, the physical layer connecting the client and server must use the same type of electrical signals to enable each to understand the other (or there must be a device to translate between them). Ensuring that the software used at the different layers is the same is accomplished by using *standards*. A standard defines a set of rules, called *protocols,* that explain exactly how hardware and software that conform to the standard are required to operate. Any hardware and software that conform to a standard can communicate with any other hardware and software that conform to the same standard. Without standards, it would be virtually impossible for computers to communicate.

Third, the major disadvantage of using a layered network model is that it is somewhat inefficient. Because there are several layers, each with its own software and packets, sending a message involves many software programs (one for each protocol) and many packets. The packets add to the total amount of data that must be sent (thus slowing down transmission), and the different software packages increase the processing power needed in computers. Because the protocols are used at different layers and are stacked on top of one another (take another look at Figure 1-4), the set of software used to understand the different protocols is often called a *protocol stack*.

NETWORK STANDARDS

The Importance of Standards

Standards are necessary in almost every business and public service entity. For example, before 1904, fire hose couplings in the United States were not standard, which meant a fire department in one community could not help in another community. The transmission of electric current was not standardized until the end of the nineteenth century, so customers had to choose between Thomas Edison's direct current (DC) and George Westinghouse's alternating current (AC).

The primary reason for standards is to ensure that hardware and software produced by different vendors can work together. Without networking standards, it would be difficult—if not impossible—to develop networks that easily share information. Standards also mean that customers are not locked into one vendor. They can buy hardware and software from any vendor whose equipment meets the standard. In this way, standards help to promote more competition and hold down prices.

The use of standards makes it much easier to develop software and hardware that link different networks because software and hardware can be developed one layer at a time.

The Standards-Making Process

There are two types of standards: *formal* and *de facto*. A formal standard is developed by an official industry or government body. For example, there are formal standards for applications such as Web browsers (e.g., HTML), for network layer software (e.g., IP), data link layer software (e.g., Ethernet IEEE 802.3), and for physical hardware (e.g., V.90 modems). Formal standards typically take several years to develop, during which time technology changes, making them less useful. The race between Netscape and Microsoft in Web browsers is a good example. Just as a new standard for HTML is developed, Netscape and Microsoft add new features to their browsers that do not conform to the standard, starting a new round of the standards development process.

De facto standards are those that emerge in the marketplace and are supported by several vendors but have no official standing. For example, Microsoft Windows is a product of one company and has not been formally recognized by any standards organization, yet it is a de facto standard. In the communications industry, de facto standards often become formal standards once they have been widely accepted.

The formal *standardization process* has three stages: specification, identification of choices, and acceptance. The *specification* stage consists of developing a nomenclature and identifying the problems to be addressed. In the *identification of choices* stage, those working on the standard identify the various solutions and choose the optimum solution from among the alternatives. *Acceptance,* which is the most difficult stage, consists of defining the solution and getting recognized industry leaders to agree on a single, uniform solution. As with many other organizational processes that have the potential to influence the sales of hardware and software, standards-making processes are not immune to corporate politics and the influence of national governments.

International Organization for Standardization   One of the most important standards-making bodies is the *International Organization for Standardization (ISO),*[2] which makes technical recommendations about data communication interfaces (see www.iso.ch). ISO is based in Geneva, Switzerland. The membership is composed of the national standards organizations of each ISO member country. In turn, ISO is a member of the International Telecommunications Union (ITU), whose task is to make technical recommendations about telephone, telegraph, and data communication interfaces on a worldwide basis. ISO and ITU usually cooperate on issues of telecommunication standards, but they are mutually independent standards-making bodies and they are not required to agree on the same standards.

International Telecommunications Union—Telecommunications Group   The Telecommunications Group (ITU-T) is the technical standards-setting organization of the United Nations ITU, which is also based in Geneva (see www.itu.int). ITU is composed of representatives from about 200 member countries. Membership was originally focused on just the public telephone companies in each country, but a major reorganization in 1993 changed this, and ITU now seeks members among public- and private-sector organizations who operate computer or communications networks (e.g., RBOCs) or build software and equipment for them (e.g., AT&T).

American National Standards Institute   The *American National Standards Institute* (ANSI) is the coordinating organization for the U.S. national system of standards for both technology and nontechnology (see www.ansi.org). ANSI has about 1,000 members from both public and private organizations in the United States. ANSI is a standardization organization, not a standards-making body, in that it accepts standards developed by other organizations and publishes them as American standards. Its role is to coordinate the development of voluntary national standards and to interact with ISO to develop national standards that comply with ISO's international recommendations. ANSI is a voting participant in the ISO and the ITU-T.

Institute of Electrical and Electronics Engineers   The *Institute of Electrical and Electronics Engineers (IEEE)* is a professional society in the United States whose Standards Association (IEEE-SA) develops standards (see standards.ieee.org). The IEEE-SA is

---

[2] You're probably wondering why the abbreviation is *ISO,* not *IOS.* Well, *ISO* is a word (not an acronym) derived from the Greek *isos,* meaning "equal." The idea is that with standards, all are equal.

MANAGEMENT FOCUS *1-3*

HOW NETWORK PROTOCOLS BECOME STANDARDS

There are many standards organizations around the world, but perhaps the best known is the Internet Engineering Task Force (IETF). IETF sets the standards that govern how much of the Internet operates.

The IETF, like all standards organizations, tries to seek consensus among those involved before issuing a standard. Usually, a standard begins as a protocol (i.e., a language or set of rules for operating) developed by a vendor (e.g., HTML [Hypertext Markup Language]). When a protocol is proposed for standardization, the IETF forms a working group of technical experts to study it. The working group examines the protocol to identify potential problems and possible extensions and improvements, then issues a report to the IETF.

If the report is favorable, the IETF issues a request for comment (RFC) that describes the proposed standard and solicits comments from the entire world. Most large software companies likely to be affected by the proposed standard prepare detailed responses. Many "regular" Internet users also send their comments to the IETF.

The IETF reviews the comments and possibly issues a new and improved RFC, which again is posted for more comments. Once no additional changes have been identified, it becomes a proposed standard.

Usually, several vendors adopt the proposed standard and develop products based on it. Once at least two vendors have developed software based on it and it has proven successful in operation, the proposed standard is changed to a draft standard. This is usually the final specification, although some protocols have been elevated to Internet standards, which usually signifies mature standards not likely to change.

The process does not focus solely on technical issues; almost 90 percent of the IETF's participants work for manufacturers and vendors, so market forces and politics often complicate matters. One former IETF chairperson who worked for a hardware manufacturer has been accused of trying to delay the standards process until his company had a product ready, although he and other IETF members deny this. Likewise, former IETF directors have complained that members try to standardize every product their firms produce, leading to a proliferation of standards, only a few of which are truly useful.

SOURCE: "How Networking Protocols Become Standards," *PC Week*, March 17, 1997; "Growing Pains," *Network World*, April 14, 1997.

---

probably most known for its standards for LANs. Other countries have similar groups; for example, the British counterpart of IEEE is the Institution of Electrical Engineers (IEE).

Internet Engineering Task Force   The IETF sets the standards that govern how much of the Internet will operate (see www.ietf.org). The IETF is unique in that it doesn't really have official memberships. Quite literally anyone is welcome to join its mailing lists, attend its meetings, and comment on developing standards. The role of the IETF and other Internet organizations is discussed in more detail in Chapter 9; also, see "How Network Protocols Become Standards" in this chapter.

Common Standards

There are many different standards used in networking today. Each standard usually covers one layer in a network. Figure 1-5 outlines some of the most commonly used standards. At this point, these models are probably just a maze of strange names and acronyms to you, but by the end of the book, you will have a good understanding of each of these. Figure 1-5 provides a brief road map for some of the important communication technologies we will discuss in this book.

Layer	Common Standards
5. Application layer	HTTP, HTML (Web) MPEG, H.323 (audio/video) IMAP, POP (e-mail)
4. Transport layer	TCP (Internet) SPX (Novell LANs)
3. Network layer	IP (Internet) IPX (Novell LANs)
2. Data link layer	Ethernet (LAN) PPP (dial-up via modem)
1. Physical layer	RS-232C cable (LAN) Category 5 cable (LAN) V.92 (56-Kbps modem)

FIGURE 1-5   Some common data communications standards. HTML = Hypertext Markup Language; HTTP = Hypertext Transfer Protocol; IMAP = Internet Message Access Protocol; IP = Internet Protocol; IPX = internetwork package exchange; LAN = local area network; MPEG = Motion Picture Experts Group; POP = Post Office Protocol; PPP = Point-to-Point Protocol; SPX = sequenced packet exchange; TCP = Transmission Control Protocol.

For now, there is one important message you should understand from Figure 1-5: For a network to operate, many different standards must be used simultaneously. The sender of a message must use one standard at the application layer, another one at the transport layer, another one at the network layer, another one at the data link layer, and another one at the physical layer. Each layer and each standard is different, but all must work together to send and receive messages.

Either the sender and receiver of a message must use the same standards or, more likely, there are devices between the two that translate from one standard into another. Because different networks often use software and hardware designed for different standards, there is usually a lot of translation between different standards.

FUTURE TRENDS

By the year 2010, data communications will have grown faster and become more important than computer processing itself. Both go hand in hand, but we have moved from the computer era to the communication era. There are three major trends driving the future of communications and networking. All are interrelated, so it is difficult to consider one without the others.

Pervasive Networking

Pervasive networking means that communication networks will one day be everywhere; virtually any device will be able to communicate with any other device in the world. This is true in many ways today, but what is important is the staggering rate at which we will eventually be able to transmit data. Figure 1-6 illustrates the dramatic changes, over the years, in the amount of data we can transfer. For example, in 1980, the capacity of a traditional telephone-based network (e.g., one that would allow you to dial up another computer from your home) was about 300 bits per second (bps). In relative terms, you could picture this as a pipe that would enable you to transfer one speck of dust every second. By the 1990s, we were routinely transmitting data at 9,600 bps, or about a grain of sand every second. By 2000, we were able to transmit either a pea (modem at 56 Kbps) or a Ping-Pong ball (DSL [digital subscriber line] at 1.5 Mbps) every second over that same telephone line. In the very near future, we will have the ability to transmit 40 Mbps using wireless technologies—or in relative terms, about one basketball per second. A new laser-based wireless technology promises data rates of 10 Gbps in not so distant future—the relative equivalent of a one-car garage per second.

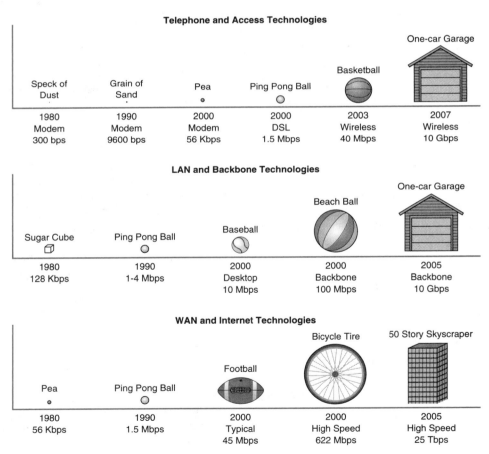

FIGURE 1-6 Relative capacities of telephone, local area network (LAN), backbone network (BN), wide area network (WAN), and Internet circuits. DSL = Digital Subscriber Line.

Between 1980 and 2000, LAN and Backbone technologies increased capacity from about 128 Kbps (a sugar cube per second) to 10 Mbps (a baseball) or 100 Mbps (a beach ball; see Figure 1-6). In only a few years, backbones routinely will be running at 10 Gbps, or the relative equivalent of a one-car garage per second.

The changes in WAN and Internet circuits has been even more dramatic (see Figure 1-6). From a typical size of 56 Kbps in 1980 to the 622 Mbps of a high-speed circuit in 2000, most experts now predict a high-speed WAN or Internet circuit will be able to carry 25 Tbps (25 terabits, or 25 trillion bits per second) in a few years—the relative equivalent of a skyscraper 50 stories tall and 50 stories wide. Our sources at IBM Research suggest that this may be conservative; they predict a capacity of 1 Pbps (1 petabit, or 1 quadrillion bits per second [1 million billion]), which is the equivalent of a skyscraper 300 stories tall and 300 stories wide in Figure 1-6. To put this in perspective in a different way, in the July 2000, the total size of the Internet was estimated to be 500 petabits (i.e., adding together every file on every computer in the world that was connected to the Internet). In other words, just *one* 1-Pbps circuit could download the entire contents of today's Internet in less than 10 minutes. Of course, no computer in the world today could store that much information—or even just 1 second's worth of the data transfer.

The term *broadband communication* has often been used to refer to these new high-speed communication circuits. *Broadband* is a technical term that refers to a specific type of data transmission that is used by one these circuits (i.e., DSL). However, its true technical meaning has become overwhelmed by its use in the popular press to refer to high-speed circuits in general. Therefore, we too, will use it to refer to circuits with data speeds of 1 Mbps or higher.

The initial costs of the technologies used for these broadband circuits will be very high, but competition will gradually drive down the cost. The challenge for businesses will be how to use them. When we have the capacity to transmit virtually all the data anywhere we want over a high-speed, low-cost circuit, how will we change the way businesses operate? Economists have long talked about the globalization of world economies. Data communications has made it a reality.

The Integration of Voice, Video, and Data

A second key trend is the integration of voice, video, and data communication, sometimes called *convergence*. In the past, the telecommunications systems used to transmit video signals (e.g., cable TV), voice signals (e.g., telephone calls), and data (e.g., computer data, e-mail) were completely separate. One network was used for data, one for voice, and one for cable TV.

This is rapidly changing. The integration of voice and data is largely complete in WANs. The IXCs, such as Sprint, provide telecommunication services that support data and voice transmission over the same circuits, even intermixing voice and data on the same physical cable. Sprint's ION service, for example, combines voice and data into one network—one that treats local calls and long-distance calls the same.

The integration of voice and data has been much slower in LANs and local telephone services. Some companies have successfully integrated both on the same network, but some still lay two separate cable networks into offices, one for voice and one for computer access.

TECHNICAL FOCUS

A CITYWIDE CONVERGENCE PROJECT

The city of Oceanside, California, had two separate networks, one for data and one for voice (i.e., telephone calls) for its 3 main office buildings and 33 smaller offices. The city now has one integrated voice and data network connecting all locations.

The integrated network is broken into three logical groups for security and redundancy, so if one part of the network fails, network traffic can roll over onto one of the two remaining groups. Each of the three network groups has a network server that is connected to the users' computers via a local area network (LAN) designed to support both data and voice traffic (using asynchronous transfer mode (ATM); see Chapter 8). Each user's phone plugs either into his or her computer or into a wall jack that runs to a 24-telephone-line phone hub that is connected into the LAN. The user's computer (or the phone hub) converts the voice phone call into computer data that travels through

the LAN and out on a backbone network (BN) to other city offices or to the phone company, where it is processed in the same manner as a traditional phone call. The network also enables video from over 140 video cameras in the police station's holding cells, parking lots, beaches, busy intersections, and so on to be easily shared.

City employees are given inexpensive traditional phones or can use headsets and screen phones on their computer. The real only change for them was having to get used to accessing PBX-style (private branch exchange–style) phone features, such as conference calling and call transfers, through their computers. And interestingly enough, the cost of the single integrated network was less than the two separate traditional networks.

SOURCE: "A Citywide Convergence Project," *Network Magazine,* February 18, 2000.

The integration of video into computer networks has been much slower, partly because of past legal restrictions and partly because of the immense communications needs of video. However, this integration is now moving quickly, owing to inexpensive video technologies. CNN, in conjunction with Intel, now offers its CNN and *Headline News* broadcasts digitally. Subscribers to this service receive the regular TV broadcasts in a format that can be transmitted over LANs. This way, users can receive the same audio and video TV images in a window on their computer.

New Information Services

A third key trend is the provision of new information services on these rapidly expanding networks. In the same way that the construction of the American interstate highway system spawned new businesses, so will the construction of worldwide integrated communications networks. The *Web* has changed the nature of computing so that now, anyone with a computer can be a publisher. You can find information on virtually anything on the Web. The problem becomes one of assessing the accuracy and value of information. In the future, we can expect information services to appear that help ensure the quality of the information they contain. Never before in the history of the human race has so much knowledge and information been available to ordinary citizens. The challenge we face as individuals and organizations is assimilating this information and using it effectively.

Today, many companies are beginning to use *application service providers (ASPs)* rather than developing their own computer systems. An ASP develops a specific system (e.g., an airline reservation system, a payroll system), and companies purchase the service, without ever installing the system on their own computers. They simply use the service, the

MANAGEMENT FOCUS *1-4*

KEEPING UP WITH TECHNOLOGY

The data communications and networking arena changes rapidly. Significant new technologies are introduced and new concepts are developed almost every year. It is therefore important for network managers to keep up with these changes.

There are at least three useful ways to keep up with change. First and foremost for users of this book is the Web site for this book, which contains updates to the book, additional sections, teaching materials, and links to useful Web sites.

Second, there are literally hundreds of thousands of Web sites with data communications and networking information. Search engines can help you find them. A good initial starting point is the telecom glossary at www.its.bldrdoc. gov/projects/telecomglossary2000.

Third, there are many useful magazines that discuss computer technology in general and networking technology in particular, including *Network Computing, Data Communications, InfoWorld, InfoWeek,* and *CIO Magazine.*

---

same way you might use a Web hosting service to publish your own Web pages rather than attempting to purchase and operate your own Web server. Some experts are predicting that by 2010, ASPs will have evolved into *information utilities.* An information utility is a company that provides a wide range of standardized information services, the same way that electric utilities today provide electricity or telephone utilities provide telephone service. Companies would simply purchase most of their information services (e.g., e-mail, Web, accounting, payroll, logistics) from these information utilities rather than attempting to develop their systems and operate their own servers.

SUMMARY

Introduction   The information society, where information and intelligence are the key drivers of personal, business, and national success, has arrived. Data communications is the principal enabler of the rapid information exchange and will become more important than the use of computers themselves in the future. Successful users of data communications, such as Wal-Mart, can gain significant competitive advantage in the marketplace.

Network Definitions   A local area network (LAN) is a group of microcomputers or terminals located in the same general area. A backbone network (BN) is a large central network that connects almost everything on a single company site. A metropolitan area network (MAN) encompasses a city or county area. A wide area network (WAN) spans city, state, or national boundaries.

Network Model   Communication networks are often broken into a series of layers, each of which can be defined separately, to enable vendors to develop software and hardware that can work together in the overall network. In this book, we use a five-layer model. The application layer is the application software used by the network user. The transport layer takes the message generated by the application layer and, if necessary, breaks it into several smaller messages. The network layer addresses the message and determines its route through the network. The data link layer formats the message to indicate where it starts and ends, decides when to transmit it over the physical media, and detects and corrects any errors that occur in transmission. The physical layer is the physical connection between the sender and receiver, including the hardware devices (e.g., computers, terminals, and modems) and physical media (e.g., cables and satellites).

Standards Standards ensure that hardware and software produced by different vendors can work together. A formal standard is developed by an official industry or government body. De facto standards are those that emerge in the marketplace and are supported by several vendors but have no official standing. Many different standards and standards-making organizations exist.

Future Trends Pervasive networking will change how and where we work and with whom we do business. As the capacity of networks increases dramatically, new ways of doing business will emerge. The integration of voice, video, and data onto the same networks will greatly simplify networks and enable anyone to access any media at any point. The rise in these pervasive, integrated networks will mean a significant increase the availability of information and new information services such as application service providers (ASPs) and information utilities.

KEY TERMS

American National Standards Institute (ANSI)
application layer
application service provider (ASP)
AT&T
backbone network (BN)
bps
broadband communications
CA*net
circuit
client
common carrier
convergence
data link layer
extranet
Federal Communications Commission (FCC)

file server
Gbps
host computer
information utility
Institute of Electrical and Electronics Engineers (IEEE)
Interexchange carrier (IXC)
International Telecommunications Union—Telecommunications Group (ITU-T)
Internet Engineering Task Force (IETF)
Internet model
Internet service provider (ISP)
intranet

Kbps
layers
local area network (LAN)
local exchange carrier (LEC)
Mbps
metropolitan area network (MAN)
monopoly
network layer
Open Systems Interconnection Reference Model (OSI model)
Pbps
peer-to-peer network
physical layer
print server
protocol

protocol stack
regional Bell operating company (RBOC)
server
standards
Tbps
Web server
wide area network (WAN)

QUESTIONS

1. How can data communications networks affect businesses?
2. Discuss three important applications of data communications networks in business and personal use.
3. Define *information lag* and discuss its importance.
4. Describe the progression of communications systems from the 1800s to the present.
5. Describe the progression of information systems from the 1950s to the present.
6. Describe the progression of the Internet from the 1960s to the present.

7. How do local area networks (LANs) differ from metropolitan area networks (MANs), wide area networks (WANs), and backbone networks (BNs)?
8. What is a circuit?
9. What is a client?
10. What is a host or server?
11. Why are network layers important?
12. Describe the seven layers in the OSI network model and what they do.
13. Describe the five layers in the Internet network model and what they do.

14. Explain how a message is transmitted from one computer to another using layers.

15. Describe the three stages of standardization.

16. How are Internet standards developed?

17. Describe two important data communications standards–making bodies. How do they differ?

18. What is the purpose of a data communications standard?

19. What are three of the largest interexchange carriers (IXCs) in North America?

20. Name two regional Bell operating companies (RBOCs). Which one(s) provide services in your area?

21. Discuss three trends in communications and networking.

22. Why has the Internet model replaced the Open Systems Interconnection Reference (OSI) Model?

23. In the 1980s when we wrote the first edition of this book, there were many, many more protocols in common use at the data link, network, and transport layers than there are today. Why do you think the number of commonly used protocols at these layers has declined? Do you think this trend will continue? What are the implications for those who design and operate networks?

24. The number of standardized protocols in use at the application layer has significantly increased since the 1980s. Why? Do you think this trend will continue? What are the implications for those who design and operate networks?

EXERCISES

1-1 Investigate the long-distance carriers (interexchange Carriers [IXCs]) and local exchange carriers (LECs) in your area. What services do they provide and what pricing plans do they have for residential users?

1-2 Discuss the issue of communications monopolies and open competition with an economics instructor and relate his or her comments to your data communication class.

1-3 Find a college or university offering a specialized degree in telecommunications or data communications and describe the program.

1-4 Describe a recent data communication development you have read about in a newspaper or magazine and how it may affect businesses.

1-5 Investigate the networks in your school or organization. Describe the important local area networks (LANs) and backbone networks (BNs) in use (but do not describe the specific clients, servers, or devices on them).

1-6 Use the Web to search the Internet Engineering Task (IETF) Web site (www.ietf.org). Describe one standard that is in the request for comment (RFC) stage.

1-7 Discuss how the revolution/evolution of communications and networking is likely to affect how you will work and live in the future.

MINI-CASES

I. Big E. Bank

Nancy Smith is the director of network infrastructure for Big E. Bank (BEB). BEB has just purchased Ohio Bank (OB), a small regional bank that has 30 branches spread over Ohio. OB has a WAN connecting five cities, in which it has branches, to OB's main headquarters in Columbus. It has a series of MANs in those cities, which in turn connect to the LANs in each of the branches. The OB network is adequate but uses very different data link, network, and transport protocols than those used by BEB's network. Smith's task is to connect OB's network with BEB's network. She has several alternatives. Alternative A is to leave the two networks separate but install a few devices in OB's headquarters to translate between the set of protocols used in BEB network and those in the OB network so that messages can flow between the two networks. Alternative B is to replace all the WAN, MAN, and LAN network components in OB's entire network so that OB uses the same protocols as BEB and the two can freely communicate. Alternative C is to replace the devices in OB's WAN (and possibly the MANs) so that each city (or each branch, if the MANs are replaced as well) can communicate with the BEB network but leave the LANs in individual branches unchanged. In this case, the device connecting the MAN (or the branch) will translate between the OB protocols and the BEB protocols. Your job is to develop a short list of pros and cons for each alternative and make a recommendation.

II. Global Consultants

John Adams is the chief information officer (CIO) of Global Consultants (GC), a very large consulting firm with offices in more than 100 countries around the world. GC is about to purchase a set of several Internet-based financial software packages that will be installed in all of their offices. There are no standards at the application layer for financial software, but several software companies that sell financial software (call them group A) use one de facto standard to enable their software to work with one another's software. However, another group of financial software companies (call them group B) use a different de facto standard. Although both groups have software packages that GC could use, GC would really prefer to buy one package from group A for one type of financial analysis and one package from group B for a different type of financial analysis. The problem, of course, is that then the two packages cannot communicate and GC's staff would end up having to type the same data into both packages. The alternative is to buy two packages from the same group—so that data could be easily shared—but that would mean having to settle for second best for one of the packages. Although there have been some reports in the press about the two groups of companies working together to develop one common standard that will enable all software to work together, there is no firm agreement yet. What advice would you give Adams?

CASE STUDY

NEXT-DAY AIR SERVICE

This is the beginning of a cumulative case study about a fictitious firm we call Next-Day Air Service (NDAS). The case study begins here in Chapter 1 and continues throughout the rest of the book. It requires you to complete tasks that are related to topics covered in each corresponding chapter of the text. The end of each chapter contains the case narrative, related figures, and a set of questions and problems. These do not have one unique solution. There are too many alternatives when dealing with LANs, WANs, MANs, BNs, and the Internet, so a real-life network design and development problem can have several workable answers.

As with any real-life problem with ambiguities or unresolved considerations, you must make your own assumptions. Feel free to read ahead or use the index to find related subjects that support your recommendations. Your instructor may provide additional guidelines regarding report formats, Web and library resources, key assumptions, and the like for the various questions and problems presented in this case study. Be sure to provide adequate justification for any recommendations you make.

(NDAS) was founded in 1985 to compete in the expanding market for overnight package deliveries. NDAS provides local pickup and delivery of these parcels and other small freight items. The founders initially restricted their efforts to the rapidly growing central Florida region.

To support its operation, NDAS purchased a facility near the Tampa International Airport. This facility consisted of a main building and a secondary building for dispatch and fleet maintenance. Because NDAS intended to expand its services throughout the southeastern United States, this facility also served as NDAS's corporate headquarters.

Between 1985 and 1992, NDAS experienced very rapid growth. As business volume increased and the company's reputation became firmly established, expansion of the facility became imperative. Consequently, NDAS purchased land adjacent to its corporate headquarters so it would have room to relocate both the maintenance shop and the company's vehicle parking lot. In addition, NDAS tripled the size of its building to accommodate its growing business. Finally, in 1994, NDAS completed the expansion of the office building to house its corporate operations.

As its business volume increased, NDAS realized it had to develop branch offices throughout its service region to continue growing. In addition to the corporate offices in Tampa, NDAS also purchased or leased facilities in several other southeastern cities, including Orlando, Miami, Atlanta, New Orleans, Dallas, and Memphis. Figure 1-7 is the NDAS map of operations.

NDAS also contracted with Chicago-based firm Overnight Delivery, Inc. (ODI) to provide overnight shipping service between Atlanta and the greater Chicago area. NDAS also entered into similar agreements with other air carriers. The purpose of these agreements was to enable NDAS to provide service throughout the United States.

As Figure 1-7 shows, connecting routes established with other carriers lead from Memphis to St. Louis and from Atlanta to Chicago and Washington, D.C. These routes allow NDAS to deliver parcels to the northeastern states and the Midwest. There are flight links out of Dallas to both Denver and Los Angeles. These two routes have been added recently to provide delivery service to the northwestern states and the West Coast, respectively. After extending its flight routes, NDAS added agents in the cities of Jacksonville, Florida; Montgomery, Alabama; Jackson, Mississippi; and Houston. To date, this is the scope of NDAS's parcel delivery operation.

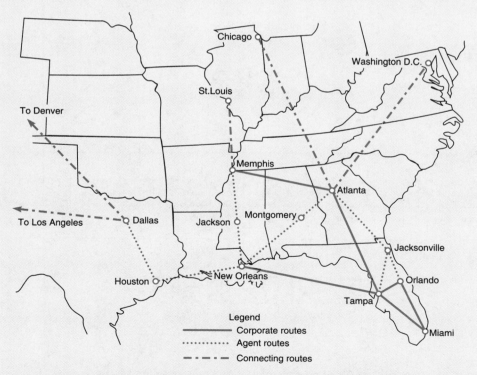

FIGURE 1-7   Next-Day Air Service map of operations.

Initially, NDAS contracted a computing services company to handle billing. As the computing power of small computers increased, however, NDAS purchased a minicomputer and took responsibility for its own data processing. The Payroll Department now runs the payroll twice monthly on this computer. Employees submit their time cards and supporting documents on the first and third Mondays of the month. The Payroll Department then prepares the paychecks for both hourly and salaried employees. The paychecks are sent via overnight delivery on the following Thursdays.

Although the Information Services/Data Processing Division, under Les Coone as acting manager, performs all data entry, processing, and check printing, John Lawson in Accounts Payable is the person who generates, reviews, and approves the reports and totals. Because so many new employees have been added at both the corporate and branch offices, a new full-time position has been added in Accounts Payable to handle the payroll and assist Lawson. The subject of paying employees weekly has been discussed as well. Figure 1-8 shows the NDAS organization chart.

The branch offices currently batch all billing data by order date and send them daily by overnight delivery to the corporate office along with other interoffice correspondence. When Information Services/Data Processing receives the packages, it enters the batches and processes them daily. The billing processing normally takes place from 48 to 96 hours after freight and parcel delivery. Once this processing has been completed, the database supports the resolution of any questions or problems associated with the billings.

Because of an increasing volume of paperwork brought about by continued business expansion, the varying complexity of the billing process, and the preferred rates being given by competitors, NDAS's corporate man-

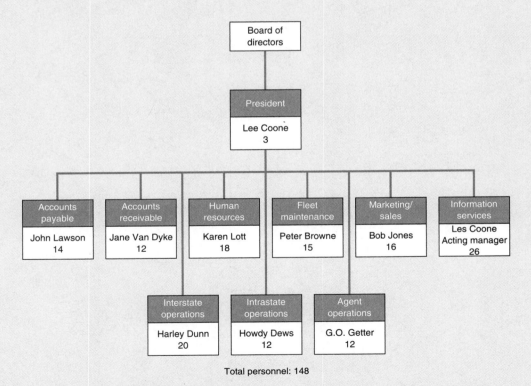

FIGURE 1-8 Next-Day Air Service organization chart showing key personnel and number of staff per area.

agement has decided to automate the billing process throughout its Florida offices. This is the first step in a series of strategic moves planned to provide online transaction processing and real-time customer information through the Internet. Management expects online transaction processing to speed the billing process and improve receivables collection time significantly. The online query system will enable agents at remote offices to obtain information such as credit status, correct delivery address, and package delivery status. The Internet component will enable customers to obtain the delivery status of packages they have sent or are expecting to receive.

The status of automation varies greatly among the various departments. The Marketing and Sales Division, headed by Bob Jones, has a computer for each account representative. All of these computers are connected to a small LAN that serves only Sales and Marketing.

The Accounts Receivable Division, headed by Jane Van Dyke, is responsible for all billing and collection activities. It recently replaced its aging minicomputer with a powerful microcomputer server. This new server provides databases for both customer billing and bad debts.

The Accounts Payable Division, led by John Lawson, maintains its own vendor database that is stored on an older minicomputer server. This database also contains the other service carriers' billings, such as those from ODI to NDAS. This division also is responsible for the payroll. It is in the process of downsizing to a powerful modern desktop computer.

The Fleet Maintenance Division has no computer capability. Its management has chosen to trace all necessary information manually. Peter Browne, the maintenance supervisor, prefers this mode of operation and has steadfastly refused to automate his division's recordkeeping processes.

Dispatch, which is part of the Fleet Maintenance Division, also processes its work manually. Dispatch currently bundles incoming packages twice daily, according to their major destination point, for overnight delivery. The bundles of packages are marked with the following information:

- DEST: City, state
- DATE: Current date
- TIME: Time package left dispatch
- NPKG: Number of individual packages in the bundle
- INIT: Initials of the person preparing the bundle

When the bundles arrive at their respective delivery points, the off-loaders mark the arrival time on the bundles' tags, write their own initials on the back of the tags, and return the tags to corporate headquarters. The packages are then delivered.

The various remote offices currently communicate with the corporate headquarters and with one another by voice mail, telephone, fax, mail, or interoffice mail, sent on company aircraft along with the daily batched transactions. There are desktop computers in each of the remote offices. However, some of the offices have Apple Macintosh computers and others use Intel-based systems. A number of managers have laptop computers, which, again, come from various computer manufacturers.

NDAS corporate management realizes that these various stages of computer support are a far cry from an integrated system. It sees the necessity for standardizing and streamlining systems, equipment, and procedures before any serious networking can be accomplished. Moreover, corporate management has stated that NDAS must enter the international package delivery market to offer full service to its major customers. Any growth plans must be able to support international operations. Management also expects that e-mail and automated package tracking will be part of the new system. In addition, management expects any system to allow for expansion into other information technology areas of networking, such as videoconferencing and use of the Internet.

As its first step in this direction, NDAS has decided to hire a new systems analyst, who will work full time to assess the current level of information system support, determine which functions should be automated, recommend the type of hardware and software systems to be installed, recommend appropriate organizational changes (if any), and, most important, determine the type of data communications support that will be required to meet the needs of NDAS's current operations and future growth.

You have been offered this position. Your experience is in information systems. Because you see the job as a remarkable opportunity to learn and grow, you accept the post. You report directly to Lee Coone, president of NDAS, and are expected to prepare your solution immediately.

Exercises

1. Briefly describe the current state of NDAS's office automation, system integration, and networking. Begin by explaining how each department uses information technology, what hardware it uses, and what functions currently are automated. Also assess which department is most in need of a network.

2. In view of the types of networks and future technologies discussed in this chapter, what kind of network would appear to be the most beneficial to NDAS? Justify your answer.

3. What are the current characteristics or practices that identify NDAS as a possible candidate for its proposed integrated data communication network?

4. Which two of the four network types (e.g., LAN) might be appropriate for NDAS?

5. When looking over the company's organization chart, you notice that the acting manager of the Information Services/Data Processing Division is also named Coone (Les Coone). Inquiring, you learn that Les is President Coone's nephew. Les has just joined NDAS. This is his first job, and he has no background in information systems, data processing, or data communications. Will this be a problem for you? If so, why? How will you handle it?

PART 2

FUNDAMENTALS

CHAPTER 2

APPLICATION LAYER

THE **APPLICATION** layer (also called layer 5) is the software that enables the user to perform useful work. The software at the application layer is the reason for having the network because it is this software that provides the business value. This chapter examines the three fundamental types of application architectures used at the application layer (host-based, client-based, client-server). It then looks at the Internet and the primary software application packages it enables: the Web, e-mail, Telnet, FTP, and Instant Messaging.

OBJECTIVES

- Understand host-based, client-based, and client-server application architectures
- Understand how the Web works
- Understand how e-mail works
- Be aware of how FTP, Telnet and instant messaging works

CHAPTER OUTLINE

INTRODUCTION

APPLICATION ARCHITECTURES

    Host-Based Architectures

    Client-Based Architectures

    Client–Server Architectures

    Choosing Architectures

INTRODUCTION

Network applications are the software packages that run in the application layer. You should be quite familiar with many types of network software, because it is these application packages that you use when you use the network. In many respects, the only reason for having a network is to enable these applications.

In this chapter, we will first discuss three basic architectures for network applications and how each those architectures affects the design of networks. Because you probably have a good understanding of applications such as the Web and word processing, we will use those as examples of different application architectures. We will then examine several common applications used on the Internet (e.g., Web, e-mail) and use those to explain how application software interacts with the networks. By the end of this chapter, you should have much better understanding of the application layer in the network model and what exactly we meant when we used the term *packet* in Chapter 1.

APPLICATION ARCHITECTURES

In Chapter 1, we discussed how the three basic components of a network (client computer, server computer, and circuit) worked together. In this section, we will get a bit more specific about how the client computer and the server computer can work together to provide application software to the users. A *application architecture* is the way in which the

TECHNICAL FOCUS *2-1*

CLIENTS AND SERVERS

There are many different types of clients and servers that can be part of a network, and the distinctions between them have become a bit more complex over time. Generally speaking, there are four types of computers that are commonly used as servers:

- A *mainframe* is a very large general-purpose computer (usually costing millions of dollars) that is capable of performing *very* many simultaneous functions, supporting *very* many simultaneous users, and storing *huge* amounts of data.

- A *minicomputer* is a large general-purpose computer (usually costing hundreds of thousands of dollars) that is capable of performing many simultaneous functions, supporting many simultaneous users, and storing large amounts of data. Minicomputers are sometimes used as database servers in client–server networks.

- A *microcomputer* is the type of computer you use. Microcomputers used as servers can range from a small microcomputer, similar to a desktop one you might use, to one costing $50,000 or more.

- A *cluster* is a group of computers (often microcomputers or workstations) linked together so that they act as one computer. Requests arrive at the cluster (e.g., Web requests) and are distributed among the computers so that no one computer is overloaded. Each computer is separate, so that if one fails, the cluster simply bypasses it. Clusters are more complex than single servers because work must be quickly coordinated and shared among the individual computers. Clusters are very scalable because one can always add one more computer to the cluster.

There are five commonly used types of clients:

- A *microcomputer* is the most common type of client today.

- A *terminal* is a device with a monitor and keyboard but no central processing unit (CPU). *Dumb terminals,* so named because they do not participate in the processing of the data they display, have the bare minimum required to operate as input and output devices (a TV screen and a keyboard). In most cases when a character is typed on a dumb terminal, it transmits the character through the circuit to the server for processing. Every keystroke is processed by the server, even simple activities such as the up arrow. *Intelligent terminals* were developed to reduce the processing demands on the server and have some small internal memory and a built-in, programmable microprocessor chip. Many simple functions, such as moving the cursor or displaying words in different colors, are done by the terminal, thus saving processing time on the server.

- A *workstation* is more powerful microcomputer designed for use in technical applications such as mathematical modeling, computer-assisted design (CAD), and intensive programming. As microcomputers become more powerful, the difference between a microcomputer and a workstation is blurring.

- A *network computer* is a designed primarily to communicate using Internet-based standards (e.g., HTTP, Java) but has no hard disk. It has only limited functionality.

- A *transaction terminal* is designed to support a specific business transactions, such as the automated teller machines (ATM) used by banks. Other examples of transaction terminals are point-of-sale terminals in a supermarket.

functions of the application layer software are spread among the clients and servers in the network.

The work done by any application program can be divided into four general functions. The first is *data storage.* Most application programs require data to be stored and retrieved, whether it is a small file such as a memo produced by a word processor or a large database such as an organization's accounting records. The second function is *data access logic,* the processing required to access data, which often means database queries in SQL (structured query language). The third function is the *application logic,* (sometimes called business logic) which also can be simple or complex, depending on the application. The fourth function is the *presentation logic,* the presentation of information to the user and the acceptance of the user's commands. These four functions, *data storage, data access logic, application logic,* and *presentation logic,* are the basic building blocks of any application.

There are many ways in which these four functions can be allocated between the client computers and the servers in a network. There are three fundamental application architectures in use today. In *host-based networks,* the server (or host computer) performs virtually all of the work. In *client-based networks,* the client computers perform most of the work. In *client–server networks,* the work is shared between the servers and clients. The client–server architecture is becoming the dominant application architecture.

Host-Based Architectures

The very first data communications networks developed in the 1960s were host-based, with the server (usually a large mainframe computer) performing all four functions. The clients (usually terminals) enabled users to send and receive messages to and from the host computer. The clients merely captured keystrokes, sent them to the server for processing, and accepted instructions from the server on what to display (Figure 2-1).

This very simple architecture often works very well. Application software is developed and stored on the one server along with all data. If you've ever used a terminal (or a microcomputer with Telnet software), you've used a host-based application. There is one point of control, because all messages flow through the one central server. In theory, there are economies of scale, because all computer resources are centralized (but more on cost later).

There are two fundamental problems with host-based networks. First, the server must process all messages. As the demands for more and more network applications grow, many servers become overloaded and unable to quickly process all the users' demands. Prioritizing users' access becomes difficult. Response time becomes slower, and network managers are required to spend increasingly more money to upgrade the server. Unfortunately, upgrades to the mainframes that usually are the servers in this architecture are "lumpy." That is, upgrades come in large increments and are expensive (e.g., $500,000); it is difficult to upgrade "a little."

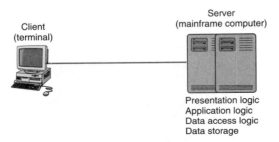

Presentation logic
Application logic
Data access logic
Data storage

FIGURE 2-1 Host-based architecture.

Client-Based Architectures

In the late 1980s, there was an explosion in the use of microcomputers and microcomputer-based LANs. Today, more than 90 percent of most organizations' total computer processing power now resides on microcomputer-based LANs, not in centralized mainframe computers. Part of this expansion was fueled by a number of low-cost, highly popular applications such as word processors, spreadsheets, and presentation graphics programs. It was also fueled in part by managers' frustrations with application software on host mainframe computers. Most mainframe software is not as easy to use as microcomputer software, is far more expensive, and can take years to develop. In the late 1980s, many large organizations had application development backlogs of 2 to 3 years; that is, getting any new mainframe application program written would take years. New York City, for example, had a 6-year backlog. In contrast, managers could buy microcomputer packages or develop microcomputer-based applications in a few months.

With client-based architectures, the clients are microcomputers on a LAN, and the server is usually another microcomputer on the same network. The application software on the client computers is responsible for the presentation logic, the application logic, and the data access logic; the server simply stores the data (Figure 2-2).

This simple architecture often works very well. If you've ever used a word processor and stored your document file on a server (or written a program in Visual Basic or C that runs on your computer but stores data on a server), you've used a client-based architecture.

The fundamental problem in client-based networks is that all data on the server must travel to the client for processing. For example, suppose the user wishes to display a list of all employees with company life insurance. All the data in the database (or all the indices) must travel from the server where the database is stored over the network circuit to the client, which then examines each record to see if it matches the data requested by the user. This can overload the network circuits because far more data is transmitted from the server to the client than the client actually needs.

Client–Server Architectures

Most organizations today are moving to client–server architectures. Client–server architectures attempt to balance the processing between the client and the server by having both do some of the logic. In these networks, the client is responsible for the presentation logic,

Client
(microcomputer)

Server
(microcomputer)

Presentation logic
Application logic
Data access logic

Data storage

FIGURE 2-2   Client-based architecture.

whereas the server is responsible for the data access logic and data storage. The application logic may either reside on the client, reside on the server, or be split between both.

Figure 2-3 shows the simplest case, with the presentation logic and application logic on the client and the data access logic and data storage on the server. In this case, the client software accepts user requests and performs the application logic that produces database requests that are transmitted to the server. The server software accepts the database requests, performs the data access logic, and transmits the results to the client. The client software accepts the results and presents them to the user. When you used a Web browser to get pages from a Web server, you used a client–server architecture. Likewise, if you've ever written a program that uses SQL to talk to a database on a server, you've used a client–server architecture.

For example, if the user requests a list of all employees with company life insurance, the client would accept the request, format it so that it could be understood by the server, and transmit it to the server. On receiving the request, the server searches the database for all requested records and then transmits only the matching records to the client, which would then present them to the user. The same would be true for database updates; the client accepts the request and sends it to the server. The server processes the update and responds (either accepting the update or explaining why not) to the client, which displays it to the user.

One of the strengths of client–server networks is that they enable software and hardware from different vendors to be used together. But this is also one of their disadvantages, because it can be difficult to get software from different vendors to work together. One solution to this problems is *middleware,* software that sits between the application software on the client and the application software on the server. Middleware does two things. First, it provides a standard way of communicating that can translate between software from different vendors. Many middleware tools began as translation utilities that enabled messages sent from a specific client tool to be translated into a form understood by a specific server tool.

The second function of middleware is to manages the message transfer from clients to servers (and vice versa) so that clients need not know the specific server that contains the application's data. The application software on the client sends all messages to the middleware, which forwards them to the correct server. The application software on the client is therefore protected from any changes in the physical network. If the network layout changes (e.g., a new server is added), only the middleware must be updated.

FIGURE 2-3 Two-tier client–server architecture.

TECHNICAL FOCUS *2-2*

A MONSTER CLIENT–SERVER ARCHITECTURE

Every spring, Monster.com, one of the largest job sites in the United States, with an average of more than 3 million visitors per month, experiences a large increase in traffic. Aaron Braham, vice president of operations, attributes the spike to college students who increase their job search activities as they approach graduation.

Monster.com has 150 Web servers and 30 database servers at its main site in Indianapolis and plans to move that to 400 over the next year by gradually growing the main site and adding a new site with servers in Maynard, Massachusetts, just in time for the spring rush. The main Web site has a set of load-balancing devices that forward Web requests to the different servers depending on how busy they are.

Braham says the major challenge is that 90 percent of the traffic is not simple requests for Web pages but rather search requests (e.g., what network jobs are available in New Mexico), which require more processing and access to the database servers. Monster.com has more than 350,000 job postings and more than 3 million résumés on file, spread across its database servers. Several copies of each posting and résumé are kept on several database servers to improve access speed and provide redundancy in case a server crashes, so just keeping the database servers in sync so that they contain correct data is a challenge.

SOURCE: "Resume Influx Tests Mettle of Job Sites' Scalability," *Internetweek,* May 29, 2000.

There are literally dozens of standards for middleware, each of which is supported by different vendors and each of which provides different functions. Two of the most important standards are Distributed Computing Environment (DCE) and Common Object Request Broker Architecture (CORBA). Both of these standards cover virtually all aspects of the client–server architecture but are quite different. Any client or server software that conforms to one of these standards can communicate with any other software that conforms to the same standard. Another important standard is Open Database Connectivity (ODBC), which provides a standard for data access logic.

Two-Tier, Three-Tier, and n-Tier Architectures   There are many ways in which the application logic can be partitioned between the client and the server. The example in Figure 2-3 is one of the most common. In this case, the server is responsible for the data and the client, the application and presentation. This is called a *two-tier architecture,* because it uses only two sets of computers, one set of clients and one set of servers.

A *three-tier architecture* uses three sets of computers, as shown in Figure 2-4. In this case, the software on the client computer is responsible for presentation logic, an application server is responsible for the application logic, and a separate database server is responsible for the data access logic and data storage.

An *n-tier architecture* uses more than three sets of computers. In this case, the client is responsible for presentation, a database server is responsible for the data access logic and data storage, and the application logic is spread across two or more different sets of servers. Figure 2-5 shows an example of an *n*-tier architecture of a groupware product called TCBWorks developed at the University of Georgia. TCBWorks has four major components. The first is the Web browser on the client computer that a user uses to access the system and enter commands (presentation logic). The second component is a Web server that responds to the user's requests, either by providing HTML pages and graphics (application logic) or

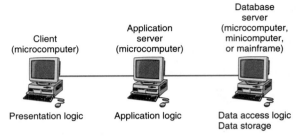

FIGURE 2-4   Three-tier client–server architecture.

by sending the request to the third component, a set of 28 C programs that perform various functions such as adding comments or voting (application logic). The fourth component is a database server that stores all the data (data access logic and data storage). Each of these four components is separate, making it easy to spread the different components on different servers and to partition the application logic on two different servers.

The primary advantage of an *n*-tier client–server architecture compared with a two-tier architecture (or a three-tier with a two-tier) is that it separates out the processing that occurs to better balance the load on the different servers; it is more scalable. In Figure 2-5, we have three separate servers, which provides more power than if we had used a two-tier architecture with only one server. If we discover that the application server is too heavily loaded, we can simply replace it with a more powerful server, or even put in two application servers. Conversely, if we discover the database server is underused, we could put data from another application on it.

There are two primary disadvantages to an *n*-tier architecture compared with a two-tier architecture (or a three-tier with a two-tier). First, it puts a greater load on the network.

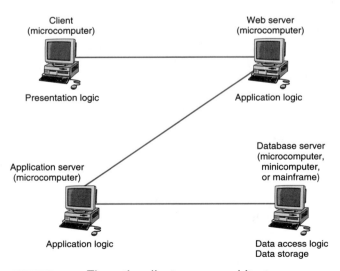

FIGURE 2-5   The *n*-tier client–server architecture.

If you compare Figures 2-3, 2-4, and 2-5, you will see that the *n*-tier model requires more communication among the servers; it generates more network traffic so you need a higher capacity network. Second, it is much more difficult to program and test software in *n*-tier architectures than in two-tier architectures because more devices have to communicate to complete a user's transaction.

Thin Clients versus Fat Clients   Another way of classifying client–server architectures is by examining how much of the application logic is placed on the client computer. A *thin-client* approach places little or no application logic on the client (e.g., Figure 2-5), whereas a *fat-client* (also called *thick-client*) approach places all or almost all of the application logic on the client (e.g., Figure 2-3). There is no direct relationship between thin and fat client and two-, three- and *n*-tier architectures. For example, Figure 2-6 shows a typical Web architecture: a two-tier architecture with a thin client. One of the biggest forces favoring thin clients is the Web.

Thin clients are much easier to manage. If an application changes, only the server with the application logic needs to be updated. With a fat client, the software on all of the clients would need to be updated. Conceptually, this is a simple task; one simply copies the new files to the hundreds of affected client computers. In practice, in can be a very difficult task.

Thin-client architectures are the wave of the future. More and more application systems are being written to use a Web browser as the client software, with Java applets (containing some of the application logic) downloaded as needed. This application architecture is sometimes called the *distributed computing model*.

Choosing Architectures

Each of the preceding architectures has certain costs and benefits, so how do you choose the "right" architecture? In many cases, the architecture is simply a given; the organization has a certain architecture, and one simply has to use it. In other cases, the organization is acquiring new equipment and writing new software and has the opportunity to develop a new architecture, at least in some part of the organization. There are at least three major sets of factors to consider (Figure 2-7).

Client
(microcomputer)

Web server
(microcomputer,
minicomputer,
or mainframe)

Presentation logic

Application logic
Data access logic
Data storage

FIGURE 2-6   The typical two-tier thin-client architecture of the Web.

	Host-Based	**Client-Based**	**Client–Server**
Cost of infrastructure	High	Medium	Low
Cost of development	Low	Medium	High
Scalability	Low	Medium	High

FIGURE 2-7   Factors involved in choosing architectures.

Cost of Infrastructure   One of the strongest forces driving companies toward client–server architectures is cost of infrastructure (the hardware, software, and networks that will support the application system). Simply put, personal computers are more than 1,000 times cheaper than mainframes for the same amount of computing power. The microcomputers on our desks today have more processing power, memory, and hard disk space than a mainframe of the early 1990s, and the cost of the microcomputers is a fraction of the cost of the mainframe. Therefore, the cost of client–server architectures is lower than that of server-based architectures, which rely on mainframes. Client–server architectures also tend to be cheaper than client-based architectures because they place less of a load on networks and thus require less network capacity.

Cost of Development   The cost of developing systems is an important factor when considering the financial benefits of client–server architectures. Developing application software for fat client–server architectures is extremely complex, and most experts believe that it costs two to three times more to develop and maintain application software for client–server architectures than it does for server-based architectures. Costs for thin-client server architectures may be less, although the tools are rather immature at this point. Developing application software for client-based architectures is usually cheaper still, because there are many graphical user interface (GUI) development tools for simple stand-alone computers that communicate with database servers (e.g., Visual Basic, Access). The cost differential may change as more companies gain experience with client–server applications, as new client–server products are developed and refined, and as client–server standards mature. However, given the inherent complexity of client–server software and the need to coordinate the interactions of software on different computers, there is likely to remain a cost difference.

Even updating the network with a new version of the software is more complicated, too. In a host-based network, there is one place in which application software is stored; to update the software, you simply replace it there. With client–server networks, you must update all clients and all servers. For example, suppose you want to add a new server and move some existing applications from the old server to the new one. All application software on all fat clients that send messages to the application on the old server must now be changed to send to the new server. Although this is not conceptually difficult, it can be an administrative nightmare.

Scalability   *Scalability* refers to the ability to increase or decrease the capacity of the computing infrastructure in response to changing capacity needs. The most scalable architecture is client–server computing because servers can be added to (or removed from) the architecture when processing needs change. For example, in a four-tier client–server architecture, one might have 10 web servers, 4 application servers, and 3 database servers. If the application servers begin to get overloaded, it is simple to add another 2 or 3 application servers.

Also, the types of hardware that are used in client–server settings (e.g., minicomputers) typically can be upgraded at a pace that most closely matches the growth of the application. In contrast, host-based architectures rely primarily on mainframe hardware that needs to be scaled up in large, expensive increments, and client-based architectures have ceilings above which the application cannot grow because increases in use and data can result in increased network traffic to the extent that performance is unacceptable.

WORLD WIDE WEB

The Web was first conceived in 1989 by Tim Berners-Lee at the European Particle Physics Laboratory (CERN) in Geneva. His original idea was to develop a database of information on physics research, but he found it difficult to fit the information into a traditional database. Instead, he decided to use a *hypertext* network of information. With hypertext, any document can contain a link to any other document.

CERN's first Web browser was created in 1990, but it was 1991 before it was available on the Internet for other organizations to use. By the end of 1992, several browsers had been created for UNIX computers by CERN and several other European and American universities, and there were about 30 Web servers in the entire world. In 1993, Marc Andreessen, a student at the University of Illinois, led a team of students that wrote Mosaic, the first graphical Web browser, as part of a project for the university's National Center for Supercomputing Applications (NCSA). By the end of 1993, the Mosaic browser was available for UNIX, Windows, and Macintosh computers, and there were about 200 Web servers in the world. In 1994, Andreessen and some colleagues left NCSA to form Netscape, and a half a dozen other startup companies introduced commercial Web browsers. Within a year, it had become clear that the Web had changed the face of computing forever. NCSA stopped development of the Mosaic browser in 1996, as Netscape and Microsoft began to invest millions to improve their browsers.

How the Web Works

The Web is a good example of a two-tier client–server architecture (Figure 2-8). Each client computer needs an application layer software package called a *Web browser.* There are many different browsers, such as Netscape Navigator and Microsoft's Internet Explorer. Each server on the network that will act as a Web server needs an application layer software package called a *Web server.* There are many different Web servers, such as those produced by Netscape, Microsoft, and Apache.

To get a page from the Web, the user must type the Internet *uniform resource locator (URL)* for the page he or she wants (e.g., www.yahoo.com) or click on a link that provides the URL. The URL specifies the Internet address of the *Web server* and the directory and name of the specific page wanted. If no directory and page are specified, the Web server will provide whatever page has been defined as the site's home page. If no server name is specified, the Web browser will presume the address is on the same server and directory as the page containing the URL.

For the requests from the Web browser to be understood by the Web server, they must use the same standard *protocol* or language. If there were no standard and each Web browser used a different protocol to request pages, then it would be impossible for a Netscape Web browser to communicate with a Microsoft Web server, for example.

The standard protocol for communication between a Web browser and a Web server is *Hypertext Transfer Protocol (HTTP).*[1] To get a page from a Web server, the web browser issues a special packet called an *HTTP request* that contains the URL and other information about the Web page requested (see Figure 2-8). Once the server receives the HTTP request, it processes it and sends back an *HTTP response,* which will be the requested page or an error message (see Figure 2-8).

This request–response dialogue occurs for every file transferred between the client and the server. For example, suppose the client requests a Web page that has two graphic images. Graphics are stored in separate files from the Web page itself using a different file format than the HTML used for the Web page (in JPEG [Joint Photographic Experts Group] format, for example). In this case, there would be three request–response pairs. First, the browser would issue a request for the Web page, and the server would send the response. Then, the browser would begin displaying the Web page and notice the two graphic files. The browser would then send a request for the first graphic and a request for the second graphic, and the server would reply with two separate HTTP responses, one for each request.

Inside an HTTP Request

The HTTP request and HTTP response are examples of the packets we introduced in Chapter 1 that are produced by the application layer and sent down to the transport, network, data link, and physical layers for transmission through the network. The HTTP response and HTTP request are simple text files that take the information provided by the application (e.g., the URL to get) and format it in a structured way so that the receiver of the message can clearly understand it.

An HTTP request from a Web browser to a Web server has three parts. The first two parts are required; the last is optional. The parts are

- The *request line,* which starts with a command (e.g., get), provides the URL and ends with the HTTP version number that the browser understands; the version

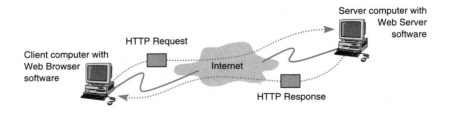

FIGURE 2-8   How the Web works.

---

[1]The formal specification for HTTP version 1.1 is provided in RFC 2616 on the IETF's Web site. The URL is www.ietf.org/rfc/rfc2616.txt.

number ensures that the Web server does not attempt to use a more advanced or newer version of the HTTP standard that the browser does not understand.

- The *request header,* which contains a variety of optional information such as the Web browser being used (e.g., Internet Explorer) and the date
- The *request body,* which contains information sent to the server, such as information that the user has typed into a form

Figure 2-9 shows an example of an HTTP request for a page on our Web server, formatted using version 1.1 of the HTTP standard. This request has only the request line and the request header, because no request body is needed for this request. This request includes the date and time of the request (expressed in Greenwich Mean Time [GMT], the time zone that runs through London) and name of the browser used (Mozilla is the code name for Netscape Navigator). The "Referrer" field means that the user obtained the URL for this web page by clicking on a link on another page, which in this case is a list of faculty at Indiana University (i.e., www.indiana.edu/~aisdept/faculty.htm). If the referrer field is blank, then it means the user typed the URL himself or herself. You can see inside HTTP headers yourself at www.rexswain.com/httpview.html.

Inside an HTTP Response

The format of an HTTP response from the server to the browser is very similar to the HTTP request. It, too, has three parts, with the first two required and the last optional:

- The *response status,* which contains the HTTP version number the server has used, a status code (e.g., *200* means "okay"; *404* means "not found"), and a reason phrase (a text description of the status code)
- The *response header,* which contains a variety of optional information, such as the Web server being used (e.g., Apache), the date, and the exact URL of the page in the response
- The *response body,* which is the Web page itself.

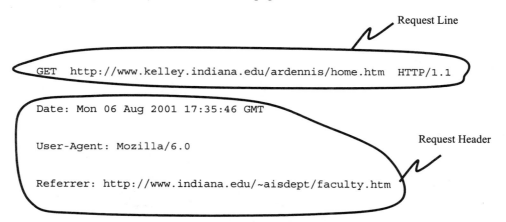

FIGURE 2-9   An example of a request from a Web browser to a Web server using the HTTP (Hypertext Transfer Protocol) standard.

Figure 2-10 shows an example of a response from our Web server to the request in Figure 2-9. This example has all three parts. The response status reports "okay," which means the requested URL was found and is included in the response body. The response header provides the date, the type of Web server software used, the actual URL included in the response body, and the type of file. In most cases, the actual URL and the requested URL are the same, but not always. For example, if you request an URL but do not specify a file name (e.g., www.indiana.edu), you will receive whatever file is defined as the home page for that server, so the actual URL will be different from the requested URL.

The response body in this example shows a Web page in *Hypertext Markup Language (HTML)*. The response body can be in any format, such as text, Microsoft Word,

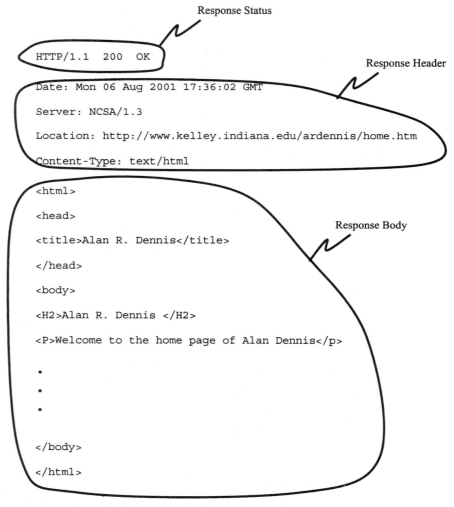

Response Status

```
HTTP/1.1   200   OK
```

Response Header

```
Date: Mon 06 Aug 2001 17:36:02 GMT

Server: NCSA/1.3

Location: http://www.kelley.indiana.edu/ardennis/home.htm

Content-Type: text/html
```

Response Body

```
<html>

<head>

<title>Alan R. Dennis</title>

</head>

<body>

<H2>Alan R. Dennis </H2>

<P>Welcome to the home page of Alan Dennis</p>

  •

  •

  •

</body>

</html>
```

FIGURE 2-10 An example of a response from a Web server to a Web browser using the HTTP standard.

MANAGEMENT FOCUS *2-1*

FREE SPEECH REIGNS ON THE INTERNET ... OR DOES IT?

In a landmark decision in 1997, the U.S. Supreme Court ruled that the sections of the 1996 Telecommunications Act restricting the publication of indecent material on the Web and the sending of indecent e-mail were unconstitutional. This means that anyone can do anything on the Internet, right?

Well, not really. The court decision affects only Internet servers located in the United States. Each country in the world has different laws that govern what may and may not be placed on servers in their country. For example, British law restricts the publication of pornography, whether on paper or on Internet servers.

Many countries such as Singapore, Saudi Arabia, and China prohibit the publication of certain political information. Because much of this "subversive" information is published outside of their countries, they actively restrict access to servers in other countries.

Other countries are very concerned about their individual cultures. In 1997, a French court convicted Georgia Institute of Technology of violating French language law. Georgia Tech operates a small campus in France that offers summer programs for American students. The information on the campus Web server was primarily in English because classes are conducted in English. This violated the law requiring French to be the predominant language on all Internet servers in France.

The most likely source of problems for North Americans lies in copyright law. Free speech does not give permission to copy from others. It is against the law to copy and republish on the Web any copyrighted material or any material produced by someone else without explicit permission. So don't copy graphics from someone else's Web site or post your favorite cartoon on your Web site, unless you want to face a lawsuit.

Adobe PDF, or a host of other formats, but the most commonly used format is HTML. HTML was developed by CERN at the same time as the first Web browser and has evolved rapidly ever since. HTML is covered by standards produced by the IETF, but Microsoft and Netscape keep making new additions to the HTML standard with every release of their browsers, so the HTML standard keeps changing. HTML is fairly easy to learn, so you can develop your own Web page. There are many Web sites with good tutorials on HTML; Yahoo lists more than a dozen. The easiest way to develop a page is to start with a page developed by someone else or to use an HTML editor.

ELECTRONIC MAIL

Electronic mail (or *e-mail*) was one of the earliest applications on the Internet and is still among the most heavily used today. With e-mail, users create and send messages to one user, several users, or all users on a *distribution list.* Most e-mail software enables users to send text messages and attach files from word processors, spreadsheets, graphics programs, and so on. Many e-mail packages also permit you to filter or organize messages by priority. For example, all messages from a particular user (e.g., your boss) could be given top priority, so they always appear at the top of your list of messages.

E-mail has several major advantages over regular mail. First, it is fast: Delivery of an e-mail message typically takes seconds or minutes, depending on the distance to the receiver. Even messages sent to other countries usually take only a few minutes or hours to deliver, compared with days for regular mail or courier services. E-mail users often call regular paper mail *snail mail* because it moves so slowly by comparison.

A second major benefit is cost. E-mail is cheaper because it costs virtually nothing to transmit the message over the network, compared with the cost of a stamp or a courier charge. E-mail is also cheaper in terms of the time invested in preparing the message. The expectations and culture of sending and receiving e-mail are different from those of sending and receiving regular letters. Regular business letters and interoffice memos are expected to be error free and formatted according to certain standards. A recent analysis of office processes estimated that it costs between $3 to $10 to prepare and send a paper letter, including printing and supply costs, clerical time, and proofreading time. In contrast, most e-mail users accept less well formatted messages, and slight typographical errors are often overlooked, so less time is spent on perfecting the appearance of the message.

E-mail can substitute for the telephone, thus allowing you to avoid *telephone tag* (the process of repeatedly exchanging voice mail messages because neither you nor the person you are trying to call is available when the other calls). A study of telephone tag in large organizations found that it took an average of three calls and messages before the parties actually got to speak to one another. E-mail can often communicate enough of a message so that the entire "conversation" will take less time than a phone call. It is particularly effective for multinational organizations, which have people working in different time zones around the world.

Several standards have been developed to ensure compatibility between different e-mail software packages. Any software package that conforms to a certain standard can send messages that are formatted using its rules. Any other package that understands that particular standard can then relay the message to its correct destination; however, if an e-mail package receives a mail message in a different format, it may be unable to process it correctly. Many e-mail packages send using one standard but can understand messages sent in several different standards. Three commonly used standards are SMTP (Simple Mail Transfer Protocol), X.400, and CMC (Common Messaging Calls). In this book, we will discuss only SMTP, but CMC and X.400 both work essentially the same way. SMTP, X.400, and CMC are different from one another (in the same way that English differs from French or Spanish), but several software packages are available that translate between them, so that companies that use one standard (e.g., CMC) can translate messages they receive that use a different standard (e.g., SMTP) into their usual standard as they first enter the company and then treat them as "normal" e-mail messages after that.

How E-Mail Works

The *Simple Mail Transfer Protocol (SMTP)* is the most commonly used e-mail standard simply because it is the e-mail standard used on the Internet.[2] E-mail works similarly to how the Web works, but it is a bit more complex. SMTP e-mail is usually implemented as a two-tier client–server application, but not always. We will first explain how the normal two-tier architecture works and then quickly contrast that with a two alternate architectures.

---

[2] The formal specification for SMTP is provided in RFC 822 on the IETF's Web site: www.ietf.org/rfc/rfc0821.txt

Two-Tier E-Mail Architecture With a two-tier client–server architecture, each client computer runs an application layer software package called a *user agent,* which is usually more commonly called an e-mail client (Figure 2-11). The are many common e-mail client software packages, such as Eudora, Outlook, and Netscape Messenger. The user creates the e-mail message using one of these e-mail clients, which formats the message into an SMTP packet that includes information such as the sender's address and the destination address.

The user agent then sends the SMTP packet to a mail server that runs a special application layer software package called a *message transfer agent,* which is more commonly called mail server software (see Figure 2-11).

This e-mail server reads the SMTP packet to find the destination address and then sends the packet on its way through the network—often over the Internet—from mail server to mail server, until it reaches the mail server specified in the destination address (see Figure 2-11). The mail transfer agent on the destination server then stores the message in the receiver's mailbox on that server. The message sits in the mailbox assigned to the user who is to receive the message until he or she checks for new mail.

The SMTP standard covers message transmission between mail servers (i.e., mail server to mail server) and between the originating e-mail client and its mail server. A different standard is used to communicate between the receiver's e-mail client and his or her mail server. Two commonly used standards for communication between e-mail client and

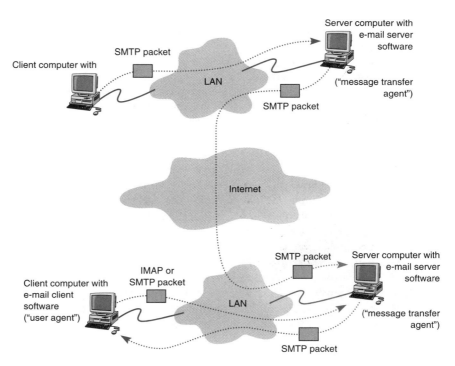

FIGURE 2-11 How SMTP (Simple Mail Transfer Protocol) e-mail works. IMAP = Internet Message Access Protocol; LAN = local area network.

mail server are *Post Office Protocol (POP)* and *Internet Message Access Protocol (IMAP)*. Although there are several important technical differences between POP and IMAP, the most noticeable difference is that before a user can read a mail message with a POP (version 3) e-mail client, the e-mail message is must be copied to the client computer's hard disk and deleted from the mail server. With IMAP, e-mail messages can remain stored on the mail server after they are read. IMAP therefore offers considerable benefits to users who read their e-mail from many different computers (e.g., home, office, computer labs) because they no longer need to worry about having old e-mail messages scattered across several client computers; all e-mail is stored on the server until it is deleted.

In our example in Figure 2-11, when the receiver next accesses his or her e-mail, the e-mail client on his or her computer contacts the mail server by sending an IMAP or POP packet that asks for the contents of the user's mailbox. In Figure 2-11, we show this as an IMAP packet, but it could just as easily be a POP packet. When the mail server receives the IMAP or POP request, it sends the original SMTP packet created by the message sender to the client computer, which the user reads with the e-mail client. Therefore, any e-mail client using POP or IMAP must also understand SMTP to create messages and to read messages it receive. Both POP and IMAP provide a host of functions that enable the user to manage his or her e-mail, such as creating mail folders, deleting mail, creating address books, and so on. If the user sends a POP or IMAP request for one of these functions, the mail server will perform the function and send back a POP or IMAP response packet that is much like an HTTP response packet.

Host-Based E-Mail Architectures   When SMTP was first developed, host-based architectures were the rule, so STMP was first designed to run on mainframe computers. If you use a text-based version of Linux or UNIX, chances are you are using a host-based architecture for your e-mail.

With this architecture, the client computer in Figure 2-11 would be replaced by a terminal that would send all of the user's keystrokes to the server for processing. The server would then send characters back to the terminal to display. All software would reside on the server. This software would take the user's keystrokes, create the STMP packet, and then send it on its way to the next mail server.

Likewise, the receiver would use a terminal that would send keystrokes to the server and receive letters back to display. The server itself would be responsible for understanding the user's commands to read a mail message and sending the appropriate characters to the user's terminal so he or she could read the e-mail message. If you had been wondering why the SMTP standard does not include the delivery of the message to the receiver's client computer, you should now understand. Because no software existed on the receiver's terminal, the SMTP standard did not include any specification about how the receiver's mail server software should display messages. Communication between the mail server and the receiver's terminal was left to the e-mail software package running on the server. Because each package and each terminal was different, no standards were developed to cover communication between the terminal and the server.

Three-Tier Client–Server Architecture   The three-tier client–server e-mail architecture uses a Web server and Web browser to provide access to your e-mail. With this architecture, you do not need an e-mail client on your client computer. Instead, you use your Web browser. This type of e-mail is sometimes called Web-based e-mail and is provided by a variety of companies such as Hotmail.

You use your browser to connect to a page on a Web server that lets you write the e-mail message by filling in a form. When you click the send button, your Web browser sends the form information to the Web server inside an HTTP request (Figure 2-12). The Web server runs a program (written in C or Perl, for example) that takes the information from the HTTP request and builds an SMTP packet that contains the e-mail message (and although not important to our example, it also sends an HTTP response back to the client). The Web server then sends the SMTP packet to the mail server, which processes the SMTP packet as though it came from a client computer. The SMTP packet flows through the network in the same manner as before. When it arrives at the destination mail server, it is placed in the receiver's mailbox.

When the receiver wants to check his or her mail, he or she uses a Web browser to send an HTTP request to a Web server (see Figure 2-12). A program on the Web server (in C or Perl, for example) processes the request and sends the appropriate IMAP (or POP)

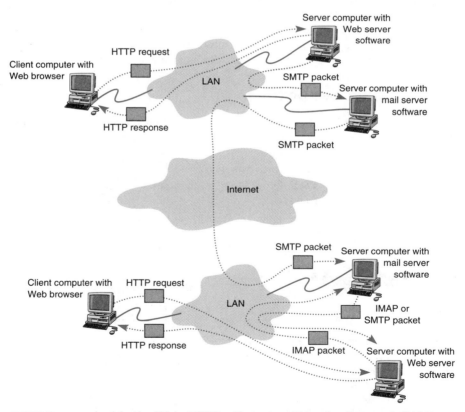

FIGURE 2-12 Inside the Web. HTTP = Hypertext Transfer Protocol; IMAP = Internet Message Access Protocol; LAN = local area network; SMTP = Simple Mail Transfer Protocol.

request to the mail server. The mail server responds with an IMAP (or POP) packet, which a program on the Web server converts into an HTTP response and sends to the client. The client then displays the e-mail message in the Web browser.

A simple comparison of Figures 2-11 and 2-12 will quickly show that the three-tier approach using a Web browser is much more complicated than the normal two-tier approach. So why do it? Well, it is simpler to have just a Web browser on the client computer rather than to require the user to install a special e-mail client on his or her computer and then set up the special e-mail client to connect to the correct mail server using either POP or IMAP. It is simpler for the user to just type the URL of the Web server providing the mail services into his or her browser and begin using mail.

It is also important to note that the sender and receiver do not have to use the same architecture for their e-mail. The sender could use a two-tier client–server architecture, and the receiver, a host-based or three-tier client–server architecture. Because all communication is standardized using SMTP between the different mail servers, how the users interact with their mail servers is unimportant. Each organization can use a different approach.

In fact, there is nothing to prevent one organization from using all three architectures simultaneously. At Indiana University, we usually access our e-mail through an e-mail client (e.g., Eudora), but we also access it over the Web because many of us travel internationally and find it easier to borrow a Web browser with Internet access than to borrow an e-mail client and set it up to use the Indiana mail server.

Inside an SMTP Packet

SMTP defines how message transfer agents operate and how they format messages sent to other message transfer agents. An SMTP packet has two parts:

- The *header,* which lists source and destination e-mail addresses (possibly in text form [e.g., "Pat Smith"]) as well as the address itself (e.g., psmith@somewhere.com), date, subject, and so on
- The *body,* which is the word *DATA,* followed by the message itself.

TECHNICAL FOCUS *2-3*

SMTP TRANSMISSION

SMTP (Simple Mail Transfer Protocol) is an older protocol, and transmission using it is rather complicated. If we were going to design it again, we would likely find a simpler transmission method. Conceptually, we think of an SMTP packet as one packet. However, SMTP mail transfer agents transmit each element within the SMTP packet as a separate packet and wait for the receiver to respond with an "OK" before sending the next element.

For example, in Figure 2-13, the sending mail transfer agent would send the *from* address and wait for an OK from the receiver. Then it would send the *to* address and wait for an OK. Then the date, and so on, with the last item being the entire message sent as one element.

Figure 2-13 shows a simple e-mail message formatted using SMTP. The header of an SMTP message has a series of fields that provide specific information, such as the sender's e-mail address, the receiver's address, date, and so on. The information in quotes on the *from* and *to* lines is ignored by SMTP; only the information in the angle brackets is used an e-mail addresse. The *message ID* field is used to provide a unique identification code so that the message can be tracked. The message body contains the actual text of the message itself.

Listserv Discussion Groups

A list server (or *Listserv*) group is a simply a mailing list of users who have joined together to discuss some topic. Listserv groups are formed around just about every topic imaginable, including cooking, skydiving, politics, education, and British comedy. Some are short lived, whereas others continue indefinitely. Some permit any member to post messages; others permit only certain members to post messages. Most businesses have Listservs organized around job functions, so that it is easy to reach everyone in a particular department.

There are two parts to every Listserv. The first part, the *Listserv processor*, processes commands such as requests to subscribe, unsubscribe, or to provide more information about the Listserv. The second part is the *Listserv mailer*. Any message send to the Listserv mailer is re-sent to everyone on the mailing list. To use a Listserv, you need to know the addresses of both the processor and the mailer.

To subscribe to a Listserv, you send an e-mail message to the Listserv processor, which adds your name to the list (see "Listserv Commands" for the message format). It is important that you send this message to the processor, not the mailer; otherwise, your subscription message will be sent to everyone on the mailing list, which might be embarrassing.

For example, suppose you want to join a Listserv on widgets that has a processor address of listerv@abc.com, and the mailer address is widget-1@abc.com. To subscribe, you send an e-mail message to listerv@abc.com containing the text: *subscribe widget-1 your name.* To send a message to everyone on this Listserv, you would e-mail your message to widget-1@abc.com.

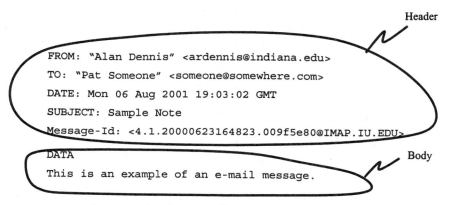

FIGURE 2-13 An example of an e-mail message using the SMTP (Simple Mail Transfer Protocol) standard.

TECHNICAL FOCUS *2-4*

LISTSERV COMMANDS

There are many different commands that can be sent to the Listserv processor to perform a variety of functions. These commands are included as lines of text in the e-mail message sent to the processor. Each command must be placed on a separate line. Some useful commands include

- SUBSCRIBE listserv-mailer-name your-name: Subscribes you to a mailing list (e.g., *subscribe maps-1 robin jones*)
- UNSUBSCRIBE listserv-mailer-name your-name: Unsubscribes you from the mailing list (e.g., *unsubscribe maps-1 robin jones*)

- HELP: Requests the Listserv to e-mail you a list of its commands
- LIST: Requests the Listserv to e-mail you a list of all Listserv groups that are available on this Listserv processor
- LIST DETAILED: Requests the Listserv to e-mail you a detailed description of all Listserv groups that are available on this Listserv processor and are public

Attachments in Multipurpose Internet Mail Extension

As the name suggests, SMTP is a simple standard that permits only the transfer of text messages. It was developed in the early days of computing, when no one had even thought about using e-mail to transfer nontext files such as graphics or word processing documents. Several standards for nontext files have been developed that can operate together with SMTP, such as *Multipurpose Internet Mail Extension (MIME),* uuencode, and binhex.

Each of the standards is different, but all work in the same general way. The MIME software, which exists as part of the e-mail client, takes the nontext file such as a PowerPoint graphic file, and translates each byte in the file into a special code that looks like regular text. This encoded section of "text" is then labeled with a series of special fields understood by SMTP as identifying a MIME encoded attachment and specifying information about the attachment (e.g., name of file, type of file). When the receiver's e-mail client receives the STMP message with the MIME attachment, it recognizes the MIME "text" and uses its MIME software (that is part of the e-mail client) to translate the file from MIME "text" back into its original format.

OTHER APPLICATIONS

There are literally thousands of applications that run on the Internet and on other networks. Most application software that we develop today, whether for sale or for private internal use, runs on a network. We could spend years talking about different network applications and still cover only a small number.

Fortunately, most network application software works in much the same way as the Web or e-mail. In this section, we will briefly discuss only three commonly used applications: File Transfer Protocol (FTP), Telnet, and instant messaging (IM).

File Transfer Protocol

File Transfer Protocol (FTP) enables you to send and receive files over the Internet. FTP works much like HTTP. FTP requires an application layer program on the client computer and a FTP server application program on a server. There are many software packages that use the FTP standard, such as WS-FTP. The user uses his or her client to send FTP requests to the FTP server. The FTP server processes these requests and sends back FTP packets containing the requested file.[3]

There are two types of FTP sites: closed and anonymous. A closed site requires users to have permission before they can connect and gain access to the files. Access is granted by providing an account name with a password. For example, a network manager or webmaster would write a Web page using software on his or her client computer and then use FTP to send it to a specific account on the Web server.

The most common type is an *anonymous FTP* site, which permits any Internet user to login using the account name of *anonymous*. When using anonymous FTP, you will still be asked for a password. It is customary to enter your Internet e-mail address as the password (e.g., smith@allstate.edu).

Many files and documents available via FTP have been compressed to reduce the amount of disk space they require. Because there are many types of data compression programs, it is possible that a file you want has been compressed by a program you lack, so you won't be able to access the file until you find the decompression program it uses. That's one of the "advantages" of the decentralized, no-rules structure of the Internet.

Telnet

Telnet enables users on one computer to log in to other computers on the Internet. Telnet requires an application layer program on the client computer and an application layer program on the server or host computer. There are many programs that conform to the Telnet standard, such as EWAN. Once Telnet makes the connection from the client to the server, you can log in to the server or host computer in the same way as you would if you dialed in with a modem; you must know the account name and password of an authorized user. Telnet can be faster or slower than a modern depending on the amount of traffic on the Internet. Modems are discussed in Chapter 3. In any event, Telnet enables you to connect to a remote computer without incurring long-distance telephone charges. Because Telnet was designed in the very early days of the Internet, it assumes your client is a dumb terminal. Therefore, when you use Telnet, you are using a host-based architecture. All keystrokes you type in the Telnet client are transferred one by one to the server computer for processing. The server processes those commands—including simple keystrokes such as up arrow or down arrow—and transfers the results back to the client computer, which displays the letters and moves the cursor as directed by the server.[4]

Telnet can be useful because it enables you to access your server or host computer without sitting at its keyboard. Most network managers use Telnet to work on servers,

---

[3] The formal specification for FTP is provided in RFC 2640 on the IETF's Web site: www.ietf.org/rfc/rfc2640.txt

[4] The formal specification for Telnet is provided in RFC 2355 and RFC 854 on the IETF's Web site. The URLs are www.ietf.org/rfc/rfc2355.txt and www.ietf.org/rfc/rfc0854.txt, respectively.

rather than physically sitting in front of them and using their keyboards. Telnet also poses a great security threat, because it means that anyone on the Internet can attempt to log in to your account and use it as he or she wishes. Two commonly used security precautions are to prohibit remote logins via Telnet unless a user specifically asks for his or her account to be authorized for it and to permit remote logins only from a specific set of Internet addresses. For example, the Web server for this book will accept Telnet logins only from computers located in the same building. Chapter 11 discusses network security.

Instant Messaging

One of the fastest growing Internet applications is *instant messaging (IM)*. With IM, you can exchange real-time typed messages or chat with your friends. Some IM software also enables you to verbally talk with your friends in the same way as you might use telephone or to use cameras to exchange real-time video in the same way you might use a videoconferencing system. Several types of IM currently exist, including ICQ and AOL Instant Messenger.

IM works in much the same way as the Web. The client computer needs an IM client software package, which communicates with an IM server software package that runs on a server. When the user connects to the Internet, the IM client software package sends an IM request packet to the IM server informing it that the user is now online. The IM client software package continues to communicate with the IM server to monitor what other users have connected to the IM server. When one of your friends connects to the IM server, the IM server sends an IM packet to your client computer so that you now know that your friend is connected to the Internet. The server also sends a packet to your friend's client computer so that he or she knows that you are on the Internet.

With the click of a button, you can both begin chatting. When you type text, your IM client creates an IM packet that is sent to the IM server (Figure 2-14). The server then retransmits packet to your friend. Several people may be part of the same chat session, in which case the server sends a copy of the packet to all of the client computers. IM also provides a way for different servers to communicate with one another, and for the client computers to communicate directly with each other.

Videoconferencing

Videoconferencing provides real-time transmission of video and audio signals to enable people in two or more locations to have a meeting. In some cases, videoconferences are held in special-purpose meeting rooms with one or more cameras and several video display monitors to capture and display the video signals (Figure 2-15). Special audio microphones and speakers are used to capture and play audio signals. The audio and video signals are combined into one signal that is transmitted though a MAN or WAN to people at the other location. Most of this type of videoconferencing involves two teams in two separate meeting rooms, but some systems can support conferences of up to eight separate meeting rooms.

The fastest-growing form of videoconferencing is *desktop videoconferencing*. Small cameras installed on top of each computer permit meetings to take place from individual offices (Figure 2-16). Special application software (e.g., CUSeeMe, Net Meeting) is installed on the client computer and transmits the images across a network to application software on a videoconferencing server. The server then sends the signals to the other

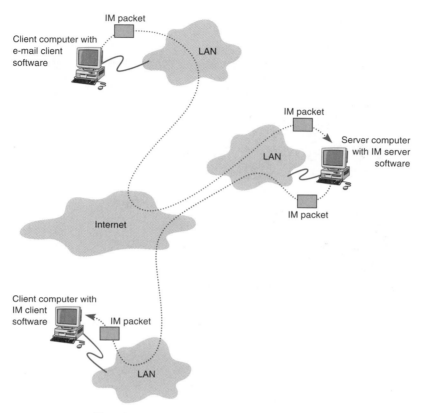

FIGURE 2-14 How instant messaging (IM) works. LAN = local area network.

FIGURE 2-15 Room-based videoconferencing.

FIGURE 2-16   Desktop videoconferencing.

client computers that want to participate in the videoconference. In some cases, the clients can communicate with one another without using the server. The cost of desktop video-conferencing ranges from less than $100 per computer for inexpensive systems to more than $4,000 for high-quality systems. Some systems have integrated conferencing software with desktop videoconferencing, enabling participants to communicate verbally and, by using applications such white boards, to attend the same meeting while they are sitting at the computers in their offices.

The key benefits of videoconferencing are the time and cost savings that can result. By using videoconferencing, meeting participants no longer need to spend time and money in travel. Videoconferencing was slow to take hold in many organizations because of its high initial installation costs (between $20,000 to $100,000 per meeting room). Today, however, most large organizations with offices in different parts of the United States or the world use it, and there is a growing demand for desktop systems; desktop systems now out-sell room-based systems three to one, but the growth has been slower than expected.

The transmission of video requires a lot of network capacity. Most videoconferenc-ing uses data compression to reduce the amount of data transmitted. Surprisingly, the most common complaint is not the quality of the video image but the quality of the voice trans-missions. Special care needs to be taken in the design and placement of microphones and speakers to ensure quality sound and minimal feedback.

Most videoconferencing systems were originally developed by vendors using differ-ent formats, so many products were incompatible. The best solution was to ensure that all hardware and software used within an organization was supplied by the same vendor and to hope that any other organizations with whom you wanted to communicate used the same equipment. Today, three standards are in common use: H.320, H.323, and MPEG-2 (also called ISO 13818-2). Each of these standards was developed by different organizations and is supported by different products. They are not compatible, although some application software packages understand more than one standard. H.320 is designed for room-to-room videoconferencing over high-speed telephone lines. H.323 is a family of standards designed for desktop videoconferencing and just simple audio conferencing over the Internet. MPEG-2 is designed for faster connections, such as a LAN or specially designed, privately operated WAN.

Webcasting is a special type of one-directional videoconferencing in which content is sent from the server to the user. The developer creates content that is downloaded as needed by the users and played by a plug-in to a Web browser. At present, there are no standards for Webcast technologies, but the products by RealNetworks.com are the de facto standards.

SUMMARY

Application Architectures   There are three fundamental application architectures. In host-based networks, the sever performs virtually all of the work. In client-based networks, the client computer does most of the work; the server is used only for data storage. In client–server networks, the work is shared between the servers and clients. The client performs all presentation logic, the server handles all data storage and data access logic, and one or both perform the application logic. Client–server networks can be cheaper to install and often better balance the network loads but are far more complex and costly to develop and manage.

World Wide Web   One of the fastest growing Internet applications is the Web, which was first developed in 1990. The Web enables the display of rich graphical images, pictures, full-motion video, and sound. The Web is the most common way for businesses to establish a presence on the Internet. The Web has two application software packages, a Web browser on the client and a Web server on the server. Web browsers and servers communicate with one another using a standard called HTTP. Most Web pages are written in HTML, but many also use other formats. The Web contains information on just about every topic under the sun, but finding it and making sure the information is reliable are major problems.

Electronic Mail   With e-mail, users create and send messages using an application-layer software package on client computers called user agents. The user agent sends the mail to a server running an application-layer software package called a mail transfer agent, which then forwards the message through a series of mail transfer agents to the mail transfer agent on the receiver's server. E-mail is faster and cheaper than regular mail and can substitute for telephone conversations in some cases. Several standards have been developed to ensure compatibility between different user agents and mail transfer agents. SMTP, POP, and IMAP are used on the Internet. X.400 and CMC are other commonly used standards.

KEY TERMS

anonymous FTP	data access logic	dumb terminal	host-based architecture
application architecture	data storage	e-mail	HTTP request
application logic	desktop video-	fat client	HTTP response
client–server architecture	conferencing	File Transfer Protocol	Hypertext Markup Language (HTML)
cluster	distributed computing	(FTP)	
Common Messaging	distribution list	H.320	Hypertext Transfer Protocol (HTTP)
Calls (CMC)	domain	H.323	

instant messaging (IM)	Netscape	Simple Mail Transfer	World Wide Web
intelligent terminal	network computer	Protocol (SMTP)	Web browser
Internet	NSFNET	snail mail	Web server
Internet Mail Access	*n*-tier architecture	Telnet	workstation
Protocol (IMAP)	Post Office Protocol	telephone tag	X.400
Listserv	(POP)	terminal	
mainframe	presentation logic	thick client	
message transfer agent	protocol	thin client	
microcomputer	request body	three-tier architecture	
minicomputer	request header	transaction terminal	
MPEG	request line	two-tier architecture	
MPEG-2	response body	uniform resource locator	
Multipurpose Internet	response header	(URL)	
Mail Extension	response status	user agent	
(MIME)	server-based architecture	videoconferencing	

QUESTIONS

1. What are the different types of application architectures?

2. Describe the four basic functions of an application software package.

3. What are the advantages and disadvantages of host-based networks versus client–server networks?

4. What is middleware, and what does it do?

5. Suppose your organization was contemplating switching from a host-based architecture to client-server. What problems would you foresee?

6. Which is less expensive: host-based networks or client–server networks? Explain.

7. Compare and contrast two-tier, three-tier, and *n*-tier client–server architectures. What are the technical differences, and what advantages and disadvantages does each offer?

8. How does a thin client differ from a fat client?

9. What is a network computer?

10. What do the following tools enable you to do: the Web, e-mail, FTP, Telnet?

11. For what is HTTP used? What are its major parts?

12. For what is HTML used?

13. Describe how a Web browser and Web server work together to send a Web page to a user.

14. How is e-mail useful?

15. Describe how mail user agents and message transfer agents work together to transfer mail messages.

16. What roles do SMTP, POP, and IMAP play in sending and receiving e-mail on the Internet?

17. What are the major parts of an e-mail message?

18. What are X.400 and CMC?

19. What is FTP, and why is it useful?

20. What is Telnet, and why is it useful?

21. What is a Listserv and how could you use it to get information?

22. Explain how instant messaging works.

23. Compare and contrast the application architecture for videoconferencing and the architecture for e-mail.

24. Which of the three application architectures for e-mail (two-tier client server, Web-based, and host-based) is "best"? Explain.

25. Some experts argue that thin-client client–server architectures are really host-based architectures in disguise and suffer from the same old problems. Do you agree? Explain.

26. You can use a Web browser to access an FTP server simply by putting *ftp://* in front of the URL (e.g., *ftp://xyz.abc.com*). If that server has FTP server software installed, then the FTP server will respond instead of the Web server. What is your browser doing differently to access the FTP server? Hint: This question is more difficult than it seems, because we haven't explained how the server knows to pass certain types of packets to the right software (i.e., HTTP requests to the Web server software and SMTP packets to the e-

mail software. At this point, don't worry about it. Linking the network to the application layer is the job of the transport layer that is explained in Chapter 5.

27. Will the Internet become an essential business tool like the telephone or will it go the way of the dinosaurs? Discuss.

EXERCISES

2-1 Investigate the use of the three major architectures by a local organization (e.g., your university). Which architecture(s) does it use most often and what does it see itself doing in the future? Why?

2-2 What are the costs of client–server versus host-based architectures? Search the Web for at least two different studies and be sure to report your sources. What are the likely reasons for the differences between the two?

2-3 Investigate the costs of dumb terminals, intelligent terminals, network computers, minimally equipped microcomputers, and top-of-the-line microcomputers. Many equipment manufacturers and resellers are on the Web, so it's a good place to start looking.

2-4 What application architecture does your university use for e-mail? Explain.

MINI-CASES

I. Deals-R-Us Brokers (Part 1)

Fred Jones, a distant relative of yours and president of Deals-R-Us Brokers (DRUB), has come to you for advice. DRUB is small brokerage house that enables its clients to buy and sell stocks over the Internet as well as place traditional orders by phone or fax. DRUB has just decided to offer a set of stock analysis tools that will help its clients more easily pick winning stocks, or so Fred tells you. Fred's information systems department has presented him with two alternatives for developing the new tools. The first alternative will have a special tool developed in C++ that clients will download onto their computers to run. The tool will communicate with the DRUB server to select data to analyze. The second alternative will have the C++ program running on the server; the client will use his or her browser interact with the server.

   a. Classify the two alternatives in terms of what type of application architecture they use.

   b. Outline the pros and cons of the two alternatives and make a recommendation to Fred about which is better.

II. Deals-R-Us Brokers (Part 2)

Fred Jones, a distant relative of yours and president of Deals-R-Us Brokers (DRUB), has come to you for advice. DRUB is small brokerage house that enables its clients to buy and sell stocks over the Internet, as well as place traditional orders by phone or fax. DRUB has just decided to install a new e-mail package. One vendor is offering an SMTP-based two-tier client–server architecture. The second vendor is offering a Web-based e-mail architecture. Fred doesn't understand either one but thinks the Web-based one should be better because, in his words, "the Web is the future."

   a. *Briefly* explain to Fred, in layperson's terms, the differences between the two.

   b. Outline the pros and cons of the two alternatives and make a recommendation to Fred about which is better.

CASE STUDY

NEXT-DAY AIR SERVICE

Bob Jones, manager of Sales and Marketing, recently read an article about the Internet in *Business Week* and has raised the issue of the Internet with President Lee Coone. Jones has asked you to help him understand the ways in which the Internet could help increase NDAS's presence in both the international and domestic markets. He is also interested in ways NDAS could make effective use of e-mail and the Web in achieving increased productivity. NDAS currently has a Web site, but it is essentially just a simple brochure that introduces NDAS.

The two most negative comments about Jones's ideas came from Peter Browne and Les Coone. Peter Browne stated that the Fleet Maintenance Division is doing just fine as it is and that one should not to "try to fix something that isn't broken." Les Coone commented that NDAS should not "jump the gun on videoconferencing; it is too early to invest in that new technology."

Exercises

President Coone has given you two tasks:

1. Prepare a brief management summary on the technical essential aspects of the Internet and the World Wide Web and how they work. Remember, the audience is not technical. The president is confused about the relationship between the World Wide Web and the Internet and often states that they are the same. Please be sure to explain this in your summary.

2. President Coone is particularly intrigued with the potential of the Internet, but he and the other members of management are not exactly sure what how NDAS can use them to improve its competitive edge. Present some alternatives. President Coone reminds you that NDAS expects to enlarge its scope in the international market. Plans call for first offerings to be services to Great Britain, France, and Germany, with later expansion to South America. President Coone wants you to involve Jones in your work on the Internet.

CHAPTER 3

PHYSICAL LAYER

THE PHYSICAL layer (also called layer 1) is the physical connection between the computers and/or devices in the network. This chapter examines how the physical layer operates. It describes the most commonly used media for network circuits and explains the basic technical concepts of how data is actually transmitted through the media. Four different types of transmission are described: digital transmission of digital data; analog transmission of digital data; digital transmission of analog voice data, and combined analog-digital transmission of digital data. You do not need an engineering-level understanding of the topics to be an effective user and manager of data communication applications. It is important, however, that you understand the basic concepts, so this chapter is somewhat technical.

OBJECTIVES

- Be familiar with the different types of network circuits and media
- Understand digital transmission of digital data
- Understand analog transmission of digital data
- Understand digital transmission of analog data
- Be familiar with analog and digital modems
- Be familiar with multiplexing

CHAPTER OUTLINE

INTRODUCTION

CIRCUITS

    Circuit Configuration

    Data Flow

    Communication Media

    Media Selection

INTRODUCTION

This chapter examines how the physical layer operates. The physical layer is the network hardware including servers, clients, and circuits, but in this chapter we focus on the circuits and on how clients and servers transmit data through them. The circuits are usually a combination of both physical media (e.g., cables, wireless transmissions) and special-purpose devices that enable the transmissions to travel through the media. Special-purpose devices such as repeaters are discussed in more detail in Chapter 4, whereas devices such as hubs, switches, and routers are discussed in Chapters 6 and 7.

The word *circuit* has two very different meanings in networking, and sometimes it is hard to understand which meaning is intended. Sometimes, we use the word *circuit* to refer to the *physical circuit*—the actual wire—used to connect two devices. In this case, we are referring to the physical media that carries the message we transmit, such as the twisted-pair wire used to connect a computer to the LAN in an office. In other cases, we are referring to a *logical circuit* used to connect two devices, which refers to the transmission characteristics of the connection, such as when we say a company has a T1 connection into the Internet. In this case, *T1* refers not to the physical media (i.e., what type of wire is used) but rather to how fast data can be sent through the connection.[1] Often, each physical circuit is also a logical circuit, but as you will see in the section on multiplexing at the end of this chapter, sometimes it is possible to have one physical circuit—one wire—carry several separate logical circuits and vice versa: have one logical circuit travel over several physical circuits.

There are two fundamentally different types of data that can flow through the circuit: *digital* and *analog.* Computers produce digital data that are binary, either on or off, 0 or 1. In contrast, telephones produce analog data whose electrical signals are shaped like the sound waves they transfer; they can take on any value in a wide range of possibilities, not just 0 or 1.

Data can be transmitted through a circuit in the same form they are produced. Most computers, for example, transmit their data through digital circuits to printers and other attached devices. Likewise, analog voice data can be transmitted through telephone networks in analog form. In general, networks designed primarily to transmit digital computer data tend to use digital transmission, and networks designed primarily to transmit analog voice data tend to use analog transmission (at least for some parts of the transmission).

Data can be converted from one form into the other for transmission over network circuits. For example, digital computer data can be transmitted over an analog telephone circuit by using a modem. A modem at the sender's computer translates the computer's digital data into analog data that can be transmitted through the voice communication circuits, and a second modem at the receiver's end translates the analog transmission back into digital data for use by the receiver's computer.

Likewise, it is possible to translate analog voice data into digital form for transmission over digital computer circuits using a device called a codec. Once again, there are two codecs, one at the sender's end and one at the receiver's end. Why bother to translate voice into digital? The answer is that digital transmission is "better" than analog transmission. Specifically, digital transmission offers five key benefits over analog transmission:

- Digital transmission produces fewer errors than analog transmission. Because the transmitted data is binary (only two distinct values), it is easier to detect and correct errors.

- Digital transmission permits higher maximum transmission rates. Fiber-optic cable, for example, is designed for digital transmission.

- Digital transmission is more efficient. It is possible to send more data through a given circuit using digital rather than analog transmission.

- Digital transmission is more secure because it is easier to encrypt.

- Finally, and most importantly, integrating voice, video and data on the same circuit is far simpler with digital transmission.

---

[1] Don't worry about what a T1 circuit is at this point. All you need to understand is that a T1 circuit is a specific type of circuit with certain characteristics, the same way we might describe gasoline as being unleaded or premium. We will discuss T1 circuits in Chapter 8.

For these reasons, most long-distance telephone circuits built by the telephone companies and other common carriers over the past decades use digital transmission. In the future, most transmissions (voice, data, and video) will be sent digitally.

In this chapter, we first describe the basic types of circuits and examine the different media used to build circuits. Then we explain how data is actually sent through these media using digital and analog transmission. Finally, we describe multiplexing, which is how several logical circuits can be combined over one physical circuit.

CIRCUITS

Circuit Configuration

Circuit configuration is the basic physical layout of the circuit. There are two fundamental circuit configurations: point-to-point and multipoint. In practice, most complex computer networks have many circuits, some of which are point-to-point and some of which are multipoint.

Figure 3-1 illustrates a *point-to-point configuration,* which is so named because it goes from one point to another (e.g., one computer to another computer). These circuits sometimes are called *dedicated circuits* because they are dedicated to the use of these two computers. This type of configuration is used when the computers generate enough data to fill the capacity of the communication circuit. When an organization builds a network using point-to-point circuits, each computer has its own circuit running from itself to the other computers. This can get very expensive, particularly if there is some distance between the computers.

Figure 3-2 shows a *multipoint configuration* (also called a *shared circuit*). In this configuration, many computers are connected on the same circuit. This means that each must share the circuit with the others, much like a party line in telephone communications. The disadvantage is that only one computer can use the circuit at a time. When one computer is sending or receiving data, all others must wait. The advantage of multipoint circuits is that they reduce the amount of cable required and typically use the available communication circuit more efficiently. Imagine the number of circuits that would be required if the network in Figure 3-2 was designed with separate point-to-point circuits. For this reason, multipoint configurations are cheaper than point-to-point configurations. Thus, multipoint configurations typically are used when each computer does not need to continuously use the entire capacity of the circuit or when building point-to-point circuits is too expensive.

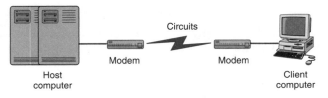

FIGURE 3-1 Point-to-point configuration.

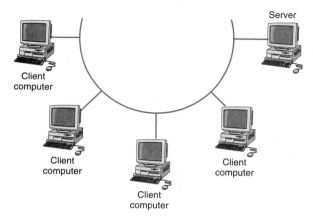

FIGURE 3-2 Multipoint configuration.

Data Flow

Circuits can be designed to permit data to flow in one direction or in both directions. Actually, there are three ways to transmit: simplex, half-duplex, and full-duplex (Figure 3-3).

Simplex is one-way transmission, such as that with radios and TVs.

Half-duplex is two-way transmission, but you can transmit in only one direction at a time. A half-duplex communication link is similar to a walkie-talkie link; only one computer can transmit at a time. Computers use *control signals* to negotiate which will send and which will receive data. The amount of time half-duplex communication takes to switch between sending and receiving is called *turnaround time* (also called retrain time or reclocking time). The turnaround time for a specific circuit can be obtained from its technical specifications (often between 20 and 50 milliseconds). Europeans sometimes use the term *simplex circuit* to mean a half-duplex circuit.

With *full-duplex* transmission, you can transmit in both directions simultaneously, with no turnaround time.

How do you choose which data flow method to use? Obviously, one factor is the application. If data always need to flow only in one direction (e.g., from a remote sensor to a host computer), then simplex is probably the best choice. In most cases, however, data must flow in both directions.

The initial temptation is to presume that a full-duplex channel is best; however, each circuit has only so much capacity to carry data. Creating a full-duplex circuit means that the available capacity in the circuit is divided—half in one direction and half in the other. In some cases, it makes more sense to build a set of simplex circuits in the same way a set of one-way streets can speed traffic. In other cases, a half-duplex circuit may work best. For example, terminals connected to mainframes often transmit data to the host, wait for a reply, transmit more data, and so on, in a turn-taking process; usually, traffic does not need to flow in both directions simultaneously. Such a traffic pattern is ideally suited to half-duplex circuits.

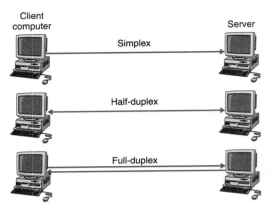

FIGURE 3-3 Simplex, half-duplex, and full-duplex transmissions.

Communication Media

The *medium* (or *media,* if there is more than one) is the physical matter or substance that carries the voice or data transmission. Many different types of transmission media are currently in use, such as copper (wire), glass or plastic (fiber-optic cable), or air (radio, infrared, microwave, or satellite). There are two basic types of media. *Guided media* are those in which the message flows through a physical media such as a twisted-pair wire, coaxial cable, or fiber-optic cable; the media "guides" the signal. *Wireless media* are those in which the message is broadcast through the air, such as infrared, microwave, or satellite.

In many cases, the circuits used in WANs are provided by the various common carriers to who sell usage of them to the public. We call the circuits sold by the common carriers *communication services.* Chapter 8 describes specific services available in North America. The following sections describe the medium and the basic characteristics of each circuit type, in the event you were establishing your own physical network, whereas Chapter 8 describes how the circuits are packaged and marketed for purchase or lease from a common carrier. If your organization has leased a circuit from a common carrier, you are probably less interested in the media used and more interested in whether the speed, cost, and reliability of the circuit meets your needs.

Guided Media One of the most commonly used types of guided media is *twisted-pair wires,* insulated pairs of wires that can be packed quite close together (Figure 3-4). Twisted pair-wires usually are twisted to minimize the electromagnetic interference between one pair and any other pair in the bundle. Your house or apartment probably has a set of two twisted-pair wires (i.e., four wires) from it to the telephone company network. One pair is used to connect your telephone; the other pair is a spare that can be used for a second telephone line. The twisted-pair wires used in LANs are usually packaged as four sets of pairs as shown in Figure 3-4, whereas bundles of several thousand wire pairs are placed under city streets and in large buildings. The specific types of twisted-pair wires used in LANs are discussed in Chapter 6.

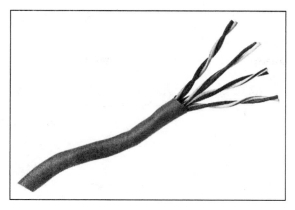

FIGURE 3-4 Twisted-pair wire.

Coaxial cable is type of guided media that is quickly disappearing (Figure 3-5). Coaxial cable has a copper core (the inner conductor) with an outer cylindrical shell for insulation. The outer shield, just under the shell, is the second conductor. Because they have additional shielding provided by their multiple layers of material, coaxial cables are less prone to interference and errors than basic low-cost twisted-pair wires. Coaxial cables cost about three times as much twisted-pair wires but offer few additional benefits other than better shielding. One can also buy specially shielded twisted-pair wire that provides the same level of quality as coaxial cable but at half its cost. For this reason, few companies are installing coaxial cable today, although some still continue to use existing coaxial cable that was installed years ago.

Although twisted-pair is the most common type of guided media, *fiber-optic cable* also is becoming widely used. Instead of carrying telecommunication signals in

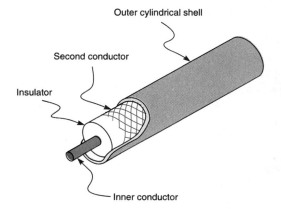

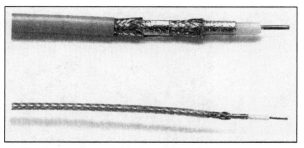

FIGURE 3-5 Coaxial cables. Thinnet and Thicknet Ethernet cables (top) and cross-sectional view (bottom).

the traditional electrical form, this technology uses high-speed streams of light pulses from lasers or LEDs (light-emitting diodes) that carry information inside hair-thin strands of glass or plastic called optical fibers. Figure 3-6 shows a fiber-optic cable and depicts the optical core, the cladding (metal coating), and how light rays travel in optical fibers.

The earliest fiber-optic systems were *multimode,* meaning that the light could reflect inside the cable at many different angles. Multimode cables are plagued by excessive signal weakening (attenuation) and dispersion (spreading of the signal so that differ-

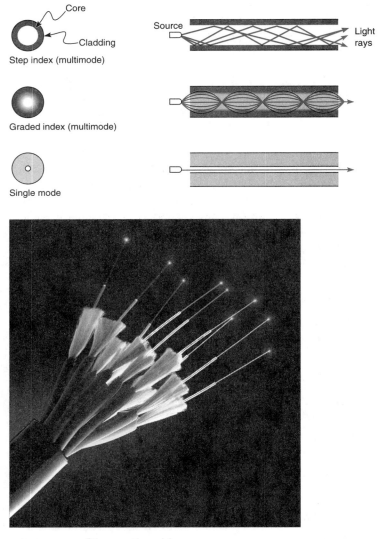

FIGURE 3-6 Fiber-optic cable.

ent parts of the signal arrive at different times at the destination). For these reasons, early multimode fiber was usually limited to about 500 meters. Graded-index multimode fiber attempts to reduce this problem by changing the refractive properties of the glass fiber so that as the light approaches the outer edge of the fiber, it speeds up, which compensates for the slightly longer distance it must travel compared with light in the center of the fiber. Therefore, the light in the center is more likely to arrive at the same time as the light that has traveled at the edges of the fiber. This increases the effective distance to just under 1,000 meters.

Single-mode fiber-optic cables transmit a single direct beam of light through a cable that ensures the light reflects in only one pattern, in part because the core diameter has been reduced from 50 microns to about 5 to 10 microns. This smaller-diameter core allows the fiber to send a more concentrated light beam, resulting in faster data transmission speeds and longer distances, often up to 100 kilometers. However, because the light source must be perfectly aligned with the cable, single-mode products usually use lasers (rather than the LEDs used in multimode systems) and therefore are more expensive.

Fiber-optic technology is a revolutionary departure from the traditional copper wires of twisted-pair cable or coaxial cable. One of the main advantages of fiber optics is that it can carry huge amounts of information at extremely fast data rates. This capacity makes it ideal for the simultaneous transmission of voice, data, and image signals. In most cases, fiber-optic cable works better under harsh environmental conditions than do its metallic counterparts. It is not as fragile or brittle, it is not as heavy or bulky, and it is more resistant to corrosion. Also, in case of fire, an optical fiber can withstand higher temperatures than can copper wire. Even when the outside jacket surrounding the optical fiber has melted, a fiber-optic system still can be used.

Wireless Media   One of the most commonly used forms of wireless media is *radio;* when people used the term *wireless,* they often mean radio transmission. Radio data transmission uses the same basic principles as standard radio transmission. Each device or computer on the network has a radio receiver/transmitter that uses a specific frequency range

MANAGEMENT FOCUS *3 - 1*

AUSTRALIA TURNS ON THE FIBER

The 2000 Olympic Games in Sydney were the most wired games in history. Telestra, the major Australian common carrier responsible for wiring the games, provided almost 1 million miles of fiber optic cable. Fiber-optic cables running at 565 Mbps were used to connect almost all of the games' venues for both video and data transmission. Only the copper cables to the more remote soccer venue ran at 45 Mbps.

Within the venues, most cable was fiber, providing at least 155 Mbps. Only a few locations used slower copper twisted-pair cable.

Data from the games ran over fiber-optic cable at 10 Gbps from Brisbane to the Sydney satellite station of Oxford Falls for broadcast around the world. A redundant connection ran across Australia from Sydney to Perth at 2.5 Gbps into Singapore and Japan to provide a backup in case the main circuit failed.

SOURCE: "Fiber Network Will Serve Sydney after Summer Olympics," *Lightwave,* August 2000.

that does not interfere with commercial radio stations. The transmitters are very low power, designed to transmit a signal only a few miles, and are often built into portable computers or handheld devices such as phones and personal digital assistants. Wireless technologies for LAN environments, such as Bluetooth and IEEE 802.11b, are discussed in more detail in Chapter 6.

Infrared transmission uses low-frequency light waves (below the visible spectrum) to carry the data through the air on a direct line-of-sight path between two points. This technology is similar to the technology used in infrared TV remote controls. It is prone to interference, particularly from heavy rain, smoke, and fog that obscure the light transmission. Infrared transmitters are quite small but are seldom used for regular communication among portable or handheld computers because of their line-of-sight transmission requirements. (However, a version of infrared has also been adopted by some portable microcomputer manufacturers to transfer data between portable computers and desktop computers at distances of less than 3 feet.) Infrared is not very common, but it is sometimes used to transmit data from building to building.

A *microwave* is an extremely high frequency radio communication beam that is transmitted over a direct line-of-sight path between any two points. As its name implies, a microwave signal is an extremely short wavelength, thus the word *micro*wave. Microwave radio transmissions perform the same functions as cables. For example, point A communicates with point B via a through-the-air microwave transmission path, instead of a copper wire cable. Because microwave signals approach the frequency of visible light waves, they exhibit the same characteristics as light waves, such as reflection, focusing, or refraction. As with visible light waves, microwave signals can be focused into narrow, powerful beams that can be projected over long distances. Just as a parabolic reflector focuses a searchlight into a beam, a parabolic reflector also focuses a high-frequency microwave into a narrow beam. As the distance between communication points increases, towers are used

TECHNICAL FOCUS *3-1*

WIRELESS COMMUNICATIONS AT YANKEE STADIUM

Food service operations at Yankee Stadium run more smoothly now than in the past, thanks to a new wireless data communications system (Figure 3-7).

Employees take orders from the stand using a handheld terminal. This terminal broadcasts a radio signal that is received by one of the three radio-base stations located behind home plate, first base, and third base. These base stations are connected via twisted-pair cable to a wireless network controller that integrates the messages from the three base stations and directs them to the other network components.

The controller directs the orders to one of the three kitchens on twisted-pair cabling, where they are printed on one of 12 small receipt printers. The order is then prepared and sent to the customer.

A network server in the main office is connected to network controller via twisted-pair cable. The server the records transactions for accounting purposes and also provides access to a credit card authorization service via a modern and outside telephone line.

SOURCE: "Food Service Without Missing the Game," *Network Computing,* October 1, 1996.

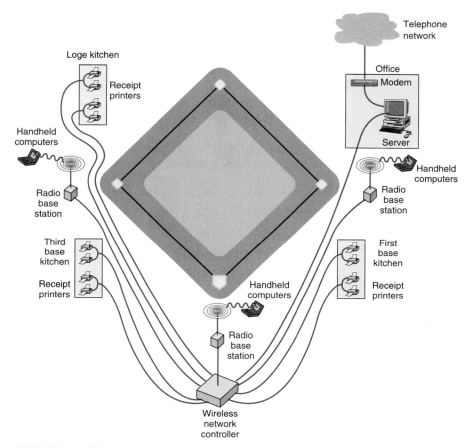

FIGURE 3-7 Wireless networking at Yankee Stadium.

to elevate the radio antennas to account for the earth's curvature and maintain a clear line-of-sight path between the two parabolic reflectors.

This transmission medium is typically used for long-distance data or voice transmission. It does not require the laying of any cable, because long-distance antennas with microwave repeater stations can be placed approximately 25 to 50 miles apart. A typical long-distance antenna might be 10 feet wide, although over shorter distances in the inner cities, the dish antennas can be less than 2 feet in diameter. The airwaves in larger cities are becoming congested because so many microwave dish antennas have been installed that they interfere with one another. This problem will force future users to seek alternative transmission media, such as radio-based wireless transmission.

Transmission via *satellite* is similar to transmission via microwave except instead transmission involving another nearby microwave dish antenna, it involves a satellite many miles up in space. Figure 3-8 depicts a geosynchronous satellite. *Geosynchronous* means that the satellite remains stationary over one point on the earth. One disadvantage of satellite transmission is the *propagation delay* that occurs because the signal has to travel out

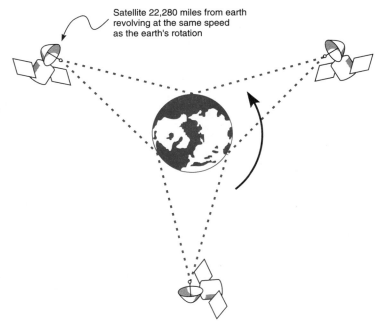

FIGURE 3-8 Satellites in operation.

into space and back to earth, a distance of many miles that even at the speed of light can be noticeable. Satellite transmission is sometimes also affected by *raindrop attenuation* when satellite transmissions are absorbed by heavy rain. It is not a major problem, but engineers need to work around it.

MANAGEMENT FOCUS *3-2*

SATELLITE COMMUNICATIONS IMPROVES PERFORMANCE

Boyle Transportation hauls hazardous materials nationwide for both commercial customers and the government, particularly the U.S. Department of Defense. The Department of Defense recently mandated that hazardous materials contractors use mobile communications systems with up-to-the-minute monitoring when hauling the department's hazardous cargoes.

After looking at the alternatives, Boyle realized that it would have to build its own system. Boyle needed a relational database at its operations center that contained information about customers, pickups, deliveries, truck location, and truck operating status. Data is distributed from this database via satellite to an antenna on each truck. Now, at any time, Boyle can notify the designated truck to make a new pickup via the bidirectional satellite link and record the truck's acknowledgment.

Each truck contains a mobile data terminal connected to the satellite network. Each driver uses a keyboard to enter information, which transmits the location of the truck. This satellite data is received by the main offices via a leased line from the satellite earth station.

This system increased productivity by an astounding 80 percent over 2 years; administration costs increased by only 20 percent.

Media Selection

Which media are best? It is hard to say, particularly when manufacturers continue to improve various media products. Several factors are important in selecting media (Figure 3-9).

- The *type of network* is one major consideration. Some media are used only for WANs (microwaves and satellite), whereas others typically are not (twisted-pair, coaxial cable, radio, and infrared), although we should note that some old WAN networks still use twisted-pair cable. Fiber-optic cable is unique in that it can be used for virtually any type of network.

- *Cost* is always a factor in any business decision. Costs are always changing as new technologies are developed and as competition among vendors drives prices down. Among the guided media, twisted-pair wire is generally the cheapest, coaxial cable is somewhat more expensive, and fiber-optic cable is the most expensive. The cost of the wireless media is generally driven more by distance than any other factor: For very short distances (several hundred meters), radio and infrared are the cheapest; for moderate distances (several hundred miles), microwave is cheapest; and for long distances, satellite is cheapest.

- *Transmission distance* is a related factor. Twisted pair wire, coaxial cable, infrared, and radio can transmit data only a short distance before the signal must be regenerated. Twisted-pair wire and radio typically can transmit up to 100 to 300 meters, and coaxial cable and infrared typically between 200 and 500 meters. Fiber optics can cable can transmit up to 75 miles, with new types of fiber-optic cable expected to reach more than 600 miles.

- *Security* is primarily determined by whether the media is guided or wireless. Wireless media (radio, infrared, microwave, and satellite) are the least secure because

Guided Media						
Media	**Network Type**	**Cost**	**Transmission Distance**	**Security**	**Error Rates**	**Speed**
Twisted Pair	LAN	Low	Short	Good	Low	Low–high
Coaxial Cable	LAN	Moderate	Short	Good	Low	Low–high
Fiber Optics	any	High	Moderate–long	Very good	Very low	High–very high

Radiated Media						
Media	**Network Type**	**Cost**	**Transmission Distance**	**Security**	**Error Rates**	**Speed**
Radio	LAN	Low	Short	Poor	Moderate	Low
Infrared	LAN, BN	Low	Short	Poor	Moderate	Low
Microwave	WAN	Moderate	Long	Poor	Low–moderate	Moderate
Satellite	WAN	Moderate	Long	Poor	Low–moderate	Moderate

FIGURE 3-9 Media summary. BN = backbone network; LAN = local area network; WAN = wide area network.

their signals are easily intercepted. Guided media (twisted pair, coaxial, and fiber optics) are more secure, with fiber optics being the most secure.

- *Error rates* are also important. Wireless media are most susceptible to interference and thus have the highest error rates. Among the guided media, fiber optics provides the lowest error rates, coaxial cable the next best, and twisted-pair cable the worst, although twisted-pair cable is generally better than the wireless media.

- *Transmission speeds* vary greatly among the different media. It is difficult to quote specific speeds for different media because transmission speeds are constantly improving and because they vary within the same type of media, depending on the specific type of cable and the vendor. In general, both twisted-pair cable and coaxial cable can provide data rates of between 1 and 100 Mbps (1 million bits per second), whereas fiber-optic cable ranges between 100 Mbps and 10 Gbps (10 billion bits per second). Radio and infrared generally provide 1 to 4 Mbps, whereas microwave and satellite range from 20 to 50 Mbps.

DIGITAL TRANSMISSION OF DIGITAL DATA

All computer systems produce binary data. For this data to be understood by both the sender and receiver, both must agree on a standard system for representing the letters, numbers, and symbols that compose messages. The coding scheme is the language that computers use to represent data.

Coding

A *character* is a symbol that has a common, constant meaning. A character might be the letter *A* or *B*, or it might be a number such as *1* or *2*. Characters also may be special symbols such as *?* or *&*. Characters in data communications, as in computer systems, are represented by groups of *bits* that are binary zeros (0) and ones (1). The groups of bits representing the set of characters that are the "alphabet" of any given system are called a *coding scheme*, or simply a *code*.

A *byte* is a group of consecutive bits that is treated as a unit or character. One byte normally is composed of 8 bits and usually represents one character; however, in data communications, some codes use 5, 6, 7, 8, or 9 bits to represent a character. For example, representation of the character *A* by a group of 7 bits (say, 1000001) is an example of coding.

There are two predominant coding schemes in use today. *United States of America Standard Code for Information Interchange (USASCII, or, more commonly, ASCII)* is the most popular code for data communications and is the standard code on most terminals and microcomputers. There are two types of ASCII; one is a 7-bit code that has 128 valid character combinations, and the other is an 8-bit code that has 256 combinations. The number of combinations can be determined by taking the number 2 and raising it to the power equal to the number of bits in the code because each bit has two possible values, a 0 or a 1. In this case $2^7 = 128$ characters or $2^8 = 256$ characters. *Extended Binary Coded Decimal Interchange Code (EBCDIC)* is IBM's standard code. This code has 8 bits, giving 256 valid character combinations.

Transmission Modes

Parallel Mode *Parallel mode* is the way the internal transfer of binary data takes place inside a computer. If the internal structure of the computer is 8-bit, then all 8 bits of the data element are transferred between main memory and the central processing unit simultaneously on 8 separate connections. The same is true of computers that use a 32-bit structure; all 32 bits are transferred simultaneously on 32 connections.

Figure 3-10 shows how all 8 bits of one character could travel down a parallel communication circuit. The circuit is physically made up of eight separate wires, wrapped in one outer coating. Each physical wire is used to send 1 bit of the 8-bit character. However, as far as the user is concerned (and the network for that matter), there is only one circuit; each of the wires inside the cable bundle simply connected to a different part of the plug that connects the computer to the bundle of wire. Compare Figure 3-10 with Figure 3-4.

Serial Mode *Serial mode* transmission means that a stream of data is sent over a communication circuit sequentially in a bit-by-bit fashion as shown in Figure 3-11. In this case, there is only one physical wire inside the bundle and all data must be transmitted over that one physical wire. The transmitting device sends one bit, then a second bit, and so on, until all the bits are transmitted. It takes n iterations or cycles to transmit n bits. Thus, serial transmission is considerably slower than parallel transmission—eight times slower in the case of 8-bit ASCII (because there are 8 bits). Compare Figure 3-11 with Figure 3-10.

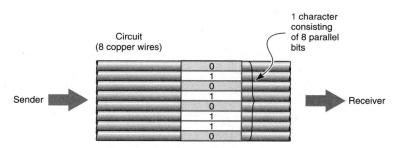

FIGURE 3-10   Parallel transmission of an 8-bit code.

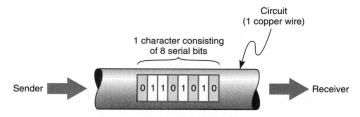

FIGURE 3-11   Serial transmission of an 8-bit code.

TECHNICAL FOCUS *3-2*

BASIC ELECTRICITY

There are two general categories of electrical current: direct current and alternating current. *Current* is the movement or flow of electrons, normally from positive (+) to negative (−). The plus (+) or minus (−) measurements are known as *polarity*. *Direct current* (DC) travels in only one direction, whereas *alternating current* (AC) travels first in one direction and then in the other direction.

A copper wire transmitting electricity acts like a hose transferring water. We use three common terms when dis-

cussing electricity. *Voltage* is defined as electrical pressure—the amount of electrical force pushing electrons through a circuit. In principle, it is the same as pounds per square inch in a water pipe. *Amperes* (amps) are units of electrical flow, or volume. This measure is analogous to gallons per minute for water. The *watt* is the fundamental unit of electrical power. It is a rate unit, not a quantity. You obtain the wattage by multiplying the volts by the amperes.

Digital Transmission

Digital transmission is the transmission of binary electrical or light pulses in that it only has two possible states, a 1 or a 0. The most commonly encountered voltage levels range from a low of +3/−3 to a high of +24/−24 volts. Digital signals are usually sent over wire of no more than a few thousand feet in length.

Figure 3-12 shows four types of digital signaling techniques. With *unipolar* signaling, the voltage is always positive or negative (like a DC current). Figure 3-12 illustrates a unipolar technique in which a signal of 0 volts (no current) is used to transmit a zero, and a signal of +5 volts is used to transmit a 1.

An obvious question at this point is this: If 0 volts means a zero, how do you send no data? This is discussed in detail in Chapter 4. For the moment, we will just say that there are ways to indicate when a message starts and stops, and when there are no messages to send, the sender and receiver agree to ignore any electrical signal on the line.

To successfully send and receive a message, both the sender and receiver have to agree on how often the sender can transmit data—that is, on the *data rate*. For example, if the data rate on a circuit is 64 Kbps (64,000 bits per second), then the sender changes the voltage on the circuit once every $1/64{,}000$ of a second and the receiver must examine the circuit once every $1/64{,}000$ of a second to read the incoming data bits.

In *bipolar* signaling, the 1's and 0's vary from a plus voltage to a minus voltage (like an AC current). The first bipolar technique illustrated in Figure 3-12 is called nonreturn to zero (NRZ) because the voltage alternates from +5 volts (indicating a 1) and −5 volts (indicating a 0), without ever returning to 0 volts. The second bipolar technique in this figure is called return to zero (RZ) because it always returns to 0 volts after each bit before going to +5 volts (for a 1) or −5 volts (for a 0). In Europe, bipolar signaling sometimes is called *double current* signaling because you are moving between a positive and negative voltage potential.

In general, bipolar signaling experiences fewer errors than unipolar signaling because the signals are more distinct. Noise or interference on the transmission circuit is less likely to cause the bipolar's +5 volts to be misread as a −5 volts than it is to cause the unipolar's 0 volts as a +5 volts. This is because changing the polarity of a current (from positive to negative, or vice versa) is more difficult than changing its magnitude.

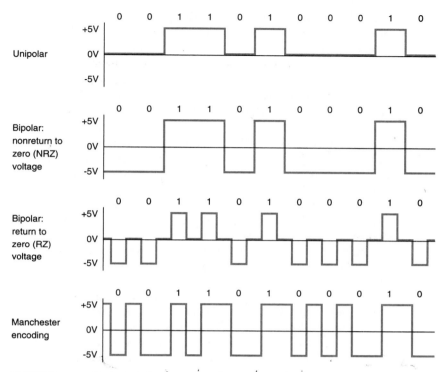

FIGURE 3-12   Unipolar, bipolar, and Manchester signals (digital).

How Ethernet Transmits Data

The most common technology used in LANs is Ethernet[2]; if you are working in a computer lab on campus, you are most likely using Ethernet. Ethernet uses digital transmission over either serial or parallel circuits, depending on which version of Ethernet you use. One version of Ethernet that uses serial transmission requires $1/10,000,000$ of a second to send one signal; that is, it transmits 10 million signals (each of 1 bit) per second. This gives a data rate of 10 Mbps, and if we assume that there are 8 bits in each character, this means that about 1.25 million characters can be transmitted per second in the circuit.

Ethernet uses *Manchester encoding.* Manchester encoding is a special type of unipolar signaling in which the signal is changed from high to low or from low to high in the middle of the signal. A change from high to low is used to represent a 0, whereas the opposite (a change from low to high) is used to represent a 1. See Figure 3-12. Manchester encoding is less susceptible to having errors go undetected, because if there is no transition in midsignal the receiver knows that an error must have occurred.

---

[2] If you don't know what Ethernet is, don't worry. We will discuss Ethernet in Chapter 5.

ANALOG TRANSMISSION OF DIGITAL DATA

Telephone networks were originally built for human speech rather than for data. They were designed to transmit the electrical representation of sound waves, rather than the binary data used by computers. There are many occasions when data need to be transmitted over a voice communications network. Many people working at home still use a modem over their telephone line to connect to the Internet.

The telephone system (commonly called *POTS* for *plain old telephone service*) enables voice communication between any two telephones within its network. The telephone converts the sound waves produced by the human voice at the sending end into electrical signals for the telephone network. These electric signals travel through the network until they reach the other telephone and are converted back into sound waves.

Analog transmission occurs when the signal sent over the transmission media continuously varies from one state to another in a wavelike pattern much like the human voice. Modems translate the digital binary data produced by computers into the analog signals required by voice transmission circuits. One modem is used by the transmitter to produce the analog signals and a second by the receiver to translate the analog signals back into digital signals.

The sound waves transmitted through the voice circuit have three important characteristics (see Figure 3-13). The first is the height of the wave, called *amplitude*. Amplitude is measured in decibels (dB). Our ears detect amplitude as the loudness or volume of sound. Every sound wave has two parts, half above the zero amplitude point (i.e., positive) and half below (i.e., negative), and both halves are always the same height.

The second characteristic is the length of the wave, usually expressed as the number of waves per second, or *frequency*. Frequency is expressed in hertz (Hz).[3] Our ears detect frequency as the pitch of the sound. Frequency is the inverse of the length of the sound wave, so that a high frequency means that that there are many short waves in a 1-second interval, whereas a low frequency means that there are fewer (but longer) waves in 1 second.

The third characteristic is the *phase,* which refers to the direction in which the wave begins. Phase is measured in the number of degrees (°). The wave in Figure 3-13 starts up

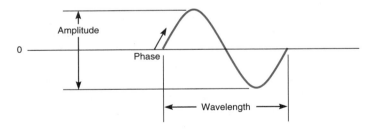

FIGURE 3-13 Sound wave.

---

[3] Hertz is the same as "cycles per second"; therefore, 20,000 Hertz is equal to 20,000 cycles per second. One hertz (Hz) is the same as 1 cycle per second. One kilohertz (KHz) is 1,000 cycles per second (kilocycles); 1 megahertz (MHz) is 1 million cycles per second (megacycles); and 1 gigahertz (GHz) is 1 billion cycles per second.

and to the right, which is defined as 0° phase wave. Waves can also start down and to the right (a 180° phase wave), and in virtually any other part of the sound wave.

Modulation

When we transmit data through the telephone lines, we use the shape of the sound waves we transmit (in terms of amplitude, frequency, and phase) to represent different data values. We do this by transmitting a simple sound wave through the circuit (called the *carrier wave*) and then changing its shape in different ways to represent a 1 or a 0. *Modulation* is the technical term used to refer to these "shape changes." There are three fundamental modulation techniques: amplitude modulation, frequency modulation, and phase modulation.

Basic Modulation   With *amplitude modulation (AM)* (also called *amplitude shift keying [ASK]*), the amplitude or height of the wave is changed. One amplitude is defined to be 0, and another amplitude is defined to be a 1. In the AM shown in Figure 3-14, the highest amplitude (tallest wave) represents a binary 1 and the lowest amplitude represents a binary 0. In this case, when the sending device wants to transmit a 1, it would send a high-amplitude wave (i.e., a loud signal). AM is more susceptible to noise (more errors) during transmission than is frequency modulation or phase modulation.

   Frequency modulation (FM) (also called *frequency shift keying [FSK]*) is a modulation technique whereby each 0 or 1 is represented by a number of waves per second (i.e., a different frequency). In this case, the amplitude does not vary. One frequency (i.e., a certain number of waves per second) is defined to be a 1, and a different frequency (a different number of waves per second) is defined to be a 0. In Figure 3-15, the higher-frequency wave (more waves per time period) equals a binary 1, and the lower frequency wave equals a binary 0.

   Phase modulation (PM) (also called *phase shift keying [PSK]*), is the most difficult to understand. *Phase* refers to the direction in which the wave begins. Until now, the waves we have shown start by moving up and to the right (this is called a 0° phase wave). Waves can also start down and to the right. This is called a phase of 180°. With phase modulation, one phase is defined to be a 0 and the other phase is defined to be a 1. Figure 3-16 shows the case where a phase of 0° is defined to be a binary 0 and a phase of 180° is defined to be a binary 1.

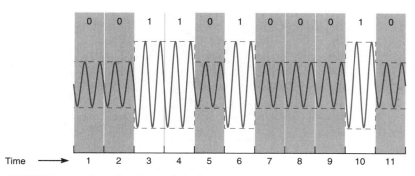

FIGURE 3-14   Amplitude modulation.

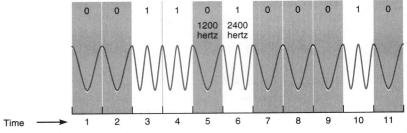

FIGURE 3-15 Frequency modulation.

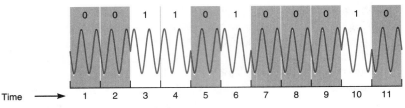

FIGURE 3-16 Phase modulation.

Sending Multiple Bits Simultaneously Each of the three basic modulation techniques (AM, FM, and PM) can be refined to send more than 1 bit at one time. For example, basic AM sends 1 bit per wave (or *symbol*) by defining two different amplitudes, one for a 1 and one for a 0. It is possible to send 2 bits on one wave or symbol by defining four different amplitudes. Figure 3-17 shows the case where the highest-amplitude wave is defined to be two bits, both 1's. The next highest amplitude is defined to mean first a 1 and then a 0, and so on.

This technique could be further refined to send 3 bits at the same time by defining 8 different amplitude levels or 4 bits by defining 16 amplitude levels, and so on. At some

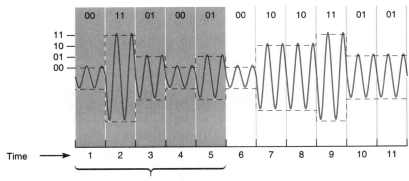

FIGURE 3-17 Two-bit amplitude modulation.

point, however, it becomes very difficult to differentiate between the different amplitudes. The differences are so small that even a small amount of noise could destroy the signal.

This same approach can be used for FM and PM. Two bits could be sent on the same symbol by defining four different frequencies, one for 11, one for 10, and so on, or by defining four phases (0°, 90°, 180°, and 270°). Three bits could be sent by defining eight frequencies or and eight phases (0°, 45°, 90°, 135°, 180°, 225°, 270°, and 315°). These techniques are also subject to the same limitations as AM; as the number of different frequencies or phases becomes larger, it becomes difficult to differentiate among them.

It is also possible to combine modulation techniques—that is, to use AM, FM, and PM techniques on the same circuit. For example, we could combine AM with four defined amplitudes (capable of sending 2 bits) with FM with four defined frequencies (capable of sending 2 bits) to enable us to send 4 bits on the same symbol.

One popular technique is *quadrature amplitude modulation* (QAM). QAM involves splitting the symbol into eight different phases (3 bits) and two different amplitudes (1 bit), for a total of 16 different possible values. Thus, one symbol in QAM can represent 4 bits.

Trellis-coded modulation (TCM) is an enhancement of QAM that combines PM and AM. TCM is unique in that it can transmit a different number of bits on each symbol. (How TCM works is beyond the scope of this book.) TCM can transmit 6, 7, 8, or 10 bits per symbol. The fastest version of TCM can average a maximum of 9.8 bits per symbol. The problem with high-speed modulation techniques such as TCM that send many bits per symbol is that they are more sensitive to imperfections in the communication circuit.

Bits Rate versus Baud Rate versus Symbol Rate   The terms *bit rate* (i.e., the number bits per second transmitted) and *baud rate* are used incorrectly much of the time. They often are used interchangeably, but they are not the same. In reality, the network designer or network user is interested in bits per second because it is the bits that are assembled into characters, characters into words and, thus, business information.

A *bit* is a unit of information. A *baud* is a unit of signaling speed used to indicate the number of times per second the signal on the communication circuit changes. Because of the confusion over the term *baud rate* among the general public, ITU-T now recommends the term *baud rate* be replaced by the term *symbol rate*. The bit rate and the symbol rate (or baud rate) are the same only when 1 bit is sent on each symbol. For example, if we use AM with two amplitudes, we send 1 bit on one symbol. Here, the bit rate equals the symbol rate. However, if we use QAM, we can send 4 bits on every symbol; the bit rate would be four times the symbol rate. If we used a 8-bit TCM, the bit rate would be eight times the symbol rate. Virtually all of today's modems send multiple bits per symbol.

Capacity of a Voice Circuit

The standard voice telephone circuit was originally designed to carry the human voice, which means that it carries sound waves only in the very narrow range of amplitudes (decibels) and frequencies (Hertz) used by human speech. Although both the available range of amplitudes and frequencies are important, for reasons that are beyond the scope of this book, it is the range of frequencies that is most important in determining the data capacity of a circuit.

The frequencies that humans can hear are between about 20 Hz and about 14,000 Hz, although some people can hear up to 20,000 Hz. The *bandwidth* is the difference between the highest and the lowest frequencies in a band or set of frequencies; thus, the bandwidth of human hearing is between 20 Hz and 14,000 Hz, or 13,880 Hz. The designers of the telephone network decided not to transmit all possible frequencies in this range but instead to transmit only the frequencies in the most commonly used range. They chose a bandwidth of 0 to 4,000 Hz, or 4,000 Hz. Some older telephone circuits have a useable bandwidth of only between 300 and 3,300 Hz, or 3,000 Hz.

It is important to note that this limit on bandwidth is imposed by the telephone and the equipment used in the telephone network. The actual capacity or bandwidth of the physical wires running into your house or apartment depends on what exact type of wires were installed and the number of miles from your house or apartment to the telephone company's office (the longer the distance, the lower the bandwidth[4]). About half of the residences and businesses in North America lie within 2 miles (or about 3 kilometers) of an end office, meaning the actual twisted-pair wire running into the residences and businesses has a usable bandwidth of 1 MHz (i.e., 1 million Hertz). Another 30 percent of residences lie between 2 and 3 miles from the end office (about 3 to 5 kilometers), at which point the usable bandwidth drops to about 300 KHz.

The data capacity of a circuit is the fastest rate at which you can send your data over the circuit in terms of the number of bits per second. The data rate is calculated by multiplying the number of bits sent on each symbol by the maximum symbol rate. As we discussed in the previous section, the number of bits per symbol depends on the modulation technique (e.g., QAM sends 4 bits per symbol).

The maximum symbol rate in any circuit depends on the bandwidth available and the signal-to-noise ratio (the strength of the signal compared with the amount of noise in the circuit). The maximum symbol rate is usually the same as the bandwidth as measured in Hertz. If the circuit is very noisy, the maximum symbol rate may fall as low as 50 percent of the bandwidth. If the circuit has very little noise, it is possible to transmit at rates up to the bandwidth.

Voice-grade lines provide a bandwidth of 4,000 Hz. Under perfect circumstances, the maximum symbol rate is therefore about 4,000 symbols per second. If we were to use basic AM (1 bit per symbol), the maximum data rate would be 4,000 bits per second (bps). If we were to use QAM (4 bits per symbol), the maximum data rate would be 4 bits per symbol × 4,000 symbols per second = 16,000 bps. Using TCM (with 6 bits per symbol), the maximum data rate would be 6 × 4000 = 24,000 bps. However, as you will see later in this chapter, it is possible to get higher data rates through a voice circuit by using other methods other than analog transmission.

How Modems Transmit Data

The *modem* (an acronym for *mo*dulator/*dem*odulator) takes the digital data from a computer in the form of electrical pulses and converts them into the analog signal that is needed for transmission over an analog voice-grade circuit. There are many different types of modems available today (Figure 3-18). For data to be transmitted between two computers

---

[4] As signals travel through the wire, they gradually lose electrical strength and fade away, the same way that sound waves gradually lose strength and are harder to hear the farther you are away. The greater the distance, the more difficult it is to process the signal and therefore the less bandwidth before noise makes the signal unreadable.

Modem Standard	Maximum Symbol Rate	Type of Signal	Maximum Bits per Symbol	Maximum Data Rate (bps)
V.22	1,200	FM	1	1,200
	2,400	FM	1	2,400
V.32	2,400	QAM	4	9,600
V.32bis	2,400	TCM	6	14,000
V.34	3,429	TCM	8.4	28,800
V.34+	3,429	TCM	9.8	33,600

FIGURE 3-18 Modem standards.

using modems, both need to use the same type of modem. Fortunately, several standards exist for modems, and any modem that conforms to a standard can communicate with any other modem that conforms to the same standard.

The *V.22* modem was one of the first widely used modem standards but is now obsolete. A V.22 modem can transmit at either 1,200 symbols per second or 2,400 symbols per second using FM to send 1 bit per symbol, resulting in a data rate of 1,200 bps or 2,400 bps (see Figure 3-18). In contrast, more modern modems use higher symbol rates and put more bits on each symbol. Because the amount of noise may limit the symbol rate and the modulation technique, V.34 modems go through a *"handshaking"* sequence when they first connect that tests the circuit and determines the optimum combination of symbol rate and modulation technique that will produce the highest data transmission rates. Therefore, although the highest data rate for a V.34+ modem is 33.6 Kbps, not all circuits will be good enough to support it.

A modem's data transmission rate is the primary factor that determines the throughput rate of data, but it is not the only factor. *Data compression* can increase throughput of data over a communication link by literally compressing the data. *V.44*, the ISO standard for data compression, uses *Lempel-Ziv encoding.* As a message is being transmitted, Lempel-Ziv encoding builds a dictionary of two-, three-, and four-character combinations that occur in the message. Anytime the same character pattern reoccurs in the message, the index to the dictionary entry is transmitted rather than sending the actual data. The reduction provided by V.44 compression depends on the actual data sent but usually averages about 6:1 (i.e., almost six times as much data can be sent per second using V.44 as without it). Thus, a V.34+ modem providing a data rate of 33.6 Kbps might provide a data rate of about 200 Kbps using V.44.

If you look carefully at Figure 3-18, you will notice that it does not include 56 Kbps modems (V.90 and V.92). These modems combine traditional analog transmission with digital transmission. Before we can explain how 56-Kbps modems work, we must first explain how digital transmission can be used to transmit analog data.

DIGITAL TRANSMISSION OF ANALOG DATA

In the same way that digital computer data can be sent over analog telephone networks using analog transmission, analog voice data be sent over digital networks using digital transmission. This process is somewhat similar to the analog transmission of digital data. A pair of special devices called *codecs* (<u>co</u>de/<u>dec</u>ode) is used in the same way that a pair of modems is used to translate the data to send across the circuit. One codec is attached to source of the signal (e.g., a telephone or the local loop at the end office) and translates the incoming analog voice signal into a digital signal for transmission across the digital circuit. A second codec at the receiver's end translates the digital data back into analog data.

Translating from Analog to Digital

Analog voice data must first be translated into a series of binary digits before they can be transmitted over a digital circuit. This is done by sampling the amplitude of the sound wave at regular intervals and translating it into a binary number. Figure 3-19 shows an example where eight different amplitude levels are used (i.e., each amplitude level is represented by three bits). The top diagram shows the original signal, and the bottom diagram, the digitized signal.

A quick glance will show that the digitized signal is only a rough approximation of the original signal. The original signal had a smooth flow, but the digitized signal has jagged "steps." The difference between the two signals is called *quantizing error*. Voice transmissions using digitized signals that have a great deal of quantizing error sound metallic or machinelike to the ear.

There are two ways to reduce quantizing error and improve the quality of the digitized signal, but neither is without cost. The first method is to increase the number of amplitude levels. This minimizes the difference between the levels (the "height" of the "steps") and results in a smoother signal. In Figure 3-19, we could define 16 amplitude levels instead of 8 levels. This would require 4 bits (rather than the current 3 bits) to represent the amplitude, thus increasing the amount of data needed to transmit the digitized signal.

No amount of levels or bits will ever result in perfect-quality sound reproduction, but in general, seven bits ($2^7 = 128$ levels) reproduces human speech adequately. Music, on the other hand, requires at least 16 bits ($2^{16} = 65,536$ levels).

The second method is to sample more frequently. This will reduce the "length" of each "step," also resulting in a smoother signal. To obtain a reasonable-quality voice signal, one must sample at least twice the highest possible frequency in the analog signal. You will recall that the highest frequency transmitted in telephone circuits is 4,000 Hz. Thus, the methods used to digitize telephone voice transmissions must sample the input voice signal at a minimum of 8,000 times per second. Sampling more frequently than this (called *oversampling*) will improve signal quality. RealNetworks.com, which produces Real Audio and other Web-based tools, sets its products to sample at 48,000 times per second to provide higher quality.

How Telephones Transmit Voice Data

When you make a telephone call, the telephone converts your analog voice data into a simple analog signal and sends it down the circuit from your home to the telephone company's network. This process is almost unchanged from the one used by Bell when he invented the telephone in 1876. With the invention of digital transmission, the common carriers (i.e., the

The signal (original wave) is quantized into 128 pulse amplitudes (PAM). In this example we have used only eight pulse amplitudes for simplicity. These eight amplitudes can be depicted by using only a 3-bit code instead of the 8-bit code normally used to encode each pulse amplitude.

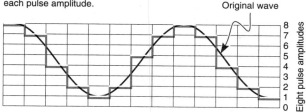

After quantizing, samples are taken at specific points to produce amplitude modulated pulses. These pulses are then coded. Because we used eight pulse levels, we only need three binary positions to code each pulse.[1] If we had used 128 pulse amplitudes, then a 7-bit code plus one parity bit would be required.

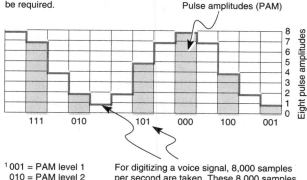

[1] 001 = PAM level 1
010 = PAM level 2
011 = PAM level 3
100 = PAM level 4
101 = PAM level 5
110 = PAM level 6
111 = PAM level 7
000 = PAM level 8

For digitizing a voice signal, 8,000 samples per second are taken. These 8,000 samples are then transmitted as a serial stream of 0s and 1s. In our case 8,000 samples times 3 bits per sample would require a 24,000 bps transmission rate. In reality, 8 bits per sample times 8,000 samples requires a 64,000 bps transmission rate.

FIGURE 3-19   Pulse amplitude modulation (PAM).

telephone companies) began converting their voice networks to use digital transmission. Today, all of the common carrier networks use digital transmission, except in the *local loop* (sometimes called the *last mile*), the wires that run from your home or business to the telephone switch that connects your local loop into the telephone network. This switch contains a codec that converts the analog signal from your phone into a digital signal. This digital signal is then sent through the telephone network until it hits the switch for local loop for the person you are calling. This switch uses its codec to convert the digital signal used inside the phone network back into the analog signal needed by that person's local loop and telephone.

There are many different combinations of sampling frequencies and numbers of bits per sample that could be used. For example, one could sample 4,000 times per second using 128 amplitude levels (i.e., 7 bits) or sample at 16,000 times per second using 256 levels (i.e., 8 bits).

The North American telephone network uses *pulse code modulation (PCM)*. With PCM, the input voice signal is sampled 8,000 times per second. Each time the input voice signal is sampled, 8 bits are generated.[5] Therefore, the transmission speed on the digital circuit must be 64,000 bps (8 bits per sample × 8,000 samples per second) to transmit a voice signal when it is in digital form. Thus, the North American telephone network is built using millions of 64 Kbps digital circuits that connect via codecs to the millions of miles of analog local loop circuits into the user's residences and businesses.

How Instant Messenger Transmits Voice Data

A 64 Kbps digital circuit works very well for transmitting voice data because it provides very good quality. The problem is that it requires a lot of capacity. Internet users who connect using modems do not have circuits that run as fast as 64 Kbps; 33.6 Kbps is more common. Therefore, they can't use PCM.

Adaptive differential pulse code modulation (ADPCM) is the alternative used by IM and many other applications that provide voice services over lower-speed digital circuits. ADPCM works in much the same way as PCM. It samples incoming voice signal 8,000 times per second and calculates the same 8-bit amplitude value as PCM. However, instead of transmitting the 8-bit value, it instead transmits the *difference* between the 8-bit value in the last time interval and the current 8-bit value (i.e., how the amplitude has *changed* from one time period to another). Because analog voice signals change slowly, these changes can be adequately represented by using only 4 bits. This means that ADPCM can be used on digital circuits that provide only 32 Kbps (4 bits per sample × 8,000 samples per second = 32,000 bps).

Several versions of ADPCM have been developed and standardized by the ITU-T. There are versions designed for 8 Kbps circuits (which send 1 bit 8,000 times per second) and 16 Kbps circuits (which send 2 bits 8,000 times per second), as well as the original 32 Kbps version. However, there is a trade-off here. Although the 32 Kbps version usually provides as good a sound quality as that of a traditional voice telephone circuit, the 8 Kbps and 16 Kbps versions provide poorer sound quality.

ANALOG–DIGITAL MODEMS

The V.34+ modem is probably the fastest analog modem that will be developed. Its symbol rate and number of bits per symbol are the fastest that are possible with traditional analog telephone technology. To get the fastest data transmission rates, 56 Kbps modems (*V.90* and *V.92* standards) had to combine analog and digital transmission.

Today's 56 Kbps modems take the basic concepts of PCM and turn them backward. If PCM needs a codec that samples 8,000 times per second and produces 8 bits in each

---

[5] Seven of those bits are used to represent the voice signal, and 1 bit is used for control purposes.

sample to accurately digitize human voice on a telephone circuit, it makes sense that the same telephone circuit can accurately transmit (and enable the receiver to recognize) up to 8 bits transmitted 8,000 times per second.

Fifty-six Kbps modems are designed to recognize an 8-bit digital symbol (one of 256 possible amplitudes, or voltages) 8,000 times per second. This gives a theoretical transmission speed of 64 Kbps. Because 1 of the bits in the PCM symbol is used for control purposes, the user can use only 7 bits. This means the maximum data rate becomes 56 Kbps (8,000 symbols × 7 bits per symbol).

Noise is a critical issue. Distinguishing among 128 different possible amplitudes (i.e., 7 bits means 128 symbols, whereas 8 bits means 256 symbols) is difficult unless the telephone line is very clear. In noisy conditions, the modem can accurately recognize fewer bits per symbol, so the number of bits per symbol must be reduced, thus reducing the data rate. It is estimated that about 20 percent of the telephone lines in North America (mostly the older rural exchanges) are too noisy to use 56 Kbps modems.

For technical reasons beyond the scope of this book, it is easier to control noise in the channel when transmitting from the server to the client than to control noise when transmitting in the opposite direction. With the older V.90 standard of 56-Kbps modems, only the "downstream" channel from server to client uses digital transmission at a maximum of 56 Kbps (slower if the circuit is noisy). "Upstream" communication from client to server uses traditional analog transmission with V.34+, which means a maximum of 33.6 Kbps.

The newer V.92 standard for 56-Kbps modems uses digital transmission both up- and downstream. The downstream provides a maximum of 56 Kbps, whereas the upstream provides a maximum of 48 Kbps.

MULTIPLEXING

Multiplexing means to break one high-speed physical communication circuit into several lower-speed logical circuits so that many different devices can simultaneously use it but still "think" that they have their own separate circuits (the multiplexer is *"transparent"*). It is multiplexing (specifically, wavelength division multiplexing [WDM], discussed later in this section) that has enabled the almost unbelievable growth in network capacity discussed in Chapter 1; without WDM, the Internet would have collapsed in the 1990s.

Multiplexing often is done in multiples of 4 (e.g., 8, 16). Figure 3-20 shows a four-level multiplexed circuit. Note that two multiplexers are needed for each circuit: one to combine the four original circuits into the one multiplexed circuit and one to separate them back into the four separate circuits.

The primary benefit of multiplexing is to save money by reducing the amount of cable or the number of network circuits that must be installed. For example, if we did not use multiplexers in Figure 3-20, we would need to run four separate circuits from the clients to the server. If the clients were located close to the server, this would be inexpensive. However, if they were located several miles away, the extra costs could be substantial.

There are four types of multiplexing: frequency division multiplexing (FDM), time division multiplexing (TDM), statistical time division multiplexing (STDM) and WDM.

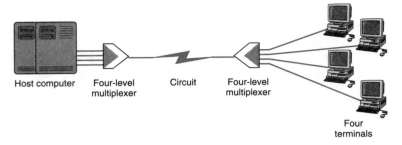

FIGURE 3-20 Multiplexed circuit.

Frequency Division Multiplexing

Frequency division multiplexing (FDM) can be described as dividing the circuit "horizon-tally" so that many signals can travel a single communication circuit simultaneously. The circuit is divided into a series of separate channels, each transmitting on a different fre-quency, much like series of different radio or TV stations. All signals exist in the media at the same time, but because they are on different frequencies, they do not interfere with each other.

Figure 3-21 illustrates the use of FDM to divide one circuit into four *channels.* Each channel is a separate logical circuit, and the devices connected to them are unaware that their circuit is multiplexed. In the same way that radio stations must be assigned separate frequencies to prevent interference, so must the signals in a FDM circuit. The *guardbands* in Figure 3-21 are the unused portions of the circuit that separate these frequencies from each other.

With FDM, the total capacity of the physical circuit is simply divided among the multiplexed circuits. For example, suppose we had a physical circuit with a data rate of 64 Kbps that we wanted to divide into four circuits. We would simply divide the 64 Kbps among the four circuits and assign each circuit 16 Kbps. However, because FDM needs guardbands, we also have to allocate some of the capacity to the guardbands, so we might

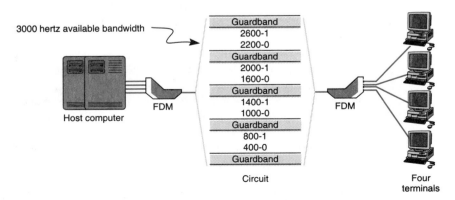

FIGURE 3-21 Frequency division multiplex (FDM) circuit.

actually end up with four circuits, each providing 15 Kbps, with the remaining 4 Kbps allocated to the guardbands. There is no requirement that all circuits be the same size, as you will see in a later section. FDM was commonly used in older telephone systems, which is why the bandwidth on older phone systems was only 3,000 Hz, not the 4,000 Hz actually available—1,000 Hz were used as guardbands, with the voice signals traveling between two guardbands on the outside of the 4,000 Hz channel.

Time Division Multiplexing

Time division multiplexing (TDM) shares a communication circuit among two or more terminals by having them take turns, dividing the circuit vertically, so to speak. Figure 3-22 shows the same four terminals connected using TDM. In this case, one character is taken from each terminal in turn, transmitted down the circuit, and delivered to the appropriate device at the far end (e.g., one character for terminal A, then one from B, one from C, one from D, another from A, another from B, and so on). Time on the circuit is allocated even when data are not be transmitted, so that some capacity is wasted when terminals are idle. TDM generally is more efficient than FDM because it does not need guardbands. Guardbands use "space" on the circuit that otherwise could be used to transmit data. Therefore, if one divides a 64-Kbps circuit into four circuits, the result would be four 16-Kbps circuits.

Statistical Time Division Multiplexing

Statistical time division multiplexing (STDM) is the exception to the rule that the capacity of the multiplexed circuit must equal the sum of the circuits it combines. STDM allows more terminals or computers to be connected to a circuit than does FDM or TDM. If you have four computers connected to a multiplexer and each can transmit at 64 Kbps, then you should have a circuit capable of transmitting 256 Kbps (4 × 64 Kbps). However, not all computers will be transmitting continuously at their maximum transmission speed. Users

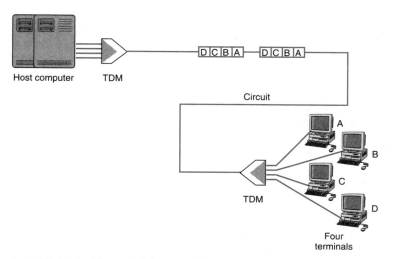

FIGURE 3-22 Time division multiplex (TDM) circuit.

typically pause to read their screens or spend time typing at lower speeds. Therefore, you do not need to provide a speed of 256 Kbps on this multiplexed circuit. If you assume that only two computers will ever transmit at the same time, 128 Kbps would be enough. STDM is called *statistical* because selection of transmission speed for the multiplexed circuit is based on a statistical analysis of the usage requirements of the circuits to be multiplexed.

The key benefit of STDM is that it provides more efficient use of the circuit and saves money. You can buy a lower-speed, less-expensive circuit than you could using FDM or TDM.

STDM introduces two additional complexities. First, STDM can cause time delays. If *all* devices start transmitting or receiving at the same time (or just more than at the statistical assumptions), the multiplexed circuit cannot transmit all the data it receives because it does not have sufficient capacity. Therefore, STDM must have internal memory to store the incoming data that it cannot immediately transmit. When traffic is particularly heavy, you may have a 1- to 30-second delay. The second problem is that because the logical circuits are not permanently assigned to specific devices as they are in FDM and TDM, the data from one device are interspersed with data from other devices. The first message might be from the third computer, the second from the first computer, and so on. Therefore, we need to add some address information to each packet to make sure we can identify the logical circuit to which it belongs. This is not a major problem, but it does increase the complexity of the multiplexer and also slightly decreases efficiency, because now we must "waste" some of the circuit's capacity in transmitting the extra address we have added to each packet.

Wavelength Division Multiplexing

Wavelength division multiplexing (WDM) is a version of FDM used in fiber-optic cables. When fiber-optic cables were first developed, the devices attached to them were designed

MANAGEMENT FOCUS *3-3*

NASA'S GROUND COMMUNICATIONS NETWORK

NASA's communications network is extensive because its operations are spread out around the world and into space. The main Deep Space Network is controlled out of the Jet Propulsion Laboratory (JPL) in California. JPL is connected to the three main Deep Space Communications Centers (DSCCs) that communicate with NASA spacecraft. The three DSCCs are spread out equidistantly around the world so that one will always be able to communicate with spacecraft no matter where they are in relation to the earth: Canberra, Australia; Madrid, Spain; and Goldstone, California.

Figure 3-23 shows the JPL network. Each DSCC has four large-dish antennas ranging in size from 85 to 230 feet (26 to 70 meters) that communicate with the spacecraft. These send and receive operational data such as telemetry, commands, tracking, and radio signals. Each DSCC also sends and receives administrative data such as e-mail, reports, and Web pages, as well as telephone calls and video.

The three DSCCs and JPL use Ethernet local area networks (LANs) that are connected to multiplexers that integrate the data, voice, and video signals for transmission. Satellite circuits are used between Canberra and JPL and Madrid and JPL. Fiber-optic circuits are used between JPL and Goldstone.

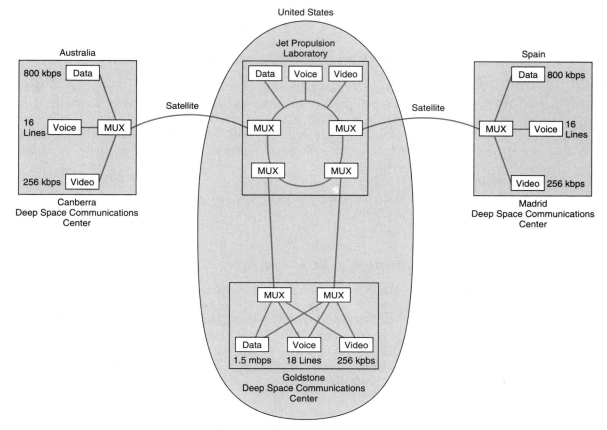

FIGURE 3-23   NASA's Deep Space Communications Centers ground communications network. MUX = multiplexer.

to use only one color of light generated by a laser or LED. With one commonly used type of fiber cable, the data rate is 622 Mbps (622 million bits per second). Until recently, the 622-Mbps data rate seemed wonderful. Then the amount of data transferred over the Internet began doubling at fairly regular intervals, and several companies began investigating how we could increase the amount of data sent over existing fiber-optic cables.

The answer, in hindsight, was obvious. Light has different frequencies (i.e., colors), so rather than building devices to transmit using only one color, why not send multiple signals, each in a different frequency, through the same fiber cable? By simply attaching different devices that could transmit in the full spectrum of light rather than just one frequency, the capacity of the existing fiber-optic cables could be dramatically increased, with no change to the physical cables themselves.

WDM works by using lasers to transmit different frequencies of light (i.e., colors) through the same fiber-optic cable. As with FDM, each logical circuit is assigned a different frequency, and the devices attached to the circuit don't "know" they are multiplexed over the same physical circuit.

Dense WDM (DWDM) is a variant of WDM that further increases the capacity of WDM by adding TDM to WDM. Today, DWDM permits up to 40 simultaneous circuits, each transmitting up to 10 Gbps, giving a total network capacity in *one* fiber optic cable of 400 Gbps (i.e., 400 billion bits per second). Remember, this is the same physical cable that until recently produced only 622 Mbps; all we've changed are the devices connected to it.

DWDM is a relatively new technique, so it will continue to improve over the next few years. As we write this, DWDM systems have been announced that provide 128 circuits, each at 10 Gbps (1.28 terabits per second (1.28 Tbps) in one fiber cable. Experts predict that DWDM transmission speeds should reach 25 Tbps (i.e., 25 trillion bits) within a few years (and possibly 1 petabit [Pbps], or 1 million billion bits per second)—all on that same single fiber-optic cable that today typically provides 622 Mbps. Once we reach these speeds, the most time-consuming part of the process is converting from the light used in the fiber cables into the electricity used in the computer devices used to route the messages through the Internet. Therefore, many companies are now developing computer devices that run on light, not electricity.

Inverse Multiplexing

Multiplexing uses one high-speed circuit to transmit a set of several lower-speed circuits. It can also be used to do the opposite. *Inverse multiplexing (IMUX)* combines several low-speed circuits to make them appear as one high-speed circuit to the user (Figure 3-24.)

One of the most common uses of IMUX is to provide *T1* circuits for WANs. T1 circuits provide data transmission rates of 1.544 Mbps by combining 24 slower-speed circuits (64 Kbps). As far as the users are concerned, they have access to one high-speed circuit, even through their data actually travels across a set of slower circuits. T1 and other circuits are discussed in Chapter 8.

Until recently, there were no standards for IMUX. If you wanted to use IMUX, you had to ensure that you bought IMUX circuits from the same vendor so both clients or hosts could communicate. Several vendors have recently adopted the *BONDING* standard (*Bandwidth on Demand Interoperability Networking Group*). Any IMUX circuit that conforms to the BONDING standard can communicate with any other IMUX circuit that conforms to the same standard. BONDING splits outgoing messages from one client or host

MANAGEMENT FOCUS *3-4*

GET MORE BANDWIDTH FOR LESS

Upstart network providers Yipes and Metromedia are among the first to offer metropolitan area network services based on wavelength division multiplexing (WDM). Both offer circuits that range from 1 Mbps up to 1 Gbps in 1-Mbps increments and cost anywhere between 10 percent and 80 percent of the cost of traditional copper-based serv-

ices. The challenge both Yipes and Metromedia face are to expand their WDM services beyond the MAN.

SOURCE: "Get More Bandwidth for Less," *Informationweek,* August 7, 2000.

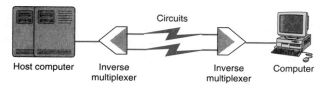

FIGURE 3-24 Inverse multiplexer.

across several low-speed telephone lines and combines incoming messages from several telephone lines into one circuit so that the client or host "thinks" it has a faster circuit.

The most common use for BONDING is for room-to-room videoconferencing. In this case, organizations usually have the telephone company install six telephone lines into their videoconferencing room that are connected to the IMUX. (The telephone lines are usually 64-Kbps ISDN telephone lines; see Chapter 8 for a description of ISDN.) When an organization wants to communicate with another videoconferencing room that has a similar six-telephone-line IMUX configuration, the first IMUX circuit uses one telephone line to call the other IMUX circuit on one of its telephone lines. The two IMUX circuits then exchange telephone numbers and call each other on the other five lines until all six lines are connected. Once the connection has been established, the IMUX circuits transmit data over the six lines simultaneously, thus giving a total data rate of 6×64 Kbps = 384 Kbps.

How DSL Transmits Data

The reason for the limited capacity on voice telephone circuits lies with the telephone and the switching equipment at the telephone company offices. The actual twisted-pair wire in the local loop is capable of providing much higher data transmission rates. *Digital subscriber line (DSL)* is one approach to changing the way data are transmitted in the local loop to provide higher-speed data transfer. DSL is a family of techniques that combines analog transmission and FDM to provide a set of voice and data circuits. There are many different types of DSL, so many in fact that DSL is sometimes called xDSL, where the x is intended to represent one of the many possible flavors. Chapter 9 examines the different types of DSL.

With DSL, a DSL modem (called *customer premises equipment [CPE]*) is installed in the customer's home or office and another DSL modem is installed at the telephone company switch closest to the customer's home or office. The modem is first an FDM device that splits the physical circuit into three logical circuits: a standard voice circuit used for telephone calls, an upstream data circuit from the customer to the telephone switch, and a downstream data circuit from the switch to the customer. TDM is then used within the two data channels to provide a set of one or more individual channels that can be used to carry different data. A combination of amplitude and phase modulation is used in the data circuits to provide the desired data rate (the exact combination depends on which flavor of DSL is used).[6] One version of DSL called G.Lite ASDL provides one voice circuit, a 1.5-Mbps downstream circuit and a 384-Kbps upstream channel.

---

[6] DSL is rapidly changing because it is so new. More information can be found from the DSL forum (www.adsl.com and www.dsllife.com) and the ITU-T under standard G.992.

SUMMARY

Circuits   Networks can be configured so that there is a separate circuit from each client to the host (called a point-to-point configuration) or so that several clients share the same circuit (a multipoint configuration). Data can flow through the circuit in one direction only (simplex), in both directions simultaneously (full duplex), or by taking turns so that data sometimes flow in one direction and then in the other (half duplex). Media are either guided, in that they travel through a physical cable (e.g., twisted-pair wires, coaxial cable, or fiber-optic cable), or wireless, in that they are broadcast through the air (e.g., radio, infrared, microwave, or satellite). The choice is important if you are building your own network; it is less important if you are leasing a circuit from a carrier who guarantees the circuit's performance. Among the guided media, fiber-optic cable can transmit data the fastest with the fewest errors and offers greater security but costs the most; twisted-pair wire is the cheapest and most commonly used. The choice of wireless media depends more on distance than on any other factor; infrared and radio are the cheapest for short distances, microwave is cheapest for moderate distances, and satellite is cheapest for long distances.

Digital Transmission of Digital Data   Digital transmission (also called baseband transmission) is done by sending a series of electrical (or light) pulse through the media. Digital transmission is preferred to analog transmission because it produces fewer errors; is more efficient; permits higher maximum transmission rates; is more secure; and simplifies the integration of voice, video, and data on the same circuit. With unipolar digital transmission, the voltage changes between 0 volts to represent a binary 0 and some positive value (e.g., +15 volts) to represent a binary 1. With bipolar digital transmission, the voltage changes polarity (i.e., positive or negative) to represent a 1 or a 0. Bipolar is less susceptible to errors. Ethernet uses Manchester encoding, which is a version of unipolar transmission.

Analog Transmission of Digital Data   Modems are used to translate the digital data produced by computers into the analog signals for transmission in today's voice communication circuits. Both the sender and receiver need to have a modem. Data is transmitted by changing (or modulating) a carrier sound wave's amplitude (height), frequency (length), or phase (shape) to indicate a binary 1 or 0. For example, in amplitude modulation, one amplitude is defined to be a 1 and another amplitude is defined to be a 0. It is possible to send more than 1 bit on every symbol (or wave). For example, with amplitude modulation, you could send 2 bits on each wave by defining four amplitude levels. The capacity or maximum data rate that an circuit can transmit is determined by multiplying the symbol rate (symbols per second) by the number of bits per symbol. Generally (but not always), the symbol rate is the same as the bandwidth, so bandwidth is often used a measure of capacity. V.44 is a data compression standard that can be combined with any of the foregoing types of modems to reduce the amount of data in the transmitted signal by a factor of up to six. Thus, a V.92 modem using V.44 could provide an effective data rate of $56,000 \times 6 = 336,000$ bps.

Digital Transmission of Analog Data   Because digital transmission is better, analog voice data is sometimes converted to digital transmission. Pulse code modulation (PCM) is the most commonly used technique. PCM samples the amplitude of the incoming voice signal 8,000 times per second and uses 8 bits to represent the signal. PCM produces a reasonable approximation of the human voice, but more sophisticated techniques are needed to adequately reproduce more complex sounds such as music.

Analog–Digital Modems   Analog–digital modems are newer modems that combine analog and digital transmission to overcome the limitations of the traditional telephone network. V.90 56-Kbps modems use analog transmission (V.34+) to transmit from the client to the server (upstream) but use digital techniques based on reversing PCM to transmit at up to 56 Kbps from the server to the client (downstream). V.92 modems use digital in both directions and can reach 48 Kbps upstream.

Multiplexers   A multiplexer is a device that combines several simultaneous low-speed circuits on one higher-speed circuit so that each low-speed circuit believes it has a separate circuit. In general, the transmission capacity of the high-speed circuit must equal or exceed the sum of the low-speed circuits. With frequency division multiplexing (FDM) each low-speed circuit is allocated a separate frequency on the high-speed circuit. Wavelength division multiplexing (WDM) is a special form of (FDM) used in fiber-optic circuits. With time division multiplexing ([TDM] the most commonly used type of multiplexing), each low-speed circuit is allocated a separate time slice on the high-speed circuit. Relying on the fact that few terminals or microcomputers transmit continuously, statistical TDM combines more low-speed circuits than the high-speed circuit can support (e.g., six 16,000-bps circuits on one 64,000 bps circuit), although problems can occur if all low-speed circuits actually transmit at once. Inverse multiplexing enables several low-speed circuits to be treated as one high-speed circuit.

KEY TERMS

56K modem
adaptive differential
    pulse code modula-
    tion (ADPCM)
American Standard
    Code for Information
    Interchange (ASCI)
amplitude
amplitude modulation
    (AM)
amplitude shift keying
    (ASK)
analog transmission
bandwidth
baud rate
bipolar
bits per second (bps)
Bandwidth on Demand
    Interoperability Net-
    working Group
    (BONDING)
carrier wave
channel
circuit
circuit configuration
coaxial cable
codec
coding

customer premises
    equipment (CPE)
cycles per second
data compression
data rate
digital subscriber line
    (DSL)
digital transmission
Extended Binary Coded
    Decimal Exchange
    (EBCDIC)
fiber-optic cable
Frequency
frequency division mul-
    tiplexing (FDM)
frequency modulation
    (FM)
frequency shift keying
    (FSK)
handshaking
Hertz (Hz)
full duplex
guardband
guided media
half duplex
infrared transmission
intelligent controller
intelligent terminal

inverse multiplexing
    (IMUX)
Lempel-Ziv encoding
local loop
logical circuit
Manchester encoding
modem
multipoint circuit
multiplexer
parallel transmission
phase
phase modulation (PM)
phase shift keying
    (ASK)
physical circuit
plain old telephone serv-
    ice (POTS)
point-to-point circuit
polarity
pulse code modulation
    (PCM)
quadrature amplitude
    modulation (QAM)
quantizing error
radio transmission
retrain time
satellite transmission
serial transmissions

simplex
statistical time division
    multiplexing
    (STDM)
switch
symbol rate
trellis-coded modulation
    (TCM)
time division multiplex-
    ing (TDM)
turnaround time
twisted pair cable
unipolar
Very Small Aperture
    Satellite (VSAT)
wavelength division
    multiplexing (WDM)
wireless media
V.22
V.32
V.32bis
V.34
V.34+
V.44
V.90
V.92

QUESTIONS

1. How does a multipoint circuit differ from a point-to-point circuit?

2. Describe the three types of data flows.

3. Describe three types of guided media.

4. Describe four types of wireless media.

5. How does analog data differ from digital data?

6. Clearly explain the differences among analog data, analog transmission, digital data, and digital transmission.

7. Explain why most telephone company circuits are now digital.

8. What is coding?

9. Briefly describe the two most important coding schemes.

10. How is data transmitted in parallel?

11. What feature distinguishes serial mode from parallel mode?

12. How does bipolar signaling differ from unipolar signaling? Why is Manchester encoding more popular than either?

13. What are three important characteristics of a sound wave?

14. What is bandwidth? What is the bandwidth in a traditional North American telephone circuit?

15. Describe how data could be transmitted using amplitude modulation.

16. Describe how data could be transmitted using frequency modulation.

17. Describe how data could be transmitted using phase modulation.

18. Describe how data could be transmitted using a combination of modulation techniques.

19. Is the bit rate the same as the symbol rate? Explain.

20. What is a modem?

21. What is quadrature amplitude modulation (QAM).

22. Explain the importance of trellis coded modulation.

24. What factors affect transmission speed?

25. Describe four common modem standards.

26. Why is data compression so useful?

27. What data compression standard uses Lempel-Ziv encoding? Describe how it works.

28. Explain how pulse code modulation (PCM) works.

29. Explain how V.90 and V.92 modems work.

30. What is the term used to describe the placing of two or more signals on a single circuit?

31. What is the purpose of multiplexing?

32. How does DSL (digital subscriber line) work?

33. Of the different types of multiplexing, what distinguishes

    a. Frequency division multiplexing (FDM)?

    b. Time division multiplexing (TDM)?

    c. Statistical time division multiplexing (STDM)?

    d. Wavelength division multiplexing (WDM)?

35. What is the function of inverse multiplexing (IMUX)?

36. If you were buying a multiplexer, why would you choose either TDM or FDM? Why?

37. Some experts argue that modems may soon become obsolete. Do you agree? Why or why not?

38. Many experts believe we have reached the maximum data rate possible on the local loop. Why might they believe this? Do you agree? Why or why not?

EXERCISES

3-1 Investigate the costs of dumb terminals, intelligent terminals, network computers, minimally equipped microcomputers, and top-of-the-line microcomputers. Many equipment manufacturers and resellers are on the Web, so it's a good place to start looking.

3-2 Investigate the different types of cabling used in your organization and where they are used (e.g., LAN, backbone network).

3-3 Three terminals (T_1, T_2, T_3) are to be connected to three computers (C_1, C_2, C_3) so that T_1 is connected to C_1, T_2 to C_2, and T_3 to C_3. All are in different cities. T_1 and C_1 are 1,500 miles apart, as are T_2 and C_2 and T_3 and C_3. The points T_1, T_2, and T_3 are 25 miles apart, and the points C_1, C_2, and C_3 also are 25 miles apart.

If telephone lines cost $1 per mile, what is the line cost for three?

3-4 A few Internet service providers in some areas now have BONDING IMUXs and offer their use to businesses wanting faster Internet access. Search the Web or call your local ISPs to see if they offer this service and if so, how much it costs.

3-5 Draw how the bit pattern 01101100 would be sent using

    a. Single-bit AM

    b. Single-bit FM

    c. Single-bit PM

    d. Two-bit AM (i.e., four amplitude levels)

e. Two-bit FM (i.e., four frequencies)

f. Two-bit PM (i.e., four different phases)

g. Single-bit AM combined with single-bit FM

h. Single-bit AM combined with single-bit PM

i. Two-bit AM combined with two-bit PM

3-6 If you had to download a 20-page paper of 40,000 bytes from your professor, approximately how long would it take to transfer it over the following modems (see Figure 3-18)? Assume that control characters add an extra 10 percent to the message.

a. V.32bis modem

b. V.34+ modem (assume it can transfer at its maximum speed)

c. V.92 modem (assume it can transfer at its maximum speed)

d. If the modem includes V.44 data compression with a 6:1 data compression ratio, what is the data rate in bits per second you would actually see in choice c above?

MINI-CASES

I. Eureka! (Part 1)

Eureka! is a telephone- and Internet-based concierge service that specializes in obtaining things that are hard to find (e.g., Superbowl tickets, first-edition books from the 1500s, Fabergé eggs). It currently employs 60 staff members who collectively provide 24-hour coverage (over three shifts). They answer the phones and respond to requests entered on the Eureka! Web site. Much of their work is spent on the phone and on computers searching on the Internet. The company has just leased a new office building and is about to wire it. What media would you suggest the company install in its office and why?

II. Eureka! (Part 2)

Eureka! is a telephone and Internet-based concierge service that specializes in obtaining things that are hard to find (e.g., Superbowl tickets, first edition books from the 1500s, Faberge eggs). It currently employs 60 staff who work 24 hours per day (over three shifts). Staff answer the phone and respond to requests entered on the Eureka! Web site. Much of their work is spent on the phone and on computers searching on the Internet. What type of connections should Eureka! consider from its offices to the outside world, in terms of phone and Internet? Outline the pros and cons of each alternative below and make a recommendation. The company has four alternatives:

1. Should it use traditional analog services, with standard voice lines, and use modems to dial into its ISP ($40 per month for each voice line plus $20 per month for each Internet access line)?

2. Should the company use standard voice lines but use DSL for its data ($60 per month per line for both services)?

3. Should the company separate its voice and data needs, using standard analog services for voice but finding some advanced digital transmission services for data ($40 per month for each voice line and $300 per month for a circuit with 1.5 Mbps of data)?

4. Should the company search for all digital services for both voice and data ($60 per month for an all-digital circuit that provides two PCM phone lines that can be used for two voice calls, one voice call and one data call at 64 Kbps, or one data call at 128 Kbps)?

CASE STUDY

NEXT-DAY AIR SERVICE

President Lee Coone has asked you to continue planning for an integrated corporate NDAS network. Ultimately, this network will link all the offices with the Tampa head office and become the foundation on which to build a sophisticated data, voice, and image communication network that includes LANs at most NDAS sites. President Coone is still not completely convinced that NDAS needs image capabilities, but he wants you to include that in your plan.

As a first step, President Coone wants you to examine the current information flow within NDAS. Figure 3–25 shows the movement of invoice information. In reality, it shows the number of packages that are transferred between offices, but each package also requires an invoice. These averages were compiled from a 2-week survey of each office. The average length of each invoice is 750 characters. Use this statistic as the basis for your computations.

Every number in the figure represents the number of packages (each of which requires an invoice) that move from the city of origin to a destination city for delivery in the latter city's delivery zone. Local deliveries are indi-

Origin \ Destination (Inbound)	Atlanta	Chicago	Dallas	Denver	Houston	Jackson	Jacksonville	Los Angeles	Memphis	Miami	Montgomery	New Orleans	Orlando	St. Louis	Tampa	Washington	Avg total pkgs/Day
Atlanta	500	400	350	15	320	100	250	100	200	300	120	250	200	120	450	400	4210
Chicago	300	N/A	400	N/A	100	50	100	N/A	200	400	70	250	300	N/A	350	N/A	2520
Dallas	250	300	800	350	450	50	150	700	300	250	50	300	150	250	300	250	4900
Denver	200	N/A	300	N/A	150	30	20	N/A	30	150	20	130	40	N/A	80	N/A	1150
Houston	150	70	450	70	N/A	20	80	70	130	120	20	230	170	120	300	10	2010
Jackson	110	N/A	120	60	120	N/A	30	N/A	220	40	30	340	110	70	210	N/A	1460
Jacksonville	130	70	130	10	80	20	N/A	30	70	200	30	50	200	10	350	30	1410
Los Angeles	150	N/A	70	N/A	80	N/A	20	N/A	150	150	N/A	30	10	N/A	110	N/A	770
Memphis	160	40	130	20	70	90	30	80	700	110	40	90	20	210	60	20	1870
Miami	330	50	70	20	30	10	160	20	40	1100	20	210	260	10	450	30	2810
Montgomery	80	10	60	N/A	40	30	20	N/A	20	30	N/A	90	20	10	30	10	450
New Orleans	120	70	160	10	120	60	30	20	70	30	60	1000	80	20	250	20	2120
Orlando	270	70	120	30	60	20	230	10	30	310	40	110	950	20	450	30	2750
St. Louis	140	N/A	70	N/A	60	20	20	N/A	310	40	20	210	40	N/A	60	N/A	990
Tampa	550	110	130	40	80	30	220	30	70	310	30	170	430	60	900	30	3190
Washington	210	N/A	20	N/A	30	N/A	70	N/A	20	40	10	30	20	N/A	40	N/A	490

FIGURE 3-25 Daily invoice (package) traffic for Next-Day Air Service.

cated in situations in which the origins and destinations are the same. For example, the intersection of the Atlanta column and the Atlanta row shows 500 local deliveries.

Invoice information is transmitted from the origin to the destination. In addition, a copy of all invoice information is transmitted to the home office in Tampa for billing. For example, every day, Los Angeles ships 150 packages to Memphis, and each one requires an invoice. This means that Los Angeles will transmit 150 750-character invoices to both Memphis and Tampa every day.

Exercises

1. President Coone is baffled about how digital information from a computer can be sent over a telephone line. Prepare a brief position paper for management explaining the way information is transferred from one computer to another over telephone lines. Keep it simple. Be sure to describe the types of modems used in data transmission over telephone circuits. Include comments on the role of data compression in increasing transmission rates. Justify the observation that as a general rule, it is best to purchase the fastest modem your communications lines can support.

2. Compute each office's number of bits sent per day (origin to destination) on the basis of the data provided in Figure 3–25. Use 10 bits per character to keep computations simple and assume all transmissions are error free. Hint: *Bits per day = Packages* $\times 750 \times 10 \times 2$.

3. How many minutes will it take for each city's modem to transmit its invoices? Use the bits per day calculated in question 2 and assume that the V.34 modems transmit at an average rate of 28,800 bps.

4. In question 3, you calculated the transmission time in minutes per day, based on a 28,800-bps modem and 10 bits per character. Now calculate the file transfer time for Atlanta to transmit all of its invoices to Tampa at the end of the workday. Why is this answer different from the time calculated for Atlanta in question 3?

5. Could all the NDAS offices transmit their invoices to Tampa between 5:00 P.M. and 6:00 P.M. each evening? How would they achieve this goal?

CHAPTER 4

DATA LINK LAYER

THE DATA link layer (also called layer 2) is responsible for moving a message from one computer or network device to the next computer or network device in the overall path from sender or receiver. It controls the way messages are sent on the physical media. Both the sender and receiver have to agree on the rules or *protocols* that govern how they will communicate with each other. A *data link protocol* determines who can transmit at what time, where a message begins and ends, and how a receiver recognizes and corrects a transmission error. In this chapter, we discuss these processes, as well as several important sources of errors.

OBJECTIVES

- Understand the role of the data link layer
- Become familiar with two basic approaches to controlling access to the media
- Become familiar with common sources of error and their prevention
- Understand three common error detection and correction methods
- Become familiar with several commonly used data link protocols

CHAPTER OUTLINE

INTRODUCTION

MEDIA ACCESS CONTROL

    Controlled Access

    Contention

    Relative Performance

ERROR CONTROL

    Sources of Errors

INTRODUCTION

In Chapter 1, we introduced the concept of layers in data communications. The data link layers sits between the physical layer (hardware such as the circuits, computers, and multi-plexers described in Chapter 3) and the network layer (that performs addressing and rout-ing, as described in Chapter 5).

The data link layer accepts messages from the network layer and controls the hard-ware that actually transmits them. The data link layer is responsible for getting a message from one computer to another without errors. The data link layer also accepts streams of bits from the physical layer and organizes them into coherent messages that it passes to the network layer.

Both the sender and receiver have to agree on the rules or *protocols* that govern how their data link layers will communicate with each other. A *data link protocol* provides three functions:

- Controls when computers transmit (*media access control*)
- Detects and corrects transmission errors (*error control*)
- Identifies the start and end of a message (*message delineation*)

MEDIA ACCESS CONTROL

Media access control refers to the need to control when computers transmit. With point-to-point full-duplex configurations, media access control is unnecessary because there are only two computers on the circuit and full duplex permits either computer to transmit at any time.

Media access control becomes important when several computers share the same communication circuit, such as a point-to-point configuration with a half-duplex configu-ration that requires computers to take turns, or a multipoint configuration in which several computers share the same circuit. Here, it is critical to ensure that no two computers attempt to transmit data at the same time—but if they do, there must be a way to recover from the problem. There are two fundamental approaches to media access control: controlled access and contention.

Controlled Access

Most computer networks managed by a host mainframe computer use controlled access. In this case, the mainframe controls the circuit and determines which clients can access media at what time. Controlled access is also common in one type of LAN.

X-ON/X-OFF *X-ON/X-OFF* is one of the oldest media access control protocols, dating back to the days of the Teletype. It was not really designed for computer networks but is still used today. X-ON/X-OFF is used only for the transmission of text messages (not binary files such as .EXE files), often on half-duplex point-to-point circuits, or between a computer and a printer.

The basic concept is simple. Computer A sends something to computer B, and computer B acknowledges that it is ready to receive it by sending an X-ON signal, which tells A to begin transmitting. Computer A periodically pauses its transmission to let computer B send a message. If B is receiving without problems, it does nothing, and A continues to transmit. If B becomes busy, it sends the X-OFF signal and A stops transmitting until B sends an X-ON signal.

Because the X-ON and X-OFF signals can be easily lost during transmission, this simple scheme can lead to confusion. More sophisticated approaches have been developed, so its use is rapidly fading.

Polling *Polling* is the process of sending a signal to a client (a computer or terminal) that gives it permission to transmit or asks it to receive. With polling, the clients store all messages that need to be transmitted. Periodically, the server (usually a mainframe computer) *polls* the client to see if it has data to send. If the client has data to send, it does so. If the client has no data to send, it responds negatively, and the server asks another client if it has data to send.

In other words, polling is analogous to a classroom situation in which the instructor calls on the students who raise their hands. The instructor acts like the server. To gain access to the media, students raise their hands and the instructor recognizes them so they can contribute. When they have finished, the instructor again takes charge and allows someone else to comment.

There are several types of polling. With *roll-call polling,* the server works consecutively through a list of clients, first polling client 1, then client 2, and so on, until all are polled. Roll-call polling can be modified to select clients in priority so that some get polled more often than others. For example, one could increase the priority of client 1 by using a polling sequence such as 1, 2, 3, 1, 4, 5, 1, 6, 7, 1, 8, 9.

Typically, roll-call polling involves some waiting because the server has to poll a client and then wait for a response. The response might be an incoming message that was waiting to be sent, a negative response indicating nothing is to be sent, or the full "time-out period" may expire because the client is temporarily out of service (e.g., it is malfunctioning or the user has turned it off). Usually, a timer "times out" the client after waiting several seconds without getting a response. If some sort of fail-safe time-out is not used, the system poll might lock up indefinitely on an out-of-service client.

With *hub polling* (often called *token passing*), one computer starts the poll and passes it to the next computer on the multipoint circuit, which sends its message and passes the poll to the next. That computer then passes the poll to the next, and so on, until it reaches the first computer, which restarts the process again.

Contention

Contention is the opposite of *controlled access*. Computers wait until the circuit is free (i.e., no other computers are transmitting) and then transmit whenever they have data to send. Contention is commonly used in Ethernet LANs.

As an analogy, suppose that you are talking with some friends. Each person tries to get the floor when the previous speaker finishes. Usually, the others yield to the first person who jumps in at the precise moment the previous speaker stops. Sometimes two people attempt to talk at the same time, so there must be some technique to continue the conversation after such a verbal collision occurs.

Relative Performance

Which media access control approach is best: controlled access or contention? There is no simple answer. The key consideration is throughput—which approach will permit the most amount of user data to be transmitted through the network.

In general, contention approaches work better than controlled approaches for small networks that have low usage. In this case, each computer can transmit when necessary, without waiting for permission. Because usage is low, there is little chance of a collision. In contrast, computers in a controlled access environment must wait for permission, so even if no other computer needs to transmit, they must wait for the poll.

The reverse is true for large networks with high usage: controlled access works better. In high-volume networks, many computers want to transmit, and the probability of a collision using contention is high. Collisions are very costly in terms of throughput because they waste circuit capacity during the collision and require both computers to retransmit later. Controlled access prevents collisions and makes more efficient use of the circuit, and although response time does increase, it does so more gradually (Figure 4-1).

The key to selecting the best access control technique is to find the crossover point between controlled and contention. Although there is no one correct answer, because it depends on how many messages the computers in the network transmit, most experts believe that the crossover point is often around 20 computers (lower for busy computers, higher for less-busy computers). For this reason, when we build shared multipoint circuits like those often used in LANs, we try to put no more than 20 computers on any one shared circuit.

ERROR CONTROL

Before learning the control mechanisms that can be implemented to protect a network from errors, you should realize that there are *human errors* and *network errors*. Human

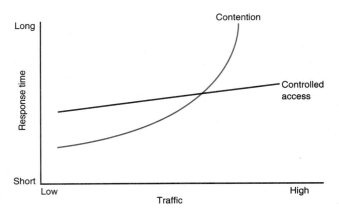

FIGURE 4-1　Relative response times.

errors, such as a mistake in typing a number, usually are controlled through the application program. Network errors, such as those that occur during transmission, are controlled by the network hardware and software.

There are two categories of network errors: *corrupted data* (data that have been changed) and *lost data*. Networks should be designed to (1) prevent, (2) detect, and (3) correct both corrupted data and lost data. We begin by examining the sources of errors and how to prevent them and then turn to error detection and correction.

Network errors are a fact of life in data communications networks. Depending on the type of circuit, they may occur every few hours, minutes, or seconds because of noise on the lines. No network can eliminate all errors, but most errors can be prevented, detected, and corrected by proper design. IXCs that provide data transmission circuits provide statistical measures specifying typical error rates and the pattern of errors that can be expected on the circuits they lease. For example, the error rate might be stated as 1 in 500,000, meaning there is 1 bit in error for every 500,000 bits transmitted.

Normally, errors appear in bursts. In a *burst error,* more than 1 data bit is changed by the error-causing condition. In other words, errors are not uniformly distributed in time. Although an error rate might be stated as 1 in 500,000, errors are more likely to occur as 100 bits every 50,000,000 bits. The fact that errors tend to be clustered in bursts rather than evenly dispersed is both good and bad. If the errors were not clustered, an error rate of 1 bit in 500,000 would make it rare for 2 erroneous bits to occur in the same character. Consequently, simple character-checking schemes would be effective at detecting errors. When errors are #ore or less evenly distrib#ted, it is not di#ficult to gras# the me#ning even when the error #ate is high, as it is in this #entence (1 charac#er in 20). But burst errors are the rule rather than the exception, often obliterating 100 or more bits at a time. This makes it more difficult to recover the meaning, so more reliance must be placed on knowledge of the message #######[1] or on special logical or numeric error detection and correction methods. The positive side is that there are long periods of error-free transmission, meaning that very few messages encounter errors.

---

[1] In case you could not guess, the word is *context.*

The error rate in transmissions sent over the dial-up network (i.e., telephone company circuits) varies from circuit to another. Dial-up lines are more prone to errors than are private dedicated lines because they have less stable transmission parameters. In some cases, users must transmit the data at a slower speed because higher transmission speeds are more error prone. Because different calls use different circuits, they usually experience different transmission conditions. A bad line is not necessarily a serious problem, because a new call may use a better line.

Sources of Errors

Line noise and *distortion* can cause data communication errors. The focus in this section is on electrical media such as twisted-pair wire and coaxial cable, because they are more likely to suffer from noise than are optical media such as fiber-optical cable. In this case, noise is undesirable electrical signals (for fiber-optic cable, it is undesirable light). Noise is introduced by equipment or natural disturbances, and it degrades the performance of a communication circuit. Noise manifests itself as extra bits, missing bits, or bits that have been "flipped" (i.e., changed from 1 to 0 or vice versa). Figure 4-2 summarizes the major sources of error and ways to prevent them. The first six sources listed there are the most important; the last three are more common in analog rather than digital circuits.

Line outages are a catastrophic cause of errors and incomplete transmission. Occasionally, a communication circuit fails for a brief period. This type of failure may be caused by faulty telephone end office equipment, storms, loss of the carrier signal, and any other failure that causes a short circuit.

White noise or *Gaussian noise* (the familiar background hiss or static on radios and telephones) is caused by the thermal agitation of electrons and therefore is inescapable. Even if the equipment were perfect and the wires were perfectly insulated from any and all external interference, there still would be some white noise. White noise usually is not a problem unless it becomes so strong that it obliterates the transmission. In this case, the strength of the electrical signal is increased so it overpowers the white noise; in technical terms, we increase the signal-to-noise ratio.

Source of Error	What Causes It	How to Prevent It
Line outages	Storms, accidents	
White noise	Movement of electrons	Increase signal strength
Impulse noise	Sudden increases in electricity (e.g., lightning)	Shield or move the wires
Cross-talk	Multiplexer guardbands too small or wires too close together	Increase the guardbands or move or shield the wires
Echo	Poor connections	Fix the connections or tune equipment
Attenuation	Gradual decrease in signal over distance	Use repeaters or amplifiers
Intermodulation noise	Signals from several circuits combine	Move or shield the wires
Jitter	Analog signals change phase	Tune equipment
Harmonic distortion	Amplifier changes phase	Tune equipment

FIGURE 4-2 Sources of errors and ways to minimize them.

Impulse noise (sometimes called *spikes*) is the primary source of errors in data communications. Impulse noise is heard as a click or a crackling noise and can last as long as $1/100$ of a second. Such a click does not really affect voice communications, but it can obliterate a group of data, causing a burst error. At 300 bps, 3 bits would be changed by a spike of $1/100$ of a second, whereas at 33,600 bits per second, 336 bits would be changed. Some of the sources of impulse noise are voltage changes in adjacent lines, lightning flashes during thunderstorms, fluorescent lights, and poor connections in circuits.

Cross-talk occurs when one circuit picks up signals in another. You experience cross-talk during telephone calls when you hear other conversations in the background. It occurs between pairs of wires that are carrying separate signals, in multiplexed links carrying many discrete signals, or in microwave links in which one antenna picks up a minute reflection from another antenna. Cross-talk between lines increases with increased communication distance, increased proximity of the two wires, increased signal strength, and higher-frequency signals. Wet or damp weather can also increase cross-talk. Like white noise, cross-talk has such a low signal strength that it normally is not bothersome.

Echoes can cause errors. Echoes are caused by poor connections that cause the signal to reflect back to the transmitting equipment. If the strength of the echo is strong enough to be detected, it causes errors. Echoes, like cross-talk and white noise, have such a low signal strength that they normally are not bothersome. Echoes can also occur in fiber-optic cables when connections between cables are not properly aligned.

Attenuation is the loss of power a signal suffers as it travels from the transmitting computer to the receiving computer. Some power is absorbed by the medium or is lost before it reaches the receiver. As the medium absorbs power, the signal becomes weaker, and the receiving equipment has less and less chance of correctly interpreting the data. This power loss is a function of the transmission method and circuit medium. High frequencies lose power more rapidly than do low frequencies during transmission, so the received signal can thus be distorted by unequal loss of its component frequencies. Attenuation increases as frequency increases or as the diameter of the wire decreases.

Intermodulation noise is a special type of cross-talk. The signals from two circuits combine to form a new signal that falls into a frequency band reserved for another signal. This type of noise is similar to harmonics in music. On a multiplexed line, many different signals are amplified together, and slight variations in the adjustment of the equipment can cause intermodulation noise. A maladjusted modem may transmit a strong frequency tone when not transmitting data, thus producing this type of noise.

Jitter may affect the accuracy of the data being transmitted because minute variations in amplitude, phase, and frequency always occur. The generation of a pure carrier signal in an analog circuit is impossible. The signal may be impaired by continuous and rapid gain and/or phase changes. This jitter may be random or periodic. Phase jitter during a telephone call causes the voice to fluctuate in volume.

Harmonic distortion usually is caused by an amplifier on a circuit that does not correctly represent its output with what was delivered to it on the input side. *Phase hits* are short-term shifts "out of phase," with the possibility of a shift back into phase.

Error Prevention

There are many techniques to prevent errors (or at least reduce them), depending on the situation. *Shielding* (protecting wires by covering them with an insulating coating) is one of

MANAGEMENT FOCUS *4 - 1*

FINDING THE SOURCE OF IMPULSE NOISE

Several years ago, the University of Georgia radio station received FCC (Federal Communications Commission) approval to broadcast using a stronger signal. Immediately after the station started broadcasting with the new signal, the campus backbone network (BN) became unusable because of impulse noise. It took 2 days to link the impulse noise to the radio station, and when the radio station returned to its usual broadcast signal, the problem disappeared.

However, this was only the first step in the problem. The radio station wanted to broadcast at full strength, and there was no good reason for why the stronger broadcast should

affect the BN in this way. After 2 weeks of effort, the problem was discovered. A short section of the BN ran above ground between two buildings. It turned out that the specific brand of outdoor cable we used was particularly tasty to squirrels. They had eaten the outer insulating coating off of the cable, making it act like an antennae to receive the radio signals. The cable was replaced with a steel-coated armored cable so the squirrels could not eat the insulation. Things worked fine when the radio station returned to its stronger signal.

the best ways to prevent impulse noise, cross-talk, and intermodulation noise. Many different types of wires and cables are available with different amounts of shielding. In general, the greater the shielding, the more expensive the cable and the more difficult it is to install.

Moving cables away from sources of noise (especially power sources) can also reduce impulse noise, cross-talk, and intermodulation noise. For impulse noise, this means avoiding lights and heavy machinery. Locating communication cables away from power cables is always a good idea. For cross-talk, this means physically separating the cables from other communication cables.

Cross-talk and intermodulation noise is often caused by improper multiplexing. Changing multiplexing techniques (e.g., from FDM to TDM) or changing the frequencies or size of the guardbands in FDM can help.

Many types of noise (e.g., echoes, white noise, jitter, harmonic distortion) can be caused by poorly maintained equipment or poor connections and splices among cables. This is particularly true for echo in fiber-optic cables, which is almost always caused by poor connections. The solution here is obvious: Tune the transmission equipment and redo the connections.

To avoid attenuation, telephone circuits have *repeaters* or *amplifiers* spaced throughout their length. The distance between them depends on the amount of power lost per unit length of the transmission line. An amplifier takes the incoming signal, increases its strength, and retransmits it on the next section of the circuit. They are typically used on analog circuits such as the telephone company's voice circuits. The distance between the amplifiers depends on the amount of attenuation, although 1- to 10-mile intervals are common. On analog circuits, it is important to recognize that the noise and distortion are *also* amplified, along with the signal. This means some noise from a previous circuit is regenerated and amplified each time the signal is amplified.

Repeaters are commonly used on digital circuits. A repeater receives the incoming signal, translates it into a digital message, and retransmits the message. Because the message is re-created at each repeater, noise and distortion from the previous circuit are not amplified. This provides a much cleaner signal and results in a lower error rate for digital circuits.

If the circuit is provided by a common carrier such as the telephone company, you can lease a more expensive *conditioned* circuit. A conditioned circuit is one that has been certified by the carrier to experience fewer errors. There are several levels of conditioning that provide increasingly fewer error at increasingly higher cost. Conditioned circuits employ a variety of the techniques described previously (e.g., shielding) to provide less noise.

Error Detection

It is possible to develop data transmission methodologies that give very high *error detection and correction* performance. The only way to do error detection and correction is to send extra data with each message. These error detection data are added to each message by the data link layer of the sender on the basis of some mathematical calculations performed on the message (in some cases, error-detection methods are built into the hardware itself). The receiver performs the same mathematical calculations on the message it receives and matches its results against the error-detection data that were transmitted with the message. If the two match, the message is assumed to be correct. If they don't match, an error has occurred.

In general, the larger the amount of error-detection data sent, the greater the ability to detect an error. However, as the amount of error-detection data is increased, the throughput of useful data is reduced, because more of the available capacity is used to transmit these error-detection data and less is used to transmit the actual message itself. Therefore, the efficiency of data throughput varies inversely as the desired amount of error detection is increased.

Three well-known *error-detection methods* are parity checking, longitudinal redundancy checking, and polynomial checking (particularly checksum and cyclic redundancy checking).

Parity Checking   One of the oldest and simplest error detection methods is *parity*. With this technique, one additional bit is added to each byte in the message. The value of this additional *parity bit* is based on the number of 1's in each byte transmitted. This parity bit is set to make the total number of 1's in the byte (including the parity bit) either an even number or an odd number. Figure 4-3 gives an example.

Assume we are using even parity with 7-bit ASCII.
The letter *V* in 7-bit ASCII is encoded as 0110101.
Because there are four 1's (an even number), parity is set to 0.
This would be transmitted as 01101010.

Assume we are using even parity with 7-bit ASCII.
The letter *W* in 7-bit ASCII is encoded as 0001101.
Because there are three 1's (an odd number), parity is set to 1.
This would be transmitted as 00011011.

FIGURE 4-3   Using parity for error detection.

A little thought will convince you that any single error (a switch of a 1 to a 0 or vice versa) will be detected by parity, but it cannot determine which bit was in error. You will know an error occurred, but not what the error was. But if *two* bits are switched, the *parity check* will not detect any error. It is easy to see that parity can detect errors only when an odd number of bits have been switched; any even number of errors cancel one another out. Therefore, the probability of detecting an error, given that one has occurred, is only about 50 percent. Many networks today do not use parity because of its low error-detection rate. When parity is used, protocols are described as having *odd parity* or *even parity*.

Longitudinal Redundancy Checking   The *longitudinal redundancy checking (LRC)* method was developed to overcome the problems with parity's low probability of detection. LRC adds one additional character, called the *block check character (BCC)*, to the end of the entire message or packet of data. The value of the BCC is determined in the same manner as the parity bit, but by counting longitudinally through the message rather than by counting vertically through each character. The first bit of the LRC is determined by counting the number of 1's in the first bits of all characters in the message and setting the first bit of the LRC to a 1 or a 0 depending on whether the sum is odd or even. The second bit of the BCC is determined by counting the number of 1's in the second bits of characters in the message, and so on for all bits in the BCC. LRC is usually used in conjunction with parity, producing an error detection rate above 98 percent for typical burst errors of 10 bits or more. LRC is less capable of detecting single-bit errors but is still much better than parity—and fortunately, single-bit errors are rare. Figure 4-4 provides an example.

Polynomial Checking   A 98 percent error-detection rate is reasonably good, but it is still not perfect. Like LRC, *polynomial checking* adds a character or series of characters, based on a mathematical algorithm, to the end of the message. There are two different types of polynomial checking: checksum and cyclical redundancy check (CRC).

With the *checksum* technique, a checksum (typically 1 byte) is added to the end of the message. The checksum is calculated by adding the decimal value of each character in

For example, suppose we were to send the message "DATA" using odd parity and LRC with 7-bit ASCII:

Letter	ASCII	Parity Bit
D	1000100	1
A	1000001	1
T	1010100	0
A	1000001	1
BCC	1101111	1

(Note that the parity bit in the BCC is determined by parity, not LRC.)

FIGURE 4-4   Using longitudinal redundancy checking (LRC) for error detection. ASCII = United States of America Standard Code for Information Interchange; BCC = block check character.

the message, dividing the sum by 255, and using the remainder as the checksum. The receiver calculates its own checksum in the same way and compares it with the transmitted checksum. If the two values are equal, the message is presumed to contain no errors. Use of checksum detects close to 95 percent of the errors for multiple-bit burst errors.

The most popular polynomial error-checking scheme is *cyclical redundancy check (CRC)*. It adds 8, 16, 24, or 32 bits to the message. With CRC, a message is treated as one long binary number, P. Before transmission, the data link layer (or hardware device) divides P by a fixed binary number, G, resulting in a whole number, Q, and a remainder, R/G. So, $P/G = Q + R/G$. For example, if $P = 58$ and $G = 8$, then $Q = 7$ and $R = 2$. G is chosen so that the remainder, R, will be either 8 bits, 16 bits, 24 bits, or 32 bits.[2]

The remainder, R, is appended to the message as the error-checking characters before transmission. The receiving hardware divides the received message by the same G, which generates an R. The receiving hardware checks to ascertain whether the received R agrees with the locally generated R. If it does not, the message is assumed to be in error.

CRC performs quite well. The most commonly used CRC codes are CRC-16 (a 16-bit version), CRC-CCITT (another 16-bit version), and CRC-32 (a 32-bit version). The probability of detecting an error is 100 percent for all errors of the same length as the CRC or less. For example, CRC-16 is guaranteed to detect errors if 16 or fewer bits are affected. If the burst error is longer than the CRC, then CRC is not perfect but is close to it. CRC-16 will detect about 99.998 percent of all burst errors longer than 16 bits, whereas CRC-32 will detect about 99.99999998 percent of all burst errors longer than 32 bits.

Error Correction via Retransmission

Once error has been detected, it must be corrected. The simplest, most effective, least expensive, and most commonly used method for error correction is retransmission. With retransmission, a receiver that detects an error simply asks the sender to retransmit the message until it is received without error. This is often called Automatic Repeat reQuest (ARQ). There are two types of ARQ: stop-and-wait and continuous.

Stop-and-Wait ARQ With *stop-and-wait ARQ,* the sender stops and waits for a response from the receiver after each data packet. After receiving a packet, the receiver sends either an *acknowledgment (ACK),* if the packet was received without error, or a *negative acknowledgment (NAK),* if the message contained an error. If it is an NAK, the sender resends the previous message. If it is an ACK, the sender continues with the next message. Stop-and-wait ARQ is by definition, a half-duplex transmission technique (Figure 4-5).

Continuous ARQ With *continuous ARQ,* the sender does not wait for an acknowledgment after sending a message; it immediately sends the next one. Although the messages are being transmitted, the sender examines the stream of returning acknowledgments. If it

---

[2] CRC is actually more complicated than this because it uses polynominal division, not "normal" division as illustrated here. Ross Willams provides an excellent tutorial on CRC at www.ross.net/crc/crcpaper.html.

Sender   Receiver

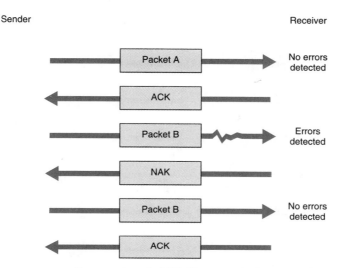

FIGURE 4-5 Stop-and-wait ARQ (Automatic Repeat reQuest). ACK = acknowledgment; NAK = negative acknowledgment.

receives an NAK, the sender retransmits the needed messages. The packets that are retransmitted may be only those containing an error (called Link Access Protocol for Modems [LAP-M]) or may be the first packet with an error and all those that followed it (called Go-Back-N ARQ). LAP-M is better because it is more efficient.

Continuous ARQ is by definition a full-duplex transmission technique, because both the sender and the receiver are transmitting simultaneously. (The sender is sending messages, and the receiver is sending ACKs and NAKs.) Figure 4-6 illustrates the flow of messages on a communication circuit using continuous ARQ. Continuous ARQ is sometimes called *sliding window* because of the visual imagery the early network designers used to think about continuous ARQ. Visualize the sender having a set of messages to send in memory stacked in order from first to last. Now imagine a window that moves through the stack from first to last. As a message it is sent, the window expands to cover it, meaning that the sender is waiting for an ACK for the message. As an ACK is received for a message, the window moves forward, dropping the message out of the bottom of the window, indicating that it has been sent and received successfully.

Both stop-and-wait ARQ and continuous ARQ are also important in providing *flow control,* which means ensuring that the computer sending the message is not transmitting too quickly for the receiver. For example, if a client computer was sending information too quickly for a server computer to store a file being uploaded, the server might run out of memory to store the file. By using ACKs and NAKs, the receiver can control the rate at which it receives information. With stop-and-wait ARQ, the receiver does not send an ACK until it is ready to receive more packets. In continuous ARQ, the sender and receiver usually agree on the size of the sliding window. Once the sender has transmitted the maximum number of packets permitted in the sliding window, it cannot send any more packets until the receiver sends an ACK.

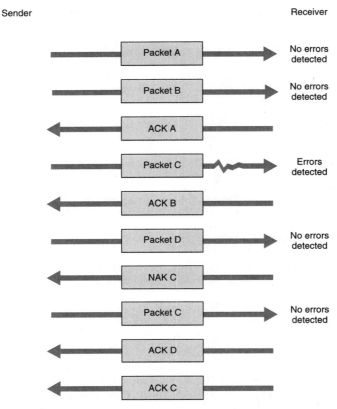

FIGURE 4-6   Continuous ARQ, (Automatic Repeat reQuest). ACK = acknowledgment; NAK = negative acknowledgment.

Forward Error Correction

Forward error correction uses codes containing sufficient redundancy to prevent errors by detecting and correcting them at the receiving end *without* retransmission of the original message. The redundancy, or extra bits required, varies with different schemes. It ranges from a small percentage of extra bits to 100 percent redundancy, with the number of error-detecting bits roughly equaling the number of data bits. One of the characteristics of many error-correcting codes is that there must be a minimum number of error-free bits between bursts of errors.

Forward error correction is commonly used in satellite transmission. A round trip from the earth station to the satellite and back includes a significant delay. Error rates can fluctuate depending on the condition of equipment, sunspots, or the weather. Indeed, some weather conditions make it impossible to transmit without some errors, making forward error correction essential. Compared with satellite equipment costs, the additional cost of forward error correction is insignificant.

TECHNICAL FOCUS

HOW FORWARD ERROR CORRECTION WORKS

To see how error-correcting codes works, consider the example of a forward error checking code in Figure 4-7, called a *Hamming code,* after its inventor, R. W. Hamming. This code is a very simple approach, capable of correcting 1-bit errors. More sophisticated techniques (e.g., Reed–Solomon) are commonly used today, but this will give you a sense of how they work.

The Hamming code associates even parity bits with unique combinations of data bits. With a 4-data-bit code as an example, a character might be represented by the data-bit configuration 1010. Three parity bits, P_1, P_2, and P_4, are added, resulting in a 7-bit code, shown in the upper half of Figure 4-7. Notice that the data bits (D_3, D_5, D_6, D_7) are 1010 and the parity bits (P_1, P_2 P_4) are 101.

As depicted in the upper half of Figure 4-7, parity bit P_1 applies to data bits D_3, D_5, and D_7. Parity bit P_2 applies to data bits D_3, D_6, and D_7. Parity bit P_4 applies to data bits D_5, D_6, and D_7. For the example, in which D_3, D_5, D_6, D_7 = 1010, P_1 must equal 1 because there is only a single 1 among D_3, D_5, and D_7 and parity must be even. Similarly,

P_2 must be 0 because D_3 and D_6 are 1's. P_4 is 1 because D_6 is the only 1 among D_5, D_6, and D_7.

Now, assume that during the transmission, data bit D_7 is changed from a 0 to a 1 by line noise. Because this data bit is being checked by P_1, P_2, and P_4, all 3 parity bits now show odd parity instead of the correct even parity. (D_7 is the only data bit that is monitored by all 3 parity bits; therefore, when D_7 is in error, all 3 parity bits show an incorrect parity.) In this way, the receiving equipment can determine which bit was in error and reverse its state, thus correcting the error without retransmission.

The lower half of the figure is a table that determines the location of the bit in error. A 1 in the table means that the corresponding parity bit indicates a parity error. Conversely, a 0 means the parity check is correct. These 0's and 1's form a binary number that indicates the numeric location of the erroneous bit. In the previous example, P_1, P_2, and P_4 checks all failed, yielding 111, or a decimal 7, the subscript of the erroneous bit.

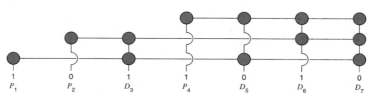

1	0	1	1	0	1	0
P_1	P_2	D_3	P_4	D_5	D_6	D_7

Checking relations between parity bits (P) and data bits (D)

0 = Corresponding parity check is correct 1 = Corresponding parity check fails			Determines in which bit the error occured
P_4	P_2	P_1	
0	0	0	no error
0	0	1	P_1
0	1	0	P_2
0	1	1	D_3
1	0	0	P_4
1	0	1	D_5
1	1	0	D_6
1	1	1	D_7

Interpreting parity bit patterns

FIGURE 4-7   Hamming code for forward error correction.

DATA LINK PROTOCOLS

In this section, we outline several commonly used data link layer protocols, which are summarized in Figure 4-8. Here we focus on message delineation, which indicates where a message starts and stops, and the various parts or *fields* within the message. For example, you must clearly indicate which part of a message or packet of data is the error-control portion; otherwise, the receiver cannot use it properly to determine if an error has occurred.

Asynchronous Transmission

Asynchronous transmission often is referred to as start-stop transmission because the transmitting computer can transmit a character whenever it is convenient, and the receiving computer will accept that character. It is typically used on point-to-point full-duplex circuits (i.e., circuits that have only two computers on them), so media access control is not a concern. If you use VT100 protocol, or connect to a UNIX or Linux computer using Telnet, chances are you are using asynchronous transmission.

With *asynchronous transmission,* each character is transmitted independently of all other characters. To separate the characters and synchronize transmission, a *start bit* and a *stop bit* are put on the front and back of *each* individual character. For example, if we are using 7-bit ASCII with even parity, the total transmission is 10 bits for each character (1 start bit, 7 bits for the letter, 1 parity bit, 1 stop bit).

Protocol	Size	Error Detection	Retransmission	Media Access
Asynchronous transmission	1	Parity	Continuous ARQ	Full Duplex
File transfer protocols				
Xmodem	132	8-bit Checksum	Stop-and-wait ARQ	Controlled Access
Xmodem-CRC	132	8-bit CRC	Stop-and-wait ARQ	Controlled Access
Xmodem-1K	1,028	8-bit CRC	Stop-and-wait ARQ	Controlled Access
Zmodem	*	32-bit CRC	Continuous ARQ	Controlled Access
Kermit	*	24-bit CRC	Continuous ARQ	Controlled Access
Synchronous protocols				
SDLC	*	16-bit CRC	Continuous ARQ	Controlled Access
HDLC	*	16-bit CRC	Continuous ARQ	Controlled Access
Ethernet	*	32-bit CRC	Stop-and wait ARQ	Contention
PPP	*	16-bit CRC	Continuous ARQ	Full Duplex

* Varies depending on the message length.
ARQ = Automatic Repeat reQuest; CRC = cyclical redundancy check; HDLC = high-level data link control; PPP = Point-to-Point Protocol; SDLC = synchronous data link control.

FIGURE 4-8 Protocol summary.

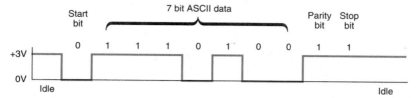

FIGURE 4-9   Asynchronous transmission. ASCII = United States of America Standard Code for Information Interchange.

The start bit and stop bit are the opposite of each other. Typically, the start bit is a 0 and the stop bit is a 1. There is no fixed distance between characters because the terminal transmits the character as soon as it is typed, which varies with the speed of the typist. The recognition of the start and stop of each message (called *synchronization*) takes place for each individual character because the *start bit* is a signal that tells the receiver to start sampling the incoming bits of a character so the data bits can be interpreted into their proper character structure. A *stop bit* informs the receiver that the character has been received and resets it for recognition of the next start bit.

When the sender is waiting for the user to type the next character, no data is sent; the communication circuit is idle. This idle time really is artificial—some signal always must be sent down the circuit. For example, suppose we are using a unipolar digital signaling technique where +5 volts indicates a 1 and 0 volts indicates a 0 (see Chapter 3). Even if we send 0 volts, we are still sending a signal, a 0 in this case. Asynchronous transmission defines the *idle signal* (the signal that is sent down the circuit when no data are being transmitted) as the same as the stop bit. When the sender finishes transmitting a letter and is waiting for more data to send, it sends a continuous series of stop bits. Figure 4-9 shows an example of asynchronous transmission.

Some older protocols have two stop bits instead of the traditional single stop bit. The use of both a start bit and a stop bit is changing; some protocols have eliminated the stop bit altogether.

Asynchronous File Transfer Protocols

Today, data transmission by microcomputers often means the transfer of data files. In general, microcomputer file transfer protocols are used on asynchronous point-to-point circuits, typically across telephone lines via a modem. All file transfer protocols have two characteristics in common. First, these protocols are designed to transmit error-free data from one computer to another. Second, because there is a large amount of data to be transmitted, it makes more sense to group the data together into blocks of data that are transmitted at the same time, rather than sending each character individually via standard asynchronous transmission. This section discusses the structure of the data blocks (also called packets or frames) used by several common protocols.

Xmodem   The *Xmodem* protocol takes the data being transmitted and divides it into blocks (Figure 4-10). Each block has a start-of-header (SOH) character, a 1-byte block number, 128 bytes of data, and a 1-byte checksum for error checking. Even though this pro-

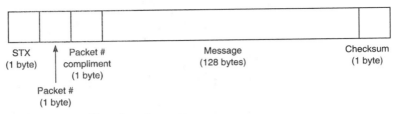

FIGURE 4-10 Xmodem format.

tocol was developed for microcomputer-to-microcomputer communications, it often is used for microcomputer-to-mainframe communications. Xmodem uses stop-and-wait ARQ.

Xmodem-CRC improves error detection accuracy of the Xmodem protocol. It replaces the checksum with a more rigorous 1-byte cyclical redundancy check (CRC-8).

Xmodem-1K increases the efficiency of Xmodem-CRC by using data blocks of 1,024 bytes instead of the 128-character blocks of the original Xmodem. Efficiency and throughput are discussed in more detail later in this chapter.

Zmodem *Zmodem* is a newer protocol and not a subset of Xmodem. It incorporates features of several protocols. It uses a more powerful error detection method (CRC-32) with continuous ARQ. Zmodem also dynamically adjusts its packet size according to communication circuit conditions to increase efficiency. Usually Zmodem is preferred to Xmodem.

Kermit *Kermit* is a very popular protocol (and yes, it is named after Kermit the Frog of *Sesame Street* fame). The Kermit protocol was developed by Columbia University, which also developed a software communication package that uses the same protocol.

Kermit is an extremely flexible protocol that can be adjusted to support a variety of different packet sizes and error-detection methods. Kermit typically uses 1,000-byte packets with CRC-24, but these are adjusted during transmission to optimize performance. It uses either stop-and-wait ARQ or continuous ARQ. It is suited especially to microcomputer-to-mainframe connections, but it works equally well with microcomputer-to-microcomputer or mainframe-to-mainframe connections. Kermit-based programs provide error-checked transfer of text and binary files using both 7- and 8-bit codes.

Synchronous Transmission

With *synchronous transmission,* all the letters or data in one group of data is transmitted at one time as a block of data. This block of data is called a *frame* or *packet,* depending on the protocol, but the meaning is the same. For example, a terminal or microcomputer will save all the keystrokes typed by the user and transmit them only when the user presses a special "transmit" key. In this case, the start and end of the entire packet must be marked, not the start and end of each letter. Synchronous transmission is often used on both point-to-point and multipoint. For multipoint circuits, each packet must include a destination address and a source address, and media access control is important.

The start and end of each packet (synchronization) sometimes is established by adding synchronization characters (SYN) to the start of the packet. Depending on the protocol, there may be anywhere from one to eight SYN characters. After the SYN characters, the transmitting computer sends a long stream of data that may contain thousands of bits. Knowing what code is being used, the receiving computer counts off the appropriate number of bits for the first character, assumes this is the first character, and passes it to the computer. It then counts off the bits for the second character, and so on.

In summary, asynchronous data transmission means each character is transmitted as a totally independent entity with its own start and stop bits to inform the receiving computer that the character is beginning and ending. Synchronous transmission means whole blocks of data are transmitted as packets after the sender and the receiver have been synchronized.

There are many protocols for synchronous transmission. They fall into three broad categories: byte-oriented protocols, bit-oriented protocols, and byte-count protocols. In this next section, we discuss four common synchronous data link protocols.

Synchronous Data Link Control *Synchronous data link control (SDLC)* is a mainframe protocol developed by IBM in 1972 that is still in use today. SDLC is a *bit-oriented protocol,* because the data contained in the frame do not have to be in 8-bit bytes. SDLC is therefore more flexible than byte-oriented protocols. It uses a controlled-access media access protocol. If you use a 3270 protocol, you're using SDLC.

Figure 4-11 shows a typical SDLC packet (or *frame,* as it is called). Each SDLC frame begins and ends with a special bit pattern (01111110), known as the *flag.* The *address field* identifies the destination. The length of the address field is usually 8 bits but can be set at 16 bits; all computers on the same network must use the same length. The *control field* identifies the kind of frame that is being transmitted, either information or supervisory. An *information frame* is used for the transfer and reception of messages, frame numbering of contiguous frames, and the like. A *supervisory frame* is used to transmit acknowledgments (ACKs and NAKs). The *message field* is of variable length and is the user's message. The *frame check sequence field* is a 32-bit CRC code (some older versions use a 16-bit CRC).

SDLC and other bit-oriented protocols suffer from a *transparency problem;* that is, the protocol is not "transparent" because it cannot automatically send all types of data with any bit patterns. It is possible that the user's data to be transmitted contains the same bit pattern as the flag (01111110). If this is not prevented, the receiver will mistakenly believe that this data marks the end of the frame and ignore all the data that follows it. The solution is called *bit stuffing.* Anytime the sender encounters five 1's in a row in the *user's data* to be transmitted, the sender "stuffs" one extra bit, a 0, into the message and continues to transmit. Anytime the receiver encounters five 1's followed by a 0 (i.e., 111110), the receiver automatically deletes the 0 and continues to process the data stream. Conversely, if the receiver encounters five 1's followed by a 1 (i.e., 111111) it knows to expect another 0 as part of the flag. This technique works, but it increases the complexity of the protocol.

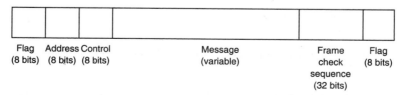

| Flag
(8 bits) | Address
(8 bits) | Control
(8 bits) | Message
(variable) | Frame
check
sequence
(32 bits) | Flag
(8 bits) |

FIGURE 4-11   SDLC (synchronous data link control) format.

High-Level Data Link Control *High-level data link control (HDLC)* is a formal standard developed by the ISO. HDLC is essentially the same as SDLC, except that the address and control fields can be longer. HDLC also has several additional benefits that are beyond the scope of this book, such as a larger sliding window for continuous ARQ. It uses a controlled-access media access protocol. One variant, Link Access Protocol–Balanced (LAP-B), uses the same structure as HDLC but is a scaled-down version of HDLC (i.e., provides fewer of those benefits mentioned that are "beyond the scope of this book").

Ethernet (IEEE 802.3) Ethernet is a very popular LAN protocol, conceived by Bob Metcalfe in 1973 and developed jointly by Digital, Intel, and Xerox in the 1970s. Since then, Ethernet has been further refined and developed into a formal standard called IEEE 802.3.[3] Ethernet is a *byte-count protocol* because instead of using special characters or bit patterns to mark the end of a packet, it includes a field that specifies the length of the message portion of the packet. Unlike SDLC and HDLC, Ethernet has no transparency problems. Any bit pattern can be transmitted, because Ethernet uses the number of bytes, not control characters, to delineate the message. Ethernet uses a contention media access protocol.

Figure 4-12 shows a typical Ethernet packet. The *destination address* specifies the receiver, whereas the *source address* specifies the sender. The *length* indicates the length in 8-bit bytes of the message portion of the packet. The *LLC control* and *SNAP control* are used to pass control information between the sender and receiver. These are often used to indicate the type of network layer protocol the packet contains (e.g., TCP/IP or IPX/SPX as described in Chapter 5). The maximum length of the message is 1,492 bytes. The packet ends with a CRC-32 *frame check sequence* used for error detection.

Point-to-Point Protocol *Point-to-Point Protocol (PPP)* is a byte-oriented protocol developed in the early 1990s that is most commonly used to dial up from home computers to an ISP. It is designed to transfer data over a point-to-point telephone line but provides an address so that it can be used on multipoint circuits. Figure 4-13 shows a PPP packet. The packet begins and ends with a *flag* (01111110). The next two fields (*address* and *control*) are generally fixed for the duration of any one connection (i.e., telephone call). The *protocol* field specifies the network layer protocol (e.g., TCP/IP, IPX/SPX). The *message* may be up to 1,500 bytes in length. PPP uses CRC-16 for error control.

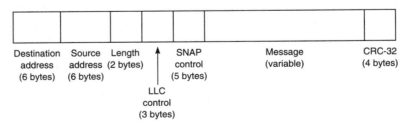

FIGURE 4-12 Ethernet packet layout. CRC = cyclical redundancy check.

---

[3] A competing version of Ethernet called Ethernet II is also available. Ethernet II and IEEE 802.3 Ethernet are similar but differ enough to be incompatible. In this book, we discuss only IEEE 802.3 Ethernet.

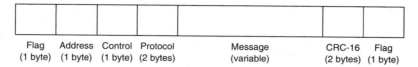

Flag (1 byte)	Address (1 byte)	Control (1 byte)	Protocol (2 bytes)	Message (variable)	CRC-16 (2 bytes)	Flag (1 byte)

FIGURE 4-13   Point-to-Point Protocol (PPP). CRC = cyclical redundancy check.

TRANSMISSION EFFICIENCY

One objective of a data communication network is to move the highest possible volume of accurate information through the network. The higher the volume, the greater the resulting network's efficiency and the lower the cost. Network efficiency is affected by characteristics of the circuits such as error rates and maximum transmission speed, as well as by the speed of transmitting and receiving equipment, the error-detection and control methodology, and the protocol used by the data link layer.

Each protocol we discussed uses some bits or bytes to delineate the start and end of each message and to control error. These bits and bytes are necessary for the transmission to occur, but they are not part of the message. They add no value to the user, but they count against the total number of bits that can be transmitted.

Each communication protocol has both information bits and overhead bits. *Information bits* are those used to convey the user's meaning. *Overhead bits* are used for purposes such as error checking and marking the start and end of characters and packets. A parity bit used for error checking is an overhead bit because it is not used to send the user's data; if you did not care about errors, the overhead error checking bit could be omitted and the users could still understand the message.

Transmission efficiency is defined as the total number of information bits (i.e., bits in the message sent by the user) divided by the total bits in transmission (i.e., information bits plus overhead bits). For example, let's calculate the transmission efficiency of asynchronous transmission. Assume we are using 7-bit ASCII. We have 1 bit for parity, plus 1 start bit and 1 stop bit. Therefore, there are 7 bits of information in each letter, but the total bits per letter is 10 (7 + 3). The efficiency of the asynchronous transmission system is 7 bits of information divided by 10 total bits, or 70 percent.

In other words, with asynchronous transmission, only 70 percent of the data rate is available for the user; 30 percent is used by the transmission protocol. If we have a communication circuit using a V.92 modem receiving 56 Kbps, the user sees an effective data rate (or throughput) of 39.2 Kbps. This is very inefficient.

We can improve efficiency by reducing the number of overhead bits in each message or by increasing the number of information bits. For example, if we remove the stop bits from asynchronous transmission, efficiency increases to $7/9$, or 77.8 percent. The throughput of a V.92 modem at 56 Kbps would increase 43.6 Kbps, which is not great but is at least a little better.

The same basic formula can be used to calculate the efficiency of asynchronous file transfer or synchronous transmission. For example, suppose we are using SDLC. The number of information bits is calculated by determining how many information characters are in the message. If the message portion of the frame contains 100 information characters and we are using an 8-bit code, then there are $100 \times 8 = 800$ bits of information. The total number of bits is the 800 information bits plus the overhead bits that are inserted for delineation and error control. Figure 4-11 shows that SDLC has a beginning flag (8 bits), an address (8 bits), a control field (8 bits), a frame check sequence (assume we use a CRC-32 with 32 bits), and an ending flag (8 bits). This is a total of 64 overhead bits; thus, efficiency is $800/(800 + 64) = 92.6$ percent. If the circuit provides a data rate of 56 Kbps, then the effective data rate available to the user is about 51.9 Kbps.

This example shows that synchronous networks usually are more efficient than asynchronous networks and some protocols are more efficient than others. The longer the message (1,000 characters as opposed to 100), the more efficient the protocol. For example, suppose the message in the SDLC example were 1,000 bytes. The efficiency here would be 99.2 percent, or $8,000/(8000 + 64)$, giving an effective data rate of about 55.6 Kbps.

This example should also show why Zmodem (with a message length of 1,024 bytes) is more efficient than Xmodem (with a message length of 128 bytes). The general rule is that the larger the message field, the more efficient the protocol.

So why not have 10,000-byte or even 100,000-byte packets to really increase efficiency? The answer is that anytime a packet is received containing an error, the entire packet must be retransmitted. Thus, if an entire file is sent as one large packet (e.g., 100K) and 1 bit is received in error, all 100,000 bytes must be sent again. Clearly, this is a waste of capacity. Furthermore, the probability that a packet contains an error increases with the size of the packet; larger packets are more likely to contain errors than are smaller ones, simply due to the laws of probability.

Thus, in designing a protocol, there is a trade-off between large and small packets. Small packets are less efficient but are less likely to contain errors and cost less (in terms of circuit capacity) to retransmit if there is an error (Figure 4-14).

Throughput is the total number of information bits received per second, after taking into account the overhead bits and the need to retransmit packets containing errors. Generally speaking, small packets provide better throughput for circuits with more errors, whereas

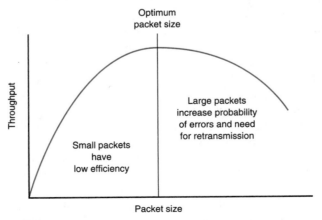

FIGURE 4-14 Packet size effects on throughput.

larger packets provide better throughput in less-error-prone networks. Fortunately, in most real networks, the curve shown in Figure 4-14 is very flat on top, meaning that there is a range of packet sizes that provide almost optimum performance. Packet sizes vary greatly among different networks, but most packet sizes tend to be between 2,000 and 4,000 bytes.

Calculating the actual *throughput* of a data communications network is complex because it depends not only on the efficiency of the data link protocol but also on the error rate and number of retransmissions that occur. *transmission rate of information bits (TRIB)* is a measure of the effective number of information bits that is transmitted over a communication circuit per unit of time. The basic TRIB equation from ANSI is shown in Figure 4-15, along with an example.

FORMULA FOR CALCULATING TRIB

$$TRIB = \frac{\text{Number of information bits accepted}}{\text{Total time required to get the bits accepted}}$$

$$TRIB = \frac{K(M - C)(1 - P)}{(M/R) + T}$$

where K = information bits per character

  M = packet length in characters

  R = data transmission rate in characters per second

  C = average number of noninformation characters per block (control characters)

  P = probability that a block will require retransmission because of error

  T = time between blocks in seconds, such as modem delay/turnaround time on half duplex, echo suppressor delay on dial-up, and propagation delay on satellite transmission. This is the time required to reverse the direction of transmission from send to receive or receive to send on a half-duplex circuit. It can be obtained from the modem specification book and may be referred to as *reclocking time*.

The following TRIB example shows the calculation of throughput assuming a 4,800-bps half-duplex circuit.

$$TRIB = \frac{7(400 - 10)(1 - 0.01)}{(400/600) + 0.025} = 3,908 \text{ bits per second}$$

where K = 7 bits per character (information)

  M = 400 characters per block

  R = 600 characters per second (derived from 4,800 bps divided by 8 bits/character)

  C = 10 control characters per block

  P = 0.01 (10^{-2}) or 1 retransmission per 100 blocks transmitted—1%

  T = 25 milliseconds (0.025) turnaround time

If all factors in the calculation remain constant except for the circuit, which is changed to full duplex (no turn-around time delays, T = 0), then the TRIB increases to 4,054 bps.

Look at the equation where the turnaround value (T) is 0.025. If there is a further propagation delay time of 475 milliseconds (0.475), this figure changes to 0.500. For demonstrating how a satellite channel affects TRIB, the total delay time is now 500 milliseconds. Still using the figures above (except for the new 0.500 delay time), we reduce the TRIB for our half-duplex satellite link to 2,317 bps, which is almost one half of the full-duplex (no turnaround time) 4,054 bps.

FIGURE 4-15 Calculating TRIB (transmission rate of information bits).

MANAGEMENT FOCUS *4-2*

SLEUTHING FOR THE RIGHT PACKET SIZE

Optimizing performance in a network, particularly a client–server network, can be difficult because few network managers realize the importance of the packet size. Selecting the right—or the wrong—packet size can have greater effects on performance than anything you might do to the server.

Standard Commercial, a multinational tobacco and agricultural company, noticed a decrease in network performance when they upgraded to a new server. They tested the effects of using packet sizes between 500 bytes to 32,000 bytes. In their tests, a packet size of 512 bytes required a total of 455,000 bytes transmitted over their network to transfer the test messages. In contrast, the 32,000-byte packets were far more efficient, cutting the total data by 44 percent to 257,000 bytes.

However, the problem with 32,000-byte packets was a noticeable response time delay because messages were saved until the 32,000-byte packets were full before transmitting.

The ideal packet size depends on the specific application and the pattern of messages it generates. For Standard Commercial, the ideal packet size appeared to be between 4,000 and 8,000. Unfortunately, not all network software packages enable network managers to fine-tune packet sizes in this way.

SOURCE: "Sleuthing for the Right Packet Size," *InfoWorld*, January 16, 1995.

SUMMARY

Media Access Control Media access control refers to controlling when computers transmit. There are three basic approaches. With roll-call polling, the server polls client computers to see if they have data to send; computers can transmit only when they have been polled. With hub polling or token passing, the computers themselves manage when they can transmit by passing a token to one other; no computer can transmit unless it has the token. With contention, computers listen and transmit only when no others are transmitting. In general, contention approaches work better for small networks that have low levels of usage, whereas polling approaches work better for networks with high usage.

Sources and Prevention of Error Errors occur in all networks. Errors tend to occur in groups (or bursts) rather than 1 bit at a time. The primary sources of errors are impulse noises (e.g., lightning), cross-talk, echo, and attenuation. Errors can be prevented (or at least reduced) by shielding the cables; moving cables away from sources of noise and power sources; using repeaters (and, to a lesser extent, amplifiers); and improving the quality of the equipment, media, and their connections.

Error Detection and Correction All error-detection schemes attach additional error-detection data, based on a mathematical calculation, to the user's message. The receiver performs the same calculation on incoming messages, and if the results of this calculation do not match the error-detection data on the incoming message, an error has occurred. Parity, LRC, and CRC are the most common error-detection schemes. The most common error-correction technique is simply to ask the sender to retransmit the message until it is received without error. A different approach, forward error correction, includes sufficient information to allow the receiver to correct the error in most cases without asking for a retransmission.

Message Delineation Message delineation means to indicate the start and end of message. Asynchronous transmission uses start and stop bits on each letter to mark where they begin and end. Synchronous techniques (e.g., SDLC, HDLC, token ring, Ethernet, PPP) or file transfer protocols (e.g., Xmodem, Zmodem, Kermit) group blocks of data together into packets or frames that use special characters or bit patterns to mark the start and end of entire messages.

Transmission Efficiency and Throughput   Every protocol adds additional bits to the user's message before sending it (e.g., for error detection). These bits are called overhead bits because they add no value to the user; they simply ensure correct data transfer. The efficiency of a transmission protocol is the number of information bits send by the user divided by the total number of bits transferred (information bits plus overhead bits). Synchronous transmission provides greater efficiency than does asynchronous transmission. In general, protocols with larger packet sizes provide greater efficiency than do those with small packet sizes. The drawback to large packet sizes is that they are more likely to be affected by errors and thus require more retransmission. Small packet sizes are therefore better suited to error-prone circuits, and large packets, to error-free circuits.

KEY TERMS

acknowledgment (ACK)
amplifier
asynchronous transmission
attenuation
Automatic Repeat reQuest (ARQ)
block check character (BCC)
burst error
checksum
contention
continuous ARQ
cyclical redundancy check (CRC)
echo
efficiency
error detection with retransmission
error prevention
error rate

Ethernet (IEEE 802.3)
even parity
flow control
forward error correction
frame
Gaussian noise
Go-Back-N ARQ
Hamming code
harmonic distortion
high-level data link control (HDLC)
hub polling
information bits
impulse noise
intermodulation noise
jitter
Kermit
Link Access Protocol–Balanced (LAP-B)
Link Access Protocol for Modems (LAP-M)

line noise
line outage
longitudinal redundancy checking (LRC)
media access control
negative acknowledgment (NAK)
odd parity
overhead bits
packet
parity bit
parity checking
Point-to-Point Protocol (PPP)
polling
polynomial checking
repeater
roll-call polling
Serial Line Internet Protocol (SLIP)
sliding window

start bit
stop-and-wait ARQ
stop bit
synchronization
synchronous data link control (SDLC)
synchronous transmission
throughput
token
token ring (IEEE 802.5)
transmission efficiency
transmission rate of information bits (TRIB)
white noise
X-ON/X-OFF
Xmodem
Zmodem

QUESTIONS

1. What does the data link layer do?
2. What is media access control, and why is it important?
3. Under what conditions is media access control unimportant?
4. Compare and contrast roll-call polling, hub polling (or token passing), and contention.
5. Which is better, hub polling or contention? Explain.
6. Define two fundamental types of errors.

7. Errors normally appear in _____, which is when more than 1 data bit is changed by the error-causing condition.
8. Is there any difference in the error rates of lower-speed lines and higher-speed lines?
9. Briefly define *noise*.
10. Describe five types of noise. Which is likely to pose the greatest problem to network managers?
11. How do amplifiers differ from repeaters?

12. What are three ways of reducing errors and the types of noise they affect?

13. Describe three approaches to *detecting* errors, including how they work, the probability of detecting an error, and any other benefits or limitations.

14. Briefly describe how even parity and odd parity work.

15. Briefly describe how polynomial checking works.

16. How does CRC work?

17. How does forward error correction work? How is it different from other error-correction methods?

18. Under what circumstances is forward error correction desirable?

19. Compare and contrast stop-and-wait ARQ and continuous ARQ.

20. Which is the simplest (least sophisticated) protocol described in this chapter?

21. How do the various types of Xmodem differ from Zmodem?

22. Describe the packet layouts for SDLC, Ethernet, and PPP.

23. What is transparency, and why is this a problem with SDLC?

24. How does SDLC overcome transparency problems?

25. Explain why Ethernet does not suffer from transparency problems.

26. Why do SDLC packets need an address?

27. What is transmission efficiency?

28. How do information bits differ from overhead bits?

29. Are stop bits necessary in asynchronous transmission? Explain using a diagram.

30. During the 1990s, there was intense competition between two technologies (10-Mbps Ethernet and 16-Mbps token ring) for the LAN market. Ethernet was promoted by a consortium of vendors, whereas token ring was primarily an IBM product, even though it was standardized. Ethernet won, and no one talks about token ring anymore. Token ring used a hub-polling–based approach. Outline a number of reasons why Ethernet might have won. Hint: the reasons were both technical and business.

EXERCISES

4-1 Draw how a series of four separate messages would be *successfully* sent from one computer to another if the first message was transferred without error, the second was initially transmitted with an error, the third was initially lost, and the ACK for the fourth was initially lost.

4-2 How efficient would a 6-bit code be in asynchronous transmission if it had 1 parity bit, 1 start bit, and 2 stop bits? (Some old equipment uses 2 stop bits.)

4-3 What is the transmission rate of information bits if you use EBCDIC (8 bits plus 1 parity bit), a 1,000-character block, 28,800-bps modem transmission speed, 20 control characters per block, an error rate of 1 percent, and a 30-millisecond turnaround time? What is the TRIB if you add a half-second delay to the turnaround time because of satellite delay?

4-4 Search the Web to find a software vendor that sells a package that supports each of the following protocols: Kermit, Zmodem, SDLC, HDLC, Ethernet, token ring, and PPP (i.e., one package that supports Kermit, another [or the same] for Zmodem, and so on).

4-5 Investigate the network at your organization (or a service offered by an IXC) to find out the average error rates.

MINI-CASES

I. Smith, Smith, Smith, and Smith

Smith, Smith, Smith, and Smith is a regional accounting firm that is putting up a new headquarters building. The building will have a backbone network that connects eight LANs (two on each floor). The company is very concerned with network errors. What advice would you give regarding the design of the building and network cable planning that would help reduce network errors?

II. Worldwide Charity

Worldwide Charity is a charitable organization whose mission is to improve education levels in developing countries. In each country where it is involved, the organization has a small headquarters and usually 5 to 10 offices in outlying towns. Staff members communicate with one another via e-mail on older computers donated to the organization. Because Internet service is not reliable in many of the towns in these countries, the staff members usually phone headquarters and use a very simple Linux e-mail system that uses a server-based network architecture. They also upload and download files. What data link layer protocols should they use for the file transfer? What range of packet sizes is likely to be used?

CASE STUDY

NEXT-DAY AIR SERVICE

The NDAs board of directors has decided that NDAS will centralize communications along two major data links (Atlanta to Tampa and New Orleans to Tampa, as shown in Figure 4-16. Both Atlanta and New Orleans have multiplexers. Although you recommended a different approach and the purchase of additional multiplexers, the board of directors would not approve further cash outlays at this time. You hear a rumor that President Les Coone suggested to several board members that developments in data communication, such as DWDM, might make added multiplexers obsolete before they could pay for themselves and that these conservative board members vetoed the funding for the additional circuits and multiplexers.

As you continue to work on the network plan, you perceive that you are becoming much more involved with the firm's strategic planning initiatives for survival. You realize that NDAS will become dependent on its communication facilities for its very existence. In other words, the communication systems at NDAS are the foundation for the firm's mission-critical applications.

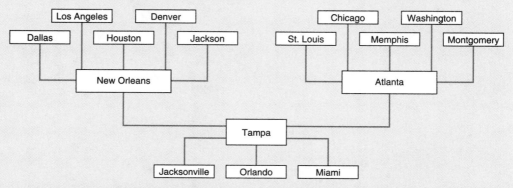

FIGURE 4-16 Next-Day Air Service's communication network circuit configuration. Both of the circuits, from New Orleans to Tampa and Atlanta to Tampa, are 64,000-bps leased circuits. All other circuits from the branch offices to the New Orleans, Atlanta, and Tampa hubs are considered capable of supporting 28,800-bps V.34 modems.

You are burdened with all sorts of thoughts about potential problems and possible errors that can threaten NDAS's communication capabilities. For example, you worry about recent major circuit and switch outages experienced by some of the leading common carriers. You recognize the fact that even though your operations were affected only slightly by these outages, someday NDAS could undergo a costly disruption of its communication network.

You do not view such a situation as a major competitive threat, because NDAS's principal competitors have similar networks, and all the parcel delivery services would be paralyzed in the event of a disastrous outage. You do, however, want to examine sources of errors in networks and find reasonable error-control mechanisms that will provide NDAS with a competitive edge. For example, are there specialized techniques that can be used for error detection and correction in NDAS communication networks? You decide to research these possibilities further and add this project to your ever-growing list of things to do.

For now, you have been asked to explore the feasibility of integrating both data and voice traffic onto a single transmission circuit. You must determine whether this is a viable option. To make this decision, you want to examine the current transmission circuits and assess their ability to handle the anticipated workload.

Exercises

1. Calculate the TRIB for the 28,800-bps circuits in the NDAS network shown in Figure 4-16. Assume an average of 1,600 characters per message, with a 1 percent probability of an erroneous transmission. The modems transmit with a 0.2-second turnaround delay. The transmissions use an 8-bit ASCII code. The transmissions using 28,800-bps modems use 1 start bit and 1 stop bit, and each message block has 10 control characters, for further error checking. Assume that the data is sent synchronously over the 28,800-bps circuits, using a 1,600-character block, but that each block has 55 control characters. Consider the transmission load data for NDAS provided in the case study for Chapter 3. Are these TRIB ratings adequate?

2. What file transfer protocols would you recommend? Be prepared to support your recommendations.

3. Prepare a brief position paper on the types of errors you can expect in the NDAS network and the steps you believe NDAS can take to prevent, detect, and correct these errors.

CHAPTER 5

NETWORK AND TRANSPORT LAYERS

THE NETWORK layer and transport layer are responsible for moving messages from end to end in a network. They are so closely tied together that they are usually discussed together. The transport layer (layer 4) performs three functions: establishing end-to-end connections (including linking the application layer to the network), addressing (finding the address of the ultimate destination computer), and packetizing (breaking long messages into smaller packets for transmission). The network layer (layer 3) performs two functions: routing (determining the next computer to which the message should be sent to reach the final destination) and addressing (finding the address of that next computer). There are several standard transport and network layer protocols that specify how packets are to be organized, in the same way that there are standards for data link layer packets. In this chapter, we look at four commonly used protocols: TCP/IP, IPX/SPX, X.25, and SNA. TCP/IP, the protocol used on the Internet, is probably the most important, so this chapter takes a detailed look at how it works.

OBJECTIVES

- Be aware of four transport/network layer protocols
- Be familiar with packetizing and linking to the application layer
- Be familiar with addressing
- Be familiar with routing
- Understand how TCP/IP works

CHAPTER OUTLINE

INTRODUCTION

TRANSPORT AND NETWORK LAYER PROTOCOLS

Transmission Control Protocol/Internet Protocol

INTRODUCTION

The transport and network layers are so closely tied together that they are almost always discussed together. For this reason, we discuss them in the same chapter. There are several different protocols that can used at the transport and network layers, in the same way there are several different data link layer protocols. TCP/IP is the most commonly used set of protocols and is well on its way to eliminating the other protocols. Therefore, this chapter focuses almost exclusively on TCP/IP.

The transport layer links the application software in the application layer with the network and is responsible for the end-to-end delivery of the message. The transport layer accepts outgoing messages from the application layer (e.g., Web, e-mail, and so on as described in Chapter 2) and packetizes and addresses them for transmission. The network layer takes the messages from the transport layer and routes them through the network by selecting the best path from computer to computer through the network (and also does addressing when needed). The network layer relies on the data link layer for error-free delivery of messages from one computer to the next. As we saw in Chapter 1, each layer in the network has its own set of protocols that are used to hold the data generated by higher layers, much like a set of *Matryoshka* (nested Russian dolls) (Figure 5-1).

The network and transport layers also accept incoming messages from the data link layer and organize them into coherent messages that are passed to the application layer. For example, a large e-mail message might require several data link layer packets to transmit. The transport layer at the sender would break the message into several smaller packets and give them to the network layer to route, which in turns gives them to the data link layer to transmit. The network layer at the receiver would receive the individual packets from the data link layer, process them, and pass them to the transport layer, which would reassemble them into the one e-mail message before giving it to the application layer.

In the this chapter, we provide a brief look at four sets of transport and network layer protocols, before turning our attention to how TCP/IP works. We first examine the transport layer functions. Addressing and routing are performed by the transport layer and net-

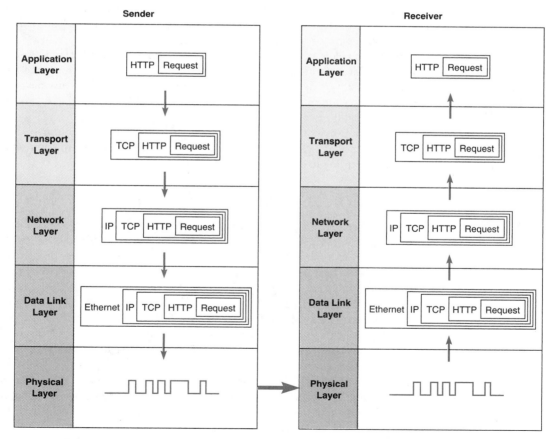

FIGURE 5-1   Message transmission using layers. HTTP = Hypertext Transfer Protocol; IP = Internet Protocol; TCP = Transmission Control Protocol.

work layers working together, so we will discuss them together rather than break them out by which part is performed by the transport layer and which by the network layer.

TRANSPORT AND NETWORK LAYER PROTOCOLS

There are many different transport/network layer protocols. Each protocol performs essentially the same functions, but each is incompatible with others unless there is a special device to translate between them. Many vendors have provide software with *multiprotocol stacks,* which means that the software supports several different transport/network protocols. The software recognizes which protocol an incoming message uses and automatically uses that protocol to process the message.

Some transport/network layer protocols (e.g., TCP/IP, IPX/SPX) are compatible with a variety of different data link layer protocols (e.g., Ethernet, frame relay) and can be used interchangeably in the same network. In other cases, network layer protocols are tightly coupled with data link layer protocols and applications and cannot easily be used with other protocols (e.g., X.25, SNA [systems network architecture]). These differences reflect the philosophy of the protocol's developers. SNA, for example, was originally developed as a complete networking architecture, designed to provide an end-to-end solution for IBM customers using entirely IBM or IBM-compatible hardware and software. TCP/IP, in contrast, was designed to be used by a variety of organizations, each of which might be using very different hardware and software, and therefore had to combine easily with many different types of data link layer protocols.

This section provides an overview of the four most commonly used network protocols: TCP/IP, IPX/SPX, X.25, and SNA. TCP/IP is the dominant protocol, and many organizations are trying to eliminate all protocols except TCP/IP.

Transmission Control Protocol/Internet Protocol

The *Transmission Control Protocol/Internet Protocol (TCP/IP)* was developed for the U.S. Department of Defense's Advanced Research Project Agency network (ARPANET) by Vinton Cerf and Bob Kahn in 1974. TCP/IP is the transport/network layer protocol used on the Internet. It is also the world's most popular network layer protocol, used by almost 70 percent of all BNs, MANs, and WANs. In 1998, TCP/IP moved past IPX/SPX as the most common protocol used on LANs.

TCP/IP allows reasonably efficient and error-free transmission. Because it performs error checking, it can send large files across sometimes unreliable networks with great assurance that the data will arrive uncorrupted. TCP/IP is compatible with a variety of data link protocols, which is one reason for its popularity.

As the name implies, TCP/IP has two parts. TCP is the transport layer protocol that links the application layer to the network layer. It performs packetizing: breaking the data into smaller packets, numbering them, ensuring each packet is reliably delivered, and putting them in the proper order at the destination.[1] IP is the network layer protocol and per-

---

[1] Some books use the terms *segmentation* instead of *packetization* and *segments* instead of *packets.* For consistency, we will use *packetization* and *packets.*

forms addressing and routing. IP software is used at each of the intervening computers through which the message passes; it is IP that routes the message to the final destination. The TCP software needs to be active only at the sender and the receiver, because TCP is involved only when data comes from or goes to the application layer.

A typical TCP packet has 192-bit header (24 bytes) of control information (Figure 5-2). Among other fields, it contains the source and destination port identifier. The destination port tells the TCP software at the destination to which the application layer program that the packet should be sent, whereas the source port tells the receiver which application layer program the packet is from. The TCP packet also provides packet sequence number so that the TCP software at the destination can assemble the packets into the correct order and make sure that no packets have been lost.

IP is the network layer protocol. Two forms of IP are currently in use. The older form is IP version 4 (IPv4), which also has a 192-bit header (24 bytes) (Figure 5-3). This header contains source and destination addresses, packet length, and packet number. IPv4 is being replaced by IPv6, which has a 320-bit header (40 bytes) (Figure 5-4). The primary reason for the increase in the packet size is an increase in the address size from 32 bits to 128 bits. Simply put, the dramatic growth in the Internet means that if the addressing format is not changed, we will run out of addresses. IPv6's simpler packet structure makes it easier to perform routing and supports a variety of new approaches to addressing and routing. The changes included in IPv6 also suggested ways to improve TCP, so a new version of TCP is currently under development.

The size of the message field depends on the data link layer protocol used. TCP/IP is commonly combined with Ethernet. Ethernet has a maximum packet size of 1,492 bytes,

Source port	Destination port	Sequence number	ACK number	Header length	Unused	Flags	Flow control	CRC–16	Urgent pointer	Options	User data
16 bits	16 bits	32 bits	32 bits	4 bits	6 bits	6 bits	16 bits	16 bits	16 bits	32 bits	Varies

FIGURE 5-2 Transmission Control Protocol (TCP) packet. ACK = acknowledgment; CRC = cyclical redundancy check.

Version number	Header length	Type of service	Total length	Indentifiers	Flags	Packet offset	Hop limit	Protocol	CRC 16	Source address	Destination address	Options	User data
4 bits	4 bits	8 bits	16 bits	16 bits	3 bits	13 bits	8 bits	8 bits	16 bits	32 bits	32 bits	32 bits	Varies

FIGURE 5-3 Internet Protocol (IP) packet (version 4). CRC = cyclical redundancy check.

Version number	Priority	Flow name	Total length	Next header	Hop limit	Source address	Destination address	User data
4 bits	4 bits	24 bits	16 bits	8 bits	8 bits	128 bits	128 bits	Varies

FIGURE 5-4 Internet Protocol (IP) packet (version 6).

so the maximum size of a TCP message field if IPv4 is used is 1492 – 24 (the size of the TCP header) – 24 (the size of the IPv4 header) = 1444.

Internetwork Packet Exchange/Sequenced Packet Exchange

Internetwork Packet Exchange/Sequenced Packet Exchange (IPX/SPX) is based on a routing protocol developed by Xerox in the 1970s. IPX/SPX is the primary network protocol used by Novell NetWare. Novell has replaced IPX/SPX with TCP/IP as its default protocol, but some organizations still use IPX/SPX.

As the name implies, IPX/SPX has two parts. IPX/SPX is similar to TCP/IP in concept but different in structure. SPX is the transport layer protocol and performs the same packetizing functions of TCP: breaking the data into smaller packets, numbering them, ensuring each packet is reliably delivered, and putting them in the proper order at the destination. IPX is the network layer protocol and performs the same routing and addressing functions as IP.

X.25

X.25 is a standard developed by ITU-T for use in WANs. It is a mature, global standard used by many international organizations. It is seldom used in North America, except by organizations with WANs that have extensive non–North American sections. X.25 also has two parts. X.3 is the transport layer protocol and performs the packetizing functions of TCP. Packet Layer Protocol (PLP) is the network layer protocol and performs the routing and addressing functions similar to IP. PLP is typically combined with LAP-B at the data link layer. ITU-T recommends that packets contain 128 bytes of application data, but X.25 can support packets containing up to 1,024 bytes.

Systems Network Architecture

Systems network architecture (SNA) is an approach to networking developed by IBM in 1974. SNA is used only on IBM and IBM-compatible mainframes (e.g., Amdahl). The major problem with SNA is that it uses proprietary nonstandard protocols, which makes it difficult to integrate SNA networks with other networks that use industry standard protocols. Routing messages between SNA networks and other networks, and even between IBM SNA networks and IBM LANs (which use industry standard protocols), requires special equipment. Most experts expect that SNA will disappear in time, either because current SNA users will switch to other products that use TCP/IP or because IBM will replace SNA protocols with TCP/IP.

TRANSPORT LAYER FUNCTIONS

The transport layer links the application software in the application layer with the network and is responsible for the end-to-end delivery of the message. One of the first issues facing the application layer is to find the numeric network address of the destination computer.

Different protocols use different methods to find this address. Depending on the protocol—and which expert you ask—finding the destination address can be classified as a transport layer function, a network layer function, a data link layer function, or an application layer function with help from the operating system. In this book, we classify it as a transport layer function, but in all honesty, understanding how it works is more important than memorizing how we classify it. The next section will discuss addressing at the network layer and transport layer together. In this section, we focus on the two unique functions performed by the transport layer: linking the application layer to the network, and packetizing.

Linking to the Application Layer

Most computers have many application layer software packages running at the same time. Users often have Web browsers, e-mail programs, word processors, and so on, in use at the same time on their client computers. Likewise, many servers act as Web servers, mail servers, FTP servers, and so on. When the transport layer receives an incoming message, the transport layer must decide to which application program it should be delivered. It makes no sense to send a Web page request to e-mail server software.

With TCP/IP, each application layer software package has a unique *port address*. Any message sent to computer must tell TCP (the transport layer software) the application layer port address that is to receive the message. Therefore, when an application layer program generates an outgoing message, it tells the TCP software its own port address (i.e., the *source port address*) and the port address at the destination computer (i.e., the *destination port address*). These two port addresses are placed in the first two fields in the TCP packet (see Figure 5-2).

Port addresses can be any 16-bit (2-byte) number. So how does a client computer sending a Web request to a Web server know what port address to use for the Web server? Simple. On the Internet, all port addresses for popular services such as the Web, e-mail, FTP, and so on, have been standardized. Any one using a Web server should set up the Web server with a port address of 80. Web browsers therefore automatically generate a port address of 80 for any Web page you click on. FTP servers use port 21, Telnet 23, SMTP 25, and so on. Network managers are free to use whatever port addresses they want, but if they use a nonstandard port number, then the application layer software on the client must specify the correct port number.[2]

Packetizing

Some messages or blocks of application data are small enough that they can be transmitted in one packet at the data link layer. However, in other cases, the application data in one "message" is too large and must be broken into several packets (e.g., Web pages, graphic images). As far as the application layer is concerned, the message should be transmitted and received as one large block of data. However, the data link layer can transmit only messages of certain lengths. It is therefore up to the sender's transport layer to break the

---

[2] One way to make a Web server private would be to use a different port number (e.g., 8080). Any Web browser wanting to access this web server would then have to explicitly include the port number in the URL (e.g., http://www.abc.com:8080).

data into several smaller packets that can be sent by the data link layer across the circuit. At the other end, the receiver's transport layer must receive all these separate packets and recombine them into one large message

Packetizing means to take one outgoing message from the application layer and break it into a set of smaller packets for transmission through the network. It also means to take the incoming set of smaller packets from the network layer and reassemble them into one message for the application layer. Depending on what the application layer software chooses, the incoming packets can either be delivered one at a time or held until all packets have arrived and the message is compete. Web browsers, for example, usually request delivery of packets as they arrive, which is why your screen gradually builds a piece at a time. Most e-mail software, on the other hand, usually requests that messages be delivered only after all packets have arrived and TCP has organized them into one intact message, which is why you usually don't see e-mail messages building screen by screen.

One of the challenges at the transport layer is deciding how big to make the packets. Remember, we discussed packet sizes in Chapter 4. When transport layer software is set up, it is told what size packets it should use to make best use of its own data link layer protocols (or it chooses the default size of 536). However, it has no idea what size is best for the destination. Therefore, the transport layer at the sender negotiates with the transport layer at the receiver to settle on the best packet sizes to use. This negotiation is done by establishing a *TCP connection* between the sender and receiver.

Connection-Oriented Routing

Connection-oriented routing sets up a *TCP Connection* (also called a *virtual circuit*) between the sender and receiver. A virtual circuit is one that *appears* to the application software to use a point-to-point circuit, even though it actually does not. In this case, the transport layer software sends a special packet (called a SYN, or synchronization characters) to the receiver requesting that a connection be established. The receiver either accepts or rejects the connection, and together, they settle on the packet sizes the connection will use.

Once the connection is established, the packets flow between the sender and receiver, following the same route through the network. (Routing is discussed in a later section in this chapter.) All packets in the same message arrive at the destination in the same order in which they were sent, so putting the packets back together again in the right order is simple. TCP uses the continuous ARQ (sliding window) technique described in Chapter 4 to make sure that all packets arrive and to provide flow control.

When the transmission is complete, the sender sends a special packet (called a FIN) to close the connection. Once the sender and receiver agree, the circuit is closed and all record of it is deleted.

Connectionless Routing

Connectionless routing means each packet is treated separately and makes its own way through the network. Unlike connection-oriented routing, no connection is established. The sender simply sends the packets as separate unrelated entities, and it is possible that different packets will take different routes through the network, depending on the type of routing used and the amount of traffic. Because packets following different routes may travel at different speeds, they may arrive out of sequence at their destination. The sender's network layer therefore puts a sequence number on each packet, in addition to information about the message stream to which the packet belongs.

The network layer must reassemble them in the correct order before passing the message to the application layer.

TCP/IP can operate either as connection-oriented or connectionless. When connection-oriented routing is desired, both TCP and IP are used. TCP establishes the virtual circuit with the destination and informs IP to route all messages along this virtual circuit. When connectionless routing is desired, the TCP packet is replaced with a User Datagram Protocol (UDP) packet. The UDP packet is much smaller than the TCP packet (only 8 bytes) because it contains only the source port, destination port, message length, and checksum.

Connectionless routing is most commonly used when the application data or message can fit into one single packet. One might expect, for example, that because HTTP requests are often very short, they might use UDP connectionless routing rather than TCP connection-oriented routing. However, HTTP always uses TCP. All of the application layer software we have discussed so far uses TCP (HTTP, SMIP, FTP, Telnet). UDP is most commonly used for control messages such as addressing (DHCP [Dynamic Host Control Protocol], discussed later in this chapter), routing control messages (RIP [Routing Information Protocol], discussed later in this chapter), and network management (SNMP [Simple Network Management Protocol], discussed in Chapter 12).

Quality of Service   *Quality of Service (QoS)* routing is a special type of connection-oriented routing in which different connections are assigned different priorities. For example, videoconferencing requires fast delivery of packets to ensure that the images and voices appear smooth and continuous; they are very time dependent, because delays in routing seriously affect the quality of the service provided. E-mail packets, on the other hand, have no such requirements. Although everyone would like to receive e-mail as fast as possible, a 10-second delay in transmitting an e-mail message does not have the same consequences as a 10-second delay in a videoconferencing packet.

With QoS routing, different *classes of service* are defined, each with different priorities. For example, a packet of a videoconferencing images would likely get higher priority than would an SMTP packet with an e-mail message and thus be routed first. When the transport layer software attempts to establish a connection (i.e., a virtual circuit), it specifies the class of service that connection requires. Each path through the network is designed to support a different number and mix of service classes. When a connection is established, the network ensures that no connections are establish that exceed the maximum number of that class on a given circuit.

QoS routing is common in certain types of networks (e.g., ATM, as discussed in Chapter 7). The Internet provides several QoS protocols that can work in a TCP/IP environment. *Resource Reservation Protocol (RSVP)* and *Real-Time Streaming Protocol (RTSP)* both permit application layer software to request connections which have certain minimum data transfer capabilities. As one might expect, RTSP is geared toward audio/video streaming applications, while RSVP is more general purpose.

RSVP and RTSP are used to create a connection (or virtual circuit) and request a certain minimum guaranteed data rate. Once the connection has been established, they use *Real-Time Transport Protocol (RTP)* to send packets across the connection. RTP contains information about the sending application, a packet sequence number, and a time stamp so that the data in the RTP packet can be synchronized with other RTP packets by the application layer software if needed.

With a name like Real-Time *Transport* Protocol, one would expect RTP to replace TCP and UDP at the transport layer. It does not. Instead, RTP is combined with UDP. (If you read the previous paragraph carefully, you noticed that RTP does not provide source and destination port addresses.) This means that each real-time packet is first created using RTP and then surrounded by a UDP packet, before being handed to the IP software at the network layer.

ADDRESSING

Before you can send a message, you must know the destination address. It is extremely important to understand that each computer has several addresses, each used by a different layer. One address is used by the data link layer, another by the network layer, and still another by the application layer.

When the users work with application software, they typically use the application layer address. For example, in Chapter 2, we discussed application software that used Internet addresses (e.g., www.indiana.edu). This is an *application layer address* (or a *server name*). When a user types an Internet address into a Web browser, the request is passed to the network layer as part of an application layer packet formatted using the HTTP protocol (Figure 5-5) (see Chapter 2).

The network layer software, in turn, uses a *network layer address.* The network layer protocol used on the Internet is IP, so this Web address (www.indiana.edu) is translated into an IP address that is 4 bytes long when using IPv4 (e.g., 129.79.127.4); see Figure 5-5. This process is similar to using a phone book to go from someone's name to his or her phone number.[3]

The network layer then determines the best route through the network to the final destination. On the basis of this routing, the network layer identifies the *data link layer address* of the next computer to which the message should be sent. If the data link layer is running Ethernet, then the network layer IP address would be translated into an Ethernet address. Chapter 3 shows that Ethernet addresses are 6 bytes in length, so a possible address might be 00-0F-00-81-14-00 (Ethernet addresses are usually expressed in hexadecimal); see Figure 5-5.

Address	Example Software	Example Address
Application layer	Web browser	www.kelley.indiana.edu
Network layer	Internet Protocol	129.79.127.4
Data link layer	Ethernet	00-0C-00-F5-03-5A

FIGURE 5-5 Types of addresses.

[3] If you ever want to find out the IP address of any computer, simply enter the command *ping,* followed by the application layer name of the computer at the DOS (Disk Operating System) prompt (e.g., ping www.indiana.edu).

Assigning Addresses

In general, the data link layer address is permanently encoded in each network card. This address is part of the hardware (e.g., Ethernet card) and can never be changed. Hardware manufacturers have an agreement that assigns each manufacturer a unique set of permitted addresses, so even if you buy hardware from different companies, they will never have the same address. Whenever you install a network card into a computer, it immediately has its own data link layer address that uniquely identifies it from every other computer in the world.

Network layer addresses are generally assigned by software. Every network layer software package usually has a configuration file that specifies the network layer address for that computer. Network managers can assign any network layer addresses they want. It is important to ensure that every computer on the same network has a unique network layer address so every network has a standards group that defines what network layer addresses can be used by each organization.

Application layer addresses (or server names) are also assigned by a software configuration file. Virtually all servers have an application layer address, but most client computers do not. This is because it is important for users to easily access servers and the information they contain, but there is usually little need for someone to access someone else's client computer. As with network layer addresses, network managers can assign any application layer address they want, but a network standards group must approve application layer addresses to ensure that no two computers have the same application layer address. Network layer addresses and application layer addresses go hand in hand, so the same standards group usually assigns both (e.g., www.indiana.edu at the application layer means 129.79.78.4 at the network layer). It is possible to have several application layer addresses for the same computer. For example, one of the Web servers in the Kelley School of Business at Indiana University is called both www.kelley.indiana.edu and pacioli.kelley.indiana.edu.

Internet Addresses No one is permitted to connect a computer to the Internet unless they use approved addresses. *ICANN (Internet Corporation for Assigned Names and Numbers)* is responsible for managing the assignment of network layer addresses (i.e., IP addresses) and application layer addresses (e.g., www.indiana.edu). ICANN sets the rules by which new *domain names* (e.g., .com, .org, .ca, .uk) are created and IP address numbers are assigned to users. ICANN also directly manages a set of Internet domains (e.g., .com, .org, .net) and authorizes private companies to become domain name registrars for those domains. Once authorized, a registrar can approve requests for application layer addresses and assign IP numbers for those requests. This means that individuals and organizations wishing to register an Internet name can use any authorized registrar for the domain they choose, and different registrars are permitted to charge different fees for their registration services. Many registrars are authorized to issue names and addresses in the ICANN managed domains, as well as domains in other countries (e.g., .ca, .uk, .au).

Several application layer addresses and network layer addresses can be assigned at the same time. IP addresses are often assigned in groups, so that one organization receives a set of numerically similar addresses for use on its computers. For example, Indiana University has been assigned the set of application layer addresses that end in .indiana.edu and .iu.edu and the set of IP addresses in the 129.79.x.x range (i.e., all IP address that start with the numbers 129.79).

One of the problems with the current address system is that the Internet is quickly running out of addresses. Although the 4-byte address of IPv4 provides more than 1 billion possible addresses, the fact that they are assigned in sets significantly limits the number of usable addresses. For example, the address ranged owned by Indiana University includes about 65,000 addresses, but we will probably not use all of them.

The IP address shortage was one of the reasons behind the development of IPv6, discussed previously. IPv6 has 16-byte addresses, meaning there are in theory about 3.2×10^{38} possible addresses—more than we can dream about. Once IPv6 is in wide use, the current Internet address system will be replaced by a totally new system based on 16-byte addresses. Most experts expect that all the current 4-byte addresses will simply assigned an arbitrary 12-byte prefix (e.g., all zeros) so that the holders of the current addresses can continue to use them.

Subnets   Each organization must assign the IP addresses it has received to specific computers on its networks. In general, IP addresses are assigned so that all computers on the same LAN have similar addresses. For example, suppose an organization has just received a set of addresses starting with 128.192.x.x. It is customary to assign all the computers in the same LAN numbers that start with the same first three digits, so the business school LAN might be assigned 128.192.56.x, which means all the computers in that LAN would have IP numbers starting with those numbers (e.g., 128.192.56.4, 128.192.56.5, and so on) (Figure 5-6). The computer science LAN might be assigned 128.192.55.x, and likewise, all the other LANs at the university and the BN that connects them would have a dif-

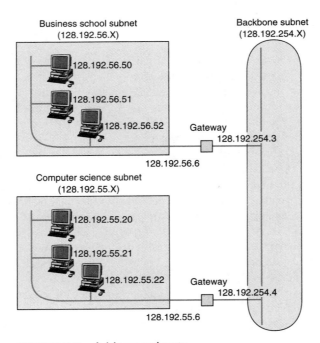

FIGURE 5-6   Address subnets.

ferent set of numbers. Each of these LANs are called a TCP/IP *subnet* because they are logically grouped together by IP number.

Although it is customary to use the first 3 bytes of the IP address to indicate different subnets, it is not required. Any portion of the IP address can be designated as a subnet by using a *subnet mask*. Every computer in a TCP/IP network is given a subnet mask to enable it to determine which computers are on the same subnet (i.e., LAN) that it is on and which computers are outside of its subnet. Knowing whether a computer is on your subnet is very important for message routing, as we shall see later in this chapter.

For example, a network could be configured so that the first 2 bytes indicated a subnet (e.g., 128.184.x.x), so all computers would be given a subnet mask giving the first 2 bytes as the subnet indicator. This would mean that a computer with an IP address of 128.184.22.33 would be on the same subnet as 128.184.78.90.

IP addresses are binary numbers, so partial bytes can also be used as subnets. For example, we could create a subnet that has IP addresses between 128.184.55.1 and 128.184.55.127, and another subnet with addresses between 128.184.55.128 and 128.184.55.254.

Dynamic Addressing   To this point, we have said that every computer knows its network layer address from a configuration file that is installed when the computer is first attached to the network. However, this leads to a major network management problem. Any time a computer is moved or its network is assigned a new address, the software on each individual computer must be updated. This is not difficult, but it is very time consuming because someone must go from office to office editing files on each individual computer.

The easiest way around this is *dynamic addressing*. With this approach, a server is designated to supply a network layer address to a computer each time the computer connects to the network. This is commonly done for client computers but usually not done for servers.

Two standards for dynamic addressing are commonly used in TCP/IP networks: *Bootstrap Protocol (bootp),* developed in 1985, and *Dynamic Host Control Protocol (DHCP),* developed in 1993. The two approaches are different but work in the same fundamental way. They do not provide a network layer address in a configuration file. Instead,

TECHNICAL FOCUS 5-1

SUBNET MASKS

Subnet masks tell computers what part of an Internet Protocol (IP) address is to be used to determine whether a destination is the same subnet or in a different subnet. A subnet mask is a 4-byte binary number that has the same format as an IP address. A 1 in the subnet mask indicates that that position is part of the subnet address. A 0 indicates that it is not.

A subnet mask of 255.255.255.0 means that the first three bytes indicate the subnet; all computers with the same first 3 bytes in their IP addresses are on the same subnet. This is because 255 expressed in binary is 11111111.

In contrast, a subnet mask of 255.255.0.0 indicates that the first 2 bytes refer to the same subnet.

Things get more complicated when we use partial-byte subnet masks. For example, 255.255.255.128 means the first 3 bytes and the next bit indicate the same subnet, because 128 in binary is 10000000. Likewise, 255.255.254.000 would indicate the first 2 bytes and 7 bits, because 254 in binary is 11111110.

there is a special software package installed on the client that instructs it to contact a bootp or DHCP server to obtain an address. In this case, when the computer is turned on and connects to the network, it first issues a broadcast bootp or DHCP message that is directed to any bootp or DHCP server that can "hear" the message. This message asks the server to assign the requesting computer a unique network layer address. The server runs a corresponding bootp or DHCP software package that responds to these requests and sends a message back to the client giving it its network layer address (and its subnet mask).

The bootp or DHCP server can be configured to assign the same network layer address to the computer (on the basis of its data link layer address) each time it requests an address, or it can *lease* the address to the computer by picking the "next available" network layer address from a list of authorized addresses. Addresses can be leased for as long as the computer is connected to the network or for a specified time limit (e.g., 2 hours). When the lease expires, the client computer must contact the bootp or DHCP server to get a new address. Address leasing is commonly used by ISPs for dial-up users. ISPs have many more authorized users than they have authorized network layer addresses because not all users can log in in at the same time. When a user logs in, his or her computer is assigned a temporary TCP/IP address that is reassigned to the next user when the first user hangs up.

Dynamic addressing greatly simplifies network management in non–dial-up networks, too. With dynamic addressing, address changes need to be made only to the bootp or DHCP server, not to each individual computer. The next time each computer connects to the network or whenever the address lease expires, the computer automatically gets the new address.

Address Resolution

To send a message, the sender must be able to translate the application layer address (or server name) of the destination into a network layer address and in turn translate that into a data link layer address. This process is called *address resolution*. There are many different approaches to address resolution that range from completely decentralized (each computer is responsible for knowing all addresses) to completely centralized (there is one computer that knows all addresses). TCP/IP uses two different approaches, one for resolving application layer addresses into IP addresses and a different one for resolving IP addresses into data link layer addresses.

Server Name Resolution   Server name resolution is the translation of application layer addresses into network layer addresses (e.g., translating an Internet address such as www.yahoo.com into an IP address such as 204.71.200.74). This is done using the *Domain Name Service (DNS)*. Throughout the Internet there are a series of computers called *name servers* that provide DNS services. These name servers run special address databases that store thousands of Internet addresses and their corresponding IP addresses. These name servers are, in effect, the "directory assistance" computers for the Internet. Anytime a computer does not know the IP number for a computer, it sends a message to the name server requesting the IP number. There are about a dozen high-level name servers that provide IP addresses for most of the Internet, with thousands of others that provide IP addresses for specific domains.

Whenever you register an Internet application layer address, you must inform the registrar of the IP address of the name server that will provide DNS information for all addresses in that name range. For example, because Indiana University owns the .indiana.edu name, it can create any name it wants that ends in that suffix (e.g., www.indiana.edu, www.kelley.indiana.edu, abc.indiana.edu). When it registers its name, it must also provide the IP address of the DNS server that it will use to provide the IP addresses for all the computers within this domain name range (i.e., everything ending in .indiana.edu). Every organization that has many servers also has its own DNS server, but smaller organizations that have only one or two servers often use a DNS server provided by their ISP. DNS servers are maintained by network managers, who update their address information as the network changes. DNS servers can also exchange information about new and changed addresses among themselves (replication).

When a computer needs to translate an application layer address into an IP address, it sends a special DNS request packet to its DNS server.[4] This packet asks the DNS server to send to the requesting computer the IP address that matches the Internet application layer address provided. If the DNS server has a matching name in its database, it sends back a special DNS response packet with the correct IP address. If that DNS server does not have that Internet address in its database, it will issue the same request to another DNS server elsewhere on the Internet.[5]

For example, if someone at the University of Toronto asked for a Web page on our server (www.kelley.indiana.edu) at Indiana University, the software on the Toronto client computer would issue a DNS request to the University of Toronto DNS server (Figure 5-7). This DNS server probably would not know the IP address of our server, so it would forward the request to the DNS root server that it knows stores addresses for the .edu domain. The .edu root server probably would not know our server's IP address either, but it would know that the DNS server on our campus could supply the address. So it would forward the request to the Indiana University DNS server, which would respond to the .edu server with a DNS response containing the requested IP address. The .edu server in turn would send it to the DNS server at the University of Toronto, which in turn would send it to the computer that requested the address.

This is why it sometimes takes a long time to access certain sites. Most DNS servers know only the names and IP addresses for the computers in their part of the network. Some store frequently used addresses (e.g., www.yahoo.com). If you try to access a computer that is far away, it may take a while before your computer receives a response from a DNS server that knows the IP address.

Once your application layer software receives an IP address, it is stored in a server address table. This way, if you ever need to access the same computer again, your computer does not need to contact a DNS server. Most server address tables are routinely deleted whenever you turn off your computer.

---

[4] DNS requests and responses are usually short, so they use UDP as their transport layer protocol. That is, the DNS request is passed to the transport layer, which surrounds them in a UDP packet before handing them to the network layer.

[5] This is called recursive DNS resolution and is the most common approach used on the Internet. DNS servers can also use iterative DNS resolution, whereby the client is told that the DNS server does not know the desired address but is given the IP address of another DNS server that can be used to find the address. Because recursive is more common, that is what we describe here.

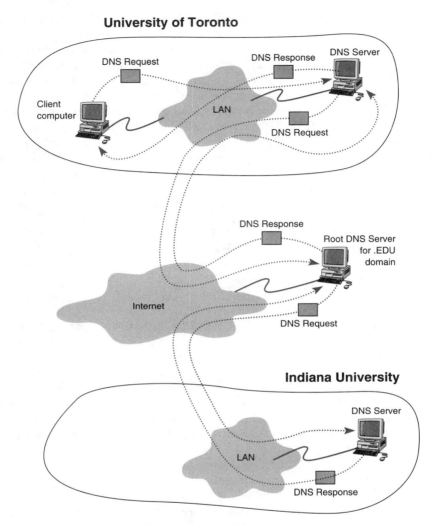

FIGURE 5-7 How the DNS system works.

Data Link Layer Address Resolution To actually send a message, the network layer software must know the data link layer address of the destination computer. The final destination may be far away (e.g., sending from Toronto to Indiana). In this case, the network layer would *route* the message by selecting a path through the network that would ultimately lead to the destination. (Routing is discussed in the next section.) The first step would be to send the message to a computer in its subnet that is the first step on this route.

To send a message to a computer in its subnet, a computer must know the correct data link layer address. In this case, the TCP/IP software sends a *broadcast message* to all computers in its subnet. A broadcast message, as the name suggests, is received and processed by all computers in the same LAN (which is usually designed to match the IP subnet). The message is a specially formatted request using *Address Resolution Protocol (ARP)* that says,

MANAGEMENT FOCUS *5-1*

OPERATOR ERROR MAKES NET GO NUTS

At 2:30 A.M. on July 17, 1997, the Internet was thrown into chaos. A computer operator at Network Solutions Inc., the company that maintained the master Domain Name Service (DNS) server for the Internet, ignored alarms on the computer, which then sent incorrect DNS information for the .com and .net domains to the 10 primary Internet DNS servers around the world.

The problem was corrected by 6:30 A.M., but it took several more hours before the corrected information was

replicated around the world to other lower-level DNS servers. By then, several million requests for Web pages and e-mail messages sent to the .com and .net domains were returned as undeliverable because of the bad DNS information.

SOURCE: "Operator Error Makes Net Go Nuts," *Atlanta Journal-Constitution,* July 18, 1997.

"Whoever is IP address xxx.xxx.xxx.xxx, please send me your data link layer address." The software in the computer with that IP address then sends an ARP response with its data link layer address. The sender transmits its message using that data link layer address. The sender also stores the data link layer address in its address table for future use.[6]

ROUTING

In many networks, there are many possible routes or paths a message can take to get from one computer to another. For example, in Figure 5-8, a message sent from computer A to computer F could travel first to computer B then to computer C to get to computer F—or it could go to computer D first and then to computer E to get to computer F.

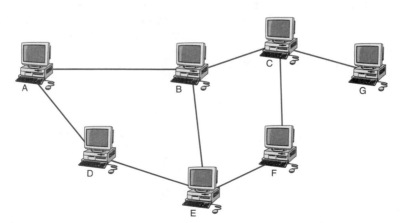

FIGURE 5-8   A typical network.

---

[6] It would be pretty reasonable at this point to guess that because ARP requests and responses are small, they use UDP in the same way that DNS requests and responses do. But they don't. Instead, ARP packets replace both the TCP/UDP and IP and are placed directly into the data link layer protocol with no transport or network layer packets.

Routing is the process of determining the route or path through the network that a message will travel from the sending computer to the receiving computer. Every computer that performs routing has a *routing table* developed by the network manager that specifies how messages will travel through the network. In its simplest form, the routing table is a two-column table. The first column lists every computer in the network, whereas the second column lists the computer to which this computer should send messages if they are destined for the computer in the first column. Figure 5-9 shows a routing table that might be used by computer B in Figure 5-8.[7]

Obviously, the Internet is more complicated than the simple network in Figure 5-8; it has millions of computers attached. How can we possibly route messages on the Internet? Well, it turns out that most parts of the Internet are connected only to a few other parts of the Internet. That is, any one part of the Internet, such as your university, is probably has only two or three connections into the Internet. When messages arrive at the computer that connects your university to the Internet, that computer must choose over which circuit to send the message. Imagine, for example, that computer B in Figure 5-8 is the computer that connects your university to the Internet and that the other computers in this figure are different parts of the Internet. Some parts of the Internet are best reached by one circuit (e.g., the part represented by computer A), whereas others are best reached via the other circuit (e.g., the part represented by computer E). In this case, the computer is told that messages sent to IP addresses in a certain range (e.g., 127.x.x.x) should go on one circuit, whereas messages to addresses is a different range (e.g., 12.x.x.x) should go on a different circuit. In some cases, computers can be reached equally well on either circuit (e.g. computer D), in which case the network manager may arbitrarily choose one circuit or configure the software to choose either circuit as it likes.

Imagine yourself as a packet that needs to travel over the Internet from the University of Texas to the University of Alberta (e.g., an HTTP request). As you leave the University of Texas on the Internet, you reach a fork in the path. A sign says *Texas this way—all other destinations straight ahead* (Figure 5-10). Although this sign does not explicitly tell you how to get to the University of Alberta, it is clear that you must you continue on straight ahead. As you reach the next fork in the path, there is another sign. Once again, your destination is not listed, but nonetheless, the direction you need to take is clear. The next sign includes your destination (Canada) in a range of destinations, so you turn down that path. The next sign

Destination	Route
A	A
C	C
D	A
E	E
F	E
G	C

FIGURE 5-9   Routing table.

---

[7] If you ever want to find out the route through the Internet from your computer to any other computer on the Internet, simply enter the command *tracert* followed by the application layer name of the computer at the DOS prompt (e.g., tracert www.indiana.edu).

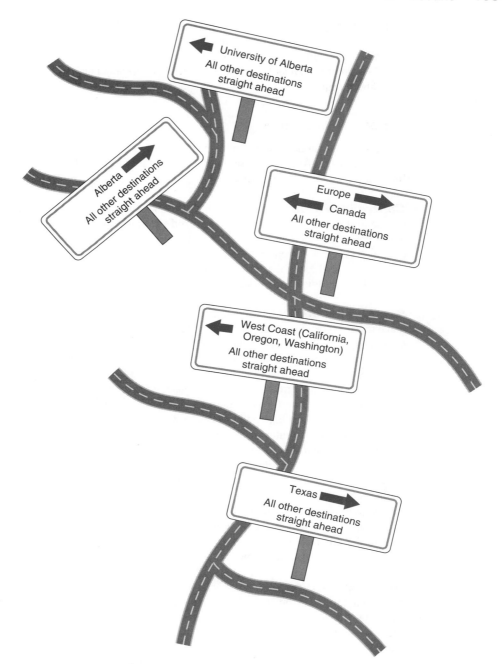

FIGURE 5-10 Internet routing.

again contains your destination (Alberta) in a range of destinations, so you take that path. At last, you see a sign to your destination. This is one way in which the Internet works.

Because routing is an important function, we often use special-purpose devices called *routers* to build and maintain the routing tables and perform routing. We will explain more about routers in Chapter 7.

Types of Routing

There are three fundamental approaches to routing: centralized routing, static routing, and dynamic routing. As you will see in the TCP/IP Example section later in this chapter, the Internet uses all three approaches.

Centralized Routing With centralized routing, all routing decisions are made by one central computer or router. Centralized routing typically is commonly used in host-based networks (see Chapter 2), and in this case, routing decisions are rather simple. All computers are connected to the central computer, so any message that needs to be routed is simply sent to the central computer, which in turn retransmits the message on the appropriate circuit to the destination.

Static Routing With decentralized routing, all computers or routers in the network make their own routing decisions following a formal routing protocol. In MANs and WANs, the routing table for each computer is developed by its individual network manager (although network managers often share information). In LANs or backbones, the routing tables used by all computers on the network are usually developed by one individual or a committee. Most decentralized routing protocols are self-adjusting, meaning that they can automatically adapt to changes in the network configuration (e.g., adding and deleting computers and circuits).

With *static routing,* routing decisions are made in a decentralized manner by individual computers or routers. The routing table is developed by the network manager, and it changes only when computers are added to or removed from the network. For example, if the computer recognizes that a circuit is broken or unusable (e.g., after the data link layer retry limit has been exceeded without receiving an acknowledgment), the computer will update the routing table to indicate the failed circuit. If an alternate route is available, it will be used for all subsequent messages. Otherwise, messages will be stored until the circuit is repaired. When new computers are added to the network, they announce their presence to the other computers, who automatically add them into their routing tables. Static routing is commonly used in networks that have few routing options that seldom change.

Dynamic Routing With *dynamic routing* (or *adaptive routing*), routing decisions are made in a decentralized manner by individual computers. It is used when there are multiple routes through a network and it is important to select the best route. Dynamic routing attempts to improve network performance by routing messages over the fastest possible route, away from busy circuits and busy computers. An initial routing table is developed by the network manager but is continuously updated by the computers themselves to reflect changing network conditions.

With *distance vector* dynamic routing, computers or routers count the number of *hops* along a route. A hop is one circuit, so that a route from one computer to another that passes through only one other computer (e.g., from A to C through B in Figure 5-8) would be two hops, whereas a route that passes through three computers (e.g., A to C via D, E, and F in Figure 5-8) would be four hops. With this approach, computers periodically (usually every 1 to 2 minutes) exchange information on the hop count and sometimes the relative speed of the circuits in route with their neighbors.

With *link state* dynamic routing, computers or routers track the number of hops in the route, the speed of the circuits in each route, and how busy each route is. In other words, rather than knowing just a route's distance, link state routing tries to determine the how fast each possible route is. Each computer or router periodically (usually every 15 to 30 minutes) exchanges this information with other computers or routers in the network, so that each computer or router has the most accurate information possible. Link state protocols are preferred to distance vector protocols in large networks because they spread more reliable routing information throughout the entire network when major changes occur in the network. They are said to *converge* more quickly.

There are two drawbacks to dynamic routing. First, it requires more processing by each computer or router in the network than does centralized routing or static routing. Computing resources are devoted to adjusting routing tables rather than to sending messages, which can slow down the network. Second, the transmission of routing information "wastes" network capacity. Some dynamic routing protocols transmit status information every minute, which can significantly reduce performance.

Routing Protocols

A routing protocol is a protocol that is used to exchange information among computers to enable them to build and maintain their routing tables. You can think of a routing protocol as the language that is used to build the signs in Figure 5-10. When new paths are added or paths are broken and cannot be used, messages are sent among computers using the routing protocol.

It can be useful to know all possible routes to a given destination. However, as a network gets quite large, knowing all possible routes becomes impractical; there are simply too many possible routes. Even at some modest number of computers, dynamic routing protocols become impractical because of the amount of network traffic they generate. For this reason, networks are often subdivided into autonomous systems of networks.

An *autonomous system* is simply a network operated by one organization, such as IBM or Indiana University or an organization that runs one part of the Internet. Remember that we said the Internet was simply a network of networks. Each part of the Internet is run by a separate organization such as AT&T, Sprint, BBN Planet, and so on. Each part of the Internet or each large organizational network connected to the Internet can be a separate autonomous system.

The computers within each autonomous system know about the other computers in that system and usually exchange routing information because the number of computers is kept to some manageable number. If an autonomous systems grows too large, it can be split into smaller parts. The routing protocols used inside an autonomous system are called *interior routing protocols.*

Protocols used between autonomous systems are called *exterior routing protocols.* Although interior routing protocols are usually designed to provide detailed routing information about all or most computers inside the autonomous systems, exterior protocols are designed to be more careful in the information they provide. Usually, exterior protocols provide information about only the preferred or the best routes rather than all possible routes.

There are many different protocols that are used to exchange routing information. Five are commonly used on the Internet: Border Gateway Protocol (BGP), Internet Control Message Protocol (ICMP), RIP, Open Shortest Path First (OSPF), and Enhanced Interior Gateway Routing Protocol (EIGRP).

Border Gateway Protocol (BGP) is a dynamic exterior routing protocol used on the Internet to exchange routing information between autonomous systems—that is, large sections of the Internet. Although BGP is the preferred routing protocol between Internet sections, it is seldom used inside companies because it is large and complex and is often hard to administer.

Internet Control Message Protocol (ICMP) is the simplest and most basic interior routing protocol on the Internet. ICMP is simply an error-reporting protocol that enables computers to report routing errors to message senders. ICMP also has a very limited ability to update routing tables.[8]

TECHNICAL FOCUS 5-2

ROUTING ON THE INTERNET

The Internet is a network of autonomous system networks. Each autonomous system operates its own interior routing protocol while using Border Gateway Protocol (BGP) as the exterior routing protocol to exchange information with the other autonomous systems in the Internet. Although there are a number of interior routing protocols, Open Shortest Path First (OSPF) is the current preferred protocol, and most organizations that run the autonomous system forming large parts of the Internet use OSPF.

Figure 5-11 shows how a small part of the Internet might operate. In this example, there are six autonomous systems (e.g., Sprint, BBN Plant), three of which we have shown in more detail. Each autonomous system has a *border router* that connects it to the adjacent autonomous systems and exchanges route information via BGP. In this example, autonomous system A is connected to autonomous system B, which in turn is connected to autonomous system C. A is also connected to C via a route through systems D and E. If someone in A wants to send a message to someone in C, the message should be routed through B because it is the fastest route. The autonomous systems must share route information via BGP so that the border routers in each system know what routes are preferred. In this case, B would inform A that there is a route through it to C (and a route to E), and D would inform A that it has a

route to E, but D would not inform A that there is a route though it to C. The border router in A would then have to decide which route to use to reach E.

Each autonomous system can use a different interior routing protocol. In this example, A and C use OSPF and B uses Routing Information Protocol (RIP). RIP is simpler, so that every minute or so, all routers broad cast route information to their neighbors. B is a rather simple network with only a few devices and routes, so RIP is probably a reasonable choice. A and C are more complex and use OSPF. Most organizations that use OSPF create a special router called a *designated router* to manage the routing information. Every 15 minutes or so, each router sends its routing information to the designated router, which then broadcasts the revised routing table information to all other routers. If no designated router is used, then every router would have to broadcast its routing information to all other routers, which would result in a very large number of messages. In the case of autonomous system C, which has seven routers, this would required 42 separate messages (seven routers each sending to six others). By using a designated router, we now have only 12 separate messages (the six other routers sending to the designated router, and the designated router sending the complete set of revised information back to the other six).

---

[8] ICMP is the protocol used by the ping command.

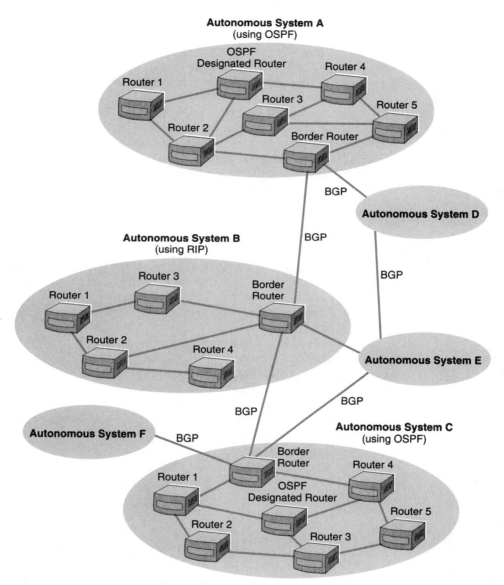

FIGURE 5-11 Routing on the Internet with Border Gateway Protocol (BGP), Open Shortest Path First (OSPF), and Routing Information Protocol (RIP).

Ro\uting Information Protocol (RIP) is a dynamic distance vector interior routing protocol that is commonly used in smaller networks, such as those operated by one organization. The network manager uses RIP to develop the routing table. When new computers are added, RIP simply counts the number of computers in the possible routes to the destination and selects the route with the least number. Computers using RIP send broadcast messages every minute or so (the timing is set by the network manager) announcing their routing status to all other computers. RIP is used by both TCP/IP and IPX/SPX.

Open Shortest Path First (OSPF) is another dynamic link state interior routing protocol that is commonly used on the Internet. It uses the number of computers in a route as well as network traffic and error rates to select the best route. OSPF is more efficient than RIP because it normally doesn't use broadcast messages. Instead, it selectively sends status update messages directly to selected computers or routers. OSPF is the preferred interior routing protocol used by TCP/IP.

Enhanced Interior Gateway Routing Protocol (EIGRP) is a dynamic link state interior routing protocol developed by Cisco and is commonly used inside organizations. EIGRP records information about a route's transmission capacity, delay, reliability, and load. EIGRP is unique in that computer or routers store their own routing table as well as the routing tables for all of their neighbors so they have a more accurate understanding of the network.

Multicasting

The most common type of message in a network is the usual transmission between two computers. One computer sends a message to another computer (e.g., a client requesting a Web page). This is called a *unicast message.* Earlier in the chapter, we introduced the concept of a *broadcast message* that is sent to all computers on a specific LAN or subnet. A third type of message called a *multicast message* is used to send the same message to a group of computers.

Consider a videoconferencing situation in which four people want to participate in the same conference. Each computer could send the same voice and video data from its camera to the computers of each of the other three participants using unicasts. In this case, each computer would send three identical messages, each addressed to the three different computers. This would work but would require a lot of network capacity. Alternately, each computer could send one broadcast message. This would reduce network traffic (because each computer would send only one message), but every computer on the network would process it, distracting them from other tasks. Broadcast messages usually are transmitted only within the same LAN or subnet, so this would not work if one of the computers was outside the subnet.

MANAGEMENT FOCUS 5-2

TOY STORY

You don't have to be a math major to figure out it's more efficient to send one file once to 200 locations than to send the 200 copies of the same file, one at a time, to each of those locations. But that's what Toys Я Us did for 10 years before multicasting.

Toys Я Us used to send software updates to its 865 stores over its satellite network one file at a time, using unicast messages. This took so much network capacity that it could be done only at night when the stores were closed. It also took so much time that not all stores could be updated on the same night. Transferring a 1-megabyte file to 250 stores took just over 6 hours.

With Internet Protocol multicasting, transferring the same 1-megabyte file now takes less than 4 minutes.

SOURCE: "Toy Story" *PC Week,* October 21, 1996.

The solution is multicast messaging. Computers wishing to participate in a multicast send a message to the sending computer or some other computer performing routing along the way using a special type packet called *Internet Group Management Protocol (IGMP)*. Each multicast group is assigned a special IP address to identify the group. Any computer performing routing knows to route all multicast messages with this IP address onto the subnet that contains the requesting computer. The routing computer sets the data link layer address on multicast messages to a matching multicast data link layer address. Each requesting computer must inform its data link layer software to process incoming messages with this multicast data link layer address. When the multicast session ends (e.g., the videoconference is over), the client computer sends another IGMP message to the organizing computer or the computer performing routing to remove it from the multicast group.

TCP/IP EXAMPLE

This chapter has discussed the functions of the transport and network layers: linking to the application layer, packetizing, addressing, and routing. In this section, we tie all of these concepts together to take a closer look at how these functions actually work using TCP/IP.

When a computer is installed on a TCP/IP network (or dials into a TCP/IP network), it must be given four pieces of network layer addressing and routing information before it can operate. This information can be provided by a configuration file, or via a bootp or DHCP server. The information is

1. Its IP address
2. A subnet mask, so it can determine what addresses are part of its subnet
3. The IP address of a DNS server, so it can translate application layer addresses into IP addresses
4. The IP address of a gateway[9] computer leading outside of its subnet, so it can route messages addressed to computers outside of its subnet (this presumes the computer is using static routing and there is only one connection from it to the outside world through which all messages must flow; if it used dynamic routing, some routing software would be needed instead)

These four pieces of information are the minimum required. A server would also need to know its application layer address.

In this section, we will use the simple network shown in Figure 5-12 to illustrate how TCP/IP works. This figure shows an organization that has four LANs connected by a BN. The BN also has a connection to the Internet. Each building is configured as a separate subnet. For example, Building A has the 128.192.98.x subnet, whereas Building B has the 128.192.95.x subnet. The BN is its own subnet: 128.192.254.x. Each building is connected to the BN via a gateway that has two IP addresses and two data link layer addresses, one for the connection into the building and one for the connection onto the BN. The organiza-

---

[9] For the moment, we will call this computer that connects to other networks a TCP/IP gateway computer. As we shall see in Chapter 7, it is probably a device called a router.

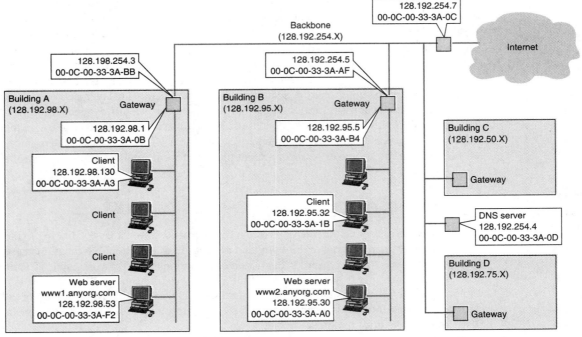

FIGURE 5-12 Example Transmission Control Protocol/Internet Protocol (TCP/IP) network.

tion has several Web servers spread throughout the four buildings. The DNS server and the gateway onto the Internet are located directly on the BN itself. For simplicity, we will assume that all networks use Ethernet as the data link layer and will only focus on Web requests at the application layer.

In the sections below, we will describe how messages are sent through the network. For the sake of simplicity, we will initially ignore the need to establish and close TCP connections. Once you understand the basic concepts, we will then add these in to complete the example.

Known Addresses, Same Subnet

Let's start with the simplest case. Suppose that a user on a client computer in Building A (128.192.98.130) requests a Web page from the Web server in the same building (www1. anyorg.com). We will assume that this computer knows the network layer and data link layer address of the Web server (e.g., it has previously requested pages from this server, so the addresses are in its address tables). Because the application layer software knows the IP address of the server, it uses its IP address, not its application layer address.

In this case, the application layer software (i.e., Web browser) passes an HTTP packet containing the user request to the transport layer software requesting a page from 128.192.98.53. The transport layer software (TCP) would take the HTTP packet, add a

TCP packet, and then hand the one packet to the network layer software (IP). The network layer software will compare the destination address (128.192.98.53) to the subnet mask (255.255.255.0) and discover that this that this computer is on its own subnet. The network layer software will then search its data link layer address table and find the matching data link layer address (00-0C-00-33-3A-F2). The network layer would then attach an IP packet and pass it to the data link layer, along with the destination Ethernet address. The data link layer would surround the packet with an Ethernet packet and transmit it over the physical layer to the web server (Figure 5-13).

The data link layer on the web server would perform error checking and send an acknowledgment back, before passing the HTTP packet with the TCP and IP packet attached to its network layer software. The network layer software (IP) would then process the IP packet, see that it was destined to this computer, and pass it to the transport layer software (TCP). This software would process the TCP packet, see that there was only one packet, and pass the HTTP packet to the Web server software.

The Web server software would find the page requested, attach an HTTP packet, and pass it to its transport layer software. The transport layer software (TCP) would break the Web page into several smaller packets, each less than 1,500 bytes in length, and attach a TCP packet (with a packet number to indicate the order) to each. Each would then go to the network layer software, get an IP packet attached that specified the IP address of the requesting client (128.192.98.130) and be given to the data link layer with the client's Ethernet address (00-0C-00-33-3A-A3) for transmission. The data link layer on the server would transmit the packets in the order in which the network layer passed them to it.

The client's data link layer software would receive the packets, perform error checking and issue an acknowledgment on each packet, and pass each to the network layer. The network layer software (IP) would check to see that the packets were destined for this computer and pass them to the transport layer software. The transport layer software (TCP) would assemble the separate data link layer packets, in order, back into one Web page, and pass each in turn to the Web browser to display on the screen.

Known Addresses, Different Subnet

Suppose this time, that the same client computer wanted to get a Web page from a Web server located somewhere in Building B (say, www2.anyorg.com). Again, assume that all addresses are known and are in the address tables of all computers. In this case, the application layer software would pass an HTTP packet to the transport layer software (TCP) with the Internet address of the destination www2.anyorg.com: 128.192.95.30. The transport layer software (TCP) would make sure that the request fit in one packet and hand it to the network layer. The

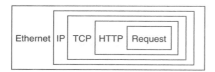

FIGURE 5-13   Packet nesting. HTTP = Hypertext Transfer Protocol; IP = Internet Protocol; TCP = Transmission Control Protocol.

network layer software (IP) would then check the subnet mask and would recognize that the Web server is located outside of its subnet. Any messages going outside the subnet must be sent to the gateway (128.192.98.1), whose job it is to process the message and send the message on its way into the outside network. The network layer software would check its address table and find the Ethernet address for the gateway. It would therefore set the data link layer address to the gateway's Ethernet address on this subnet (00-0C-00-33-3A-0B) and pass it to the data link layer for transmission. The data link layer would add the Ethernet packet and pass it to the physical layer for transmission. The data link layer would add the Ethernet packet and pass it to the physical layer for transmission.

The gateway would receive the message and its data link layer would perform error checking and send an acknowledgement before passing the message to the network layer software (IP). The network layer software would read the IP address to determine the final destination. The gateway would recognize that this address (128.192.95.30) needed to be sent to the 128.192.95.x subnet. It knows the gateway for this subnet is 128.192.254.5. It would pass the packet back to its data link layer, giving the Ethernet address of the this gateway (00-0C-00-33-3A-AF).

This gateway would receive the message (do error checking, etc.) and read the IP address to determine the final destination. The gateway would recognize that this address (128.192.95.30) was inside its 128.192.95.x subnet and would search its data link layer address table for this computer. It would then pass the packet the data link layer along with the Ethernet address of (00-0C-00-33-3A-A0) for transmission.

The www2.anyorg.com web server would receive the message and process it. This would result in a series of TCP/IP packets addressed to the requesting client (128.192.98.130). These would make their way through the network in reverse order. The Web server would recognize that this IP address is outside its subnet and would send the message to the 128.192.95.5 gateway using its Ethernet address (00-0C-00-33-3A-B4). This gateway would then send the message to the gateway for the 128.192.98.x subnet (128.192.254.3) using its Ethernet address (00-0C-00-33-3A-BB). This gateway would in turn send the message back to the client (128.192.98.130) using its Ethernet address (00-0C-00-33-3A-A3).

This process would work in the same way for Web servers located outside the organization on the Internet. In this case, the message would go from the client to the 128.192.98.x gateway, which would send it to the Internet gateway (128.192.254.7), which would send it to its Internet connection. The message would be routed through the Internet, from gateway to gateway, until it reached its destination. Then the process would work in reverse to return the requested page.

Unknown Addresses

Let's return to the simplest case (requesting a Web page from a Web server on the same subnet), only this time we will assume that the client computer does not know the network layer or data link layer address of the Web server. For simplicity, we will assume that the client knows the data link layer address of its subnet gateway, but after you read through this example, you will realize that obtaining the data link layer address of the subnet gateway is straightforward. (It is done the same way as the client obtains the data link layer address of the Web server.)

Suppose the client computer in building A (128.192.98.130) wants to retrieve a Web page from the www1.anyorg.com Web server but does not know its addresses. The Web browser realizes that it does not know the IP address after searching its IP address table and not finding a matching entry. Therefore, it issues a DNS request to the name server (128.192.254.4). The DNS request is passed to the transport layer (TCP), which attaches a TCP packet (or a UDP packet, depending on the configuration) and hands the message to the network layer.

Using its subnet mask, the network layer (IP) will recognize that the DNS server is outside of its subnet. It will attach an IP packet and set the data link layer address to its gateway's address.

The gateway will process the message and recognize that the 128.192.254.4 IP address is on the BN. It will transmit the packet using the DNS server's Ethernet address.

The name server will process the DNS request and send the matching IP address back to the client via the 128.198.98.x subnet gateway.

The IP address for the desired computers makes its way back to the application layer software, which stores it in its IP table. It then issues the HTTP request using the the the IP address for the web server (128.192.98.53) and passes it to the transport layer, which in turn passes it to the network layer. The network layer uses its subnet mask and recognizes that this computer is on its subnet. However, it does not know the Web server's Ethernet address. Therefore, it broadcasts an ARP request to all computers on its subnet, requesting that the computer whose IP address is 128.192.98.53 to respond with its Ethernet address.

This request is processed by all computers on the subnet, but only the Web server responds with an ARP packet giving its Ethernet address. The network layer software on the client stores this address in its data link layer address table and sends the original Web request to the Web server using its Ethernet address.

This process works the same for a Web server outside the subnet, whether in the same organization or anywhere in the Internet. If the Web server is far away (e.g., Australia), the process will likely involve searching more than one name server, but it is still the same process.

TCP Connections

Whenever a computer transmits data from itself to another computer, it must choose whether to use a connection-oriented service via TCP or a connectionless service via UDP. Most application layer software such as Web browsers (HTTP), e-mail (SMTP), FTP, and Telnet use connection-oriented services. This means that before the first packet is sent, the transport layer first sends a SYN packet to establish a connection. Once the connection is established, then the data packets begin to flow. Once the data is finished, the connection is closed with a FIN packet.

In the examples above, this means that the first packet sent is really a SYN packet, followed by a response from the receiver accepting the connection, and then the packets as described above. There is nothing magical about the SYN and FIN packets; they are addressed and routed in the same manner as any other TCP packets. But they do add to the complexity and length of the example.

A special word is needed about HTTP packets. When HTTP was first developed, Web browsers opened a separate TCP connection for each HTTP request. That is, when they requested a page, they would open a connection, send the single packet requesting the Web page, and close the connection at their end. The Web server would accept the connection, send as many packets as needed to transmit the requested page, and the close the connection. If the page included graphic images, the Web browser would open and close a separate connection for each request. This requirement to open and close connections for each request was time consuming and not really necessary. With the newest version of HTTP, Web browsers open one connection when they first issue an HTTP request and leave that connection open for all subsequent HTTP requests to the same server.

SUMMARY

Transport and Network Layer Protocols   Many different standard transport and network protocols exist to perform addressing (finding destination addresses), routing (finding the "best" route through the network), and packetizing (breaking large messages into smaller packets for transmission and reassembling them at the destination). All provide formal definitions for how addressing and routing are to be executed and specify packet structures to transfer this information between computers. TCP/IP, IPX/SPX, X.25, and SNA are the four most commonly used network layer protocols. TCP/IP is the most common.

Transport Layer   The transport layer (TCP) uses the source and destination port address to link the application layer software to the network. TCP is also responsible for packetizing—breaking large messages into smaller packets for transmission and resembling them at the receiver's end. When connection-oriented routing is needed, TCP establishes a connection or virtual circuit from the sender to the receiver. When connectionless routing is needed, TCP is replaced with UDP. Quality of service provides the ability to prioritize packets so that real-time voice packets are transmitted more quickly than simple e-mail messages.

Addressing   Computers can have three different addresses: application layer address, network layer address, and data link layer address. Data link layer addresses are usually part of the hardware, whereas network layer and application layer addresses are set by software. Network layer and application layer addresses for the Internet are assigned by Internet registrars. Addresses within one organization are usually assigned so that computers in the same LAN or subnet have the similar addresses, usually with the first 3 bytes the same. Subnet masks are used to indicate whether the first 2 or 3 bytes (or partial bytes) indicate the same subnet. Some networks assign network layer addresses in a configuration file on the client computer, whereas others use dynamic addressing in which a bootp or DHCP server assigns addresses when a computer first joins the network.

Address Resolution   Address resolution is the process of translating an application layer address into a network layer address or translating a network layer address into a data link layer address. On the Internet, network layer resolution is done by sending a special message to a DNS server (also called a name server) that asks for the IP address (e.g., 128.192.98.5) for a given Internet address (e.g., www.kelley.indiana.edu). If a DNS server does not have an entry for the requested Internet address, it will forward the request to another DNS server that it thinks it likely to have the address, which will either respond or forward it to another DNS server, and so on, until the address is found or it becomes clear that the address is unknown. Resolving data link layer addresses is done by sending an ARP request in a broadcast message to all computers on the same subnet that asks the computer with the requested IP address to respond with its data link layer address.

Routing   Routing is the process of selecting the route or path through the network that a message will travel from the sending computer to the receiving computer. With centralized routing, one computer performs all the routing decisions. With static routing, the routing table is developed by the network manager and remains unchanged until the network manager updates it. With dynamic routing, the goal is to improve network performance by routing messages over the fastest possible route; an initial routing table is developed by the network manager but is continuously updated to reflect changing network conditions, such as message traffic. BGP, RIP, ICMP, and OSPF are examples of dynamic routing protocols.

TCP/IP Example In TCP/IP, it is important to remember that the TCP and IP packets are created by the sending computer and never change until the message reaches its final destination. The IP packet contains the original source and ultimate destination address for the packet. The sending computer also creates a data link layer packet (e.g., Ethernet) for each message. This packet contains the data link layer address of the current computer sending the packet and the data link layer address of the next computer in the route through the network. The data link layer packet is removed and replaced with a new packet at each computer at which the message stops as it works its way through the network. Thus, the source and destination data link layer addresses change at each step along the route, whereas the IP source and destination addresses never change.

KEY TERMS

address resolution	dynamic addressing	packet exchange	router
Address Resolution Protocol (ARP)	Dynamic Host Control Protocol (DHCP)	(IPX/SPX)	routing
addressing	dynamic routing	link state routing	Routing Information Protocol (RIP)
application layer address	Enhanced Interior Gateway Routing Protocol	multicast	routing table
autonomous systems	(EIGRP)	name server	static routing
Bootstrap Protocol (bootp)	exterior routing protocol	network layer address	source port address
Border Gateway Protocol (BGP)	hop	Open Shortest Path First (OSPF)	subnet
border router	interior routing protocol	Packet Layer Protocol (PLP)	subnet mask
broadcast	Internet address classes	packetizing	systems network architecture (SNA)
connectionless routing	Internet Control Message Protocol (ICMP)	path control	transmission control
connection-oriented routing	Internet Corporation for Assigned Names and	port address	Transmission Control Protocol/Internet Protocol (TCP/IP)
data link layer address	Numbers (ICANN)	Quality of Service (QoS)	unicast
designated router	Internet Group Management Protocol	Real-Time Streaming Protocol (RTSP)	User Datagram Protocol (UDP)
destination port address	(IGMP)	Real-Time Transport Protocol (RTP)	virtual circuit
distance vector routing	internetwork packet exchange/sequenced	Resource Reservation Protocol (RSVP)	X.25
Domain Name Service (DNS)			X.3

QUESTIONS

1. What does the transport layer do?
2. What does the network layer do?
3. What are the parts of TCP/IP and what do they do? Who is the primary user of TCP/IP?
4. What are the parts of IPX/SPX and what do they do? Who is the primary user of IPX/SPX?
5. What are the parts of X.25 and what do they do? Who is the primary user of X.25?

6. What are the parts of SNA and what do they do? Who is the primary user of SNA?
7. Compare and contrast the three types of addresses used in a network.
8. How is TCP different from UDP?
9. How does TCP establish a connection?
10. What is a subnet and why do networks need them?
11. What is a subnet mask?

12. How does dynamic addressing work?

13. What benefits and problems does dynamic addressing provide?

14. What is address resolution?

15. How does TCP/IP perform address resolution for network layer addresses?

16. How does TCP/IP perform address resolution for data link layer addresses?

17. What is routing?

18. How does decentralized routing differ from centralized routing?

19. What are the differences between connectionless and connection-oriented routing?

20. What is a virtual circuit?

21. What is QoS routing and why is it useful?

22. Compare and contrast unicast, broadcast, and multicast messages.

23. Explain how multicasting works.

24. Explain how the client computer in Figure 5-12 (128.192.98.xx) would obtain the data link layer address of its subnet gateway.

25. Why does HTTP use TCP and DNS use UDP?

26. How does static routing differ from dynamic routing? When would you use static routing? When would you use dynamic routing?

27. What type of routing does a TCP/IP client use? What type of routing does a TCP/IP gateway use? Explain.

28. Why would a network manager want to have only TCP/IP as the transport/network layer protocols?

29. What is the transmission efficiency of a 10-byte Web request sent using HTTP, TCP/IP, and Ethernet? Assume the HTTP packet has 100 bytes in addition to the 10-byte URL. Hint: Remember from Chapter 4 that *efficiency = user data/total transmission size.*

30. What is the transmission efficiency of a 1,000-byte file sent in response to a Web request HTTP, TCP/IP, and Ethernet? Assume the HTTP packet has 100 bytes in addition to the 1,000-byte file. Hint: Remember from Chapter 4 that *efficiency = user data/total transmission size.*

31. What is the transmission efficiency of a 5,000-byte file sent in response to a Web request HTTP, TCP/IP, and Ethernet? Assume the HTTP packet has 100 bytes in addition to the 5,000-byte file. Assume that the maximum packet size is 1,200 bytes. Hint: Remember from Chapter 4 that *efficiency = user data/total transmission size.*

EXERCISES

5-1 What network layer protocols are used by your organization's BN? Why?

5-2 Would you recommend dynamic addressing for your organization? Why?

5-3 Use the Web to explore the differences between bootp and DHCP. Which is likely to become more popular? Why?

5-4 Look at your network layer software (either on a LAN or dial-in) and see what options are set—but don't change them! You can do this by using the RUN command to run winipcfg. How do these match the fundamental addressing and routing concepts discussed in this chapter?

5-5 Suppose a client computer (128.192.95.32) in building B in Figure 5-12 would requests a large Web page on the server in building A (www1.anyorg.com). Assume that the client computer has just been turned on and does not know any addresses other than those in its configuration tables. Assume that all gateways and Web servers know all network layer and data link layer addresses.

  a. Explain what messages would be sent and how they would flow through the network to deliver the Web page request to the server.

  b. Explain what messages would be sent and how they would flow through the network as the Web server sent the requested page to the client.

  c. Describe, but do not explain in detail, what would happen if the Web page contained several graphic images (e.g., GIF (Graphics Interchange Format) or JPEG files).

MINI-CASES

I. Fred's Donuts

Fred's Donuts is large regional bakery company that supplies baked goods (e.g., doughnuts, bread, pastries) to cafeterias, grocery stores, and convenience stores in three states. The company has five separate bakeries and office complexes spread over the region and wants to connect the five locations. Unfortunately, the network infrastructure at the five locations has grown up separately and thus there are three different network/transport layer protocols in use (TCP/IP, SPX/IPX, and SNA). How can the company connect the locations that use different protocols together? (Hint: This was briefly discussed in Chapter 1.) Should the company continue to use the three different protocols or move to one protocol, and if the latter, which one? Explain.

II. Central University

Suppose you are the network manager for Central University, a medium-size university with 13,000 students. The university has 10 separate colleges (e.g., business, arts, journalism), 3 of which are relatively large (300 faculty and staff members, 2,000 students, and 3 buildings) and 7 of which are relatively small (200 faculty and staff, 1,000 students, and 1 building). In addition, there are another 2,000 staff members who work in various administration departments (e.g., library, maintenance, finance) spread over another 10 buildings. There are 4 residence halls that house a total of 2,000 students. Suppose the university has the 128.100.xxx.xxx address range on the Internet. How would you assign the IP addresses the various subnets? How would you control the process by which IP addresses are assigned to individual computers? You will have to make some assumptions to answer both questions, so be sure to state your assumptions.

CASE STUDY

NEXT-DAY AIR SERVICE

As you continue to work on the data communications network plans for NDAS, you realize that it is imperative for you to gain a broader base of management and staff support for the new network and for the additional investment in information technology.

Many of the board members and staff at NDAS have little or no understanding of data communications and are therefore unwilling to support or fund developments in this area. You discuss this matter with Bob Jones, who has become one of your major backers since you helped him understand the workings of the Internet and the World Wide Web. NDAS's home page and inquiry–response system on the Internet is now considered an industry model. Bob Jones suggests a training session on data communications basics for management and staff. The training should not be too technical, but should be technical enough so that management and staff can understand and appreciate just what occurs, what equipment is needed, what is important, how much it will cost, and how to be sure it is working properly. Jones is also confused about the TCP/IP protocol used on the Internet and hopes you will clarify that for him in the training session. He reminds you that your position paper on how computer data are transferred over telephone lines was well received by President Coone and NDAS top management. "Use that approach," he suggests.

You bring the idea of a training session up with President Coone. He is very interested, but he wants you to consider a series rather than a single session. The initial training topic will be network concepts. President Coone confesses that the concept of a network is a mystery to him. He schedules the first session for next Tuesday, just before the monthly management meeting. You will have 30 minutes.

It is clear that you have a great deal riding on this session. It will be your first contact with several key top and middle managers. If the session is a success, it will be much easier for you to get their support. You call Bob Jones to thank him for suggesting a training session. Bob recommends that you use a presentation software package like Microsoft's PowerPoint to prepare bullet charts as the basis for the presentation. You must start work on your preparations immediately.

Exercises

1. Review the topics in this chapter. Prepare an agenda for your training session. The agenda should be an outline, showing topics and subtopics with enough detail to allow the reader to follow. Remember Bob Jones's advice on what the management and staff will want and expect from your session.

2. Jones calls to warn you that the new manager of International Services Division, Sally Wong, will be present at the training session. She wants to be sure any new data communications system will be able to handle international messaging. Jones suggests that you include material in the session on how adherence to standards can ensure smooth integration of the NDAS data communication with overseas systems. You agree. Present a review of standards and standardizing groups for data communications. Which standards do you consider most important for NDAS? Be prepared to defend your view.

3. Jones also reminds you that he needs a straightforward, simple, and understandable explanation of the Internet TCP/IP protocol. Prepare a bullet chart that describes the key concepts of TCP/IP.

4. You have just finished your preparations when President Coone's secretary calls to tell you that IBM sales representatives have asked President Coone for an appointment to discuss SNA and how it can be used at NDAS. Because IBM is a valued customer of NDAS, President Coone feels he must pay attention to their request. However, he wants you to send him a brief memo covering the differences between SNA and TCP/IP before he responds to IBM. Prepare the memo, including in it your observations of SNA's importance in the development of a data communications system at NDAS.

PART 3

NETWORK
TECHNOLOGIES

CHAPTER 6

LOCAL AREA NETWORKS

THE PRECEDING chapters provided a fundamental understanding of the five basic layers in a typical network. This chapter draws together these concepts to describe a basic LAN. We first summarize the major components of a LAN and then describe the three most commonly used LAN technologies (traditional Ethernet, switched Ethernet, and wireless Ethernet), as well as two new wireless technologies. The chapter ends with a discussion of how to improve LAN performance. In this chapter, we focus only on the basics of LANs; the next chapter describes how LANs and BNs are used together.

OBJECTIVES

- Be aware of the roles of LANs in organizations
- Understand the major components of LANs
- Understand traditional Ethernet LANs
- Understand switched Ethernet LANs
- Understand wireless Ethernet LANs
- Be aware of other wireless LAN technologies
- Be familiar with how to improve LAN performance

CHAPTER OUTLINE

INTRODUCTION

Most large organizations have numerous LANs connected by BNs. These LANs also provide access to a variety of servers, mainframe computers, and the Internet. In this chapter, we discuss the fundamental components of a LAN, along with three technologies commonly used in LANs—traditional Ethernet (IEEE 802.3), switched Ethernet, and wireless Ethernet (IEEE 802.11). There used to be many different types of LAN technologies, such as Token Ring and ARCnet (Attached Resources Computer network), but gradually the world has changed so that Ethernet dominates. Today, very few organizations consider any LAN technology other than Ethernet. Together, traditional Ethernet and its switched and wireless cousins account for almost 95 percent of all LANs installed today.

Why Use a LAN?

There are two basic reasons for developing a LAN: information sharing and resource sharing. *Information sharing* refers to having users access the same data files, exchange information via e-mail, or use the Internet. For example, a single purchase order database might be maintained so all users can access its contents over the LAN. (Many information-sharing applications were described in Chapter 2.) The main benefit of information sharing is improved decision making, which makes it generally more important than resource sharing.

Resource sharing refers to one computer sharing a hardware device (e.g., printer) or software package with other computers on the network, to save costs. For example, suppose we have 30 computers on a LAN, each of which needs access to a word processing package. One option is to purchase 30 copies of the software and install one on each computer. This would use disk space on each computer and require a significant amount of staff time to perform the installation and maintain the software, particularly if the package were updated regularly.

An alternative is to install the software on the network for all to use. This would eliminate the need to keep a copy on every computer and would free up disk space. It would also simplify software maintenance because any software upgrades would be installed once on the network server; staff members would no longer have to upgrade all computers.

In most cases, not all users would need to access the word processing package simultaneously. Therefore, rather than purchasing a license for each computer in the network, you could instead purchase 10 licenses, presuming that only 10 users would simultaneously use the software. Of course, the temptation is to purchase only one copy of the software and permit everyone to use it simultaneously. The cost savings would be significant, but this is illegal. Virtually all software licenses require one copy to be purchased for each simultaneous user. Most companies and all government agencies have policies forbidding the violation of software licenses, and many fire employees who knowingly violate them.

One approach to controlling the number of copies of a particular software package is to use *LAN metering software* that prohibits using more copies of a package than there are installed licenses. Many software packages now sell LAN versions that do this automatically, and a number of third-party packages are also available.

Nonetheless, the *Software Publishers Association (SPA)* in Washington, D.C., estimates that about 40 percent of all the software in the world is used illegally—an annual total of more than $13 billion. North America has the lowest rate of software piracy (28 percent). Although piracy has been on the decline, it still exceeds 75 percent in many parts of the world, with the exception of western Europe (43 percent), Australia (32 percent), New Zealand (35 percent), and Japan (41 percent).

The SPA has recently undertaken an aggressive *software audit* program to check the number of illegal software copies on LANs. Whistle-blowers receive rewards from SPA, and the violating organizations and employees are brought to court. The SPA will work with companies that voluntarily submit to an audit, and it offers an audit kit that scrutinizes networks in search of software sold by SPA members (see http://www.spa.org).

Dedicated-Server versus Peer-to-Peer LANs

One common way to categorize LANs is by whether they have a dedicated server or whether they operate as a peer-to-peer LAN without a dedicated server. This chapter focuses primarily on dedicated-server LANs because they account for more than 90 percent of all installed LANs, although many of the issues are also common in peer-to-peer networks.

Dedicated Server Networks   As the name suggests, a *dedicated-server LAN* has one or more computers that are permanently assigned to being the network servers. These servers enable users to share files and often are also used to share printers. A dedicated-server LAN can connect with almost any other network, can handle very large files and databases, and uses sophisticated LAN software. Moreover, high-end dedicated-server LANs can be easily interconnected to form enterprisewide networks or, in some cases, can replace a host mainframe computer. Generally speaking, the dedicated servers are powerful microcomputers or minicomputers. Sometimes servers are organized into a large set of servers on one part of the network called a *server farm.* Server farms can range from tens to hundreds of servers.

In a dedicated-server LAN, the server's usual operating system (e.g., Windows) is replaced by a network operating system (e.g., Novell NetWare, Windows NT). Special-purpose network communication software is also installed on each client computer and is the link between the client computer's operating system and the network operating system on the server. This set of communication software provides the data link layer and network layer protocols that allow data transmissions to take place. Three software components must work together and in conjunction with the network hardware to enable communications: the network operating system in the dedicated server, the network communication software on the client, and the application software that runs on the server and client computers.

A LAN can have many different types of dedicated servers, such as mail servers, database servers, and Web servers, as discussed in Chapter 2. Three other common types are file servers, print servers, and remote-access servers (RASs).

File servers allow many users to share the same set of files on a common, shared disk drive. The hard disk volume can be of any size, limited only by the size of the disk storage itself. Files on the shared disk drive can be made freely available to all network users, shared only among authorized users, or restricted to only one user.

Print servers handle print requests on the LAN. By offloading the management of printing from the main LAN file server or database server, print servers help reduce the load on them and increase network efficiency. Print servers have traditionally been separate computers, but many vendors now sell "black boxes" that perform all the functions of a print server at a much less than the cost of a stand-alone computer.

Remote-access servers (RASs) enable users to dial into and out of the LAN by telephone. A RAS lets users dial into the LAN and perform all the same functions as though they were physically connected to the LAN itself. RASs are best for applications that move only small amounts of information and do not require high speed beyond the limited capabilities of regular voice-grade telephone lines. (LANs typically provide data transmission rates of between 10 and 100 Mbps, whereas telephone lines typically provide between only 28.8 and 128 Kbps).

Peer-to-Peer Networks   *Peer-to-peer networks* do not require a dedicated server. All computers run network software that enables them to function both as clients and as servers.

Authorized users can connect to any computer in the LAN that permits access and use its hard drives and printer as though it were physically attached to their own computers. Peer-to-peer networks often are slower than dedicated server networks because if you access a computer that is also being used by its owner, it slows down both the owner and the network.

In general, peer-to-peer LANs have less capability, support a more limited number of computers, provide less sophisticated software, and can prove more difficult to manage than dedicated-server LANs. However, they are cheaper both in hardware and software. Peer-to-peer LANs are most appropriate for sharing resources in small LANs.

LAN COMPONENTS

There are six components in a traditional LAN (Figure 6-1). The first two are the client computer and the server (but see the section above on peer-to-peer networks). Clients and servers have been discussed in Chapter 2, so they will not be discussed further here. The other components are network interface cards (NICs), network cables, hubs, and network operating system. In recent years, a new form of LAN called switched Ethernet has become popular that uses switches instead of hubs; the role of switches is discussed in a later section.

Network Interface Cards

The *network interface card (NIC)* is used to connect the computer to the network cable and is one part of the physical layer connection among the computers in the network. Many computers come with a NIC built in, but sometimes a separate NIC must be installed. Some laptops have a special port that enables network cards to be installed without physically opening them (i.e., PCMCIA [Personal Computer Memory Card International Association] slot).

Network Cables

Each computer must be physically connected by network cable to the other computers in the network. Just as highways carry all kinds of traffic, the perfect cabling system also

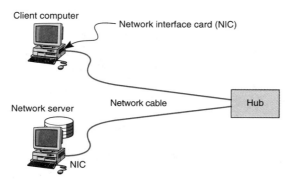

FIGURE 6-1 Local area network components.

should be able to carry all kinds of electronic transmissions within the building. But in practice, it isn't that simple. The selection of a LAN can be influenced greatly by the type of cable that already exists in the building where the LAN is to be installed.

Most LANs are built with *unshielded twisted-pair (UTP)* wires, *shielded twisted-pair (STP),* coaxial cable, or fiber-optic cable (although fiber-optic cable is far more commonly used in BNs, which are discussed in the next chapter). Wireless LANs run on infrared or radio frequencies, eliminating the need for cables. (Common cable standards are discussed on the next page. We should add that these cable standards specify the minimum quality cable required; it is possible, for example, to use category 5 UTP wire for a 10Base-T Ethernet.)

Many LANs use a combination of STP and UTP wire. Although initially it appeared that twisted-pair would not be able to meet long-term capacity and distance requirements, today this is one of the leading LAN cabling technologies. Its low cost and the availability of shielded wiring make it very useful.

Coaxial cable used to be the most common type of LAN cable, but today, it is less commonly used than UTP or STP wire. By definition, coaxial cable is shielded because its outer conductor is also a shield. Coaxial cable is physically larger than twisted-pair wire, weighing anywhere between 20 and 90 pounds per 1,000 feet, which can be detrimental in an overhead ceiling, especially if it collapses because of the cable's weight! Coaxial cable is also not as flexible as twisted-pair wire, so it is sometimes harder to install in older buildings not designed for computer cabling.

Fiber-optic cable is even thinner than UTP wire and therefore takes far less space when cabled throughout a building. It also is much lighter, weighing less than 10 pounds per 1,000 feet. Because of its high capacity, fiber-optic cabling is perfect for BNs, although it is beginning to be used in LANs.

Although most LANs use only one type of cable, it is possible to buy devices that permit different types of cable to be connected together. A *BALUN (bal*anced*/un*balanced) is a small device about .5 inch in diameter and 3 inches long that connects twisted-pair cabling with coaxial cable. One end has a standard twisted-pair connection and the other has a standard screw-in coaxial connector lead. Similar devices are available to connect fiber-optic cable to twisted-pair wire and coaxial cable, but they are significantly larger and more expensive because they must convert between electricity and light.

Network Hubs

Network *hubs* serve two purposes. First, they provide an easy way to connect network cables. A hub can be thought of as a junction box, permitting new computers to be connected to the network as easily as plugging a power cord into an electrical socket (Figure 6-2). Each connection point where a cable can be plugged in is called a *port*. Each port has a unique number.

Simple hubs are commonly available in 4-, 8-, 16-, and 24-port sizes, meaning that they provide anywhere between 4 and 24 ports into which network cables can be plugged. When no cables are plugged in, the signal bypasses the unused port. When a cable is plugged into a port, the signal travels down the cable as though it were directly connected to the cables attached to the hub. Some hubs also enable different types of cables to be connected and perform the necessary conversions (e.g., twisted-pair wire to coaxial cable, coaxial cable to fiber-optic cable).

TECHNICAL FOCUS *6-1*

COMMONLY USED NETWORK CABLE STANDARDS

Name	Type	Maximum Data Rate (Mbps)	Often Used By	Cost[1] ($/foot)
Category 1[2]	UTP[7]	1	Modem	.04
Category 2	UTP	4	Token Ring-4[3]	.35
Category 3	UTP	10	10Base-T Ethernet	.05
Category 4	STP[8]	16	Token Ring-16[3]	.60
Category 5	UTP	100	100Base-T Ethernet	.07
Category 5	STP	100	100Base-T Ethernet	.16
Category 5e[4]	UTP	100	1,000Base-T Ethernet	.13
Category 6[5]	UTP	200	1,000Base-T Ethernet	.18
Category 7[5]	STP	600	1,000Base-T Ethernet	.30
RG-58	Coaxial	10	10Base-2 Ethernet	.20
RG-8	Coaxial	10	10Base-5 Ethernet	.90
X3T9.5	Fiber	100	FDDI[6]	.35

Notes

1. These costs are approximate costs for cable only (no connectors). They often change but will give you a sense of the relative differences in costs among the different options.
2. Category 1 is standard voice-grade twisted-pair, wires but it can also be used to support low-speed analog data transmission.
3. Token ring is an old local area network technology seldom used today.
4. Category 5e is an improved version of category 5 that has better insulation and a center plastic pipe inside the cable to keep the individual wires in place and reduce noise from cross-talk, so that it is better suited to 1000Base-T.
5. The standards for categories 6 and 7 have not been finalized. The category 6 standard has fluctuated between 200 Mbps and 250 Mbps.
6. FDDI (fiber distributed data interface) is a backbone technology discussed in the next chapter.
7. UTP is unshielded twisted-pair wire.
8. STP is shielded twisted-pair wire.

Second, hubs can act as repeaters or amplifiers. Signals can travel only so far in a network cable before they attenuate and can no longer be recognized. (Attenuation was discussed in Chapter 4.) All LAN cables are rated for the maximum distance they can be used (typically 100 meters for twisted-pair wire, 200 to 500 meters for coaxial cable, and

FIGURE 6-2 Network hub.

several kilometers for fiber-optic cable) Any LAN that spans more than these distances—and most LANs do—must use hubs with repeaters or amplifiers.

In the early days of LANs, it was common practice to install network cable wherever it was convenient. Little long-term planning was done. Hubs were placed at random intervals to meet the needs of the few users, and cable was laid where it was convenient. The exact placement of the cables and hubs was often not documented, making future expansion more difficult—you had to find the cable and a hub before you could add a new user.

With today's explosion in LAN use, it is critical to plan for the effective installation and use of LAN cabling. The cheapest point at which to install network is during the construction of the building; adding cable to an existing building can cost significantly more. Indeed, the costs to install cable (i.e., paying those doing the installation and additional construction) are usually substantially more than the cost of the cable itself, making it expensive to reinstall the cable if the cable plan does not meet the organization's needs.

Most buildings under construction today have a separate LAN cable plan, as they have plans for telephone cables and electrical cables. The same is true for older buildings in which new LAN cabling is being installed. Most cable plans are similar in style to electrical and telephone plans. Each floor has a telecommunications wiring closet that contains one or more network hubs. Cables are run from each room on the floor to this wiring closet. It is common to install 20 to 50 percent more cables than you actually need, to make future expansion simple. Any reconfiguration or expansion can be done easily by adding a network hub and connecting the unused cables in the wiring closet. This saves the difficulty and expense of attempting to locate network hubs and installing new cables.

MANAGEMENT FOCUS **6-1**

CABLE PROBLEMS AT THE UNIVERSITY OF GEORGIA

Like many organizations, the Terry College of Business at the University of Georgia is headquartered in a building built before the computer age. When local area network cabling was first installed in the early 1980s, no one foresaw the rapid expansion that was to come. Cables and hubs were installed piecemeal to support the needs of the handful of early users.

The network eventually grew far beyond the number of users it was designed to support. The network cable plan gradually became a complex, confusing, and inefficient mess of cables. There was no logical pattern for the cables, and there was no network cable plan. Worse still, no one knew where all the cables and hubs were physically located. Before a new user was added, a network technician had to open up a ceiling and crawl around to find a

hub. Hopefully, the hub had an unused port to connect the new user, or else the technician would have to find another hub with an empty port.

To complicate matters even more, asbestos was discovered. Now network technicians could not open the ceiling and work on the cable unless asbestos precautions were taken. This meant calling in the university's asbestos team and sealing off nearby offices. Installing a new user to the network (or fixing a network cable problem) now took 2 days and cost $2,000.

The solution was obvious. The university spent $400,000 to install new category 5 twisted-pair cable to every office and to install a new high-speed fiber-optic backbone network between network segments.

Network Operating Systems

The *network operating system (NOS)* is the software that controls the network. Every NOS provides two sets of software: one that runs on the network server(s) and one that runs on the network client(s). The server version of the NOS provides the software that performs the functions associated with the data link, network, and application layers and usually the computer's own operating system. The client version of the NOS provides the software that performs the functions associated with the data link and the network layers and must interact with the application software and the computer's own operating system. Most NOSs provide different versions of their client software that run on different types of computers, so that Windows computers, for example, can function on the same network as Apples. In most cases (e.g., Windows, UNIX), the client NOS software is included with the operating system itself.

NOS Server Software   The NOS server software enables the file server, print server, or database server to operate. It addition to handling all the required network functions, it acts as the application software by executing the requests sent to it by the clients (e.g., copying a file from its hard disk and transferring it to the client, printing a file on the printer, executing a database request and sending the result to the client). NOS server software replaces the normal operating system on the server. By replacing the existing operating system, it provides better performance and faster response time because a NOS is optimized for its limited range of operations.

NOS Client Software   The NOS software running at the client computers provides the data link layer and network layer. To work effectively with the application software, the

---

MANAGEMENT FOCUS *6-2*

MANAGING NETWORK CABLING

You must consider a number of items when installing cables or when performing cable maintenance. You should:

- Perform a physical inventory of any existing cabling systems and document those findings in the network cable plan.
- Properly maintain the network cable plan. Always update cable documentation immediately on installing or removing cable or hub. Insist that any cabling contractor provide "as-built" plans that document where the cabling was actually placed, in case of minor differences from the construction plan.
- Establish a long-term plan for the evolution of the current cabling system to whatever cabling system will be in place in the future.

- Obtain a copy of the local city fire codes and follow them. For example, cables used in airways without conduit need to be plenum-certified (i.e., covered with a fire-retardant jacket).
- Conceal all cable as much as possible to protect them from damage and for security reasons.
- Properly number and mark both ends of all cable installations as you install them. If a contractor installs cabling, always make a complete inspection to ensure that all cables are labeled.

NOS must also work together with the client's own operating system. Most operating systems today are designed with networking in mind. For example, Windows provides built-in software that will enable it to act as a client computer with a Novell NetWare server or a Windows NT server.

Network Profiles A *network profile* specifies what resources on each server are available on the network for use by other computers and which devices or people are allowed what access to the network. The network profile normally is configured when the network is established and remains in place until someone makes a change. In a LAN, the server hard disk may have various resources that can or cannot be accessed by a specific network user (e.g., data files, printers). Furthermore, a password may be required to grant network access to the resources.

If a device such as a hard disk on one of the network's computers is not included on the network profile, it cannot be used by another computer on the network. For example, if you have a hard disk (C) on your computer and your computer is connected to this LAN but the hard disk is not included on the network profile assignment list, then no other computer can access it.

In addition to profiling disks and printers, there must be a *user profile* for each person who uses the LAN, to add some security. Each device and each user is assigned various access codes, and only those users who log in with the correct code can use a specific device. Most LANs keep audit files to track who uses which resource. Security is discussed in Chapter 10.

TRADITIONAL ETHERNET (IEEE 802.3)

Almost all LANs installed today use some form of *Ethernet*. Ethernet was originally developed by DEC, Xerox, and Intel but has since become a standard formalized by the (IEEE)

TECHNICAL FOCUS *6-2*

STORAGE AREA NETWORKS AND NETWORK ATTACHED STORAGE

New ideas and new terms emerge rapidly in data communications and networking. In recent years, a variant on the local area network (LAN) has emerged. A *storage area network (SAN)* is a LAN devoted solely to data storage. When the amount of data to be stored exceeds the practical limits of servers, the SAN plays a critical role. The SAN has set of high-speed storage devices and servers that are networked together using a very high speed network (often using a technology called *fibre channel* that runs over a series of multi-gigabit point-to-point fiber-optic circuits). Servers are connected into the normal LAN and to the SAN, which is usually reserved for servers. When data are needed, clients send the request to a server on the LAN, which obtains the information from the devices on the SAN and then returns it to the client.

The devices on the SAN may be a large set of database servers or a set of network-attached disk arrays. In other cases, the devices may be *network-attached storage devices (NASs)*. A NAS is not a general-purpose computer like a sever that runs a server operating system (e.g., NT, Linux) but instead is specially designed to just respond to requests for files and data. A NAS device has a small processor and a large amount of disk storage and is designed solely to respond to data requests. NAS can also be attached to LANs, where they function as a fast database server.

as IEEE 802.3.[1] The IEEE 802.3 version of Ethernet is slightly different than the original version but the differences are minor. Likewise, another version of Ethernet has also been developed that differs slightly from the 802.3 standard. In this section, we describe traditional Ethernet, which is sometimes called *shared Ethernet*.

Topology

Topology is the basic geometric layout of the network—the way in which the computers on the network are interconnected. It is important to distinguish between a logical topology and a physical topology. A *logical topology* is how the network works conceptually, much like a logical data flow diagram (DFD) or logical entity relation diagram (ERD) in systems analysis and design or database design. A *physical topology* is how the network is physically installed, much like a physical DFD or physical ERD.

Ethernet's logical topology is a bus topology. All computers are connected to one half-duplex circuit running the length of the network that is called the bus. The top part of Figure 6-3 shows Ethernet's logical topology. All messages from any computer flow onto the central cable (or bus) and through it to all computers on the LAN. Every computer on

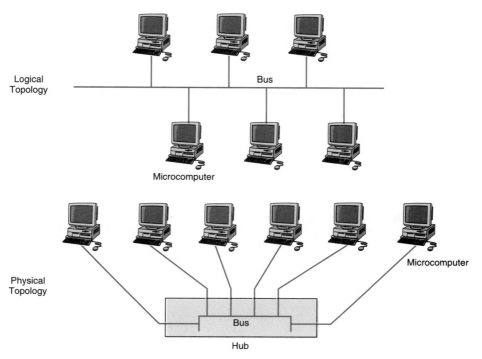

FIGURE 6-3 Ethernet topology.

---

[1] The formal specification for Ethernet is provided in the 802.3 standard on the IEEE standards Web site. The URL is http://grouper.ieee.org/groups/802/3.

the bus receives *all* messages sent on the bus, even those intended for other computers. Before processing incoming messages, the Ethernet software on each computer checks the data link layer address and processes only those messages addressed to that computer.

The bottom part of Figure 6-3 shows the physical topology of an Ethernet LAN when a hub is used. From the outside, an Ethernet LAN *appears* to be a star topology, because all cables connect to the central hub. Nonetheless, it is logically a bus.

Most Ethernet LANs span sufficient distance to require several hubs. In this case, the hubs are connected via cable in the same manner as any other connection in the network (Figure 6-4).

Media Access Control

When several computers share the same communication circuit, it is important to control their access to the media. If two computers on the same circuit transmit at the same time, their transmissions will become garbled. These collisions must be prevented, or if they do occur, there must be a way to recover from them. This is called media access control.

Ethernet uses a contention-based media access control technique called *Carrier Sense Multiple Access with Collision Detection (CSMA/CD)*. CSMA/CD, like all contention-based techniques, is very simple in concept: Wait until the circuit is free and then transmit. Computers wait until no other devices are transmitting, then transmit their data. As an analogy, suppose you are talking with a small group of friends (four or five people). As the discussion progresses, each person tries to grab the floor when the previous speaker finishes. Usually, the other members of the group yield to the first person who jumps right after the previous speaker.

Ethernet's CSMA/CD protocol can be termed ordered chaos. As long as no other computer attempts to transmit at the same time, everything is fine. However, it is possible

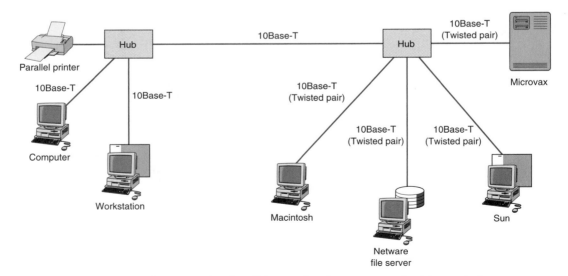

FIGURE 6-4 An example of an Ethernet local area network with two hubs.

that two computers located some distance from one another can both listen to the circuit, find it empty, and begin to simultaneously. This simultaneous transmission is called a *collision*. The two messages collide and destroy each other.

The solution to this is to listen while transmitting, better known as *collision detection (CD)*. If the NIC detects any signal other than its own, it presumes that a collision has occurred and sends a jamming signal. All computers stop transmitting and wait for the circuit to become free before trying to retransmit. The problem is that the computers that caused the collision could attempt to retransmit at the same time. To prevent this, each computer waits a random amount of time after the colliding message disappears before attempting to retransmit. Chances are both computers will choose a different random amount of time and one will begin to transmit before the other, thus preventing a second collision. However, if another collision occurs, the computers wait a random amount of time before trying again. This does not eliminate collisions completely, but it reduces them to manageable proportions.

Types of Ethernet

Figure 6-5 summarizes the many different types of Ethernet. The original Ethernet specification was a 10-Mbps data rate using thick coaxial cable, called *10Base-5* (or Thicknet), capable of running 500 meters between hubs. A new version, *10Base-2* (called Thinnet), soon appeared that used thinner, cheaper coaxial cable (which ran up to 200 meters). *10Base-T* runs on very cheap twisted-pair cable up to 100 meters. It was the 10Base-T standard that revolutionized Ethernet and made it the most popular type of LAN in the world. The extremely low cost of 10Base-T made it very inexpensive compared to its foremost competitor, Token Ring. 10Base-T is probably the most common form of Ethernet in use today, although *100Base-T* is also growing rapidly.

Three new types of Ethernet have been introduced: *1000Base-T* (which runs at 1 Gbps and is sometimes called 1 GbE), *10 GbE* (which runs at 10 Gbps), and *40 GbE* (which runs at 40 Gbps). They can use Ethernet's traditional half-duplex approach, but most are configured to use full duplex. Each also is designed to run over fiber-optic cables, but some may also use traditional twisted-pair wire cables (e.g., Cat 5, Cat 5e). For example,

Name	Maximum Data Rate	Cables
10Base-5	10 Mbps	Coaxial
10Base-2	10 Mbps	Coaxial
10Base-T	10 Mbps	UTP cat 3, UTP cat 5
100Base-T	100 Mbps	UTP cat 5, fiber
1000Base-T	1 Gbps	UTP cat 5, UTP cat 5e, UTP cat 6, fiber
10 GbE	10 Gbps	UTP cat 5e, UTP cat 6, UTP cat 7, fiber
40 GbE	40 Gbps	fiber

FIGURE 6-5   Types of Ethernet. UTP = unshielded twisted-pair.

MANAGEMENT FOCUS *6-3*

GIGABIT ETHERNET MAPS THE HUMAN GENOME

Fall 2000 saw the publishication of an initial working draft of the human genome (the basic genetic makeup of the human body). Gigabit Ethernet played a key role.

Incyte Genomics, major player in the project, had been using 100Base-T but found its networks crumbling under the need to move an average of 70 terabits of data a day over its networks among its 1,300 high-power servers. It replaced more than 500 of its most heavily used circuits with 1000Base-T. Many of those circuits use time division multiplexing to combine several physical 1000Base-T circuits into 4- to 6-Gbps logical circuits.

SOURCE: "Genome Project Meets Gigabit Ethernet," *Network World,* September 18, 2000.

---

four common versions of 1000Base-T are *1000Base-LX* and *1000Base-SX,* which both use fiber-optic cable, running up to 440 meters and 260 meters, respectively; *1000Base-T,* which runs on four pairs of category 5 twisted-pair cable, but only up to 100 meters[2]; and *1000Base-CX,* which runs up to 24 meters on one category 5 cable. Similar versions of 10 GbE and 40 GbE that use different media are also available.

Some organizations use *10/100 Ethernet,* which is a hybrid that uses either 10Base-T or 100Base-T. 10/100 Ethernet NICs have the ability to run at either 10Base-T or 100Base-T, depending on how they are configured. 10/100 autosense hubs (and switches, as we will discuss shortly) detect the signal transmitted by the client's NIC and will use 10 Mbps or 100 Mbps, depending on which the client uses. 10/100 is useful in the short term as organizations move from 10Base-T to 100base-T or if they are uncertain where they want to use which standard.

SWITCHED ETHERNET

Switched Ethernet is identical to traditional Ethernet, except that a switch replaces the hub (see Figure 6-6). In traditional shared Ethernet, all devices share the same multipoint circuit and must take turns using it. When a message is sent from one computer to another, it enters the hub, and the hub retransmits it to *all* the computers attached to the hub (Figure 6-6). Each computer looks at the Ethernet address on incoming packets, and if the address on the packet does not match its address, it discards the packet. This process ensures that no two computers transmit at the same time, because they are always listening and do not transmit when they are receiving a message, even if the message is not addressed to them. If the hub did not send the message to all computers, a computer could begin transmitting at the same time as an another computer and never be aware of it.

---

[2] It would be reasonable to think that 1000BaseT would require 10 category 5 cables because $10 \times 100\text{Mps} = 1000$ Mbps. However, it is possible to push 100-Mbps cables to faster speeds over shorter distances. Therefore, the category 5 flavor of 1000Base-T uses only 4 pairs of category 5 (i.e. 8 wires) running at 125 Mbps, but over shorter distances than would be normal for 100Base-T. A special form of category 5 cable (called category 5e) has been developed to meet the special needs of 1000Base-T. This same approach is used to run 10 GbE over category 5.

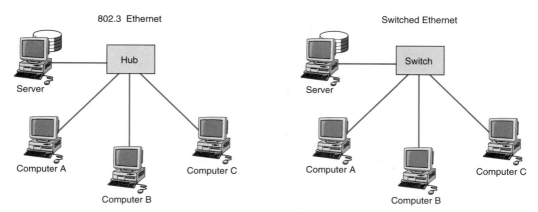

FIGURE 6-6   802.3 Ethernet versus switched Ethernet.

Topology

With switched Ethernet, the hub is replaced by a *switch* (see Figure 6-6). This type of switch is often called a *workgroup switch* because it is designed to support a small set of computers (often 16 to 24) in one LAN. From the outside, the switch looks almost identical to a hub, but inside, it is very different. A switch is designed to manage a set of separate point-to-point circuits. That means that each circuit connected to a switch is *not* shared with any other devices; only the switch and the attached computer use it. The physical topology looks essentially the same as Ethernet's physical topology: a star. On the inside, the logical topology is a set of separate point-to-point circuits, also a star.

When a switch receives a packet from a computer, it looks at the address on the packet and retransmits the packet only on the circuit connected to that computer, not to all circuits as a hub would. For example, in Figure 6-6, if computer A sends a packet to the switched destined for computer C, the switch retransmits it only on the circuit connected to computer C.

So how does a switch know which circuit is connected to what computer? The switch uses a *forwarding table* that is very similar to the routing tables discussed in Chapter 5. The table lists the Ethernet address of the computer connected to each port on the switch. When the switch receives a packet, it compares the destination address on the packet to the addresses in its forwarding table to find the port number on which it needs to transmit the packet. Because the switch uses the Ethernet address to decide which port to use and because Ethernet is a data link layer or layer-2 protocol, this type of switch is called a *layer-2 switch*. In the next chapter, we describe other types of switches.

When switches are first turned on, their forwarding tables are empty; they do not know what Ethernet address is attached to what port. Switches *learn* addresses to build the forwarding table. When a switch receives a packet, it reads the packet's data link layer source address and compares this address to its forwarding table. If the address is not in the forwarding table, the switch adds it, along with port on which the message was received.

If a switch receives a packet with a destination address that is not in the forwarding table, the switch must still send the packet to the correct destination. In this case, it must retransmit the packet to all ports, except the one on which the packet was received. In this case, the attached computers, being Ethernet and assuming they are attached to a hub, will simply ignore all messages not addressed to them. The one computer for whom the message is addressed will recognize its address and will process the message, which includes sending an ACK or a NAK back to the sender. When the switch receives the ACK or NAK, it will add this computer's address and the port number on which the ACK or NAK was received to its forwarding table and then send the ACK or NAK on its way.

So, for the first few minutes until the forwarding table is complete, the switch acts like a hub. But as its forwarding table becomes more complete, it begins to act more and more like a switch. In a busy network, it takes only a few minutes for the switch to learn most addresses and match them to port numbers.

Media Access Control

Each of the circuits connected to the switch is a separate point-to-point circuit connecting the switch to one computer (or another network device, such as another switch). The switch and the attached computer (or other network device) must share this circuit. Media access control is done in the same manner as traditional Ethernet: Each computer (or device) listens before it transmits, and if no one is transmitting, it transmits.

Unlike a hub, in which all attached cables form one shared circuit so that the hub can process only one packet at a time (forcing all attached computers to wait until the one packet is transmitted and it is someone else's turn), a switch is built so that it can simultaneously send or receive packets on *all* the attached circuits. In Figure 6-6, computer A could be sending a packet to the server at the same time as computer B sends one to computer C.

It is possible that two computers may attempt to transmit a packet to the same computer at the same time. For example, both A and B send a packet to C. In this case, the switch chooses which packet to transmit first (usually, the first packet it receives is sent first) and temporarily stores all other packets for that circuit in its internal memory. When the packet is finished and the circuit is again free, the switch then retransmits (or forwards) the temporarily stored packets.

Performance Benefits

In planning a network, it is generally accepted that traditional hub-based 10Base-T LANs can run effectively only to about 50 percent of their capacity. Once the total amount of traffic exceeds 50 percent, so many collisions occur that response time becomes unacceptable. This would mean, for example, that a standard hub-based LAN using 10Base-T is really only capable of providing a total network capacity of only 5 Mbps. This capacity is shared by all computers on the LAN. So if we had 10 computers on one 10Base-T hub, this would mean that on average, each computer could realistically use about 500 Kbps on average.

As speeds increase, packets take less time to transmit on the circuit and the probability of collisions decreases. Tests have shown that 100Base-T can run close to 90 percent of capacity with few problems.

Switched Ethernet dramatically improves network performance because each computer has its own dedicated point-to-point circuit, rather than the one common shared multipoint circuit in traditional hub-based Ethernet. Because there are only two devices on each point-to-point circuit (e.g., the switch and a computer), the probability of a collision is lower. We do not yet have extensive experience with Ethernet switches, but the some experts believe we can effectively use up to about 95 percent of the switched Ethernet capacity before performance becomes a problem. So each 10Base-T switched circuit effectively has a maximum capacity of about 9.5 Mbps. Therefore, if we have 10 computers on one 10base-T switch, this would mean that on average, each computer could realistically use about 9.5 Mbps, giving a total network capacity of about 95 Mbps.

In most LANs, the majority of network traffic is to and from the server, or to and from the connection from the LAN to the BN (the gateway in TCP/IP terminology used in Chapter 5, or more commonly, a device called a router, as discussed in Chapter 7). In most LANs, this circuit is the network bottleneck. Each computer is transmitting at 10 Mbps, but if the circuit to the server is also 10 Mbps, there is often a traffic jam. The solution to this is to use a 10/100 switch, which provides 10-Mbps circuits to the client computers but a 100-Mbps circuit to the server or BN. Although traffic jams will still occur, the higher speed on the bottleneck circuit will mean they will clear up much more quickly.

WIRELESS ETHERNET (IEEE 802.11)

Wireless LANs form a very small percentage of LANs in operation today, but their use is growing rapidly. Wireless LANs transmit data through the air using radio or infrared transmission rather than through coaxial cable, twisted pair, or fiber-optic cable. Until recently, there were few widely accepted standards for wireless LANs, and as a result, equipment from different vendors could not be used in the same network. Over the past few years, however, several standards for wireless LANs have emerged, as have new terms: *wireless LAN (WLAN)* and *local area wireless network (LAW).*

The IEEE 802.11 standard will likely become the dominant standard for WLANs. It is very similar to Ethernet, with a few differences. Most importantly, IEEE 802.11 systems are easily connected into Ethernet LANs and translate between IEEE 802.3 Ethernet and IEEE 802.11 wireless. For this reason, IEEE 802.11 is usually called *wireless Ethernet,* although its official name is wireless LAN. IEEE 802.11 is rapidly evolving.[3]

Topology

The logical and physical topologies of wireless Ethernet are the same as those of traditional Ethernet. It is both a physical star and a logical bus (Figure 6-7). A central wireless *access point (AP)* is a radio transmitter that plays the same role as a hub in traditional Ethernet. All devices in the WLAN use the same radio frequencies, so the WLAN functions as a shared media LAN in the same manner as traditional Ethernet: Computers must take turns using the one circuit. Because the system uses radio waves, the signal travels in all directions from the AP. The maximum range from the AP to the computers is determined by the amount of interference (e.g., concrete walls) but is typically 100 to 500 feet.

---

[3] For more information, see the IEEE standards site at http://grouper.ieee.org/groups/802/11 and the site for the Wireless Ethernet Compatibility Alliance at www.wirelessethernet.org.

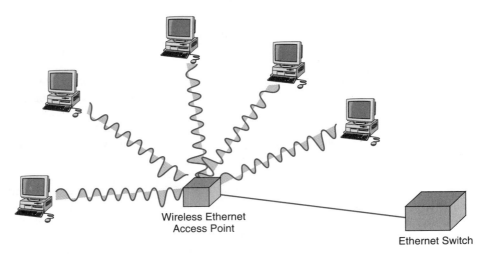

FIGURE 6-7 A wireless Ethernet access point connected into an Ethernet Switch.

The computers on the WLAN have a NIC inside the computer that is connected to an external transmitter that communicates with the AP (Figure 6-8). The external transmitter transmits radio signals to a receiver that acts like a network hub and enables wireless computers to communicate with each other and with traditional wired networks.

Usually a set of APs are installed, so that there is complete wireless coverage in some area, enabling users to roam from AP to AP. When configured with a wireless network, a set of laptops or Palm-based devices becomes an effective way to enable workers to walk through a facility and have constant network access at any point (e.g., warehouse, hospital, airport).

One potential problem is security. Because anyone within range of a WLAN can receive transmissions, eavesdropping is a serious threat. IEEE 802.11 encrypts all transmissions using a 40-bit encryption scheme so that only those computers that have the key can decode and read the messages. However, as will be discussed in Chapter 10, a 40-bit key is not terribly good.

Media Access Control

Media access control in wireless Ethernet is *Carrier Sense Multiple Access with Collision Avoidance (CSMA/CA),* which is similar to the CSMA/CD used by traditional Ethernet. With CSMA/CA, computers listen before they transmit, and if no one else is transmitting, they transmit. Detecting collisions is more difficult in wireless transmission than in transmission over wires, so wireless Ethernet attempts to avoid collisions to a greater extent than traditional Ethernet. CSMA/CA can use two approaches simultaneously to media access control.

Physical Carrier Sense Method The first media access control method is the *physical carrier sense method* because it is based on the ability of computers to physically listen before they transmit. Each packet in CSMA/CA is sent using stop-and-wait ARQ (see

A

B

FIGURE 6-8   a. Radio hub. **b.** Radio PCMCIA (Personal Computer Memory Card International Association) network interface card (NIC) for portable computers.

Chapter 4). After the sender transmits one packet, it immediately stops and waits for an ACK from the receiver before attempting to send another packet. When the receiver of a packet detects the end of the packet in a transmission, it waits a fraction of a second to make sure the sender has really stopped transmitting, then immediately transmits an ACK (or an NAK). The original sender can then send another packet, stop and wait for an ACK, and so on.

While the sender and receiver are exchanging packets and ACKs, other computers may also want to transmit. So when the sender ends its transmission, why doesn't some other computer begin transmitting before the receiver can transmit an ACK? The answer is that the physical carrier sense method is designed so that the time the receiver waits after the transmission ends before sending an ACK is significantly less than the time a computer must listen to determine no one else is transmitting before initiating a new transmission. Thus, the time interval between a transmission and the matching ACK is so short that no other computer has the opportunity to begin transmitting.

Virtual Carrier Sense Method The second media access control technique is called the *virtual carrier sense method,* because it does not rely on the physical media. The physical carrier sense method works well in traditional Ethernet, because every computer on the shared circuit receives every transmission on the shared circuit. However, in a wireless environment, this is not always true. A computer at the extreme edge of the range limit from the AP on one side may not receive transmissions from a computer on the extreme opposite edge of the AP's range limit. In Figure 6-7, both computers may be within range of the AP but not be within range of each other. In this case, if one computer transmits, another computer on the opposite edge may not sense the other transmission and thus may transmit at the same time, causing a collision at the AP. This is called the *hidden node problem,* because the computer at the opposite edges of the WLAN are hidden from each other.

When the hidden node problem exists, the AP is the only device guaranteed to be able communicate with all computers on the WLAN. Therefore, the AP must manage the shared circuit using a controlled access technique, not the contention-based approach of traditional Ethernet (see Chapter 4). With this approach, any computer wishing to transmit first sends a request to transmit (RTS) to the AP, which may or may not be heard by all computers. The RTS requests permission to transmit and to reserve the circuit for the sole use of the requesting computer for a specified time period. If no other computer is transmitting, the AP responds with a clear to transmit (CTS) specifying the amount of time for which the circuit is reserved for the requesting computer. All computers hear the CTS and remain silent for the specified time period.

The virtual carrier sense method is optional. It can be used always, never, or just for packets exceeding a certain size, as set by the LAN manager. From Chapter 4, you should remember that controlled access methods provide poorer performance in low-traffic networks and better performance in high-traffic networks, so unlike its traditional Ethernet cousin, a WLAN using this controlled access approach may provide a higher percentage of available capacity to the attached devices, perhaps as high as 90 percent.

Types of Wireless Ethernet

Two basic types of Wireless Ethernet have been defined: IEEE 802.11b, which is the most common today, and 802.11a, which is the high speed alternative.

MANAGEMENT FOCUS *6-4*

T.G.I. WIRELESS

Employees at T.G.I. Friday's restaurants must juggle plenty of constantly changing information, such as table availability, waiting lists, and orders. When guests arrive at the door, the host or hostess enters the party's name and the number of guests in the party in the waiting-list system at the kiosk at the front door, which is networked with the main server. When a table of the appropriate size becomes available, the system highlights the party's name and the host/hostess seats the party.

When the restaurant becomes busy, the kiosk becomes a bottleneck and sometimes tables sit empty while the waiting list gets longer. New restaurant have added a pen-based

system that communications with the waiting-list system via a wireless local area network in addition to the standard wired kiosk. The pen-based system provides a second access point to the system but also enables the host/hostess to walk around the restaurant and enter data directly from the table area, rather than having to walk to the front door to enter the data. The wireless system not only reduced the wait time but actually was cheaper than installing a second wired kiosk.

SOURCE: "Wireless LAN Makes for Better Service at Restaurant Chain," Wireless-nets.com, November 2000.

IEEE 802.11b IEEE 802.11b in turn has two basic forms. *Direct-sequence spread-spectrum (DSSS)* systems transmit signals through a wide spectrum of radio frequencies simultaneously (in the 2.4-GHz band). The signal is divided into many different parts and sent on different frequencies simultaneously. Because several radio devices could be operating in these same frequency bands (not just wireless LANs but also cordless phones), devices add a special code to each bit transmitted that uniquely identifies the signal and enables the intended receiver to identify it.

Frequency-hopping spread-spectrum (FHSS) systems transmit signals through the same wide spectrum of radio frequencies but use each frequency in turn. A short burst of data is sent on one frequency (usually less than half a second) and then the sender changes to another pseudorandom frequency and broadcasts another burst of data before changing to another frequency, and so on. The transmitter and receiver are synchronized so that they both know which frequencies will be used at which point. This approach minimizes jamming and eavesdropping because it is difficult for an outside listener to know what frequencies will be used next.

The FHSS version provides speeds of 1 Mbps and 2 Mbps. The DSSS version provides speeds of 1 Mbps, 2 Mbps, 5.5 Mbps, and 11 Mbps. A DSSS 20-Mbps version is under development. Because greater distance from the computer to the AP can weaken the signal, making interference from microwave ovens, cordless phones, and baby monitors a major problem, both FSSS and DSSS have the ability to automatically seek changes in speeds. In good conditions at close range, for example, DSSS may provide 11 Mbps, but as the distance increases between the AP and the computer, or if interference increases, the transmission rate may back down to 1 Mbps.

It is important to remember that both versions are shared media implementations, meaning that all devices in the WLAN share the one logical circuit. So if the WLAN has 10 computers and the speed is reduced to 1 Mbps because of inference, there may be noticeable response time delays. In this example, if we assume a 90 percent throughput rate (assuming controlled access), this would mean that each computer has a speed of about 90 Kbps.

IEEE 802.11a As we write this, the IEEE 802.11a standard has not been completely defined, but it should be by the time you read this. IEEE 802.11a is expected to operate in the 5-GHz range, meaning that it is capable of much higher transmission speeds but also will likely be more susceptible to interference. The initial standard will likely provide a raw data rate of 54 Mbps but will probably average only 27 Mbps in practice.

OTHER WIRELESS TECHNOLOGIES

There are two other wireless technologies that may become more common: infrared technologies and Bluetooth.

Infrared Wireless LANs

In general, *infrared wireless* LANs are less flexible than radio-based IEEE 802.11 WLANs because most require a direct line of sight between the transmitters and receivers in the same manner as your TV remote control. Transmitters and receivers are usually mounted in fixed positions to ensure the line of sight, so most infrared LANs are wireless only between the hubs. The NICs inside the computers are connected via traditional wires to a network hub that contains the transmitter (Figure 6-9). The hubs use wireless transmission to communicate from hub to hub.

The primary advantage of a wireless LAN is the reduction in wiring. Infrared-based LANs are sometimes used for communication between buildings where installing underground cable would be expensive. In an old building where wiring is difficult and costs are extremely high, wireless LANs offer a low-cost alternative by enabling communication without the installation of cables. Most infrared wireless systems provide 1 to 4 Mbps, but some provide 100 Mbps or more.

A new version of infrared, called diffuse infrared, operates without a direct line of sight by bouncing infrared light around a room. Most diffuse infrared systems have extremely short ranges (usually only 50 to 75 feet) and will operate only in the same room because the light cannot travel through walls.

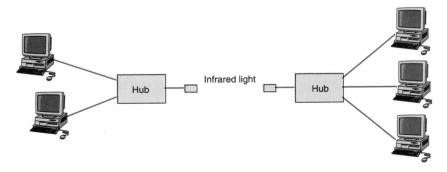

FIGURE 6-9 Infrared transmission between network hubs.

MANAGEMENT FOCUS *6-5*

NO MORE PIGEONS

When the city of Walnut Creek, California, needed to connect its LANs, a wireless system seemed obvious. Most of its buildings were in the downtown area, separated only by a city street. Rather than laying cable or leasing circuits from the telephone company, the city decided to install a point-to-point infrared wireless system on top of city hall. The system would simply shoot infrared signals to the nearby buildings, providing a simple 1.5-Mbps circuit.

However, it didn't work that way. Fog blocked the signal. Heavy trucks driving along the main street bounced the infrared hubs, interrupting the signal. Worse still,

pigeons regularly walked in front of the hubs and blocked the signal. The system was down 80 percent of the time. A new solution was needed.

Walnut Creek turned to radio-based wireless, which is less susceptible to interference. The infrared system was replaced with a series of radio access points, and the network turned back on. So far, it has worked perfectly.

SOURCE: "A Wireless LAN Unfettered by Pigeons," *Internetweek,* October 1998.

Bluetooth

Bluetooth is strikingly different from the wireless LAN technologies discussed above. Its goal is to provide seamless networking of devices in a very small area (up to 30 feet, soon to increase to about 300 feet). Bluetooth is an unofficial standard but may soon be standardized as IEEE 802.15.

Bluetooth devices are small (about .33 inch square) and cheap (currently priced at about $30 but expected to quickly to drop to $4 or even lower). A Bluetooth network is called a *piconet* and consists of no more than eight devices but can be linked to other piconets to form a larger network. A typical application might be to connect a mouse to a computer, to connect a telephone headset to a base unit (up to three digital voice circuits can be in use simultaneously), or to link your Palm handheld computer with your car so that your car door unlocks and automatically opens as you approach.

Bluetooth provides a 1-Mbps shared circuit, but its data link protocol is inefficient, so it provides only a 780-Kbps throughput. It uses FHSS in the same crowded 2.4-Ghz range used by IEEE 802.11b, so interference with 802.11b devices can significantly reduce throughput in both the Bluetooth and 802.11b networks. It uses controlled access media access control, with one device, called a master, polling the other devices, called slaves.

IMPROVING LAN PERFORMANCE

When LANs had only a few users, performance was usually very good. Today, however, when most computers in an organization are on LANs, performance can be a problem. Performance is usually expressed in terms of throughput (the total amount of user data transmitted in a given time period). In this section, we discuss how to improve throughput. We focus on dedicated-server networks because they are the most commonly used type of LANs, but many of these concepts also apply to peer-to-peer networks.

To improve performance, you must locate the *bottleneck,* the part of the network that is restricting the data flow. Generally speaking, the bottleneck will lie in one of two places.

The first is the network server. In this case, the client computers have no difficulty sending requests to the network server, but the server lacks sufficient capacity to process all the requests it receives in a timely manner. The second location is the network circuit, often the circuit connecting the LAN to the corporate BN. In this case, the server can easily process all the client requests it receives, but the circuit lacks enough capacity to transmit all the requests to server. It is also possible that the bottleneck could lie in the client computers themselves (e.g., they are receiving data too fast for them to process it), but this is extremely unlikely—unless, of course, you are still using old computers!

The first step in improving performance, therefore, is to identify whether the bottleneck lies in the circuit or the server. To do so, you simply watch the utilization of the server during periods of poor performance. If the server utilization is high (e.g., 60 to 100 percent), then the bottleneck is the server; it cannot process all the requests it receives in a timely manner. If the server utilization is low during periods of poor performance (e.g., 10 to 40 percent), then the problem lies with the network circuit; the circuit cannot transmit requests to the server as quickly as necessary. Things become more difficult if utilization is in the midrange (e.g., 40 to 60 percent). This suggests that the bottleneck may shift between the server and the circuit depending on the type of request, and it suggests that both should be upgraded to provide the best performance.

Now we will focus attention on ways to improve the server and the circuit to remove bottlenecks. These actions address only the supply side of the equation—that is, increasing the capacity of the LAN as a whole. The other way to reduce performance problems is to attack the demand side: reduce the amount of network use by the clients, which we also discuss. Figure 6-10 provides a performance checklist.

Performance Checklist

Increase Server Performance
- Software
- Fine-tune the network operating system settings
- Hardware
- Add more servers and spread the network applications across the servers to balance the load
- Upgrade to a faster computer
- Increase the server's memory
- Increase the number and speed of the server's hard disk(s)
- Upgrade to a faster network interface card

Increase Circuit Capacity
- Upgrade to a faster circuit
- Segment the network

Reduce Network Demand
- Move files from the server to the client computers
- Increase the use of disk caching on client computers
- Change user behavior

FIGURE 6-10 Improving local area network performance.

Improving Server Performance

Improving server performance can be approached from two directions simultaneously: software and hardware.

Software   The NOS is the primary software-based approach to improving network performance. Some NOSs are faster than others, so replacing the NOS with a faster one will improve performance.

Each NOS provides a number of software settings to fine-tune network performance. Depending on the number, size, and type of messages and requests in your LAN, different settings can have a significant effect on performance. The specific settings differ by NOS but often include things such as the amount of memory used for disk caches, the number of simultaneously open files, and the amount of buffer space.

Hardware   One obvious solution if your network server is overloaded is to buy a second server (or more). Each server is then dedicated to supporting one set of application software (e.g., one handles e-mail, another handles the financial database, and another stores customer records). The bottleneck can be broken by carefully identifying the demands each major application software package places on the server and allocating them to different servers.

Sometimes, however, most of the demand on the server is produced by one application that cannot be split across several servers. In this case, the server itself must be upgraded. The first place to start is with the server's CPU. Faster CPUs mean better performance. If you are still using an old computer as a LAN server, this may be the answer; you probably need to upgrade to the latest and greatest. Clock speed also matters; the faster, the better. Most computers today also come with CPU-cache (a very fast memory module directly connected to the CPU). Increasing the cache will increase CPU performance.

A second bottleneck is the amount of memory in the server. Increasing the amount of memory increases the probability that disk caching will work, thus increasing performance.

A third bottleneck is the number and speed of the hard disks in the server. The primary function of the LAN server is to process requests for information on its disks. Slow hard disks give slow network performance. The obvious solution is to buy the fastest disk drive possible. Even more importantly, however, is the number of hard disks. Each computer hard disk has only one read/write head, meaning that all requests must go through this one device. By using several smaller disks rather than one larger disk (e.g., five 20-gigabyte disks rather than one 100-gigabyte disk), you now have more read/write heads, each of which can be used simultaneously, dramatically improving throughput. A special type of disk drive called *RAID (redundant array of inexpensive disks)* builds on this concept and is typically used in applications requiring very fast processing of large volumes of data, such as multimedia. Of course, RAID is more expensive than traditional disk drives, but costs have been shrinking. RAID can also provide fault tolerance, which is discussed in Chapter 10.

A fourth bottleneck is the NIC itself. Simply put, some NICs are faster than others. Some NICs provide built-in CPUs to perform some of the network functions usually handled by the server (much like front-end processors in mainframe networks). Others provide memory and cache to improve the access time to and from the network.

Several vendors sell special-purpose network servers that are optimized to provide extremely fast performance. Many of these provide RAID and use *symmetric multipro-*

cessing (SMP) that enables one server to use up to 16 CPUs. Each of these CPUs may be an Intel chip such as Pentium, or may be based on reduced instruction set computing (RISC). Such servers provide excellent performance but cost more than a standard micro-computer (often $20,000 to $50,000).

Improving Circuit Capacity

Improving the capacity of the circuit means increasing the volume of simultaneous mes-sages the circuit can transmit from network clients to the server(s). One obvious approach is simply to buy a bigger circuit. For example, if you are now using a traditional hub-based 10Base-T LAN, upgrading to 100Base-T or switched 10Base-T will improve capacity.

The other approach is to segment the network. If there is more traffic on a LAN than the network circuit and media access protocol can handle, the solution is divide the LAN into several smaller segments. Breaking a network into smaller parts is called *network seg-mentation.* By carefully identifying how much each computer contributes to the demand on the server and carefully spreading those computers to different network segments, one can often break a network bottleneck.

Figure 6-11 presents an example in which each network segment is connected into the same server. Most servers can support up to as many as 16 separate networks or network seg-ments, simply by adding one NIC into the server for each network. As the number of NICs in the server increase, however, the server spends more of its processing capacity monitoring and managing the NICs and has less capacity left to process client requests. Most experts rec-ommend no more than three or four NICs per server. There are two ways to create more net-work segments: one is to use more servers, each dedicated to one or more segments, and the other is to use a BN to connect different segments. BNs are discussed in the next chapter.

Reducing Network Demand

Upgrading the server hardware and software, choosing a different LAN protocol, or seg-menting the LAN are all strategies to increase network capacity. Performance also can be improved by attempting to reduce the demand on the network.

One way to reduce network demand is to move files to client computers. Heavily used software packages that continually access and load modules from the network can place unusually heavy demands on the network. Although user data and messages are often only a few kilobytes in size, today's software packages can be many megabytes in size. Placing even one or two such applications on client computers can greatly improve net-work performance (although this can create other problems, such as increasing the diffi-culty in upgrading to new versions of the software).

Another way is to increase the use of disk-caching software on the client machines to reduce the client's need to access disk files stored on the server. For example, most Web browsers store Web pages in their cache so that they can access previously used pages from their hard disks without accessing the network.

Because the demand on most LANs is uneven, network performance can be improved by attempting to move user demands from peak times to off-peak times. For example, early morning and after lunch are often busy times when people check their e-mail. Telling net-work users about the peak times and encouraging them to change their habits may help;

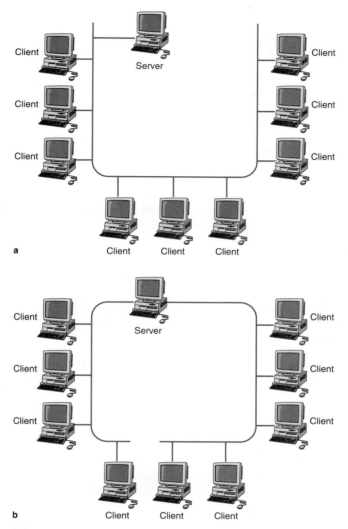

FIGURE 6-11   a. Before network segmentation. **b.** After segmentation.

however, in practice, it is often difficult to get users to change. Nonetheless, finding one application that places a large demand on the network and moving it can have a significant impact (e.g., printing several thousand customer records after midnight).

SUMMARY

Why use a LAN?   The two basic reasons for developing a LAN are information sharing and resource sharing. *Information sharing* refers to business needs that require users to access the same data files, exchange information via e-mail, or search the Internet for information, as discussed in

Chapter 2. *Resource sharing* refers to one computer sharing a hardware device (e.g., printer) or software package with other computers on the network. The main benefit of resource sharing is cost savings, whereas the main benefit of information sharing is improved decision making.

Dedicated-Server versus Peer-to-Peer Networks   A dedicated-server LAN has one computer that acts as the network server. It can connect with almost any other network, handle very large databases, and use sophisticated LAN software. Moreover, high-end dedicated-server LANs can be interconnected easily to form enterprisewide networks or, in some cases, replace the host mainframe central computer. Common types of dedicated servers include Web servers, application servers, file servers, database servers, print servers, and remote access servers All computers on a peer-to-peer LAN run special network software that enables them to function both as a client and as a server.

LAN Components   The NIC enables the computer to be physically connected to the network cable and provides the physical layer connection among the computers in the network. Most LANs use UTP wires, STP wires, coaxial cable, and/or fiber-optic cable. Network hubs provide an easy way to connect network cables and act as repeaters or amplifiers. Most new buildings built today have a separate LAN cable plan, just as they have plans for telephone cables and for electrical cables. The NOS is the software that performs the functions associated with the data link and the network layers and interacts with the application software and the computer's own operating system. Every NOS provides two sets of software: one that runs on the network server(s), and one that runs on the network client(s). A network profile specifies what resources on each server are available for network use by other computers and which devices or people are allowed what access to the network.

Ethernet (IEEE 802.3)   Ethernet, the most commonly used LAN in the world uses a logical bus topology that has a shared multipoint circuit used by all attached computers and devices, although the physical appearance of the network is a star. It uses a contention-based technique media access technique called CSMA/CD. There are many different types of Ethernet that use different network cabling (e.g., 10Base-2, 10Base-5, 10Base-T, 100Base-T, 1,000Base-T, 10 GbE).

Switched Ethernet   With switched Ethernet, a switch replaces the hub, but otherwise, all other components are identical. The switch provides a series of separate point-to-point circuits to the attached devices, so that no device needs to wait for another device before it transmits. When a packet arrives at the switch, the switch reads the Ethernet address and then forwards the packet to the one destination computer. Switched Ethernet has considerably better performance than traditional Ethernet because computers do not have to share circuits with other computers.

Wireless Ethernet (IEEE 802.11)   Wireless Ethernet is a small but growing form of Ethernet that provides data speeds of 1 to 11 Mbps via radio transmission. Wireless Ethernet has a radio transmitter AP that acts like a hub, so it provides a bus-oriented shared multipoint circuit like that of traditional Ethernet. It uses a similar contention-based media access control approach as traditional Ethernet, but it also has the ability to provided more controlled access by permitting stations to reserve time to transmit to prevent collisions. The current wireless Ethernet (called IEEE 802.11b) comes in several flavors, including DSSS, which transmits signals simultaneously through set of radio frequencies, and FHSS, which transmits signals through the same set of frequencies but uses each frequency in turn. A new version, called IEEE 802.11a, is under development and promises speeds of about 54 Mbps.

Other Wireless Technologies   Infrared wireless requires a direct line of sight and is useful only in fixed locations from hub to hub. Bluetooth is a new technology designed to permit devices to communicate using point-to-point circuits over very short distances (e.g., 30 feet).

Improving LAN Performance   Every LAN has a bottleneck, a narrow point in the network that limits the number of messages that can be processed. Generally speaking, the bottleneck will lie in either the network server or the network circuit. Server performance can be improved with a faster NOS that provides better disk caching and disk elevatoring, by buying more servers and spreading applications among them or by upgrading the server's CPU, memory, NIC, and the speed and number of its hard disks. Circuit capacity can be improved by using faster technologies (100Base-T rather than

10Base-T) and by segmenting the network into several separate LANs. Overall LAN performance also can be improved by reducing the demand for the LAN by moving files off the LAN, using disk caching on the client computers, and by shifting users' routines.

KEY TERMS

access point (AP)
BALUN
Bluetooth
bottleneck
bus topology
cabling
cable plan
Carrier Sense Multiple
    Access with Collision
    Avoidance
    (CSMA/CA)
Carrier Sense Multiple
    Access with Collision
    Detection
    (CSMA/CD)
coaxial cable
collision
collision avoidance (CA)
collision detection (CD)
database server
dedicated server
direct-sequence spread-
    spectrum (DSSS)
Ethernet
fiber channel
fiber-optic cable
file server

forwarding table
frequency-hopping
    spread-spectrum
    (FHSS)
hidden node problem
hub
IEEE 802.3
IEEE 802.11
information sharing
infrared wireless
LAN management soft-
    ware
LAN metering software
layer-2 switch
local area wireless net-
    work (LAW)
logical carrier sense
    method
logical topology
network-attached stor-
    age (NAS)
network interface card
    (NIC)
network operating
    system (NOS)
network profile
network segmentation

network server
PCMCIA (Personal
    Computer Memory
    Card International
    Association) slot
peer-to-peer network
physical carrier sense
    method
physical topology
piconet
print server
port
redundant array of inex-
    pensive disks (RAID)
resource sharing
remote-access server
    (RAS)
server farm
shared Ethernet
shielded twisted-pair
    (STP)
software audit
software piracy
Software Publishers
    Association (SPA)
storage area network
    (SAN)

store and forward
switch
switched Ethernet
symmetric multi-
    processing (SMP)
Thicknet
Thinnet
topology
transceiver
twisted-pair wiring
unshielded twisted-pair
    (UTP) wiring
user profile
virtual carrier sense
    method
wireless Ethernet
wireless LAN (WLAN)
workgroup switch
1 GbE
10 GbE
40 GbE
10Base-2
10Base-5
10Base-T
100Base-T
1000Base-T
10/100 Ethernet

QUESTIONS

1. Define *local area network.*

2. What are the distinguishing features of a LAN?

3. What are two reasons for developing LANs?

4. What is the function of LAN metering software?

5. Discuss the legal issue of using single-computer license software on networks.

6. Discuss why it is important for organizations to enforce policies restricting use of employee-owned hardware and software and unauthorized copies of software.

7. In some LANs, most of the computers talk with the server, but others use no server. What are these two approaches called?

8. Describe at least three types of servers.

9. What is a NIC? What is a hub?

10. What media do LANs normally use?

11. What is the purpose of a BALUN?

12. Compare and contrast category 5 UTP, category 5e UTP, and category 5 STP.

13. What is a cable plan and why would you want one?

14. What does a NOS do? What are the major software parts of a NOS?

15. What is the most important characteristic of a NOS?

16. What is a network profile?

17. What is Ethernet? How does it work?

18. How does a logical topology differ from a physical topology?

19. Briefly describe how CSMA/CD works.

20. Why should CSMA/CD networks be built so that no more than 50 percent of their capacity is dedicated to actual network traffic?

21. Explain the terms *10Base-2, 10Base-T, 100Base-T, 1000Base-T, 10 GbE,* and *10/100 Ethernet.*

22. How does switched Ethernet differ from traditional Ethernet?

23. How do layer-2 Ethernet switches know where to send the packets they receive? Describe how switches gather and use this knowledge.

24. What are the primary advantages and disadvantages of switched Ethernet?

25. What is the topology of wireless Ethernet and how does it work?

26. Explain how the two approaches to media access control work in CSMA/CA.

27. How do DSSS WLANs differ from FHSS WLANs?

28. What are the primary advantages and disadvantages of infrared wireless LANs?

29. Explain how Bluetooth works.

30. What is a bottleneck, and how can you locate one?

31. Describe four ways to improve network performance on the server.

32. Describe four ways to improve network performance on the circuit.

33. Why does network segmentation improve LAN performance?

34. It is said that hooking some computers together with a cable does not make a network. Why?

35. Some people believe Bluetooth is a revolution, whereas others see it as being similar to our current short-range infrared communication between computer devices. What do you think? *Is* Bluetooth a revolution?

36. Given the dramatic changes ahead in WLANs (e.g., IEEE 802.11a), would you install a WLAN today? Explain.

37. If IEEE 802.11a is widely available in the next few years, what are the implications for networks of the future? Will 10Base-T still be around, or will we eliminate wired offices?

EXERCISES

6-1 Survey the LANs used in your organization. Are they Ethernet, switched Ethernet, or some other standard? Why?

6-2 Document one LAN (or LAN segment) in detail. What devices are attached, what cabling is used, and what is the topology? What does the cable plan look like?

6-3 You have been hired by a small company to install a simple LAN for their 18 Windows computers. Develop a simple LAN and determine the total cost; that is, select the cables, hubs/switches, and NICs and price them.

MINI-CASES

I. Designing a New Ethernet

One important issue in designing Ethernet lies in making sure that if a computer transmits a packet, any other computer that attempts to transmit at the same time will be able to hear the incoming packet before it stops transmitting, or else a collision might go unnoticed. For example, assume that we are on earth and send an Ethernet packet over a very long piece of Category 5 wire to the moon. If a computer on the moon starts transmitting at the same time as we do on earth and finishes transmitting before our packet arrives at the moon, there will be a collision, but neither computer will detect it; the packets will be garbled, but no one will know why. So, in designing Ethernet, we must make sure that the length of cable in the LAN is shorter than the length of the shortest possible message that can be sent. Otherwise, a collision could go undetected.

1. Let's assume that the smallest possible message is 64 bytes. If we use 10Base-T, how long (in feet or meters) is a 64-byte message? Hint: You can assume that the electricity in the cable travels at approximately 200 million meters per second but after factoring in the delays due to the devices the real transmission rate is closer to 40 million meters per second.
2. If we use 10 GbE, how long (in feet or meters) is a 64-byte message?
3. The answer in question 2 is the maximum sum of all cable laid in a hub-based Ethernet LAN or the maximum distance that any single cable could run from a switch to one attached computer in a switched Ethernet LAN. How would you overcome the problem implied by this?

II. Pat's Petunias

You have been called in as a network consultant by your cousin Pat who operates a successful mail-order flower business. She is moving to a new office and wants to install a network for her telephone operators, who take phone calls and enter orders into the system. The number of operators working varies depending on the time of day and day of the week. On slow shifts, there are usually only 10 operators, whereas at peak times, there are 50. She has bids from different companies to install (1) a traditional shared Ethernet 10Base-T network, (2) a switched Ethernet 10Base-T network, or (3) a switched Ethernet 100Base-T network. She wants you to give her some sense of the relative performance of the three alternatives so she can compare that with their different costs.

CASE STUDY

NEXT-DAY AIR SERVICE

Sally Wong is excited about installing a new LAN as a key element of the new International Services Division. She wants you to assist her in developing a plan and proposal for a departmental LAN. You see this as an opportunity to build a model LAN within NDAS. You can start from the beginning with new equipment and procedures. Wong is very well respected in the company. NDAS is committed to moving strongly into the international arena. A successful LAN (or for that matter, an unsuccessful one) in her department will get a great deal of attention at NDAS.

Now you need to revisit the issue of LAN protocols and configurations so that you can make a final recommendation. Other issues that need to be considered at this time include the LAN's cabling, installation, security, anticipated growth, and access—who or which remote offices can access the LAN. You also need to consider the operational and managerial procedures that will have to be adopted to ensure successful operation of the department LAN. And, of course, there are cost considerations.

Wong is excited about starting off with a LAN in her department. She has told you that her group will be using specialized software and creating a departmental database of customers and vendors. The group will initially consist of eight people but is expected to grow rapidly to twice that number.

Exercises

1. Which is best for the International Services Division, a dedicated-server network or peer-to-peer LAN? Explain your choice.

2. Draw a network plan that includes the general layout of the LAN (computers, servers, cables, hubs/switches) and recommend what type of LAN to install (e.g., 10Base-2, 10Base-T, switched 10Base-T, wireless Ethernet 802.11b). Justify your recommendation.

3. Sally Wong has heard horror stories about LAN bottlenecks. Prepare a brief discussion of LAN bottlenecks and what can be done to improve LAN performance.

4. What safeguards do you recommend for NDAS to control the use of illegal copies of software on the LANs?

CHAPTER 7

BACKBONE NETWORKS

THIS **CHAPTER** examines backbone networks (BNs) that are used to link LANs together and to link BNs to WANs. We begin with the various types of devices used in BNs and discuss several backbone architectures. We then turn to two technologies designed primarily for use in the BN (ATM and fiber distributed data interface [FDDI]). The chapter ends with a discussion of how to improve BN performance and of the future of BNs.

OBJECTIVES

- Understand the internetworking devices used in BNs
- Understand several common backbone architectures
- Be aware of FDDI
- Be familiar with ATM
- Be aware of ways to improve BN performance

CHAPTER OUTLINE

INTRODUCTION

The driving force behind networking is the shift toward an information-based business economy and the Internet. Most business organizations realize that information must be stored, retrieved, analyzed, acted on, and shared with others at a moment's notice. Without an enterprisewide network or an Internet connection, moving information from one department LAN to another or to customers is difficult.

Interconnecting the organization's diverse networks is critical. A *backbone network (BN)* is a high-speed network that connects many networks. BNs typically use higher-speed circuits to interconnect a series of LANs and provide connections to other BNs, MANs, WANs, and the Internet. A backbone that connects many BNs spanning several nearby buildings for a single organization is often called a *campus network*. A BN also may called be an *enterprise network* if it connects all networks within a company, regardless of whether it crosses state, national, or international boundaries.

We begin this chapter by describing several commonly used devices in the BN and then showing how those can be used to create different backbone architectures with different performance capabilities. Next, we focus on the high-speed network technologies often used in BNs.

BACKBONE NETWORK COMPONENTS

There are two basic components to a BN: the network cable, and the hardware devices that connect other networks to the BN. The cable is essentially the same as that used in LANs, except that it is usually fiber optic to provide higher data rates. The hardware devices can be computers or special-purpose devices that just transfer messages from one network to another. These include bridges, routers, and gateways (Figure 7-1).

Device	Operates At	Packets	Physical Layer	Data Link Layer	Network Layer
Bridge	Data link layer	Filtered using data link layer addresses	Same or different	Same	Same
Router	Network layer	Routed using network layer addresses	Same or different	Same or different	Same
Gateway	Network layer	Routed using network layer addresses	Same or different	Same or different	Same or different

FIGURE 7-1 Backbone network devices.

Bridges

Bridges operate at the data link layer. They connect two or more network segments that use the *same* data link and network protocol. They understand only data link layer protocols and addresses. They may connect the *same or different* types of cable. Bridges are similar to the layer-2 switches discussed in the last chapter in that they use the data link layer address to forward packets between network segments (Figure 7-2). Like switches, they learn addresses by reading the source and destination addresses. As layer-2 switches have become more powerful, bridges have become obsolete, although they are still in use in older networks.

Routers

Routers operate at the network layer. Routers connect two or more network segments that use the *same or different* data link protocols but the *same* network protocol. They may con-

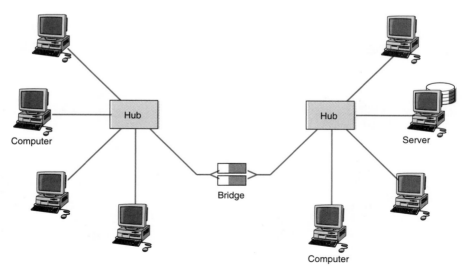

FIGURE 7-2 Use of bridges to connect local area network segments.

nect the *same or different* types of cable. Routers are the "TCP/IP gateways" that we first introduced in Chapter 5. Routers strip off the data link layer packet and process the network layer packet. Routers forward only those messages that need to go to other networks, on the basis of their network layer address (Figure 7-3).

Routers may be "black boxes," computers with several NICs, or special network modules in computers or other devices. In general, they perform more processing on each message than bridges and therefore operate more slowly.

One major feature of a router is that it can choose the "best" route between networks when there are several possible routes between them. Because a router knows its own location, as well as the packet's final destination, it looks in a routing table to identify the best route or *path*.

One other important difference between a router and a bridge is that router processes only those messages that are specifically addressed to it. Bridges process all messages that appear on the network and forward them to the appropriate network on the basis of on their data link layer address. Bridges simply forward the message unchanged onto the other network. In contrast, because routers operate at the network layer, the router's data link layer must first recognize that the incoming message is specifically addressed to the router at the data link layer level, before the message it is passed to the network layer for processing. The router will then process the message by building an entirely new data link layer packet, then transmit it on the other network.

The router attempts to make no changes to the network layer packet and user data it receives. (As noted previously, it creates a new data link layer packet.) Sometimes, however, changes are needed, such as when the maximum data link layer packet size on one network is different from another, which forces the router to split a message into several smaller messages for transmission.

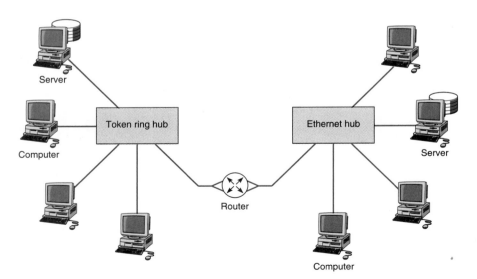

FIGURE 7-3 Use of routers to connect local area networks.

Gateways

Gateways operate at the network layer and use network layer addresses in processing messages. Gateways are more complex than bridges or routers because they are the interface between two or more dissimilar networks. Gateways connect two or more networks that use the *same or different* (usually different) data link and network protocols. They may connect the *same or different* types of cable. Some gateways operate at the application layer as well. Gateways process only those messages explicitly addressed to them (i.e., using their data link layer address) and route those messages that need to go to other networks (Figure 7-4).

Gateways translate one network layer protocol into another, translate data link layer protocols, and open sessions between application programs, thus overcoming both hardware and software incompatibilities. More complex gateways even take care of such tasks as code conversion (e.g., converting from ASCII into EBCDIC). A gateway may be a stand-alone computer with several NICs and special software or a front-end processor connected to a mainframe computer.

One of the most common uses of gateways is to enable LANs that use TCP/IP and Ethernet to communicate with IBM mainframes that use SNA. In this case, the gateway converts the microcomputer LAN transmissions into a transmission that looks like it came from a smart terminal. The gateway provides both the basic system interconnection and the necessary translation between the protocols in both directions. Without this SNA gateway on the LAN, each microcomputer would have to have its own SNA hardware and software in addition to the TCP/IP and Ethernet hardware and software (e.g., software to make the

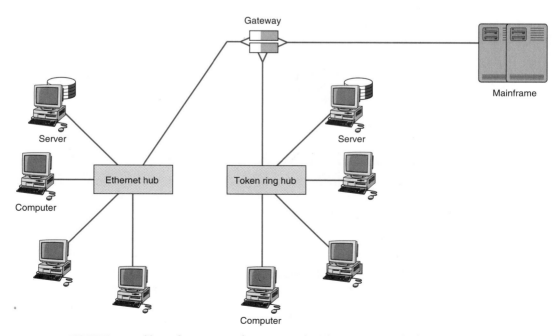

FIGURE 7-4 Use of gateways to connect local area networks and a mainframe.

microcomputer act like an IBM 3270 terminal, 3270 hardware emulation card, coaxial cable, and mainframe controller port). The SNA gateway eliminates the need for additional hardware for the microcomputer, and it requires only one connection to the client computer because all data are sent through the LAN.

A Caveat

One warning is in order. The terminology used in the marketplace may differ substantially from that in the preceding discussion. Many new types of bridges, switches, and routers are being developed, so that one vendor's "bridge" may actually provide the functions of a "router."

Multiprotocol routers can understand several different network layer protocols. If they receive a message in one protocol, they process it and send it out using the same protocol. The most common multiprotocol routers understand both TCP/IP and IPX/SPX and are commonly used in Novell LANs connected through the BN to the Internet. They enable the LAN to use IPX/SPX internally or for communications to other Novell LANs inside the organizations, and simultaneously to use TCP/IP for Internet access. Some vendors' "multiprotocol routers" translate between different network layer protocols (usually TCP/IP and IPX/SPX) so, technically, they are gateways.

Brouters are devices that combine the functions of both bridges and routers. These operate at both the data link and network layers. A brouter connects both same data-link-type network segments and different data-link ones. Like a bridge, it examines the data link layer addresses of all messages on the network (not just those addressed to it) and forwards them as needed to other networks. At the same time, any messages explicitly addressed to it using its data link layer address are routed. The advantage of brouters is that they are as fast as bridges for same data link type networks but can also connect different data link type networks.

Layer-3 switches function in the same way as layer-2 switches discussed previously, but they switch messages on the basis of their network layer address (usually IP address). These switches provide the best of both switches and routers. They can be used in place of routers but provide the benefits of traditional layer-2 switches: much faster transmission and more simultaneously active ports than routers.

BACKBONE NETWORK ARCHITECTURES

While there are an infinite number of ways in which network designers can build backbone networks, there are really only four fundamental architectures that can be combined in different ways. These four architectures are routed backbone (routers that move packets on the basis of network layer addresses), bridged backbones (bridges that move packets on the basis of data link layer addresses), collapsed backbones (switches that move packets based on data link layer addresses), and virtual LANs (switches that move packets through LANs that are built virtually, not using physical location).

These four architectures are mixed and matched to build sets of BNs. Before we discuss these four architectures, we first must discuss the way in which network designers think about backbone designs and how to combine them; that is, the different layers of backbones that exist in most organizations today.

Backbone Architecture Layers

Network designers often think about three distinct technology layers[1] when they design BNs. The layer closest to the users is the *access layer,* the technology used in the LANs attached to the BN as described in the previous chapter (e.g., 100Base-T, switched 10Base-T, wireless Ethernet) (Figure 7-5). Although the access layer is not part of the BN, the technologies used in the LANs (or access layer) can have major impacts on the design of the backbone.

The *distribution layer* is the part of the backbone that connects the LANs together. This is the part of the backbone that contains the "TCP/IP gateways" described in Chapter 5. It usually runs throughout one building.

The *core layer* is the part of the backbone that connects the different BNs together, often from building to building. The core layer is technologies used in the campus network or the enterprise network. Some small organizations are not large enough to have a core layer; their backbone spans only the distribution layer. Other organizations are large enough that they have a core network at several locations that are in turn connected by WANs.

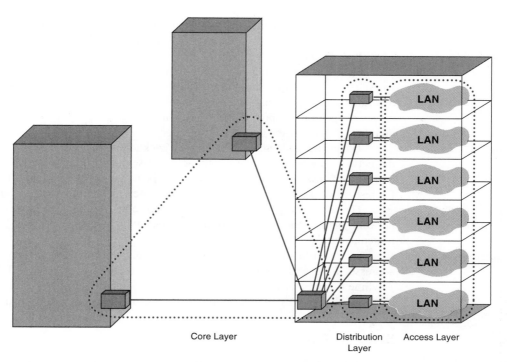

Core Layer   Distribution   Access Layer
Layer

FIGURE 7-5 Backbone network design layers. LAN = local area network.

---

[1] Try not to confuse the five basic layers in the network model (application layer, transport layer, and so on) with the layers of backbone technology we are describing here. They are different. We would have preferred to use a different word than *layer* to describe these, but unfortunately, that is the term used in industry.

In the sections that follow, we describe the four basic BN architectures and discuss at which layer they are often used. We will focus on TCP/IP networks when comparing these four architectures. We assume that you are comfortable with the material on TCP/IP in Chapter 5; if you are not, you may want to go back and review the last section of the chapter, entitled TCP/IP Example, before you continue reading.

Routed Backbone

Routed backbones move packets along the backbone on the basis of their network layer address (i.e., layer-3 address). The most common form of routed backbone uses a bus topology (e.g., using Ethernet 100Base-T). Routed backbones are sometimes called subnetted backbones or hierarchical backbones and are most commonly used to connect different buildings within the same campus network (i.e., at the core layer).

Figure 7-6 illustrates a routed backbone used at distribution layer (because it is simpler to explain how routed backbones work using the distribution layer than using the core layer). A routed backbone is the basic backbone architecture we used to illustrate how TCP/IP worked in Chapter 5. There are a series of LANs (access layer) connected by routers or layer-3 switches to a single shared-media BN. Each of the LANs are a separate subnet. Message traffic stays within each subnet unless it specifically needs to leave the subnet to travel elsewhere on the network, in which case the network layer address (e.g., TCP/IP) is used to move the packet.

Each LAN is usually a separate entity, relatively isolated from the rest of the network. There is no requirement that all LANs share the same data link layer. One LAN can use Ethernet, whereas another uses another technology. Each LAN can contain its own server designed to support the users on that LAN, but users can still easily access servers on other LANs over the backbone as needed.

The primary advantage of the routed backbone is that it clearly segments each part of the network connected to the backbone. Each segment (usually a LAN or another backbone) has its own subnet addresses that can be managed by a different network manager. Each segment off the backbone also can use different data link layer technologies.

There are two primary disadvantages to routed backbones. First, the routers in the network impose time delays. Routing takes more time than bridging or switching, so routed networks can sometimes be slower.

Second, routed networks require a lot of management. Establishing separate subnet addresses for each LAN is time consuming and requires a large set of TCP/IP addresses. Anytime a computer is moved from one LAN to another, it must be reconfigured (unless the network is using dynamic addressing, which imposes costs of its own).

Bridged Backbone

Bridged backbones move packets along the backbone on the basis of their data link layer address (i.e., layer-2 address). The most common form also uses a bus topology. They were common in the distribution layer, but their use is declining; few organizations install bridged networks, because they have major performance problems, as we shall shortly see. Bridged backbones are sometimes called flat backbones.

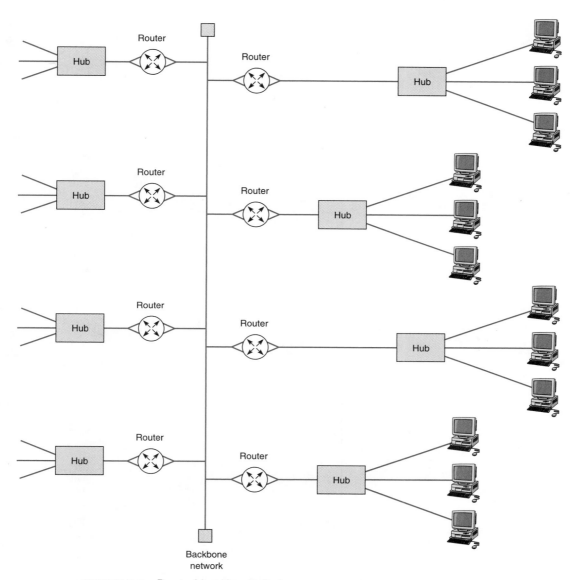

FIGURE 7-6   Routed backbone design.

Figure 7-7 illustrates a distribution layer bridged backbone with a bus topology. This figure shows the same series of LANs as in Figure 7-6, but now the LANs are connected by bridges or layer-2 switches to the single shared-media BN. As you can see, a bridged backbone looks very similar to a routed backbone. With a bridged backbone, however, the entire network (backbone and all connected network segments) are on the same subnet. All

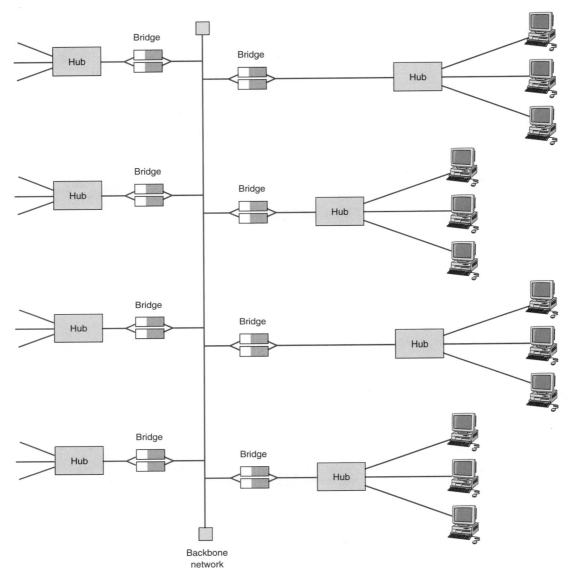

FIGURE 7-7 Bridged backbone design.

LANs are part of the same overall network and all must have the same data link layer protocol. This is in sharp contrast to the routed backbone, in which the LANs are isolated and may be different.

Bridged backbones have several distinct advantages and disadvantages compared with routed backbones. First, because bridges tend to be less expensive than routers, they are often cheaper. Second, they are usually simpler to install because the network manager does not need to worry about building many different subnets and assigning a whole variety of different subnet masks and addresses in each part of the network. However, because the backbone and all attached networks are considered part of the same subnet, it is more difficult to permit different individuals to manage different parts of the network (e.g., LANs); a change in one part of the network has the potential to significantly affect all other parts. Also, it is possible to run out of IP addresses if the entire network has many computers.

The single most important problem is network speed. Bridging is faster than routing, so one might expect the bridged backbone to be faster. For small networks, this is true. For large networks, it is not. Bridged backbones are slower than routed backbones. Because bridged backbones and all networks connected to them are part of the same subnet, broadcast messages (e.g., address requests) must be permitted to travel everywhere in the backbone. This means, for example, that a computer in one LAN attempting to find the data link layer address of a server in the same LAN will issue a broadcast message that will travel to every computer on every LAN attached to the backbone. (In contrast, on a routed backbone, such messages would never leave the LAN in which they originated.)

There are many different types of broadcast messages other than address requests (e.g., a printer reporting it is out of paper, a server about to be shut down). These broadcast messages quickly use up network capacity in a large bridged network. The result is slower response times for the user. In a small network, the problems are not as great, because there are fewer computers to issue such broadcast messages.

Collapsed Backbone

Collapsed backbones are probably the most common type of BN used in the distribution layer (i.e., within a building); most new building BNs designed today use collapsed backbones. They also are making their way into the core layer as the campus backbone, but routed backbones still remain common.

Collapsed backbone networks use a star topology with one device, usually a switch, at its center. Figure 7-8 shows a collapsed backbone connecting the same series of LANs. Here, the backbone circuit and set of routers or bridges is replaced by one switch and a set of circuits to each LAN. The collapsed backbone has more cable but fewer devices. There is no backbone cable. The "backbone" exists only in the switch, which is why this is called a collapsed backbone.

There are two major advantages to collapsed backbones. First, performance is improved. With the routed or bridged backbone BN, the backbone circuit was shared among many LANs (eight LANs, in the case of Figure 7-8); each had to take turns sending messages. With the collapsed backbone, each connection into the switch is a separate point-to-point circuit. The switch enables simultaneous access, so that several LANs can send messages to other LANs at the same time. Throughput is increased significantly, often by 200 to 600 percent, depending on the number of attached LANs and the traffic pattern.

Second, there are far fewer networking devices in the network. In Figure 7-8, one switch replaces eight routers. This reduces costs and greatly simplifies network management. All the key backbone devices are in the same physical location, and all traffic must flow through the switch. If something goes wrong or if new cabling is needed, it can all be done in one place.

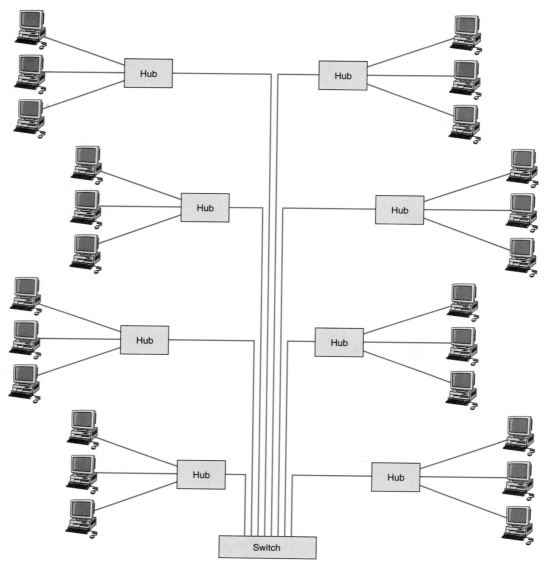

FIGURE 7-8 Collapsed backbone network design.

Collapsed backbones have two relatively minor disadvantages. First, they use more cable, and the cable must be run longer distances, which often means that fiber-optic cables must be used. Second, if the switch fails, so does the entire BN. However, if the reliability of the switch has the same reliability as the reliability of the routers in Figure 7-6, then there is less chance of an failure (because there are fewer devices to fail). For most organizations, these disadvantages are outweighed by benefits offered by collapsed backbones.

Rack-Based Collapsed Backbones   Most organizations now use collapsed backbones in which all network devices for one part of the building are physically located in the same room, often in a *rack* of equipment. This form of collapsed backbone is shown graphically in Figure 7-9. This has the advantage of placing all network equipment in one place for easy maintenance and upgrade, but it does require more cable. In most cases, the cost of the cable itself is only a small part of the overall cost to install the network, so the

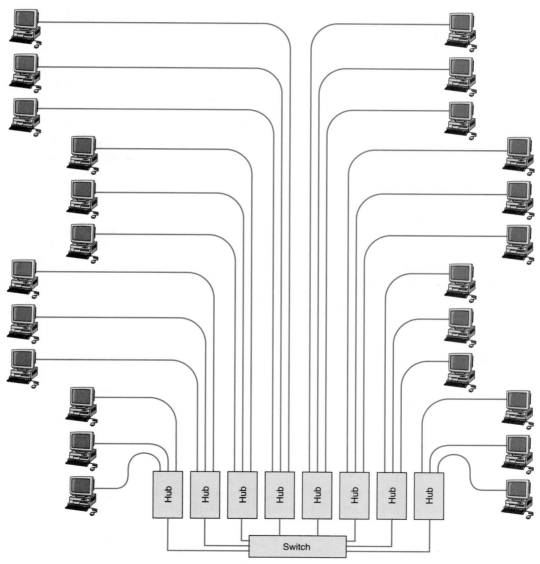

FIGURE 7-9   Rack-based Collapsed backbone network design.

cost is greatly outweighed by the simplicity of maintenance and the flexibility it provides for future upgrades.

The room containing the rack of equipment is sometimes called the *main distribution facility (MDF)* or central distribution facility (CDF) (Figure 7-10). The cables from all computers and devices in the area served by the MDF (often hundreds of cables) are run into the MDF room. Once in the run, they are connected into the various devices. The devices in the rack are connected among themselves using very short cables called *patch cables*.

With rack-based equipment, it becomes simple to move computers from one LAN to another. In the traditional routed backbone design as shown in Figure 7-6, for example, all the computers in the same general physical location are connected to the same hub and thus share the capacity of the hub. Although this often works well, it can cause problems if many of the computers on the hub are high-traffic computers. For example, in Figure 7-6, if all the busy computers on the network are located in the upper left area of the figure, the hub in this area may become a severe bottleneck.

With an MDF, all cables run into the MDF. If one hub becomes overloaded, it is straightforward to unplug the cables from several high-demand computers from the overloaded hub and plug them into one or more less-busy hubs. This effectively spreads the traffic around the network more efficiently and means that network capacity is no longer tied to the physical location of the computers; computers in the same physical area can be connected into very different network segments.

Chassis-Based Collapsed Backbones Sometimes a *chassis switch* is used instead of a rack. A chassis switch enables users to plug *modules* directly into the switch. Each module is a certain type of network device. One module might be a 16-port 10Base-T hub, another might be a router, whereas another might be an 4-port 100Base-T switch, and so on. The switch is designed to hold a certain number of modules and has a certain internal capacity, so that all the modules can be active at one time. For example, a switch with five 10Base-T hubs, two 10Base-T switches (with 8 ports each), a 100Base-T switch (with 4 ports), and a 100Base-T router would have to have an internal switching capacity of at least 710 Mbps ([5 × 10 Mbps] + [2 × 8 × 10 Mbps] + [4 × 100 Mbps] + 100 Mbps = 710 Mbps).

The key advantage of chassis switches is their flexibility. It becomes simple to add new modules with additional ports as the LAN grows and to upgrade the switch to use new technologies. For example, if you want to add gigabit Ethernet or ATM (discussed below), you simply lay the cable and insert the appropriate module into the switch.

FIGURE 7-10 An MDF with rack-mounted equipment. A layer-2 chassis switch with six 100Base-T modules (center of photo) connects to four 24-port 10Base-T switches. The chassis switch is connected to the campus backbone using 100Base-F over fiber optic cable. The cables from each room are wired into the rear of the patch panel (shown at the top of the photo), with the ports on the front of the patch panel labeled to show which room is which. Patch cables connect the patch panel ports to the ports on the switches.

MANAGEMENT FOCUS **7 - 1**

CENTRAL PARKING COLLAPSES

Central Parking, based in Nashville, operates 4,500 parking lots and 100 offices in 42 states and 13 countries. Its rapid growth had brought its headquarters backbone network to its knees; network outages occurred daily as the network routinely hit its maximum capacity.

The new network uses one layer-3 switch as a collapsed backbone for its core layer (Figure 7-11). This switch manages traffic for 42 IP subnets, through a series of 48-gigabit Ethernet circuits (most of which are fiber optic, but a few use category 6 cable), and 48 10/100 Ethernet circuits over category 6 cable. Central Parking's 20 main servers are connected directly to the switch as a server farm.

Two other layer-2 switches act the distribution layer and access layer for almost 200 desktop PCs using 10/100 Ethernet over category 6 cable. These switches are connected to the core switch via multiple gigabit over fiber circuits, so that the circuits between the switches do not become bottlenecks.

Several routers provide distribution layer backbones to Central's offices around the world through a series of wide area networks and the Internet.

SOURCE: "Central Parking Puts the Brakes on Network Downtime," *Network Magazine,* November 2000.

Virtual LAN

For many years, the design of LANs remained relatively constant. However, in recent years, the introduction of high-speed switches has begun to change the way we think about LANs. Switches offer the opportunity to design radically new types of LANs. Most large organizations today have traditional LANs, but many are considering the *virtual LAN (VLAN),* a new type of LAN–BN architecture made possible by intelligent, high-speed switches.

VLANs are networks in which computers are assigned to LAN segments by software rather than by hardware. In the section above, we described how in rack-based collapsed BNs a computer could be moved from one hub to another by unplugging its cable and plugging it into a different hub. VLANs provide the same capability via software so that the network manager does not have to unplug and replug physical cables to move computers from one segment to another.

VLANs are often faster and provide greater opportunities to manage the flow of traffic on the LAN and BN than do the traditional LAN and routed BN architecture. However, VLANs are significantly more complex, so they usually are used only for large networks. There are two basic approaches to designing VLANs: single-switch VLANs and multiswitch VLANs.

Single-Switch VLAN   A *single-switch VLAN* means that the VLAN operates only inside one switch. The computers on the VLAN are connected into the one switch and assigned by software into different VLANs (Figure 7-12). The network manager uses special software to assign the dozens or even hundreds of computers attached to the switch to different VLAN segments. The VLAN segments function in the same way as physical LAN segments; the computers in the same VLAN act as though they are connected to the same physical switch or hub. For example, broadcast messages sent by computers in a VLAN segment are sent only to the computers on the same VLAN. VLANs can be designed so that they act as though computers are connected via hubs (i.e., several computers share

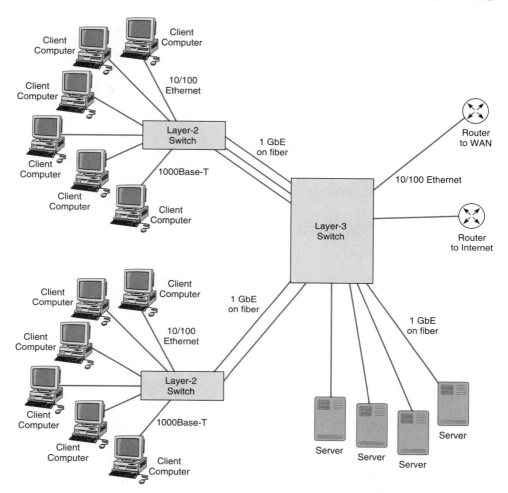

FIGURE 7-11 Central Parking's collapsed backbone.

a given capacity and must take turns using it) or via workgroup switches (i.e., all computers in the VLAN can transmit simultaneously). Although switched circuits are preferred to the shared circuits of hubs, VLAN switches with the capacity to provided a complete set of switched circuits for hundreds of computers are more expensive than those that permit shared circuits.

We should also note that it is possible to have just one computer in a given VLAN. In this case, that computer has a dedicated connection and does not need to share the network capacity with any other computer. This is commonly done for servers.

There are four ways in which computers attached to VLAN switches can be assigned to the specific VLANs inside them. The first approach, used by *port-based VLANs* (also called *layer-1 VLANs*), uses the physical layer port number on the front of the VLAN switch to assign computers to VLAN segments. Each computer is physically cabled into a

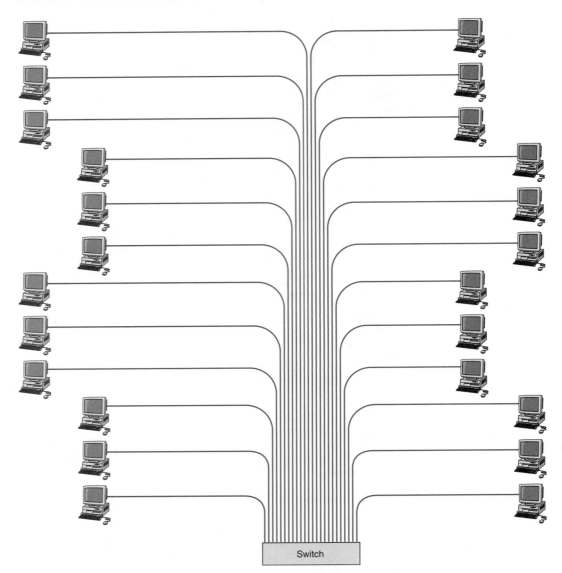

FIGURE 7-12   VLAN-baseed Collapsed backbone network design.

specific port on the VLAN switch. The network manager uses special software provided by the switch manufacturer to instruct the switch as to which ports are assigned to which VLAN. This means that the network manager must know which computer is connected to which port.

The second approach, used by *MAC-based VLANs* (also called *layer 2-VLANs*), uses the data link layer address (or media access control address) to form the VLANs. The network manager uses special software to instruct the switch which incoming data link layer addresses are assigned to which VLAN segment. The advantage of a layer-2 VLAN is that they are simpler to manage when computers are moved. If a computer is moved in a layer-1 VLAN, then the network manager must reconfigure the switch to keep that computer in the same VLAN because the computer has moved from one port to another. With a layer-2 VLAN, no reconfiguration is needed. Although the computer may have moved from one port to another, it is the permanently assigned data link layer address that is used to determine which VLAN the computer is on.

The third approach, used by *IP-based VLANs* (also called *layer-3 VLANs*), uses the network layer address to form the VLANs. As before, the network administrator uses special software to instruct the switch as to which network layer addresses are assigned to which VLAN. Layer-3 VLANs reduce the time spent reconfiguring the network when computers move in the same way as layer-2 VLANs. Layer-3 VLANs tend to be a bit slower at processing each message than layer-2 VLANs because processing layer-3 protocols is slightly slower than processing layer-2 protocols.

The fourth approach, used by *application-based VLANs* (also called *policy-based VLANs* or *layer-4 VLANs*), uses the type of application indicated by the port number in the TCP packet in combination with the network layer addresses to form the VLAN groups. As before, the network administrator uses special software to instruct the switch as to which types of packets from which addresses are assigned to which VLAN. This process is very complex because the network manager must decide on a variety of different factors in forming the VLANs. The advantage is a very precise allocation of network capacity. Now VLANs can be formed to allocate a certain amount of network capacity for Web browsing to certain individuals, so much to Web browsing for others, so much to transaction processing, and so on. In this way, the network manager can restrict the amount of network capacity used by potentially less productive applications (e.g., Web surfing) and thus provide much better allocation of resources.

Multiswitch VLAN A *multiswitch VLAN* works the same way as a single-switch VLAN, except that now several switches are used to build the VLANs (Figure 7-13). In this case, the switches must be able to send packets among themselves in a way that identifies the VLAN to which the packet belongs. There are two approaches to this.

The first approach is to use a proprietary protocol that encapsulates the packet (i.e., a protocol that is not standard but instead is used only by specific companies). In this case, when a packet needs to go from one VLAN switch to another VLAN switch, the first switch puts a new VLAN packet around the outside of the Ethernet packet. The VLAN packet contains the VLAN information and is used to move the packet from switch to switch within the VLAN network. When the packet arrives at the final destination switch, the VLAN packet is stripped off and the unchanged Ethernet packet inside is sent to the destination computer.

The other approach is to modify the Ethernet packet itself to carry the VLAN information. IEEE 802.1q is an emerging standard that inserts 16 bytes of VLAN information into the normal IEEE 802.3 Ethernet packet. In this case, when a packet needs to go from one VLAN switch to another VLAN switch, the first switch replaces the incoming Ethernet packet with an 802.1q packet that contains all the information in the original 802.3 Ethernet packet, plus 16 bytes of VLAN information. The additional VLAN information is used to move the packet from switch to switch within the VLAN network. When the packet arrives at the final destination switch, the IEEE 802.1q packet is stripped off and replaced

FIGURE 7-13   Multi-switch VLAN-based Collapsed backbone network design.

with a new Ethernet packet that is identical to the one with which it entered the VLAN and is sent to the destination computer.

BACKBONE TECHNOLOGIES

Many of the same high-speed technologies used in LANs are often used in BNs (e.g., 100Base-T, 1,000Base-T). However, two technologies originally developed for use in MANs and WANs have also been refined for use in BNs: FDDI and ATM.

MANAGEMENT FOCUS *7-2*

VLAN NETWORK AT IONA

IONA Technologies, Inc., a 600-person software developer of enterprise middleware, took advantage of its relocation to Waltham, Massachusetts, to redesign its network infrastructure. The new network, designed to support 230 users in one office complex, uses a multiswitch virtual local area network (VLAN) architecture.

IONA has 27 access-layer VLAN switches located close to its users—built into their cubicle walls, to be exact. Up to 24 users are connected to each access-layer switch, using a mixture of 10/100 Ethernet and 1000Base-T over copper cables (e.g., category 5e) (Figure 7-14). Each of the

first-level switches are connected via gigabit Ethernet over fiber to a central set of 5 VLAN switches that form the core of the network. IEEE 802.1q is used to communicate among the access-layer switches and the distribution-layer switches.

Because both the access-layer switches and distribution-layer switches are modular, it is easy for IONA to upgrade when technologies change.

SOURCE: "Middleware Maker Future-Proofs LAN Infrastructure," *Packet,* Cisco Systems, Inc., second quarter, 2000.

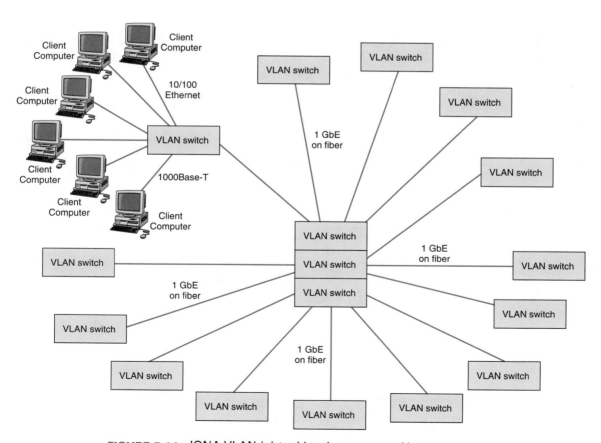

FIGURE 7-14   IONA VLAN (virtual local area network).

Fiber-Distributed Data Interface

The *fiber distributed data interface* (*FDDI*, pronounced *fĭd-ē*) is a set of standards originally designed in the late 1980s for use in MANs (ANSI X3T9.5). FDDI has since made its way into BNs and, in some limited cases, into the LAN itself. FDDI was once seen as the logical replacement for Ethernet, but its future will probably be limited to specialized applications as gigabit Ethernet and ATM (discussed below) become more popular.

Topology FDDI is a ring network that operates at 100 Mbps over a fiber-optic cable. The FDDI standard assumes a maximum of 1,000 stations (i.e., computers, devices) and a 200-kilometer (124-mile) path that requires a repeater every 2 kilometers. FDDI uses two counter-rotating rings called the *primary ring* and the *secondary ring*. Data traffic normally travels on the primary ring. The secondary ring mainly serves as a backup circuit.

All computers on an FDDI network are connected to the primary ring. Some computers are also connected to the secondary ring. Thus, there are two types of FDDI computers: the *dual-attachment station (DAS)* on both rings and the *single-attachment station (SAS)* on just the primary ring (Figure 7-15).

If the cable in the FDDI ring is broken, the ring can still operate in a limited fashion. The DAS nearest to the break reroutes traffic from the primary ring onto the secondary ring. Because the secondary ring is running in the opposite direction, the data travels back around the ring. The DAS nearest the break, on the opposite side of the break, receives the data on the secondary ring and reroutes it back onto the primary ring. In Figure 7-16, for example, there is a break in the ring between computers F and G. Because both are DAS, G can reroute traffic from H on the primary ring back to A on the secondary ring. The data

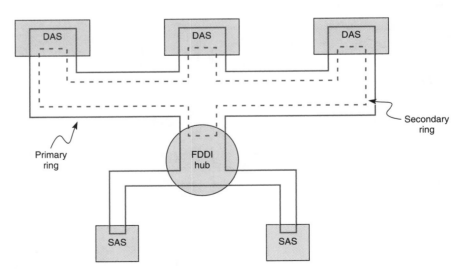

DAS: Dual-attachment station
SAS: Single-attachment station

FIGURE 7-15 Optical cable topology for an FDDI (fiber-distributed data interface) local area network. The FDDI has two rings. Data traffic normally travels on the primary ring.

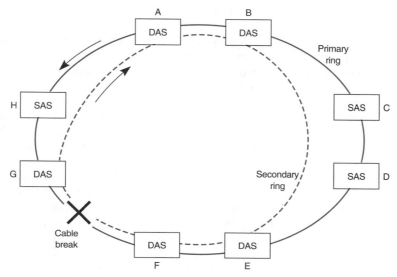

FIGURE 7-16 Managing a broken circuit. DAS = dual-attachment station; SAS = single-attachment station.

will travel along the secondary ring from A to B to E to F. F will then reroute the traffic back to E on the primary ring, from where it will flow back on the primary ring to G (F to E to D to C to B to A to H to G).

Media Access Control The FDDI media access control scheme uses a controlled-access token-passing system. No computer on the network can transmit until it receives then token, a prespecified bit pattern. The token flows through the network from computer to computer. If a computer has a packet to transmit, it waits until it receives the token, attaches the packet it wishes to the token, and retransmits the token with the packet. When a computer receives the token, it look to see if it contains any packets addressed to it, processes them if necessary, and sends the token to the next computer in the ring, unless it has a packet to transmit. The token can contain several packets, each addressed to different computers.

Because FDDI uses a controlled-access technique, it can support a greater percentage of active computers and devices than can contention-based approaches like Ethernet. Tests suggest that FDDI remains reliable and provides adequate response time until it almost reaches saturation at 100 Mbps.

Types of FDDI There is one type of FDDI in addition to the basic FDDI described above, which uses fiber-optic cable. *Copper distributed data interface (CDDI)* uses the same topology and media-access protocol as FDDI but uses category 5 twisted-pair cable instead of fiber-optic cable. It is identical to FDDI in every other way.

Asynchronous Transfer Mode

Asynchronous transfer mode (ATM) is a technology originally designed for use in WANs that is now often used in BNs. Because it is standardized, it is simple to connect ATM

BNs into ATM WANs run by common carriers such as AT&T. ATM is sometimes called cell relay.

ATM backbone switches typically provide point-to-point full-duplex circuits at 155 Mbps (for a total of 310 Mbps) or 622 Mbps (1.24 Gbps total) from switch to switch. Although originally designed to run on fiber-optic cable, some versions of ATM can run on category 5e twisted-pair cables (although the cables cannot be run as far as they would be for 100Base-T).

ATM is a switched network but differs from switched Ethernet in four important ways. First, ATM uses fixed-length packets (or "cells") of 53 bytes (a 5-byte header containing addressing and QoS information, plus 48 bytes of user data). The small fixed-length packets make switching much faster because it is so simple it can be done in hardware—and hardware switching is substantially faster than software switching.

Second, ATM provides no error correction on the user data. (Error checking is provided on the 5-byte header, and if an unrecoverable error is detected, the packet is discarded.) All other types of data link layer protocols we have discussed in this book perform error checking at each computer in the network. Any errors in transmission are corrected immediately, so that the network layer and application software can assume error-free transmission. However, this error control is one of the most time-consuming processes at the data link layer. By not checking for errors, ATM devices can run significantly faster. However, it is up to software at the source and destination to perform error correction and to control for lost messages.

Third, ATM uses a very different type of addressing from traditional data link layer protocols (e.g., Ethernet) or network layer protocols (e.g., IP). Ethernet and IP assign permanent addresses to each computer so that all messages sent to the same computer use the same address. ATM does not use permanent addresses. Instead, ATM defines a *virtual channel (VC)* (sometimes called a *virtual circuit,* although this is not the preferred name) between each sender and receiver, and all packets use the virtual circuit identifier as the address. Each VC identifier has two parts, a path number and a circuit number within that path. Each ATM switch contains a VC table that lists all VCs known to that switch (analogous to a routing table in IP). Because there are potentially thousands of VCs and because each switch knows only those VCs in its VC table, a given VC identifier is used only between one switch and the next.

When an ATM packet arrives at a switch, the switch looks up the packet's VC identifier in its VC table to determine where to send it and what VC identifier should be used when the packet is transmitted on the outgoing circuit. Figure 7-17, for example, shows two switches, each with four ports (or physical circuits). When an incoming packet arrives, the switch looks up the packet's VC identifier in the circuit table, switches the packet to the outgoing port, and changes the VC identifier the packet had when it arrived to a new VC identifier used by the switch at its destination. For example, a packet arriving at switch A via port 1 with a VC identifier of 1,10 would be transmitted out on port 4 to switch B and would be given a new VC identifier of 3,15.

ATM is connection-oriented, so all packets travel in order through the VC. A VC can be either a *permanent virtual circuit (PVC)* (i.e., defined when the network is established or modified) or a *switched virtual circuit (SVC)* (i.e., defined temporarily for one transmission and deleted when the transmission is completed).[2] ATM provides a separate control

---

[2] You will notice a slight change in terminology: *VC* is virtual **channel,** whereas *PVC* is *permanent virtual **circuit.*** The reasons are arbitrary and historical. As you will see in the next chapter, the term *PVC* has the same meaning in X.25 WANs, and because X.25 was developed before ATM, ATM has simply adopted the same terminology.

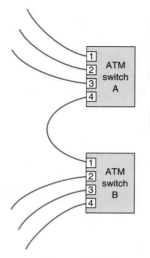

Switch A Circuit Table

Incoming Port	Incoming Circuit	Outgoing Port	Outgoing Circuit
1	1,10	4	3,15
2	3,18	1	2,10
2	2,11	4	2,11
3	4,10	2	3,26
3	4,11	2	1,18
4	5,10	1	4,21

FIGURE 7-17   Addressing and forwarding with asynchronous transfer mode virtual circuits.

circuit that is used for nondata communication between devices, such as the setup and takedown of an SVC.

The fourth major difference between ATM and other collapsed backbone technologies such as switched Ethernet is that ATM prioritizes transmissions on the basis of QoS. You may recall that Chapter 5 briefly discussed QoS routing. With QoS routing or QoS switching, different *classes of service* are defined, each with different priorities. Each virtual circuit is assigned a specific class of service when it is first established. ATM defines five service classes (see ATM Classes of Service) that enable the network to prioritize transmissions. For example, circuits containing voice transmissions receive higher priority than circuits containing e-mail transmissions, because delays in voice transmissions can seriously affect transmission quality, whereas delays in e-mail transmission are less important. If an ATM switch becomes overloaded and it receives a traffic on a low-priority circuit, it will store the packet for later transmission or simply refuse the request until it has sufficient capacity.

ATM and Traditional LANs   ATM uses a very different type of protocol than do traditional LANs. It has a small 53-byte fixed-length packet and is connection oriented (meaning that devices establish a virtual channel before transmitting). Ethernet uses larger variable-length packets and is typically connectionless. To use ATM in a BN that connects traditional Ethernet LANs, some translation must be done to enable the LAN packets to flow over the ATM backbone. There are two approaches to this, LANE and MPOA.

With *LAN Emulation (LANE),* the data link layer packets from the LAN are left intact; they are broken into 48-byte blocks and surrounded by ATM packets. This process is called *encapsulation* and is done by an *edge switch.* The packets flow through the ATM network and are reassembled at an edge switch at the other end before being transmitted into the destination LAN (Figure 7-18). The use of ATM is transparent to users because LANE leaves the original data link layer packets intact and uses the packet's data link layer address to forward the message through the ATM network.

Translating from Ethernet into ATM (and vice versa) is not simple. First, the Ethernet address must be translated into an ATM VC identifier for the PVC or SVC that leads from the edge switch to the edge switch nearest the destination. This is done through a process similar to that of using a broadcast message on a subnet to locate a data link layer address (see Chapter 5). ATM is a switched point-to-point network, so it lacks a simple built-in ability to issue broadcast messages. LANE enables the transmission of broadcast messages, but to date, it has been problematic.

Once the VC address for the destination data link layer address has been found, it can be used to transmit the packet through the ATM backbone. However, if no PVC is currently defined from the edge switch to the destination edge switch, then the edge switch must establish a new SVC.

Once the VC is ready, the LAN packet is broken into the series of ATM cells and transmitted over the ATM backbone using the ATM VC identifier. The destination edge switch then reassembles the ATM cells into the LAN packet and forwards it to the appropriate device.

This process is not without cost. The resolution of the Ethernet address into an ATM VC identifier, the setup of the SVC (if necessary), and the packetization and reassembly of

TECHNICAL FOCUS *7-1*

ATM CLASSES OF SERVICE

Asynchronous transfer mode (ATM) provides five classes of service that each receive different priorities in traveling though the network:

- *Constant bit rate (CBR)* means that the circuit must provide a constant, predefined data rate at all times, much like having a point-to-point physical circuit between the devices. Whenever a CBR circuit is established, ATM guarantees that the switch can provide the circuit; the sum of all CBR circuits at one switch cannot exceed its capacity, even if they are all not active simultaneously. In some ways, CBR is like time division multiplexing, discussed in Chapter 3. CBR was originally designed to support voice transmissions.

- *Variable bit rate—real time (VBR-RT)* means that the data transmission rate in the circuit will vary but that all cells received must be switched immediately on arrival because the devices (or people) on the opposite ends of the circuit are waiting for the transmission and expect to receive it in a timely fashion. Each VBR-RT

circuit is assigned a standard transmission rate but can exceed it. If the cells in a VBR-RT circuit arrive too fast to transmit, they are lost. Most voice traffic today uses VBR-RT rather CBR.

- *Variable bit rate—nonreal time (VBR-NRT)* means that the data transmission rate in the circuit will vary and that the application is tolerant of delays.

- *Available bit rate (ABR)* means that the circuit can tolerate wide variation in transmission speeds and many delays. ABR circuits have lower priority than VBR-NRT circuits. They receive the lowest amount of guaranteed capacity but can use whatever capacity is available (i.e., not in use by CBR, VBR-RT, and VBR-NRT circuits).

- *Unspecified bit rate (UBR)* means that the circuit has no guaranteed data rate but that data are transported when capacity is available. When the network is busy, UBR packets are the first to be discarded. Using UBR is a bit like flying standby on an airline.

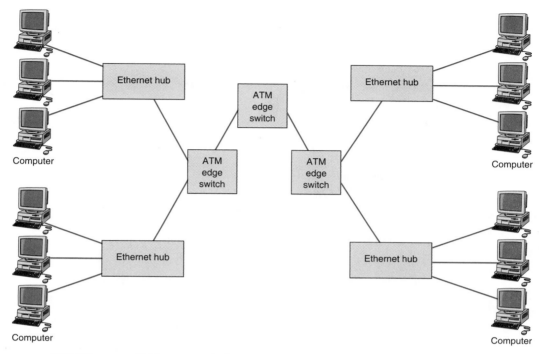

FIGURE 7-18   ATM encapsulation.

the LAN packets to and from ATM cells can impose quite a delay. Recent tests of ATM edge switches suggest that even though they are capable of transmitting at 155 Mbps, the encapsulation delays can reduce performance significantly.

Multiprotocol over ATM (MPOA) is an extension to LANE. MPOA uses the network layer address (e.g., IP address) in addition to the data link layer address. If the packet destination is in the same subnet, MPOA will use data link layer addresses in the same manner as LANE. If the packet is addressed to a different subnet, MPOA will use the network layer address to forward the packet. In this case, the ATM backbone is operating somewhat similarly to a network of brouters. In an ATM MPOA network, a series of *route servers* (also called MPOA servers or MPSs) are provided that perform the somewhat the same function as DNS servers in TCP/IP networks (see Chapter 5): Route servers translate network layer addresses (e.g., IP addresses) into ATM virtual circuit identifiers.

IMPROVING BACKBONE PERFORMANCE

The method for improving the performance of BNs is similar to that for improving LAN performance. First, find the bottleneck, then solve it (or, more accurately, move the bottleneck somewhere else). You can improve the performance of the network by improving the performance of the computers and other devices in the network, by upgrading the circuits between computers, and by changing the demand placed on the network (Figure 7-19).

Performance Checklist

Increase Computer and Device Performance

- Change to a more appropriate routing protocol (either static or dynamic)
- Buy devices and software from one vendor
- Reduce translation between different protocols
- Increase the devices' memory

Increase Circuit Capacity

- Upgrade to a faster circuit
- Add circuits

Reduce Network Demand

- Change user behavior
- Reduce broadcast messages

FIGURE 7-19   Improving backbone network performance.

Improving Computer and Device Performance

The primary functions of computers and devices in BNs are routing and protocol transla-tions. If the devices and computers are the bottleneck, routing can be improved with faster devices or a faster routing protocol. Static routing is accomplished faster than dynamic routing (see Chapter 5) but obviously can impair circuit performance in high-traffic situa-tions. Dynamic routing is usually used in WANs and MANs because there are many possi-ble routes through the network. BNs often have only a few routes through the network, so dynamic routing may not be too helpful, because it will delay processing and increase the network traffic because of the status reports sent through the network. Static routing will often simplify processing and improve performance.

FDDI and ATM require the translation or encapsulation of Ethernet packets before they can flow through the backbone. Translating protocols (FDDI) typically require more processing than does encapsulation (ATM), so encapsulation can improve performance if the backbone devices are the bottleneck. In either case, though, the additional processing slows the devices connecting the BN to the attached LANs. One obvious solution is to use the same protocols in the backbone and the LANs. If you have Ethernet LANs, gigabit Eth-ernet backbones can reduce processing at the connecting devices.

Most backbone devices are store-and-forward devices. One simple way to improve performance is to ensure that they have sufficient memory. If they don't, the devices will lose packets, requiring them to be retransmitted.

Improving Circuit Capacity

If network circuits are the bottlenecks, there are several options. One is to increase overall circuit capacity (e.g., by going from 100Base-T Ethernet to gigabit Ethernet). Another option is to add additional circuits alongside heavily used ones so that there are several cir-cuits between some devices (as in Figure 7-11). Circuit capacity can also be improved by replacing a shared-circuit backbone with a switched-circuit backbone (e.g., by replacing Ethernet with switched Ethernet.

In many cases, the bottleneck on the circuit is only in one place—the circuit to the server. A switched network that provides the usual 10 Mbps to the client computers but a faster circuit to the server (e.g., 100Base-T) can improve performance at very little cost. All one needs to do is replace the Ethernet hub with a switch and change one NIC in the server.

Reducing Network Demand

One way to reduce network demand is to restrict applications that use a lot of network capacity, such as desktop videoconferencing, medical imaging, or multimedia. In practice, it is often difficult to restrict users. Nonetheless, finding one application that places a large demand on the network and moving it can have a significant impact.

Much network demand is caused by broadcast messages, such as those used to find data link layer addresses (see Chapter 5). Some application software packages and NOS modules written for use on LANs also use broadcast messages to send status information to all computers on the LAN. For example, broadcast messages inform users when printers are out of paper, or when the server is running low on disk space. When used in a LAN, such messages place little extra demand on the network because every computer on the LAN gets every message.

This is not the case for switched LANs or LANs connected to BNs, because messages do not normally flow to all computers. Broadcast messages can consume a fair amount of network capacity. In many cases, broadcast messages have little value outside their individual LAN. Therefore, some switches, bridges, and routers can be set to filter broadcast messages so that they do not go to other networks. This reduces network traffic and improves performance.

THE BEST PRACTICE BACKBONE

The past few years have seen radical changes in the backbone, both in terms of new technologies (e.g., ATM, gigabit Ethernet) and in architectures (e.g., collapsed backbones, VLANs). In the early 1990s, the most common best practice backbone architecture was the routed backbone, connected to a series of 10Base-T hubs in the LAN. Bridged backbones were a close second, although most organizations were even then moving away from them. For many years, experts predicted that FDDI or ATM would be the best practice backbone technology and that there was a good chance that ATM would gradually move into the LAN.

Today, the generally accepted best practice is to use Ethernet-based collapsed backbones with switched Ethernet in the LAN. With the arrival of gigabit Ethernet and its cousins (10 GbE and 40 GbE), suddenly the usefulness of ATM and FDDI with their inherently complex protocols becomes questionable. Although ATM will continue to play an important role in the WAN (as we will see in the next chapter), we believe that Ethernet will dominate the LAN and backbone.

If this is true, then there are some clear implications for the future of network design. The ideal network design is likely to be a mix of layer-2 and layer-3 Ethernet switches.[3] Figure 7-20 shows one likely design. The access layer (i.e., the LANs) uses 10/100 layer-2

---

[3] We thank our friends at Cisco Systems, Inc., the market leader in LANs and backbone networking, for helping us think about this.

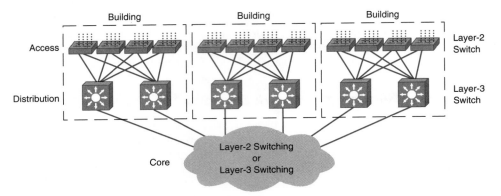

FIGURE 7-20   A best practice network design.

Ethernet switches running on Cat 5e or Cat 6 twisted-pair cables to provide flexibility for today's common 10Base-T and tomorrow's 100Base-T, with category 6 enabling a move to 1000Base-T. The distribution layer uses layer-3 Ethernet switches that use 100Base-T or, more likely, 1000Base-T (over fiber or category 6 or 7) to connect to the access layer. To provide good reliability, some organizations may provide redundant switches, so if one fails, the backbone continues to operate. The core layer uses layer-3 Ethernet switches running 10 GbE or 40 GbE over fiber.

SUMMARY

Network Components   There are two basic components to a BN: the network cable and the hardware devices that connect other networks to the backbone. The cable is essentially the same as the used in LANs, except that it is usually fiber optic to provide higher data rates. The hardware devices include bridges, routers, gateways, and switches. Bridges connect two LAN segments that use the same data link and network protocol and forward only those messages that need to go to other network segment. Routers connect two or more LANs that use the same or different data link protocols but employ the same network protocol. Gateways connect two or more LANs that use the same or different data link and network protocols (usually different). Layer-2 switches are similar to bridges, whereas layer-3 switches are similar to routers.

Backbone Architectures   Network designers often think about three distinct technology layers when designing backbones. The access layer is the LAN, the distribution layer connects the LANs together, and the core layer connects the distribution-layer BNs together. The distribution layer is usually a backbone within a building, whereas the core layer often connects buildings and is sometimes called the campus network. A routed backbone uses a set of routers or layer-3 switches to connect LANs together and moves messages using layer-3 addresses. A bridged backbone uses set of bridges or layer-2 switches to connect LANs together and moves messages using layer-2 addresses. A collapsed backbone uses one device, usually a layer-2 or layer-3 switch to connect the LANs. A VLAN uses layer-2 or layer-3 switches to build logical or virtual LANs that enable the network manager to assign capacity separate from physical location.

FDDI   FDDI is a token-passing ring network that operates at 100 Mbps over a fiber-optic cable arranged in two rings that can continue to operate if they are cut.

ATM ATM is a packet-switched technology originally designed for use in WANs. ATM uses 53-byte fixed-length packets with no error control of full-duplex 155 Mbps or 622 Mbps point-to-point circuits. ATM enables QoS and uses virtual circuits rather than permanently assigning addresses to devices. To use ATM in a BN that connects LANs, some conversion must be done on the LAN packets to enable them to flow over the ATM backbone. With LANE, an ATM edge switch encapsulates the Ethernet (or token ring) packet, leaving the existing data link layer packet intact, and transmits it on the basis of data link layer addresses. MPOA is an alternative that can use network-layer addresses for transmission.

Selecting a Backbone Selecting a BN for an organization is difficult because new products and completely new technologies are constantly being introduced. There are several factors to consider. Throughput is the amount of user data the network can transmit. In general, switched networks are faster than shared networks. There have been few throughput differences found among the high-speed multipoint technologies, although for heavy-traffic networks with large packet sizes, FDDI outperformed 100Base-T. Among switched networks, the best determinant of throughput is the data transmission rate, although full duplex may help on heavily used circuits or circuits to servers. New technologies (e.g., switched networks) are often harder to manage, but switched networks often are more flexible. It appears that switched networks are the way of the future. The type of application may also influence the choice of network: ATM is well suited to voice and video, although new QoS capabilities in TCP/IP and gigabit Ethernet may reduce ATM's advantage.

KEY TERMS

access layer
application-based
   VLAN
asynchronous transfer
   mode (ATM)
backbone network (BN)
bridge
bridged backbone
brouter
campus network
chassis switch
classes of service
collapsed backbone
copper distributed data
   interface (CDDI)

core layer
distribution layer
dual-attachment station
   (DAS)
edge switch
encapsulation
enterprise network
fiber distributed data
   interface (FDDI)
gateways
IEEE 802.1q
IP-based VLAN
LAN Emulation
   (LANE)
layer-1 VLAN

layer-2 switch
layer-2 VLAN
layer-3 switch
layer-3 VLAN
layer-4 VLAN
MAC-based VLAN
main distribution facility
   (MDF)
module
multiprotocol over ATM
   (MPOA)
multiprotocol router
multiprotocol switch
multiswitch VLAN
patch cables

permanent virtual circuit
   (PVC)
policy-based VLAN
port-based VLAN
rack
routed backbone
router
single-attachment sta-
   tion (SAS)
single-switch VLAN
switched virtual circuit
   (SVC)
virtual channel (VC)
virtual circuit
virtual LAN (VLAN)

QUESTIONS

1. Compare and contrast bridges, routers, and gateways.
2. How does a bridge differ from a layer-2 switch?
3. How does a router differ from a layer-3 switch?
4. Under what circumstances would you want to use a brouter?
5. Under what circumstances would you want to use a multiprotocol router?
6. What is an enterprise network?
7. What are the three technology layers important in backbone design?

8. Explain how routed backbones work.
9. Explain how bridged backbones work.
10. Explain how collapsed backbones work.
11. What are the key advantages and disadvantages among bridged, routed, and collapsed backbones?
12. Compare and contrast rack-based and chassis-switch–based collapsed backbones.
13. What is a module, and why are modules important?
14. Explain how single-switch VLANs work.
15. Explain how multiswitch VLANs work.
16. Explain the differences among layer-1, -2, -3, and -4 VLANs.
17. What is IEEE 802.lq?
18. Which backbone architecture is the most flexible? Why?
19. How does FDDI operate?
20. What is the difference between a DAS and an SAS?
21. Discuss four important characteristics of ATM.
22. How does ATM perform addressing?
23. How can ATM be used to link Ethernet LANs?
24. What is encapsulation, and how does it differ from translation?
25. How can you improve the performance of a BN?
26. Why are broadcast messages important?
27. Which has greater throughput: FDDI or switched 100Base-T Ethernet?
28. How does a FDDI LAN carry an Ethernet packet?
29. How does ATM LANE carry an Ethernet packet?
30. What are the preferred technologies used in the three technology layers in backbone design?
31. What are the preferred architectures used in the three technology layers in backbone design?
32. What do you think is the future of ATM and FDDI?
33. Some experts are predicting that Ethernet will move into the WAN. What do you think?

EXERCISES

7-1 Survey the BNs used in your organization. Do they use Ethernet, ATM, or some other technology? Why?

7-2 Document one BN in detail. What devices are attached, what cabling is used, and what is the topology? What networks does the backbone connect?

7-3 You have been hired by a small company to install a backbone to connect four 10base-T Ethernet LANs (each using one 24-port hub) and to provide a connection to the Internet. Develop a simple backbone and determine the total cost (i.e., select the backbone technology and price it, select the cabling and price it, select the devices and price them, and so on. Prices are available at www.datacommwarehouse.com, but use any source that is convenient. For simplicity, assume that category 5, category 5e, category 6, and fiber-optic cable have a fixed cost per circuit to buy and install, regardless of distance, of $80, $100, $250, and $400, respectively.

MINI-CASES

I. Pat's Engineering Works

Pat's Engineering Works is a small company that specializes in complex engineering consulting projects. The projects typically involve one or two engineers who do data-intensive analyses for companies. Because so much data are needed, the projects are stored on the company's high-capacity server but moved to the engineers' workstations for analysis. The company is moving into new offices and wants you to design its network. It has a staff of 8 engineers (which is expected to grow to 12 over the next 5 years), plus another 8 management and clerical employees who also need network connections but whose needs are less intense. Design the network. Be sure to include a diagram.

II. Hospitality Hotel

Hospitality Hotel is a luxury hotel that whose guests are mostly business travelers. To improve its quality of service, it has decided to install network connections in each of its 600 guest rooms and 12 conference meeting rooms.

Last year, the hotel upgraded its own internal networks to switched 10Base-T, but it wants to keep the public network (i.e., the guest and meeting rooms) separate from its private network (i.e., its own computer systems). Your task is to design the network for the public network; do not worry about how to connect the two networks together (that's the job of another consultant). Design the public network. Be sure to include a diagram.

CASE STUDY

NEXT-DAY AIR SERVICE

There are now four new LANs at NDAS's Tampa headquarters, and President Coone says he is getting requests for new LANs "from all over the place, even from Peter Browne of the Fleet Maintenance Division!" You notice that he seems to be a bit upset over this situation. He says that Les Coone, now manager of the Information Service/Data Processing Division (no longer acting manager) has complained that things are "getting out of control." Instead of going through a planned, orderly movement to an integrated NDAS data communications network, everyone wants to move their departments to new LANs, all at once.

It is clear that President Coone is worried. Although he did not say it, he implied that things are getting out of control in your area—data communications. And it was, in a way, your fault for encouraging many departments to ask President Coone for new LANs.

You talk to Bob Jones about the problem. He says that you don't want to get President Coone upset with you. He suggests that the best thing to do is to show President Coone that the system will "talk together" and that you have everything under control. You resolve to do this immediately, and you set up an appointment with President Coone.

Exercises

1. Figure 7-21 shows a facility map of the NDAS headquarters. Assume that there are LANs in four department offices (Data Processing, Accounts Payable, Information Services, and Agent Operations) and at Fleet Maintenance and Dispatch in the secondary building. What type of BN do you recommend for NDAS headquarters? Be prepared to justify your recommendation. Remember to consider the expected growth of the company.

2. Price the network you have designed. Prices are available at http://www.datacommwarehouse.com, but use any source that is convenient. For simplicity, assume that Cat 5, Cat 5e, Cat 6, and fiber-optic cable have a fixed cost per circuit to buy and install, regardless of distance, of $80, $100, $250, and $400, respectively.

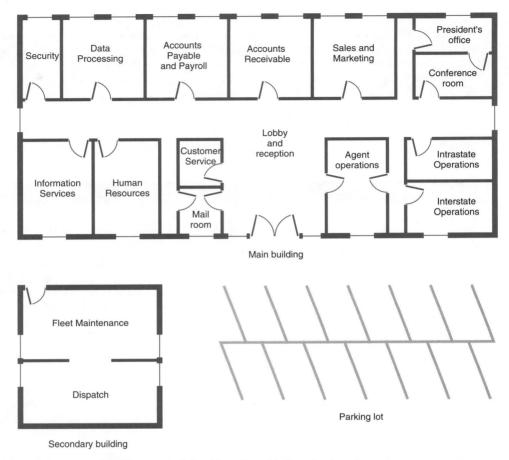

FIGURE 7-21 Facility map of the Next-Day Air Service headquarters.

CHAPTER 8

METROPOLITAN AND WIDE AREA NETWORKS

MOST ORGANIZATIONS do not build their own metropolitan or long-distance communication circuits, preferring instead to lease them from common carriers or to use the Internet. Therefore, this chapter focuses on the MAN/WAN architectures and telecommunications services offered by common carriers for use in MANs and WANs, not the underlying technology that the carriers use to provide them. We discuss the four principal types of MAN and WAN services that are available: circuit-switched services, dedicated-circuit services, packet-switched services, and virtual private network (VPN) services. We conclude by discussing how to improve MAN and WAN performance and how to select services to build MANs and WANs.

OBJECTIVES

- Understand circuit-switched services and architectures
- Understand dedicated-circuit services and architectures
- Understand packet-switched services and architectures
- Understand VPN services and architectures
- Be familiar with how to improve MAN and WAN performance

CHAPTER OUTLINE

INTRODUCTION

CIRCUIT-SWITCHED NETWORKS

    Basic Architecture

    Plain Old Telephone Service

    ISDN

INTRODUCTION

Metropolitan area networks (MANs) typically span between 3 and 30 miles and connect BNs and LANs. MANs also provide dial-in and dial-out capability to LANs, BNs, and mainframes and access to the Internet. WANs connect BNs and MANs across longer distances, often hundreds or thousands of miles.

The communication media used in MANs and WANs were described in Chapter 3 (e.g., twisted-pair, wirecoaxial cable, fiber optics, microwave, satellite, infrared). Although some organizations build their own MANs and WANs using these media, most do not. Most organizations cannot afford to lay long stretches of cable, build microwave towers, or lease satellites. Instead, most rent or lease circuits from *common carriers* such as AT&T, Bell Canada, Ameritech, BellSouth, and so on. As a customer, you do not lease physical cables per se; you simply lease circuits that provide certain transmission characteristics. The carrier decides whether it will use twisted-pair, coaxial, fiber optics, or other media for its circuits.

In this chapter, we examine the MAN and WAN architectures and technologies from the viewpoint of a network manager, rather than that of a common carrier. We focus less on internal operations and how the specific technologies work, and more on how these services are offered to network managers and how they can be used to build networks, because most network managers are less concerned with how the services work and most concerned with how they can use them effectively.

Likewise, we will focus on MAN and WAN services in North America, because the majority of our readers are in North America. Although there are many similarities in the way data communications networks and services have evolved in different countries, there also are many differences. Most countries have a federal government agency that regulates data and voice communications. In the United States, the agency is the *Federal Communications Commission (FCC);* in Canada it is the *Canadian Radio-Television and Telecommunications Commission (CRTC).* Each state or province also has its own *public utilities commission (PUC)* to regulate communications within its borders.

A *common carrier* is a private company that sells or leases communication services and facilities to the public. Common carriers are profit-oriented, and their primary products are services for voice and data transmissions, both over traditional wired circuits as well as cellular services. Common carriers often supply a broad range of computer-based services, such as the manufacturing and marketing of specialized communication hardware and software. A common carriers that provides local telephone services (e.g., BellSouth) is commonly called a *local exchange carrier (LEC),* whereas one that provides long-distance services (e.g., AT&T) is commonly called an *interexchange carrier (IXC).* As the LECs move into the long-distance market and IXCs move into the local telephone market, this distinction may disappear.

CIRCUIT-SWITCHED NETWORKS

Circuit-switched networks are the oldest and simplest approach to MAN and WAN circuits. These services operate over the *public switched telephone network (PSTN);* that is, the telephone networks operated by the common carriers such as AT&T, Ameritech, Bell-South, and so on. When you telephone someone, you are using the PSTN. The first service we will discuss is the standard dial-up service you use when you call an ISP with a modem—but first we need to discuss the basic architecture shared by all circuit-switched services.

Basic Architecture

Circuit-switched services use a *cloud architecture.* The users lease connection points (e.g., telephone lines) into the common carrier's network, which is called the *cloud*[1] (Figure 8-1). A person (or computer) dials the telephone number of the destination computer and establishes a temporary circuit between the two computers. The computers exchange data, and when the task is complete, the circuit is disconnected (e.g., by hanging up the phone).

---

[1] It is called a cloud because what happens inside the common carrier's network is hidden from view. Network managers really don't care how the common carrier switches the circuit inside their network, just as long as the network is fast, accurate, and reliable.

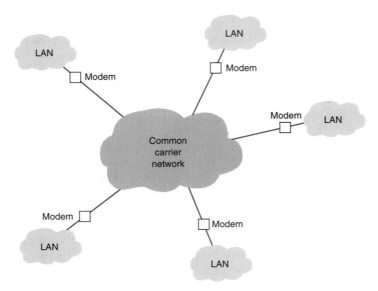

FIGURE 8-1 Dialed circuit services. LAN = local area network.

This architecture is very flexible. Circuits can be established as needed between any computers attached to the cloud at any point. However, data can be transmitted only while a circuit is established, and only to the one location it connects to. If a computer needs to send data to a number of other locations, a series of temporary circuits must be established with and later disconnected from each location, one after another. In general, only a limited number of circuits can be established from or to any one location at a time (e.g., each location has only so many telephone lines).

Cloud-based designs are simpler for the organization because they move the burden of network design and management inside the cloud from the organization to the common carrier. Network managers do not need to worry about the amount of traffic sent between each computer; they just need to specify the amount of traffic entering and leaving each computer and buy the appropriate size and number of connections into the PSTN. However, this comes at a price. Cloud-based designs can be more expensive because users must pay for each connection into the network and pay on the basis of the amount of time each circuit is used. Cloud-based designs are often used when network managers are uncertain of network demand, particularly in a new or rapidly growing network.

There are two basic types of switched-circuit services in use today: POTS and ISDN.

Plain Old Telephone Service

Plain old telephone service (POTS) is the name for the common dial-up services you've probably used at one time or another. To use POTS, you need to lease a circuit into the network (i.e., a telephone line) and install special equipment (i.e., a modem) to enable your computer to talk to the PSTN. To transfer data to and from another computer on the network, you instruct your modem dial the other computer's telephone. Once the modem in you computer connects to the modem at the other end, you can transfer data back and forth. When you are done, you hang up and can then call another computer if you wish. Today, POTS is most commonly used to connect to the Internet, but you can also use it to communicate directly with a private non-Internet server.

POTS may use different circuit paths between the two computers each time a number is dialed. Some circuits have more noise and distortion than others, so the quality and maximum data transmission rate can vary.

Charges for direct dialing are based on the distance between the two telephones (in miles) and the number of minutes the connection is used. Data communications users pay the same rate as voice communications users. In general, most local calls are free, but this depends on the type of local telephone service you have purchased. Long-distance calls are charged at the rate for which you have contracted with your long-distance carrier.

Wide area telephone services (WATSs) are special-rate services that allows calls for both voice communications and data transmission to be purchased in large quantities. For example, you might purchase 100 hours of usage per month for one fixed rate and be charged so many dollars per hour thereafter.

ISDN

The first generation of *integrated services digital network (ISDN)* combines voice, video, and data over the same digital circuit. Because there is a newer version of ISDN, the original version is occasionally called *narrowband ISDN,* but we will just use the term *ISDN.* ISDN is widely available from a number of common carriers in North America.

To use ISDN, users first need to lease connection points in the PSTN, which are telephone lines just like POTS. Next, they must have special equipment to connect their computers (or networks) into the PSTN. Users need an ISDN *network terminator* (NT-1 or NT-2) that functions much like a hub, and a NIC (called a *terminal adapter* [TA] or even an "ISDN modem") in all computers attached to the NT-1/NT-2. In most cases, the ISDN service appears identical to the regular dialed telephone service, with the exception that usually (but not always), each device attached to the NT-1/NT-2 needs a unique *service profile identifier (SPID)* to identify it. To connect to another computer using ISDN, you dial that computer's telephone number using the ISDN NIC in much the same way as you would with a modem on a regular telephone line.

ISDN has long been more of a concept than a reliable service in North America. It has been available since the late 1970s, although it has not been widely adopted. Its largest problems are a lack of standards and a lack of interest from common carriers. Acceptance of ISDN has also been slowed because equipment vendors and common carriers have conflicting interpretations of the ISDN standards, and because the data rates it offers are low compared with newer services. Skeptics claim that *ISDN* actually stands for "*I s*till *d*on't know," "*I s*till *d*on't *N*eed it" or "*It s*till *d*oes *n*othing." ISDN offers two types of "normal" or narrowband service, plus one emerging higherspeed broadband service.

Basic Rate Interface *Basic rate interface (BRI)* (sometimes called basic access service or *2B+D*) provides a communication circuit with two 64-Kbps digital transmission channels (called B channels) and one 16-Kbps control signaling channel (called a D channel). The two B channels handle digitized voice, data, and image transmissions, providing a total of 128 Kbps. The D channel is used for control messages such as acknowledgments, call setup and termination, and other functions such as automatic number identification. Some common carriers sell just one single 64-Kbps channel to those customers needing less capacity than full BRI.

One advantage of BRI is that it can be installed in many existing telephone locations without adding any new cable. If the connection from the customer's telephone to the common carrier's end office is less than 3.5 miles, the ISDN line can use the existing two pairs of twisted-pair wires. The only changes are the end connections at the customer's location and at the carrier's end office. If the connection is longer than 3.5 miles, then new cable will have to be laid.

Primary Rate Interface   *Primary rate interface (PRI)* (also called primary access service or *23B+D*) is typically offered to commercial customers. It consists of 23 64-Kbps B channels plus 1 64-Kbps D channel. PRI has almost same capacity as a T1 circuit (1.544 Mbps). In Europe, PRI is defined as 30 B channels plus 1 D channel, making interconnection between America and Europe difficult.

Broadband Integrated Services Digital Network   *Broadband ISDN (B-ISDN)* is emerging type of ISDN that is very different than narrowband ISDN—so different, in fact, that it really is not ISDN. It is a circuit-switched service, but B-ISDN uses ATM to move data from one end point to the other. B-ISDN is backward-compatible with narrowband ISDN, which means it can accept narrowband BRI and PRI transmissions. B-ISDN currently defines three services. The first is a full-duplex channel that operates at 155.52 Mbps; the second provides a full-duplex channel that operates at 622.08 Mbps; and the third is an asymmetrical service with two simplex channels, one from the subscriber at 155.52 Mbps and one from the host to the subscriber at 622.08 Mbps. The first two services are intended for normal bidirectional information exchange. The third (asymmetrical) service is intended to be used for information distribution services such as digital broadcast television.

DEDICATED CIRCUIT NETWORKS

There are three main problems with POTS and ISDN circuit-switched networks. First, each connection goes through the regular telephone network on a different circuit. These circuits may vary in quality, meaning that although one connection will be fairly clear, the next call may be noisy. Second, the data transmission rates on these circuits are usually low. Generally speaking, transmission rates range from 28.8 Kbps to 56 Kbps for dialed POTS circuits to 128 Kbps to 1.5 Mbps for ISDN circuits. Third, you usually pay per use for circuit-switched services. One alternative is to establish a dedicated circuit network, in which the user leases circuits from the common carrier for his or her exclusive use 24 hours per day, 7 days per week.

Basic Architecture

With a dedicated-circuit network, you lease circuits from common carriers. All connections are point to point, from one building in one city to another building in the same or a different city. The carrier installs the circuit connections at the two end points of the circuit and makes the connection between them. The circuits still run through the common carrier's cloud, but the network behaves as if you have your own physical circuits running from one point to another (Figure 8-2).

Once again, the user leases the desired circuit from the common carrier (specifying the physical end points of the circuit) and installs the equipment needed to connect computers and devices (e.g., routers or switches) to the circuit. This equipment may be multiplexers or a *channel service unit* (CSU) and/or a *data service unit (DSU);* a CSU/DSU is the WAN equivalent of a NIC in a LAN.

Unlike circuit-switched services that typically use a pay-per-use model, dedicated circuits are billed at a flat fee per month and the user has unlimited use of the circuit. Once you sign a contract, making changes can be expensive because it means rewiring the buildings and signing a new contract with the carrier. Therefore, dedicated circuits require more care in network design than do switched circuits, both in terms of locations and the amount of capacity you purchase.

There are three basic architectures used in dedicated-circuit networks: ring, star, and mesh. In practice, most networks use a combination of architectures. For example, a *distributed star architecture* has a series of star networks that are connected by a mesh or ring architecture.

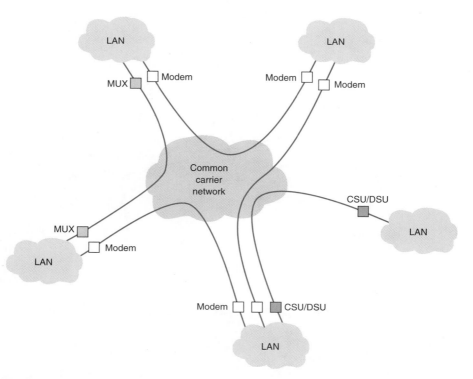

FIGURE 8-2 Dedicated circuit services. CSU = channel service unit; DSU = data service unit; MUX = multiplexer.

Ring Architecture A *ring architecture* connects all computers in a closed loop, with each computer linked to the next (Figure 8-3). The circuits are full-duplex or half-duplex circuits, meaning that messages flow in both directions around the ring. Computers in the ring may send data in one direction or the other, depending on which direction is the shortest to the destination.

One disadvantage of the ring topology is that messages can take a long time to travel from the sender to the receiver. Messages usually travel through several computers and circuits before they reach their destination, so traffic delays can build up very quickly if one circuit or computer becomes overloaded. A long delay in any one circuit or computer can have significant impacts on the entire network.

In general, the failure of any one circuit or computer in a ring network means that the network can continue to function. Messages are simply routed away from the failed circuit or computer in the opposite direction around the ring. However, if the network is operating close to its capacity, this will dramatically increase transmission times because the traffic on the remaining part of the network may come close to doubling (because all traffic originally routed in the direction of the failed link will now be routed in the opposite direction through the longest way around the ring).

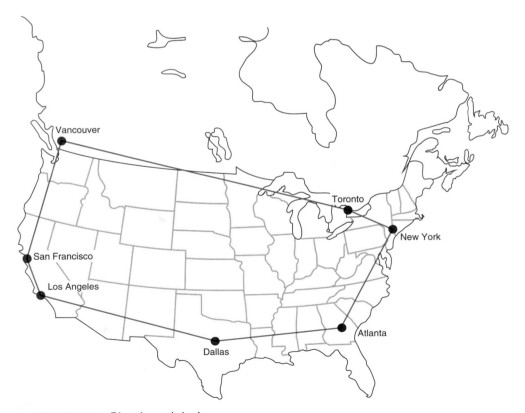

FIGURE 8-3 Ring-based design.

Star Architecture   A *star architecture* connects all computers to one central computer that routes messages to the appropriate computer (Figure 8-4). The star topology is easy manage because the central computer receives and routes all messages in the network. It can also be faster than the ring network because any message needs to travel through at most two circuits to reach its destination, whereas messages may have to travel through far more circuits in the ring network. However, the star topology is the most susceptible to traffic problems because the central computer must process all messages on the network. The central computer must have sufficient capacity to handle traffic peaks or it may become overloaded and network performance will suffer.

In general, the failure of any one circuit or computer affects only the one computer on that circuit. However, if the central computer fails, the entire network fails because all traffic must flow through it. It is critical that the central computer be extremely reliable.

Mesh Architecture   In a *full-mesh architecture,* every computer is connected to every other computer (Figure 8-5a). Full-mesh networks are seldom used because of the extremely high cost. *Partial-mesh architecture,* in which many, but not all, computers are connected, is far more common (Figure 8-5b). Most WANs use partial-mesh topologies. Partial-mesh architectures are usually just called *mesh architectures* for short.

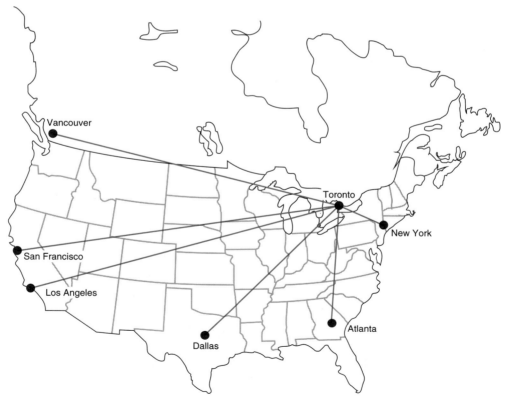

FIGURE 8-4   Star-based design.

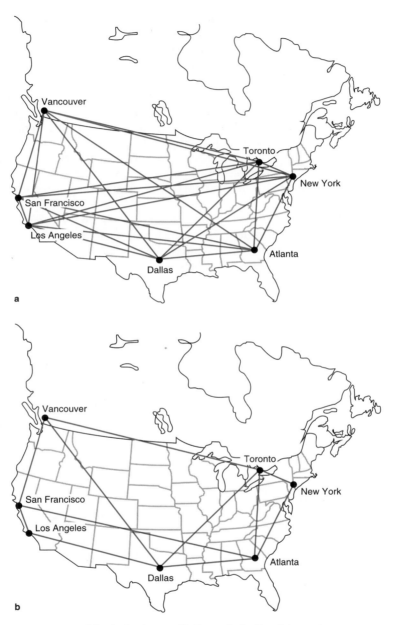

FIGURE 8-5 Mesh design: **a.** Full mesh. **b.** Partial mesh.

The effects of the loss of computers or circuits in a mesh network depend entirely on the circuits available in the network. If there are many possible routes through the network, the loss of one or even several circuits or computers may have few effects beyond the specific computers involved. However, if there are only few circuits in the network, the loss of even one circuit or computer may seriously impair the network.

In general, mesh networks combine the performance benefits of both ring networks and star networks. Mesh networks usually provide relative short routes through the network (compared with ring networks) and provide many possible routes through the network to prevent any one circuit or computer from becoming overloaded when there is a lot of traffic (compared with star networks, in which all traffic goes through one computer).

The drawback is that mesh networks use decentralized routing so that each computer in the network performs its own routing. This requires more processing by each computer in the network than in star or ring networks. Also, the transmission of network status information (e.g., how busy each computer is) "wastes" network capacity.

There are two types of dedicated-circuit services in common use today: T carrier services and synchronous optical network (SONET) services. Both T carrier and SONET have their own data link protocols, which are beyond the focus of this chapter.

T Carrier Services

T carrier circuits are the most commonly used form of dedicated circuit services in North America today. As with all dedicated-circuit services, you lease a dedicated circuit from one building in one city to another building in the same or different city. Costs are fixed amount per month, regardless of how much or how little traffic flows through the circuit. There are several types of T carrier circuits (Figure 8-6).

A *T1 circuit* (also called a DS1 circuit) provides a data rate of 1.544 Mbps. T1 circuits can be used to transmit data but often are used to transmit both data and voice. In this case, inverse TDM provides 24 64-Kbps circuits.[2] Digitized voice using PCM requires a 64-Kbps circuit (see Chapter 3), so a T1 circuit enables 24 simultaneous voice channels. Most common carriers make extensive use of PCM internally and transmit most of their voice telephone calls in digital format using PCM, so you will see many digital services offering combinations of the standard PCM 64-Kbps circuit.

A *T2 circuit,* which transmits data at a rate of 6.312 Mbps, is an inverse multiplexed bundle of four T1 circuits. A *T3 circuit* allows transmission at a rate of 44.736 Mbps, although most articles refer to this rate as 45 megabits per second. This is equal to the capacity of 28 T1 circuits. T3 circuits are becoming popular as the transmission medium

T Carrier Designation	DS Designation	Speed
FT1	DS0	64 Kbps
T1	DS1	1.544 Mbps
T2	DS2	6.312 Mbps
T3	DS3	44.736 Mbps
T4	DS4	274.176 Mbps

FIGURE 8-6   T carrier services.

---

[2] If you multiply 24 circuits by 64 Kbps per circuit, you will get 1.536 Mbps, not 1.544 Mbps. This is because some of the 1.544-Mbps circuit capacity is used by the common carrier for control signals used to frame the data (i.e., mark the start and stop of packets).

SONET Designation	SDH Designation	Speed
OC-1		51.84 Mbps
OC-3	STM-1	155.52 Mbps
OC-9	STM-3	466.56 Mbps
OC-12	STM-4	622.08 Mbps
OC-18	STM-6	933.12 Mbps
OC-24	STM-8	1.244 Gbps
OC-36	STM-12	1.866 Gbps
OC-48	STM-16	2.488 Gbps
OC-192	STM-64	9.953 Gbps

FIGURE 8-7   SONET (synchronous optical network) and SDH (synchronous digital hierarchy) services. OC = optical carrier (level); STM = synchronous transport module.

for corporate MANs and WANs because of their higher data rates. At low speed, these T3 circuits can be used as 672 different 64-Kbps channels or voice channels. A *T4 circuit* transmits at 274.176 Mbps, which is equal to the capacity of 178 T1 circuits.

Fractional T1 sometimes called *FT1,* offers portions of a 1.544-Mbps T1 circuit for a fraction of its full cost. Many (but not all) common carriers offer sets of 64 Kbps DS-0 channels as FT1 circuits. The most common FT1 services provide 128 Kbps, 256 Kbps, 384 Kbps, 512 Kbps, and 768 Kbps.

Synchronous Optical Network

The *synchronous optical network (SONET)* is the American standard (ANSI) for high-speed dedicated-circuit services. The ITU-T recently standardized an almost identical service that easily interconnects with SONET, under the name *synchronous digital hierarchy (SDH).*

SONET transmission speeds begin at the OC-1 level (optical carrier level 1) of 51.84 Mbps. Each succeeding rate in the SONET fiber hierarchy is defined as a multiple of OC-1, with SONET data rates defined as high as OC-192, or about 10 Gbps. Figure 8-7 presents the other major SONET and SDH services. Each level above OC-1 is created by IMUX. Notice that the slowest SONET transmission rate (OC-1) of 51.84 Mbps is slightly faster than the T3 rate of 44.376 Mbps. Although not yet available in all locations, SONET/SDH is available in most large cities worldwide.

PACKET-SWITCHED NETWORKS

Packet-switched networks are quite different from the two types of networks discussed previously. For both circuit-switched and dedicated-circuit networks, a circuit was established between the two communicating computers. This circuit provided a guaranteed data transmission capability that was available for use by only those two computers.

MANAGEMENT FOCUS *8-1*

CAREGROUP'S DEDICATED CIRCUIT NETWORK

CareGroup Healthcare System operates six hospitals in the Boston area and uses a metropolitan area network (MAN) and wide area network to connect them together to share clinical data (Figure 8-8). The three major hospitals have relatively high data needs and therefore are connected to one another and the main data center via a MAN that uses a set of SONET OC-1 circuits in a ring architecture.

The other three hospitals, with lower data needs, are connected to the data center via a set of T3 circuits in a star architecture. The data center also has a T3 connection into the Internet to enable its 3,000 or so doctors to access clinical data from their private practice offices or from home.

SOURCE: "Using the Web to Extend Patient Care," *Network World*, May 29, 2000.

For example, if computer A is to transmit data using an ISDN BRI connection to computer B, the connection at both A and B must be available. Once in use for this transmission, it is assigned solely to that transmission. No other transmission is possible until the circuit is closed. So, for example, if computer C attempts to reach computer B, it will have to wait until the circuit is closed. In contrast, packet-switched services enable multiple connections to exist simultaneously between computers over the same physical circuit, just like LANs and BNs.

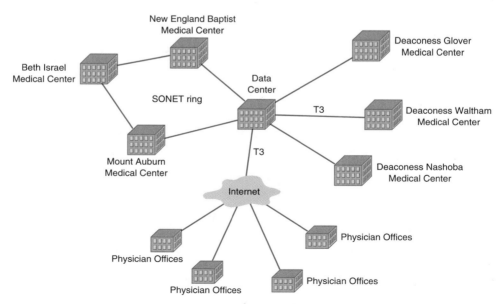

FIGURE 8-8 CareGroup's metropolitan and wide area networks. SONET = synchronous optical network.

Basic Architecture

With packet-switched services, the user again buys a connection into the common carrier cloud (Figure 8-9). The user pays a fixed fee for the connection into the network (depending on the type and capacity of the service) and is charged for the number of packets transmitted.

The user's connection into the network is a *packet assembly/disassembly device (PAD)*, which can be owned and operated by the customer or by the common carrier. The PAD converts the sender's data into the network layer and data link layer packets used by the packet network and sends them through the packet-switched network. At the other end, another PAD reassembles the packets back into the network layer and data link layer protocols expected by the destination and delivers it to the appropriate computer. The PAD also compensates for differences in transmission speed between sender and receiver; for example, the circuit at the sender might be 1.5 Mbps, whereas the receiver only has a 64-Kbps circuit.

Packet-switched networks enable packets from separate messages with different destinations to be *interleaved* for transmission, unlike switched circuits and dedicated circuits. Packet switching is popular because most data communications consist of short bursts of data with intervening spaces that usually last longer than the actual burst of data. Packet switching takes advantage of this characteristic by interleaving bursts of data from many users to maximize use of the shared communication network. Figure 8-10 shows a packet-switching connection between six different cities. The little boat-shaped figures (shown on the communication circuits) represent individual packets from separate messages.

Although the packets in one data stream may mix with several other data streams during their journey, it is unlikely that packets from two different data streams will travel together during the entire length of their transmission. The two communicating computers

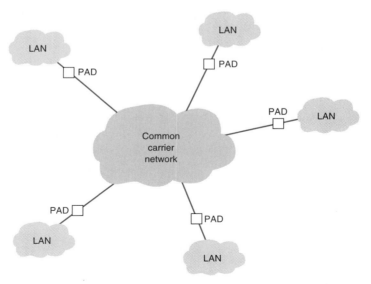

FIGURE 8-9 Packet-switched services. LAN = local area network; PAD = packet assembly/disassembly device.

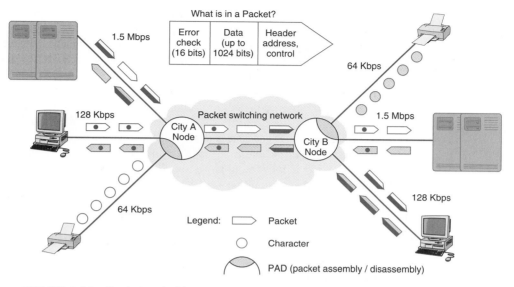

FIGURE 8-10   Packet-switching concepts.

do not need to know through which intermediate devices their data are routed, because the packet network takes care of it by either of two methods.

The first method, called *datagram,* is a connectionless service. It adds a destination address and sequence number to each packet, in addition to information about the data stream to which the packet belongs. In this case, a route is chosen for each packet as it is accepted into the packet network. Each packet may follow a different route through the network. At the destination address, the sequence number tells the network how to reassemble the packets into a continuous message. The sequence number is necessary because different routes may deliver packets at different speeds, so data packets often arrive out of sequence. Few networks today use datagrams for data transfer.

The second and more common routing method is a connection-oriented approach called a *virtual circuit.* In this case, the packet-switched network establishes what appears to be one end-to-end circuit between the sender and receiver. All packets for that transmission take the same route over the virtual circuit that has been set up for that particular transmission. The two computers believe they have a dedicated point-to-point circuit, but in fact, they do not.

Virtual circuits are usually *permanent virtual circuits (PVC),* which means that they are defined for frequent and consistent use by the network. They do not change unless the network manager changes the network. Some common carriers also permit the use of *switched virtual circuits (SVC),* although this is not usual. Changing PVCs is done using software, but common carriers usually charge each time a PVC is established or removed. It often takes days or weeks to create or take down PVCs, although this is mostly due to poor management by common carriers, rather than due to technology issues, so this may change.

Because most network managers build packet-switched networks using PVCs, *most packet-switched networks behave like dedicated-circuit networks.* At first glance, the basic architecture in Figure 8-9 looks very similar to the cloud mesh of switched-circuit services, and in fact, they are very similar, because data can move from any computer attached to the cloud to any other on the cloud. However, because virtually all data-intensive networks use PVCs, this means that the network is actually built using virtual circuits that are the software equivalent of the hardware-based dedicated circuits.

Most common carriers permit users to specify two different types of data rates that are negotiated per connection and for each PVC as it is established. The *committed information rate (CIR)* is the data rate the PVC must guarantee to transmit. If the network accepts the connection, it guarantees to provide that level of service. Most connections also specify a *maximum allowable rate (MAR),* which is the maximum rate that the network will attempt to provide, over and above the CIR. The circuit will attempt to transmit all packets up to the MAR, but all packets that exceed the CIR are marked as *discard eligible (DE).* If the network becomes overloaded, DE packets are discarded. So although users can transmit more data than the CIR, they do so at a risk of lost packets and the need to retransmit them.

Packet-switched services are often provided by different common carriers than the one from which organizations get their usual telephone and data services. Therefore, organizations often lease a dedicated circuit (e.g., T1) from their offices to the packet-switched network *point of presence* (POP). The POP is the location at which the packet-switched network (or any common carrier network, for that matter) connects into the local telephone exchange.

There are five types of packet switched services: X.25, ATM, frame relay, switched multimegabit data service (SMDS) and Ethernet/IP packet networks.

X.25

The oldest packet switched service is *X.25,* a standard developed by ITU-T. X.25 offers datagram, SVC, and PVC services. As discussed in Chapter 5, X.25 uses the LAP-B data link layer protocol and the PLP network-layer protocol. When packets arrive at the PAD, connecting the user's network to the packet-switched network, their data link (e.g., Ethernet) and network layer (e.g., IP) packets are removed and PLP and LAP-B are packets substituted. Packets are moved through the X.25 network in much the same way as in TCP/IP networks, with the LAP-B packet error checked and replaced at each hop in the network. When they arrive at the edge of the X.25 network, new destination protocols (e.g., Ethernet, IP) are created and the message is sent on its way. X.25 is sometimes called a *reliable packet service* because it provides complete error checking and guaranteed delivery on all packets transmitted.

Although widely used in Europe, X.25 is not widespread in North America. The primary reason is its transmission speed. For many years, the maximum speed into North American X.25 networks was 64 Kbps, but this has increased to 2.048 Mbps, which is the European standard for ISDN. However, for many users, 2.048 Mbps is still not fast enough.

Asynchronous Transfer Mode

Asynchronous transfer mode (ATM), also standardized, is a newer technology than X.25. ATM for BNs was discussed in the previous chapter. ATM for the MAN and WAN is essentially the same.

ATM is similar to X.25 in that is provides packet-switched services, but it has four distinct operating characteristics that differ from X.25. First, ATM performs encapsulation of packets, so packets are delivered unchanged through the network.

Second, ATM provides no error control in the network; error control is the responsibility of the source and destination (ATM is considered an unreliable packet service). Because the user's data link packet remains intact, it is simple for the devices at the edge of the ATM network to check the error-control information in the packet to ensure that no errors have occurred and to request transmission of damaged or lost packets. Figure 8-11 illustrates the difference in error control between X.25 networks and ATM networks. The left side shows that when a X.25 packet leaves its source A and moves through node B, to node C, to node D, and finally to destination E, each intermediate node acknowledges the packet as it passes. The right side of the figure shows how a ATM packet moves through node B, node C, node D, and on to destination E. When destination E receives the packet correctly, a single acknowledgment is sent back through the nodes to source A, as shown by the numbers *5,6,7,* and *8.* For this reason, ATM networks are called *unreliable packet services.* Some common carriers have started using the term *fast packet services* instead to refer to these services that do not provide error control— it sounds better for marketing!

Third, ATM provides extensive QoS information that enables the setting of very precise priorities among different types of transmissions: high priority for voice and video, lower priority for e-mail.

Finally, ATM is scalable; it is easy to multiplex basic ATM circuits into much faster ATM circuits. Most common carriers offer ATM circuits that provide the same data transmission rates as SONET: 51.84 Mbps, 466.56 Mbps, 622.08 Mbps, and so on up to OC-768 (39 Gbps). New versions called T1 ATM (1.544 Mbps) and T3 ATM (45 Mbps) are also available.

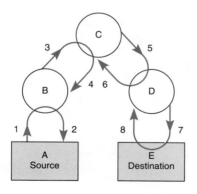
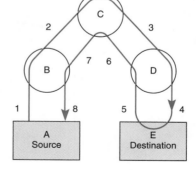

X.25 packet network   ATM packet network

FIGURE 8-11 Asynchronous transfer mode (ATM) compared with X.25 packet switching. With X.25, each node sends an acknowledgment immediately on receiving a packet. With ATM, the final destination sends an acknowledgment, making this technique faster than the X.25 technique.

MANAGEMENT FOCUS *8-2*

DIGITAL ISLAND'S GLOBAL NETWORK

Digital Island was formed in 1995 to provide network services for global e-business applications. Its clients include many large global corporations, such as Master-Card, Sega, AOL, MTV, ZDNet, and Cisco.

Digital Island's network is organized as a distributed star network (Figure 8-12). Its six major data centers (Silicon Valley, New York, London, Hong Kong, Tokyo, and Honolulu) are connected via a global ATM network using

a mesh architecture of OC-3 and higher permanent virtual circuits. Each of the data centers in turn are connected to a variety of other sites and networks, both client sites and Digital Island offices, over a mix of dedicated lines, including FT1, T1 and T3.

SOURCE: "Digital Island," Cisco Systems, Inc., www.cisco.com.

Frame Relay

Frame relay, just recently standardized, is an even newer packet-switching technology that transmits data faster than X.25 but slower than ATM; it has sometimes been called a poor man's ATM. Like ATM, frame relay performs encapsulation of packets, so packets are delivered unchanged through the network. Like ATM, it is an unreliable packet service

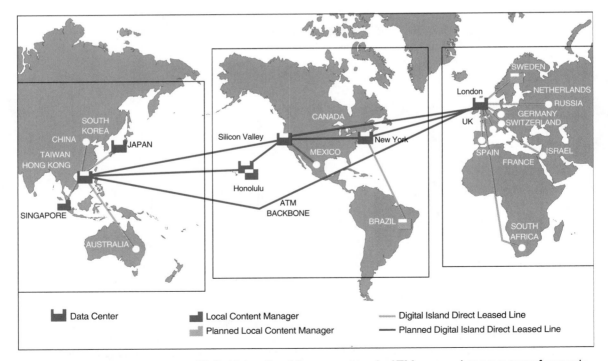

FIGURE 8-12 Digital Island's wide area network. ATM = asynchronous transfer mode.

because it does not perform error control.[3] It is up to the software at the source and destination to perform error correction and to control for lost messages.

Frame relay does not yet provide QoS capabilities, but this is under development. Different common carriers offer frame relay networks with different transmission speeds. Most offer a range of CIR speeds that include 56 Kbps, 128 Kbps, 256 Kbps, 384 Kbps, 1.544 Mbps, 2.048 Mbps, and 45 Mbps.

Switched Multimegabit Data Service

Switched multimegabit data service (SMDS) is an unreliable packet service like ATM and frame relay. Like ATM and frame relay, SMDS does not perform error checking; the user is responsible for error checking. As with ATM and frame relay, SMDS encapsulates incoming packets and

SMDS is not yet standardized. At present, most (but not all) RBOCs and some IXCs offer it. SMDS was originally aimed at MANs, particularly the interconnection of LANs. Recently, it has also made its way into the WAN environment. RBOCs offer SMDS at a variety of transmission rates, ranging from 56 Kbps up to 44.376 Mbps. There are no widely accepted standards, so transmissions rates vary by carrier. The future of SMDS is uncertain because it is not standardized and offers no clear advantages over frame relay.

Ethernet/IP Packet Networks

Although we have seen rapid increases in capacities and sharp decreases in costs in LAN and BN technologies, changes in MAN and WAN services offered by common carriers have seen only modest changes over the past decade. That changed in 2000 with the introduction of several Internet startups (e.g., Yipes) offering *Ethernet/IP packet networks.*

Most organizations today use Ethernet and IP in the LAN and BN environment. Yet, the four MAN/WAN packet network services (X.25, ATM, frame relay, and SMDS) discussed above use different layer-2 protocols. Any LAN or BN traffic, therefore, must be translated or encapsulated into a new protocol and destination addresses generated for the new protocol. This takes time, slowing network throughput. It also adds complexity, meaning that companies must add staff knowledgeable in the different MAN/WAN protocols, software, and hardware these technologies require.

Each of the four preceding packet services uses the traditional PSTN and thus are provided by the common carriers such as AT&T and BellSouth. In contrast, Ethernet/IP packet networks bypass the PSTN; companies offering Ethernet/IP packet networks have laid their own gigabit Ethernet fiber-optic networks in large cities. When an organization signs up for service, the packet network company installs new fiber-optic cables from their city-wide MAN backbone into the organization's office complex and connects it to an Ethernet switch. The organization simply plugs its network into its Ethernet switch and begins using the service. All traffic entering the packet network must be Ethernet, using IP.

---

[3] Frame relay does have a CRC-16 field in the packet layout to permit error correction, but as we write this, few common carriers have implemented error control. Frame relay networks do perform error checking but simply discard packets with errors; they do not generate NAKs and ask for retransmission.

MANAGEMENT FOCUS *8-3*

YIPES AND THE LAW

As a preeminent high-tech law firm, Fenwick & West LLP understands the importance of the Internet. For many years, Fenwick & West relied on T1 circuits and a frame relay cloud to connect its offices. However, the network was saturated; staff members often resorted to express-mailing floppies rather than using e-mail or file transfer protocol.

Staff members at Fenwick & West guessed that they needed to raise their wide area network's capacity to match that of their 10Base-T local area network (i.e., 10 Mbps). They began by looking to add more T1 lines, but at $1,500 to $2,500 per circuit (depending on office loca-

tion), adding multiple T1s into each office was very expensive. They also considered T3 circuits, but these ranged from $18,000 to $30,000 per month.

Then they contacted Yipes to learn more about Ethernet/IP services. The price, a flat $6,000 per month for 10 Mbps, was noticeably less. The simplicity of connecting into their existing Ethernet and Internet Protocol backbone was also attractive, as was the flexibility of being able to increase or decrease capacity in 1-Mbps increments.

SOURCE: "Look Beyond T1 and DS-3 to Managed Optical IP Network," *Communications News,* September 2000.

Currently, Ethernet/IP packet network services offer CIR speeds of 1 Mbps to 1 Gbps, in 1-Mbps increments at about one quarter the cost of traditional packet-switched networks. Because this is an emerging technology, we should see many changes in the next few years.

VIRTUAL PRIVATE NETWORKS

A new type of network architecture has emerged with the rise of the Internet. A *virtual private network (VPN)* provides the equivalent of a private packet-switched network over the public Internet.[4] It involves establishing a series of PVCs that run over the Internet, so that the network acts like a set of dedicated circuits over a private packet network.

Basic Architecture

With a VPN, you first lease an Internet connection at whatever access rate and access technology you choose for each location you want to connect. For example, you might lease a T1 circuit from a common carrier that runs from your office to your *Internet service provider (ISP).* You pay the common carrier for the circuit and the ISP for Internet access. Then you connect a VPN device (a specially designed router or switch) to each Internet access circuit to provide access from your networks to the VPN. The VPN devices enable you to create PVCs through the Internet that are called *tunnels* (Figure 8-13).

The VPN device at the sender takes the outgoing packet and encapsulates it with a protocol that is used to move it through the tunnel to the VPN device on the other side (see "Virtual Private Network Encapsulation" later in this chapter for a detailed description of this

---

[4] Some common carriers and third-party vendors are now providing VPN services that use their own networks rather than the Internet, but by far the majority of VPN services are Internet-based. In the interest of simplicity, we will focus on Internet-based VPN services.

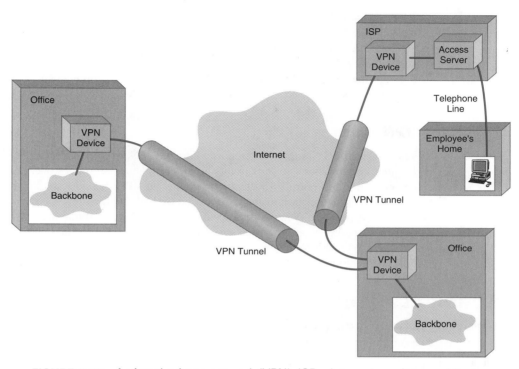

FIGURE 8-13   A virtual private network (VPN). ISP = Internet service provider.

process). The VPN device at the receiver strips off the VPN packet and delivers the packet to the destination network. The VPN is transparent to the users; it appears as though a traditional packet-switched network PVC is in use. The VPN is also transparent to the ISP and the Internet as a whole; there is a simply a stream of Internet packets moving across the Internet.

VPNs operate either at layer 2 or layer 3. A *layer-2 VPN* uses the layer 2 packet (e.g., Ethernet) to select the VPN tunnel and encapsulates the entire packet, starting with the layer-2 packet. A *layer-3 VPN* uses the layer-3 packet (e.g., IP) to select the VPN tunnel and encapsulates the entire packet, starting with the layer-3 packet; that it, it discards the incoming layer-2 packet and generates an entirely new layer-2 packet at the destination.

The primary advantages of VPNs is low cost and flexibility. Because they use the Internet to carry messages, the major cost is Internet access, which is inexpensive compared with the cost of circuit-switched services, dedicated-circuit services, and packet-switched services from a common carrier. Likewise, anywhere you can establish Internet service, you can quickly put in a VPN.

There are two important disadvantages. First, traffic on the Internet is unpredictable. Sometimes packets travel quickly, but at other times, they take a long while to reach their destination. Although some VPN vendors advertise QoS capabilities, these apply only in the VPN devices themselves; on the Internet, a packet is a packet (at least until Internet 2 becomes more common—see the next chapter). Second, because the data travels on the Internet, security is always a concern. Most VPN networks encrypt the packet at the source

VPN device before it enters the Internet and decrypt the packet at the destination VPN device. (See Chapter 10 for more on encryption.)

At present, there are several different approaches to providing VPN services, each supported by different sets of companies and each moving down the path to standardization. For the moment, it is important to build VPNs using equipment and services from one set of vendors.

VPN Types

Three types of VPN are in common use: intranet VPN, extranet VPN, and access VPN. An *intranet VPN* provides virtual circuits between organization offices over the Internet. The center section of Figure 8-13 illustrates an intranet VPN. Each location has a VPN device that connects the location to another location through the Internet.

An *extranet VPN* is the same as an intranet VPN, except that the VPN connects several different organizations, often customers and suppliers, over the Internet.

An *access VPN* enables employees to access an organization's networks from a remote location. Employees have access to the network and all the resources on it in the

TECHNICAL FOCUS *8-1*

VIRTUAL PRIVATE NETWORK ENCAPSULATION

When a virtual private network (VPN) device sends packets through an Internet tunnel, it must first encapsulate (i.e., surround) the existing packet with a VPN packet that provides information to the receiving VPN, so do that it knows how to process the packet. This encapsulation is conceptually simple and works in much the same way as ATM or frame relay. However, because the packets must travel over the Internet, things become a bit more complex.

At present, there are several competing approaches to managing VPNs, so there are several incompatible VPN protocols used by different vendors. Layer-2 tunneling protocol (L2TP) is an emerging standard for use by layer-2 access VPNs.

Suppose a user is sending e-mail message through an access VPN into the corporate network. The user connects to a VPN device at an internet service provider via a modem over a dial-up circuit (i.e., plain old telephone service). The e-mail client software on the user's computer generates a Simple Mail Transfer Protocol (SMTP) packet at the application layer. The transport and network layers in the client computer add Transmission Control Protocol (TCP) and Internet Protocol (IP) packets, respectively. Point-to-Point Protocol (PPP) is the most commonly used dial-up data link layer protocol, so the packet that arrives

at the VPN device is a PPP packet, containing an IP packet, containing a TCP packet, containing an SMTP packet with the e-mail message (see the upper left corner of Figure 8-14).

The VPN device encrypts the incoming packet and encapsulates it with the VPN protocol, L2TP. Now the packet is ready for transmission on the Internet. The protocol on the Internet is TCP/IP, so the VPN device now encapsulates the VPN packet with an IP packet that specifies the IP address of the destination VPN device. Each circuit on the Internet is simply a T1, T3, ATM OC-48, or some other circuit. Each of these circuits has its own data link protocol. So the VPN device then surrounds the IP packet with the appropriate packet for the specific Internet circuit the message will use (e.g., T1; see Figure 8-14).

The message travels through the Internet and arrives at the destination VPN device at the corporate network, perhaps arriving with a different data link layer packet, depending on the type of connection the corporation has with the Internet (e.g., T3). The VPN device strips off the data link layer packet and the IP packet and processes the L2TP packet. It then decrypts the PPP packet and sends it to the corporate access server for processing. As far as the access server is concerned, the packet arrived from a directly connected dial-up circuit (see Figure 8-14).

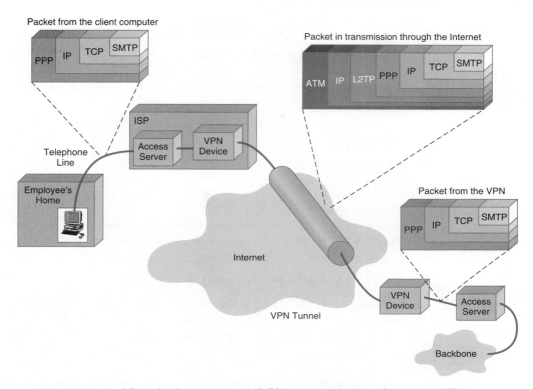

FIGURE 8-14   Virtual private network (VPN) encapsulation of packets. ATM = asynchronous transfer mode; IP = Internet Protocol; L2TP = layer-2 tunneling protocol; PPP = Point-to-Point Protocol; SMTP = Simple Mail Transfer Protocol; TCP = Transmission Control Protocol.

same way as employees physically located on network. The upper right part of Figure 8-13 shows an access VPN. The user connects to a local ISP that supports the VPN service via POTS, ISDN, or other circuit. The VPN device at the ISP accepts the user's log-in, establishes the tunnel to the VPN device at the organization's office, and begins forwarding packets over the Internet. An access VPN provides a less expensive connection than having a national toll-free phone number that connects directly into large sets of modems at the organization's office. Compared with a typical ISP-based remote connection, the access VPN is secure connection than simply sending packets over the Internet.

IMPROVING MAN/WAN PERFORMANCE

Improving the performance of MANs and WANs is handled in the same way as improving LAN performance. You begin by checking the devices in the network, by upgrading the circuits between the computers, and by changing the demand placed on the network (Figure 8-15).

Performance Checklist

Increase Computer and Device Performance
- Upgrade devices
- Change to a more appropriate routing protocol (either static or dynamic)

Increase Circuit Capacity
- Analyze message traffic and upgrade to faster circuits where needed
- Check error rates

Reduce Network Demand
- Change user behavior
- Analyze network needs of all new systems
- Move data closer to users

FIGURE 8-15 Improving performance of metropolitan and local area networks.

Improving Device Performance

In some cases, the key bottleneck in the network is not the circuits; it is the devices that provide access to the circuits (e.g., routers). One way to improve network performance is to upgrade the devices and computers that connect backbones to the WAN. Most devices are rated for their speed in converting input packets to output packets (called *latency*). Not all devices are created equal; some vendors produce devices with lower latencies than others.

Another strategy is to examining the routing protocol, either static or dynamic. Dynamic routing will increase performance in networks that have many possible routes from one computer to another and in which message traffic is "bursty"—that is, in which traffic occurs in spurts, with many messages at one time, and few at others. But dynamic routing imposes an overhead cost by increasing network traffic. In some cases, the traffic and status information sent between computers accounts for more than 50 percent of all WAN message traffic. This is clearly a problem, because it drastically reduces the amount of network capacity available for users' messages. Dynamic routing should use no more than 10 to 20 percent of the networks' total capacity.

Improving Circuit Capacity

The first step is to analyze the message traffic in the network to find which circuits are approaching capacity. These circuits then can be upgraded to provide more capacity. Less-used circuits can be downgraded to save costs. A more sophisticated analysis involves examining *why* circuits are heavily used. For example, in Figure 8-3, the circuit from San Francisco to Vancouver may be heavily used, but much traffic on this circuit may not originate in San Francisco or be destined for Vancouver. It may, for example, be going from Los Angeles to Toronto, suggesting that adding a circuit here would improve performance to a greater extent than upgrading the San Francisco-to-Vancouver circuit.

The capacity may be adequate for most traffic but not for meeting peak demand. One solution may be to add a circuit-switched or packet-switched service that is used only when demand exceeds circuit capacity. The use of a service as a backup for heavy traffic provides the best of both worlds. The lower-cost dedicated circuit is used constantly, and the backup service is used only when necessary to avoid poor response times.

Sometimes a shortage of capacity may be caused by a faulty circuit. As circuits deteriorate, the number of errors increases. As the error rate increases, throughput falls because more messages have to be retransmitted. Before installing new circuits, monitor the existing ones to ensure that they are operating properly or ask the common carrier to do it.

Reducing Network Demand

There are many ways to reduce network demand. One simple step is to require a network impact statement for all new application software developed or purchased by the organization. This focuses attention on the network impacts at any early stage in application development. Another simple approach is to use data compression techniques for all data in the network.

Another, sometimes more difficult, approach is to shift network usage from peak or high-cost times to lower-demand or lower-cost times. For example, the transmission of detailed sales and inventory reports from a retail store to headquarters could be done after the store closes. This takes advantage of off-peak rate charges and avoids interfering with transmissions requiring higher priority, such as customer credit card authorizations.

The network can be redesigned to move data closer to the applications and people who use them. This also will reduce the amount of traffic in the network. Distributed database applications enable databases to be spread across several different computers. For example, instead of storing customer records in one central location, you could store them according to region.

THE BEST PRACTICE MAN/WAN

At the end of the last chapter, we presented a best practice BN/LAN architecture for the future. It seems fitting, therefore, that we should do the same at the end of this chapter on MANs and WANs. However, it is not as easy in this case. The relatively stable environment enjoyed by the MAN/WAN common carriers is facing sharp challenges by VPNs at the low end and Ethernet/IP packet networks at the high end. As larger information technology and equipment firms begin to enter the VPN and Ethernet/IP packet network markets, we should see some major changes in the industry and in the available services and costs.

We also need to point out that the technologies in this chapter are used primarily to connect different corporate locations. Technologies primarily used for Internet access (e.g., DSL, cable modem) are discussed in the next chapter.

Figure 8-16 summarizes the major technologies available today for the MAN and WAN and five factors important in building a network. The first factor is simply the type of service, whether circuit-switched, dedicated, packet-switched, or VPN. The second is the data rate each service can be expected to provide. The next considers the cost of the service relative to its data capacity. The next is the reliability of the service in terms of its ability to predictably send messages as expected; VPNs are of low reliability because they use the unpredictable Internet. The final factor is the ease with which the technology can be integrated into a LAN and BN environment.

Type of Service	Approximate Data Rates	Relative Cost	Reliability	Network Integration
Circuit-switched services				
POTS	28.8–56 Kbps	Low	High	Difficult
ISDN	64 Kbps–1.5 Mbps	Moderate	Moderate	Difficult
Broadband ISDN	155–622 Mbps	High	Low	Difficult
Dedicated-circuit services				
T Carrier	64 Kbps–274 Mbps	Moderate	High	Moderate
SONET	52 Mbps–10 Gbps	High	High	Moderate
Packet-switched services				
X.25	56 Kbps–2 Mbps	Moderate	High	Difficult
Frame relay	56 Kbps–45 Mbps	Moderate	Moderate	Moderate
SMDS	56 Kbps–45 Mbps	Moderate	Low	Difficult
Ethernet/IP	1 Mbps–1 Gbps	Low	High	Simple
ATM	52 Mbps–10 Gbps	High	Moderate	Moderate
VPN services				
VPN	56 Kbps–2 Mbps	Very low	Low	Moderate

FIGURE 8-16 Metropolitan area network and local area network services. ATM = asynchronous transfer mode; IP = Internet Protocol; ISDN = integrated services, digital network; POTS = plain old telephone service; SMDS = switched multimegabit data service; SONET = synchronous optical network; VPN = virtual private network.

A few patterns should be apparent in looking at the figure. For small, manually operated MANs and WANs with low data transmission needs, POTS dial-up services are a reasonable alternative. However, because most of this type of network is used for Internet access, we really need to wait to the next chapter before drawing conclusions.

For networks with moderate data transmission needs (64 Kbps to 2 Mbps), there are several distinct choices. If cost is more important than reliability, then a VPN is probably a good choice. If you need flexibility in the location of your network connections and you are not completely sure of the volume of traffic you will have between locations, frame relay is probably a good choice. If you have a mature network with predictable demands, then T carrier services is probably a good choice.

For high-traffic networks (2 Mbps to 1 Gbps), the new Ethernet/IP packet networks seem to be a dominant choice. Some organizations may prefer the more mature—and therefore proven—SONET or ATM technologies, depending on whether the greater flexibility of packet services provides value or a dedicated circuit makes more sense.

Unless their data needs are stable, network managers often start with more flexible packet-switched services and move to the usually cheaper dedicated-circuit services once their needs have become clear and an investment in dedicated services is safer. In other cases, network managers sometimes add a packet network service over the top of a network built with dedicated circuits to handle peak data needs; data usually travel over the dedicated-circuit network, but when it becomes overloaded with traffic, the extra traffic is routed to the packet network.

SUMMARY

Circuit-Switched Networks   Circuit-switched services enable you to define the end points of the WAN, without specifying all the interconnecting circuits through carrier's cloud. The user dials the number of the destination computer to establish a temporary circuit, which is disconnected when the data transfer is complete. POTS is traditional dial-up service. BRI ISDN provides a communication circuit with two 64-Kbps digital transmission channels and one 16-Kbps control channel. PRI ISDN consists of 23 64-Kbps data channels and one 64-Kbps control channel. Broadband ISDN, not yet widely available, offer much faster data speeds ranging up to 622 Mbps.

Dedicated-Circuit Networks   A dedicated circuit is leased from the common carrier for exclusive use 24 hours per day, 7 days per week. Faster and more noise-free transmissions are possible, but you must carefully plan the circuits you need because changes can be expensive. The three common architectures are ring, star, and mesh. T carrier circuits have a set of digital services ranging from FT1 (64 Kbps) to T1 (1.544 Mbps) to T4 (274 Mbps). A SONET uses fiber optics to provide services ranging from OC-1 (51 Mbps) to OC-12 (622 Mbps).

Packet-Switched Networks   Packet switching is technique in which messages are split into small segments. The user buys a connection into the common carrier cloud and pays a fixed fee for the connection into the network and for the number of packets transmitted. X.25 is an older, traditional service that provides slower service (up to 2 Mbps) but guarantees error-free delivery. ATM does not perform error control, and it offers data rates up to 622 Mbps. Frame relay is a newer packet-switching service with higher data rates (up to 45 Mbps), but it does not perform error control. SMDS is an nonstandardized service that offers data rates up to 45 Mbps. Ethernet/IP packet networks use Ethernet and IP to transmit packets at speeds between 1 Mbps and 1 Gbps.

VPN Networks   A VPN provides a packet service network over the Internet. The sender and receiver have VPN devices that enable them to send data over the Internet in encrypted form through a VPN tunnel. Although VPNs are inexpensive, traffic delays on the Internet can be unpredictable.

Improving MAN/WAN Performance   One can improve network performance by improving the speed of the devices themselves, and by using a better routing protocol. Analysis of network usage can show what circuits need to be increased or decreased in capacity, what new circuits need to be leased, and when additional switched circuits may be needed to meet peak demand. Performance may also be improved by reducing network demand by including a network usage analysis for all new application software, using data compression, shifting usage to off-peak times, establishing priorities for some applications, or redesigning the network to move data closer to those who use it.

The Ideal MAN/WAN   For small, manually operated MANs and WANs with low data transmission needs, POTS dial-up services are a reasonable alternative. For networks with moderate data transmission needs (64 Kbps to 2 Mbps), a VPN is a good choice if cost is more important than reliability; otherwise, frame relay or T carrier services are good choices. For high-traffic networks (2 Mbps to 1 Gbps), the new Ethernet/IP packet networks seem to be a dominant choice, although some organizations may prefer the more mature SONET or ATM technologies. Unless their data needs are stable, network managers often start with more flexible packet-switched services and move to the usually cheaper dedicated-circuit services once their needs have become clear and an investment in dedicated services is safer.

KEY TERMS

2B+D	discard eligible (DE)	maximum allowable rate	reliable packet services
23B+D	distributed star	(MAR)	ring architecture
access VPN	architecture	mesh	service profile identifier
available bit rate (ABR)	Ethernet/IP packet net-	mesh architecture	(SPID)
asynchronous transfer	work	narrowband ISDN	star architecture
mode (ATM)	extranet VPN	network terminator	switched multimegabit
basic rate interface (BRI)	fast packet services	(NT-1, NT-2)	data service (SMDS)
broadband ISDN	Federal Communica-	packet assembly/disas-	switched virtual circuit
(B-ISDN)	tions Commission	sembly (PAD)	(SVC)
Canadian Radio-Televi-	(FCC)	packet-switched services	synchronous digital hier-
sion and Telecommu-	fractional T1 (FT1)	permanent virtual circuit	archy (SDH)
nications	frame relay	(PVC)	synchronous optical net-
Commission (CRTC)	integrated services digi-	plain old telephone serv-	work (SONET)
channel service unit/data	tal network (ISDN)	ice (POTS)	T carrier circuit
service unit	Internet service provider	point of presence (POP)	T1, T2, T3, T4 circuits
(CSU/DSU)	(ISP)	primary rate interface	terminal adapter (TA)
circuit-switched services	interexchange carrier	(PRI)	unreliable packet
cloud	(IXC)	public switched tele-	services
cloud architecture	intranet VPN	phone network	virtual circuit
committed information	latency	(PSTN)	virtual private network
rate (CIR)	layer-2 VPN	public utilities commis-	(VPN)
common carrier	layer-3 VPN	sion (PUC)	wide area telephone
datagram	local exchange carrier	regional Bell operating	service (WATS)
dedicated-circuit services	(LEC)	company (RBOC)	X.25

QUESTIONS

1. What are common carriers, local exchange carriers, and interexchange carriers?

2. Who regulates common carriers and how is it done?

3. Explain how a cloud architecture works.

4. What is POTS?

5. How does ISDN work?

6. Compare and contrast BRI, PRI, and B-ISDN.

7. What is a 2B+D? Define it.

8. How does broadband ISDN differ from narrowband ISDN?

9. Compare and contrast circuit-switched services, dedicated-circuit services, and packet-switched services.

10. Is a WAN that uses dedicated circuits easier or hard to design than one that uses dialed circuits? Explain.

11. Compare and contrast ring architecture, star architecture, and mesh architecture.

12. What are the most commonly used T carrier services? What data rates do they provide?

13. Distinguish among T1, T2, T3, and T4 circuits.

14. Describe SONET. How does it differ from SDH?

15. How do packet-switching services differ from other WAN services?

16. How is a virtual circuit distinguished from other circuits?

17. Where does packetizing take place?

18. What does a packet contain?

19. How does a reliable packet service differ from an unreliable packet service?

20. How do datagram services differ from virtual circuit services?

21. How does an SVC differ from a PVC?

22. Compare and contrast X.25, frame relay, ATM, SMDS, and Ethernet/IP packet networks.

23. Which likely to be the longer-term winner, X.25, frame relay, ATM, SMDS, or Ethernet/IP packet networks?

24. Explain the differences between CIR and MAR.

25. How do VPN services differ from common carrier services?

26. Explain how VPN services work.

27. Compare the three types of VPN.

28. How can you improve WAN performance?

29. Describe five important factors in selecting WAN services.

30. Is the Yipes service a major change in the future of networking or a fly-by-night service?

31. Are there any MAN/WAN technologies that you would avoid if you were building a network today? Explain.

32. Suppose you joined a company that had a WAN composed of SONET, T carrier services, ATM, and frame relay, each selected to match a specific network need for a certain set of circuits. Would you say this was a well-designed network? Explain.

EXERCISES

8-1 Find out the data rates and costs of T carrier and ISDN services in your area.

8-2 Find out the data rates and costs of packet-switched and circuit-switched services in your area.

8-3 Examine Figure 8-8. What other options did Care-Group likely consider? Explain the tradeoffs among the different services available. What services would you have selected?

8-4 Examine Figure 8-12. What other options did Digital Island likely consider? Explain the tradeoffs among the different services available. What services would you have selected?

8-5 Fenwick & West LLP choose to use Yipes. Explain the tradeoffs among the different services available. What services would you have selected?

MINI-CASES

I. Cookies Are Us

Cookies Are Us runs a series of 100 cookie stores across the Midwestern United States and central Canada. At the end of each day, the stores express-mail a diskette or two of sales and inventory data to headquarters, which uses the data to ship new inventory and plan marketing campaigns. The company has decided to move to a WAN. What type of a WAN architecture and WAN service would you recommend?

II. MegaCorp

MegaCorp is large manufacturing firm that operates 5 factories in Dallas, 4 factories in Los Angeles, and 5 factories in Albany, New York. It operates a tightly connected order management system that coordinates orders, raw materials, and inventory across all 14 factories. What type of WAN architecture and WAN service would you recommend?

CASE STUDY

NEXT-DAY AIR SERVICE

President Coone and the board of directors are focusing on the kinds of communication facilities NDAS will need over the next several years. The current WAN uses POTS dial-up circuits to connect the remote offices to Atlanta and New Orleans and private leased circuits to connect these two hubs to Tampa. Figure 1-6 shows the current NDAS offices.

President Coone meets with you to discuss the future of communications for NDAS. He believes that NDAS needs a network that can be expanded readily without having a major impact on the way the company conducts its routine business. He assumes that NDAS will continue its rapid growth pattern, and he wants a recommendation on what steps may be necessary to enable NDAS to meet the competition. NDAS considers the Mississippi River as the east–west dividing line for the continental United States. The projected growth trends are as follows:

1. Western United States: Traffic volumes will increase by 400 percent over the next 3 years, and one additional office will be opened every 4 months.

2. Eastern United States: Traffic volumes will increase by 300 percent over the next 3 years, and one additional office will be opened every 6 months.

3. International market: Traffic volumes will increase by 100 percent each year over the next 3 years, and additional offices will be opened in London, Paris, Rome, Berlin, Madrid, Bogotá, and Caracas.

Exercises

1. With your knowledge of NDAS's network, what service would you recommend for the future to connect the remote offices to the hubs at Atlanta and New Orleans and the hubs to the corporate office in Tampa? Will the current facilities be adequate?

2. President Coone has just informed you that NDAS is considering placing several new offices in Chicago and Los Angeles. Each office would have its own LAN. What factors would determine the use of a MAN to connect NDAS's offices in a single city together?

CHAPTER 9

THE INTERNET

THIS CHAPTER examines the Internet in more detail to explain how it works and why it is a network of networks. This chapter also examines Internet access technologies, such as DSL and cable modem, as well as the possible future of the Internet in the form of Internet 2.

OBJECTIVES

- Understand the overall design of the Internet
- Be familiar with DSL, cable modem, and Wireless Application Protocol
- Be familiar with Internet 2

CHAPTER OUTLINE

INTRODUCTION

The Internet is the most used network in the world, but it is also one of the least understood. There is no one network that is *the* Internet. Instead, the Internet is a network of networks—a set of separate and distinct networks operated by various national and state government agencies, nonprofit organizations, and for-profit corporations. The Internet exists only to the extent that these thousands of separate networks agree to use Internet protocols and to exchange data packets among one another.

The Internet is simultaneously a strict, rigidly controlled club in which deviance from the rules is not tolerated and a freewheeling open marketplace of ideas. All networks that connect to the Internet must rigidly conform to an unyielding set of standards for the transport and network layers; without these standards, data communication would not be possible. At the same time, content and new application protocols are developed freely and without restriction, and quite literally anyone in the world is allowed to comment on proposed changes.

In this chapter, we first explain how the Internet really works and look inside one of the busiest intersections on the Internet, the Chicago Network Access Point, at which about 100 separate Internet networks meet to exchange data. We then turn our attention to how you as an individual can access the Internet and what the Internet may look like in the future.

HOW THE INTERNET WORKS

Basic Architecture

The Internet is hierarchical in structure. At the top are the very large national *Internet service providers (ISPs),* such as BBN Planet and Sprint, that are responsible for large Internet networks. These *national ISPs* connect together and exchange data at *network access points* (NAPs) (Figure 9-1).

In the early 1990s, when the Internet was still primarily run by the U.S. National Science Foundation (NSF), the NSF established four main NAPs in the United States to connect the major national ISPs. When the NSF stopped funding the Internet, the companies running these NAPs began charging the national ISPs for connections, so today the NAPs in the United States are all commercial enterprises run by various common carriers such as Ameritech and Sprint. As the Internet has grown, so, too, has the number of NAPs; today there are about a dozen NAPs in the United States, with many more spread around the world.

NAPs were originally designed to connect only national ISPs. These national ISPs in turn provide services for their customers and also to regional ISPs such as BellSouth and EarthLink. These regional ISPs rely on the national ISPs to transmit their messages to

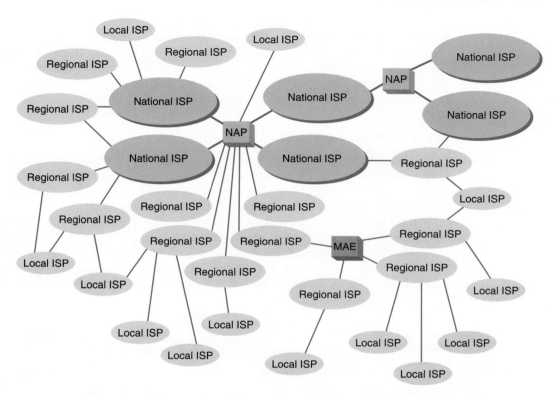

FIGURE 9-1 Basic Internet architecture. ISP = Internet service provider; MAE = metropolitan area exchange; NAP = network access point.

national ISPs in other countries. Regional ISPs, in turn, provide services to their customers and to local ISPs, who sell Internet access to individuals. As the number of ISPs grew, a new form of NAP called a metropolitan area exchange (MAE) emerged. MAEs are smaller versions of NAPs and typically link a set of regional ISPs whose networks come together in major cities (see Figure 9-1). Today there are about 50 MAEs in the United States.

Because most NAPs, MAEs, and ISPs now are run by commercial firms, many of the early restrictions on who could connect to whom have been lifted. Indiana University, for example, which might be considered a local ISP because it provides Internet access for about 40,000 individuals, has a direct connection into the Chicago NAP, as do several other universities and large corporations. Regional and local ISPs often will have several connections into other national, regional, and local ISPs to provide backup connections in case one Internet connection fails. In this way, they are not dependent on just one higher-level ISP.

In general, ISPs at the same level do not charge one other for transferring messages they exchange across a NAP or MAE. That is, a national ISP does not charge another national ISP to transmit its messages, and a regional ISP does not charge another regional ISP. This is called *peering*. It is peering that makes the Internet work and has led to the belief that the Internet is free. This is true to some extent, but higher-level ISPs normally charge lower-level

ISPs to transmit their data (e.g., a national will charge a regional, and a regional will charge a local). And of course, a local ISP will charge individuals like us for access!

In Figure 9-1, each of the ISPs are *autonomous systems,* as defined in Chapter 5. Each ISP is responsible for running its own interior routing protocols and for exchanging routing information via the BGP exterior routing protocol at NAPs and MAEs and any other connection points between individual ISPs.

Connecting to an ISP

Each of the ISPs is responsible for running its own network that forms part of the Internet. ISPs make money by charging customers to connect to their part of the Internet. Local ISPs charge individuals for dial-up access, whereas national and regional ISPs (and sometimes local ISPs) charge larger organizations for higher-speed access.

Each ISP has one or more *points-of-presence* (POP). A POP is simply the place at which the ISP provides services to its customers. To connect into the Internet, a customer must establish a circuit from his or her location into the ISP POP. For individuals, this is often done using a modem over a traditional telephone line using the PPP protocol (Figure 9-2). This call connects to the modem pool at the ISP and from there to

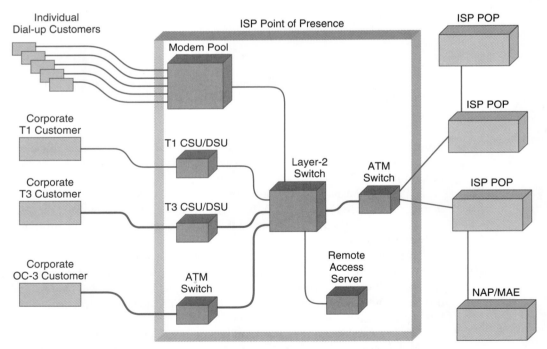

FIGURE 9-2 Inside an Internet service provider (ISP) point-of-presence. ATM = asynchronous transfer mode; CSU = channel service unit; DSU = data service unit; ISP = Internet service provider; MAE = metropolitan area exchange; NAP = network access point.

a *remote-access server (RAS),* which checks the user ID and password to make sure the caller is a valid customer. Once logged in, the user can begin sending TCP/IP packets from his or her computer over the phone to the POP. Figure 9-2 shows a POP using a collapsed BN with a layer-2 switch. The POP backbone can take many forms, as we discussed in Chapter 7.

There are many other types of Internet access that ISPs can provide. In the next section, we will discuss newer Internet access technologies such as DSL, cable modem, and Wireless Application Protocol (WAP). Customers with needs for more network capacity simply lease a higher-capacity circuit. Figure 9-2 shows customers with T1, T3, and ATM OC-3 connections into the ISP POP. It is important to note that the customer must pay for both Internet access (paid to the ISP) and for the circuit connecting from their location to the POP (usually paid to the local exchange carrier (e.g., BellSouth, Ameritech), but sometimes the ISP also can provide circuits). For a T1 connection, for example, a company might pay the local exchange carrier $1,000 per month to provide the T1 circuit from its offices to the ISP POP and also pay the ISP $2,000 per month to provide the Internet access.

As Figure 9-2 shows, the ISP POP is connected in turn to the other POPs in the ISP's network. Any messages destined for other customers of the same ISP would flow within the ISP's own network. In most cases, the majority of messages are destined outside of the ISP's network and thus must flow through it to the nearest NAP/MAE, and from there, into some other ISP's network.

TECHNICAL FOCUS *9-1*

INSIDE THE CHICAGO NETWORK ACCESS POINT

The Chicago network access point (NAP) is one of the busiest NAPs in the world. As we write this in mid-2001, it processes an average of about 4 gigabits of data per second. You can check its URL (see below) to see the current average.

More 100 different Internet service providers (ISPs), including national ISPs (e.g., BBN Planet and Sprint), regional ISPs (e.g., Michigan's Merit network), and local ISPs (e.g., Indiana University), as well as ISPs in other countries (e.g., Germany's Tiscali network, and the Singapore Advanced Research and Education Network), exchange traffic at the Chicago NAP. At present, roughly half the connections are asynchronous transfer mode (ATM) OC-3, a few are ATM OC-12, and the rest are T3. Pricing starts at about $4,000 per month for T3. (Remember, this only for Internet access; the ISPs must also lease a T3 circuit from their closest point-of-presence (POP) to the NAP.)

The NAP currently uses a large Cisco ATM switch that connects the more than 100 separate ISP networks (Figure 9-3). The ISP networks exchange IP packets through the NAP. They also exchange routing information through the Border Gateway Protocol (BGP) exterior routing protocol. Normally, the border router at each ISP simply generates BGP packets and sends them to the border routers at the other ISPs connected to the NAP. The Chicago NAP has so many ISPs that this is impossible. Because there are about 100 ISPs, each ISP would send messages to about 100 other ISPs, meaning a total of about 1 million BGP packets moving through the NAP every few minutes.

Instead, the Chicago NAP uses a route server in much the same way large networks based on OSPF (Open Shortest Path First) used designated routers (see "Routing on the Internet" in Chapter 5). The border router in each ISP sends BGP packets just to the NAP route server. The route server consolidates the routing information and then sends BGP packets back to each border router. This results in more efficient processing and only 200 messages every few minutes.

SOURCE: www.nap.aads.net/main.html.

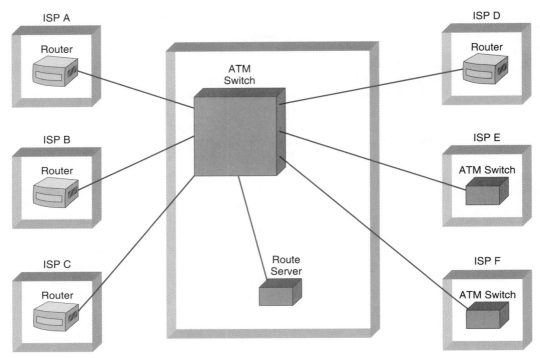

FIGURE 9-3 Inside the Internet's Chicago network access point. ATM = asynchronous transfer mode; ISP = Internet service provider.

This can be less efficient than one might expect. For example, suppose you are connected to the Internet via a local ISP in Minneapolis and request a Web page from another organization in Minneapolis. A short distance, right? Maybe not. If the other organization uses a different local ISP, which in turn uses a different regional ISP, the message may have to travel all the way to the Chicago NAP before it can move between the two separate parts of the Internet.

The Internet Today

Figure 9-4 shows the Internet networks of three ISPs in North America. CAIS and CompuServe are regional ISPs in the United States; iSTAR Internet is a national ISP in Canada. This figure shows that iSTAR and CAIS meet and peer in London, Ontario, whereas CAIS and CompuServe meet and peer at the Chicago NAP. Each ISP runs its own set of circuits. CompuServe, for example, runs mostly T3 circuits (45 Mbps) in its network, whereas CAIS uses a mix of T3 and ATM OC-12 circuits (622 Mbps). In contrast, iSTAR uses a mix of T1 circuits (1.5 Mbps).

Today, the backbone circuits of the major U.S. national ISPs operate at ATM OC-12 (622 Mbps). Most of the largest national ISPs (e.g., Sprint, Cable & Wireless) plan to convert their principal backbones to OC-192 (10 Gbps) by the end of 2001. A few are now

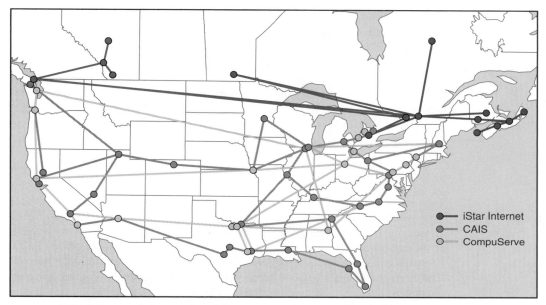

FIGURE 9-4   A few national Internet service providers in North America.

experimenting with OC-768 (80 Gbps), and several are in the planning stages with OC-3072 (160 Gbps). This is good, because the amount of Internet traffic has been growing rapidly. The Internet traffic in 2001 hit a peak of 2.5 Tbps and is expected to grow to a peak of 35 Tbps by 2005.

As traffic increases, ISPs can add more and faster circuits relatively easily, but where these circuits come together at NAPs and MAEs, bottlenecks are becoming more common. Network vendors such as Cisco and Juniper are making larger and larger switches capable of handling these high-capacity circuits, but it is a daunting task. When circuit capacities increase by 100 percent, switch manufacturers also must increase their capacities by 100 percent. It is simpler to go from a 622 mbps circuit to a 10 Gbps circuit than to go from a 20 Gbps switch to a 200 Gbps switch

The Internet is constantly changing, so by the time you read this, CAIS, CompuServe, and iSTAR will likely have added extra circuits. An up-to-date map of the major ISPs whose networks make up large portions of the Internet is available at www.caida.org/tools/visualization/mapnet (just click on "run mapnet").

INTERNET ACCESS TECHNOLOGIES

There are many ways in which individuals and organizations can connect to an ISP. Most people today use 56-Kbps dial-up modems over telephone lines. As we discussed in the preceding section, many organizations lease T1 or T3 lines into their ISPs. There are several newer technologies such as DSL and cable modem that are designed to provide faster access from an individual or organization to the ISP. These technologies are commonly called *broadband technologies* because they provide higher-speed communications than traditional modems.[1]

It is important to understand that Internet access technologies are used only to connect from one location to an ISP. Unlike the MAN and WAN technologies in the previous chapter, Internet access technologies cannot be used for general-purpose networking from any point to any point. In this section, we discuss four principal Internet access technologies (DSL, cable modem, fixed wireless, and mobile wireless) and also discuss some future technologies that may become common.

DSL

Digital subscriber line (DSL) is a family of point-to-point technologies designed to provide high-speed data transmission over traditional telephone lines.[2] The reason for the limited capacity on traditional telephone circuits lies with the telephone and the switching equipment at the end offices. The actual cable in the *local loop* from a home or office to the telephone company end office is capable of providing much higher data transmission rates. So conversion from traditional telephone service (POTS) to DSL usually requires just changing the telephone equipment, not rewiring the local loop, which is what has made it so attractive.

Architecture   DSL uses the existing local loop cable but places different equipment on the customer premises (i.e., the home or office) and in the telephone company end office. The equipment that is installed at the customer location is called the *customer premises equipment (CPE)*. Figure 9-5 shows one common type of DSL installation. (There are other forms.) The CPE in this case includes a *line splitter* that is used to separate the traditional voice telephone transmission from the data transmissions. The line splitter directs the telephone signals into the normal telephone system so that if the DSL equipment fails, voice communications are unaffected.

The line splitter also directs the data transmissions into a *DSL modem,* which is sometimes also called a DSL router. As you will recall from Chapter 3, this is both a modem and an FDM multiplexer. The DSL modem produces Ethernet 10BaseT packets so it can be connected directly into a computer or to a router and hub so that it can serve the needs of a small network.

Figure 9–5 also shows the architecture within the local carrier's end office (i.e., the telephone company office closest to the customer premises). The local loops from many customers enter and are connected to the main distribution facility (MDF). The MDF works like the CPE line splitter; it splits the voice traffic from the data traffic and directs the voice traffic to the voice telephone network and the data traffic to the *DSL access multiplexer (DSLAM)*. The DSLAM demultiplexes the data streams and converts them into ATM data, which are then distributed to the ISPs. Some ISPs are collocated, in that they

[1] *Broadband* is a technical term that means "analog transmission" (see Chapter 3). The new broadband technologies often use analog transmission, so they were called broadband. However, the term *broadband* has been corrupted in common usage, so that to most people, it usually means "high speed."

[2] DSL is rapidly changing because it is so new. More information can be found from the DSL forum (www.adsl.com, www.dsllife.com) and the ITU-T under standard G.992.

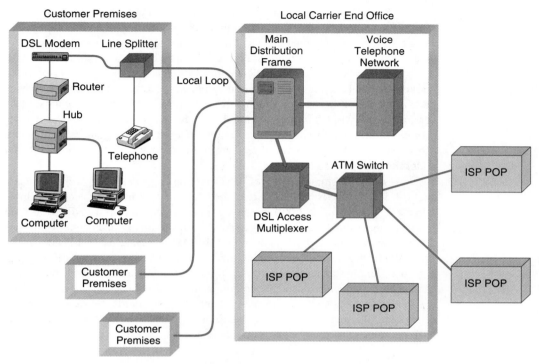

FIGURE 9-5 Digital subscriber line (DSL) architecture. ATM = asynchronous transfer mode; ISP = Internet service provider; POP = point-of-presence.

have their POPs physically in the telephone company end offices. Other ISPs have their POPs located elsewhere.

Types of DSL DSL services are relatively new, and they are not available in all locations. In general, DSL services have advanced more quickly in Canada (and Europe, Australia, and Asia) than in the United States, owing to their newer telephone networks from the end offices to the customer.

There are many different types of DSL. The most common type of DSL in use today is *asymmetric DSL (ADSL)*. ADSL uses frequency division multiplexing to create three separate channels over the one local loop circuit. One channel is the traditional voice telephone circuit. A second channel is a relatively high speed simplex data channel downstream from the carrier's end office to the customer. The third channel is a slightly slower duplex data channel primarily used for upstream from the customer to the carrier's end office.[3] ADSL is called asymmetric because its two data channels have different speeds. Each of the two data channels are further multiplexed using time division multiplexing so they can be further subdivided.

---

[3]Because the second data channel is intended primarily for upstream data communication, many authors imply that this is a simplex channel, but it is actually a set of half duplex channels.

The size of the two digital channels depends on the distance from the CPE to the end office. The shorter the distance, the higher the speed, because with a shorter distance, the circuit suffers less attenuation and higher-frequency signals can be used, providing a greater bandwidth for modulation. Figure 9-6 lists the common types of ADSL.

ADSL providers face a challenge in selecting what type of ADSL to offer in a given market. On one hand, customers want the highest speed access possible. However, because there is a trade-off between speed and distance, if an ADSL provider chooses a high-speed version, they have just limited the number of customers they can serve because a significant proportion of households in the United States are long distances from the nearest end office. Most ADSL providers have therefore chosen the T1 level of ADSL and offer it under the trademarked name of G.Lite ASDL.

A second common type of DSL is *very-high-data-rate digital subscriber line (VDSL)*. VDSL is asymmetric DSL service designed for use over very short local loops of at most 4,500 feet, with 1,000 feet being more typical. It also uses FDM to provide three channels: the normal analog voice channel, an upstream digital channel, and a downstream digital channel. Figure 9-7 lists the types of VDSL we anticipate will become common.

VDSL has not yet been standerdized, and five separarte standards groups are working on different standards. Therefore, the exact data speeds and channels are likely to change as manufacturers, telephone companies, and ITU-T gain more experience and as the standards groups attempt to merge competing standards. Several companies are also developing symmetric versions of VDSL in which upstream and downstream channels have the same capacity. We expect major changes to VDSL.

Cable Modems

One alternative to DSL is the *cable modem,* a digital service offered by cable television companies. As with DSL, cable modem technology is relatively new. There are several competing standards, but the *Data over Cable Service Interface Specification (DOCSIS)* standard is the dominant one. DOCSIS is not a formal standard but is the one used by most vendors of *hybrid fiber coax (HFC)* networks (i.e., cable networks that use both fiber-optic and coaxial cable). As with DSL, these technologies are changing rapidly.[4]

Type	Maximum Length of Local Loop	Maximum Downstream Rate	Maximum Upstream Rate
T1	18,000 feet	1.5 Mbps	384 Kbps
E1*	16,000 feet	2.0 Mbps	384 Kbps
T2	12,000 feet	6.1 Mbps	384 Kbps
E2*	9,000 feet	8.4 Mbps	640 Kbps
* E1 and E2 are the European standard services similar to T1 and T2 services in North America.			

FIGURE 9-6 Asymmetric digital subscriber line data rates.

[4] More information can be found at cablemodem.com and cable-modems.org.

Type	Maximum Length of Local Loop	Maximum Downstream Rate	Maximum Upstream Rate
1/4 OC-1	4,500 feet	12.96 Mbps	1.6 Mbps
1/2 OC-1	3,000 feet	25.92 Mbps	2.3 Mbps
OC-1	1,000 feet	51.84 Mbps	2.3 Mbps

FIGURE 9-7   Data rates for very-high-data-rate digital subscriber line. OC = optical carrier.

Architecture   Cable modem architecture is very similar to DSL—with one very important difference. DSL is a point-to-point technology, whereas cable modems use *shared* multipoint circuits. With cable modems, each user must compete with other users for the available capacity. Furthermore, because the cable circuit is a multipoint circuit, all messages on the circuit go to all computers on the circuit. If your neighbors were hackers, they could modify their software to read all messages that travel over the cable, including yours.

Figure 9-8 shows the most common architecture for cable modems. The cable TV circuit enters the customer premises through a cable splitter that separates the data trans-

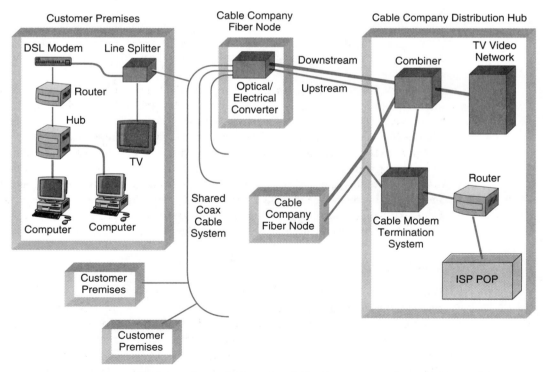

FIGURE 9-8   Cable modem architecture. ISP = Internet service provider; POP = point-of-presence.

missions from the TV transmissions and sends the TV signals to the TV network and the data signals to the cable modem. The cable modem (both a modem and frequency division multiplexer) translates from the cable data into 10baseT Ethernet packets, which then be directed into a computer to into a router and hub for distribution in a small network.

The cable TV cable entering the customer premises is a standard coxial cable that is shared by anywhere from 300 to 1,000 customers, depending on the cable company that installed the cable. These 300 to 1,000 customers share the available data capacity, but of course, not all customers who have cable TV will choose to install cable modems. This coax cable runs to a *fiber node,* which has an optical-electrical (OE) converter to convert between the coaxial cable on the customer side and fiber-optic cable on the cable TV company side. Each fiber node serves as many as half a dozen separate coaxial cable runs.

The fiber nodes are in turn connected to the cable company *distribution hub* (sometimes called a headend) through two separate circuits, an upstream circuit and a downstream circuit. The upstream circuit, containing data traffic from the customer, is connected into a *cable modem termination system (CMTS).* The CMTS contains a series of cable modems/multiplexers and converts the data from cable modem protocols into protocols needed for Internet traffic, before passing them to a router connected to an ISP POP. Often, the cable company is an Internet regional ISP, but sometimes it just provides Internet access to a third-party ISP.

The downstream circuit to the customer contains both ordinary video transmissions from the cable TV video network and data transmissions from the Internet. Downstream data traffic enters the distribution hub from the ISP POP and is routed through the CMTS, which produces the cable modem signals. This traffic is then sent to a *combiner,* which combines the Internet data traffic with the ordinary TV video traffic and sends it back to the fiber node for distribution.

Types of Cable Modems There are few widely used standards in the cable modem industry, because unlike the telephone system, each cable TV company was able to build very different HFC cable plants because each cable company was a separate entity with no need to connect to other cable TV networks. In theory, cable modems can provide downstream speeds of 27 to 55 Mbps and upstream speeds of 2 to 10 Mbps, depending on the exact nature and quality of the HFC cable plant. In practice, most cable systems do not offer speeds at this rate. Today, typical downstream speeds range between 1.5 and 2 Mbps and typical upstream speeds range between 200 Kbps and 2 Mbps. However, as cable modems become more common and as certain standards emerge as dominant standards, we should see a consolidation in the types of cable modem services offered.

Fixed Wireless

The most popular type of *fixed wireless* is *wireless DSL,* which requires a line of sight between the communicating transmitters. For this reason, it has limited application, because it requires tall buildings or towers to be effective. The most common use today is to provide Internet access to multi-tenant buildings such as remote office buildings, apartment buildings, and hotels. Transmitters are used to connect the building to the ISP, and DSL is used inside the building to connect to the wireless transceiver (Figure 9-9).

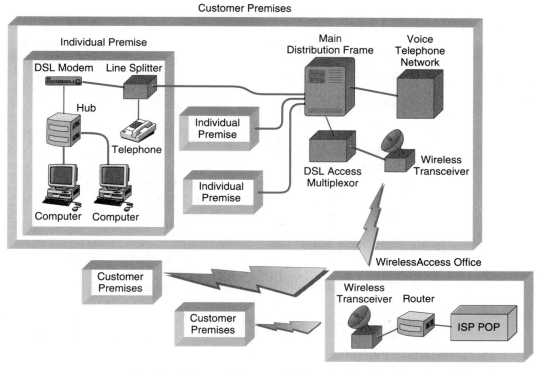

FIGURE 9-9   Fixed wireless architecture. DSL = digital subscriber line; POP = point-of-presence.

Fixed wireless comes in both point-to-point and multipoint versions. The point-to-point version is designed to connect only two locations and is often used as backbone between buildings owned by the same organization. The multipoint version is sometimes called point-to-multipoint because there is one central receiver and all other locations communicate only with it. The multipoint version is designed as an alternative to DSL and cable modems and is intended for use by an ISP supporting a small number of customers. Like cable modems, the circuit is a shared circuit, so users must compete for the shared capacity, but most installations are limited to a few dozen users. Data transmission for both versions ranges from 1.5 to 11 Mbps, depending on the vendor.

Other fixed wireless technologies such as *satellite* are also available. Satellite technologies use the satellite for downstream transmissions (from the ISP to the customer) but use traditional dial-up modems for upstream transmissions. Although satellite technology has been available for several years, but it has never become really popular.

Mobile Wireless

Mobile wireless technologies enable users to access the Internet from any location where there is mobile wireless service. Widespread mobile wireless Internet access is probably the next major change in the networking. Mobile wireless Internet access technologies exist today (e.g., cell phone connections), but most are slow compared with wired access, whether DSL, cable modem, or simply a dial-up modem. The WLAN technologies discussed in Chapter 6 (Bluetooth, 802.11b) are primarily intended for use inside one organization, although some are being installed in public places such as airports for open access to the Internet. In this section, we will focus on what we believe will be the most common mobile wireless technology—at least until new high-speed mobile wireless technologies become more common.

Wireless Application Protocol (WAP) provides a set of application and network protocols called the *Wireless Application Environment (WAE)* to support mobile wireless Internet applications. WAP is designed to enable the use of normal Web application on computers and devices with small display screens operating over low-speed wireless connections. Figure 9-10 shows the basic WAP architecture.

The WAP client (a mobile phone, palm computer, or laptop computer) runs special WAP software called a WAE user agent. This software generates WAE requests that are similar in many ways to HTTP requests and transmits them wirelessly to a WAP gateway. A transceiver at the WAP gateway passes the requests to a *wireless telephony application (WTA)* server. This server responds to the requests and, if the client has requested a Web page on the Internet, sends a WAE request to a *WAP proxy*. The WAP proxy translates the WAE request into HTTP and sends it over the Internet to the desired Web server.

This Web server responds to the request and sends back to the WAP proxy an HTTP response that contains HTML, jpeg, and other Internet application protocols. The WAP proxy in turn translates these into their WAE equivalents and sends them to the WTA server, which sends them to the client.

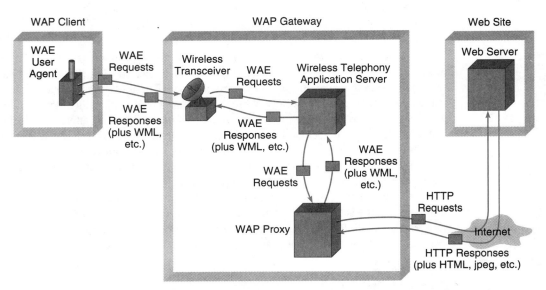

FIGURE 9-10 Mobile wireless architecture for Wireless Application Protocol (WAP) applications. HTML = Hypertext Markup Language; HTTP = Hypertext Transfer Protocol; WAE = Wireless Application Environment; WML = Wireless Markup Language.

MANAGEMENT FOCUS *9-1*

BANKING ON WIRELESS APPLICATION PROTOCOL

SkandiaBanken, a leading Swedish Internet bank, provides retail banking services to over 350,000 clients. The bank operates entirely via the Internet, having no traditional branches. Customers communicate with the bank through the Web, e-mail, telephones, and now Wireless Application Protocol (WAP) technology.

SkandiaBanken chose to implement WAP to provide customers with safe and easy access to their financial data from wherever in the world. Customers can securely view their deposit and credit card accounts, execute their credit card payments, make balance inquiries, and pay their bills. Users of the mobile service may also check the foreign exchange, gold, and treasury bill rates, as well as access information on the bank's range of financial products. There is even location-based information available, such as city guides, restaurant reviews, movies, theaters, museums, art galleries, libraries and other important facilities.

SOURCE: "Financial Institutions Worldwide Use Infinite WAP Server to Offer Mobile Banking," Infinite.com, January 21, 2001.

Future Technologies

Internet access technologies are one of the fastest growth areas in networking, so there are several new technologies that have the potential to become important alternatives to DSL, cable modems, and wireless technologies. In this section, we focus on two up-and-coming technologies: Ethernet and passive optical networking (PON).

Passive Optical Networking   *Passive optical networking* (PON), sometimes called *fiber-to-the-home (FTTH),* is exactly what it sounds like: running fiber-optic cable into the home. The traditional set of hundreds of copper telephone lines that run from the telephone company switch office is replaced by one fiber-optic cable that is run past each house or office in the neighborhood. Data is transmitted down the signal fiber cable using WDM, providing hundreds or thousands of separate channels. At each subscriber location, a fiber splitter separates the channels belonging to that location and runs them into an optical electrical converter, which then connects to a 10BaseT hub.

This approach is called passive optical because the splitters require no electrical current and thus are quicker and easier to install than traditional electrical-based hubs and repeaters. However, because they are passive, the optical signal fades quickly, giving a maximum length of about 10 miles.

Each single fiber has a capacity of about 155 Mbps, which must be allocated among the subscribers. This means about 1.5 Mbps if there are 100 subscribers per fiber, or 15 Mbps if there are only 10 subscribers. At present, there are no standards for PON and FTTH, but several vendors have joined together to develop standards. The larger problem, of course, is the cost of laying miles and miles of fiber-optic cable.

Ethernet to the Home   Perhaps the most exciting possibility is Ethernet to the home. If we were to start over and design an entirely new network for Internet access from home, we would probably start with Ethernet, because of its low cost and popularity in organizational LANs. Using common protocols would make the whole task of networking much simpler for everyone involved.

Pioneered by Yipes.com, such an approach is exactly what is being used in several major U.S. cities. With this approach, the common carrier installs a TCP/IP router with 10BaseT or 100BaseT connections into the customer's network and a Ethernet fiber on the other. The IP/Ethernet traffic moves from the router into the carrier's Ethernet MAN and then onto the Internet.

Although this approach is also limited because of the cost of providing Ethernet fiber to the customer, we believe this has great potential. Because conversions between protocols are not required at the customer site, connecting to the network is much simpler than with other Internet access technologies.

INTERNET GOVERNANCE

Because the Internet is a network of networks, no one organization operates the Internet. The closest thing the Internet has to an owner is the *Internet Society (ISOC)* (www.isoc. org). ISOC is an open-membership professional society with more than 175 organizational and 8,000 individual members in over 100 countries and including corporations, government agencies, and foundations that have created the Internet and its technologies. Because membership in ISOC is open, anyone, including students, is welcome to join and vote on key issues facing the Internet.

The ISOC mission is to ensure "the open development, evolution and use of the Internet for the benefit of all people throughout the world."[5] ISOC works in three general areas: public policy, education, and standards. In terms of public policy, ISOC participates in the national and international debates on important issues such as censorship, copyright, privacy, and universal access. ISOC delivers training and education programs targeted at improving the Internet infrastructure in developing nations. The most important ISOC activity lies in the development and maintenance of Internet standards. ISOC works through four interrelated standards bodies: Internet Engineering Task Force (IETF), Internet Engineering Steering Group (IESG), Internet Architecture Board (IAB), and Internet Research Task Force (IRTF).

The *Internet Engineering Task Force (IETF)* (www.ietf.org) is a large open international community of network designers, operators, vendors, and researchers concerned with the evolution of the Internet architecture and the smooth operation of the Internet. IETF works through a series of working groups, which are organized by topic (e.g., routing, transport, security). The requests for comment (RFCs) that form the basis for Internet standards are developed by the IETF and its working groups.

Closely related to the IETF is the *Internet Engineering Steering Group (IESG)*. The IESG is responsible for technical management of IETF activities and the Internet standards process. It administers the process according to the rules and procedures that have been ratified by the ISOC trustees. The IESG is directly responsible for the actions associated with entry into and movement along the Internet "standards track," including final approval of specifications as Internet standards. Each IETF working group is chaired by a member of the IESG.

---

[5] See www.isoc.org/isoc/mission.

TECHNICAL FOCUS *9-1*

REGISTERING AN INTERNET DOMAIN NAME

Until the 1990s, there was only a moderate number of computers on the Internet. One organization was responsible for registering domain names (sets of application layer addresses) and assigning IP addresses for each top level domain (e.g., .COM). Network Solutions, for example, was the sole organization responsible for domain name registrations for the .COM, .NET and .ORG domains. In the October of 1998, the *Internet Corporation for Assigned Names and Numbers* (ICANN) was formed to assume responsibility for the IP address space and domain name system management.

In the spring of 1999, ICANN established the Shared Registration System (SRS) that enabled many organizations to perform domain name registration and address assignment using a shared database. More than 80 organizations are now accredited by ICANN as a registrar and are permitted to use the SRS. Each registrar has the right to assign names and addresses in one or more top level domains. For a list of registrars and the domains they serve, see www.internic.com.

If you want to register a new domain name and obtain an IP address, you can contact any accredited registrar for that top level domain. One of the oldest privately operated registrars is register.com. Each registrar follows the same basic process for registering a name and assigning an address, but each may charge a different amount for their services. In order to register an name, you must first check to see if it is available (i.e., that no one else has registered it). If the name has already been registered, you can find out who owns it and perhaps attempt to buy it from them.

If the domain name is available, you will need to provide the IP address of the DNS server that will be used to store all IP addresses in the domain. Most large organizations, have their own DNS servers, but small companies and individuals often use the DNS of their ISP.

Whereas the IETF develops standards and the IESG provides the operational leadership for the IETF working groups, the *Internet Architecture Board (IAB)* provides strategic architectural oversight. The IAB attempts to develop conclusions on strategic issues (e.g., top-level domain names, use of international character sets) that can be passed on as guidance to the IESG or turned into published statements or simply passed directly to the relevant IETF working group. In general, the IAB does not produce polished technical proposals but rather tries to stimulate action by the IESG or the IETF that will lead to proposals that meet general consensus. The IAB appoints the IETF chairperson and all IESG members, from a list provided by the IETF nominating committee. The IAB also adjudicates appeals when someone complains that the IESG has failed.

The *Internet Research Task Force (IRTF)* operates much like the IETF, through small research groups focused on specific issues. Whereas IETF working groups focus on current issues, IRTF research groups work on long-term issues related to Internet protocols, applications, architecture, and technology. The IRTF chairperson is appointed by the IAB.

Internet 2

The Internet is changing. New applications and access technologies are being developed at lighting pace. But these innovations do not change the fundamental structure of the Internet; it has evolved more slowly because the core technologies (TCP/IP) are harder to change gradually; it is difficult to change one part of the Internet without changing the attached parts.

Many organizations in many different countries are working on dozens of different projects in an attempt to design new technologies for the next version of the Internet.[6] The two primary American projects working on the future Internet got started at about the same time in 1996. The U.S. National Science Foundation provided $100 million to start the *Next Generation Internet (NGI)* program, which developed the *very-high-performance Backbone Network Service (vBNS)* now run by MCI WorldCom, and 34 universities got together to start what turned into the *University Corporation for Advanced Internet Development (UCAID)*, which developed the *Abilene network,* commonly called *Internet 2.* In 1997, the Canadian government established the *Advanced Research and Development Network Operations Center (ARDNOC),* which developed *CA*net 3,* the Canadian project on the future Internet.[7]

Figure 9-11 shows the major high-speed circuits in the Internet 2's Abilene network, NGI's vBNS network, and ARDNOC's CA*net 3 network. This figure is a shapshot of these networks as of 2001; these networks will have changed by the time you read this. These circuits, mostly SONET and ATM OC-48 circuits running at 2.4 Gbps, plus a few SONET or ATM OC-12 (622 Mbps), are the major high-speed circuits in these networks.

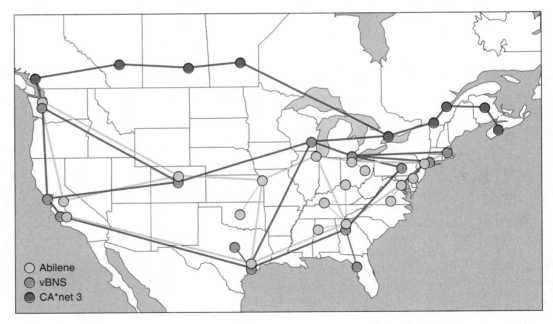

FIGURE 9-11 Gigapops and high-speed backbones of Internet 2/Abilene, very-high-performance Backbone Network Service (vBNS), and CA*net 3.

[6] For a listing of several major international projects, see www.startap.net.

[7] For more information on these projects, see www.internet2.org, www.vbns.org, www.ucaid.edu/abilene, and www.canet3.org.

MANAGEMENT FOCUS *9-2*

INSIDE THE PACIFIC/NORTHWEST GIGAPOP

The Pacific/Northwest Gigapop is located in Seattle, Washington, and is run by the University of Washington and University Corporation for Advanced Internet Development (i.e., Internet 2). It provides OC-48 (2.4-Gbps) connections to several high-speed networks such as Abilene, CA*net 3, Microsoft, and the High Speed Connectivity Consortium (HSCC), which is funded by the U.S. Department of Defense. It also provides a network access point for these high-speed networks to connect to lower-speed networks of the traditional Internet, such as those

run by Sprint, AT&T, and UUNET, as well as a number of universities in the Pacific Northwest.

The basic structure of the gigapop is a set of four high-speed switches, connected to two high-speed routers (Figure 9-12). High-speed networks, such as Abilene, connect directly into this set of six core devices, whereas lower-speed networks connect into the core via a set of routers.

SOURCE: www.pnw-gigapop.net.

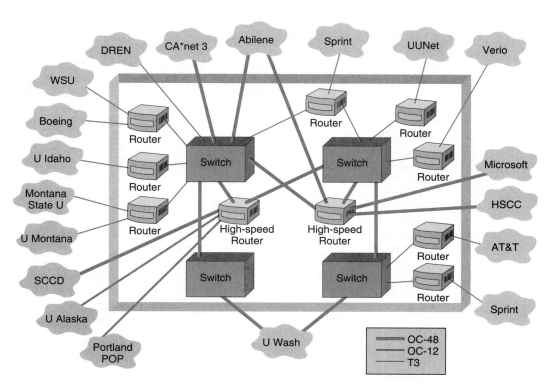

FIGURE 9-12 Inside the Pacific/Northwest Gigapop. DREN = Defense Research Engineering; HSCC = High Speed Connectivity Consortium; OC = optical carrier.

Each of the networks have a set of access points called *gigapops,* so named because they provide a point-of-presence at gigabit speeds. Although traditional Internet NAPs provide connections between networks at T1, T3, OC-1, OC-3, and—occasionally—OC-12 speeds, gigapops are designed to provide access at much higher speeds so that different networks can exchange data at much higher rates of speed. Gigapops also usually provide a wider range of services than traditional NAPs that are primarily just layer-2 data exchange points.

Besides providing very high speed Internet connections, these networks are intended to experiment with new protocols that one day may end up on in the future Internet. For example, most of these networks run IPv6 as the primary network layer protocol, rather than IPv4. Most are also working on new ways to provide QoS and multicasting. Some, such as Internet 2, are also working on developing new applications for a high-speed Internet, such as tele-immersion and videoconferencing.

SUMMARY

How the Internet Works   The Internet is a set of separate networks, ranging from large national ISPs to midsize regional ISPs to small local ISPs that connect with one another at NAPs and MAEs. NAPs and MAEs charge the ISPs to connect, but similar-size ISPs usually do not charge each other to exchange data. Each ISP has a set of points-of-presence through which it charges its users (individuals, businesses, and smaller ISPs) to connect to the Internet. Users connect to a POP to get access to the Internet. This connection may be via a dial-up modem over a telephone line or via a higher-speed circuit such as a T1.

DSL   DSL enables users to connect to an ISP POP over a standard point-to-point telephone line. The customer installs a DSL modem that connects via Ethernet to his or her computer system. The modem communicates with a DSLAM at the telephone company office, which sends the data to the ISP POP ADSL is the most common type of DSL and often provides 1.5 Mbps downstream and 384 Kbps upstream. VDSL is a faster version that runs over short distances and has speeds up to 51.8 Mbps.

Cable Modem   Cable modems use a shared multipoint circuit that runs through the cable TV cable. They also provide the customer with a modem that connects via Ethernet to his or her computer system. The modem communicates with a CMTS at the cable company office, which sends the data to the ISP POP. The DOCSIS standard is the dominant standard, but there are no standard data rates today. Typical downstream speeds range between 1.5 and 2 Mbps, and typical upstream speeds range between 200 Kbps and 2 Mbps.

Wireless   Fixed wireless systems provide DSL-like speeds over a single line-of-sight wireless circuit to a multitenant building. Inside the building, DSL is used to provide service to a large number of users over the existing phone lines. Mobile wireless uses cellular telephone technologies to provide access to small hand-held devices using WAP. WAP translates from traditional Internet protocols such as HTTP and HTML into their WAE equivalents for use in the small devices.

Internet Governance   The closet the Internet has to an owner is the ISOC, which works on public policy, education, and Internet standards. Standards are developed through four related organizations governed by ISOC. The IETF develops the actual standards through a series of working groups. The IESG manages IETF activities. The IAB sets long-term strategic directions, whereas the IRTF works on future issues through working groups in much the same way as the IETF.

Internet 2   There are many different organizations currently working on the next generation of the Internet, including the Abilene network, vBNS, and CA*net 3. Although each is working in a slightly different fashion, all join together with one another and parts of the regular Internet at gigapops (gigabit points of presence).

KEY TERMS

Abilene network
Advanced Research and
  Development Net-
  work Operations
  Center (ARDNOC)
asymmetric DSL
  (ADSL)
autonomous systems
broadband technologies
cable modem
cable modem termina-
  tion system (CMTS)
CA*net 3
customer premises
  equipment (CPE)
Data over Cable Service
  Interface Specifica-
  tion (DOCSIS)
digital subscriber line
  (DSL)
distribution hub
DSL access multiplexer
  (DSLAM)

DSL modem
fiber-to-the-home
  (FTTH)
fixed wireless
G.Lite ASDL
hybrid fiber coax (HFC)
Internet Architecture
  Board (IAB)
Internet Corporation for
  Assigned Names and
  Numbers (ICANN)
Internet Engineering
  Steering Group
  (IESG)
Internet Engineering
  Task Force (IETF)
Internet Research Task
  Force (IRTF)
Internet service provider
  (ISP)
Internet Society (ISOC)
Internet 2
line splitter

local ISP
local loop
main distribution facility
  (MDF)
metropolitan area
  exchange (MAE)
mobile wireless
national ISP
network access point
  (NAP)
Next Generation Internet
  (NGI)
optical-electrical (OE)
  converter
Passive optical network-
  ing (PON)
peering
point-of-presence (POP)
regional ISP
remote-access server
  (RAS)
request for comment
  (RFC)

University Corporation
  for Advanced Internet
  Development
  (UCAID)
very-high-data-rate digi-
  tal subscriber line
  (VDSL)
very-high-performance
  Backbone Network
  Service (vBNS)
WAP proxy
Wireless Application
  Environment (WAE)
Wireless Application
  Protocol (WAP)
wireless telephony
  application (WTA)
  server
wireless DSL
Yipes

QUESTIONS

1. What is the basic structure of the Internet?

2. Explain how the Internet is a network of networks.

3. Compare and contrast an NAP and a MAE.

4. What is a POP?

5. Explain one reason why you might experience long response times in getting a Web page from a server in your own city.

6. What type of circuits are commonly used to build the Internet today? What type of circuits are commonly used to build Internet 2?

7. Compare and contrast cable modem and DSL.

8. Explain how DSL works.

9. How does a DSL modem differ from a DSLAM?

10. Explain how ADSL works.

11. Explain how VDSL works.

12. Compare and contrast ADSL and VDSL.

13. Explain how a cable modem works.

14. What is a OE converter? A CMTS?

15. Which is better, cable modem or DSL? Explain.

16. Explain how one type of fixed wireless called wireless DSL works.

17. Compare and contrast mobile wireless and fixed wireless.

18. Explain how WAP works.

19. What are some future technologies that might change how we access the Internet?

20. What is PON, and how does it work?

21. Explain how Yipes.com works.

22. What are the principal organizations responsible for Internet governance, and what do they do?

23. How is the IETF related to the IRTF?

24. What are two principal American organizations working on the future of the Internet?

25. What is Internet 2?

26. What is a gigapop?

27. There are many different organizations working on their vision of a high-speed Internet. Is this good or bad? Would we be better off just having one organization working on this and coordinating the work?

28. Today, there is no clear winner in the competition for higher-speed Internet access. What technology or technologies do you think will dominate in 2 years' time? Why?

29. Some experts believe that in 5 years, the modem will have disappeared. What do you think?

30. Many experts predicted that small, local ISPs would disappear as regional and national ISPs began offering local access. This hasn't happened. Why?

EXERCISES

9-1 Describe the current network structure of the Abilene network, the vBNS network, and the CA*net 3 network.

9-2 Provide the service details (e.g., pricing) for at least two high-speed Internet access service providers in your area.

9-3 Many people are wiring their homes for 10BaseT or 100BaseT. Suppose a friend who is building a house asks you what—if any—network to put inside the house and what Internet access technology to use. What would you recommend?

MINI-CASES

I. Cathy's Collectibles

Your cousin Cathy runs a part-time business out of her apartment. She buys and sells collectibles such as antique prints, baseball cards, and cartoon cells and has recently discovered the Web with its many auction sites. She has begun buying and selling on the Web by bidding on collectibles at lesser-known sites and selling them at a profit at more well-known sites. She downloads and uploads lots of graphics (pictures of the items she's buying and selling). She is getting frustrated with the slow Internet access she has with her 56-Kbps dial-up modem and asks you for advice. DSL is available at a cost of $60 per month for 1.5 Mbps down and 384 Kbps up. Cable modem service is available for a cost of $50 per month for 1.5 Mbps down and 640 Kbps up. Wireless DSL is available in her apartment building for $45 per month for 1.5 Mbps down and 256 Kbps up. Explain the differences in these services and make a recommendation.

II. Surfing Sam

Sam likes to surf the Web for fun, to buy things, and to research for his classes. Suppose the same Internet access technologies are available as in mini-case I above. Explain the differences in these services and make a recommen-

NEXT-DAY AIR SERVICE

President Coone has asked you to put NDAS "on the Internet." You interpret this to mean getting a Web site up and running and putting Internet access technologies into the NDAS offices.

Exercises

1. With your knowledge of NDAS's network, what types of Internet access technologies (e.g., dial-up modem, DSL, cable modem, wireless) would you recommend for Atlanta, New Orleans, and the corporate office in Tampa?

2. There are several options for creating the Web site. The first would be for NDAS to develop it in-house on its own Web server and purchase an ISDN, T1, or similar access from its offices into an ISP's POP. Another approach would be for NDAS to outsource the Web server to a company that specializes in Web hosting (e.g., IBM) and pay so much per month on the basis of on the Web site traffic but to develop and manage the content on the Web site itself. A third option would be to outsource the whole Web site, both hosting and content development and maintenance. Outline the advantages and disadvantages of each approach and make a recommendation.

PART 4

NETWORK MANAGEMENT

CHAPTER 10

NETWORK SECURITY

THIS CHAPTER describes why networks need security and how to provide it. The first step in any security plan is risk assessment: understanding the key assets that need protection and assessing the threats to each. There are a variety of steps that can be taken to prevent, detect, and correct security problems due to disruptions, destruction, and disaster, and unauthorized access.

OBJECTIVES

- Be familiar the major threats to network security
- Be familiar with how to conduct a risk assessment
- Understand how to prevent, detect, and correct disruptions, destruction, and disaster
- Understand how to prevent, detect, and correct unauthorized access

CHAPTER OUTLINE

Introduction

    Why Networks Need Security

    Types of Security Threats

    Network Controls

Risk Assessment

    Develop a Control Spreadsheet

    Identify and Document the Controls

    Evaluate the Network's Security

Controlling Disruption, Destruction, and Disaster

    Preventing Disruption, Destruction, and Disaster

INTRODUCTION

Both business and government were concerned with security long before the need for computer-related security was recognized. They always have been interested in the physical protection of assets through means such as locks, barriers, and guards, but the introduction of computer processing, large databases, and the Internet has increased the need for security.[1] Approximately 90 percent of the respondents to the 2000 Computer Security Institute/FBI Computer Crime and Security Survey reported that they had detected security breaches in the last 12 months. Almost 75 percent reported they suffered a measurable financial loss because of the security problem, with the average loss being just under $1 million. *InformationWeek* estimates that worldwide annual losses due to security problems exceeds $1.6 trillion.

For many people, security means preventing unauthorized access, such as preventing hackers from breaking into their computers. Security is more than that, however. It also includes being able to recover from temporary service problems (e.g., a circuit breaks) or from natural disasters (e.g., fire, earthquake). Figure 10-1 shows some threats to a computer center, the data communication circuits, and the attached computers.

Why Networks Need Security

In recent years, organizations have become increasingly dependent on data communication networks for their daily business communications, database information retrieval, distributed data processing, and the internetworking of LANs. The rise of the Internet with opportunities to connect computers anywhere in the world has significantly increased the potential vulnerability of the organization's assets. Emphasis on network security also has increased as a result of well-publicized security break-ins and as government regulatory agencies have issued security-related pronouncements.

The losses associated with the security failures can be huge. The average loss of about $1 million sounds large enough, but this is just the tip of the iceberg. The potential loss of consumer confidence from a well-publicized security break-in can cost much more in lost business. More important than these losses, however, are the potential losses from the disruption of application systems that run on computer networks. As organizations have come to depend on computer systems, computer networks have become "mission

---

[1] There are many good security sites, including www.cert.org and www.infosyssec.net.

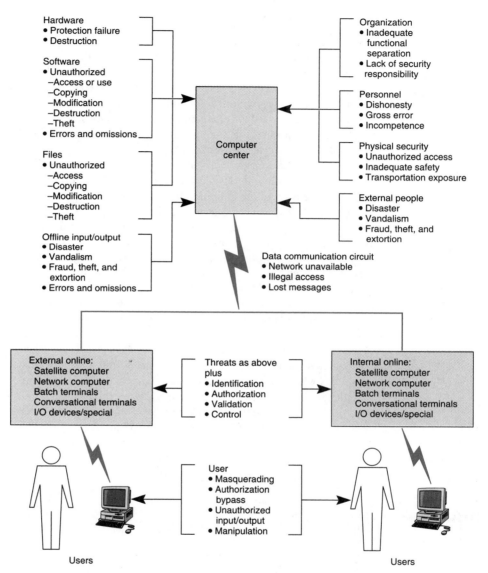

FIGURE 10-1   Some threats to a computer center, the data communication circuits, and the client computers.

critical." Bank of America, one of the largest banks in the United States, estimates that it would cost the bank $50 million if its computer networks were unavailable for 24 hours. Other large organizations have produced similar estimates. The value of the data stored on most organizations' networks and the value provided by the application systems in use far exceeds the cost of the network themselves. For this reason, the primary goal of network security is to protect the organization's data and application software.

Types of Security Threats

In general, network security threats can be classified into one of two categories: (1) disruption, destruction, and disaster; and (2) unauthorized access.

Disruptions are the loss of or reduction in network service. Disruptions may be minor and temporary. For example, a network switch might fail or a circuit may be cut, causing part of the network to cease functioning until the failed component can be replaced. Some users may be affected, but others are not. Some disruptions may also be caused by or result in the *destruction* of data. For example a virus may destroy files, or the "crash" of a hard disk may cause files to be destroyed. Other disruptions may be catastrophic. Natural (or human-made) *disasters* may occur that destroy host computers or large sections of the network. For example, fires, floods, earthquakes, mudslides, tornadoes, and terrorist attacks can destroy large parts of the buildings and networks in their path.

Unauthorized access is often viewed as hackers' gaining access to organizational data files and resources from across the Internet. However, most unauthorized access incidents involve employees. Unauthorized access may have only minor effects. A curious intruder may simply explore the system, gaining knowledge that has little value. A more serious intruder may be a competitor bent on industrial espionage who could attempt to gain access to information on products under development or the details and price of a bid on a large contract. Worse still, the intruder could change files to commit fraud or theft or could destroy information to injure the organization.

Although computer security is improving, so, too, are the number and frequency of problems. The *Computer Emergency Response Team (CERT)* at Carnegie Mellon University (whose mission is to work with the Internet community to respond to computer security problems, raise awareness of computer security issues, and prevent security breaches) was established by the U.S. Department of Defense in 1988 after a virus (called the Internet Worm) shut down almost 10 percent of the computers on the Internet. In 1989, its first full year of operation, the CERT responded to 137 incidents. In 2000, CERT responded to 21,756 incidents. The number of Internet security incidents reported to CERT has doubled every year for the last few years (Figure 10-2).

MANAGEMENT FOCUS *10-1*

BREAKING INTO WESTERN UNION.COM

On September 9, 2000, a hacker broke into the Web site of Western Union, a money transfer company that enables customers to send money over the Internet, and stole credit card numbers for 15,700 customers. Western Union quickly reported the theft to its customers and to the National Bankcard Association so that the card numbers could not be used. No attempts to use the stolen card numbers were made.

The security problem was caused by human error. The Web site was revised earlier in the week, and staff members mistakenly left a file unprotected, creating a security breach that enabled the hacker to enter the site. A routine performance audit found the break-in and staff members immediately shut down the site. It took 5 days before the site was repaired and security tightened. Not counting the actual cost to fix the problem or the loss in reputation, experts estimated that the 5-day outage had cost Western Union more than $1 million in lost business.

SOURCE: "Western.Union.com Back Online after Theft of Credit-Card Data," *ComputerWorld,* September 14, 2000.

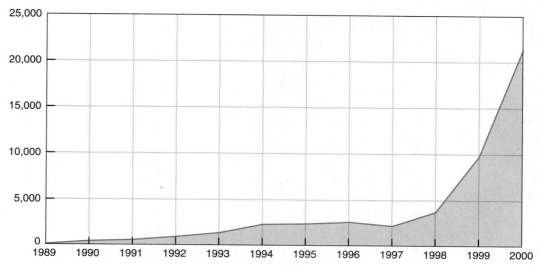

FIGURE 10-2 Number of incidents reported to CERT (Computer Emergency Response Team). SOURCE: CERT Statistics, www.cert.org/stats/cert_stats.html.

Part of the reason for the increase is the increasing availability of sophisticated tools for breaking into networks. Just a few years ago, a hacker wanting to break into a network needed to have some expertise. Today, even inexperienced hackers can obtain hacking tools from a Web site and immediately begin trying to break into networks. Fortunately, laws have begun to catch up with the rapidly changing Internet. Breaking into a computer in the United States—even without causing damage—is a federal crime punishable by a fine and/or imprisonment.

Network Controls

Developing a secure network means developing *controls*. Controls are mechanisms that reduce or eliminate the threats to network security. There are three types of controls that *prevent, detect,* and *correct* whatever might happen to the organization through the threats faced by its computer-based systems.

Preventive controls mitigate or stop a person from acting or an event from occurring. For example, a password can prevent illegal entry into the system or a second set of circuits can prevent a network from crashing. Preventive controls also act as a deterrent by discouraging or restraining someone from acting or proceeding because of fear or doubt. For example, a guard or a security lock on a door may deter an attempt to gain illegal entry.

Detective controls reveal or discover unwanted events. For example, software that looks for illegal network entry or a virus can detect these problems. They also document an event, a situation, or a trespass, providing evidence for subsequent action against the individuals or organizations involved or to enable corrective action to be taken. For example, the same software that detects the problem must report it immediately so that someone or some automated process can take corrective action.

Corrective controls remedy an unwanted event or a trespass. Either computer programs or humans verify and check data to correct errors or fix a security breach so it will not recur in the future. Controls also can aid recovery from network errors or disasters. For example, software can recover and restart the communication circuits automatically when there is a data communication failure.

The remainder of this chapter discusses the various controls that might be used to prevent, detect, and correct threats. We also present a control spreadsheet and risk analysis methodology for identifying the threats and their associated controls. The control spreadsheet provides a data communications network manager with a good view of the current threats and any controls that are in place to mitigate the occurrence of threats.

Nonetheless, it is important to remember that it is not enough to just establish a series of controls; someone or some department must be accountable for the control and security of the network. This includes being responsible for the developing controls, ensuring they are operating effectively, and determining when they need to be updated or replaced.

Controls must reviewed periodically to be sure that they are still useful. They also should be verified and tested. Verifying ensures that the controls are present, and testing determines whether the controls are working as originally specified.

It is also important to recognize that there may be occasions in which a person must override a control. This may be when the network or one of its software or hardware subsystems is not operating properly and controls must be suspended temporarily. Such overrides should be tightly controlled, and there should be a formal procedure to document this occurrence should it happen.

RISK ASSESSMENT

One key step in developing a secure network is to conduct a *risk assessment*. This assigns levels of risk to various threats to the network security by comparing the nature of the threats to the controls designed to reduce them. It is done by developing a control spreadsheet and then rating the importance of each risk. This section provides a brief summary of this process.[2]

Develop a Control Spreadsheet

To be sure that the data communications network and microcomputer workstations have the necessary controls and that these controls offer adequate protection, it is best to build a *control spreadsheet* (Figure 10-3). Threats to the network are listed across the top, and the network assets are listed down the side. The center of the spreadsheet incorporates all the controls that *currently* are in the network. This will become the benchmark on which to base future security reviews.

Assets   The first step is to identify the assets on the network. An *asset* is something of value and can be either hardware or software. Probably the most important asset on a net-

[2] For a detailed risk-assessment procedure, see the OCTAVE method developed by CERT at www. cert.org/octave.

Threats Assets (with Priority)	Disruption, Destruction, Disaster				Unauthorized Access			
	Fire	Flood	Power Loss	Circuit Failure	Virus	External Intruder	Internal Intruder	Eaves-drop
(92) Mail server								
(90) Web server								
(90) DNS server								
(50) Computers on sixth floor								
(50) Sixth-floor LAN circuits								
(80) Building A backbone								
(70) Router in building A								
(30) Network software								
(100) Client database								
(100) Financial database								
(70) Network technical staff								

FIGURE 10-3 Sample control spreadsheet with some assets and threats. DNS = Domain Name Service; LAN = local area network.

work is the organization's data. For example, suppose someone destroyed a mainframe worth $10 million. The mainframe could be replaced, simply by buying a new one. It would be expensive, but the problem would be solved in a few weeks. Now suppose someone destroyed all the student records at your university so that no one know what courses anyone had taken or what grades anyone had received. The cost would far exceed the cost of replacing a $10 million computer. The lawsuits alone would easily exceed $10 million, the cost of hiring a staff to find and reenter paper records would be enormous, and the reentry certainly would take more than a few weeks. Figure 10-4 summarizes some typical assets.

An important type of asset is the *mission-critical application.* A mission-critical application is an information system that is literally critical to the survival of the organization. It is an application that cannot be permitted to fail, and if it does fail the network staff drops everything else to fix it. For example, for an Internet bank that has no brick and mortar branches, the Web site is a mission critical application. If the Web site crashes, the bank cannot conduct business with its customers. Mission-critical applications are usually clearly identified so their importance is not overlooked.

Once you have a list of assets, they should be evaluated on the basis of their importance. There will rarely be enough time and money to protect all assets perfectly, so it is important to focus the organization's attention on the most important ones.

Threats A *threat* to the data communications network is any potential adverse occurrence that can do harm, interrupt the systems using the network, or cause a monetary loss to the organization. Although threats may be listed in generic terms (e.g., theft of data, destruction of data), it is better to be specific and use actual data from the organization being assessed (e.g., theft of customer credit card numbers, destruction of the inventory database).

Hardware	• Servers, such as mail servers, web servers, DNS servers, DHCP servers, and LAN file servers • Client computers • Devices such as hubs, switches, and routers
Circuits	• Locally operated circuits such LANs and backbones • Contracted circuits such as MAN and WAN circuits • Internet access circuits
Network software	• Server operating systems and system settings • Applications software such as mail server and Web server software
Client software	• Operating systems and system settings • Application software such as word processors
Organizational data	• Databases with organizational records
Mission-critical applications	• For example, for an Internet bank, its Web site is mission critical

FIGURE 10-4 Types of assets. DNS = Domain Name Service; DHCP = Dynamic Host Control Protocol; LAN = local area network; MAN = metropolitan area network; WAN = wide area network.

Once the threats are identified, they can be ranked on their probability of occurrence. Figure 10-5, based on several different surveys, summarizes the most common threats and their likelihood of occurring. The actual probability of a threat to your organization depends on your business. An Internet bank, for example, is more likely to be a target of fraud than is a restaurant with a simple Web site. Nonetheless, Figure 10-5 provides some general guidance.

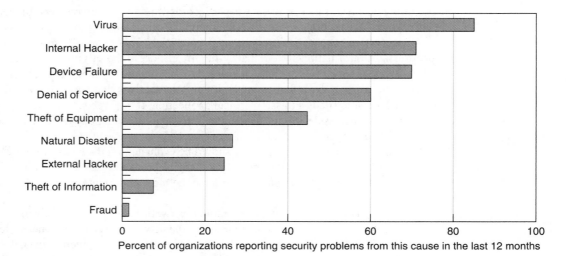

Percent of organizations reporting security problems from this cause in the last 12 months

FIGURE 10-5 Common threats.

There are two important messages from Figure 10-5. First, the most common threat is probably not the one that first came to your mind when we started talking about security; most people first think of a hacker breaking in over the Internet. Instead, the most common threat is viruses, experienced by 85 percent of organizations each year; that is, for an average organization, there is an 85 percent chance that they will be subjected to a virus attack in the next year. In fact, if we look at the relative probabilities, we can see that the chance of disruption, destruction or disaster (virus, device failure, theft of equipment, or natural disaster) is greater than the chance of unauthorized access. Thus, the greatest security risk is not a hacker, but some other problem causing a network outage.

The second important message is that the greatest hacking threat is not from the outside intruder coming at you over the Internet but rather from your own employees. More than 70 percent of organizations reported encountering security breaches caused by employees, compared with only 25 percent reporting security breaches caused by outsiders. Thus, the greatest hacking risk is from inside; for every outside attack, there are on, average, three inside attacks.

Identify and Document the Controls

Once the specific assets and threats have been identified, you can begin working on the network *controls*. A control is something that mitigates or stops a threat or protects an asset. During this step, you identify the current in-place controls and list them in the cell for each asset and threat. Begin by considering the asset and the specific threat, and then describe each control that prevents, detects, or corrects that threat. The description of the control (and its role) is placed in a numeric list, and the control's number is placed in the cell. For example, assume 24 controls have been identified as being in use. Each one is described, named, and numbered consecutively. The numbered list of controls has no ranking attached to it: the first control is number 1 just because it is the first control identified.

Figure 10-6 shows a partially completed spreadsheet. The assets and their priorities are listed as rows, with threats as columns. Each cell lists one or more controls that protects one asset against one threat. For example, in the first row, the mail server is currently protected from a fire threat by a halon fire suppression system, and there is a disaster recovery plan in place. The placement of the mail server above ground level protects against flood, and the disaster recovery plan helps here, too.

Evaluate the Network's Security

The last step in using a control spreadsheet is to evaluate the adequacy of the existing controls and the resulting degree of risk associated with each threat. On the basis of this assessment, priorities can be established to determine which threats must be addressed immediately. Assessment is done by reviewing each set of controls as it relates to each threat and network component. The objective of this step is to answer the specific question "Are the controls adequate to effectively prevent, detect, and correct this specific threat?"

The assessment can be done by the network manager, but it is better done by a team of experts chosen for their in-depth knowledge about the network and environment being

Threats Assets (with Priority)	Distribution, Destruction, Disaster					Unauthorized Access		
	Fire	Flood	Power Loss	Circuit Failure	Virus	External Intruder	Internal Intruder	Eavesdrop
(92) Mail server	1, 2	1, 3	4	5, 6	7, 8	9, 10, 11	9, 10	
(90) Web server	1, 2	1, 3	4	5, 6	7, 8	9, 10, 11	9, 10	
(90) DNS server	1, 2	1, 3	4	5, 6	7, 8	9, 10, 11	9, 10	
(50) Computers on sixth floor	1, 2	1, 3			7, 8	10, 11	10	
(50) Sixth-floor LAN circuits	1, 2	1, 3						
(80) Building A backbone	1, 2	1, 3		6				
(70) Router in building A	1, 2	1, 3				9	9	
(30) Network software					7, 8	9, 10, 11	9, 10	
(100) Client database					7, 8	9, 10, 11	9, 10	
(100) Financial database					7, 8	9, 10, 11	9, 10	
(70) Network technical staff	1	1						

Controls

1. Disaster recovery plan
2. Halon fire system in server room; sprinklers in rest of building
3. Not on or below ground level
4. Uninterruptable power supply (UPS) on all major network servers
5. Contract guarantees from interexchange carriers
6. Extra backbone fiber cable laid in different conduits
7. Virus checking software present on the network
8. Extensive user training about viruses and reminders in monthly newsletter
9. Strong password software
10. Extensive user training about password security and reminders in monthly newsletter
11. Application-layer firewall

FIGURE 10-6   Sample control spreadsheet with some assets, threats, and controls. DNS = Domain Name Service; LAN = local area network.

reviewed. This team, known as the *Delphi team,* is composed of three to nine key people. Key managers should be team members because they deal with both the long-term and day-to-day operational aspects of the network. More importantly, their participation means the final results can be implemented quickly, without further justification, because they make the final decisions affecting the network.

CONTROLLING DISRUPTION, DESTRUCTION, AND DISASTER

Disruption, destruction, and disaster are interruptions in network service or loss of data due to network failure. In this section, we discuss controls that attempt to prevent, detect, and correct for these threats.

Preventing Disruption, Destruction, and Disaster

The key principle in preventing disruption, destruction, and disaster—or at least reducing their impact—is *redundancy*. Redundant hardware that automatically recognizes failure and intervenes to replace the failed component can mask a failure that would otherwise result in a service disruption. Redundancy can be built into any network component.

Using Redundant Hardware   The most common example of redundancy is an *uninterruptable power supply (UPS)*. A UPS is a separate battery-operated power supply unit that can supply power for minutes (or even hours) in the event of a power loss. The UPS is installed on the network server so that in the event of a power failure, the server continues to operate until power is restored or until the UPS battery becomes low. When the UPS battery begins to weaken, many UPSs can send a special message to the server, enabling it to start a normal shutdown.

You can also buy a special-purpose *fault tolerant server* that contains many redundant components to prevent failure. One common strategy, *disk mirroring,* uses a second redundant disk for every disk on the server. Every data item written to the primary disk is automatically duplicated on the mirrored disk. If the primary disk fails, the mirrored disk automatically takes over, with no observable effects on any network applications. This

MANAGEMENT FOCUS *10-2*

MICROSOFT DISRUPTION, PART 1

Microsoft's Web sites and the Web sites of affiliated companies such as MSN.com, MSNBC.com, Expedia.com, Carpoint.com, and Hotmail.com together form the third most visited Internet domain. All were down for about 22 hours in January 2001 owing to a technician's mistake.

Although the problem was caused by one individual's mistake, a poor network design is really to blame. Microsoft had placed all four of its Domain Name Service (DNS) servers on the same network segment, meaning they were connected to the Internet via the same set of routers. The technician loaded incorrect routing table information into the routers on the network, and thus, no messages could reach any of the DNS servers. Without

DNS servers, no one could locate IP addresses for the entire Microsoft family of sites. If Microsoft had just placed some of the DNS servers on different network segments, the problem could have been avoided.

The routing information was eventually corrected and the DNS were servers back up, but experts estimate that Microsoft lost more than $4 million in advertising revenue during the 22-hour outage. Much more was lost through sales at Expedia.com and other sales-oriented sites.

Source: "Microsoft's 'Incredibly Embarrassing' Week," Yahoo.com, January 26, 2001.

concept can be extended to include disk controllers (called *disk duplexing*), so that even if the disk controller fails, the server continues to operate.

Redundancy can be applied to other network components as well. For example, additional client computers, circuits, or devices (e.g., routers, bridges, multiplexers) can be installed to ensure that the network remains operational should any of these components fail. The last control point is the network personnel and equipment in the network control center, which oversees network management and operation, the test equipment, reports, documentation, and the like.

Preventing Natural Disaster   Natural disasters can be huge: An entire site can be destroyed. Even if redundant components are present, often the scope of the loss is such that returning the network to operation is extremely difficult. The best solution is to have a completely redundant network that duplicates every network component but is in a separate location.

Generally speaking, preventing natural disasters is difficult. How do you prevent an earthquake? There are, however, some practical commonsense steps that can be taken to prevent the full the impact of disasters. The most fundamental principle is to decentralize the network resources. Don't store all critical data on the same server or even multiple servers in the same building (or even in the same part of the country). By decentralizing critical data, you can eliminate the chance that a huge natural disaster can destroy all your data resources.

Other steps depend on the type of disaster to be prevented. For example, to reduce the risks due to flooding, do not locate key network components in basement rooms near rivers or oceans. To reduce risks from fire, install halon fire suppression systems in rooms containing important network equipment. To reduce the risks from terrorist attacks, keep secret the location of key network components and protect them with security guards.

Preventing Theft   In some cases, the disruption is intentional. One often overlooked security risk is theft. Computers and network devices are commonly stolen. There is a good secondhand market for such equipment, making these items valuable to steal. Several industry sources estimate that about $1 billion is lost each year through theft of computers and related equipment. Any security plan should include an evaluation of ways to prevent people from stealing equipment, such as the use of security cables to connect computers to desks and private security guards.

Preventing Viruses   Special attention also must be paid to preventing computer *viruses*. Viruses cause unwanted events—some are harmless (such as nuisance messages); others are serious (such as the destruction of data). In most cases, disruptions or the destruction of data are local and affect only a small number of components (although the failure of one WAN or BN circuit may affect many computers). Such disruptions are usually fairly easy to deal with; the failed component is replaced or the virus is removed and the network continues to operate.

Most viruses attach themselves to other programs or to special parts on disks. As those files execute or are accessed, the virus spreads. *Macro viruses,* viruses that are contained in documents or spreadsheet files, can spread when an infected file simply is opened. Macro viruses are the fastest growing type of virus, accounting for more than 75 percent of all virus problems. Some viruses change their appearances as they spread, making detection more difficult.

The best way to prevent the spread of viruses is to not copy or download files of unknown origin, or at least to check every file you do copy or download. Many antivirus software packages are available to check disks and files to ensure that they are virus free. Always check all diskettes and files for viruses before using them—even those from friends! Researchers estimate that six new viruses are developed every day, so it is important to frequently update the virus information files that are provided by antivirus software.

Preventing Denial-of-Service Attacks   Another special case is the *denial-of-service (DoS) attack*. With a DoS attack, a hacker attempts to disrupt the network by flooding the network with messages so that the network cannot process messages from normal users. The simplest approach is to flood a Web server, mail server, and so on, with incoming messages. The server attempts to respond to these, but there are so many messages that it cannot.

One might expect that it would be possible to filter messages from one source IP so that if one user floods the network, the messages from this person can be filtered out before they reach the Web server being targeted. This could work, but most hackers use tools that enable them to put false source IP addresses on the incoming messages so that it is impossible to quickly recognize a message as a real message or a DoS message.

A *distributed denial-of-service attack (DDoS)* is a even more disruptive. With a DDoS attack, the hacker breaks into and takes control of many computers on the Internet (often several hundred to several thousand) and plants software on them called a *DDoS agent*. The hacker then uses software called a *DDoS handler* to control the agents. The handler issues instructions to the computers under the hacker's control, which simultaneously begin sending messages to the target site. In this way, the target is deluged with mes-

MANAGEMENT FOCUS *10-3*

SECURITY MEANS NEVER HAVING TO SAY, "I LOVE YOU"

On May 4, 2000, the "I Love You" e-mail virus swept the world. Frank Wood, chief operations officer of the New Mexico State Highway Department (NMSHD), was in a meeting when he received an emergency call from his Santa Fe office informing him that the NMSHD network was decimated.

The "I Love You" virus spread through the e-mail system, deleting files and then e-mailing itself to others in the infected user's address book. Wood estimates that NMSHD's engineering group alone had more than 50,000 files infected.

The first step was to shut down the entire network—for 2 days. Wood's team first removed the virus from the central e-mail servers and then installed special antivirus software to prevent the virus from reinfecting the servers. Then the remaining 100 servers were scanned and cleaned. Once the network was turned on, the 1,750 client computers were scanned and cleaned. After one week, NMSHD was back at 90 percent.

Computer Economics, a research firm, puts the worldwide cost of the "I Love You" virus at $6.7 billion for the first 5 days.

SOURCE: "Security Means Never Having to Say, 'I Love You'" *InfoWorld,* July 10, 2000.

TECHNICAL FOCUS *10-1*

INSIDE A DENIAL-OF-SERVICE ATTACK

A denial-of-service (DoS) attack typically involves the misuse of standard TCP/IP protocols or connection processes so that the target for the DoS attack responds in a way designed to create maximum trouble. Five common types of attacks include:

- **Smurf attacks:** The network is flooded with Internet Control Message Protocol (ICMP) echo requests (i.e., pings) that have a broadcast destination address and a faked source address of the intended target. Because it is a broadcast message, every computer on the network responds to the faked source address, so that the target is overwhelmed by responses. Because there are often dozens of computers in the same broadcast domain, each smurf message generates dozens of messages at the target.
- **Fraggle attacks:** A fraggle attack is similar to a smurf attack, except that it uses User Datagram Protocol (UDP) echo requests instead of ICMP echo requests.

- **TCP SYN floods:** The target is swamped with repeated SYN requests to establish a TCP connection, but when the target responds (usually to a faked source address), there is no response. The target continues to allocate TCP control blocks, expecting each of the requests to be completed, and gradually runs out of memory.
- **UNIX process table attacks:** These are similar to a TCP SYN flood, but instead of being flooded with TCP SYN packets, the target is swamped by UNIX open connection requests that are never completed. The target opens connections and gradually runs out of memory.
- **Finger of death attacks:** These are similar to the TCP SYN flood, but instead the target is swamped by finger requests that are never disconnected.

SOURCE: "Web Site Security and Denial of Service Protection," www.nwfusion.com, February 2, 2001.

sages from many different sources, making it harder to identify the DoS messages and greatly increasing the number of messages hitting the target.

At present, there is little an individual firm can do to prevent DoS and DDoS attacks. One possibility is to set up many different servers around the world as some companies have done (see Microsoft Disruption, Part 2). Other companies are experimenting with new intrusion detection systems that monitor for DoS attacks; these systems are discussed later in this chapter. Another possibility under discussion by the Internet community as a whole is to require ISPs to verify that all incoming messages they receive from their customers have valid source IP addresses. This would prevent the use of faked IP addresses and enable users to easily filter out DoS messages from a given address. It would make virtually impossible for a DoS attack to succeed and much harder for a DDoS attack to succeed. Many ISPs are beginning to impose security restrictions on the small to medium sized businesses that are often the unwitting accomplices in DDoS attacks because of their poor security, such as requiring firewalls to prevent unauthorized access. (Firewalls are discussed later in this chapter.)

Detecting Disruption, Destruction, and Disaster

Major problems need to be quickly recognized. As we will discuss in Chapter 12, one function of network management software is to alert network managers to problems so these can be corrected. Some intelligent network servers even can be programmed to send

MANAGEMENT FOCUS *10-4*

MICROSOFT DISRUPTION, PART 2

Microsoft has come under a number of distributed denial-of-service (DDoS) attacks over the years, but the one in January 2001 was the one that provoked Microsoft to redesign its network.

The attack was a clever one. The hackers gained control of a large number of computers and planted DDoS software that they launched on cue. The DDoS targeted not Microsoft's Web servers or mail servers but something more important that had been overlooked: Microsoft's Domain Name Service (DNS) servers. Microsoft runs four DNS servers responsible for providing IP addresses for its vast array of Web sites such as Microsoft.com, MSN.com, MSNBC.com, and Hotmail.com. By poor design, Microsoft had placed all four DNS servers on the same network segment, meaning that the DDoS attack could be concentrated on one network segment. The DDoS attack focused on the routers for the DNS network segment and brought them to a crawl on several occasions before Microsoft was able to redesign the network to put the DNS servers on separate segments.

Microsoft also contracted with Akamai.com to reduce the chance of this happening again. Akamai.com has approximately 8,000 Web servers spread around the world, most located at major ISPs. These Web servers contain the pages most commonly used by its many customers, such as Microsoft, Barnes & Noble, and Lands' End. When a user requests a page from one of Akamai.com's customers, the page is provided from the Akamai.com server closest to the customer, rather than from the customer's own server. If the Akamai.com server does not have the page, then the HTTP request continues on its way to the customer's site. In this way, many of the most popular pages on the Web are provided from servers closer to the user, thus reducing the response time—and reducing traffic on the Web—which helps everyone.

SOURCE: "Under Attack, Microsoft Outsources Web Security," Yahoo.com, January 29, 2001.

---

an alarm to a pager if necessary. The organization's disaster procedures should include notifying the network managers as soon as possible.

Detecting minor disruptions and destruction can be more difficult. A network drive may develop bad spots that remain unnoticed unless the drive is routinely checked. Likewise, a network cable may be partially damaged by hungry squirrels, resulting in intermittent problems. These types of problems require ongoing monitoring. The network should routinely log fault information to enable network managers to recognize minor service problems before they become major ones. In addition, there should be a clear procedure by which network users can report problems.

Correcting Disruption, Destruction, and Disaster

Disaster Recovery Plan A critical element in correcting problems is the *disaster recovery plan,* which should address various levels of response to a number of possible disasters and should provide for partial or complete recovery of all data, application software, network components, and physical facilities. A complete disaster recovery plan covering all these areas is beyond the scope of this text. Figure 10-7 provides a summary of many key issues.

The most important elements of the disaster recovery plan are *backup and recovery controls* that enable the organization to recover its data and restart its application software

Elements of a Disaster Recovery Plan

A good disaster recovery plan should include

- The name of the decision-making manager who is in charge of the disaster recovery operation. A second manager should be indicated in case the first manager is unavailable.
- Staff assignments and responsibilities during the disaster
- A preestablished list of priorities that states what is to be fixed first
- Location of alternative facilities operated by the company or a professional disaster recovery firm and procedures for switching operations to those facilities using backups of data and software
- Recovery procedures for the data communication facilities (backbone network, metropolitan area network, wide area network, and local area network), servers, and application systems. This includes information on the location of circuits and devices, whom to contact for information, and the support that can be expected from vendors, along with the name and telephone number of the person at each vendor to contact.
- Action to be taken in case of partial damage or threats such as bomb threats, fire, water or electrical damage, sabotage, civil disorders, and vendor failures
- Manual processes to be used until the network is functional
- Procedures to ensure adequate updating and testing of the disaster recovery plan
- Storage of the data, software, and the disaster recovery plan itself in a safe area where they cannot be destroyed by a catastrophe. This area must be accessible, however, to those who need to use the plan.

FIGURE 10-7 Elements of a disaster recovery plan.

should some portion of the network fail. The simplest approach is to routinely make backup copies of all organizational data and software and to store these backup copies off-site at a different location. Most organizations make daily backups of all critical information, with less important information (e.g., e-mail files) backed up weekly.

Backups ensure that important data is safe. However, it does not guarantee the data can be used. The disaster recovery plan should include a documented and tested approach to recovery, going from the backups to an operating application software system. The recovery plan should have specific goals for different types of disasters. For example, if the main database server was destroyed, how long should it take the organization to have the software and data back in operation by using the backups? Conversely, if the main data center was completely destroyed, how long should it take? The answers to these questions have very different implications for costs. Having a spare network server or a server with extra capacity that can be used in the event of the loss of the primary server is one thing. Having a spare data center ready to operate within 12 hours (for example) is an entirely different proposition.

Although many organizations have a disaster recovery plan, only a few test their plans. A *disaster recovery drill* is much like a fire drill in that it tests the disaster recovery plan and provides staff members the opportunity to practice little-used skills to see what works and what doesn't work before a disaster happens and the staff members must use the plan for real. Without regular disaster recovery drills, the only time a plan is tested is when it must be used.

MANAGEMENT FOCUS *10-5*

FIRM ON ALERT WITH DISASTER RECOVERY SWAT TEAM

Northrop Grumman, an aerospace company, has devised a disaster recovery plan as rigorous as those followed by banking institutions. Daily backup of all mainframe and local area network data is the norm at Northrop, and should computer or network facilities face critical failure, the company's 34-step disaster recovery plan outlines an organized sequence of action. Northrop has compiled an inventory of all its manufacturing and business applications, assigning a priority to each.

Some elements of Northrop's disaster recover checklist are

- Take inventory of all hardware and software and prioritize applications in terms of how quickly they must be recovered
- Establish company-owned, off-site data processing and backup site or contract with a disaster recovery service
- Develop network configuration documentation as well as document recovery guidelines and procedures
- Implement a simulation and testing program

Storage of backup tapes off-site is a daily ritual at Northrop, with the company using several different vendors. If Northrop's data center were disabled, the storage site would be instructed to transfer tapes to the firm's disaster recovery contractor, SunGard Recovery Services. Northrop employees can start data processing and transfer data over a T1 line to any site selected as the company's remote operations center, where employees can continue working.

When problems hit a Northrop facility, the first calls to action go out to the vice president of information systems and the disaster recovery director. Then, team leaders are called on to size up the damage, providing an assessment checklist that helps the security director decide whether to attempt to recover on site or from one of Northrop's remote facilities or to declare a disaster and go to SunGard or to use some combination of the two.

SOURCE: "Firm on Alert with Disaster Recovery SWAT Team," *Network World,* December 5, 1994.

Disaster Recovery Outsourcing   Most large organizations have a two-level disaster recovery plan. When they build networks, they build enough capacity and have enough spare equipment to recover from a minor disaster such as loss of a major server or portion of the network (if any such disaster can truly be called minor). This is the first level. Building a network that has sufficient capacity to quickly recover from a major disaster such as the loss of an entire data center is beyond the resources of most firms. Therefore, most large organizations rely on professional disaster recovery firms to provide this second level support for major disasters.

Many large firms outsource their disaster recovery efforts by hiring *disaster recovery firms* that provide a wide range of services. At the simplest, disaster recovery firms provide secure storage for backups. Full services include a complete networked data center that clients can use when they experience a disaster. Once a company declares a disaster, the disaster recovery firm immediately begins recovery operations using the backups stored on site and can have the organization's entire data network back in operation on the disaster recovery firm's computer systems within hours. Full services are not cheap, but compared with the potential millions of dollars that can be lost per day from the inability to access critical data and application systems, these systems quickly pay for themselves in time of disaster.

MANAGEMENT FOCUS *10-6*

DISASTER RECOVERY HITS HOME

"The building is on fire" were the first words she said as I answered the phone. It was just before noon, and one of my students had called me from her office on the top floor of the business school at the University of Georgia. The roofing contractor had just started what would turn out to be the worst fire in more than 20 years, although we didn't know it then. I had enough time to gather up the really important things from my office on the ground floor (memorabilia, awards, and pictures from 10 years in academia) when the fire alarm went off. I didn't bother with the computer; all the files were backed up off-site.

Ten hours, 100 firefighters, and 1.5 million gallons of water later, the fire was out. Then our work began. The fire had completely destroyed the top floor of the building, including my 20-computer networking lab. Water had severely damaged the rest of the main part of the building, including my office, which, I learned later, had been flooded by almost 2 feet of water at the height of the fire. My computer, and virtually all the computers in the building, were so damaged by the water that they were unusable.

My personal files were unaffected by the loss of the computer in my office; I simply used the backups and continued working—after making new backups and giving them to a

friend to store at his house. The Web server I managed had been backed up to another server on the opposite side of campus 2 days before (on its usual weekly backup cycle), so we had lost only 2 day's worth of changes. In less than 24 hours, our Web site was operational; I had our server's files mounted on the university library's Web server and redirected the university's DNS server to route traffic from our old server address to our new temporary home.

Unfortunately, the rest of our network did not fare as well. Our primary Web server had been backed up to tape the night before, and although the tapes were stored off-site, the tape drive was not; the tape drive was destroyed and no one else on campus had a one that could read our tapes. It took five days to get a replacement and reestablish the Web site. Within 30 days, we were operating from temporary offices with a new network, and 90 percent of the office computers and their data had been successfully recovered.

Living through a fire changes a person. I'm more careful now about backing up my files, and I move ever so much more quickly when a fire alarm sounds. But I still can't get used to the rust that is slowly growing on my "recovered" computer.

Alan Dennis

CONTROLLING UNAUTHORIZED ACCESS

Unauthorized access is the second main type of security problem, and the one that tends to receive the most attention. No one wants an intruder breaking into his or her network.

There are four types of intruders who attempt to gain unauthorized access to computer networks. The first are casual hackers who have only a limited knowledge of computer security. They simply cruise along the Internet trying to access any computer they come across. Their unsophisticated techniques are the equivalent of trying doorknobs, and, until recently, only those networks that left their front doors unlocked were at risk. Unfortunately, there are now a variety of hacking tools available on the Internet that enable even novices to launch sophisticated intrusion attempts. Novice hackers who use such tools are sometimes called *script kiddies.*

The second type of intruders are experts in security but are motivated by the thrill of the hunt. They break into computer networks because they enjoy the challenge and enjoy showing off for friends or embarrassing the network owners. These intruders prefer to be called *crackers*—not hackers—and often have a strong philosophy against ownership of data and software. Most cause little damage and make little attempt to profit from their exploits, but those who do can cause major problems.

The third type of intruder is the most dangerous—the professional hacker who breaks into corporate or government computers for specific purposes, such as espionage, fraud, or intentional destruction. The U.S. Department of Defense (DOD), which routinely monitors attacks against U.S. military targets, has until recently concluded that most attacks are individuals or small groups of hackers in the first two categories. Although some of their attacks have been embarrassing (e.g., defacement of some military and intelligence Web sites), there have been no serious security risks. However, in the late 1990s, the DOD noticed a small but growing set of intentional attacks that it classifies as exercises, exploratory attacks designed to test the effectiveness of certain weapons. Therefore, the DOD established an *information warfare* program and a new organization responsible for coordinating the defense of military networks under the U.S. Space Command.

The fourth type of intruder is also very dangerous. These are organization employees who have legitimate access to the network but who gain access to information they are not authorized to use. This information could be used for their own personal gain, sold to competitors, or fraudulently changed to give the employee extra income. Most security breaches are caused by this type of intruder.

Preventing Unauthorized Access

The key principle in preventing unauthorized access is to be *proactive*. This means routinely testing your security systems before an intruder does. Many steps can be taken to prevent unauthorized access to organizational data and networks, but no network is completely safe. The best rule for high security is to do what the military does: Do not keep

---

MANAGEMENT FOCUS *10-7*

CYBERWAR IN THE MIDDLE EAST

While Israelis and Palestinians have been slugging it out on the ground with guns and stones, others have gone into battle with mouse and modem. Although cyberattacks are not new, this is the first conflict in which two sides have fought each other in such an organized way over the Internet. The most common attacks are of two types, both fairly primitive.

The first is the equivalent of scrawling graffiti on a poster: Someone breaks into an "enemy" Web site and defaces it. Israeli supporters, for example, broke into several Hezbollah-related Web sites, planting Israeli flags and other material on their pages. Palestinian supporters retaliated by defacing the Israel Institute of Technology Web site.

The second is the denial-of-service attack. Israeli supporters, for example, crashed Albawaba.com, a Jordanian-based portal site, by deluging its chat room with large image files. In return, Palestinian supporters attacked Netvision, the Israeli Internet service provider (ISP) that hosts Web sites for the Knesset, the foreign ministry, and the defense forces. Netvision service became extremely slow for a couple of weeks and ordinary subscribers had difficulty logging on.

In reality, there is no evidence that these crude attacks have caused lasting damage, but a more sophisticated attack hit the American–Israel Public Affairs Committee (AIPAC), a pro-Israel lobbying group. The attacker not only defaced the site but also downloaded the credit card details for 700 people—including a Republican senator—who had subscribed to AIPAC via the Internet.

In the crude form that it takes in the Middle East conflict, there is no sign that cyberwar is doing much to advance the cause of either side. However, we have yet to see the full weight of a government's resources deployed in a cyberattack.

SOURCE: "Cyber-Attacks," *The Guardian,* November 30, 2000.

extremely sensitive data online. Data that needs special security are stored in computers isolated from other networks. There are eight general security areas related to preventing unauthorized access: a security policy, user profiles, physical security, dial-in security, firewalls, network address translation, security holes, and encryption.

Security Policy In the same way that a disaster recovery plan is critical to controlling risks due to disruption, destruction, and disaster, a *security policy* is critical to controlling risk due to unauthorized access. The security policy should clearly define the important assets to be safeguarded and the important controls needed to do that. It should a section devoted what employees should and should not do. It should contain a clear plan for routinely training employees—particularly end users with little computer expertise—on key security rules and a clear plan for routinely testing and improving the security controls in place (Figure 10-8).

One of the most common ways for hackers to break into a system, even master hackers, is through *social engineering*—breaking security simply by asking. For example, hackers routinely phone unsuspecting users and, imitating someone such as a technician or senior manager, ask for a password. Unfortunately, too many users simply provide the requested information. Most security experts no longer test for social-engineering attacks; they know from experience that social engineering will eventually succeed in any organization and therefore assume that hackers can gain access at will to normal user accounts. Training end users not to divulge passwords may not eliminate social-engineering attacks, but it may reduce its effectiveness so that hackers give up and move on to easier targets.

Elements of a Security Policy

A good security policy should include

- The name of the decision-making manager who is in charge of security
- An incident-reporting system and a rapid-response team to respond to security breaches in progress
- A risk assessment with priorities as to which assets are most important
- Effective controls placed at all major access points into the network to prevent or deter access by external agents
- Effective controls placed within the network to ensure that internal users cannot exceed their authorized access
- Use of minimum number of controls possible to reduce management time and to provide the least inconvenience to users
- An acceptable use policy that explains to users what they can and cannot do, including guidelines for accessing others' accounts, password security, e-mail rules, and so on
- A procedure for monitoring changes to important network components (e.g., routers, DNS servers)
- A plan to routinely train users regarding security policies and build awareness of security risks
- A plan to routinely test and update all security controls that includes monitoring of popular press and vendor reports of security holes
- An annual audit and review of the security practices

FIGURE 10-8 Elements of a security policy.

User Profiles The basis of network access is the *user profile* for each user's *account* that is assigned by the network manager. Each user's profile specifies what data and network resources he or she can access and the type of access (read only, write, create, delete). Gaining access to an account can be based on what you know, what you have, or what you are. The most common approach is what you know, usually a password. Before users can log in, they need to enter a password. Unfortunately, passwords are often poorly chosen, enabling intruders to guess them and gain access.

More and more systems are requiring users to enter a password in conjunction with something they have, such as a *smart card*. A smart card is a card about the size of a credit card that contains a small processing chip and a memory chip. This card can be read by a smart device; to gain access to the network, the user must present both the card and the password. Intruders must have access to both before they can break in. The best example of this is the automated teller machine (ATM) network operated by your bank. Before you can gain access to you account, you must have both your ATM card and the access number.

In high-security applications, users may be required to present something they are, such as a finger, hand, or the retina of one eye for scanning by the system. These *biometric systems* scan the user to ensure that the user is the sole individual authorized to access the network account. Although most biometric systems are developed for high-security users, several low-cost biometric systems are now on the market. The most popular biometric system is the fingerprint scanner. Several vendors sell devices the size of a mouse that can scan a user's fingerprint for less than $100. Other technologies include facial scans via small desktop video-

MANAGEMENT FOCUS *10-8*

SELECTING PASSWORDS

The keys to users' accounts are passwords; each account has a unique password chosen by the user. The problem is that passwords are often chosen poorly and not changed regularly. Many network managers require users to change passwords periodically (e.g., every 90 days), but this does not ensure that users choose good passwords.

A good password is one that the user finds easy to remember but is difficult for potential intruders to guess. Several studies have found that about three quarters of passwords fall into one of four categories:

- Names of family members or pets
- Important numbers in the user's life (e.g., Social Security number, birthday)
- Words in a dictionary, whether an English or other language dictionary (e.g., *cat, hunter, supercilious, gracias, ici*)
- Keyboard patterns (e.g., *QWERTY, ASDF*)

The best advice is to avoid these categories because such passwords can be guessed easily. Better choices are passwords that

- Are meaningful to the user but no one else
- Are at least seven characters long
- Are made of two or more words that have several letters omitted (e.g., *pplepi [apple pie]*) or are the first letters of the words in a prhase that is not in common usage (e.g., no song lyrics), such as *hapwicac (hot apple pie with ice cream and cheese)*
- Include characters such as numbers or punctuation marks in the middle of the password (e.g., *1hapwic,&c* for *one hot apple pie with ice cream, and cheese*)
- Include some uppercase and lowercase letters (e.g., *1HAPwic,&c*)

For more information, see www.securitystats.com/tools/password.asp.

conferencing cameras and retina scans by more sophisticated devices. Although some banks have begun using fingerprint devices for customer access to their accounts over the Internet, such devices have not become widespread, which we find a bit puzzling. The fingerprint method is unobtrusive and means users no longer have to remember arcane passwords.

User profiles can limit the allowable log-in days, time of day, physical locations, and the allowable number of incorrect log-in attempts. Some will also automatically log off a user if that person has not performed any network activity for a certain length of time (e.g., the user has gone to lunch and has forgotten to log off the network). Regular security checks throughout the day when the user is logged in can determine whether a user is still permitted access to the network. For example, the network manager might have disabled the user's profile while the user is logged in, or the user's account may have run out of funds.

Creating accounts and profiles is simple. When a new staff member joins an organization, that person is assigned a user account and profile. One security problem is the removal of user accounts when someone leaves an organization. Often, network managers are not informed of the departure and accounts remain in the system. For example, a recent examination of the user accounts at the University of Georgia found 30 percent belonged to staff members no longer employed by the university. If the staff member's departure was not friendly, there is a risk that he or she may attempt to access data and resources and use them for personal gain or destroy them to get back at the organization. Many systems permit the network manager to assign expiration dates to user accounts to ensure that unused profiles are automatically deleted or deactivated, but these actions do not negate the need to notify network managers about an employee's departure.

It is important to screen and classify both users and data. Some organizations, especially in government, assign different security clearance levels to users as well as to data, thus permitting users to see only what they need to know.

The impact of any security software packages that restrict or control access to files, records, or data items should be reviewed. Independent of the data communications software, these packages may offer a unique password and identification for each user and allow access only to the specific functions assigned to that user. Some packages also offer additional features, such as file security and layers of passwords to the record or field level, terminal security, transaction security, batch reports on all activity, automatic sign-off of unattended terminals, and immediate online notification of security violations.

Adequate user training on network security should be provided through self-teaching manuals, newsletters, policy statements, and short courses. A well-publicized security campaign may deter potential intruders.

Physical Security One important element of security is *physical security,* preventing outside intruders from gaining access to the organization's offices or network equipment facilities. Both main and remote physical facilities should be secured adequately and have the proper controls. Good security requires implementing the proper access controls so that only authorized personnel can enter closed areas where network equipment is located or access the network. The network components themselves also have a level of physical security. Computers can have locks on their power switches or passwords that disable the screen and keyboard. Network circuits can be locked by having the network manager disable them after hours.

Proper security education, background checks, and the implementation of error and fraud controls are important. In many cases, the simplest means for gaining access is to become employed as a janitor and access the network at night. In some ways, this is easier than the previous methods because the intruder only has to insert a listening device or computer into the organization's network to record messages. Two areas are vulnerable to this type of unauthorized access: network cabling and network devices.

Network cables are the easiest target for eavesdropping because they often run long distances and usually are not regularly checked for tampering. The cables owned by the organization and installed within its facility are usually the first choice for eavesdropping. It is 100 times easier to tap a local cable than it is to tap an interexchange channel, because it is extremely difficult to identify the specific circuits belonging to any one organization in a highly multiplexed switched interexchange circuit operated by a common carrier. Local cables should be secured behind walls and above ceilings, and telephone equipment and switching rooms (wiring closets) should be locked and their doors equipped with alarms. The primary goal is to control physical access by employees or vendors to the connector cables and modems. This includes restricting their access to the wiring closets in which all the communication wires and cables are connected.

Certain types of cable can impair or increase security by making eavesdropping easier or more difficult. Obviously, any wireless network is at extreme risk for eavesdropping because anyone in the area of the transmission can easily install devices to monitor the radio or infrared signals. Conversely, fiber-optic cables are harder to tap, thus increasing security. Some companies offer armored cable that is virtually impossible to cut without special tools. Other cables have built-in alarm systems. The U.S. Air Force, for example, uses pressurized cables that are filled with gas. If the cable is cut, the gas escapes, pressure drops, and an alarm sounds.

Physical protection of the network's local loop and interexchange telephone circuits is the responsibility of the common carrier. You cannot do much about it, except to audit the telephone company's physical security procedures and possibly encrypt the data before it leaves your building to go out onto the public network. All local loops leaving the building should be physically secured and out of harm's way to prevent physical damage or an easy telephone tap. Formal procedures should exist to help identify breaches of security or illegal entries to the network.

Network devices such as controllers, hubs, and bridges should be secured in a locked wiring closet. As discussed in Chapter 6, all messages within a given LAN are actually received by all computers on the LAN, although they process only those messages addressed to them. It is rather simple to install a *sniffer program* that records all messages received for later (unauthorized) analysis. A computer with a sniffer program could then be plugged into an unattended hub or bridge to eavesdrop on all message traffic. A *secure hub* makes this type of eavesdropping more difficult by requiring a special authorization code to be entered before new computers can be added.

Dial-In Security   Any organization that permits staff members to access its network via dial-in modems opens itself to a broader range of intruders. Some dial-up modem controls include changing the modem telephone numbers periodically, keeping telephone numbers confidential, and requiring the use of computers that have an electronic identification chip for all dial-up ports.

Another common strategy is to use a *call-back modem.* In this case, the user dials the organization's modem's telephone number and logs in to to his or her account. Once the user enters the correct password, the modem automatically hangs ups and dials the user's modem's telephone number. In this way, unauthorized intruders cannot access others' accounts because the host computer or communications server will permit access only via modems calling from prespecified numbers. The drawback to this is that only one remote telephone number can be defined for each account. If users have several locations from which they wish to have access (e.g., the user's home and remote office), call-back modems won't work. In recent years, this technique been extended to use automatic number identification (ANI). The network manager can specify several telephone numbers authorized to access each account. When a user successfully logs onto an account, the source of incoming phone call is identified using ANI, and if it is one of the authorized numbers, the log-in is accepted; otherwise, the host computer or communications server disconnects the call.

Neither call-back modemsn or ANI permits users who frequently travel (e.g., sales representatives) to have secure dial-in access. Such users often call from hotel rooms and have no knowledge of telephone numbers in advance. One solution is to use *one-time passwords.* The user connects into the network as usual, and after the user's password is accepted, the system generates a one-time password. The user must enter this password to gain access; otherwise, the connection is terminated. The user can receive this one-time password in a number of ways. Some systems send the password to the user's pager. Other systems provide the user with a unique number that must be entered into a separate hand-held device (called a *token* system), which in turn displays the password for the user to enter. To gain access, an intruder must know the user's account name and password and have access to the user's pager or password device.

Firewalls   With the increasing use of the Internet, it becomes important to prevent unauthorized access to the network from intruders on other networks. The obvious solution is to disconnect any computer or network containing confidential information from the Internet, which is often not a practical solution. In many cases, organizations are disconnecting unneeded applications to improve security. For example, a Web server often does not need e-mail, so network managers often remove e-mail software to reduce the number of entry points that a hacker has into the network. A firewall is another solution.

A *firewall* is a router or special-purpose computer that examines packets flowing into and out of a network and restricts access to the organization's network. The network is designed so that a firewall is placed on every network connection between the organization and the Internet (Figure 10-9). No access is permitted except through the firewall. Some firewalls have the ability to detect and prevent DoS attacks, as well as unauthorized access attempts. Two commonly used types of firewalls are packet-level firewalls and application-level firewalls.

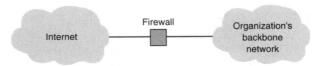

FIGURE 10-9   Using a firewall to protect networks.

TECHNICAL FOCUS *10-2*

BASIC CONTROL PRINCIPLES OF A SECURE NETWORK

- The less complex a control, the better.
- A control's cost should be equivalent to the identified risk. It often is not possible to ascertain the expected loss, so this is a subjective judgment in many cases.
- Preventing a security incident is always preferable to detecting and correcting it after it occurs.
- An adequate system of internal controls is one that provides "just enough" control to protect the network, taking into account both the risks and costs of the controls.
- Automated controls (computer-driven) always are more reliable than manual controls that depend on human interaction.
- Controls should apply to everyone, not just a few select individuals.
- When a control has an override mechanism, make sure that it is documented and that the override procedure has its own controls to avoid misuse.
- Institute the various security levels in an organization on the basis of need to know. If you do not need to know, you do not need to access the network.
- The control documentation should be confidential.
- Names, uses, and locations of network components should not be publicly available.
- Controls must be sufficient to ensure that the network can be audited. This means there should be transaction trails and historical records.
- When designing controls, assume that you are operating in a hostile environment.

- Always convey an image of high security by providing education and training.
- Make sure the controls provide the proper separation of duties. This applies especially to those who design and install the controls and those who are responsible for everyday use and monitoring.
- It is desirable to implement entrapment controls in networks to identify hackers who gain illegal access.
- When a control fails, the network should default to a condition in which everyone is denied access. A period of failure is when the network is most vulnerable.
- Controls should still work even when only one part of a network fails. For example, if a backbone network fails, all local area networks (LANs) connected to it should still be operational, with their own independent controls providing protection.
- Don't forget the LAN. Security and disaster recovery planning has traditionally focused on host mainframe computers and wide area networks. However, LANs now play an increasingly important role in most organizations but are often overlooked by central site network managers.
- Always have insurance as the last resort should all controls fail.
- Always assume your opponent (a hacker) is smarter than you.

A *packet-level firewall* examines the source and destination address of every network packet that passes through it. It allows into or out of the organization's networks only those packets that have acceptable source and destination addresses. In general, the addresses are examined only at the transport layer (TCP port ID) and network layer (IP address). Each packet is examined individually, so the firewall has no knowledge of what the user is attempting to do. It simply chooses to permit entry or exit on the basis of the contents of the packet itself. This type of firewall is the simplest and least secure because it does not monitor the contents of the packets or why they are being transmitted and typically does not log the packets for later analysis.

Some packet-level firewalls are vulnerable to *IP spoofing*. The goal of an intruder using IP spoofing is to send packets to a target computer requesting certain privileges be granted to some user (e.g., setting up a new account for the intruder or changing access permission or password for an existing account). Such a message would not be accepted by the target computer unless it can be fooled into believing that the request is genuine.

IP spoofing is done by changing the source address on incoming packets from their real IP address to an IP address inside the organization's network. Seeing a valid internal address, the firewall lets the packets through to their destination. The destination computer believes the packets are from a valid internal user and processes them. Typically, IP spoofing is more complex than this, because such changes often require a dialogue between the computers. Because the target computer believes it is talking to an internal computer, it directs its messages to it, not to the intruders' computer. Intruders therefore have to guess at the nature and timing of these messages, so that they can generate more spoofed messages that appear to be responses to the target computer's messages. In practice, expert intruders have enough knowledge to have a reasonable chance of getting this right.

Many firewalls have had their security strengthened since the first documented case of IP spoofing occurred in December 1994. For example, some firewalls automatically delete any packets arriving from the Internet that have internal source addresses. However, IP spoofing still remains a problem, because not all packet-level firewalls prevent it.

An *application-level firewall* acts as an intermediate host computer between the Internet and the rest of the organization's networks. This kind of firewall is generally more complicated to install and manage than is a packet-level one. Anyone wishing to access the organization's networks from the Internet must log in to this firewall and can access only the information he or she is authorized for, based on the firewall account profile he or she accesses. This places an additional burden on users who must now remember an additional set of passwords. With application-level firewalls, any access that has not been explicitly authorized is prohibited. In contrast, with a packet-level firewall, any access that has not been disabled is permitted.

TECHNICAL FOCUS *10-3*

HOW PACKET-LEVEL FIREWALLS WORK

Remember from Chapter 5 that TCP/IP networks such as the Internet use TCP packets and IP packets. IP packets provide the source and destination IP addresses. TCP packets provide application-layer port numbers that indicate the application-layer software to which the packet should be sent. For example, the Web uses port 80, Telnet uses port 23, and File Transfer Protocol (FTP) uses port 21.

Packet-level firewalls enable the network administrator to establish a series of rules that define what packets should be allowed to pass through and what packets should be deleted. Suppose, for example, that the organization had a Web server with an IP address of 128.192.55.55 that was for internal use only. The administrator could define a rule on the firewall that instructed the firewall to delete any packet from the Internet that listed 128.192.55.55 as a destination. In this case, the firewall simply needs to examine the destination address.

Suppose, however, that the organization had a Web server (128.192.44.44) that was intended to be available to Internet users. However, to prevent anyone on the Internet from making changes to the server, the organization wants to prevent any Telnet, FTP, or other similar packets from reaching the server. In this case, the administrator could define a rule that instructed the firewall to permit TCP packets with a destination port address of 80 and a destination IP address of 128.192.44.44 to pass through. A second rule would instruct the firewall to delete any packets with any other port number and that destination IP address.

In many cases, special programming code must be written to permit the use of application software unique to the organization (as opposed to commercial off-the-shelf software such as that for e-mail, which is built into the firewall). Many application-level firewalls prohibit external users from uploading executable files. In this way, intruders (or authorized users) cannot modify any software unless they have physical access to the firewall. Some firewalls refuse changes to their software unless the changes are made by the vendor. Other firewalls also actively monitor their own software and automatically disable outside connections if they detect any changes.

Network Address Translation *Network address translation (NAT)* is the process of translating between one set of private addresses inside a network and a set of public addresses outside the network. NAT is transparent, in that no computer notices that it is being done. Although NAT can be done for several reasons, the primary reason today is security.

The *NAT proxy server* uses an address table to translate the private IP addresses used inside the organization into proxy IP addresses used on the Internet. When a computer inside the organization accesses a computer on the Internet, the proxy server changes the source IP address in the outgoing IP packet to its own address. It also sets the source port number in the TCP packet to a unique number that it uses as an index into its address table to find the IP address of the actual sending computer in the organization's internal network. When the external computer responds to the request, it addresses the message to the proxy server's IP address. The proxy server receives the incoming message and, after ensuring the packet should be permitted inside, changes the destination IP address to the private IP address of the internal computer and changes the TCP port ID to the correct port ID before transmitting it on the internal network.

This way, systems outside the organization never see the actual internal IP addresses and thus they think there is only one computer on the internal network. Some organizations also increase security by using illegal internal addresses. For example, if the organization has been assigned the Internet 128.192.55.X address domain, the NAT proxy server would be assigned an address such as 128.192.55.1. Internal computers, however, would *not* be assigned addresses in the 128.192.55.X subnet. Instead, they would be assigned unauthorized Internet addresses such as 10.3.3.55. (Addresses in the 10.X.X.X domain are not assigned to organizations but instead are reserved for special purposes.) Because these internal addresses are never used on the Internet but are always converted by the proxy server, this poses no problems for the users. However, even if intruders discovered the actual internal IP address, it would be impossible for them to reach the internal address from the Internet because the addresses could not be used to reach the organization's computers.

NAT proxy servers work very well and are replacing traditional firewalls. They do, however, slow message transfer between internal networks and the Internet. They also require a separate DNS server for use by external users on the Internet and a separate internal DNS server for use on the internal networks. Because an organization's own employees are the greatest risk for unauthorized access, many organizations use internal firewall to prevent employees in one part of an organization from accessing resources in a different part.

Many organizations use a combination of NAT proxy servers and packet-level and application-level firewalls (Figure 10-10). Packet-level firewalls are used as an initial screen from the Internet into a network devoted solely to servers intended to provide public access

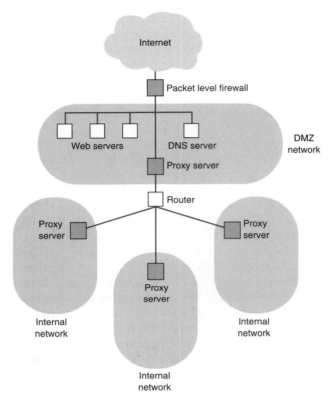

FIGURE 10-10   A typical network design using firewalls.

(e.g., Web servers, public DNS servers). This network is sometimes called the DMZ (demil-itarized zone) because it contains the organization's servers but does not provide complete security for them. This packet-level firewall will permit Web requests and similar access to the DMZ network servers, but will deny FTP access to these servers from the Internet because no one except internal users should have the right to modify the servers. This DMZ network contains a proxy server that provides access to the organization's internal networks. Each major portion of the organization's internal networks has its own proxy server to grant (or deny) access on the basis of rules established by that part of the organization.

While firewalls and NAT proxy servers were originally designed for large corpora-tions who are most often the targets of hackers, they are becoming increasingly important for individuals as well. With the arrival of broadband Internet access technologies, such as cable modem and DSL, residential computers are more vulnerable to attack because they are always on the Internet whenever they are powered on. Thus it is easier for hackers to attack them now than when they were only occasionally connected to the Internet over dial-up services. As DDoS attacks become more common, hackers are more frequently try-ing to break-in to less heavily protected residential computers to install DDoS agents to aid in their attacks. Many inexpensive routers intended for home use with cable modem and DSL services now provide NAT.

Security Holes   Even with physical security, dial-in security, firewalls, and NAT, a network may not be safe because of *security holes.* A security hole is simply a bug that permits unauthorized access. Many commonly used operating system have major security holes well known to potential intruders. Many security holes have been documented, and patches are available from vendors to fix them, but network managers may be unaware of all the holes or simply forget to regularly update their systems with new patches.

A complete discussion of security holes is beyond the scope of the book. Many security holes are highly technical—for example, sending a message designed to overflow a network buffer, thereby placing a short command into a very specific memory area that unlocks a user profile. Others are rather simple but not obvious. For example, the hacker sends a message that lists the server's address as both the sender and the destination, so the server repeatedly sends messages to itself until it crashes.

Once a security hole is discovered, it is quickly circulated through the Internet. The race begins between hackers and security teams; hackers share their discovery with other hackers and security teams share the discovery with other security teams. CERT is the central clearinghouse for major Internet-related security holes, so the CERT team quickly responds to reports of new security problems and posts alerts and advisories on the Web and e-mails them to those who subscribe to its service. The developer of the software with the security hole usually works quickly to fix the security hole and produces a *patch* that corrects the hole. This patch is then shared with customers so they can download it and apply it to their systems to prevent hackers from exploiting the hole to break in. The problem is that many network managers do not routinely respond to such security threats by immediately downloading and installing the patch. Often, it takes many months for patches to be distributed to most sites.[3]

Other security holes are not really holes but simply policies adopted by computer vendors that open the door for security problems, such as computer systems that come with a variety of preinstalled user accounts. These accounts and their initial passwords are well documented and known to all potential intruders. This wouldn't be a problem if network managers didn't sometimes forget to change the passwords on these well-known accounts, thus enabling a hacker to slip in.

The U.S. government requires certain levels of security in the operating systems and network operating systems it uses for certain applications. The minimum level of security is C2. Most major operating systems (e.g., Windows) provide at least C2. Most widely used systems are striving to meet the requirements of much higher security levels, such as B2. Very few systems meet the highest levels of security (A1 and A2).

Symmetric Encryption   One of the best ways to prevent unauthorized access is *encryption,* which is a means of disguising information by the use of mathematical rules known as *algorithms.*[4] Actually, *cryptography* is the more general and proper term. *Encryption* is the process of disguising information, whereas *decryption* is the process of

---

[3] For an example of one CERT advisory posted about problems with the most common DNS server software used on the Internet, see www.cert.org/advisories/CA-2001-02.html. The history in this advisory shows that it took about 8 months for the patch for the previous advisory in this family (issued in November 1999) to be installed on most DNS servers around the world.

[4] For more information on cryptography, see www.rsasecurity.com/rsalabs/faq.

TECHNICAL FOCUS *10-4*

EXPLOITING A SECURITY HOLE

To exploit a security hole, the hacker has to know it's there. So how does a hacker find out? It's simple in the era of automated tools.

First, the hacker has to find the servers on a network. The hacker could start by using network-scanning software to systematically probe every IP address on a network to find all the servers on the network. At this point, the hacker has narrowed the potential targets to a few servers.

Second, the hacker needs to learn what services are available on each server. To do this, he or she could use port-scanning software to systematically probe every port on a given server. This would reveal which ports are in use and thus what services the server offers. For example, if the server has software that responds to port 80, it is a Web server, whereas if it responds to port 25, it is a mail server.

Third, the hacker would begin to seek out the exact software and version number of the server software providing each service. For example, suppose the hacker decides to target mail servers. There is a variety of tools that can probe the mail server software and, on the basis of how the server software responds to certain messages, determine which manufacturer and version number of software is being used.

Finally, once the hacker knows which package and version number the server is using, the hacker uses tools designed to exploit the known security holes in the software. For example, some older mail server software packages do not require users to authenticate themselves (e.g., by a user ID and password) before accepting Simple Mail Transfer Protocol (SMTP) packets for the mail server to forward. In this case, a hacker could create SMTP packets with fake source addresses and use the server to flood the Internet with spam (i.e., junk mail). In another case, a certain version of a well-known e-commerce package enabled users to pass operating system commands to the server simply by including a UNIX pipe symbol (|) and the command to name a file name to be uploaded; when the system opened the uploaded file, it also executed the command attached to it.

---

restoring it to readable form. When information is in readable form, it is called *plaintext*; when in encrypted form, it is called *ciphertext*.

There are two fundamentally different types of encryption: symmetric and asymmetric. A *symmetric algorithm* is one in which the key used to encrypt a message is the *same* as the one used to decrypt it. An *asymmetric algorithm* is one in which the key used to decrypt is *different* from the one used to encrypt it. In this section, we discuss symmetric encryption; the next section is devoted to asymmetric encryption.

A symmetric encryption system (also call single-key encryption) has two parts: the algorithm itself and the *key,* which personalizes the algorithm by making the transformation of data unique. Two pieces of identical information encrypted with the same algorithm but with different keys produce completely different ciphertexts. When using most encryption systems, communicating parties must share this key. If the algorithm is adequate and the key is kept secret, acquisition of the ciphertext by unauthorized personnel is of no consequence to the communicating parties.

Good encryption systems do not depend on keeping the algorithm secret. Only the keys need to be kept secret. The key is a relatively small numeric value (in terms of the number of bits). The larger the key, the more secure the encryption, because large "key space" protects the ciphertext against those who try to break it by *brute-force attacks*—which are simply trying every possible key. There should be a large enough number of possible keys that an exhaustive brute-force attack would take inordinately long or would cost more than the value of the encrypted information.

Because the same key is used to encrypt and decrypt, symmetric algorithms can cause problems with *key management*; keys must be shared among the senders and receivers very carefully. Before two computers in a network to can communicate using encryption, both must have the same key. This means that both computers can then send and read any messages that use that key. Companies often do not want one company to be able to read messages they send to another company, so this means that there must be a separate key used for communication with each company. These keys must be recorded but kept secure so that they cannot be stolen. Because the algorithm is known publicly, the disclosure of the key means the total compromise of encrypted messages. Managing this system of keys can be challenging.

One commonly used symmetric encryption algorithm is the *Data Encryption Standard (DES),* which was developed in the mid-1970s by the U.S. government in conjunction with IBM. DES is maintained by the National Institute of Standards and Technology (NIST). The most common form of DES uses a 56-bit key but can be broken by brute-force attacks. In a recent test using a special decryption supercomputer, 56-bit DES was broken in 56 hours. In another attempt, this same computer, working with the help of 10,000 microcomputers distributed over the Internet, broke 56-bit DES in 22 hours. DES is no longer recommended for government use, although the commercial sector continues to use it for less important messages.

Another commonly used symmetric encryption algorithm is *RC4,* developed by Ron Rivest of RSA Data Security, Inc. RC4 can use a key up to 256 bits long but most commonly uses a 40-bit key. It is faster to use than DES but suffers from the same problems from brute-force attacks: It can be broken by a determined attacker.

Triple DES (3DES) is a newer standard that is harder to break. As the name suggest, it involves using DES three times, usually with three different keys to produce the encrypted text,[5] which produces a stronger level of security, because it has a total of 168 bits as the key (i.e., 3×56 bits).

The NIST's new *Advanced Encryption Standard (AES)* is designed to replace DES and 3DES with the *Rijndael* (pronounced "rain doll") *algorithm,* developed by two Flemish researchers.[6] AES will have key sizes of 128, 192, and 256 bits. NIST estimates that using the most advanced computers and techniques available today, cracking AES by brute force would require about 150 trillion years. As computers and techniques improve, the time requirement will drop, but AES seems secure for the foreseeable future; the original DES lasted 20 years, so AES may have a similar life span.

Today, the U.S. government considers encryption to be a weapon and regulates its export in the same way it regulates the export of machine guns or bombs. Present rules prohibit the export of encryption techniques with keys longer than 56 bits (for some algorithms, 64 bits and 168 bits are permitted), although exports to Canada and the European Union are permitted, and American banks and Fortune 100 companies are now permitted to use more powerful encryption techniques in their foreign offices. This policy made

---

[5] There are several versions of 3DES. One version (called 3DES-EEE) simply encrypts the message three times with different keys, as one would expect. Another version (3DES-EDE) encrypts with one key, decrypts with a second key (i.e., reverse-encrypts), and then encrypts with a third key. There are other variants, as you can imagine.

[6] It was developed by Joan Daemen and Vincent Rijmen. It was Rijmen's doctoral dissertation. For more information on Rijndael, see csrc.nist.gov/encryption/aes/rijndael.

sense when only U.S. companies had the expertise to develop powerful encryption software. Today, however, many companies outside the United States are developing encryption software that is more powerful than U.S. software that is limited by these rules. Therefore, the U.S. software industry is lobbying the government to change the rules so that it can successfully compete overseas.[7]

Public Key Encryption The most popular form of *public key encryption* (also called asymmetric encryption) is *RSA,* which was invented at Massachusetts Institute of Technology in 1977 by Ron Rivest, Adi Shamir, and Leonard Adleman. The inventors of the initial algorithm founded RSA Data Security in 1982, and many companies have licensed the RSA patented technique. The patent expired in 2000, so many new companies have entered the market and public key software has dropped in price. The RSA technique forms the basis for today's *public key infrastructure (PKI).*

Public key encryption is inherently different from symmetric single-key systems like DES. Because public key encryption is asymmetric, there are two keys. One key (called the *public key*) is used to encrypt the message and a second, very different *private key* is used to decrypt the message. Keys are often 512 or 1,024 bits in length.

Public key systems are based on one-way functions. Even though you originally know both the contents of your message and the public encryption key, once it is encrypted by the one-way function, the message cannot be decrypted without the private key. One-way functions, which are relatively easy to calculate in one direction, are impossible to "uncalculate" in the reverse direction. Public key encryption is one of the most secure encryption techniques available, excluding special encryption techniques developed by national security agencies.

Public key encryption greatly reduces the key management problem. Each user has its public key that is used to encrypt messages sent to it. These public keys are widely publicized (e.g., listed in a telephone book–style directory)—that's why they're called *public* keys. In addition, each user has a private key that decrypts only the messages that were encrypted by its public key. This private key is kept secret. The net result is that if two parties wish to communicate with one another, there is no need to exchange keys beforehand. Each knows the other's public key from the listing in a public directory and can communicate encrypted information immediately. The key management problem is reduced to the on-site protection of the private key.

Figure 10-11 illustrates how this process works. All public keys are published in a directory. When organization A wants to send an encrypted message to organization B, it looks through the directory to find its public key. It then encrypts the message using B's public key. This encrypted message is then send through the network to organization B, which decrypts the message using its private key.

Public key encryption also permits *authentication* (or *digital signatures*). When one user sends a message to another, it is difficult to legally prove who actually sent the message. Legal proof is important in many communications, such as bank transfers and buy/sell orders in currency and stock trading, which normally require legal signatures. Public key encryption algorithms are invertable, meaning that text encrypted with either key can be decrypted by the other. Normally, we encrypt with the public key and decrypt

---

[7] The rules have been changed several times in recent years, so for more recent information, see www.bxa.doc.gov/Encryption.

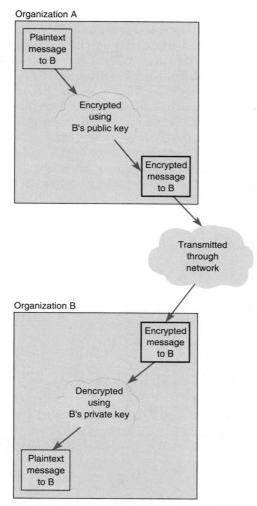

Organization A

Plaintext
message
to B

Encrypted
using
B's public key

Encrypted
message
to B

Transmitted
through
network

Organization B

Encrypted
message
to B

Dencrypted
using
B's private key

Plaintext
message
to B

FIGURE 10-11   Secure transmission with public key encryption.

with the private key. However, it is possible to do the inverse: Encrypt with the private key and decrypt with the public key. Because the private key is secret, only the real user could use it to encrypt a message. Thus, a digital signature or authentication sequence is used as a legal signature on many financial transactions. This signature is usually the name of the signing party plus other *key contents* such as unique information from the message (e.g., date, time, or dollar amount). This signature and the other key contents are encrypted by the sender using the private key. The receiver uses the sender's public key to decrypt the signature block and compares the result to the name and other key contents in the rest of the message to ensure a match.

Figure 10-12 illustrates how authentication can be combined with public encryption to provide a secure and authenticated transmission. The plaintext message is first encrypted using organization A's private key and then encrypted using organization's B public key. It is then transmitted to B. Organization B first decrypts the message using its private key. It sees that part of the message (the key contents) is still in ciphertext, indicating it is an authenticated message. B then decrypts the key contents part of the message using A's public key to produce the plaintext message. Because only A has the private key that matches A's public key, B can safely assume that A sent the message.

The only problem with this approach lies in ensuring that the person or organization who sent the document with the correct private key is actually the person or organization claimed. Anyone can post a public key on the Internet, so there is no way of knowing for sure who that person actually is. For example, it would be possible for someone other than organization A in this example to claim to be organization A when in fact that someone is an imposter.

This is where the Internet's PKI becomes important.[8] The PKI is a set of hardware, software, organizations, and policies designed to make public key encryption work on the Internet. PKI begins with a *certificate authority (CA)*, which is a trusted organization that can vouch for the authenticity of the person or organization using authentication (e.g.,

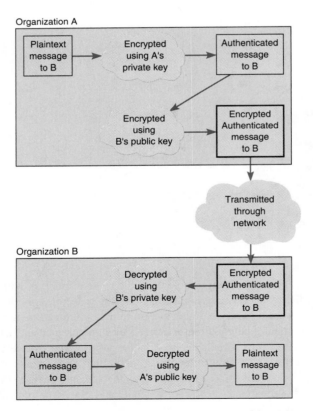

FIGURE 10-12 Authenticated and secure transmission with public key encryption.

[8] For more on the PKI, see www.ietf.org/internet-drafts/draft-ietf-pkix-roadmap-06.txt.

VeriSign). A person wanting to use a CA registers with the CA and must provide some proof of identify. There are several levels of certification, ranging from a simple confirmation from valid e-mail address to a complete police-style background check with an in-person interview. The CA issues a digital *certificate* that is the requestor's public key encrypted using the CA's private key as proof of identify. This certificate is then attached to the user's e-mail or Web transactions in addition to the authentication information. The receiver then verifies the certificate by decrypting it with the CA's public key—and must also contact the CA to ensure that the user's certificate has not been revoked by the CA.

For higher-security certifications, the CA requires that a unique "fingerprint" be issued by the CA for each message sent by the user. The user submits the message to the CA, who creates the unique fingerprint by combining the CA's private key with the message's authentication key contents. Because the user must obtain a unique fingerprint for each message, this ensures that the CA has not revoked the certificate between the time it was issued and the time the message was sent by the user.

Pretty Good Privacy (PGP) is a freeware public key encryption package developed by Philip Zimmermann that is often used to encrypt e-mail. Users post their public key on Web pages, for example, and anyone wishing to send them an encrypted message simply cuts and pastes the key off the Web page into the PGP software, which encrypts and sends the message.[9] There are also a variety of PGP key servers around the Internet that enable you to search for and extract someone's public key using their e-mail address (e.g., pgp5.ai.mit.edu)

Secure Sockets Layer (SSL) is an encryption protocol widely used on the Web. SSL operates between the application-layer software and the transport layer (in what the OSI model calls the presentation layer). SSL encrypts outbound packets coming out of the application layer before they reach the transport layer and decrypts inbound packets coming out of the transport layer before they reach the application layer. With SSL, the client and the server start with a handshake for PKI authentication and for the server to provide its public key and preferred encryption technique to the client (usually RC4, DES, or 3DES). The client then generates a key for this encryption technique, which is sent to the server encrypted with the server's public key. The rest of the communication then uses this encryption technique and key.

IP Security Protocol (IPSec) is another widely used encryption protocol. IPSec differs from SSL in that SSL is focused on Web applications, whereas IPSec can be used with a much wider variety of application-layer protocols. IPSec sits between IP at the network layer and TCP/UDP at the transport layer. IPSec can use a wide variety of encryption techniques, so the first step is to the sender and receiver to establish the technique and key to be used. This is done using *Internet Key Exchange (IKE)*. Both parties generate a random key and send to the other using an encrypted authenticated PKI process, then put these two numbers together to produce the key.[10] The encryption technique is also negotiated between the two, often being DES or 3DES. Once the keys and technique have been established, IPSec can begin transmitting data.

---

[9] For example, Cisco posts the public keys it uses for security incident reporting on its Web site. You will find a link to the Cisco PGP Public keys near the bottom of the page at: www.cisco.com/warp/public/707/sec_incident_response.shtml. For more information on PGP, see www.pgpi.org and www.pgp.com.

[10] This is done using the Diffie–Hellman process; see www.rsasecurity.com/rsalabs/faq/3-6-1.html.

IPSec can operate in either transport mode or tunnel mode. In *transport mode,* IPSec encrypts just the IP payload, leaving the IP packet header unchanged so it can be easily routed through the Internet. In this case, IPSec adds an additional packet (either an authentication header [AH] or an encapsulating security payload [ESP]) at the start of the IP packet that provides encryption information for the receiver.

In *tunnel mode,* IPSec encrypts the entire IP packet and must therefore add an entirely new IP packet that contains the encrypted packet, as well as the IPSec AH or ESP packets. In tunnel mode, the newly added IP packet just identifies the IPSec encryption agent at the destination, not the final destination; once the IPSec packet arrives at the encryption agent, the encrypted packet is decrypted and sent on its way. In tunnel mode, attackers can learn only the end points of the tunnel, not the ultimate source and destination of the packets.

Detecting Unauthorized Access

The previous section focused on preventing unauthorized access. Although one hopes that these techniques are successful, the possibility of a security break-in still remains. Therefore, networks sometimes need an *intrusion detection system (IDS).*

There are three general types of IDS, and many network managers choose to install all three. The first type is a *network-based IDS.* With a network-based IDS, *IDS sensors* are placed on key network circuits. An IDS sensor is simply a device running a special operating system that monitors all network packets on that circuit and reports intrusions to an *IDS management console.*

The second type of IDS is the *host-based IDS,* which, as the name suggests, is a software package installed on a host or server. The host-based IDS monitors activity on the server and the incoming circuits and reports intrusions to the IDS management console. An

MANAGEMENT FOCUS *10-9*

ANATOMY OF A FRIENDLY HACK

If you've seen the movie *Sneakers,* you know that there are professional security firms that organizations can hire to break in to their own networks to test security. BABank was about to launch a new online banking service, so it hired such a firm to test its security before the launch. The bank's system failed the security test.

The security team began by mapping the bank's network. It used DNS searches, sniffer software, network security analysis software (e.g., SATAN), and dialing software to test for dial-in ports. The mapping process found a computer running an old mail program with a known security hole and a bunch of maintenance accounts with unchanged passwords. The team then used social engineering to gain passwords to several high-privilege accounts. Once into to these computers, the team used password-cracking software to find passwords on these computers and ultimately gain the administrator passwords on several servers and routers.

At this point, the team transferred $1,000 into their test account. They could have transferred more, but the security point was made. Finally, the team launched a successful denial-of-service attack that crashed the online banking system.

SOURCE: *Network World,* February 2, 1998.

application-based IDS is a specialized form of host-based IDS that just monitors one application on the server, often a Web server.

There are two fundamental techniques that these three type of IDS can use to determine that an intrusion is in progress; most IDS use both techniques. The first technique is *misuse detection,* which compares monitored activities with signatures of known attacks. Whenever an attack signature is recognized, the IDS issues an alert and discards the suspicious packets. The problem, of course, is keeping the database of attack signatures up to date as new attacks are invented.

The second fundamental technique is *anomaly detection,* which works well in stable networks by comparing monitored activities with the "normal" set of activities. When a major deviation is detected (e.g., a sudden flood of ICMP ping packets, an unusual number of failed log-ins to the network manager's account), the IDS issues an alert and discards the suspicious packets. The problem, of course, is false alarms when situations arise that produce valid network traffic that is different from normal (e.g., on a heavy trading day on Wall Street, E-trade receives a larger-than-normal volume of messages).

IDSs are often used in conjunction with other security tools such as firewalls (Figure 10-13). In fact, some firewalls are now including IDS functions. One problem is that the

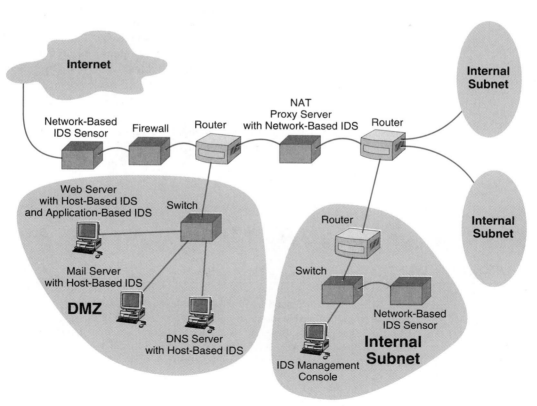

FIGURE 10-13   Intrusion detection system (IDS). DMZ = demilitarized zone. NAT = network address translation.

IDS and its sensors and management console are a prime target for hackers. Whatever IDS is used, it must be very secure against attack. Some organizations deploy redundant IDS from different vendors (e.g., a network-based IDS from one vendor and a host-based IDS from another) to decrease the chance that the IDS can be hacked.

Correcting Unauthorized Access

Although IDS monitoring is important, it has little value unless there is a clear plan for responding to a security breach in progress. Every organization should have a clear response planned if a break-in is discovered. Many large organizations have emergency response "SWAT" teams ready to be called into action if a problem is discovered. The best example is CERT, the Internet's emergency response team. CERT has helped many organizations establish such teams.

Responding to an intrusion can be more complicated than it at first seems. For example, suppose the IDS detects a DoS attack from a certain IP address. The immediate reaction could be to discard all packets from that IP address; however, in the age of IP spoofing, the attacker could fake the address of your best customer and trick you into discarding packets from it.

Once an intrusion has been detected, the first step is to identify how the intruder gained unauthorized access and prevent others from breaking in the same way. Some organizations will simply choose to close the door on the hacker and fix the security problem Other organizations may take a more aggressive response by logging the intruder's activities and working with police to catch the individuals involved. Once identified, the hacker will be charged with criminal activities, and/or sued in civil court.

A whole new area called *computer forensics* has recently opened up. Computer forensics is the use of computer analysis techniques to gather evidence for criminal and/or civil trials. The basic steps of computer forensics are similar to those of traditional forensics, but the techniques are different. First, identify potential evidence. Second, preserve evidence by making backup copies and use those copies for all analysis. Third, analyze the evidence. Finally, prepare a detailed legal report for use in prosecutions.

MANAGEMENT FOCUS *10-10*

SNAPPING A HONEY TRAP

After a 6-month investigation, British police arrested three men with links to organized crime who attempted to rob an online bank, London's Egg PLC. The men exploited a security hole in the bank's application software that enabled them to open multiple accounts and apply for multiple credit cards and loans.

After discovering the security hole, the bank choose to pursue and prosecute the intruders. First, however, the bank closed the hole to other would-be thieves but permit-

ted the three men to continue with their activities. Working with police, the bank installed special software to monitor and track the thieves. Once enough evidence had been collected, Britain's National Crime Squad swooped in and arrested them.

SOURCE: "U.K. police catch e-bank robbers," *Computer World,* August 23, 2000.

Although criminal law has been slow to keep up with the Internet, most industrialized countries now have criminal laws under which hackers can be prosecuted. Companies are sometimes tempted to launch counterattacks (or counterhacks) against intruders, but this can be illegal.

Many organizations have taken their own steps to snare intruders by using *entrapment* techniques. The objective is to divert the hackers' attention from the real network to an attractive server that contains only fake information. This server is often called a *honey pot*. The honey pot server contains highly interesting fake information, available only through illegal intrusion, to "bait" the intruder. The honey pot server has sophisticated tracking software to monitor access to this information that allows the organization and law enforcement officials to trace and legally document the intruder's actions. Possession of this information then becomes final legal proof of the intrusion.

SUMMARY

Types of Security Threats   In general, network security threats can be classified into one of two categories: (1) disruption, destruction, and disaster; and (2) unauthorized access. Disruptions are usually minor and temporary. Some disruptions may also be caused by or result in the destruction of data. Natural (or human-made) disasters may occur that destroy host computers or large sections of the network. Unauthorized access refers to intruder's (external hackers or organizational employees) gainining unauthorized access to files. Intruders may gain knowledge, change files to commit fraud or theft, or destroy information to injure the organization.

Risk Assessment   Developing a secure network means developing controls that reduce or eliminate threats to the network. Controls prevent, detect, and correct whatever might happen to the organization when its computer-based systems are threatened. The first step in developing a secure network is to conduct a risk assessment. This is done by identifying the key assets and threats and comparing the nature of the threats to the controls designed to protect the assets. A control spreadsheet lists the assets, threats, and controls, which a network manager uses to assess the level of risk.

Controlling Disruption, Destruction, and Disaster   The key principle in controlling these threats—or at least reducing their impact—is redundancy. Redundant hardware that automatically recognizes failure and intervenes to replace the failed component can mask a failure that would otherwise result in a service disruption. Special attention needs to be given to preventing computer viruses and DoS attacks. Generally speaking, preventing disasters is difficult, so the best option is a well-designed disaster recovery plan that includes backups and sometime a professional disaster recovery firm.

Controlling Unauthorized Access   The key principle in controlling unauthorized access is to be proactive in routinely testing and upgrading security controls. Contrary to popular belief, unauthorized intruders are usually organization employees, not external hackers. There are eight general areas to preventing unauthorized access: a security policy, user profiles, physical security, dial-in security, firewalls, network address translation, security holes, and encryption. The basic principle in detecting unauthorized access is using an intrusion detection system to monitor for known attacks and/or to look for anything out of the ordinary. The intrusion system should trigger a rapid-response team once an intrusion is detected.

KEY TERMS

account
Advanced Encryption
    Standard (AES)
anomaly detection
application-based IDS
application-level firewall
asset
asymmetric algorithm
authentication
backup controls
biometric system
block cipher
brute-force attack
call-back modem
certificate
certificate authority (CA)
ciphertext
Computer Emergency
    Response Team
    (CERT)
computer forensics
control principles
control spreadsheet
controls
cracker
Data Encryption Stan-
    dard (DES)

decryption
delphi team
denial-of-service (DoS)
    attack
digital signature
disaster recovery drill
disaster recovery firm
disaster recovery plan
disk mirroring
distributed denial-of-
    service (DDoS) attack
DDoS agent
DDoS handler
eavesdropping
encryption
entrapment
fault-tolerant server
firewall
hacker
honey pot
host-based IDS
IDS management
    console
IDS sensor
information warfare
Internet Key Exchange
    (IKE)

intrusion detection sys-
    tem (IDS)
IP Security Protocol
    (IPSec)
IPSec transport mode
IPSec tunnel mode
IP spoofing
key
Key escrow
key management
macro virus
mission-critical
    application
misuse detection
NAT proxy server
network address transla-
    tion (NAT)
network-based IDS
one-time password
packet-level firewall
password
patch
physical security
plaintext
Pretty Good Privacy
    (PGP)
private key

public key
public key encryption
public key infrastructure
    (PKI)
RC4
recovery controls
redundancy
Rijndael algorithm
risk assessment
RSA
script kiddies
secure hub
Secure Sockets Layer
    (SSL)
security hole
security policy
smart card
sniffer program
social engineering
symmetric algorithm
Triple DES (3DES)
uninterruptable power
    supply (UPS)
user profile
Threat
token
virus

QUESTIONS

1. What factors have brought about increased emphasis on network security?

2. Briefly outline the steps required to complete a risk assessment.

3. Name at least six assets that should have controls in a data communications network.

4. What are some of the criteria that can be used to rank security risks?

5. What is the primary principle of controlling disruption, destruction, disaster?

6. What is the primary principle of controlling unauthorized access?

7. What is the purpose of a disaster recovery plan? What are five major elements of a typical disaster recovery plan?

8. What are the most common security threats? What are the most critical?

9. What is a computer virus?

10. How can one reduce the risk of natural disaster?

11. Explain how a DoS attack works.

12. How does a DoS attack differ from a DDoS attack?

13. What is a disaster recovery firm? When and why would you establish a contract with them?

14. Reread Microsoft Disruption, Part 1 and Microsoft Disruption, Part 2, which discussed the security problems experienced by Microsoft. Which disruption had the greatest impact? What are the implications for security?

15. People who attempt unauthorized access can be classified into four different categories. Describe them.

16. What are five major elements of a security policy?

17. What is social engineering?

18. What is a token (in the security meaning of the word, not the medium access control meaning of the word)? A smart card?

19. Explain how a biometric system can improve security.

20. What is a security hole, and how do you fix it?

21. What is a sniffer?

22. Describe the purpose of a call-back modem.

23. Describe the three general ways of restricting access to a network.

24. What do you think are the three most important security controls that can be placed on a network? Why?

25. What is a firewall?

26. What are the differences between the different types of firewalls?

27. What is IP spoofing?

28. What is a NAT proxy server, and how does it work?

29. Compare and contrast symmetric and asymmetric encryption.

30. Is it possible first to encrypt with a public key and then to decrypt with a private (secret) key, as well as first to encrypt with the private key and then to decrypt that message with the public key?

31. Describe how symmetric encryption and decryption work.

32. Describe how asymmetric encryption and decryption work.

33. What is key management?

34. How does DES differ from 3DES? From RC4? From AES?

35. Compare and contrast DES and public key encryption.

36. Explain how authentication works.

37. What is a certificate authority?

38. How does PGP differ from SSL?

39. How does SSL differ from IPSec?

40. Compare and contrast IPSec tunnel mode and IPSec transfer mode.

41. What is an intrusion detection system?

42. Compare and contrast a network-based IDS, a host-based IDS, and an application-based IDS.

43. How does IDS anomaly detection differ from misuse detection?

44. What is computer forensics?

45. What is a honey pot?

46. A few security consultants have said that broadband and wireless technologies are their best friends. Explain.

47. Some experts argue that CERT's posting of security holes on its Web site causes more security break-ins than it prevents and should be stopped. What are the pros and cons on both sides of this argument? What do you think?

48. If you had the ability to invent a fabulous new security tool, what would it be?

49. Suppose you started working as a network manager at a medium-size firm with an Internet presence and discovered that the previous network manager had done a terrible job of network security. Which four security controls would be your top priority? Why?

50. Although it is important to protect all servers, some servers are more important than others. What server is the most important to protect and why?

EXERCISES

10-1 Conduct a risk assessment of your organization's networks. Some information may be confidential, so report what you can.

10-2 Investigate and report on the activities of CERT.

10-3 Investigate the capabilities and costs of three firewall products.

10-4 Investigate the capabilities and costs of three IDSs.

10-5 Investigate the capabilities and costs of three encryption software packages.

MINI-CASES

I. Belmont State Bank

Belmont State Bank is a large bank with hundreds of branches that are connected to a central computer system. Some branches are connected over dedicated circuits, and others use the dial-up telephone network. Each branch has a variety of client computers and ATMs connected to a server. The server stores the branch's daily transaction data and transmits it several times during the day to the central computer system. Tellers at each branch use a four-digit numeric password, and each teller's computer is transaction-coded to accept only its authorized transactions. Perform a risk assessment.

II. Western Bank

Western Bank is a small family-owned bank with six branches spread over one county. It has decided to move onto the Internet with a Web site that permits customers to access their accounts and pay bills. Design the key security hardware and software the bank should use.

CASE STUDY

NEXT-DAY AIR SERVICE

The president of NDAS has just read a newspaper article about a recent security break-in at a major clothing company and rushed down to Les Coone's office to understand if it could happen to NDAS. The hackers broke into their Web site and left insulting messages on their home page. Les has turned to you to prepare an analysis of NDAS security.

Exercises

1. Prepare a report outlining the major security threats faced by NDAS. Be sure to identify those that you think are major threats and those that are minor threats.
2. Prepare a partial risk assessment for NDAS that includes their major assets, threats, and controls. You will need to make some reasonable assumptions.
3. Develop a set of security controls, for use in the NDAS main office and for its Web site, designed to control risks due to disruption, destruction, and disaster.
4. Develop a set of security controls, for use in the NDAS main office and for its Web site, designed to control risks due to unauthorized access.

CHAPTER 11

NETWORK DESIGN

NETWORK MANAGERS perform two key tasks: (1) designing new networks and network upgrades and (2) managing the day-to-day operation of existing networks. This chapter examines network design. Network design is an interative process in which the designer examines users' needs, develops an initial set of technology designs, assesses their cost, and then revisits the needs analysis until the final network design emerges.

OBJECTIVES

- Be familiar with the overall process of designing and implementing a network
- Be familiar with techniques for developing a logical network design
- Be familiar with techniques for developing a physical network design
- Be familiar with network design principles

CHAPTER OUTLINE

INTRODUCTION

Most organizations today have networks, which means that most network design projects are the design of upgrades or extensions to existing networks, rather than the construction of entirely new networks. Even the network for an entirely new building is likely to be integrated with the organization's existing BN or WAN, so even new projects can be seen as extensions of existing networks. Nonetheless, network design is very challenging.

The Traditional Network Design Process

The *traditional network design process* follows a very structured systems analysis and design process similar to that used to build application systems. First, the network analyst meets with users to identify user needs and the application systems planned for the network. Second, the analyst develops a precise estimate of the amount of data that each user will send and receive and uses this to estimate the total amount of traffic on each part of the network. Third, the circuits needed to support this traffic plus a modest increase in traffic are designed and cost estimates are obtained from vendors. Finally, 1 or 2 years later, the network is built and implemented.

This traditional process, although expensive and time consuming, works well for static or slowly evolving networks. Unfortunately, networking today is significantly different from what it was when the traditional process was developed. Three forces are making the traditional design process less appropriate for many of today's networks.

First, the underlying technology of the client and server computers, networking devices, and the circuits themselves is changing very rapidly. In the early 1990s, mainframes dominated networks, the typical client computer was an 8-MHz 386 with 1 megabyte (MB) of random access memory (RAM) and 40 MB of hard disk space, and a typical circuit was a 9,600-bps mainframe connection or an amazingly fast 1-Mbps LAN. Today, client computers and severs are significantly more powerful, and circuit speeds of 100 Mbps and 1 Gbps are common. We now have more processing capability and network capacity than ever before; both are no longer scarce commodities that we need to manage carefully.

Second, the growth in network traffic is immense. The challenge is not in estimating today's user demand but in estimating its rate of growth. In the early 1990s, e-mail and the Web were novelties primarily used by university professors and scientists. In the past, network demand essentially was driven by predictable business systems such as order processing. Today, much network demand is driven by less predictable user behavior, such as e-mail and Web searches. Many experts expect the rapid increase in network demand to continue, especially as video, voice, and multimedia applications become commonplace on networks. At a 10 percent growth rate, user demand on a given network will increase by one third in 3 years. At 20 percent, it will increase by about 75 percent in 3 years. At 30 percent, it will double in less than 3 years. A minor mistake in estimating the growth rate can lead to major problems. With such rapid growth, it is no longer possible to accurately predict network needs for most networks. In the past, it was not uncommon for networks to be designed to last for 5 to 10 years. Today, most network designers use a 3-year planning horizon.

Finally, the balance of costs have changed dramatically over the past 10 years. In the early 1990s, the most expensive item in any network was the hardware (circuits, devices, and servers). Today, the most expensive part of the network is the staff members who design, operate, and maintain it. As the costs have shifted, the emphasis in network design in no longer on minimizing hardware cost (although it is important); the emphasis today is on designing networks to reduce the staff time needed to operate them.

The traditional process minimizes the equipment cost by tailoring the equipment to a careful assessment of needs but often results in a mishmash of different devices with different capabilities. Two resulting problems are that staff members need to learn to operate

MANAGEMENT FOCUS *11-1*

THE END OF ARCHITECTURE

All good things must end. After a century of predictability, the telephone network as we know it is fading into oblivion. Lulled to sleep by relatively predictable voice and data traffic forecasts, interexchange carriers (IXCs) set a timetable for a gradual replacement of existing networks with faster all-ATM, (asynchronous transfer mode) network architectures. Their leisurely replacement timetable ran smack into a brick wall.

Huge increases in data traffic, primarily due to the booming growth of the Internet, have caused IXCs to throw out the nicely planned replacements of their core telephone networks. Rather than investing in all-ATM architectures whose main benefit is the ability to handle voice, data, and video on the same circuits, IXCs are building "overlay networks." Overlay networks coexist with the primary core voice networks and support separate services

in an attempt to keep up with the demand. One set of overlay networks, for example, is designed to support Internet traffic, another carries frame relay wide area network traffic, another carries switched multimegabit data services, and so on.

The core telephone network is gradually changing from a centrally designed and managed hierarchical network to a decentralized set of networks, much the same changes that have been seen in the office environment as decentralized client–server local area networks have replaced the centralized host-based mainframe systems. The key challenges now facing IXCs are how to manage this huge— and rapidly growing—collection of distinct networks and how to route traffic from one network to another.

Source: "The End of Architecture," *tele.com*, September 1996.

and maintain many different devices and that it often takes longer to perform network management activities because each device may use slightly different software.

Today, the cost of staff time is far more expensive than the cost of equipment. Thus, the traditional process can lead to a false economy—save money now in equipment costs but pay much more over the long term in staff costs.

The Building-Block Network Design Process

Some organizations still use the traditional process to network design, particularly for those applications for which hardware or network circuits are unusually expensive (e.g., WANs that cover long distances through many different countries). However, many other organizations now use a simpler approach to network design that we call the *building-block process*. The key concept in the building-block process is that networks that use a few standard components throughout the network are cheaper in the long run than networks that use a variety of different components on different parts of the network.

Rather than attempting to accurately predict user traffic on the network and build networks to meet those demands, the building-block process instead starts with a few standard components and uses them over and over again, even if they provide more capacity than is needed. The goal is simplicity of design. This strategy is sometimes called "narrow and deep" because a very narrow range of technologies and devices are used over and over again (very deeply throughout the organization). The result is a simpler design process and a more easily managed network built with a smaller range of components.

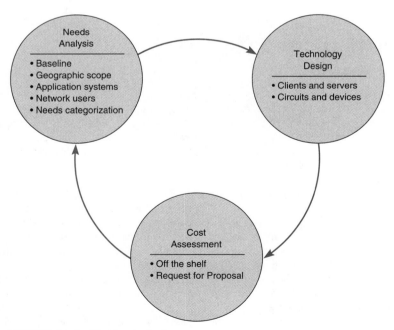

FIGURE 11-1 Network design.

In this chapter, we focus on the building-block process to network design. The basic design process involves three steps that are performed repeatedly: needs analysis, technology design, and cost assessment (Figure 11-1). This process begins with *needs analysis,* during which the designer attempts to understand the fundamental current and future network needs of the various users, departments, and applications. This is likely to be an educated guess at best. Users and applications are classified as typical or high volume. Specific technology needs are identified (e.g., the ability to dial in with current modem technologies).

The next step, *technology design,* examines the available technologies and assesses which options will meet users' needs. The designer makes some estimates about the network needs of each category of user and circuit in terms of current technology (e.g., 10Base-T, 100Base-T, 1000Base-T) and matches needs to technologies. Because the basic network design is general, it can easily be changed as needs and technologies change. The difficulty, of course, lies in predicting user demand so one can define the technologies needed. Most organizations solve this by building more capacity than they expect to need and by designing networks that can easily grow and then closely monitoring growth so they expand the network ahead of the growth pattern.

In the third step, cost assessment, the relative costs of the technologies are considered. The process then cycles back to the needs analysis, which is refined using the technology and cost information to produce a new assessment of users' needs. This in turn triggers changes in the technology design and cost assessment and so on. By cycling through these three processes, the network design settles on the final network design (Figure 11-2).

MANAGEMENT FOCUS *11-2*

WHY NETWORK PROJECTS FAIL

CIMI Corporation surveyed almost 300 organizations about the key success factors in network design. These 300 organizations reported on 1,370 network design projects. Of these, 475 (35 percent) were considered complete successes and 125 (9 percent) were considered complete failures. The rest (56 percent) were only partial successes.

Network managers reported that the key problems leading to failure in the 125 failed projects were as follows (multiple answers were permitted):

- Needs analysis problems
    - Had requirements that were incomplete or inaccurate: 64 percent
    - Encountered a significant change in business requirements as the network was installed: 30 percent

- Technology design problems
    - Bought the wrong equipment or services—often the right technology but the wrong products or features: 99 percent
    - Encountered vendor misrepresentation—the products and/or services did not work as promised: 38 percent
- Overall problems with the design process
    - Lacked network design skills internally and did not use external consultants or systems integrators: 34 percent
    - Used external network consultants or systems integrators who bungled the project: 32 Percent

SOURCE: "Why Projects Fail," *Network World,* July 7, 1997.

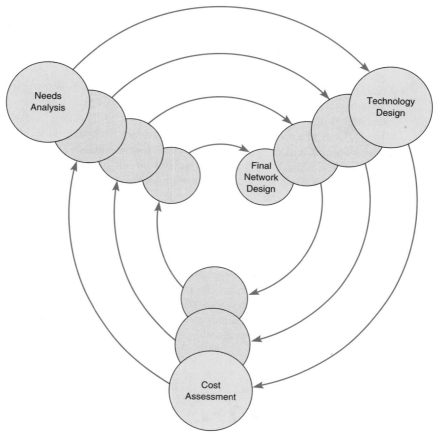

FIGURE 11-2 The cyclical nature of network design.

NEEDS ANALYSIS

The goal of the needs analysis is to understand why the network is being built and what users and applications it will support. In many cases, the network is being designed to improve poor performance or enable new applications to be used. In other cases, the network is upgraded to replace unreliable or aging equipment or to standardize equipment so that only one type of equipment, one protocol (e.g., TCP/IP, Ethernet), or one vendor's equipment is used everywhere in the network.

Often, the goals in network design are slightly different between LANs and BNs on the one hand and MANs and WANs on the other. In the LAN and BN environment, the organization owns and operates the equipment and the circuits. Once they are paid for, there are no additional charges for usage. However, if major changes must be made, the organization will need to spend additional funds. In this case, most network designers tend to err on the side of building too big a network—that is, building in more capacity than they expect to need.

In contrast, in most MANs and WANs, the organization leases circuits from a common carrier and pays for them on monthly or per-use basis. Understanding capacity becomes more important in this situation because additional capacity comes at a noticeable cost. In this case, most network designers tend to err on the side of building too small a network, because they can lease additional capacity if they need it—but it is much more difficult to cancel a long-term contract for capacity they are not using.

Much of the needs analysis may already have been done, because most network design projects today are network upgrades rather than the design of entirely new networks. In this case, there is already a fairly good understanding of the existing traffic in the network and, most importantly, of the rate of growth of network traffic. It is important to gain an understanding of the current operations (application systems and messages). This step provides a *baseline* against which future design requirements can be gauged. It should provide a clear picture of the present sequence of operations, processing times, work volumes, current communication network (if one exists), existing costs, and user/management needs. Whether the network is a new network or a network upgrade, the primary objective of this stage is to define (1) the geographic scope of the network and (2) the users and applications that will use it.

The goal of the needs analysis step is to produce a *logical network design,* which is a statement of the network elements needed to meet the needs of the organization. The logical design does not specify technologies or products to be used (although any specific requirements are noted). Instead, it focuses on the fundamental functionality needed, such as a high-speed access network, which in the technology design stage will be translated into specific technologies (e.g., switched 100Base-T).

Geographic Scope

The first step in needs analysis is to break the network into three conceptual parts on the basis of their geographic and logical scope: the access layer, the distribution layer, and the core layer, as first discussed in Chapter 7.[1] The *access layer* is the technology that is closest to the user—the user's first contact with the network—and is often a LAN or a dial-up connection over a MAN. The *distribution layer* is the next part of the network that connects the access layer to the rest of the network, such as the BN(s) in a specific building. The *core layer* is the innermost part of the network, the part that connects the different distribution-layer networks to each other, such as the primary BN on a campus or a set of MAN or WAN circuits connecting different offices together. As the name suggests, the core layer is usually the busiest, most important part of the network. Not all layers are present in all networks; small networks, for example, may not have a distribution layer, because their core may the BN that directly connects the parts of the access layer together.

Within each of these parts of the network, the network designer must then identify some basic technical constraints. For example, if the access layer is a MAN, in that the users need to connect to the network over the public telephone network, this provides some constraints on the technologies to be used; one could not use 100Base-T Ethernet, for example. Likewise, if the access layer is a LAN, it would be silly to consider using T1 circuits.

---

[1] It is important to understand that these three layers refer to geographic parts of the network, not the five conceptal layers in the network model, such as application layer, transport layer, and so on.

Sometimes, the current network infrastructure also imposes constraints. For example, if we are adding a new building to an existing office complex that used 100Base-T in the access-layer LANs, then we will probably choose to use 100Base-T for the access layer in the new building. Likewise, if we are running a dial-up ISP, we will probably need to support the V.90 and V.92 modems of our customers. All such constraints are noted.

It is easiest to start with the highest level, so most designers begin by drawing a network diagram for any WANs with international or countrywide locations that must be connected. A diagram that shows the logical network going between the locations is sufficient. Details such as the type of circuit and other considerations will be added later. Next, the individual locations connected to the WAN are drawn, usually in a series of separate diagrams, but for a simple network, one diagram may be sufficient.

At this point, the designers gather general information and characteristics of the environment in which the network must operate. For example, they determine whether there are any legal requirements, such as local, state/provincial, federal, or international laws, regulations, or building codes, that might affect the network.

Figure 11-3 shows an the initial drawing of a network design for an organization with offices in four areas connected to the core network, which is a WAN. The Toronto location, for example has a distribution layer (a BN) connecting three distinct access-layer LANs, which could be three distinct LANs in the same office building. Chicago has a similar structure, with the addition of a fourth access part that connects to the Internet; that is, the organization has only one Internet connection, so all Internet traffic must be routed through the core network to the Chicago location. The Atlantic Canada network section has two distinct access layer parts; one is a LAN and one access layer is a MAN (e.g., dial-up). The New York network section is more complex, having its own core network component (a BN connected into the core WAN), which in turn supports three distribution layer BNs. Each of these support several access-layer LANs

Application Systems

Once the basic geographic scope is identified, the designers must review the list of applications that will use the network and identify the location of each. This information should be added to the emerging network diagrams. This process is called baselining. Next, those applications that are expected to use the network in the future are added.

In many cases, the applications will be relatively well defined. Specific internal applications (e.g., payroll) and external applications (e.g., Web servers) may already be part of the "old " network. However, it is important to review the organization's long-range and short-range plans concerning changes in company goals, strategic plans, development plans for new products or services, projections of sales, research and development projects, major capital expenditures, possible changes in product mix, new offices that must be served by the communications network, security issues, and future commitments to technology. For example, a major expansion in the number of offices or a major electronic commerce initiative will have a significant impact on network requirements.

It also is helpful to identify the hardware and software requirements of each application that will use the network and, if possible, the protocol each application uses (e.g., HTTP over TCP/IP, Windows file access to a Novell file server over SPX/IPX). This knowledge helps now and will be particularly useful later when developing technological

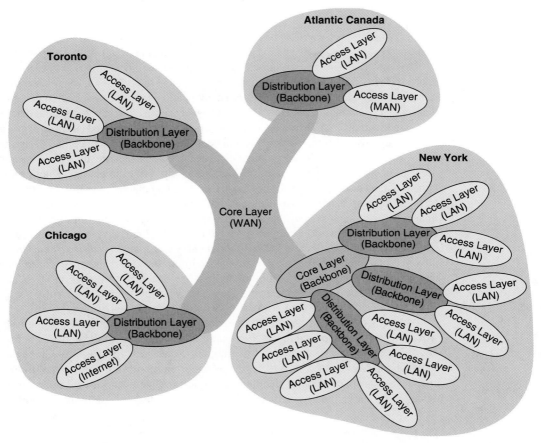

FIGURE 11-3 Geographic scope. LAN = local area network; MAN = metropolitan area network; WAN = wide area network.

solutions. For example, if the main financial application payroll runs on an IBM mainframe, the network may need to support SNA traffic and provide a gateway to translate it into more standard TCP/IP protocols.

Network Users

In the past, application systems accounted for the majority of network traffic. Today, much network traffic is produced by the discretionary use of the Internet. Applications such as e-mail and the Web are generating significant traffic, so the network manager is no longer in total control of the network traffic generated on his or her networks. This is likely to continue in the future as network-hungry applications such as desktop videoconferencing become more common. Therefore, in addition to understanding the applications, you must also assess the number and type of users that will generate and receive network traffic and identify their location on the emerging network diagram.

Categorizing Network Needs

At this point, the network has been designed in terms of geographic scope, application systems, and users. The next step is to assess the relative amount of traffic generated in each part of the network. With the traditional design approach, this involves considerable detailed analysis. With the building-block approach, the goal is provide some rough assessment of the relative magnitude of network needs. Each application system is assessed in general terms to determine the amount of network traffic it can be expected to generate today and in the future, compared with other applications. Likewise, each user is categorized as either a typical user or a high-traffic user. These assessments will be refined in the next stage of the design process.

This assessment can be problematic, but the goal is some relative understanding of the network needs. Some simple rules of thumb can help. For example, applications that require large amounts of multimedia data or those that load executables over the network are likely to be high-traffic applications. Applications that are time sensitive or need constant updates (e.g., financial information systems, order processing) are likely to be high-traffic applications.

Once the network requirements have been identified, they also should be organized into *mandatory requirements, desirable requirements,* and *wish-list requirements.* This information enables the development of a minimum level of mandatory requirements and a negotiable list of desirable requirements that are dependent on cost and availability. For example, desktop videoconferencing may be a wish-list item, but it will be omitted if it increases the cost of the network beyond what is desired.

At this point, the local facility network diagrams are prepared. For really large network, there may be several levels. For example, the designer of the network in Figure 11-3 might choose to draw another set of diagrams, one each for Toronto, Chicago, Atlantic Canada, and New York. Conversely, the designer might just add more detail to Figure 11-3 and develop separate, more detailed, diagrams for New York. The choice is up to the designer, provided the diagrams and supporting text clearly explain the network's needs.

Deliverables

The key deliverable for the needs assessments stage are a set of logical network diagrams, showing the applications, circuits, clients, and servers in the proposed network, each categorized as either typical or high traffic. The logical diagram is the conceptual plan for the network and does not consider the specific physical elements (e.g., routers, switches, circuits) that will be used to implement the network.

Figure 11-4 shows the results of a needs assessment for one of the New York parts of the network from Figure 11-3. This figure shows the distribution and access parts in the building with the series of six access LANs connected by one distribution BN, which is in turn connected to a campus-area core BN. One of the six LANs is highlighted as a high-traffic LAN, whereas the others are typical. Three mandatory applications are identified that will be used by all network users: e-mail, Web, and file sharing. One wish-list requirement (desktop video conferencing) is also identified for a portion of the network.

TECHNOLOGY DESIGN

Once the needs have been defined in the logical network design, the next step is to develop a *physical network design* (or set of possible designs). The physical network design starts

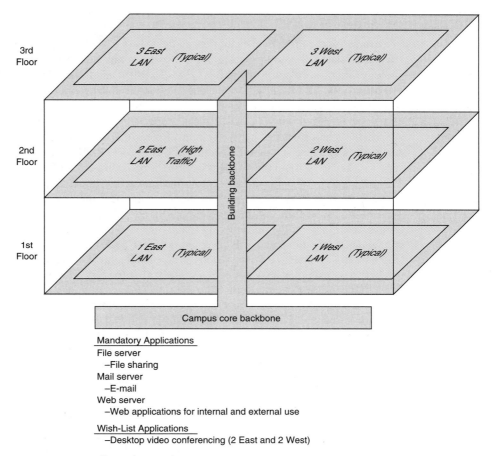

Mandatory Applications
File server
 –File sharing
Mail server
 –E-mail
Web server
 –Web applications for internal and external use

Wish-List Applications
 –Desktop video conferencing (2 East and 2 West)

FIGURE 11-4 Sample needs assessment.

with the client and server computers needed to support the users and applications. If the network is a new network, new computers will need to be purchased. If the network is an existing network, the servers may needed to be upgraded to the newest technology. Once these are designed, then the circuits and devices connecting them are designed.

Designing Clients and Servers

The idea behind the building-block approach is to specify the computers needed in terms of some standard units. Typical users are allocated the base-level client computers, as are servers supporting typical applications. Users and servers for applications needing more powerful computers are assigned some advanced computer. As the specifications for computers rapidly improve and costs drop (usually every 4 months), today's typical user may receive the type of computer originally intended for the advanced user when the network is actually implemented, and the advanced users may end up with a computer not available when the network was designed.

Designing Circuits and Devices

The same is true for network circuits and devices (e.g., hubs, routers, switches). There are two interrelated decisions in designing network circuits and devices: the fundamental technology and protocols (e.g., Ethernet, ATM, TCP/IP), and the capacity of each circuit (e.g., 10 Mbps, 100 Mbps, 1,000 Mbps). These are interrelated, because each technology offers different circuit capacities.

Designing the circuit capacity means *capacity planning,* estimating the size and type of the standard and advanced network circuits for each type of network (LAN, BN, WAN). For example, should the standard LAN circuit be 10Base-T, 100Base-T, or 10/100 switched Ethernet? Likewise, should the standard BN circuit be 100Base-T, 1000Base-T, or ATM OC-3?

This requires some assessment of the current and future *circuit loading* (the amount of data transmitted on a circuit). This analysis can focus on either the *average* circuit traffic or the *peak* circuit traffic. For example, in an online banking network, traffic volume peaks usually are in the midmorning (bank opening) and just prior to closing. Airline and rental car reservations network designers look for peak message volumes before and during holidays or other vacation periods, whereas telephone companies normally have their highest peak volumes on Mother's Day. Designing for peak circuit traffic is the ideal.

The designer usually starts with the total characters transmitted per day on each circuit or, if possible, the maximum number of characters transmitted per 2-second interval if peaks must be met. You can calculate message volumes by counting messages in a current network and applying some estimated growth rate. If an existing network is in place, network monitors/analyzers (see Chapter 12) may be able to provide an actual circuit character count of the volume transmitted per minute or per day.

A good rule of thumb is that 80 percent of this circuit loading information is easy to gather. The last 20 percent needed for very precise estimates is extremely difficult and expensive to find. However, precision usually is not a major concern because of the stairstep nature of communication circuits and the need to project future needs. For example, the difference between 10Base-T and 100Base-T is quite large, and assessing which level is needed for typical traffic does not require a lot of precision. Forecasts are inherently less precise than understanding current network traffic. The *turnpike effect* results when the network is used to a greater extent than was anticipated because it is available, is very efficient, and provides new services. The annual growth factor for network use may vary from 5 to 50 percent and, in some cases, may exceed 100 percent for high-growth organizations.

Although no organization wants to overbuild its network and pay for more capacity than it needs, in most cases, upgrading a network costs 50 to 80 percent more than building it right the first time. Few organizations complain about having too much network capacity, but being under capacity can cause significant problems. Giving the rapid growth in network demand and the difficulty accurate predicting it, most organizations intentionally overbuild (build more capacity into their network they plan to use), and most end up using this supposedly unneeded capacity within 3 years.

Network Design Tools

Network modeling and design tools can perform a number of functions to help in the technology design process. With most tools, the first step is to enter a diagram or model of the existing network or proposed network design. Some modeling tools require the user to create the network diagram from scratch. That is, the user must enter all of the network components by hand, placing each server, client computer, and circuit on the diagram and defining what each is (e.g., 10Base-T, frame relay circuit with a 1-Mbps committed information rate).

Other tools can "discover" the existing network; that is, once installed on the network, they will explore the network to draw a network diagram. In this case, the user provides some starting point, and the modeling software explores the network and automatically draws the diagram itself. Once the diagram is complete, the user can then change it to reflect the new network design. Obviously, a tool that can perform network discovery by itself is most helpful when the network being designed is an upgrade to an existing network and when the network is very complex.

Once the diagram is complete, the next step is to add information about the expected network traffic and see if the network can support the level of traffic that is expected. *Simulation* is used to model the behavior of the communication network. Simulation is a mathematical technique in which the network comes to life and behaves as it would under real conditions: Applications and users generate and respond to messages, the simulator tracks the number of packets in the network and the delays encountered at each point in the network.

Simulation models may be tailored to the user's needs by entering parameter values specific to the network at hand (e.g., this computer will generate an average of three 100-byte packets per minute). Alternatively, the user may prefer to rely primarily on the set of average values provided by the network.

Once the simulation is complete, the user can examine the results to see the estimated response times and throughout. It is important to note that these network design tools provide only estimates, which may vary from the actual results. At this point, the user can change the network design, in an attempt to eliminate bottlenecks, and rerun the simulation. Good modeling tools not only produce simulation results but also highlight poten-

MANAGEMENT FOCUS *11-3*

MAKING PREDICTIONS AT MTV

MTV Networks (MTVN) creates innovative programming for MTV, VH1, Nickelodeon, Nick at Night, and TV Land, as well as other networks. MTVN operates more than 80 offices worldwide, in the United States, Canada, Latin America, Australia, Europe, and Asia. Because of its reliance on an extensive wide area network (WAN), predicting network performance and designing the WAN to support peak data flows was very important.

MTVN first used CACI's Predictor to model its current WAN. It then captured network usage data from a set of test users for several new network-intensive applications soon to be used throughout MTVN's network. It added this information into the model developed by Predictor and performed a series of what-if analyses to see the effect of widespread use of these applications on overall network performance. In this way, MTV can anticipate the effects of new applications and upgrade its networks, before users begin using the new application systems and encountering problems.

SOURCE: "What's My Line," *Communications News,* September 1999.

tial trouble spots (e.g., servers, circuits, or devices that experienced long response times). The very best tools offer suggestions on how to overcome the problems that the simulation identified (e.g., network segmentation, increasing from T1 to T3).

Deliverables

The key deliverable is a set of one or more physical network designs. Most designers like to prepare several physical designs so they can trade off technical benefits (e.g., performance) against cost. In most cases, the critical part is the design of the network circuits and devices. In the case of a new network designed from scratch, it is also important to define the client computers with care, because these will form a large portion of the total cost of the network. Usually, however, the network will replace an existing network and only a few of the client computers in the existing network will be upgraded.

Figure 11-5 shows a physical network design for the simple network in Figure 11-4. In this case, a switched 10/100Base-T collapsed backbone is used in the distribution layer, and switched 10Base-T Ethernet has been chosen as the standard network for typical users in the access layer. High-traffic users (2 East) will used switched 10/100Base-T. All LAN cabling will be category 5 cable so that all users can easily move to 100 Mbps in the future. The building backbone will be connected directly into the campus backbone using a router. The building backbone will use fiber-optic cable to enable the possible future addition of desktop videoconferencing.

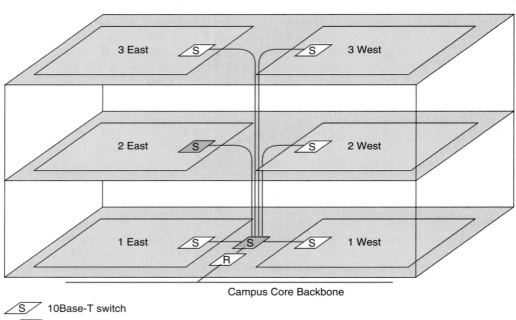

FIGURE 11-5 Physical network design.

COST ASSESSMENT

The purpose of this step is to assess the costs of various physical network design alternatives produced in the previous step. The main items are the costs of software, hardware, and circuits. These three factors are all interconnected and must be considered along with the performance and reliability required. All factors are interrelated with regard to cost.

Estimating the cost of a network is quite complex because many factors are not immediately obvious. Some of the costs that must be considered are

- Circuit costs, including costs of circuits provided by common carriers or the cost of purchasing and installing your own cable
- Internetworking devices such as switches and routers
- Hardware costs, including server computers, NICs, hubs, memory, printers, uninterruptible power supplies, and backup tape drives
- Software costs for network operating system, application software, and middleware
- Network management costs, including special hardware, software, and training needed to develop a network management system for ongoing redesign, monitoring, and diagnosing of problems
- Test and maintenance costs for special monitoring equipment and software, plus the cost of onsite spare parts
- Costs to operate the network

Request for Proposal

Although some network components can be purchased off the shelf, most organizations develop a *request for proposal (RFP)* before making large network purchases. RFPs specify what equipment, software, and services are desired and ask vendors to provide their best prices. Some RFPs are very specific about what items are to be provided in what time frame. In other cases, items are defined as mandatory, important, or desirable, or several scenarios are provided and the vendor is asked to propose the best solution. In a few cases, RFPs specify generally what is required and the vendors are asked to propose their own network designs. Figure 11-6 provides a summary of the key parts of an RFP.

Once the vendors have submitted their proposals, the organization evaluates them against specified criteria and selects the winner(s). Depending on the scope and complexity of the network, it is sometimes necessary to redesign the network on the basis of the information in the vendors' proposals.

One of the key decisions in the RFP process is the scope of the RFP. Will you use one vendor or several vendors for all hardware, software, and services? Multivendor environments tend to provide better performance because it is unlikely that one vendor makes the best hardware, software, and services in all categories. Multivendor networks also tend to be less expensive because it is unlikely that one vendor will always have the cheapest hardware, software, and services in all product categories.

Multivendor environments can be more difficult to manage, however. If equipment is not working properly and it is provided by two different vendors, each can blame the other for the problem. In contrast, a single vendor is solely responsible for everything.

Information in a Typical Request for Proposal
- Background information
    - Organizational profile
    - Overview of current network
    - Overview of new network
    - Goals of new network
- Network requirements
    - Choice sets of possible network designs (hardware, software, circuits)
    - Mandatory, desirable, and wish-list items
    - Security and control requirements
    - Response-time requirements
    - Guidelines for proposing new network designs
- Service requirements
    - Implementation time plan
    - Training courses and materials
    - Support services (e.g., spare parts on site)
    - Reliability and performance guarantees
- Bidding process
    - Time schedule for the bidding process
    - Ground rules
    - Bid evaluation criteria
    - Availability of additional information
- Information required from vendor
    - Vendor corporate profile
    - Experience with similar networks
    - Hardware and software benchmarks
    - Reference list

FIGURE 11-6   Request for proposal.

Selling the Proposal to Management

One of the main problems in network design is obtaining the support of senior management. To management, the network is simply a cost center, something on which the organization is spending a lot of money with little apparent change. The network keeps on running just as it did the year before.

The key to gaining the acceptance of senior management lies in speaking management's language. It is pointless to talk about upgrades from 10 Mbps to 100 Mbps on the backbone, because this terminology is meaningless from a business perspective. A more compelling argument is to discuss the growth in network use. For example, a simple graph that shows network usage growing at 25 percent per year, compared with network budget growing at 10 percent per year, presents a powerful illustration that the network costs are well managed, not out of control.

Likewise, a focus on network reliability is an easily understandable issue. For example, if the network supports a mission-critical system such as order processing or moving point-of-sale data from retail stores to corporate offices, it is clear from a business perspective that the network must be available and performing properly, or the organization will lose revenue.

Deliverables

There are three key deliverables for this step. The first is an RFP that goes to potential vendors. The second deliverable, after the vendor has been selected, is the revised physical network diagram (e.g., Figure 11-5) with the technology design complete. Exact products and costs are specified at this point (e.g., a layer-3 switch with four 16-port 10Base-T modules). The third deliverable is the business case that provides support for the network design, expressed in business objectives.

SUMMARY

Traditional Network Design   The traditional network design approach follows a very structured systems analysis and design process similar to that used to build application systems. It attempts to develop precise estimates of network traffic for each network user and network segment. Although this is expensive and time consuming, it works well for static or slowly evolving networks. Unfortunately, computer and networking technology is changing very rapidly, the growth in network traffic is immense, and hardware and circuit costs are relatively less expensive than they used to be. Therefore, use of the traditional network design approach is decreasing.

Building-Block Approach to Network Design   The building-block approach attempts to build the network using a series of simple building predefined components, resulting in a simpler design process and a more easily managed network built with a smaller range of components. The basic process involves three steps that are performed repeatedly. Needs analysis involves developing a logical network design that includes the geographic scope of the network and a categorization of current and future network needs of the various network segments, users, and applications as either typical or high traffic. The next step, technology design, results in a set of one or more physical network designs. Network design and simulation tools can play an important role in selecting the technology that typical and high-volume users, applications, and network segments will use. The final step, cost assessment, gathers cost information for the network, usually through an RFP that specifies what equipment, software, and services are desired and asks vendors to provide their best prices. One of the keys to gaining acceptance by senior management of the network design lies in speaking management's language (cost, network growth, and reliability), not the language of the technology (Ethernet, ATM, and DSL).

KEY TERMS

access layer	cost assessment	needs analysis	technology design
baseline	desirable requirements	needs categorization	traditional network
building-block process	distribution layer	physical network design	design process
capacity planning	geographic scope	request for proposal	turnpike effect
circuit loading	logical network design	(RFP)	wish-list requirements
core layer	mandatory requirements	simulation	

QUESTIONS

1. What are the keys to designing a successful data communications network?
2. How does the traditional approach to network design differ from the building-block approach?
3. Describe the three major steps in current network design.
4. What is the most important principle in designing networks?
5. Why is it important to analyze needs in terms of both application systems and users?
6. Describe the key parts of the technology design step.
7. How can a network design tool help in network design?
8. On what should the design plan be based?
9. What is an RFP, and why do companies use them?
10. What are the key parts of an RFP?
11. What are some major problems that can cause network designs to fail?
12. What is a network baseline, and when is it established?
13. What issues are important to consider in explaining a network design to senior management?
14. What is the turnpike effect and why is it important in network design?
15. Why do you think some organizations were slow to adopt a building-block approach to network design?
16. For what types of networks are network design tools most important? Why?

EXERCISES

11-1 What factors might cause peak loads in a network? How can a network designer determine if they are important, and how are they taken into account when designing a data communications network?

11-2 Collect information about two network design tools and compare and contrast what they can and cannot do.

MINI-CASES

I. Computer Dynamics
Computer Dynamics is a microcomputer software development company that has a 300-computer network. The company is located in three adjacent five-story buildings in an office park, with about 100 computers in each building. The current network is a poorly designed mix of Ethernet and token ring (Ethernet in two buildings and token ring in the other). The networks in all three buildings are heavily overloaded, and the company anticipates significant growth in network traffic. There is currently no network connection among the buildings, but this is one objective in building the new network. Describe the network you would recommend and how it would be configured with the goal of to building a new network that will support the company's needs for the next 3 years with few additional investments. Be sure to include the devices and type of network circuits you would use. You will need to make some assumptions, so be sure to document your assumptions and explain why you have designed the network in this way.

II. Drop and Forge
Drop and Forge is a small manufacturing firm with a 60-computer network. The company has one very large manufacturing plant with an adjacent office building. The office building houses 50 computers, with an additional 10 computers in the plant. The current network is an old 1-Mbps Ethernet that will need to be completely replaced. Describe the network you would recommend and how it would be configured. The goal is to build a new network that will support the company's needs for the next 3 years with few additional investments. Be sure to include the devices and type of network circuits you would use. You will need to make some assumptions, so be sure to document your assumptions and explain why you have designed the network in this way.

III. AdviceNet

AdviceNet is a consulting firm with offices in Toronto, New York, Los Angeles, Dallas, and Atlanta. The firm currently uses the Internet to transmit data, but its needs are growing and it is concerned over the security of the Internet. The firm wants to establish its own private WAN. Consultants in all offices are frustrated at the current 56-Kbps modems they use for Internet access, so the firm believes that it needs faster data transmission capabilities. The firm has no records of data transmission, but it believes that the New York and Toronto offices send and receive the most data. The firm is growing by 20 percent per year and expects to open offices in Vancouver and Chicago within the next 1 or 2 years. Describe two alternatives for the network and explain what choice you would make under what assumptions.

CASE STUDY

NEXT-DAY AIR SERVICE

The holding company that owns NDAS has just purchased a regional trucking company called Sunshine Trucking (ST). NDAS believes that ST offers a way build revenues in an area in which it has experience (package delivery), even though ST will not operate directly with NDAS. ST focuses on large commercial shipments (e.g., food products for wholesalers, packaged goods for department stores).

At present, ST has a very poor data communications network. Because you have done such a good job on the NDAS network, President Coone offers your expertise to ST to help design a new network.

ST operates three regional shipping hubs: Miami, Dallas, and Atlanta. Each of these regional hubs is responsible for taking shipping requests from customers and scheduling pickups and deliveries. Each regional hub has a about four dozen computers that will need to be networked to each other and onto a WAN. The computers access the network server (a Novell file server) and the corporate minicomputer (see below) almost constantly. The current network is an old 1-Mbps Ethernet that needs to be completely replaced because it can no longer handle the network traffic. The regional hubs communicate with one another fairly regularly via dial-up modems, usually a dozen times an hour. The staff members are irritated at having to constantly dial up and hang up for each connection. Sometimes modems are left connected for long periods of time each day.

The Atlanta hub also houses the corporate head office and therefore has an additional 20 computers for use by corporate staff. This office also has the corporate minicomputer that processes all accounting data (a UNIX computer). There has been some discussion about establishing a corporate Web site, but no plans have been made.

ST has a series of seven local offices for short-term storage, truck maintenance, and managing the local drivers: Houston, New Orleans, Jackson, Birmingham, Tallahassee, Charlotte, and Memphis. Each regional office has 5 to 10 computers that are not networked but that need to be networked to one another and to the WAN. These computers have fairly minimal networking requirements. At present, each local office sends data to the corporate minicomputer at the end of each day by sending one diskette via overnight courier (NDAS). ST would like to automate this process so that it can transmit the data via a network. ST also would like to enable the local offices to communicate with all the regional hubs (and perhaps with one another) but do not anticipate needing to send a large amount of data.

Exercises

1. What WAN would you recommend for ST? Describe each circuit you would recommend in terms of the technology (e.g., dial-up modem) and data rate (e.g., 56-Kbps modem).

2. What LANs and/or BNs would you recommend for the three regional hubs (including Atlanta, which has the corporate office)? In your answer, include the devices you would install.

3. What LANs and/or BNs would you recommend for the seven local offices? In your answer, include the devices you would install.

CHAPTER 12

NETWORK MANAGEMENT

NETWORK MANAGERS perform two key tasks: (1) designing new networks and network upgrades and (2) managing the day-to-day operation of existing networks. This chapter examines day-to-day network management, discussing the things that must be done to ensure that the network functions properly. We discuss the network management organization and the basic functions that a network manager must perform to operate a successful network.

OBJECTIVES

▓ Understand what is required to manage the day-to-day operation of networks,
▓ Be familiar with the network management organization,
▓ Understand configuration management,
▓ Understand performance and fault management,
▓ Be familiar with end user support,
▓ Be familiar with cost management,
▓ Understand the role and functions of network management software,
▓ Be familiar with several types of network management hardware tools.

CHAPTER OUTLINE

Introduction

Organizing the Network Management Function

    The Shift to LANs and the Internet

    Integrating LANs, WANs, and the Internet

    Integrating Voice and Data Communications

INTRODUCTION

Network management is the process of operating, monitoring, and controlling the network to ensure it works as intended and provides value to its users. The primary objective of the data communications function is to move application-layer data from one location to another in a timely fashion and to provide the resources that allow this transfer to occur. This transfer of information may take place within a single department, between departments in an organization, or with entities outside the organization across private networks or the Internet.

Without a well-planned, well-designed network and without a well-organized network management staff, operating the network becomes extremely difficult. Unfortunately, many network managers spend most of their time *firefighting*—dealing with breakdowns and immediate problems. If managers do not spend enough time on planning and organizing the network and networking staff, which are needed to predict and prevent problems, they are destined to be reactive rather than proactive in solving problems.

In this chapter, we examine the network management function. We begin by examining the job of the network manager and how the network management function can be organized within companies. We then break down the activities that network managers perform into four basic functions: configuration management (knowing what hardware and software are where), performance and fault management (making sure the network operates as desired), end user support (assisting end users), and cost management (minimizing the cost of providing network services). In practice, it is difficult to separate the network manager's job into these four neat categories, but these are useful ways to help understand what a network manager does. The chapter concludes with a discussion of the many different types of network management tools that are available to support the network manager.

ORGANIZING THE NETWORK MANAGEMENT FUNCTION

Communication and networking functions present special organizational problems because they are both centralized and decentralized. The developers, gatherers, and users of data are typically decentralized. The need for communications and networking affects every business function, so the management of voice and data communications has traditionally been highly centralized. Networks and mainframe servers were "owned" and operated by centralized IT departments that were used to controlling every aspect of the IT and communication environment.

The Shift to LANs and the Internet

Since the late 1980s, this picture has changed dramatically. There has been an explosion in the use of microcomputer-based networks. In fact, more than 90 percent of most organizations' total computer processing power (measured in millions of instructions per seconds)

MANAGEMENT FOCUS *12-1*

WHAT DO NETWORK MANAGERS DO?

If you were to become a network manager, some of your responsibilities and tasks would be to

- Manage the day-to-day operations of the network
- Provide support to network users
- Ensure the network is operating reliably
- Evaluate and acquire network hardware, software, and services
- Manage the network technical staff
- Manage the network budget, with emphasis on controlling costs
- Develop a strategic (long-term) networking and voice communications plan to meet the organization's policies and goals

- Keep abreast of the latest technological developments in computers, data communications devices, network software, and the Internet
- Keep abreast of the latest technological developments in telephone technologies and metropolitan area and local area network services.
- Assist senior management in understanding the business implications of network decisions and the role of the network in business operations

now resides on microcomputer-based LANs. This trend is continuing; since the early 1990s, the number of computers attached to LANs has grown by almost 40 percent *per year*. Today, the host mainframe computer will provides less than 10 percent of the organization's total computing power, although the number of Internet-based servers (e.g., Web servers, mail servers) has grown dramatically.

Although the management of host-based mainframe networks will always be important, the future of network management lies in the successful management of multiple clients and servers communicating over LANs, BNs, and the Internet. Many LANs and Web servers were initially designed and implemented by individual departments as separate networks and applications, whose goals were to best meet the needs of their individual owners, not to integrate with other networks and applications.

Today, the critical issue is the integration of all organizational networks and applications. Because each LAN was developed by a different department within the organization, not all LANs use the same architecture (e.g., shared 10Base-T versus switched 10Base-T, routed backbone versus collapsed backbone, TCP/IP versus IPX/SPX). Having different protocols and technologies means that routers or gateways must be used to connect the different LANs to organizational backbones and mainframe and that network managers and technicians must be familiar with many types of networks. The more different types of network technology used, the more complex network management becomes.

MANAGEMENT FOCUS *12-2*

FIVE KEY MANAGEMENT TASKS

Planning activities require
- Forecasting
- Establishing objectives
- Scheduling
- Budgeting
- Allocating resources
- Developing policies

Organizing activities require
- Developing organizational structure
- Delegating
- Establishing relationships
- Establishing procedures
- Integrating the smaller organization with the larger organization

Directing activities require
- Initiating activities
- Decision making
- Communicating
- Motivating

Controlling activities require
- Establishing performance standards
- Measuring performance
- Evaluating performance
- Correcting performance

Staffing activities require
- Interviewing people
- Selecting people
- Developing people

Integrating LANs, WANs, and the Internet

The key to integrating LANs, WANs, and the Internet into one overall organization network is for both LAN/Web and WAN managers to recognize that they no longer have the power they once had. No longer can network managers make independent decisions without considering their impacts on other parts of the organization's network. There must be a single overall communications and networking goal that best meets the needs of the entire organization. This will require some network managers to compromise on policies that are not in the best interest of their own departments or networks.

The central data communication network organization should have a written charter that defines its purpose, operational philosophy, and long-range goals. These goals must conform both to the parent organization's information processing goals and to its own departmental goals. Along with its long-term policies, the organization must develop individual procedures with which to implement the policies. Individual departments and LAN/Web managers must be free to implement their own policies and procedures that guide the day-to-day tasks of network staff.

Integrating Voice and Data Communications

Another major organizational challenge is the prospect of combining the voice communication function with the data communication function. Traditionally, voice communications were handled by a manager in the facilities department who supervised the telephone switchboard systems and also coordinated the installation and maintenance of the organization's voice telephone networks. By contrast, data communications traditionally were handled by the IT department because the staff installed their own communication circuits as the need arose, rather than coordinating with the voice communications staff.

This separation of voice and data worked well over the years, but now changing communication technologies are causing enormous pressures to combine these functions. These pressures are magnified by the high cost of maintaining separate facilities, the low efficiency and productivity of the organization's employees because there are two separate network functions, and the potential political problems within an organization when neither manager wants to relinquish his or her functional duties or job position. A key factor in voice–data integration might turn out to be the elimination of one key management position and the merging of two staffs.

There is no perfect solution to this problem because it must be handled in a way unique to each organization. Depending on the business environment and specific communication needs, some organizations may want to combine these functions, whereas others may find it better to keep them separate. We can state unequivocally that an organization that avoids studying this situation might be promoting inefficient communication systems, lower employee productivity, and increased operating costs for its separate voice and data networks.

In communications, we are moving from an era in which the computer system is the dominant IT function to one in which communications networks are the dominant IT function. In some organizations, the total cost of both voice and data communications will equal or exceed the total cost of the computer systems.

MANAGEMENT FOCUS *12-3*

KEY NETWORK MANAGEMENT SKILLS

What skills do network managers see as important? A survey of more than 350 network managers identified the following skills:

Very important skills
- Network design
- Project management
- Knowledge of TCP/IP
- Knowledge of routing technologies

Moderately important skills
- Capacity planning
- Knowledge of Web technologies
- Knowledge of Windows NT

- Knowledge of UNIX
- Knowledge of Novell NetWare

Less important skills
- Knowledge of asynchronous transfer mode
- Knowledge of frame relay
- Knowledge of integrated services digital network
- Knowledge of Notes/Domino

SOURCE: "Making the Best of a Difficult Situation," *Communications Week,* July 1, 1996.

CONFIGURATION MANAGEMENT

Configuration management means managing the network's hardware and software configuration and documenting it (and ensuring it is updated as the configuration changes).

Configuring the Network and Client Computers

One of the most common configuration activities is adding and deleting user accounts. When new users are added to the network, they are usually categorized as being a member of some group of users (e.g., faculty, students, accounting department, personnel department). Each user group has its own access privileges, which define what file servers, directories, and files they can access and provide a standard log-in script. The log-in script specifies what commands are to be run when the user first logs in (e.g., setting default directories, connecting to public disks, running menu programs).

Another common activity is updating the software on the client computers attached the network. Every time a new application system is developed or updated (or, for that matter, when a new version is released), each client computer in the organization must be updated. Traditionally, this has meant that someone from the networking staff has had to go to each client computer and manually install the software, either from diskettes/CDs or by downloading over the network. For a small organization, this is time consuming but not a major problem. For a large organization with hundreds or thousands of client computers (possibly with a mixture of Windows and Apples), this can be a nightmare.

Electronic software distribution (ESD), sometimes called *desktop management,* is one solution to the configuration problem. ESD enables network managers to install software on client computers over the network without physically touching each client computer. Most ESD packages provide application-layer software for the network server and all client computers. The server software communicates directly with the ESD application software on the clients and can be instructed to download and install certain application packages on each client at some predefined time (e.g., at midnight on a Saturday).

ESD software greatly reduces the cost of configuration management over the long term because it eliminates the need to manually update each and every client computer. It also automatically produces and maintains accurate documentation of all software installed on each client computer and enables network managers to produce a variety of useful reports. However, ESD increases costs in the short term because it costs money (typically $50 to $100 per client computer) and requires network staff to manually install it on each client computer. Desktop Management Interface (DMI) is the emerging standard in ESD software.

Documenting the Configuration

Configuration documentation includes information about network hardware, network software, user and application profiles, and network documentation. The most basic information about network hardware is a set of network configuration diagrams that document the number, type, and placement of network circuits (whether organization owned or leased from a common carrier), network servers, network devices (e.g., hubs, routers), and client computers. For most organizations, this is a large set of diagrams: one for each LAN, BN, MAN, and WAN. Figure 12-1 shows is a diagram of network devices in one office location.

These diagrams must be supplemented by documentation on each individual network component (e.g., circuit, hub, server). Documentation should include the type of device, serial number, vendor, date of purchase, warranty information, repair history, telephone number for repairs, and any additional information or comments the network manager wishes to add. For example, it would be useful to include the dial-in numbers for communication servers, contact names and telephone numbers for the individual network managers responsible for each separate LAN within the network, and common carrier circuit control telephone contact index and log. (Whenever possible, establish a national account with the common carrier rather than dealing with individual common carriers in separate states and areas.)

A similar approach can be used for network software. This includes the network operating system and any special-purpose network software. For example, it is important to record which network operating system and which version or release date is installed on each network server. The same is true of application software. As discussed in Chapter 6 on LANs, sharing software on networks can greatly reduce costs, although it is important to ensure that the organization is not violating any software license rules.

Software documentation can also help in negotiating site licenses for software. Many users buy software on a copy-by-copy basis, paying retail price for each copy. It may be cheaper to negotiate the payment of one large fee for an unlimited use license for widely used software packages instead of paying on a per-copy basis.

The third type of documentation is the user and application profiles, which should be automatically provided by the network operating system or additional vendor or third-party software agreements. These should enable the network manager to easily identify the files and directories to which each user has access and each user's access rights (e.g., read-

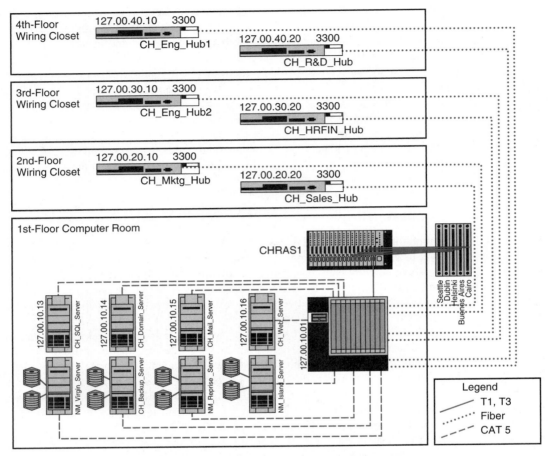

FIGURE 12-1 Network configuration diagram. SOURCE: netViz.

only, edit, delete). Equally important is the ability to access this information in the "opposite" direction; that is, to be able to select a file or directory and obtain a list of all authorized users and their access rights.

In addition, other documentation must be routinely developed and updated pertaining to the network. This includes network hardware and software manuals, application software manuals, standards manuals, operations manuals for network staff, vendor contracts and agreements, and licenses for software. The documentation should include details about performance and fault management (e.g., preventive maintenance guidelines and schedules, disaster recovery plan, and diagnostic techniques), end user support (e.g., applications software manuals, vendor support telephone numbers), and cost management (e.g., annual budgets, repair costs for each device). The documentation should also include any legal requirements to comply with local or federal laws, control, or regulatory bodies.

PERFORMANCE AND FAULT MANAGEMENT

Performance management means ensuring the network is operating as efficiently as possible, whereas *fault management* means preventing, detecting, and correcting faults in the network circuits, hardware, and software (e.g., a broken hub or improperly installed software). Fault management and performance management are closely related, because any faults in the network reduce performance. Both require *network monitoring,* which means keeping track of the operation of network circuits and devices to ensure they are functioning properly and to determine how heavily they are used.

Network Monitoring

Most large organizations and many smaller ones use *network management software* to monitor and control their networks. One function provided by these systems is to collect operational statistics from the network devices. For small networks, network monitoring is often done by one person, aided by a few simple tools (discussed later in this chapter). These tools collect information and send messages to the network manager's computer.

In large networks, network monitoring becomes more important. Large networks that support organizations operating 24 hours a day are often mission critical, which means a network problem can have serious business consequences. For example, consider the impact of a network failure for an IXC such as AT&T or for the air traffic control system. These networks often have a dedicated *network operations center (NOC)* that is responsible for monitoring and fixing problems. Such centers are staffed by a set of skilled network

MANAGEMENT FOCUS *12-4*

RIDING THE STORM AT WEATHER.COM

Mark Ryan, chief technology officer of weather.com, the Web counterpart of The Weather Channel, has more to worry about than getting wet when he sees a storm approaching. He has to consider whether a flood of visitors will overwhelm his information technology infrastructure.

Weather.com has unique requirements. The content is dynamic, usage spikes are unpredictable, and visitors demand instant access or will head elsewhere on the Web. Most companies can scale their network infrastructure gradually to well-known peaks (e.g., the Christmas rush for e-commerce sites), but weather.com is not so fortunate. For example, it had to scale from a low of 4 million to 5 million page views per day to a peak of 19 million to 22 million, over a single 2-day period in the face of a major storm.

Weather.com used an initial strategy of "just throw hardware at it" to meet the rapidly growing demands

over its first few years. The result was a hodgepodge of different systems, which produced a network management nightmare. The solution was a narrow and deep strategy: weather.com put in the identical hardware, wherever possible. Rather than use expensive high-performance hardware, custom-tailored to different jobs, weather.com has standardized on many more less expensive Linux servers all configured in the same way. Page load times have dropped from a high of 18 to 25 seconds to a fairly consistent 2 seconds—even during hurricane season, when weather.com averages 15 million page views per day.

SOURCE: "Riding the Storm," *Intelligent Enterprise,* February 16, 2001.

technicians that use sophisticated network management software. When a problem occurs, the software immediately detects the problems and sends an alarm to the NOC. Staff members in the NOC diagnose the problem and can sometimes fix the problem from the NOC (e.g., restarting a failed device). Other times, when a device or circuit fails, they must change routing tables to route traffic away from the device and inform the common carrier or dispatch a technician to fix or replace it.

The parameters monitored by a network management system fall into two distinct categories: physical network statistics and logical network information. Gathering statistics on the *physical network parameters* includes monitoring the operation of the network's modems, multiplexers, circuits linking the various hardware devices, and any other network devices. Monitoring the physical network consists of keeping track of circuits that may be down and tracing malfunctioning devices. *Logical network parameters* include performance measurement systems that keep track of user response times, the volume of traffic on a specific circuit, the destination of data routed across various networks, and any other indicators showing the level of service provided by the network.

Some types of management software operate passively, collecting the information and reporting it back to the central NOC. Others are active, in that they routinely send test messages to the servers or application being monitored (e.g., an HTTP Web page request) and record the response times.[1]

MANAGEMENT FOCUS *12-5*

LONG NIGHT ON THE NET WATCH

At an hour when most network personnel are asleep, Walter Snider and Willie Williams are huddled over a network management console in railroad giant CSX Corporation's network operations center (NOC) trying to determine why a circuit between Jacksonville and Baltimore is down. The problem becomes urgent when the dispatcher tells the Snider the outage will delay trains if it is not fixed soon.

A quick check of the circuit shows it is fine. The multiplexer ports on both ends pass tests, too. Williams becomes convinced that the dispatcher has reported the wrong circuit number and begins checking other circuits out of Baltimore. He quickly finds one that does not respond, reboots the multiplexer, and the circuit begins working. He calls the dispatcher who reports that the circuit is working again.

The night shift is the quietest shift at CSX's network control center in Jacksonville, which gives network personnel the chance to learn new skills and identify network improvements. However, staff members need the greatest range of skills and have more autonomy to solve problems. Unlike their daytime counterparts, they have a harder time reaching managers and other network personnel for help. Although CSX policy requires the NOC to contact network managers and support personnel in the event of a major problem, no one likes to wake up colleagues.

At 4:00 A.M., 5 hours after beginning the shift, Williams notices an alarm go off, indicating the failure of a major circuit in the Washington area. He begins to zero in on the trouble spot when the circuit comes back up. "Probably just line noise or a power surge," he says, and returns to his doughnut and coffee.

SOURCE: "Long Night on the Net Watch," *Network World,* February 9, 1998.

---

[1] Two examples of performance tracking on the Internet that provide a simple overview are www.InternetTrafficReport.com and www.my.keynote.com/MyKeynote/mykeynote.asp.

Performance tracking is important because it enables the network manager to be proactive and respond to performance problems before users begin to complain. Poor network reporting leads to an organization that is overburdened with current problems and lacks time to address future needs. Management requires adequate reports if it is to address future needs.

Failure Control Function

Failure control requires developing a central control philosophy for problem reporting, whether the problems are first identified by the NOC or by users calling in to the NOC or a help desk. Whether problem reporting is done by the NOC or the help desk, the organization should maintain a central telephone number for network users to call when any problem occurs in the network. As a central troubleshooting function, only this group or its designee should have the authority to call hardware or software vendors or common carriers.

Many years ago, before the importance (and cost) of network management was widely recognized, most networks ignored the importance of fault management. Network devices were "dumb" in that they did only what they were designed to do (e.g., routing packets) but did not provide any network management information.

For example, suppose a network interface card fails and begins to randomly transmit garbage messages. Network performance immediately begins to deteriorate because these random messages destroy the messages transmitted by other computers, which need to be retransmitted. Users notice a delay in response time and complain to the network support group, which begins to search for the cause. Even if the network support group suspects a failing network card (which is unlikely unless such an event has occurred before), locating the faulty card is very difficult and time consuming.

Most network managers today are installing *managed devices* that perform their functions (e.g., routing, switching) and also record data on the messages they process. These data can be sent to the network manager's computer when the device receives a special control message requesting the data, or it can send an *alarm* message to the network

MANAGEMENT FOCUS *12-6*

TECHNICAL REPORTS

Technical reports that are helpful to network managers are those that provide summary information, as well as details that enable the mangers to improve the network. Technical details include

- Circuit use
- Usage rate of critical hardware such as host computers, front-end processors, and servers
- File activity rates for database systems
- Usage by various categories of client computers

- Response time analysis per circuit or per computer
- Voice versus data usage per circuit
- Queue-length descriptions, whether in the host computer, in the front-end processor, or at remote sites
- Distribution of traffic by time of day, location, and type of application software
- Failure rates for circuits, hardware, and software
- Details of any network faults

manager's computer if the device detects a critical situation. In this way, network faults and performance problems can be detected and reported by the devices themselves before they become serious. In the case of the failing network card, a managed device could record the increased number of retransmissions required to successfully transmit messages and inform the network management software of the problem. A managed hub or switch might even be able to detect the faulty transmissions from the failing network card, disable the incoming circuit so that the card could not send any more messages, and issue an alarm to the network manager. In either case, finding and fixing the fault is much simpler, requiring minutes, not hours.

Numerous software packages are available for recording fault information. The reports they produce are known as *trouble tickets*. The software packages assist the help desk personnel so they can type the trouble report immediately into a computerized failure analysis program. They also automatically produce various statistical reports to track how many failures have occurred for each piece of hardware, circuit, or software package. Automated trouble tickets are better than paper because they allow management personnel to gather problem and vendor statistics. There are four main reasons for trouble tickets: problem tracking, problem statistics, problem-solving methodology, and management reports.

Problem tracking allows the network manager to determine who is responsible for correcting any outstanding problems. This is important because some problems often are forgotten in the rush of a very hectic day. In addition, anyone might request information on the status of a problem. The network manager can determine whether the problem-solving mechanism is meeting predetermined schedules. Finally, the manager can be assured that all problems are being addressed. Problem tracking also can assist in problem resolution. Are problems being resolved in a timely manner? Are overdue problems being flagged? Are all resources and information available for problem solving?

Problem statistics are important because they are a control device for the network managers as well as for vendors. With this information, a manager can see how well the network is meeting the needs of end users. These statistics also can be used to determine whether vendors are meeting their contractual maintenance commitments. Finally, they help to determine whether problem-solving objectives are being met.

Problem prioritizing helps ensure that critical problems get priority over less important ones. For example, a network support staff member should not work on a problem on

TECHNICAL FOCUS

ELEMENTS OF A TROUBLE REPORT

When a problem is reported, the trouble log staff members should record the following:

- Time and date of the report
- Name and telephone number of the person who reported the problem
- The time and date of the problem (and the time and date of the call)

- Location of the problem
- The nature of the problem
- When the problem was identified
- Why and how the problem happened

one client computer if an entire circuit with dozens of computers is waiting for help. Moreover, a manager must know whether problem-resolution objectives are being met. For example, how long is it taking to resolve critical problems?

Management reports are required to determine network availability, product and vendor reliability (mean time between failures), and vendor responsiveness. Without them, a manager has nothing more than a "best guess" estimate for the effectiveness of either the network's technicians or the vendor's technicians. Regardless of whether this information is typed immediately into an automated trouble ticket package or recorded manually in a bound notebook-style trouble log, the objectives are the same.

The purposes of the trouble log are to record problems that must be corrected and to keep track of statistics associated with these problems. For example, the log might reveal that there were 37 calls for software problems (3 for one package, 4 for another package, and 30 for a third software package), 26 calls for modems evenly distributed among two vendors, 49 calls for client computers, and 2 calls to the common carrier that provides the network circuits. These data are valuable when the design and analysis group begins redesigning the network to meet future requirements.

Performance and Failure Statistics

There are many different types of failure and recovery statistics that can be collected. The most obvious performance statistics are those discussed above: how many packets are being moved on what circuits and what the response time is. Failure statistics also tell an important story.

One important failure statistic is *availability,* the percentage of time the network is available to users. It is calculated as the number of hours per month the network is available divided by the total number of hours per month (i.e., 24 hours per day $\times$ 30 days per month = 720 hours). The *downtime* includes times when the network is unavailable because of faults and to routine maintenance and network upgrades. Most network managers strive for 99 to 99.5 percent availability, with downtime scheduled after normal working hours.

The *mean time between failures (MTBF)* is the number of hours or days of continuous operation before the component fails. Obviously, devices with higher MTBF are more reliable.

When faults occur, and devices or circuits go down, the *mean time to repair (MTTR)* is the average number of minutes or hours until the failed device or circuit is operational again. The MTTR is composed of these separate elements:

$$MTTRepair = MTTDiagnose + MTTRespond + MTTFix$$

The *mean time to diagnose (MTTD)* is the average number of minutes until the root cause of the failure is correctly diagnosed. This is an indicator of the efficiency of problem management personnel in the NOC or help desk who receive the problem report.

The *mean time to respond (MTTR)* is average number of minutes or hours until service personnel arrive at the problem location to begin work on the problem. This is a valuable statistic because it indicates how quickly vendors and internal groups respond to emergencies. Compilation of these figures over time can lead to a change of vendors or internal management policies or, at the minimum, can exert pressure on vendors who do not respond to problems promptly.

Finally, after the vendor or internal support group arrives on the premises, the last statistic is the *mean time to fix (MTTF)*. This figure tells how quickly the staff is able to correct the problem after they arrive. A very long time to fix in comparison with the time of other vendors may indicate faulty equipment design, inadequately trained customer service technicians, or even the fact that inexperienced personnel are repeatedly sent to fix problems.

The MTBF can be influenced by the original selection of vendor-supplied equipment. The MTTD relates directly to the ability of network personnel to isolate and diagnose failures and can often be improved by training. The MTTR (respond) can be influenced by showing vendors or internal groups how good or bad their response times have been in the past. The MTTF can be affected by the technical expertise of internal or vendor staff and the availability of spare parts on site.

Another set of statistics that should be gathered are those collected daily by the network operations group, which uses network management software. These statistics record the normal operation of the network, such as the number of errors (retransmissions) per communication circuit. Statistics also should be collected on the daily volume of transmissions (characters per hour) for each communication circuit, each computer, or whatever is appropriate for the network. It is important to closely monitor usage rates, the percentage of the theoretical capacity that is being used. These data can identify computers/devices or communication circuits that have higher-than-average error or usage rates, and they may be used for predicting future growth patterns and failures. A device or circuit that is approaching maximum usage obviously needs to be upgraded.

Such predictions can be accomplished by establishing simple *quality-control charts* similar to those used in manufacturing. Programs use an upper control limit and a lower control limit with regard to the number of blocks in error per day or per week. Notice how Figure 12-2 identifies when the common carrier moved a circuit from one microwave channel to another (circuit B), how a deteriorating circuit can be located and fixed before it goes through the upper control limit (circuit A) and causes problems for the users, or how a temporary high rate of errors (circuit C) can be encountered when installing new hardware and software.

TECHNICAL FOCUS *12-1*

MANAGEMENT REPORTS

Management-oriented reports that are helpful to network managers and their supervisors provide summary information for overall evaluation and for network planning and design. Details include

- Graphs of daily/weekly/monthly usage, number of errors, or whatever is appropriate to the network
- Network availability (uptime) for yesterday, the last 5 days, the last month, or any other specific period
- Percentage of hours per week the network is unavailable because of network maintenance and repair

- Fault diagnosis
- Whether most response times are less than or equal to 3 seconds for online real-time traffic
- Whether management reports are timely and contain the most up-to-date statistics
- Peak volume statistics as well as average volume statistics per circuit
- Comparison of activity between today and a similar previous period

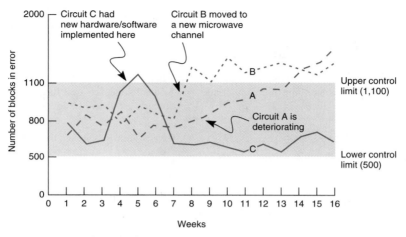

FIGURE 12-2 Quality control chart for circuits.

Improving Performance

The chapters on LANs, BNs, MANs, and WANs discussed several specific actions that could be taken to improve network performance for each of those types of networks. There are also several general activities that cut across the different types of networks.

Policy-Based Management A new approach to managing performance is policy-based management. With *policy-based management,* the network manager uses special software to set priority policies for network traffic that take effect when the network becomes busy. For example, the network manager might say that order processing and videoconferencing get the highest priority (order processing because it is the lifeblood of the company and videoconferencing because poor response time will have the greatest impact on it). The policy management software would then configure the network devices using the QoS capabilities in TCP/IP and/or ATM to give these applications the highest priority when the devices become busy.

Server Load Balancing Load balancing, as the name suggests, means to allocate incoming requests for network services (e.g., Web requests) across a set of equivalent servers so that the work is spread fairly evenly across all devices. With load balancing, a separate load-balancing server (sometimes called a virtual server), or a router or switch with special load-balancing software, allocates the requests among a set of identical servers using a simple round-robin formula (requests go to each server one after the other in turn) or more complex formulas that track how busy each server actually is. If a server crashes, the load balancer stops sending requests to it and the network continues to operate without the failed server.

Service-Level Agreements More organizations establish *service-level agreements (SLAs)* with their common carriers and Internet service providers. An SLA specifies the exact

TECHNICAL FOCUS *12-2*

INSIDE A SERVICE-LEVEL AGREEMENT

There are many elements to a solid service-level agreement (SLA) with a common carrier. Some of the important ones include

- Network availability, measured over a month as the percentage of time the network is available (e.g., [total hours – hours unavailable]/total hours) should be at least 99.5 percent
- Average round-trip permanent virtual circuit (PVC) delay, measured over a month as the number of seconds it takes a message to travel over the PVC from sender to receiver, should be less than 110 milliseconds, although some carriers will offer discounted services for SLA guarantees of 300 milliseconds or less
- PVC throughput, measured over a month as the number of outbound packets sent over a PVC divided by

the inbound packets received at the destination (not counting packets over the committed information rate, which are discard eligible), should be above 99 percent—ideally, 99.99 percent
- Mean time to respond, measured as a monthly average of the time from inception of trouble ticket until repair personnel are on site, should be 4 hours or less
- Mean time to fix, measured as a monthly average of the time from the arrival of repair personnel on-site until the problem is repaired, should be 4 hours or less

SOURCE: "Carrier Service-Level Agreements," International Engineering Consortium Tutorial, www.iec.org, February 2001.

type of performance and fault conditions that the organization will accept. For example, the SLA might state that network availability must be 99 percent or higher and that the MTBF for T1 circuits must be 120 days or more. In many cases, SLA includes maximum allowable response times. The SLA also states what compensation the service provider must provide if it fails to meet the SLA. Some organizations are also starting to use an SLA internally to clearly define relationships between the networking group and its organizational "customers."

END USER SUPPORT

Providing end user support means solving whatever problems users encounter while using the network. There are three main functions within end user support: resolving network faults, resolving user problems, and training. We have already discussed how to resolve network faults, and now we focus on resolution of user problems and on end user training.

Resolving Problems

Problems with user equipment (as distinct from network equipment) usually stem from three major sources. The first is a failed hardware device. These are usually the easiest to fix. A network technician simply fixes the device or installs a new part.

The second type of problem is a lack of user knowledge. These problems can usually be solved by discussing the situation with the user and taking that person through the process step by step. This is the next easiest type of problem to solve and can often be done by e-mail or over the telephone.

The third type of problem is a one with the software, software settings, or an incompatibility between the software and network software and hardware. In this case, there may be a bug in the software or the software may not function properly on a certain combination of hardware and software. Solving these problems may be difficult because they require expertise with the specific software package in use and sometimes require software upgrades from the vendor.

Resolving either type of software problem begins with a request for assistance from the help desk. Requests for assistance are usually handled in the same manner as network faults. A trouble log is maintained to document all incoming requests and the manner in which they are resolved. The staff member receiving the request attempts to resolve the problem in the best manner possible. Staff members should be provided with the set of standard procedures or scripts for soliciting information from the user about problems. In large organizations, this process may be supported by special software.

There are often several levels to the problem-resolution process. The first level is the most basic. All staff members working at the help desk should be able to resolve most of the these. Most organizations strive to resolve between 75 and 85 percent of requests at this first level in less than an hour. If the request cannot be resolved, it is escalated to the second level of problem resolution. Staff members who handle second-level support have specialized skills in certain problem areas or with certain types of software and hardware. In most cases, problems are resolved at this level. Some large organizations also have a third level of resolution in which specialists spend many hours developing and testing various solutions to the problem, often in conjunction with staff members from the vendors of network software and hardware.

Providing End User Training

End user training is an ongoing responsibility of the network manager. Training is a key part in the implementation of new networks or network components. It is also important to have an ongoing training program because employees may change job functions and new employees require training to use the organization's networks.

Training usually is conducted through in-class or one-on-one instruction and through the documentation and training manuals provided. In-class training should focus on the 20 percent of the network functions that the user will use 80 percent of the time instead of attempting to cover all network functions. By getting in-depth instruction of the fundamentals, users become confident about what they need to do. The training should also explain how to locate additional information from training manuals, documentation, or the help desk.

COST MANAGEMENT

As the demand for network services grows, so do their costs. Effective and efficient management of data communications networks is important because more and more organizational resources are being spent on networks. In this section, we examine the major sources of costs and discuss several ways to reduce them.

Sources of Costs

The *total cost of ownership (TCO)* is a measure of how much it costs per year to keep one computer operating. TCO includes the cost of repair parts, software upgrades, and support staff members to maintain the network, install software, administer the network (e.g., create user IDs, backup user data), provide training and technical support, and upgrade hardware and software. It also includes the cost of time "wasted" by the user when problems occur or when the user is attempting to learn new software.

Several studies over the past few years by Gartner Group, Inc. (a leading industry research firm) suggest that the TCO of a computer is astoundingly high. Most studies suggest that the TCO for typical Windows computers on a network is about $10,000 *per computer per year.* In other words, it costs almost five times as much *each year* to operate a computer than it does to purchase it in the first place. Other studies by firms such as IBM and *InformationWeek* (an industry magazine) have produced TCO estimates of between $8,000 and $12,000 per year, suggesting that the Gartner Group's estimates are reasonable.

Although TCO has been accepted by many organizations, other firms argue against the practice of including "wasted" time in the calculation. For example, using the Gartner Group approach, the TCO of a coffee machine is more than $50,000 per year—not counting the cost of the coffee or supplies. The assumption that getting coffee "wastes" 12 minutes per day times 5 days per week yields 1 hour per week, or about 50 hours per year, of wasted time. If you assume the coffeepot serves 20 employees who have an average cost of $50 per hour (not an unusually high number), you have a loss $50,000 per year.

Some organizations, therefore, prefer to focus on costing methods that examine only the direct costs of operating the computers, omitting softer costs such as "wasted" time. Such measures, often called *network cost of ownership (NCO)* or real cost of ownership, have found that network management costs (TCO without "wasted" time) range between $1,500 and $3,500 *per computer per year.* The typical network management group for a 100-user network would therefore have an annual budget of about $150,000 to $350,000. The most expensive item is personnel (network managers and technicians), which typically accounts for 50 to 70 percent of total costs. The second most expensive cost item is WAN circuits, followed by hardware upgrades and replacement parts.

There is one very important message from this pattern of costs. Because the largest cost item is personnel time, the primary focus of cost management lies in designing networks and developing policies to reduce personnel time, not to reduce hardware cost. Over the long term, it makes more sense to buy more expensive equipment if it can reduce the cost of network management.

Figure 12-3 shows the average breakdown of personnel costs by function. The largest time cost (where staff members spend most of their time) is systems management, which includes configuration, fault, and performance management tasks that focus on the network as a whole. The second largest item is end user support.

Network managers often find it difficult to manage their budgets because networks grow so rapidly. They often find themselves having to defend ever-increasing requests for more equipment and staff. To counter these escalating costs, many large organizations have adopted *charge-back policies* for users of WANs and mainframe-based networks. (A charge-back policy attempts to allocate the costs associated with the network to specific users.) These users must "pay" for their network usage by transferring part of their budget

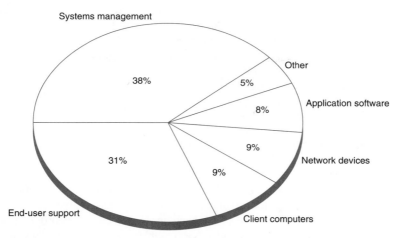

FIGURE 12-3 Network management personnel costs.

allocations to the network group. Such policies are seldom used in LANs, making one more potential cultural difference between network management styles.

Reducing Costs

Given the huge amounts in TCO or even the substantial amounts spent in NCO, there is considerable pressure on network managers to reduce costs. Figure 12-4 summarizes five steps to reduce network costs.

The first and most important step is to develop standards for client computers, servers, and network devices (i.e., switches, routers). These standards define one configuration (or a small set of configurations) that are permitted for all computers and devices. Standardizing hardware and software makes it easier to diagnose and fix problems. Also, there are fewer software packages for the network support staff members to learn. The downside, of course, is that rigid adherence to standards reduces innovation.

The second most important step is automate as much of the network management process as possible. ESD can significantly reduce the cost to upgrade when new software is released. It also enables faster installation of new computers and faster recovery when software needs to be reinstalled and helps enforce the standards policies. Dynamic address assignment (e.g., DHCP; see Chapter 5) can reduce time spent on managing TCP/IP addresses. The use of network management software to identify and diagnose problems can significantly reduce time spent in performance and fault management. Likewise, help desk software can cut the cost of the end support function.

A third step is to do everything possible to reduce the time spent installing new hardware and software. The cost of a network technician's spending half a day to install and configure new computers is often $300 to 500. ESD is an important step to reducing costs, but careful purchasing can also go a long way. The installation of standard hardware and software (e.g., Microsoft Office) by the hardware vendor can significantly reduce costs.

> **Five Steps to Reduce Network Costs**
> - Develop standard hardware and software configurations for client computers and servers.
> - Automate as much of the network management function as possible by deploying a solid set of network management tools.
> - Reduce the costs of installing new hardware and software by working with vendors.
> - Centralize help desks.
> - Move to thin-client architectures.

FIGURE 12-4   Reducing network costs.

Likewise, careful monitoring of hardware failures can quickly identify vendors of less reliable equipment who can be avoided in the next purchasing cycle.

Traditionally, help desks have been decentralized into user departments. The result is a proliferation of help desks and support staff members, many of whom tend to be generalists rather than specialists in one area. Many organizations have found that centralizing help desks enables them to reduce the number of generalists and provide more specialists in key technology areas. This results in faster resolution of difficult problems. Centralization also makes it easier to identify common problems occurring in different parts of the organization and take actions to reduce them.

Finally, many network experts argue that moving to thin-client architectures, particularly those using network computers or just Web browsers on the client (see Chapter 2), can significantly reduce costs. Although network computers cost slightly less than traditional computers, the real saving lies in the support costs. Because they are restricted to a narrow set of functions and generally do not permit software installations, they become much easier to manage. TCO and NCO drop by 20 to 40 percent. However, there is not a lot of software available for network computers today, although this will change. Most organizations anticipate using network computers selectively, in areas where application

MANAGEMENT FOCUS *12-7*

OUTSOURCING NETWORK MANAGEMENT AT NASA

After a 1998 survey of 11 NASA installations found a network cost of ownership (NCO) of just under $3,000 per desktop per year, NASA decided to outsource the network support for its desktops to focus on its core competency: space flight. So far, NASA has outsourced the management of 27,000 desktops to third parties. Reducing NCO was not the only driving force behind the decision, but it was the most important one.

Because of its mission priorities, NASA has a real mix of desktop technologies, including seven very different types of Windows, Apple, and UNIX computers. After a tough competition, NASA approved seven firms to provide

network management service, such as Computer Sciences Corporation, Wang, and Federal Data Corp. Local NASA managers can select which of the seven vendors to use. Prices range from $1,800 to $2,200 per computer per year, depending on the level of service desired. This has resulted in a clear drop in operating expenses, as well as better service. NASA now has a well-documented network configuration, one phone number to call for service, and total certainty of the cost of operating its desktops.

SOURCE: "Every Last Dime," *CIO Magazine,* November 15, 2000.

software is well defined and can easily be restricted (e.g., receptionists, clerks, help desks, order processing).

NETWORK MANAGEMENT TOOLS

Network managers tools to help them perform their various functions. Most tools can be classified as being primarily hardware or primarily software, although in practice any software tool needs to be supported by hardware.

Network Management Software

Network management software is designed to provide automated support for some or all of the network management functions. There are dozens of network management tools available. Some software tools support configuration management, some support performance and fault management, and some attempt to do both. Some tools have modules to aid the help desk in providing end user support.

Types of Network Management Software
There are three fundamentally different types of network management software. *Device management software* (sometimes called point management software) is designed to provide information about the specific devices on a network. They enable the network manager to monitor important devices such as servers, routers, and gateway and typically report configuration information, traffic volumes, and error conditions for each device. Figure 12-5 shows some sample displays from a device management package running at Indiana University. This figure shows the amount of traffic over the last few days and weeks in terms of inbound traffic and outbound traffic. Users can "drill down" to get more specific information and analyses on each segment by clicking on any graph. This tool is available on the Web at resnet.indiana.edu/resnetstats.html so you can investigate the network structure and performance today.

System management software (sometimes called enterprise management software or a network management framework) adds two additional functions on top of device management. First, system management software provides the same configuration, traffic, and error information as do device management systems, but it also provides ESD. Second, and most important, system management software can analyze the device information to diagnose patterns, not just display individual device problems. This is important when a critical device fails (e.g., a router into a high-traffic building). With device management software, all of the devices that depend on the failed device will attempt to send warning messages to the network administrator. One failure often generates several dozen problem reports, called an *alarm storm,* making it difficult to quickly pinpoint the true source of the problem. The dozens of error messages are symptoms that mask the root cause. System management software tools correlate the individual error messages into a pattern to find the true cause, which is called *root cause analysis,* and then report the pattern to the network manager. Rather than first seeing pages and pages of error messages, the network manage instead is informed of the root cause of the problem. Figure 12-6

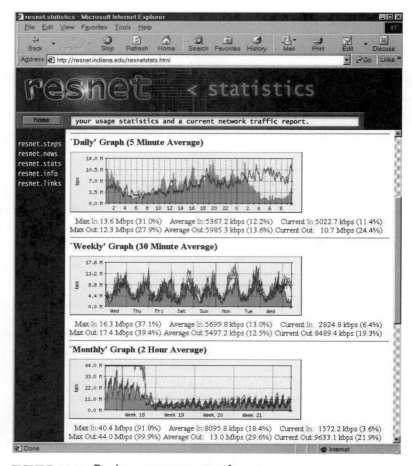

FIGURE 12-5 Device management software.

shows a sample from HP OpenView. This tool is available on the Web at www.openview.hp.com/products/vpis/seetrybuy/Product_HTML-265.asp.

Application management software also builds on the device management software, but instead of monitoring systems, it monitors applications. In many organizations, there are mission-critical applications that should have priority over other network traffic. For example, real-time order-entry systems used by telephone operators need priority over e-mail. Application management systems track delays and problems with application-layer packets and inform the network manager if problems occur and if these packets for priority applications experience important delays.

Simple Network Management Protocol One important problem is ensuring that hardware devices from different vendors can understand and respond to the messages sent by the network management software of other vendors. By this point in this book, the

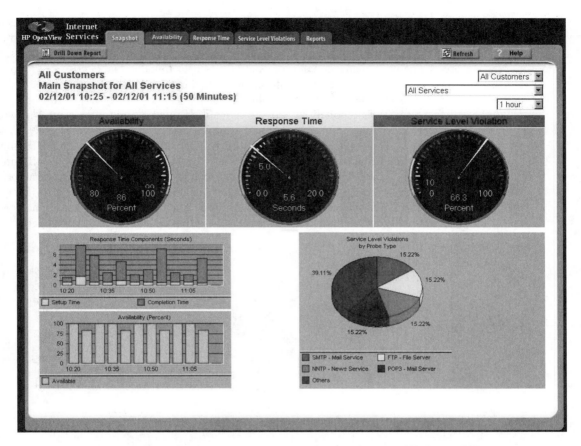

FIGURE 12-6   Network management software. SOURCE: HP OpenView.

solution should be obvious: standards. A number of formal and de facto standards have been developed for network management. These standards are application-layer protocols that define the type of information collected by network devices and the format of control messages that the devices understand.

The two most commonly used network management protocols are *Simple Network Management Protocol (SNMP)* and *Common Management Interface Protocol (CMIP)*. Both perform the same basic functions but are incompatible. SNMP is the Internet network management standard, whereas CMIP is a newer protocol developed by the International Standards Organization. SNMP is the most commonly used today, although most of the major network management software tools understand both SNMP and CMIP and can operate with hardware that uses either standard.

SNMP originally was developed to control and monitor the status of network devices on TCP/IP networks, but now it is available for other network protocols (e.g., IPX/SPX). Each SNMP device (e.g., router, gateway, server) has an *agent* that collects information about itself and the messages it processes, and it stores that information in a central database called the *management information base (MIB)*. The network manager's management station that runs the network management software has access to the MIB. Using this software, the network manager can send control messages to individual devices or groups of devices asking them to report the information stored in their MIB.

Most SNMP devices have the ability for *remote monitoring (RMON)*. Most first-generation SNMP tools reported all network monitoring information to one central network management database. Each device would transmits update to its MIB to the server every few minutes, greatly increasing network traffic. RMON SNMP software enables MIB information to be stored on the device itself or on distributed *RMON probes* that store MIB information closer to the devices that generate it. The data is not transmitted to the central server until the network manager requests the data, thus reducing network traffic (Figure 12-7).

Network information is recorded on the basis of data link layer protocols, network-layer protocols, and application-layer protocols, so that network managers can get a very

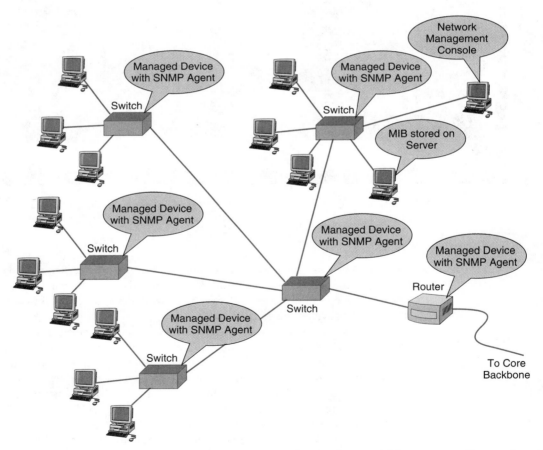

FIGURE 12-7 Network Management with Simple Network Management Protocol (SNMP). MIB = management information base.

clear picture of the exact types of network traffic in the network. Statistics are also collected on the basis of network addresses so the network manager can see how much network traffic any particular computer is sending and receiving. A wide variety of *alarms* can be defined, such as instructing a device to send a warning message if certain items in the MIB exceed certain values (e.g., if circuit use exceeds 50 percent). SNMP also supports PKI encryption and authentication.

As the name suggests, SNMP is a simple protocol with a limited number of functions. One problem with SNMP is that many vendors have defined their own extensions to it, so the network devices sold by a vendor may be SNMP compliant, but the MIBs they produce contain additional information that can be used only by network management software produced by the same vendor. Therefore, although SNMP was designed to make it easier to manage devices from different vendors, in practice, this is not always the case.

Network Management Hardware

Most network management hardware is used to test circuits. Testing is divided into analog testing, digital testing, and protocol testing. *Analog testing* involves troubleshooting on the analog side of the modem on the communication circuits supplied by common carriers. *Digital testing* is aimed primarily at testing digital communication circuits. *Protocol testing* focuses on testing the various sign-on/sign-off procedures, checking the content of packets or frames, examining message transmission times, and other items related to software protocols.

Monitors and analyzers generally are test sets that allow the operator to simulate specific message streams to test devices, communication circuits, or other workstations. A monitor resembles a portable microcomputer. Protocol analyzers offer both data and protocol analysis for TCP/IP, SNA, X.25, HDLC, T1, frame relay, and the like. Most of today's line monitors and network analyzers use microprocessor chips to perform sophisticated network tests. In other cases, microcomputers with special software handle the required network testing and monitoring.

Analog and digital test sets are found on any network that uses modems in conjunction with telephone company circuits. Most networks require both analog and digital test sets. These devices also resemble portable microcomputers, complete with a video screen and keyboard for data entry.

Patch panels provide an electrical connection to all parts of the network. At the minimum, they provide centralized access to each network communication circuit. They are large panels with a number of plugs or connectors that can be cross-connected between different communication circuits. Cross-patching permits the immediate replacement of a failed circuit with a spare.

Data recorders do not always perform tests. They are used to tap into communication circuits and store on disk pertinent activities about various circuits. Basically, they are a monitor for collecting and analyzing data and printing out reports. They resemble portable microcomputers.

Handheld test sets are the least expensive and simplest type of network equipment. They can be inserted between two network devices to test voltages or to send and receive various test patterns of bits to isolate errors. They also are used to determine whether there is a problem with the cables.

Breakout Box The most basic level of data communication monitoring and test equipment is analog test equipment. The *breakout box* is the next level up. It is a handheld device that can be plugged into a modem's digital side to determine the voltage values for the circuit.

Bit-Error Rate Tester The *bit-error rate tester (BERT)* is a somewhat more sophisticated than a breakout box because it sends a known pseudorandom pattern over the communication circuit. When this pattern is reflected back, the BERT compares it to the transmitted pattern and calculates the number of bit errors that occurred on the communication circuit. Various test patterns are used, and common pattern lengths are 63, 511, 2,047, and 63,511 bits. The odd numbers allow simple circuitry in this test equipment.

Bit-error rate (BER) measurements can be made with this type of equipment. A BER is the number of bits received in error divided by the total number of bits received. Service personnel use BER measurements to tune the communication circuit and to make a subjective evaluation as to the quality of a specific circuit or channel. BER cannot be related directly to throughput because error distribution is not taken into account. Assume that 1,000 one-bit errors occur during a time interval of 1,000 seconds. If the errors are distributed evenly (one per second), the effect on throughput will be disastrous; however, if all the errors occur in a single second, the effect will be minimal.

Block-Error Rate Tester A *block-error rate tester (BKERT)*, calculates *the block-error rate (BKER),* which is the number of received blocks that contain at least 1 bit error divided by the total number of blocks received. A BKER is more closely related to throughput than is a BER. Assume that a BKER measurement has been made and that the BKER value is 10^2 (1/100). This means that of every 100 blocks received, 1 contained an error; therefore, you would expect to see one retry for every 100 blocks transmitted (a 1 percent error rate).

Another error rate parameter used only for digital networks is *error-free seconds* (EFS). It is similar to BKER, except that it indicates the probability of success rather than failure and that the block size is the number of bits transmitted in a 1-second time period. For example, for a 4,800-bps channel, the 1-second block would contain 4,800 bits.

Fiber Identifier The *fiber identifier* is for locating a particular nonworking fiber without interrupting service on a fiber-optic network. (Remember that a fiber cable may contain a bundle of 72 or 144 glass or plastic fibers.) The fiber identifier consists of a transmitter that injects a light signal; a detector that induces a low stress on the fibers, allowing them to be searched without damage; and a receiver that emits an audible and visual signal when the fiber in question has been identified. The detector is a wandlike device that detects the signal at splice locations as it is passed near the splice. Because splices leak light, these are the points at which illegal taps would be inserted.

Cable Analyzer The *cable analyzer* checks LAN cabling for signal continuity, pulse distortion, parity, conductivity, connectivity, polarity reversals, and excessive noise in the data stream. It also can test to ensure that the cable meets the standards for that type of cable.

Protocol Analyzer/Data Line Monitor   Today, protocol analyzers and data line monitors all tend to do the same things. Recognizing this overlap, however, we can distinguish between them by their original purpose. A *data line monitor* traces network activity and response time analysis on a specific circuit. It also checks the actual data. *Protocol analyzers* decode messages on the circuit to allow you to see the content (bits) of a frame or packet during its transmission. Users can capture data in an external tape storage or internal memory, print it, or freeze the most current data on the video screen. A protocol analyzer shows when a carriage return or a line feed occurs, as well as when a communication control code is transmitted. The technician can count the bits within a packet or frame and identify each field and its contents.

Protocol analyzers also measure the responses of all hardware in the network and determine whether the network equipment is meeting specifications. In addition, they can print the captured information or trap information when certain character sequences appear on the send or receive communication circuits. Some analyzers offer performance monitoring operations to help evaluate specific areas of network performance such as response time and circuit use.

These devices may be active or passive. *Active analyzers/monitors* can generate data, are interactive on the circuit, and can emulate various terminals because they are programmable. *Passive analyzers/monitors* merely monitor and collect data to be examined later. It should be noted that this test equipment, especially active analyzers, can be a security risk because of its ability to generate data, interactively place it on a communication circuit, and do this while emulating another terminal.

A typical analyzer can monitor data, trap and count data for gathering communication circuit statistics, offer a video screen and printer, poll various stations, offer BERT capabilities, work with both asynchronous and synchronous systems, analyze various protocols, and possess breakout box capabilities. Several vendors sell the hardware and software needed to turn a microcomputer into a limited version of a protocol analyzer, data line monitor, and BERT tester.

Automated Test Equipment   *Automated test equipment* consists of hardware and specialized software packages. All have built-in microprocessor chips and programmable testing features. You should note that the programs able to do this testing also can be housed within the host mainframe computer or a remote computer somewhere out in the network. Furthermore, the telephone companies offer centralized automated testing equipment for monitoring your network.

Automated testing equipment performs diagnostic testing, polling, statistics gathering, protocol emulation, measurement of bandwidth efficiency, self-diagnosis of its own circuits, analog and digital circuit testing, testing of centralized and remote switches, and automatic restart and recovery in case of disaster.

SUMMARY

Integrating LANs, WANs and the Internet   Today, the critical issue is the integration of all organizational networks. The keys to integrating LANs, WANs, and the Web into one overall organization network are for WAN managers to recognize that LAN/Web managers can make independent decisions and for LAN/Web managers to realize that they need to work within organizational standards.

Integrating Voice and Data Communications   Another major challenge is combining voice communications with data and image communications. This separation of voice and data worked well for years, but changing communication technologies are generating enormous pressures to combine them. A key factor in voice–data integration might turn out to be the elimination of one key management position and the merging of two staffs into one.

Configuration Management   Configuration management means managing the network's hardware and software configuration and documenting it (and ensuring the documentation is updated as the configuration changes). The most common configuration management activity is adding and deleting user accounts. The most basic documentation about network hardware is a set of network configuration diagrams, supplemented by documentation on each individual network component. A similar approach can be used for network software. ESD plays a key role in simplifying configuration management by automating and documenting the network configurations. User and application profiles should be automatically provided by the network and ESD software. There are variety of other documentation that must be routinely developed and updated, including users' manuals and organizational policies.

Performance and Fault Management   Performance management means ensuring the network is operating as efficiently as possible. Fault management means preventing, detecting, and correcting any faults in the network circuits, hardware, and software. The two are closely related because any faults in the network reduce performance and because both require network monitoring. Today, most networks use a combination of smart devices to monitor the network and issue alarms and a help desk to respond to user problems. Problem tracking allows the network manager to determine problem ownership or who is responsible for correcting any outstanding problems. Problem statistics are important because they are a control device for the network operators as well as for vendors.

Providing End User Support   Providing end user support means solving whatever network problems users encounter. Support consists of resolving network faults, resolving software problems, and training. Software problems often stem from lack of user knowledge and fundamental problems with the software or an incompatibility between the software and the network's software and hardware. There are often several levels to problem resolution. End user training is an ongoing responsibility of the network manager. Training usually has two parts: (1) in-class instruction and (2) the documentation and training manuals that the user keeps for reference.

Cost Management   As the demand for network services grows, so does its cost. The TCO for typical networked computers is about $10,000 per year per computer, far more than the initial purchase price. The network management cost (omitting "wasted" time) is between $1,500 and $3,500 per year per computer. The largest single cost item is staff salaries. The best way to control rapidly increasing network costs is to reduce the amount of time taken to perform network management functions, often by automating as many routine ones as possible.

Network Management Software   Network Management Software is designed to provide automated support for any or all of the network management functions. Device management software provides information about devices. Systems management software provides ESD and analyzes the device-level information to provide more useful network-level information. Application management software tracks information about mission-critical applications that run on the network. Managed network devices perform their functions and also record data on the messages they process. These data can be sent to the network manager's computer when the device receives a special control message. If the device detects a critical situation, it can send a special control message (called an alarm) to the network manager's computer. The two most commonly used network management protocol standards are SNMP and CMIP.

Network Management Hardware Tools   There five basic categories of test equipment. Monitors and analyzers allow the operator to simulate specific message streams to test devices, communication circuits, or other workstations. Analog and digital test sets are found on any network that uses modems in conjunction with telephone company circuits. Patch panels provide electrical connection to all parts of the network. Data recorders tap into communication circuits and store on disk pertinent activities about various circuits. Handheld test sets can be inserted between two network devices to test voltages or to send and receive various test patterns of bits to isolate errors.

KEY TERMS

active analyzers/monitors
agent
alarm
alarm storm
analog testing
analyzer
application management
    software
automated test equipment
availability
bit-error rate (BER)
bit-error rate tester
    (BERT)
block-error rate (BKER)
block-error rate tester
    (BKERT)
breakout box
cable analyzer
charge-back policy
Common Management
    Interface Protocol
    (CMIP)

data line monitor
data recorders
desktop management
device management
    software
digital testing
downtime
electronic software dis-
    tribution (ESD)
error-free seconds (EFS)
fiber identifier
firefighting
handheld test set
help desk
load balancing
logical network
    parameters
managed device
management informa-
    tion base (MIB)
mean time between
    failures (MTBF)

mean time to diagnose
    (MTTD)
mean time to fix
    (MTTF)
mean time to repair
    (MTTR)
mean time to respond
    (MTTR)
monitor
network cost of owner-
    ship (NCO)
network documentation
network management
network management
    software
network operations
    center (NOC)
passive analyzer/
    monitor
patch panel
physical network
    parameters

policy-based
    management
problem statistics
problem tracking
protocol analyzer
protocol testing
quality-control chart
remote monitorning
    (RMON)
RMON probe
root cause analysis
service-level agreement
    (SLA)
Simple Network Man-
    agement Protocol
    (SNMP)
system management
    software
total cost of ownership
    (TCO)
trouble ticket
Uptime

QUESTIONS

1. What are some differences between LAN and WAN management?
2. What is firefighting?
3. Why is combining voice and data a major organizational challenge?
4. Describe what configuration management encompasses.
5. People tend to think of software when documentation is mentioned. What is documentation in a network situation?
6. What is electronic software delivery, and why is it import?
7. What is performance and fault management?
8. What does a help desk do?
9. What do trouble tickets report?
10. Several important statistics related to network uptime and downtime are discussed in this chapter. What are they, and why are they important?
11. What is an SLA?

12. How is network availability calculated?

13. What is problem escalation?

14. What are the primary functions of end user support?

15. What is TCO?

16. Why is the TCO so high?

17. How can network costs be reduced?

18. What do network management software systems do, and why are they important?

19. Discuss three types of network management software.

20. What is the SNMP?

21. What is RMON?

22. What are the five categories of network test equipment?

23. What is the purpose of a fiber identifier?

24. How is a cable analyzer used?

25. What is a protocol analyzer?

26. How does network cost of ownership differ from total cost of ownership? Which is the most useful measure of network costs from the point of view of the network manager? Why?

27. Why do some organizations choose to install device management software, and others, system management software?

28. Authentication and encryption were added to SNMP only in the last few years. Why do think this is the case?

29. Many organizations do not have a formal trouble reporting system. Why do you think this is the case?

30. Early in the chapter, there is a box entitled Key Network Management Skills. Compare and contrast the skills labeled "very important" with those labeled "moderately important" and "less important." What patterns do you notice? Why do you think there are such patterns.

EXERCISES

12-1 What factors might cause peak loads in a network? How can a network manager determine if they are important and how are they taken into account when designing a data communications network?

12-2 Today's network managers face a number of demanding problems. Investigate and discuss three major issues.

12-3 Investigate the latest versions of SMNP and RMON and describe the functions that have been added in the latest version of the standard.

12-4 Investigate and report on the purpose, relative advantages, and relative disadvantages of two network management software tools (e.g., OpenView, Tivoli TME).

12-5 Research the networking budget in your organization and discuss the major cost areas. Discuss several ways of reducing costs over the long term.

MINI-CASES

I. Mary's Manufacturing

Mary's Manufacturing is a small manufacturing company that has a network with eight LANs (each with about 20 computers on them using switched 10Base-T) connected via 100Base-T over fiber-optic cable into a core switch (i.e., a collapsed BN). The switch is connected to the company's ISP over a fractional T1 circuit. Most computers are used for order processing and standard office applications, but some are used to control the manufacturing equipment in the plant. The current network is working fine and there have been no major problems, but Mary is wondering whether she should invest in network management software. It will cost about $5,000 to replace the current hardware with SNMP-capable hardware. Mary can buy SNMP device management software for $2,000 or spend $7,000 to buy SNMP system management software. Should Mary install SNMP, and if so, which software should she buy? Why?

II. Network Simulator

The Web site for this book has a network simulator that shows what a network management system for a small company might look like. The simulator shows a series of network alerts that indicate problems in network. Identify the problems and state how would you fix them.

CASE STUDY

NEXT-DAY AIR SERVICE

The NDAS network system is finally in place and operating. President Coone has assigned operational control of the network to the Information Services/Data Processing Division. He believes this is reasonable and justified because of the division's data processing responsibilities and experience in operating data communications equipment. In addition, his nephew, Les Coone, is running that department and has expressed considerable interest in data communications.

The Human Resources Division originally set up the telephone system, because—at the time—no one else was interested in doing it. As a result, Human Resources, headed by Karen Lott, controls the voice and facsimile communication system for the company.

One recurring problem is that two division heads disagree on which department should be responsible for dealing with the common carriers. Each division believes it should be the contact for dealing with the common carriers, and each thinks the other is stopping it from assuming its rightful place within the organization.

Because of your excellent past performance, President Coone has asked you to study certain organizational issues pertaining to the control and operation of both voice and data communications. He wants you to analyze the operations of both divisions and propose a method for streamlining the organization and fixing the problem. This analysis should address the possibility of combining the voice and data communication responsibilities under a single manager. You may propose any reorganization that seems appropriate. Be sure to consider economies of scale when submitting any recommendations. President Coone reminds you that you were a staunch advocate of video conferencing. He wants you to include video and image transmission considerations in your analysis.

You should also consider the type of individual that should manage this reorganization. Some of the factors to evaluate are the traits and characteristics needed for successful leadership, the ability to understand current systems, the ability to handle both data and voice networks, and the ability to analyze and manage future growth. The results of this evaluation will help determine whether such an individual exists within NDAS or whether the firm needs to hire someone from outside the organization.

Another little problem occurred last week when DNAS experienced its first network line failure. President Coone had to ask Karen Lott to determine what failed on the circuit. After fiddling with the problem for an hour and a half, she finally called the modem vendor, who then took 3 hours to get to the Tampa headquarters building. The good news is that the vendor's maintenance employee swapped a new circuit card into the failed modem and had it fixed in 15 minutes. Needless to say, President Coone was not happy!

Exercises

1. If the responsibilities for managing communications were to be consolidated into one division, which one would you choose, and why? Base your answer on your knowledge of the communication management responsibilities exercised by both the Human Resources and Information Services Divisions.

2. Review the organization chart for NDAS, as shown in Figure 1-8, and then develop an organization chart that reflects a realignment of the responsibilities for communications. Show separate organizational entities for both data processing and communications. Consider the pros and cons of creating a new communications manager position. Discuss the reasons why NDAS should promote someone from within the company to fill this new position. Now discuss the contrary reasons why NDAS should hire someone from outside the organization for this position. Which method would you take? Why?

3. Sketch out a simple network management system for NDAS. What software and hardware support would you recommend? Be sure you can justify the information items collected and reported for this system, as well as your software and hardware recommendations.

GROUPWARE

Groupware is software that helps groups of people to work together more productively. This is a very broad definition, but it is difficult to find a more specific one that includes all the different types of groupware applications. Groupware applications are often organized using a two-by-two grid (Figure A-1). Groupware permits people in different places to communicate either at the same time (like a telephone) or at different times. Groupware also can be used to improve communication and decision making among those who work together in the same room, either at the same time or at different times.

Groupware allows people to exchange ideas, debate issues, make decisions, and write reports without actually having to meet face-to-face. Even when groups do meet in the same room at the same time, groupware can improve the meetings. There are many advantages of groupware, but the most important is its ability to help groups make decisions faster, particularly in situations in which it is difficult for group members to meet in the same room at the same time.

This section examines three popular types of groupware: discussion groups, document-based groupware (e.g., Lotus Notes), and group support systems. However, the lines between these different types of groupware are rapidly disappearing, as Notes, for example, incorporates discussion capabilities.

Discussion Groups

Discussion groups are collections of users who have joined together to discuss some topic. Discussion groups are formed around just about every topic imaginable, including cooking, skydiving, politics, education, and British comedy. Some are short lived, whereas others continue indefinitely. Two are commonly used for business: Usenet newsgroups and Listservs.

Usenet Newsgroups *Usenet newsgroups* are the most formally organized of the discussion groups. Establishing a new one requires a vote of all interested people on the Internet. If enough people express interest, the new topic is established.

The newsgroups are just a series of discussions about each topic. The Usenet newsgroups are a set of huge bulletin boards on which anyone who wishes can read and post messages. The Usenet "newsfeed" of the discussions within each of these groups is available to all computers on the Internet (about 70 megabytes of new messages each *day*). Some network managers choose not to provide access to all topics. For example, some universities to not provide access to the more sexually explicit newsgroups.

	Same time	Different time
Same place	Group support systems	Group support systems
Different place	Video teleconferencing Desktop video teleconferencing	Electronic mail Discussion groups Document-based groupware

FIGURE A-1 Different types of groupware

The exact commands to gain access to these newsgroups varies from computer to computer. The general process is to subscribe to a specific topic or set of topics. Once you have subscribed, then each time you access the newsgroups, you are informed of any new messages added to the topics. You can then read these messages and respond to them by adding your own message.

Listservs A listserver (or *Listserv*) group is similar in concept to the Usenet newsgroups but is generally less formal. Anyone with the right e-mail server software can establish a Listserv, which is simply a mailing list. One part, the *Listserv processor,* processes commands such as requests to subscribe, unsubscribe, or to provide more information about the Listserv. The second part is the *Listserv mailer.* Any message send to the Listserv mailer is re-sent to everyone on the mailing list. To use a Listserv, you need to know the addresses of both the processor and the mailer.

To subscribe to a Listserv, you send an e-mail message to the Listserv processor, which adds your name to the list. It is important that you send this message to the processor, not the mailer; otherwise, your subscription message will be sent to everyone on the mailing list, and you may feel embarrassed.

For example, you can join the Listserv on group support systems. The processor address is listerv@uga.cc.uga.edu and the mailer address is gss-1@uga.cc.uga.edu. To subscribe, you send an e-mail message to listerv@uga.cc.uga.edu containing the text: subscribe_gss_1_yourname. To send a message to everyone on this Listserv, you would e-mail your message to gss-1@uga.cc.uga.edu.

Listservs generally are more focused than the Usenet news groups and have fewer members. They are harder to find than the Usenet newsgroups because literally anyone can create one. There is no centrally managed list of Listservs, although many Listservs keep track of some Listservs on other Listservs. To get a list of some of the most popular Listservs, send an e-mail message to any Listserv with the message *list global.*

Document-Based Groupware

One of the problems with e-mail is that it lacks a structured way to support an ongoing discussion. Each mail message is a separate item, unrelated to other messages. It is possible to group and file e-mail messages into separate file folders, but there is no overall way to integrate them.

Lotus Notes (also called Domino), a document database designed to store and manage large collections of text and graphics, was the first product to provide a solution. Documents can have different sections and can be organized into a hierarchical structures of sections, documents, and folders. Lotus Notes can be used as a computer bulletin board to support ongoing discussions. Several topics and subtopics can be created, and everyone in the organization (or selected individuals) can be given access. For example, a topic area about data communications could be created. Users could ask questions about problems they face, contribute advice, or post new company policies. These individuals can add messages to the different topics and read those contributed by others. Messages can be easily linked so that it is clear which messages are related to which others.

Lotus Notes can also be used to organize a discussion among a certain people, such as a project team working to improve manufacturing quality. Notes might reduce the amount of time the team spent in face-to-face meetings, because many of the issues might be discussed before the meeting actually started. Notes also could be used to replace standard word processors in preparing the team's reports. Each team member could use Notes to write a portion of the report, which could then be passed to other team members for editing or comments.

Lotus Notes can also automate certain document-based processes (called *workflow automation*). For example, insurance claims require people from several different parts of an insurance company to work together to process the claim. One person might handle the initial claim, which would then be passed to an insurance adjuster to finish a report. Another person would process the payment. All this paperwork could be replaced if Lotus Notes were used to prepare and pass the documents from one person to another.

One of Notes' greatest strengths is its *replication* abilities. *Replication* is the automatic sharing of information among servers when information changes. For example, Notes servers can be set to replicate the information they contain with any other Notes server on the network, so that a change to a document on one server will automatically be shared with all other servers that contain that same document.

More than 2 million people worldwide now use Lotus Notes, a fact that has not escaped the notice of other software vendors. Microsoft has introduced Microsoft Exchange to compete with Notes. At present, there are no standards for this type of groupware software, but more and more vendors are using Web browsers as their client software so that anyone with Web access can use their groupware server.

Group Support Systems

Both e-mail and document-based groupware are designed to support individuals and groups working in different places and different times. Neither is very suited to support the needs of groups working together at the same time in the same place. Likewise, both e-mail and document-based groupware provide support for the exchange of text, but neither provides more advanced tools for helping groups make decisions.

Group support systems (GSSs) are software tools designed to improve group decision making. Most GSSs are used in special-purpose meeting rooms that provide each group member with a networked computer, plus large-screen video projection systems that act as electronic blackboards. These rooms are equipped with special-purpose GSS software that enables participants to communicate, propose ideas, analyze options, evaluate alternatives, and so on. Typically, a meeting facilitator assists the group.

In the GSS meeting, group members can discuss issues verbally as they could in any meeting room; however, they can also use the computers to type ideas and information, which are then shared with all other group members via the network. At first glance, it may seem strange to ask people who are sitting next to each other to type their ideas, because typing is slower than talking. For small groups, typing adds little value.

For large groups, however, typing ideas is faster than talking because only one person can speak at a time. Very few people get a chance to talk, so their ideas and opinions can be overlooked. For example, in a traditional meeting, if 10 people participate equally for 1 hour, each spends 6 minutes talking and 54 minutes listening (or at least not contributing). This is a very inefficient use of time. Typing ideas into a GSS allows everyone the same opportunity to contribute and collects ideas much faster.

In addition, GSSs enable users to make anonymous comments. Without anonymity, certain participants may withhold ideas because they fear their ideas may not be well received. Anonymity can help participant overcome pressure to conform to the views of the group majority or more senior participants, whether that pressure is or is not intended.

These systems also provide tools to support voting and ranking of alternatives, so that more structured decision-making processes can be used. Studies of GSSs have shown that its use can reduce the amount of time taken to make decisions by 50 to 80 percent. At present, there are no standards for GSSs, so products from different vendors are not compatible. As with document groupware above, more vendors are using the Web browser as their client software so that virtually anyone can access their groupware server.

Managing in a Groupware World

Groupware dramatically changes the way people interact. Communication is simpler and faster. Anyone can communicate directly with anyone else, organizational rules permitting. Improved communication can provide large paybacks in increased productivity, especially when you consider that the primary task of most office workers (e.g., consultants, accountants, managers) is the processing and communication of information. A study of 65 Lotus Notes users conducted by International Data Corp. found an average 3-year return on investment of 179 percent.

Nonetheless, groupware's ability to greatly improve communication can also create problems. Hewlett-Packard's 97,000 employees exchange about 20 million electronic mail messages each month—an average of about 10 messages per person per business day. At Sun Microsystems, the average is 120 messages per person per day. Managing in this glut of information can be difficult. Identifying priorities and not being distracted by less important issues are key to success; otherwise, you can drown in an endless sea of communication.

Social norms are one of the greatest limiting factors in the widespread use of groupware technologies, because the technology changes faster than the people who use it. Many organizations use groupware as a means to exchange information and knowledge among their staff. The problem is, most organizations using groupware in this way do not reward people for contributing their expertise. Contributing information and helping others is important to help the organization achieve its goals, but it takes time from the person contributing the information and slows down their performance. This sets up conflicting goals for employees: Do I do my work or help others do theirs?

ELECTRONIC COMMERCE

Almost all large and medium-size companies use the Internet. Many are actively using it for *electronic commerce*—doing business on the Internet. Making money, however, is still a risky proposition. Some businesses are making a profit, but others have quickly failed. This is also true for businesses in the "real" world; only about 20 percent of new businesses are still operating 5 years later.

In the early days of the California gold rush, it wasn't the prospectors who got rich; it was the people selling the steamship tickets, denim clothing, and pickaxes. Likewise, the fastest way to make money from the Internet may be to sell products and services to those trying to strike it rich. One of the most profitable niches today is providing consulting, tools, training, and services for electronic commerce, rather than actually doing it. For this reason, much business use of the Internet is not for making money per se; rather, it is to find information, improve communications, and provide information—most of the same reasons that individuals use the Internet.

Many people automatically focus on the retail aspects of electronic commerce—that is, on selling products to individuals. However, that is just one small part of electronic commerce. The fastest-growing and soon-to-be largest segment of electronic commerce is business-to-business selling. In this section, we look at the types of sites on the Web that support electronic commerce and why companies and individuals want electronic commerce. There are many other ways to support electronic commerce, such as using FTP to share files. However, we believe that as Web browsers mature and include FTP and other functions, the Web will gradually become the most important.

There are four major ways in which the Web can be used to support electronic commerce: electronic store, electronic marketing, information/entertainment provider, and customer service. Most Web sites focus on just one approach, but it is possible to combine all four in one Web site. The most common type of Web site is electronic marketing. Today, less than 10 percent of corporate Web sites provide electronic stores, but this percentage is expected to grow rapidly over the next few years.

Electronic Store

The most obvious approach to electronic commerce is an *electronic store*. With an electronic store, a company develops the Internet equivalent of a local store or a mail-order catalogue. It develops a Web site that lists all of the products and services it wishes to sell and enables customers to purchase them by calling a toll-free number or by using the Internet

391

itself. There is some concern about transmitting credit-card information over the Internet because this information can be copied by any computer through which the message flows, making it easy to steal information. Although this is possible, the risk of having credit-card information stolen on the Internet is much less than having it stolen by a regular thief or unscrupulous store owner.

There are many examples of electronic stores. Many existing catalogue companies such as Lands' End have opened Web sites that operate in much the same manner as their traditional catalogues. Other entrepreneurs have opened electronic stores to compete with traditional stores. There are dozens of online travel agents (such as Travelocity) and online bookstores (such as Amazon.com) that provide products and services in direct competition to local stores. Electronic stores have lower overhead costs than traditional stores because they do not have physical stores with lots of employees and because they usually carry little or no inventory; all orders are shipped directly from the manufacturer. Electronic stores do, however, have higher shipping costs because they ship purchases to each customer individually rather than in bulk to stores.

One of the more interesting electronic stores is that run by Boeing. Boeing sells millions of spare parts each year to the 700 or so airlines that use its airplanes. Boeing now operates a electronic store that enables these airlines to purchase spare parts through the Web. This has improved customer service, because now a customer anywhere in the world can order a needed part directly from Boeing 24 hours a day. Surprisingly, this has also enabled Boeing to reduce costs and speed up delivery. The Boeing electronic store is a closed site (an extranet), which means that only Boeing customers can access it—so unless you own an airline, you won't be able to order a new engine for a 777.

Because there are few additional costs to providing more information on the Web (unlike a catalogue in which each page adds to the cost), electronic stores can provide much information. Electronic stores can also add value by providing dynamic information. Dell Computer, for example, sells computers that can be configured in many different ways (e.g., different-size hard disks, more or less memory). A static catalogue or magazine advertisement can list only a few configurations. The Dell electronic store enables customers to specify such things as exact hard drive size and amount of memory and get a price quote for the exact computer they want. It is simple for customers to price many different configurations, something that is not possible in a static paper medium. As an aside, Dell sells almost $1 billion of computers per year from its Web site alone—a staggering indication of the importance of the Web to Dell and to other computer companies.

One problem is verifying that the transaction is accurate and is from whom it claims to be from. Suppose your electronic banker receives a message instructing the bank to transfer $10,000 into another account. The banker must ensure that the message actually came from your account (there are ways to mask a true address) and that you actually sent it (a hacker could have stolen your password). This is becoming possible with some new security tools discussed in Chapter 12 but will remain an issue for many years.

A variation on the electronic store is the *electronic mall*. An electronic mall is a collection of electronic stores. The mall usually provides all the computer infrastructure needed for electronic commerce and advertises the mall to potential customers. In return, the stores pay the mall a monthly fee or some percentage of sales. One of the reasons for the success of real shopping malls is that location is extremely important for retail sales; if you are not near other stores, it is hard to attract customers. On the Web, location is unimportant. It is as simple to click to an electronic store in the United States or Canada as it is to one in England or Australia. Many electronic malls have closed because they cannot attract enough electronic stores to become profitable.

Electronic Marketing Site

A second common approach is the *electronic marketing site.* This type of site supports the sales process but does not make actually sales. The goal is to attract and keep customers. The most common type of electronic commerce site is the electronic marketing site. The Web sites of the major automobile manufacturers in the North America are good examples. These sites provide a wealth of information about their cars, complete with technical details and photographs. Customers can view these pages and obtain information without going to the dealer, but they cannot buy a car over the Web. The goal of these Web sites is to encourage the user visit a local dealer, who will then make the sale. One Toyota dealer estimates that he sells two or three cars per month (that he would not otherwise have sold) because of Toyota's Web page. Although the numbers sound small, this translates into more than $150 million per year in North America alone—a rather substantial payback for one Web site.

Many companies use electronic marketing sites to provide newsletters with information on latest products and tips on how to use them. IBM and Microsoft, for example, use the Web to provide information on the latest versions of their software and on products that have been announced but not yet released. Other companies enable potential customers to sign up for notification of new product releases. Amazon.com, for example, will notify you the next time your favorite author publishes a new book.

Electronic marketing is cheaper in many ways than traditional print, direct mail, TV, or radio marketing. Electronic marketing costs no more than other media to develop, but unlike print, direct mail, TV, and radio, there are no costs to sending the information to the consumer. It is also easier to customize the presentation of information to a potential customer because the Web is interactive. In contrast, the other media are fixed once they are developed and provide the same marketing approach to all who see it.

Information/Entertainment Provider

As the name suggests, an *information/entertainment provider* supplies information and/or entertainment. The key difference between electronic stores and information/entertainment providers is the nature of the products. Electronic stores provide physical goods and services (e.g., flowers, airline tickets), whereas information/entertainment providers provide intangible things. The key difference between electronic marketing sites and information/entertainment providers is the nature of the information. Electronic marketing sites focus on the products and services of one company; their goal is to increase sales. Information/entertainment providers provide information from many sources; their goal is to help their user. Some of the most common information/entertainment providers are the search engines discussed above.

Information/entertainment providers can be very broad or very focused in topic coverage and can present information in a variety of media. For example, many national magazines and newspapers have gone on the Web. Most of these provide broad coverage of a wide range of topics. Other information/entertainment providers provide very narrowly focused information and advice about specific topics (e.g., sports scores, movie reviews, used car prices).

The information provided by these information/entertainment providers can take many forms. Typically, the information has been text or graphic. Over the past year, several radio and TV stations have moved onto the Web, providing broadcasts of audio and video in much the same way as they do in their traditional media. The Web also offers new forms of entertainment. Virtual reality, for example, enables new multiplayer interactive games that are not available in any other media. Several studies have noticed a slight drop in TV viewing among longtime users of the Web, suggesting that for some people, the Web may replace some of their traditional sources of entertainment.

Most Web users expect information to be free, so most information/entertainment providers do not charge for access, although a few require subscriptions just like magazines before they will let anyone into their site. Many national newspapers initially tried to charge for subscriptions, but most dropped fees after failing to generate enough interest. Several narrowly focused information/entertainment providers have been very successful in charging fees because the information they provide has a clear value to those who subscribe.

Like their print counterparts, information/entertainment providers generate revenue by selling advertising. Web advertising has been slow to build, but most experts believe that it will quickly grow as more businesses come to understand how to use the Web as one part of their marketing strategies. As one might expect, the largest advertisers on the Web are computer and telecommunications companies such as IBM, Microsoft, AT&T, and MCI, but many of the world's largest advertisers, such as automobile manufacturers (e.g., General Motors) and package goods firms (e.g., Proctor and Gamble), have begun to advertise on the Web.

Customer Service Site

A *customer service site* provides a variety of information for customers after they have purchased a product or service. For example, Dell provides more than 30,000 Web pages of technical support information, service information, and *frequently asked questions (FAQs)* on its Web sites. Rather than telephoning the company during business hours—and possibly having to wait for a customer service representative—customers can now access the most commonly needed information 24 hours a day. Many software companies post updates to software on their Web sites so that customers can download the newest versions of software or updates that fix problems.

FedEx has been one of the leading innovators in the use of the Web for customer service. The company's Web site enables customers to track the packages they have sent. When a customer enters a package number, the Web site provides specific information about the current location of the package and when it was delivered (or when it is scheduled for delivery). Dell also provides an online order tracking system, so customers can quickly find out the status of their order. This service receives about 15,000 requests per day, meaning 15,000 fewer telephone calls for the customer service staff.

Customer service sites benefit both the company and its customers. They enable the customer to more quickly access needed information and provide support 24 hours a day.

They also often reduce the number of staff members needed by automating many of the routine information requests that previously needed to be handled an employee. Many companies are now extending the customer service by offering information targeted to suppliers, partners, and employees. Many of the same concepts apply and many of the same benefits are realized.

CELLULAR TECHNOLOGY

Cellular technology is becoming increasingly popular. Its most common use is to provide *cellular telephone* services, but the cellular network is also being used more and more often by data communications devices such as pagers and personal digital assistants (PDAs).

Cellular technology is a form of high frequency radio in which antennas are spaced strategically throughout a metropolitan area. A service area or city is divided into many cells, each with its own antenna. This arrangement generally provides subscribers with reliable mobile telephone service of a quality almost that of a hardwired telephone system. Users (voice or data transmission) dial or log in to the system, and their voices or data are transmitted directly from their automobile, home, or place of business to one of these antennas. In this way, the cellular system replaces the hardwired local loop.

This system is intelligent. For example, as you drive your automobile across the service area or city, you move away from one antenna and closer to another. As the signal weakens at the first antenna, the system automatically begins picking up your signal at the second antenna. Transmission is switched automatically to the closest antenna without communication being lost.

When you speak on a cellular telephone, anyone might be listening to your conversation. Cellular telephone calls are transmitted over the 870- to 890-MHz frequency bands, which are easily accessible by today's scanners. These devices can scan the frequencies and stop and listen in at the specific frequency your call is using. Even though federal law says it is illegal to manufacture scanners for this frequency range or to use them to listen in on a cellular telephone call, it is virtually impossible to enforce this law because thousands of people own scanners.

Cellular telephone fraud is also becoming a problem. Unscrupulous people purchase a cellular telephone and remove its security EPROM (erasable programmable read-only memory) and replace it with "thumbwheel" EPROM substitutes. They do this by turning the wheels at random until they discover some other person's cellular telephone security code, at which point they can begin making calls on that code—at least until that person receives the next telephone bill. Some of the more sophisticated fraud perpetrators use scanners and laptop microcomputers to find large numbers of cellular telephone codes automatically. As yet, this type of fraud is not very common, but owners of cellular telephones should check their bills immediately. Also, remember that you pay for both incoming and outgoing cellular airtime. Thus, you pay not only for calls you make but also for those other people make to you.

A pager may be better for incoming calls than a cellular telephone if you want to save money and also have more security. For security reasons, you should not provide cellular telephone numbers to strangers. Instead, you should provide a beeper number for others to call you, and then you call them back on the cellular telephone. This procedure is more secure and eliminates the cost of incoming cellular calls.

The real future of cellular technology is based on the philosophy of dividing the entire United States, or even the world, into cells so a person can call from anywhere to anywhere. It would be easy to interconnect the cells of the entire United States with the cells of, say, France by using either satellite communications or fiber-optic undersea cables.

CONNECTOR CABLES

When a message leaves the microcomputer or terminal and begins to move onto the network, the first component it encounters is the *connector cable* between the microcomputer (or terminal) and the circuit. When people discuss connector cables, the focus is on the standards (such as RS232 or RS449).

RS232 (DB-25)/RS449 (DB-9)

When people talk about connector cables, they frequently refer to them as a *RS232, DB-25, RS449,* or *DB-9.* This is because each connector cable is based on a specified standard. Calling the connector by its standard designation allows everyone to know precisely which connector is being discussed.

The RS232 standard is the most frequently mentioned. It was first issued in 1962, and its third revision, RS232C, was issued in 1969. The RS232D standard was issued in 1987 to expand on RS232C. The RS232D standard also is known as the EIA-232-D.

The RS232 connector cable that is the standard interface for connecting *data terminal equipment (DTE)* to *data circuit terminating equipment (DCE).* The newer RS232D is specified as having 25 wires and using the DB-25 connector plug like the one used on microcomputers. If this connector cable is attached to a microcomputer, people may refer to it simply as DB-25; if it is not attached to a microcomputer, they may refer to it as the RS232 interface.

DTE comprises the data source, the data sink, or both. In reality, it is any piece of equipment at which a data communications path begins or ends, such as a terminal. (DCE) provides all the functions required to establish, maintain, and terminate a connection. This includes signal conversion and coding between the DTE and the common carrier's circuit, including the modem. A modem is DCE.

Figure A-2 shows a picture of the RS232D interface plug and describes each of its 25 protruding pins. It is the standard connector cable (25 wires/pins) that passes control signals and data between the terminal (DTE) and the modem (DCE). This standard has been supplied by the Electronic Industries Association (EIA). Outside the United States, this RS232D connector cable is known as the V.24 and V.28. The V.24 and V.28 standards have been accepted by the international standards group known as the ITU-T. These standards provide a common description of what the signal coming out of and going into the serial port of a computer or terminal looks like electrically. Specifically, RS232 provides for a signal changing from a nominal +12 volts to a nominal −12 volts. The standard also defines the cables and connectors used to link data communications devices. This is the cable that connects the modem to your microcomputer.

The RS232 has a maximum 50-foot cable length, but it can be increased to 100 feet or more by means of a special low-capacitance, extended-distance cable. This is not

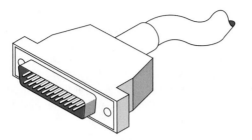

Pin	Circuit Name
1	Shield
2	Transmitted data
3	Received data
4	Request to send
5	Clear to send
6	DCE ready
7	Signal ground
8	Received line signal detector
9	(Reserved for testing)
10	(Reserved for testing)
11	(Unassigned)
12	Secondary received line signal detector/data signal rate select (DCE source)
13	Secondary clear to send
14	Secondary transmitted data
15	Transmitter signal element timing (DCE source)
16	Secondary received data
17	Receiver signal element timing (DCE source)
18	Local loopback
19	Secondary request to send
20	DTE ready
21	Remote loopback/signal quality detector
22	Ring indicator
23	Data signal rate select (DTE/DCE source)
24	Transmitter signal element timing (DTE source)
25	Text mode

FIGURE A-2   RS232 cable specifications. DCE = data circuit terminating equipment;
DTE = data terminal equipment.

advised, however, because some vendors may not honor maintenance agreements if the
cable is lengthened beyond the 50-foot standard.

In illustration, we present the cable distances for Texas Instruments' products. The
cable length of the RS232 varies according to the speed at which you transmit. For Texas
Instruments, the connector cable length can be up to 914 meters (1 meter = 1.1 yards)
when transmitting at 1,200 bps, 549 meters when transmitting at 2,400 bps, 244 meters
when transmitting at 4,800 bps, and 122 meters when transmitting at 9,600 bps. When end

users operate equipment at maximum distances, it is important to remember that they must meet the restrictions on all types of equipment used, including the electrical environment, cable construction, and cable wiring. This means that when you want to operate at a maximum cable distance, you must contact the terminal and/or modem vendors to obtain their maximum cable distance before you proceed.

The RS449 standard has been adopted as U.S. Federal Standard 1031. The RS449 is shown in Figure A-3. A 4,000-foot cable length can be used, there are 37 pins instead of 25

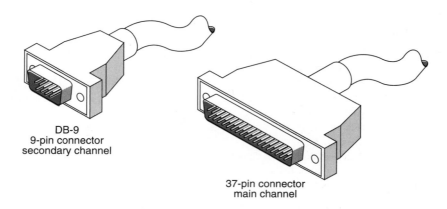

DB-9
9-pin connector
secondary channel

37-pin connector
main channel

37-Pin Connector				9-Pin Connector	
Pin	**First Segment Assignment Function**	**Pin**	**Second Segment Assignment Function**	**Pin**	**Function**
1	Shield	20	Receive common	1	Shield
2	Signaling rate indicator	21	(Unassigned)	2	Secondary receiver
3	(Unassigned)	22	Send data ready	3	Secondary send data
4	Send data	23	Send timing	4	Secondary receive data
5	Send timing	24	Receive data	5	Signal ground
6	Receive data	25	Request to send	6	Receive common
7	Request to send	26	Receive timing	7	Secondary request to send
8	Receive timing	27	Clear to send	8	Secondary clear to send
9	Clear to send	28	Terminal in service	9	Send common
10	Local loopback	29	Data mode		
11	Data mode	30	Terminal ready		
12	Terminal ready	31	Receiver ready		
13	Receiver ready	32	Select standby		
14	Remote loopback	33	Signal quality		
15	Incoming call	34	New signal		
16	Select frequency/signaling rate selector	35	Terminal timing		
17	Terminal timing	36	Standby indicator		
18	Test mode	37	Send common		
19	Signal ground				

FIGURE A-3 RS449 cable specifications.

(useful for digital transmission), and various other circuit functions have been added, such as diagnostic circuits and digital circuits. In addition, secondary channel circuits (reverse channel) have been put into a separate 9-pin connector known as a DB-9. The serial port on your microcomputer may be either a DB-9 or a DB-25.

For some of the new features, look at pin 32 (Select standby). With this pin, the terminal can instruct the modem to use an alternate standby network such as changing from a private leased line to a public packet network, either for backup or simply to access another database not normally used. In other words, a terminal can be connected to two different networks, and the operator can enter a keyboard command to switch the connection from one network to another. With regard to loopback (pins 10 and 14), the terminal can allow basic tests without special test equipment or the manual exchanging of equipment or cables.

With microcomputers, the RS232 and RS449 also are referred to as D-type connectors. The RS232 may be called a DB-25, and the 9-pin RS449 may be called a DB-9. Look at Figure A-4 to see the microcomputer pin configurations for these two connectors.

There are also X.20 and X.21 interface cables. The *X.20* interface is for asynchronous communications, and the *X.21* is for synchronous communications. Each is based on only 15 pins (wires) connecting the DTE and the DCE; the presence of fewer pins requires an increased intelligence in both the DTE and the DCE. X.20 and X.21 are international standards intended to provide an interface with the X.25 packet switching networks discussed elsewhere in this book.

Another option that may become available in the near future is a fiber-optic cable in place of the standard RS232 electrical cables. Currently, by using fiber-optic cable, we can locate a terminal 1,000 meters (3,280 feet) from a host mainframe computer. With a 1,000-meter fiber-optic cable, these products can communicate at speeds ranging from 19,200 bps to twice that speed. Therefore, you get not only greater distance (1,000 meters) but also greater speed. This may be another example in which fiber optics eventually will replace electronics.

The *high-speed serial interface (HSSI)* is beginning to appear in new products. HSSI defines the physical and electrical interface between the DTE and the DCE equipment. It was developed by Cisco Systems of Menlo Park, California, and T3plus of Santa Clara, California. They have submitted it to the American National Standards Institute, which also formalized the EIA-232 and V.35 standards. HSSI allows data transfers over the connector cable at 52 million bps, whereas RS-449 cannot handle more than 10 million bps. HSSI is a 50-pin connector using shielded twisted-pair cabling.

Null Modem Cable Connections

Null modem cables allow transmission between two microcomputers that are next to each other (6 to 8 feet apart) without using a modem. If you discover that the diskette from your microcomputer will not fit into another one, that transmitting over telephone lines is impossible, or that you cannot transmit data easily from one microcomputer to another for any reason, then it is time to get a null modem cable.

First, bring the two microcomputers close together. Next, obtain a null modem cable (more on the pin connections shortly). The cable runs from the serial communication port on the first microcomputer to the serial communication port on the second one. The cable is called a *null* modem cable because it eliminates the need for a modem. You can either

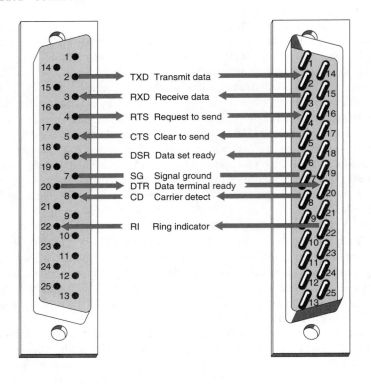

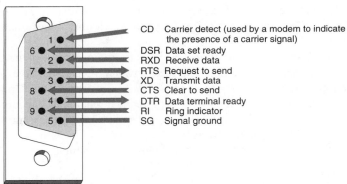

FIGURE A-4   Pin configurations.

build a null modem cable or buy one from any microcomputer store. Null modem connector blocks are available to connect between two cables you already own.

To transfer data between two microcomputers, just hook the null modem cable between them and call up one of the computers by using the communication software you normally use. To do so, put one microcomputer in answer mode and use the other one to call it, but skip the step of dialing the telephone number. After the receiving computer has answered that it is ready, the data can be sent, just as you would on a normal long-distance dial-up connection.

With null modem cables, a higher bits per second rate is accomplished easily; transmission can be 9,600 bps, for example. This may be a great advantage for high-volume data transfers from microcomputer to microcomputer because your modem might limit transmission to 1200 bps or less. Basically, a null modem cable switches pins 2 and 3 (Transmit and Receive) of the RS232 connector plug.

Data Signaling/Synchronization

Let us look at *data signaling* or *synchronization* as it occurs on a RS232 connector cable. Figure A-5 shows the 13 most frequently used pins of the 25-pin RS232 connector cable. A microcomputer is on the left side of the figure and a modem is on the right.

Do you ever wonder what happens when you press the "send" key to transmit synchronous data? When a synchronous block of data is sent, the microcomputer and the modem raise and lower electrical signals (plus and minus voltages of electricity) between themselves over the RS232 connector. This usually is a nominal +12 or −12 volts. For example, a modem with a RS232 interface might indicate that it is on and ready to operate

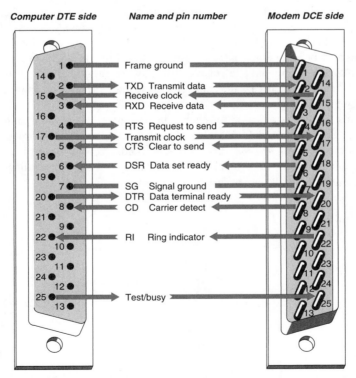

FIGURE A-5 Data signaling with RS232 cables. DCE 1-1 data circuit terminating equipment; DTE 1-1 data terminal equipment.

by raising the signal on pin 6, *Data Set ready.* (*Data set* is an older term for a modem.) When a call comes in, the modem shows the microcomputer that the telephone line is ringing by raising a signal on pin 22, the *Ring indicator.* Raising a signal means putting +12 volts on the wire or pin. The microcomputer may then tell the modem to answer the call by raising a signal on pin 20, *Data terminal ready.* After the modems connect, the modem may indicate the connection status to the microcomputer by raising a signal on pin 8, *Carrier detect.* At the end of the session, the microcomputer may tell the modem to drop the telephone call (release the circuit) by lowering the signal on pin 20, *Data terminal ready.* The *Request to send* and *Clear to send* signals go over pins 4 and 5, respectively, which are used in half-duplex modems to manage control of the communication channel. Incidentally, some of these basic procedures may vary slightly from one manufacturer to another.

Follow the pins and signal direction arrows in Figure A-5 as we discuss an example that handles the flow of a block of synchronous data. When the microcomputer operator presses the "send" key to transmit a block of data, pin 4, *Request to send,* transmits the signal from the microcomputer to the modem. This informs the modem that a block of data is ready to be sent. The modem then sends a *Clear to send* signal back to the microcomputer by using pin 5, thus telling the microcomputer that it can send a synchronous block of data.

The microcomputer now outpulses a serial stream of bits that contain two 8-bit SYN characters in front of the message block. A SYN character is 0110100 (decimal 22 in ASCII code). This bit stream passes over the connector cable to the modem using pin 2, *Transmit data.* The modem then modulates this data block to convert it from the digital signal (plus and minus voltages of electricity) to an analog signal (discussed in the next section). From the modem, the data go out onto the local loop circuit between your business premises and the telephone company central office. From there, it goes to the long-distance IXC and the receiving end's telephone company central office. Then it moves to the local loop, into the modem, across the connector cable, and into the host mainframe computer at the other end of the circuit.

This process is repeated for each synchronous message block in half-duplex transmission. The data signaling that takes place between the microcomputer and the modem involves the *Request to send, Clear to send,* and *Transmit data* pins. Accurate timing between blocks of data is critical in data signaling and synchronization. If this timing is lost, the entire block of data is destroyed and must be retransmitted.

SYSTEMS NETWORK ARCHITECTURE

IBM developed its own architecture and protocols for networking, called *systems network architecture (SNA)*. SNA describes an integrated structure that provides for all modes of data communications and on which new data communication networks can be planned and implemented. SNA is similar to the OSI model in concept but is different in implementation; SNA is not OSI compliant.

The major problem with SNA is that it uses proprietary nonstandard protocols at the network layer and above. This means that it is difficult to integrate SNA networks with other networks that use industry standard network layer protocols. Routing messages between SNA networks and other networks, and even between IBM SNA networks and IBM LANs (which use industry standard protocols) requires special equipment. In many cases, network managers using both IBM SNA and IBM LANs have built two separate networks into the same offices, laying two sets of cable to each location, one for SNA, one for the LAN a newer form of SNA (APPN) [advanced peer-to-peer networking]) that uses industry standard protocols, as discussed next. In a 1995 survey of mainframe network managers, 68 percent said that SNA and APPN were not important to their future plans (9 percent said they were critical and 23 percent said they were important).

SNA is built around four basic principles. *First,* SNA encompasses distributed functions in which many network responsibilities can be moved from the central computer to other network components, such as remote concentrators. *Second,* it describes paths between the end users (programs, devices, or operators) of the data communications network separately from the users themselves, thus allowing network configuration modifications or extensions without affecting the end users. *Third,* it uses the principle of device independence, which permits an application program to communicate with an input–output device without regard to any unique device requirements. This also allows application programs and communication equipment to be added or changed without affecting other elements of the communication network. *Fourth,* SNA uses both logical and physical standardized functions and protocols for the communication of information between any two points. This means there can be *one* architecture for general-purpose and industry terminals of many varieties and *one* network protocol.

The appropriate place to begin understanding the SNA concept is to look at it from the viewpoint of the end user. The end user (terminal operator) talks to the network through what is called a *logical unit (LU)*. These logical units are implemented as program code or microcode (firmware), and they provide the end user with a point of access to the network. The program code or microcode can be built into the terminal or implemented into an intelligent terminal controller, concentrator, or remote front end.

Before one end user of a SNA network can communicate with any other end user, each of their respective LUs must be connected in a mutual relationship called a *session.* Because a session joins two LUs, it is called a *LU-LU session.* The terminal user enters the request to talk to another terminal, and the network's software connects the two LUs.

The exchange of data by end users is subject to a number of procedural rules that the LUs specify before beginning the exchange of information. These procedural rules specify how the session is to be conducted, the frame size, the amount of data to be sent by one end user before the other end user replies, actions to be taken if errors occur, the transmission speed, sequencing, what route the frame will take, what to do if the circuit fails, and the like.

Each LU in a network is assigned a network name. Before a session begins, the SNA network determines the network address that corresponds to each LU network name. This scheme allows one end user (for example, a terminal operator) to establish communication with another end user (for example, an application program) without having to specify where that end user is located in the network. These network names and addresses are used for addressing messages.

The flow of data between users moves between two logical units in a session. This flow moves as a bit sequence carried in an SDLC frame and generally is referred to as a *message unit.* The message unit also contains the network addresses of the LU that originated the message and the LU that is to receive the message. These are the basic protocols at work.

A session between a pair of LUs is initiated when one of them (the end user) issues a *Request to send* message. Once a session has been activated between a pair of LUs, they can begin to exchange data. This is where the SDLC protocol handles the movement of data to have an orderly data flow. A session between a pair of LUs is deactivated when one of them sends a deactivation request or when some other outside event—intervention by a network operator or failure at some other part of the network—interrupts the session.

The logical organization of a SNA network, regardless of its physical configuration, is divided into two broad categories of components: network addressable units and path control network.

Network Addressable Units

Network addressable units (NAUs) are sets of SNA components that provide services enabling end users to send data through the network and helping network operators perform network control and management functions. Physically, NAUs are hardware and programming components within terminals, intelligent controllers, and front-end processors. NAUs communicate with one another through the path control network (discussed in the next section).

There are three kinds of NAUs in SNA. The first one, the LU, has already been introduced. The second is the *physical unit (PU),* which is a set of SNA components that provides services to control communication links, terminals, intelligent controllers, front-end processors, and host computers. Each terminal, intelligent controller, front-end processor, and the like contains a PU that represents that particular device to the SNA network. The third kind of NAU is the *system services control point (SSCP).* This also is a set of SNA components, but its duties are broader than those of the PUs and LUs. PUs and LUs represent machine resources and end users, whereas the SSCP manages the entire SNA network or a significant part of it called a *domain.* A SSCP controls many other devices.

Just as sessions exist between LUs, sessions can exist between other kinds of NAUs, such as an *SSCP-LU, SSCP-PU,* or *SSCP-SSCP session.* In a family, the mother, father, and children are all PUs. You conduct an LU session when speaking with your father, mother, sister, or brother, but your mother or father is the SSCP controlling the children's LUs.

SNA defines a *node* as a point within the SNA network that contains SNA components. For example, each terminal, intelligent controller, and front-end processor that is designed into the SNA specifications can be a node.

An expanded definition of a node is any microcomputer, minicomputer, mainframe computer, or database that constitutes a point on the network at which data might be stored, forwarded, input into the network, or removed from the network as output. Depending on which vendor's literature you read, a node might be referred to as a *station,* an *intelligent microprocessor-based device,* a *terminal,* or a *workstation.*

Each SNA node contains a PU that represents that node and its resources to the SSCP. When the SSCP activates a session with a PU (SSCP-PU session), it makes the node (terminal, intelligent controller, or front-end processor) containing that PU an active part of the SNA network. It is convenient to think of a SNA node as being a terminal, intelligent controller or a front-end processor within the network. Certainly, more powerful nodes also can be a SSCP.

Path Control Network

Remember that the logical organization of SNA is divided into two broad categories of components: NAUs and the path control network. The *path control network* provides for routing and flow control. LUs must establish a path before a LU-LU session can begin. Each SSCP, PU, and LU has a different network address, which identifies it to other NAUs as well as to the path control network. Path control provides for the following:

- Virtual routing so all sessions can send their messages by different routes
- Transmission priorities
- Multiple links to maximize throughput
- Message pacing (flow control) to keep a fast transmitter from drowning a slow receiver
- Ability to detect and recover from errors as they occur
- Facilities to handle disruption because of a circuit failure
- Facilities to inform network operators when there is a disruption in the network

The path control network has two layers: the *path control layer* and the *data link control layer* (similar to layers 2 and 3 in the OSI model). Routing and flow control are provided by the path control layer, whereas transmitting data over individual links is provided by the data link control layer, which uses SDLC.

Telecommunication Access Programs

Access to SNA networks is controlled by a series of telecommunications access programs, including telecommunications access method (TCAM) virtual telecommunications access method (VTAM), network control program (NCP), and customer information control program (CICS). Each provides certain functions, although there is some overlap among the four. All are not used at the same time.

Telecommunications Access Method   The *telecommunications access method (TCAM)* provides the basic functions needed for controlling data communications circuits. It provides facilities for polling terminals, transmitting and receiving messages, detecting errors, automatically retransmitting erroneous messages, translating code, dialing and answering calls, logging transmission errors, allocating blocks of buffer storage, and performing online diagnostics to facilitate the testing of terminal equipment. It supports asynchronous terminals, synchronous communications, and audio response units. Residing in the host computer, TCAM's most significant features are those for network control and system recovery. An operator control facility also provides network supervision and modification.

TCAM handles the data communications in a network that uses a high degree of multiprogramming. Unlike the prior basic data communication software, TCAM has its own control program that commands and schedules traffic-handling operations. In some cases, it can handle an incoming message by itself without passing it to an application program—for example, routing a message to another terminal in a message switching system. TCAM also provides status reporting on terminals, lines, and queues. It has significant recovery and serviceability features to increase the security and availability of the data communications network. The checkpoint and restart facilities are very good. TCAM has prewritten routines for checkpointing, logging, date and time stamping, sequence numbering and checking, message interception and rerouting, and error message transmission, and it supports a separate master terminal for the data communications network operator.

Virtual Telecommunications Access Method   The *virtual telecommunications access method (VTAM)* is the data communications software package that complements IBM's advanced hardware and software. It resides in the host computer. VTAM manages a network structured on SNA principles. It directs the transmission of data between the application programs in the host computer and the components of the data communication network. It operates with front-end processors. The basic services performed by VTAM include establishing, controlling, and terminating access between the application programs and the terminals. It moves data between application programs and terminals and permits application programs to share communication circuits, communication controllers, and terminals. In addition, VTAM controls the configuration of the entire network, creates virtual connections, and permits the network to be monitored and altered.

When VTAM establishes sessions, one end of the session is understood to be the host, and the other, the terminal. VTAM makes the mainframe the primary end of the session and the remote terminal the secondary end. In technical terms, the host program is said to be the *primary logical unit (PLU),* and the terminal or microcomputer is considered to be the *secondary logical unit (SLU).* Only the PLU can start a session, end the session, and perform key aspects of error recovery. When personal computers are linked to SNA hosts, they are considered to be SLUs just like terminals.

VTAM can be the sole telecommunication access method in the host, or it can operate in conjunction with the NCP (described next), which allows some of the network control functions to be offloaded to the front-end processor.

Network Control Program   The *network control program (NCP)* is a telecommunication access method located in the front-end processors that control IBM's SDLC communications between host computers and remote terminals. (SDLC is the protocol developed for SNA by IBM.) It also works with host resident VTAM software to route information through networks. NCP routes data and controls data flow between the front-end processor and any other network resources. These other network resources can be the host mainframe computer or an intelligent control unit located either locally or at the remote end of the communication link. IBM's primary NCP is the advanced communication function/network control program (ACF/NCP). Network control programs reside in the front-end processor, primarily in IBM's 3704, 3705, 3725, and 3745. NCP is *not* a replacement for TCAM or VTAM; it provides an interface with TCAM and VTAM by taking over some of their functions and moving them to the front end.

NCP can handle polling, error detection, error recovery, and intermediate routing. It provides some flow control (such as various types of message pacing), prevents network congestion, provides internetwork communication, and insulates VTAM from being overburdened by having to speak to an excessive number of other protocols. NCP version 5 supports dial-up lines and improves support for multipoint lines. It also supports SDLC's PU 2.1 functionality, enabling the front-end processor to initiate sessions with remote terminals. With NCP version 5, one front-end processor can communicate with other front-end processors via an IBM Token Ring network. It includes load balancing across network bridges and backbone rings, port swapping, backup capabilities, and remote controller support. NCP is IBM's effort to move the telecommunication access method software out from the host mainframe to the front-end processor. NCP is the only one of these five telecommunication access programs that actually resides in a front-end processor; all the others reside in the host mainframe.

Customer Information Control System   Some functions overlap between the telecommunication access programs such as TCAM and *customer information control system (CICS)* (a teleprocessing monitor), both of which reside in the host computer. IBM's front end has its own program called the NCP (this also is a telecommunication access program). TCAM and NCP overlap; therefore, functions such as polling/selecting can be performed from either the host computer or the front-end processor.

Teleprocessing monitors such as CICS are software programs that directly relieve the host computer's operating system of many tasks involved in handling message traffic between the host and the front end or the host and other internal CPU software packages (such as the host database management system). Generally speaking, teleprocessing monitors perform such functions as message handling, access methods, task scheduling, and system recovery. The teleprocessing monitor acts as the interface with the telecommunication access programs on one side and with all of the host computer's software on the other side. Teleprocessing monitors must be the interface with various operating systems, computer architectures, database management systems, security software packages, and application programs.

CICS is the world's most widely used mainframe teleprocessing monitor. It may not be perfect, but even IBM's direct competitors implicitly acknowledge that CICS has few alternatives. Whatever comes along to supplant it will be an evolving CICS rather than a totally new replacement. CICS is a table-driven teleprocessing program that offers 64 layers or systems it can service. Like any other teleprocessing monitor, CICS runs in conjunction with the host computer's operating system. CICS takes over the communication-related tasks that previously were handled by the operating system, thus allowing the operating system to concentrate on other control tasks or application programs.

CICS also offers an additional level of security. It can accommodate a unique password and identification for each terminal operator and allow access only to the specific functions assigned to that operator password and/or terminal identifier. It can assign highly sensitive functions to a specific terminal or a group of terminals. Some security features might be security sign-on fields, darkened password fields, and a complete log of terminal sign-ons, including any security violations.

Other tasks conducted by teleprocessing monitors such as CICS are logging of all messages (both input and output), accounting procedures for cost control, restart and recovery procedures in case of failure, utility features that perform special maintenance tasks, and queue management of both inbound and outbound message queues, as well as the ability to place priorities on messages and/or queues. A teleprocessing monitor should be able to interact with multiple front-end processors, terminals, microcomputers, and various data communications transmission speeds. The monitor provides input–output job task queue management, various methods of instituting priorities for certain transactions or jobs, file and database management, application program management, task and resource control, restart and recovery procedures in case of failure, and special utilities that carry out tasks often enough to warrant establishing them as a utility feature (OSI model layer 6). It keeps track of accounting features and operating statistics and isolates various programs or parts of the system from other programs or parts of the system. In other words, a teleprocessing monitor can be considered a mini operating system with data communications interfaces.

APPN and the "New" SNA

A newer part of IBM's systems network architecture is *advanced peer-to-peer networking (APPN)*. This approach supports peer-to-peer communication between two or more network devices in which either side can initiate sessions. No *primary–secondary* relationship exists, and either side is able to poll or answer to polls. Before the introduction of peer-to-peer communications, a primary–secondary relationship always existed where only one of the two nodes could initiate or start a communication session.

IBM has a new form of SNA that provides two important advantages over the traditional SNA. First, the "new" SNA supports a variety of industry standard network and data link protocols,. This will solve many of the problems that now exist in integrating SNA networks with other networks. Second, the host computer does not have to mediate the connection between the two end user terminals or computers. This allows microcomputers to speak as equals to the host mainframe computer and eliminates the bonds of IBM microcomputer-to-mainframe emulation that confine the microcomputer to terminal status in its communications with host mainframes.

TOKEN RING

Token Ring was originally developed by IBM and has since been standardized by IEEE as IEEE 802.5. As with Ethernet, the 802.5 version is slightly different than the original version developed by IBM. Use of token ring is declining as Ethernet becomes more popular.

Topology

As the name suggests, Token Ring uses a *ring topology*. A ring topology connects all computers on the LAN in one closed-loop circuit with each computer linked to the next. Messages pass around the ring, in one direction only, to each computer in turn. Each computer receives messages intended for all computers, but each processes only those messages addressed to itself; it transmits other messages to the next computer in the ring.

The *physical topology* of a token ring LAN is a star—because all cables flow into the central hub—but it is truly a ring, with messages passing from one computer to the next. Most Token Ring LANs span sufficient distance to require several hubs. In this case, the hubs are connected via two cables like any other connection in the network.

Media Access Control

All computers in a Token Ring LAN share the same common circuit, so it is essential that access to the media be controlled by the data-link layer. Token Ring uses a controlled-access technique called token passing.

The *token-passing* access method can be compared to a relay race in which the track belongs to you as long as you have the baton. When your run is finished, you hand the baton to the next runner. In a token-passing network, the baton is the *token,* a short electronic message that is generated when the network is started.

The token moves between the computers on the network in a predetermined sequence (much like hub polling). A computer with a message to transmit waits until it receives what is called a *free token*—that is, one available for use. The computer then changes the free token into a *busy token* and attaches its message to it, then retransmits it on the circuit to the next computer in the sequence. Should that computer want to transmit a message, it must wait, because the token is busy. It simply forwards the message with the busy token to the next computer in sequence. When the token and message arrive at the destination computer, that computer copies the data in the message, sets the ACK bit (or NAK if there was an error in transmission), and the message continues around the ring, making a complete round trip back to the transmitting computer. The transmitting computer then removes the message and inserts a new free token on the ring. Most token-passing methods restrict the maximum number of messages that a computer can transmit before it must issue a free token and permit other computers to send messages. This ensures that no one computer monopolizes the circuit.

One problem with token-passing protocols is dealing with "lost" tokens. Suppose the computer that has the token crashes before it can retransmit it, or suppose a computer that has just transmitted a message (and marked the token as busy) crashes before it can receive an ACK and create a free token. In this case, the token is "lost" because no other computer on the network can use the token. Unless some action is taken, the entire network will cease to function.

The solution is to designate one computer in the network to be the *token monitor*. If no token circulates through the network for a certain length of time or if a busy token circulates too often, the token monitor will create a new free token (and destroy the busy token if necessary). Unfortunately, the problem is not that simple, because the computer that crashed (causing the lost token) could be the token monitor itself. Therefore, there is a backup token monitor to ensure the first token monitor is operating; it steps in if the primary token monitor malfunctions.

Types of Token Ring

There are two common types of Token Ring. The original token ring was Token Ring 4, operating at 4 Mbps over UTP wire. The newer token ring is Token Ring 16, which operates at 16 Mbps over higher-quality twisted-pair cable.

APPENDIX **G**

TCP/IP GAME

Introduction

The purpose of this game is to help you better understand how messages are transmitted in TCP/IP-based computer networks. Players are organized into five-person teams that represent different computers in the network. Each person in the team assumes the role of one layer of software or hardware on that computer (e.g., data link layer) and works with the others to send messages through the network.

General Rules

1. This is a team game. The class will be broken into a set of five-member teams, with each team being one computer in the communications network. Each person in the team will role-play one layer in the computer, either the application layer, the transport layer, the network layer, the data link layer, or the physical layer.

2. Messages will be created by the application layer and passed to the transport layer. The transport layer will break the message into several smaller messages if necessary and pass them to the network layer. The network layer will address and route the message and pass the message to the data link layer. The data link layer will format the message and perform error control (which will involve sending ACKs and NAKs) and pass the message to the physical layer for transmission. The physical layer will transmit the message to the physical layer of the destination computer. Messages are sent using the forms in Figure A-6. Be sure to make lots of copies the forms before the game starts.

3. Each layer will have a set of instructions to follow to ensure the messages are sent and received properly. Follow them carefully. These instructions explain what you are to write on the message forms. Never write anything on the message form in an area used by another layer.

4. At some point, someone will make a mistake. If you receive a message that contains an error, hand it back to the person who gave it to you and explain the error to that person.

5. And remember, the game is meant to be fun, too!

SMTP	From	To	Message	┊	
				┊	

TCP	Sequence Number	User Data	
	of		

IP	Final Destination	Next Node	User Data	

Ethernet	Source	Destination	Control	Message #	Error	User Data	

FIGURE A-6   Forms for the TCP/IP game.

Application Layer

Activities

1. Send messages to other computers

2. Respond to messages from other computers

Tools Needed
- Several blank SMTP forms
- List of messages
- Network map (Figure A-7 shows an example; the instructor will draw one for your class.)
- A blank piece of paper

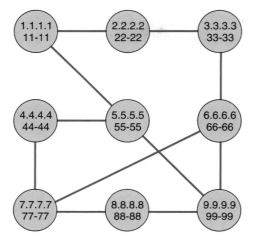

FIGURE A-7   Sample network map.

Sending Outgoing Messages   To send a message, you must

1. Find a blank SMTP packet.

2. Write the *IP address* of your computer in the **From** box.

3. Use the network map to select a computer as the destination for this message. Write the *IP address* of the destination computer in the **To** box. Don't send all your messages to one computer; we want to even out the messages. Try to send a few messages to computers close to you and a few to computers far away.

4. Write the message you wish to send in the **Message** box. To make the message simple to understand, please use a hyphen (-) to indicate spaces between words. Select a message from the list of messages (see below). Try to have at least one hyphen in the message (this is to help the data link layer do error control) or add one at the end or at the start if you must.

5. Write the message and the name of the computer to which you send the message on the blank piece of paper. This will help you understand the responses you get to your messages.

6. Pass the message to the transport layer.

Responding to Incoming Messages   Eventually, you will receive an incoming message from the transport layer that was sent to you by some other computer asking you a question. To respond to the message, you will send a message that answers the question. Follow the same steps above to send a message, but in step 4, write your answer in the **Message** box. For example, if the message you received asked what your favorite color was, you might write *red* or *blue* in the **Message** box.

List of Messages   Here are a list of messages you can send. Remember to use a hyphen instead of a space to separate the words. Rather than writing the entire message, you can omit the words *What is your.*

- What is your favorite color?
- What is your birthday?
- What is your phone number?
- What are your favorite holidays?
- What is your favorite car?

Transport Layer

Activities

1. Accept outgoing SMTP messages from the application layer, packetize them, and pass them to the network layer.

2. Accept incoming messages from the network layer and, if they are made up of several packets, assemble the entire SMTP message before passing it to the application layer.

Tools Needed

- TCP forms
- Tape

Accepting Outgoing Messages from the Application Layer
Every few minutes, the application layer will hand you an outgoing message to transmit. To transmit them, you must

1. Break the SMTP message into smaller packets. Tear the SMTP packet into two parts at the dotted line. If there is writing on both parts, then you must send each part as a separate message. If the second half of the SMTP packet has no writing on it, throw it away and ignore it.
2. Find one or two blank TCP packets.
3. Fill in the **Sequence Number** box. If there is only one part of the SMTP packet, write "1 of 1" in the **Sequence Number** box. If there are two parts of the SMTP packet, write "1 of 2" on the first TCP packet and "2 of 2" on the second TCP packet.
4. Tape the SMTP packet(s) to the TCP packet(s) over the **User Data** space. (The packet(s) will be too big to fit, but don't worry about it.)
5. Pass the TCP + SMTP packet(s) to the network layer.

Accepting Incoming Messages from the Network Layer
Every few minutes, the network layer will hand you an incoming message. To process it, you must

- **If the message is complete (that is, if the** Sequence Number **box says "1 of 1"):**

1. Take the TCP packet off of the SMTP packet and throw away the TCP packet.
2. Pass the SMTP packet to the application layer.

- **If the message is not complete (that is, if the** Sequence Number **box says "1 of 2"):**

1. Wait for the second part of the message to arrive.
2. Take the TCP packets off of both SMTP packets and throw away the TCP packets.
3. Tape the two parts of the SMTP packet back together.
4. Pass the SMTP packet to the application layer.

Network Layer

Activities

1. Accept messages from the transport layer, route them, and pass them to the data link layer.
2. Accept messages from the data link layer and, if they are addressed to you, pass them to the transport layer; if they are not addressed to you, route them and pass them back to the data link layer

Tools Needed

- IP forms
- Tape
- Network map

Accepting Outgoing Messages from the Transport Layer   Every few minutes, the transport layer will hand you an outgoing message to transmit. To transmit them, you must

1. Find a blank IP packet.

2. Address the message by writing the IP address in the **To** box of the SMTP packet into the **Final Destination** box of the IP packet.

3. Route the message by finding the next computer in the network map to which the message should be sent and writing its Ethernet address in the **Next Node** box. If your computer is directly connected to the final destination computer, the next node is the same as the final destination. If your computer is not directly connected to the destination, you must select the best route that the message should follow and specify one of the computers to which you are connected.

4. Tape the TCP + SMTP packet to the IP packet over the **User Data** space. (It will be too big to fit, but don't worry about it.)

5. Pass the IP + TCP + SMTP packet to the data link layer.

Accepting Incoming Messages from the Data Link Layer   Every few minutes, the data link layer will hand you a message to process. You must

- **If the message is addressed to you (that is, if the** Final Destination **box in the IP packet lists your IP address):**

1. Remove the IP packet from the SMTP + TCP packet and throw the IP packet away.

2. Pass the SMTP + TCP packet to the transport layer.

- **If the message is not addressed to you (that is, if the** Final Destination **box in the IP packet lists someone else's IP address):**

1. Scratch out or erase the address in the **Next Node** box.

2. Route the message by finding the next computer in the network map to which the message should be sent in and writing its data link layer address in the **Next Node** box. If your computer is directly connected to the destination computer, the next node is the same as the destination. If your computer is not directly connected to the destination, you must select the best route that the message should follow and specify one of the computers to which you are connected.

3. Pass the message to the data link layer.

Data Link Layer

Activities

1. Accept outgoing messages from the network layer, format them, add error-control information, and pass them to the physical layer.

2. Accept incoming messages from the physical layer. If they are data messages and contain no errors, send an ACK and pass them to the network layer. If they are data messages with an error, send an NAK. If they are an ACK, destroy the message they acknowledge. If they are an NAK, retransmit the original message.

Tools Needed

- Ethernet forms
- Tape
- Network map
- Some blank pieces of paper. You will discover that you are receiving and storing many different types of messages. To help you organize those messages, we suggest that before you begin, you use three blank pieces of paper to create three message storage piles:
- Label one pile **Messages from the Network Layer**.
- Label the second pile **Messages from the Physical Layer**.
- Label the third pile **Messages Transmitted**.

Accepting Outgoing Messages from the Network Layer   Every few minutes, the network layer will hand you a message to transmit. If you receive more messages from the network layer than you can process right away, put them in the **Messages from the Network Layer** pile until you can process them. For each message, you must

1. Find a blank Ethernet packet.
2. Format the message for the physical layer by writing your Ethernet address in the **Source** box. Copy the Ethernet address in the **Next Node** box in the IP packet into the **Destination** box. Write an asterisk (*) in the **Control** box.
3. Number the message. Write a two-digit number in the **Message Number** box. This should be *01* for the first message you send, *02* for the second, and so on. Use the blank piece of paper to help you remember what numbers you have used.
4. Add error-control information. Most error control is very sophisticated, but in this game, we'll use something very simple. Count the number of hyphens in the user data (the SMTP packet, the TCP packet and the IP packet [but not the Ethernet packet]) and write this number in the **Error** box on the Ethernet packet.
5. Tape the SMTP + TCP + IP packet to the Ethernet packet over the **User Data** space. (It will be too big to fit, but don't worry about it.)

6. Pass the message to the physical layer. In a few moments, the physical layer will return the packet to you. *Save it* in the **Messages Transmitted** pile!

Accepting Incoming Messages from the Physical Layer Every few minutes, the physical layer will hand you a message to process. If you receive more messages than you can process right away, put them in the **Messages from the Physical Layer** pile. These messages will either be data messages, ACKs, or NAKs. Each is processed differently.

- **If the** Control **box contains an asterisk (*), this is a data message. Do the following:**

1. Perform error checking. Count the number of hyphens in the user data (the SMTP packet, the TCP packet, and the IP packet [but not the Ethernet packet]). If this number is the same as the number in the **Error** box, no errors have occurred. If they are different, an error has occurred.

2. If no errors have occurred, you must send an ACK to the sender and send the incoming message to the next layer:

    a. Find a blank Ethernet packet.

    b. Write your Ethernet address in the **Source** box. Write the Ethernet address contained in the **Source** box of the incoming message in the **Destination** box of your message. (This ACK message is going to the sender of the original message.) Write *ACK* in the **Control** box. Write the two-digit number contained in the **Message Number** box of the incoming message in the **Message Number** box.

    c. Pass the outgoing ACK message to the physical layer.

    d. Remove the Ethernet packet from the incoming message and throw the Ethernet packet away.

    e. Pass the incoming SMTP + TCP +IP packet to the network layer.

3. If an error has occurred, you must send a NAK to the sender and discard the incoming message:

    a. Find a blank Ethernet packet.

    b. Write your Ethernet address in the **Source** box. Write the Ethernet address contained in the **Source** box of the incoming message in the **Destination** box of your message. (This NAK message is going to the sender of the original message.) Write *NAK* in the **Control** box. Write the two-digit number contained in the **Message Number** box of the incoming message in the **Message Number** box.

    c. Pass the outgoing NAK message to the physical layer.

    d. Throw away the incoming message containing the error.

- **If the** Control **box contains an ACK, this is an ACK message. Do the following:**

1. Find the original message you sent, in the **Messages Transmitted** pile, that has the same message number as the ACK.

2. Destroy the original message and the ACK.

- **If the** Control **box contains an NAK, this is an NAK message. Do the following.**

1. Find the original message you sent, in the **Messages Transmitted** pile, that has the same message number as the NAK.

2. Give the original message to the physical layer to transmit again. In a few moments, the physical layer will return the packet to you. *Save it* in the **Messages Transmitted** pile.

3. Destroy the NAK.

Physical Layer

Activities

1. Accept messages from the data link layer and pass them to the physical layer of the computer to which they are to go, possibly introducing a transmission error.

2. Accept messages from the physical layer of other computers and pass them to the data link layer.

Tools Needed

- Ethernet forms
- IP forms
- TCP forms
- SMTP forms
- Network map
- Transmission forms
- Two coins

Accepting Messages from the Data Link Layer   Every few minutes, the data link layer will hand you a message to transmit. These messages will either be data messages or control messages (ACKs or NAKs). Each is processed differently.

- **If the** Control **box contains an asterisk (*), this is a data message. Do the following:**

1. Determine if there will be an error in transmission by tossing two coins; if they are both heads, you will introduce an error.

2. Copy the entire contents of the message packet onto new forms; that is, copy the SMTP packet to a new SMTP packet, the TCP packet to a new TCP packet, the IP packet to a new IP packet, and the Ethernet packet to a new Ethernet packet. If you are to introduce an error, omit all the data in the SMTP **Message** box. Be sure to tape the packets together in the right order.

3. Pass the copied SMTP + TCP + IP + Ethernet packet to the physical layer of the computer whose address is listed in the **Destination** box.

4. Pass the original SMTP + TCP + IP + Ethernet packet back to the data link layer and make sure that that person understands that you are giving back the message that he/she just gave you to transmit.

- **If the** Control **box contains an ACK or an NAK, this is a control message. Do the following:**

1. Simply pass the Ethernet packet to the physical layer of the computer whose address is listed in the **Destination** box. Things are complicated enough without ACKs and NAKs getting destroyed.

Accepting Messages from the Physical Layer of Another Computer
Every few minutes, the physical layer of another computer will hand you a message. Simply hand the message to the data link layer.

Note to Instructors

Background   This games helps students *really* understand what the various layers actually do and how they must work together to send a message. Reading about it is one thing; having to perform a simple version of the function is something else altogether. Experiential learning can be an extremely powerful tool. I have noticed a distinct improvement in students' understanding of this material since I have begun using the game.

The game is an extremely simplified version of what happens in a real TCP/IP network. Nonetheless, it can be complicated. Students have to work together and sometimes make mistakes. Ideally, students will recognize mistakes themselves and will help one another learn. Participation is key to the learning objectives. It's also key to making a somewhat dry conceptual set of issues, more real—and more fun.

When I teach the course, I usually use this game after I complete Chapter 5, **The Network and Transport Layers.** At this point students will have learned everything they need to know to run the game, and it will reinforce the material

Preparing to Teach the Game

This game contains all the materials you will need to run the game, except a set of coins and paper (which you can rely on students to have), enough tape for each group (bring several rolls), and a network map (which you draw on the board just before the game starts). You will also have to make copies of the four types of packets. It takes an average of three SMTP, TCP, and IP forms and four Ethernet forms for each message, so you will need a lot of them. I usually plan on the class sending about 10–15 messages per team; for a 40 person class, this means you will need 250–350 SMTP, TCP, and IP forms and 350–500 Ethernet forms.

I have found from experience that it takes the students a little while to catch onto the game. Be sure to tell the students to read the game before they come to class.

Teaching the Game

It usually takes 20 minutes before the game gets going. The first step is to organize the class into five-person teams. Each team represents one computer in the network. If there are more than five people in a team, have two people play the data link layer; if there are less than five, then combine the application, transport and/or network layers.

Draw the network map on the board. The map will have a circle to represent each team (i.e., computer). Try to draw the circles to represent the actual physical placement of the teams within the classroom. Inside each circle, write

- The IP address (e.g., 1.1.1.1). Arbitrarily choose a number for each team but keep it short and easy to remember.
- The Ethernet address (e.g., 11-11). Arbitrarily choose a number for each team but keep it short and easy to remember. It helps if it matches the IP address in some way. Be sure to have at least one hyphen in the address to help reinforce the error-control concepts.

Next, connect the computers (i.e., teams) by drawing lines (i.e., circuits) between the circles. Don't draw in all possible circuits, because you want some teams to have to route messages through other teams to reach their final destination. Likewise, don't put too few circuits, or else all messages will take a long time to send.

Do a simple example. Walk through the sending of one message on the board and have the students follow by replicating each step you do for one of their own messages. Once the message has reached the physical layer on the next computer, I turn the students loose and let them play. I usually walk around the classroom answering questions and listening in on discussions as the game progresses.

Because each layer performs a unique function, it is useful to have each student play each layer if time permits. I try to have students rotate layers after 15 minutes. I keep the game going so that the students playing one layer need to explain to the person taking over their layer what is going on and how to play. The easiest way to rotate is downward; that is, the person playing the application layer moves to the transport layer, and so on.

Discussion Questions   After each person has had the opportunity to play several layers, it is useful to ask what the students have learned. This gives you the opportunity to reinforce the concepts the game was designed to teach. Some possible discussion questions are

1. Why are standards important?
2. How could you improve network performance by changing the topology?
3. What layer is the busiest? How could you improve network performance by changing the protocol at this layer?

GLOSSARY

A

Abilene network: The Abilene network is the part of Internet 2 that is run by Indiana University.

access layer: The access layer is the part of a network that connects clients or servers to the rest of the network. It is often a LAN.

access point (AP): The part of the wireless LAN that connects the LAN to other networks.

ACK: *See* **acknowledgment (ACK)**.

acknowledgment (ACK): A character indicating a positive acknowledgment that a message has been received correctly.

ACM: Association for Computing Machinery. The ACM is an association of computer professionals.

acronym: A word formed from the initial letters or groups of letters of words in a phrase. An example is the word *laser,* which means *l*ight *a*mplification by *s*timulated *e*mission of *r*adiation.

address: A coded representation of the destination of data or of its originating source. For example, multiple computers on one communication circuit must each have a unique data link layer address.

address resolution: The process of determining the lower-layer address from a higher-layer address. For example, IP address resolution means determining the IP address from the application-layer address, whereas data link layer address resolution means determining the data link layer address from an IP address.

Address Resolution Protocol (ARP): The network-layer protocol standard for data link layer address resolution requests.

ADSL: *See* **asymmetric DSL (ADSL)**.

Advanced Encryption Standard (AES): A new single-key encryption standard authorized by NIST that replaces DES. It uses the Rijndael (pronounced "rain doll") algorithm and has key sizes of 128, 192 and 256 bits. NIST estimates that using the most advanced computers and techniques available today, it will require about 150 trillion years to crack AES by brute force.

Advanced Research and Development Network Operations Center (ARDNOC): The agency funded by the Canadian government to develop new Internet 2 technologies and protocols.

AES: *See* **Advanced Encryption Standard (AES)**.

American National Standards Institute (ANSI): The principal standards-setting body in the United States. ANSI is a nonprofit, nongovernmental organization supported by more than 1,000 trade organizations, professional societies, and companies. It belongs to the ITU-T CCITT and the ISO.

American Standard Code for Information Interchange: *See* **ASCII**.

Amplifier: A device used to boost the strength of a signal. Amplifiers are spaced at intervals throughout the length of a communication circuit to increase the distance a signal can travel. *See also* **repeater**.

Amplitude Modulation: *See* **modulation, amplitude**.

Analog: Pertaining to representation by means of continuously variable quantity, such as varying frequencies. Physical quantities such as temperature are continuous variable and therefore are "analog."

analog signal: A signal in the form of a continuously varying quantity such as amplitude, which reflects variations in the loudness of the human voice.

analog transmission: Transmission of a continuously variable signal as opposed to a discrete on/off signal. The traditional way of transmitting a telephone or voice signal is analog.

ANI: *See* **automatic number identification (ANI)**.

anonymous FTP: *See* **File Transfer Protocol (FTP)**.

ANSI: *See* **American National Standards Institute (ANSI).**

AP: *See* **access point (AP).**

API: Application Program Interface. API is the way IBM links incompatible equipment for microcomputer-to-mainframe links. API allows applications on microcomputers and mainframes to speak directly to each other at the application software level, even though the equipment is from different vendors.

Apple Talk: A set of communication protocols that defines networking for Apple computers. Rarely used today.

application service provider (ASP): An application service develops an application system (e.g., an airline reservation system, a payroll system) and companies purchase the service, without ever installing the software on their own computers. They simply use the service, the same way you might use a Web hosting service to publish your own Web pages rather than attempting to purchase and operate your own Web server.

ARCnet: Attached Resource Computing network. A proprietary token-bus LAN developed by the Datapoint Corporation.

ARDNOC: *See* **Advanced Research and Development Network Operations Center (ARDNOC).**

ARPANET: One of the early packet-switching networks. ARPANET was developed by the U.S. Department of Defense Advanced Research Projects Agency. It was the predecessor of the Internet.

ARP: *See* **Address Resolution Protocol (ARP).**

ARQ: Automatic Repeat reQuest. A system employing an error-detecting code so conceived that any error initiates a repetition of the transmission of the incorrectly received message.

ASCII: American Standard Code for Information Interchange. Pronounced "ask-e." An eight-level code for data transfer adopted by the ANSI to achieve compatibility among data devices.

asymmetric DSL (ADSL): A data link layer technology that provides high-speed ("broadband") communication over traditional telephone lines. A DSL modem is used to provide three channels: a traditional voice channel, an upstream channel for communicating from the client to the ISP (often at speeds of 64 to 640 Kbps), and a downstream channel for communicating from the ISP to the client (often at speeds of 640 Kbps to 6 Mbps).

asynchronous transfer mode (ATM): A communication switch that handles interface speeds ranging from 25 million to 622 million bps. It multiplexes data streams onto the same BN by using cell relay techniques. ATM switches can handle multimedia traffic, such as data, graphics, voice, and video.

asynchronous transmission: Transmission in which each information character is individually synchronized, usually by start and stop bits. The gap between each character is not a fixed length. *Compare with* **synchronous transmission**.

ATM: *See* **asynchronous transfer mode (ATM)**. In banking, an **automated teller machine**.

attenuation: As a signal travels through a circuit, it gradually attenuates, or loses power. Expressed in decibels, attenuation is the difference between the transmitted and received power caused by loss of signal strength through the equipment, communication circuits, or other devices.

authentication: A security method of guaranteeing that a message is genuine, that it has arrived unaltered, and that it comes from the source indicated.

automatic number identification (ANI): The process whereby a long-distance common carrier provides its customers with a visual display of an incoming caller's telephone number.

Automatic Repeat reQuest: *See* **ARQ.**

B

backbone network (BN): A large network to which many networks within an organization are connected. It usually is a network that interconnects all networks on a single site, but it can be larger if it connects all the organization's terminals, microcomputers, mainframes, LANs, and other communication equipment.

BALUN: balanced/unbalanced. An impedance-matching device to connect balanced twisted-pair cabling with unbalanced coaxial cable.

Bandwidth: The difference between the highest and lowest frequencies in a band. For example, a voice-grade circuit has a 4,000-Hz bandwidth. In common usage, *bandwidth* refers to circuit capacity; when people say they need more bandwidth, they need a higher transmission speed.

basic rate interface (BRI): In ISDN, two 64,000-bps B circuits for data transmission and one 16,000-bps D circuit for signaling (2 B+D). Also called basic rate access. *See also* **primary rate interface (PRI)**.

baud: Unit of signaling speed. Now obsolete and replaced by the term *symbol rate.* The speed in baud is the number of signal elements per second. If each signal represents only 1 bit, *baud* is the same as *bits per second (bps).* When each signal contains more than 1 bit, *baud* does not equal *bps.*

BCC: *See* **block check character (BCC).**

BER: bit-error rate. The number of bits received in error divided by the total number of bits received. An indicator of circuit quality.

BERT: bit-error rate testing. Testing a data line with a pattern of bits that are compared before and after the transmission to detect errors.

BGP: *See* **Border Gateway Protocol (BGP).**

Binary: A number system using only the two symbols 0 and 1 that is especially well adapted to computer usage because 0 and 1 can be represented as "on" and "off," respectively or as negative charges and positive charges, respectively. The binary digits appear in strings of 0's and 1's.

bipolar transmission: A method of digital transmission in which binary 0 is sent as a negative pulse and binary 1 is sent as a positive pulse.

Bit: 1. An abbreviation of the term *binary digit.* 2. A single pulse in a group of pulses. 3. A unit of information capacity.

bit-error rate (BER): *See* **BER.**

bit-error rate testing (BERT): *See* **BERT.**

bit rate: The rate at which bits are transmitted over a communication path, normally expressed in bits per second (bps). The bit rate should not be confused with the data signaling rate (*baud*), which measures the rate of signal changes being transmitted. *See also* **bps.**

bit stream: A continuous series of bits being transmitted on a transmission line.

bits per second (bps): *See* **bps.**

BKER: Block-error rate. The number of blocks received in error divided by the total number of blocks received.

BKERT: Block-error rate testing. Testing a data link with groups of information arranged into transmission blocks for error checking.

Block: Sets of contiguous bits or bytes that make up a message, frame, or packet.

block check character (BCC): The character(s) at the end of a binary synchronous communications (BSC) message used to check for errors.

block-error rate (BKER): *See* **BKER.**

block-error rate testing (BKERT): *See* **BKERT.**

Bluetooth: A standard for short-distance wireless communication.

BN: *See* **backbone network (BN).**

BOC: *See* **RBOC.**

BONDING: BONDING (Bandwidth on Demand Interoperatibility Networking Group) is an inverse multiplexing proposal for combining several 56-Kbps or 64-Kbps circuits into one higher-speed circuit.

Border Gateway Protocol (BGP): A network-layer standard protocol used to exchange route information between routers using dynamic decentralized routing. Used only between different TCP/IP autonomous systems (i.e., major sections of the Internet).

bps: Bits per second. The basic unit of data communication rate measurement. Usually refers to rate of information bits transmitted. *Contrast with* **baud** and **bit rate.**

BRI: *See* **basic rate interface (BRI).**

bridge: A device that connects two similar networks using the same data link and network protocols. *Compare with* **gateway, router,** and **brouter.**

broadband circuit: An analog communication circuit.

broadband communications: Originally, the term referred to analog communications, but it has become corrupted in common usage so that it now usually means high-speed communications networks, typically Internet access technologies with access speeds of 1 Mbps or higher.

broadband Ethernet: The 10Broad36 version of Ethernet IEEE 802.3, meaning that it transmits at 10 million bps in broadband with a maximum distance of 3,600 meters.

broadcast routing: *See* **decentralized routing.**

brouter: A piece of hardware that combines the functions of a bridge and a router. *See also* **bridge** and **router.**

brute-force attack: A way of breaking an encrypted message by trying all possible values of the key.

buffer: A device used for the temporary storage of data, primarily to compensate for differences in data flow rates (for example, between a terminal and its transmission circuit) but also as a security measure to allow retransmission of data if an error is detected during transmission.

burst error: A series of consecutive errors in data transmission. Refers to the phenomenon on communication circuits in which errors are highly prone to occurring in groups or clusters.

bus: A transmission path or circuit. Typically an electrical connection with one or more conductors in which all attached devices receive all transmissions at the same time.

byte: A small group of data bits that is handled as a unit. In most cases, it is an 8-bit byte and it is known as a *character.*

C

call-back modem: When a user calls a host computer, the modem disconnects the call after receiving the password and calls back to the caller's predefined telephone number to establish a connection.

CA*net 3: CA*net 3 is the Canadian network that forms part of Internet 2.

carrier: An analog signal at some fixed amplitude and frequency that then is combined with an information-bearing signal to produce an intelligent output signal suitable for transmission of meaningful information. *Also called carrier wave* or **carrier frequency**.

carrier frequency: The basic frequency or pulse repetition rate of a signal bearing no intelligence until it is modulated by another signal that does impart intelligence.

Carrier Sense Multiple Access: *See* **CSMA/CA** and **CSMA/CD**.

CCITT: *See* **Consultative Committee on International Telegraph and Telephone (CCITT)**. Now obsolete and renamed **International Telecommunications Union—Telecommunications (ITU-T)**.

CD: 1. Collision detection in the CSMA (Carrier Sense Multiple Access) protocol for LANs. 2. Carrier detect occurs when a modem detects a carrier signal to be received.

central office: The switching and control facility set up by the local telephone company (common carrier) where the subscriber's local loop terminates. Central offices handle calls within a specified geographic area, which is identified by the first three digits of the telephone number. *Also called* an **end office** or **exchange office**.

Central processing unit (CPU): *See* **CPU**.

CENTREX: A widespread telephone company switching service that uses dedicated central office switching equipment. CENTREX CPE is where the user site also has customer premises equipment (CPE).

CERT: *See* **Computer Emergency Response Team (CERT)**.

certificate authority (CA): A CA is a trusted organization that can vouch for the authenticity of the person or organization using authentication (e.g., VeriSign). A person wanting to use a CA registers with the CA an must provide some proof of identify. CA issues a digital certificate that is the requestor's public key encrypted using the CA's private key as proof of identify that can be attached to the user's e-mail or Web transactions.

channel: 1. A path for transmission of electromagnetic signals. *Synonym for* **line** or **link**. *Compare with* **circuit**. 2. A data communications path. Circuits may be divided into subcircuits.

character: A member of a set of elements used for the organization, control, or representation of data. Characters may be letters, digits, punctuation marks, or other symbols. *Also called* a **byte**.

cheapnet: *See* **thin Ethernet**.

checking, echo: A method of checking the accuracy of transmitted data in which the received data are returned to the sending end for comparison with the original data.

checking, parity: *See* **parity check**.

checking, polynomial: *See* **polynomial checking**.

circuit: The path over which the voice, data, or image transmission travels. Circuits can be twisted-wire pairs, coaxial cables, fiber-optic cables, microwave transmissions, and so forth. *Compare with* **channel**, **line**, and **link**.

circuit switching: A method of communications whereby an electrical connection between calling and called stations is established on demand for exclusive use of the circuit until the connection is terminated.

cladding: A layer of material (usually glass) that surrounds the glass core of an optical fiber. Prevents loss of signal by reflecting light back into the core.

client: The input–output hardware device at the user's end of a communication circuit. There are three major categories of clients: microcomputers, terminals, and special-purpose terminals.

cluster controller: A device that controls the input–output operations of the cluster of devices (microcomputers, terminals, printers, and so forth) attached to it. Also called a *terminal controller.* For example, the 3274 Control Unit is a cluster controller that directs all communications between the host computer and remote devices attached to it.

CMIP: *See* **Common Management Interface Protocol (CMIP)**.

coaxial cable: An insulated wire that runs through the middle of a cable. A second braided wire surrounds the insulation of the inner wire like a sheath. Used on LANs for transmitting messages between devices.

code: A transformation or representation of information in a different form according to some set of preestablished conventions. *See also* **ASCII** and **EBCDIC**.

codec: A codec translates analog voice data into digital data for transmission over computer networks. Two codecs are needed—one at the sender's end and one at the receiver's end.

code conversion: A hardware box or software that converts from one code to another, such as from ASCII to EBCDIC.

collapsed backbone network: In a collapsed BN, the set of routers in a typical BN is replaced by one switch and a set of circuits to each LAN. The collapsed backbone has more cable but fewer devices. There is no backbone cable. The "backbone" exists only in the switch.

collision: When two computers or devices transmit at the same time on a shared multipoint circuit, their signals collide and destroy each other.

common carrier: An organization in the business of providing regulated telephone, telegraph, telex, and data communications services, such as AT&T, MCI, Bell-South, and NYNEX. This term is applied most often to U.S. and Canadian commercial organizations, but sometimes it is used to refer to telecommunication entities, such as government-operated suppliers of communication services in other countries. *See also* **PTT**.

Common Management Interface Protocol (CMIP): CMIP is a network management system that monitors and tracks network usage and other parameters for user workstations and other nodes. It is similar to SNMP, but it is more complete and is better in many ways.

communication services: A group of transmission facilities that is available for lease or purchase.

comparison risk ranking: The process by which the members of a Delphi team reach a consensus on which network threats have the highest risk. It produces a ranked list from high risk to low risk.

component: One of the specific pieces of a network, system, or application. When these components are assembled, they become the network, system, or application. Components are the individual parts of the network that we want to safeguard or restrict by using controls.

compression: *See* **data compression**.

Computer Emergency Response Team (CERT): The job of CERT, located at Carnegie Mellon University, is to respond to computer security problems on the Internet, raise awareness of computer security issues, and prevent security breaches. It was established by the U.S. Department of Defense in 1988 after a virus shut down almost 10 percent of the computers on the Internet. Many organizations are starting their own computer emergency response teams, so the term is beginning to refer to any response team, not just the one at Carnegie Mellon University.

concentrator: A device that multiplexes several low-speed communication circuits onto a single high-speed trunk. A remote data concentrator (RDC) is similar in function to a multiplexer but differs because the host computer software usually must be rewritten to accommodate the RDC. RDCs differ from statistical multiplexes because the total capacity of the high-speed outgoing circuit, in characters per second, is equal to the total capacity of the incoming low-speed circuits. On the other hand, output capacity of a statistical multiplexer (stat mux) is less than the total capacity of the incoming circuits.

conditioning: A technique of applying electronic filtering elements to a communication line to improve the capability of that line so it can support higher data transmission rates. *See also* **equalization**.

configuration: The actual or practical layout of a network that takes into account its software, hardware, and cabling. Configurations may be multidrop, point-to-point, LANs, and the like. By contrast, a topology is the geometric layout (ring, bus, star) of the configuration. Topologies are the building blocks of configurations. *Compare with* **topology**.

connectionless routing: Connectionless routing means each packet is treated separately and makes its own way through the network. It is possible that different packets will take different routes through the network depending on the type of routing used and the amount of traffic.

connection-oriented routing: Connection-oriented routing sets up a virtual circuit (one that appears to use point-to-point circuit switching) between the sender and receiver. The network layer makes one routing decision when the connection is established, and all packets follow the same route. All packets in the same message arrive at the destination in the same order in which they were sent.

Consultative Committee on International Telegraph and Telephone (CCITT): An international organization that sets worldwide communication standards. Its new name is **International Telecommunications Union—Telecommunications (ITU-T)**.

contention: A method by which devices on the same shared multipoint circuit compete for time on the circuit.

control: A mechanism to ensure that the threats to a network are mitigated. There are two levels of controls: system-level controls and application-level controls.

control character: A character whose occurrence in a particular context specifies some network operation or function.

control spreadsheet: A two-dimensional matrix showing the relationship between the controls in a network, the threats that are being mitigated, and the components that are being protected. The controls listed in each cell represent the specific control enacted to reduce or eliminate the exposure.

core layer: The core layer is the central part of a network that provides access to the distribution layer. It is often a very fast BN that runs through the center of a campus or office complex.

COS: Corporation for Open Systems. An organization of computer and communications equipment vendors and users formed to accelerate the introduction of products based on the seven-layer OSI model. Its primary interest is the application layer (layer 7) of the OSI model and the X.400 e-mail standard.

CPE: *See* **customer premises equipment (CPE)**.

CPU: central processing unit.

CRC: Cyclical redundancy check. An error-checking control technique using a specific binary prime divisor that results in a unique remainder. It usually is a 16- to 32-bit character.

CSMA/CA: Carrier Sense Multiple Access (CSMA) with Collision Avoidance (CA). This protocol is similar to the Carrier Sense Multiple Access (CSMA) with Collision Detection (CD) protocol. Whereas CSMA/CD sends a data packet and then reports back if it collides with another packet, CSMA/CA sends a small preliminary packet to determine whether the network is busy.

If there is a collision, it is with the small packet rather than with the entire message. CA is thought to be more efficient because it reduces the time required to recover from collisions.

CSMA/CD: Carrier Sense Multiple Access (CSMA) with Collision Detection (CD). A system used in contention networks. The network interface unit listens for the presence of a carrier before attempting to send and detects the presence of a collision by monitoring for a distorted pulse.

customer premises equipment (CPE): Equipment that provides the interface between the customer's CENTREX system and the telephone network. It physically resides at the customer's site rather than the telephone company's end office. *CPE* generally refers to voice telephone equipment instead of data transmission equipment.

cyclical redundancy check (CRC): *See* **CRC**.

D

data: 1. Specific individual facts or a list of such items. 2. Facts from which conclusions can be drawn.

data circuit terminating equipment (DCE): *See* **DCE**.

data compression: The technique that provides for the transmission of fewer data bits without the loss of information. The receiving location expands the received data bits into the original bit sequence. *See also* **compression**.

Data Encryption Standard (DES): *See* **DES**.

Data over Cable System Interface Specification (DOCSIS): A de facto data link layer standard for transmitting data via a cable modem using Ethernet-like protocols.

Data-over-Voice (DOV): When data and voice share the same transmission medium. Data transmissions are superimposed over the voice transmission.

data terminal equipment (DTE): *See* **DTE**.

datagram: A datagram is a connectionless service in packet-switched networks. Each packet has a destination and sequence number and may follow a different route through the network. Different routes may deliver packets at different speeds, so data packets often arrive out of sequence. The sequence number tells the network how to reassemble the packets into a continuous message.

dB: *See* **decibel (dB)**.

DCE: Data circuit terminating equipment. The equipment (usually the modem) installed at the user's site that provides all the functions required to establish, maintain, and terminate a connection, including the signal conversion and coding between the data terminal equipment (DTE) and the common carrier's line.

DDoS attack: *See* **distributed denial-of-service (DDoS) attack**.

decentralized routing: With decentralized routing, all computers in the network make their own routing decisions. There are three major types of decentralized routing. With static routing, the routing table is developed by the network manager and remains unchanged until the network manager updates it. With dynamic routing, the goal is to improve network performance by routing messages over the fastest possible route; an initial routing table is developed by the network manager but is continuously updated to reflect changing network conditions, such as message traffic. With broadcast routing, the message is sent to all computers, but it is processed only by the computer to which it is addressed.

decibel (dB): A tenth of a bel. A unit for measuring relative strength of a signal parameter such as power and voltage. The number of decibels is ten times the logarithm (base 10) of the ratio of the power of two signals, or ratio of the power of one signal to a reference level. The reference level always must be indicated, such as 1 milliwatt for power ratio.

dedicated circuit: A leased communication circuit that goes from your site to some other location. It is a clear, unbroken communication path that is yours to use 24 hours per day, 7 days per week. Also called a *private circuit* or **leased circuit**.

delay distortion: A distortion on communication lines that is caused because some frequencies travel more slowly than others in a given transmission medium and therefore arrive at the destination at slightly different times. Delay distortion is measured in microseconds of delay relative to the delay at 1,700 Hz. This type of distortion does not affect voice, but it can have a serious effect on data transmissions.

delay equalizer: A corrective device for making the phase delay or envelope delay of a circuit substantially constant over a desired frequency range. *see also* **equalizer**.

Delphi group: A small group of experts (three to nine people) who meet to develop a consensus when it may be impossible or too expensive to collect more accurate data. For example, a Delphi group of communication experts might assemble to reach a consensus on the various threats to a communication network, the potential dollar losses for each occurrence of each threat, and the estimated frequency of occurrence for each threat.

denial of service (DoS) attack: A DoS attempts to disrupt the network by flooding the network with messages so that the network cannot process messages from normal users.

DES: Data Encryption Standard. Developed by IBM and the U.S. National Institute of Standards, this widely used single-key encryption algorithm uses a 64-bit key.

desktop video conferencing: With desktop video conferencing, small cameras are installed on top of each user's computer so that participants can hold meetings from their offices.

DHCP: *See* **Dynamic Host Control Protocol (DHCP)**.

digital signal: A discrete or discontinuous signal whose various states are discrete intervals apart, such as +15 volts and −15 volts.

digital subscriber line (DSL): A data link layer technology that provides high-speed ("broadband") communication over traditional telephone lines. A DSL modem is used to provide three channels: a traditional voice channel, an upstream channel for communicating from the client to the ISP (often at speeds of 64 to 640 Kbps), and a downstream channel for communicating from the ISP to the client (often at speeds of 640 Kbps to 6 Mbps).

distortion: The unwanted modification or change of signals from their true form by some characteristic of the communication line or equipment being used for transmission—for example, delay distortion and amplitude distortion.

distortion types: 1. *Bias:* A type of distortion resulting when the intervals of modulation do not all have exactly their normal durations. 2. *Characteristic:* Distortion caused by transient disturbances that are present in the transmission circuit because of modulation. 3. *Delay:* Distortion occurring when the envelope delay of a circuit is not consistent over the frequency range required for transmission. 4. *End:* Distortion of start–stop signals. The shifting of the end of all marking pulses from their proper positions in relation to the beginning of the start pulse. 5. *Jitter:* A type of distortion that results in the intermittent shortening or lengthening of the signals. This distortion is entirely random in nature and can be caused by hits on the line.

6. *Harmonic:* The resultant process of harmonic frequencies (due to nonlinear characteristics of a transmission circuit) in the response when a sinusoidal stimulus is applied.

distributed denial of service (DDoS) attack: With a DDoS attack, a hacker breaks into and takes control of many computers on the Internet (often several hundred to several thousand) and uses them to launch the DoS attack from thousands of computers at the same time.

distribution layer: The distribution layer is the part of a network that connects the access layer to other access layers and to the core layer. It is often a BN in a building.

DNS: *See* **Domain Name Service (DNS)**.

DOCSIS: *See* **Data over Cable System Interface Specification (DOCSIS)**.

Domain Name Service (DNS): A server that provides a directory used to supply IP addresses for application-layer addresses—that is, a server that performs IP address resolution.

DoS attack: *See* **denial of service (DoS) attack**.

download: The process of loading software and data into the nodes of a network from the central node. Downloading usually refers to the movement of data from a host mainframe computer to a remote terminal or microcomputer.

DPSK: Differential phase shift keying. *See* **modulation, phase**.

DSL: *See* **digital subscriber line (DSL)**.

DTE: Data terminal equipment. Any piece of equipment at which a communication path begins or ends, such as a terminal.

duplexing: An alternative to the process of mirroring, which occurs when a database server mirrors or backs up the database with each transaction. In mirroring, the server writes on two different hard disks through two different disk controllers. Duplexing is more redundant and therefore even safer than mirroring, because the database is written to two different hard disks on two different disk circuits. *Compare with* **mirroring**.

Dynamic Host Control Protocol (DHCP): A network-layer protocol standard used to supply TCP/IP address information using dynamic address assignment.

dynamic routing: *See* **decentralized routing**.

E

e-mail: *See* **electronic mail (e-mail)**.

EBCDIC: Extended Binary Coded Decimal Interchange Code. A standard code consisting of a set of 8-bit characters used for information representation and interchange among data processing and communication systems. Very common in IBM equipment.

echo cancellation: Used in higher-speed modems to isolate and filter out (cancel) echoes when half-duplex transmissions use stop and wait ARQ (Automatic Repeat reQuest) protocols. Needed especially for satellite links.

echo checking: *See* **checking, echo**.

echo suppressor: A device for use in a two-way telephone circuit (especially circuits over 900 miles long) to attenuate echo currents in one direction caused by telephone currents in the other direction. This is done by sending an appropriate disabling tone to the circuit.

ECMA: *See* **European Computer Manufacturers Association (ECMA)**.

EDI: *See* **Electronic Data Interchange (EDI)**.

EIA: *See* **Electronic Industries Association (EIA)**.

Electronic Data Interchange (EDI): Electronic Data Interchange for Administration, Commerce, and Transport. Standardizes the electronic interchange of business documents for both ASCII and graphics. Endorsed by the ISO. Defines major components of the ANSI X.12 EDI standard.

Electronic Industries Association (EIA): Composed of electronic manufacturers in the United States. Recommends standards for electrical and functional characteristics of interface equipment. Belongs to the ANSI. Known for the RS232 interface connector cable standard.

electronic mail (e-mail): A networking application that allows users to send and receive mail electronically.

electronic software distribution (ESD): ESD enables network managers to install software on client computers over the network without physically touching each client computer. ESD client software is installed on each client and enables an ESD server to to download and install certain application packages on each client at some predefined time (e.g., at midnight on a Saturday).

emulate: Computer vendors provide software and hardware emulators that accept hardware and software from other vendors and enable them to run on their hardware or software.

encapsulation: A technique in which a frame from one network is placed within the data field of the frame in another network for transmission on the second network. For example, it enables a message initiated on a coaxial cable-based Ethernet LAN to be transmitted over an ATM fiber optic–based network and then placed onto another Ethernet LAN at the other end.

encryption: The technique of modifying a known bit stream on a transmission circuit so that to an unauthorized observer, it appears to be a random sequence of bits.

end office: The telephone company switching office for the interconnection of calls. *See also* **central office**.

envelope delay distortion: A derivative of the circuit phase shift with respect to the frequency. This distortion affects the time it takes for different frequencies to propagate the length of a communication circuit so that two signals arrive at different times.

equalization: The process of reducing frequency and phase distortion of a circuit by introducing time differences to compensate for the difference in attenuation or time delay at the various frequencies in the transmission band.

equalizer: Any combination (usually adjustable) of coils, capacitors, or resistors inserted in the transmission circuit or amplifier to improve its frequency response.

error control: An arrangement that detects the presence of errors. In some networks, refinements are added that correct the detected errors, either by operations on the received data or by retransmission from the source.

ESD: *See* **electronic software distribution (ESD)**.

Ethernet: A LAN developed by the Xerox Corporation. It uses coaxial cable or twisted-pair wires to connect the stations. It was standardized as **IEEE 802.3**.

European Computer Manufacturers Association (ECMA): Recommends standards for computer components manufactured or used in Europe. Belongs to the International Organization for Standardization (ISO).

exchange office: *See* **central office**.

exposure: The calculated or estimated loss resulting from the occurrence of a threat, as in "The exposure from theft could be $42,000 this year." It can be either tangible and therefore measurable in dollars or intangible and therefore not directly measurable in dollars. *See also* **comparison risk ranking**.

Extended Binary Coded Decimal Interchange Code (EBCDIC): *See* **EBCDIC**.

extranet: Using the Internet to provide access to information intended for a selected set of users, not the public

at large. Usually done by requiring a password to access a selected set of Web sites.

F

FCC: *See* **Federal Communications Commission (FCC)**.

FCS: *See* **frame check sequence (FCC)**.

FDDI: *See* **fiber distributed data interface (FDDI)**.

FDM: Frequency division multiplexing. *See* **multiplexer**.

feasibility study: A study undertaken to determine the possibility or probability of improving the existing system within a reasonable cost. Determines what the problem is and what its causes are and makes recommendations for solving the problem.

FEC: *See* **forward error correction (FEC)**.

Federal Communications Commission (FCC): A board of seven commissioners appointed by the U.S. president under the Communication Act of 1934, having the power to regulate all interstate and foreign electrical communication systems originating in the United States.

FEP: *See* **front-end processor (FEP)**.

fiber distributed data interface (FDDI): A Token Ring-like LAN technology that permits transmission speeds of 100 million bps using fiber-optic cables (ANSI standard X3T9.5).

fiber-optic cable: A transmission medium that uses glass or plastic cable instead of copper wires.

fiber optics: A transmission technology in which modulated visible lightwave signals containing information are sent down hair-thin plastic or glass fibers and demodulated back into electrical signals at the other end by a special light-sensitive receiver.

File Transfer Protocol (FTP): FTP enables users to send and receive files over the Internet. There are two types of FTP sites: closed (which require users to have an account and a password) and anonymous (which permit anyone to use them).

firewall: A firewall is a router, gateway, or special-purpose computer that filters packets flowing into and out of a network. No access to the organization's networks is permitted except through the firewall. Two commonly used types of firewalls are packet level and application level.

firmware: A set of software instructions set permanently or semipermanently into a read-only memory (ROM).

flow control: The capability of the network nodes to manage buffering schemes that allow devices of different data transmission speeds to communicate with each other.

forward error correction (FEC): A technique that identifies errors at the received station and automatically corrects those errors without retransmitting the message.

fractional T1 (FT1): A portion of a T1 circuit. A full T1 allows transmission at 1,544,000 bps. A fractional T1 circuit allows transmission at lower speeds of 384,000, 512,000, or 768,000 bps. *See also* **T carrier**.

frame: Generally, a group of data bits having bits at each end to indicate the beginning and end of the frame. Frames also contain source addresses, destination addresses, frame type identifiers, and a data message.

frame check sequence (FCS): Used for error checking. FCS uses a 16-bit field with cyclical redundancy checking for error detection with retransmission.

frame relay: Frame relay is a type of packet-switching technology that transmits data faster than X.25 standard. The key difference is that unlike X.25 networks, frame relay does not perform error correction at each computer in the network. Instead, it simply discards any messages with errors. It is up to the application software at the source and destination to perform error correction and to control for lost messages.

Frequency: The rate at which a current alternates, measured in Hertz, kilohertz, megahertz, and so forth. Other units of measure are cycles, kilocycles, or megacycles; *hertz* and *cycles per second* are synonymous.

frequency division multiplexing (FDM): *See* **multiplexer**.

frequency modulation: *See* **modulation, frequency**.

frequency shift keying (FSK): *See* **FSK**.

front-end processor (FEP): An auxiliary processor that is placed between a computer's CPU and the transmission facilities. This device normally handles housekeeping functions like circuit management and code translation, which otherwise would interfere with efficient operation of the CPU.

FSK: Frequency shift keying. A modulation technique whereby 0 and 1 are represented by a different frequency and the amplitude does not vary.

FTP: *See* **File Transfer Protocol (FTP)**.

full duplex: The capability of transmission in both directions at one time. *Contrast with* **half duplex** and **simplex**.

G

gateway: A device that connects two dissimilar networks. Allows networks of different vendors to communicate by translating one vendor's protocol into another. *See also* **bridge**, **router**, and **brouter**.

Gaussian noise: *See* **noise, Gaussian**.

Gbps: Gigabit per second; 1 Gbps is equal to 1 billion bps.

GHz: Gigahertz; 1 GHz is equal to 1 billion cycles per second in a frequency.

gigabyte: One billion bytes.

G.Lite: One de facto standard form of ADSL.

guardband: A small bandwidth of frequency that separates two voice-grade circuits. Also, the frequencies between subcircuits in FDM systems that guard against subcircuit interference.

H

hacker: A person who sleuths for passwords to gain illegal access to important computer files. Hackers may rummage through corporate trash cans looking for carelessly discarded printouts.

half duplex: A circuit that permits transmission of a signal in two directions but not at the same time. *Contrast with* **full duplex** and **simplex**.

Hamming code: A forward error correction (FEC) technique named for its inventor.

handshaking: Exchange of predetermined signals when a connection is established between two data set devices. This is used to establish the circuit and message path.

HDLC: *See* **high-level data link control (HDLC)**.

Hertz (Hz): Same as cycles per second; for example, 3,000 Hz is 3,000 cycles per second.

high-level data link control (HDLC): A bit-oriented protocol in which control of data links is specified by series of bits rather than by control characters (bytes).

home page: A home page is the main starting point or page for a World Wide Web entry.

host computer: The computer that lies at the center of the network. It generally performs the basic centralized data processing functions for which the network was designed. The host used to be where the network communication control functions took place, but today these functions tend to take place in the front-end processor or further out in the network. *Also called* a *central computer.*

hotline: A service that provides direct connection between customers in various cities using a dedicated circuit.

HTML: Web text files or pages use a structural language called HTML (Hypertext Markup Language) to store their information. HTML enables the author to define different type styles and sizes for the text, titles, and headings, and a variety of other formatting information. HTML also permits the author to define links to other pages that may be stored on the same Web server or on any Web server anywhere on the Internet.

hub: Network hubs act as junction boxes, permitting new computers to be connected to the network as easily as plugging a power cord into an electrical socket, and provide an easy way to connect network cables. Hubs also act as repeaters or amplifiers. Hubs are sometimes also called concentrators, multistation access units, or transceivers.

Hypertext Markup Language (HTML): *See* **HTML**.

Hz: *See* **Hertz (Hz)**.

I

IAB: *See* **Internet Architecture Board (IAB)**.

IANA: *See* **Internet Assigned Numbers Authority (IANA)**.

ICMP: *See* **Internet Control Message Protocol (ICMP)**.

idle character: A transmitted character indicating "no information" that does not manifest itself as part of a message at the destination point.

IDS: *See* **intrusion detection system (IDS)**.

IEEE: *See* **Institute of Electrical and Electronics Engineers (IEEE)**. IEEE has defined numerous standards for LANs and BNs; see Chapters 8 and 10.

IESG: Internet Engineering Steering Group.

IETF: Internet Engineering Task Force.

IMAP: *See* **Internet Mail Access Protocol (IMAP)**.

impulse noise: *See* **noise, impulse**.

in-band signaling: The transmission signaling information at some frequency or frequencies that lie within a carrier circuit normally used for information transmission.

Institute of Electrical and Electronics Engineers (IEEE): A professional organization for engineers in the United States. Issues standards and belongs to the ANSI and the ISO.

integrated services digital network (ISDN): *See* **ISDN**.

interexchange circuit (IXC): A circuit or circuit between end offices (central offices).

interLATA: Circuits that cross from one LATA (local access and transport area) into another.

intermodulation distortion: An analog line impairment whereby two frequencies create a third erroneous frequency, which in turn distorts the data signal representation.

International Organization for Standardization (ISO): *See* **ISO**.

International Telecommunications Union—Telecommunications (ITU-T): An International organization that sets worldwide communication standards. Its old name was **Consultative Committee on International Telegraph and Telephone (CCITT)**.

Internet: The information superhighway. The network of networks that spans the world, linking more than 20 million users.

Internet Architecture Board (IAB): IAB provides strategic architectural oversight (e.g., top-level domain names, use of international character sets) that can be passed on as guidance to the IESG or turned into published statements or simply passed directly to the relevant IETF working group. The IAB does not produce polished technical proposals but rather tries to stimulate action by the IESG or the IETF that will lead to proposals that meet general consensus. The IAB appoints the IETF chair and all IESG members.

Internet Assigned Numbers Authority (IANA): IANA governs the assignment of IP numbers.

Internet Control Message Protocol (ICMP): A simple network layer protocol standard intended to exchange limited routing information between routers. Most commonly known as a ping, after the DOS and UNIX command.

Internet Engineering Steering Group (IESG): The IESG is responsible for technical management of IETF activities and the Internet standards process. It administers the process according to the rules and procedures and is directly responsible for the actions associated with entry into and movement along the Internet "standards track," including final approval of specifications as Internet standards. Each IETF working group is chaired by a member of the IESG.

Internet Engineering Task Force (IETF): IETF is a large, open international community of network designers, operators, vendors, and researchers concerned with the evolution of the Internet architecture and the smooth operation of the Internet. IETF operates through a series of working groups, which are organized by topic (e.g., routing, transport, security). The requests for comment (RFCs) that form the basis for Internet standards are developed by the IETF and its working groups.

Internet Mail Access Protocol (IMAP): An application-layer protocol standard that covers communication between an e-mail client and an e-mail server.

Internet Research Task Force (IRTF): IRTF operates much like the IETF, through small research groups focused on specific issues. Although IETF working groups focus on current issues, IRTF research groups work on long-term issues related to Internet protocols, applications, architecture, and technology. The IRTF chair is appointed by the IAB.

Internet service provider (ISP): ISPs offer connections to the Internet. Some access providers charge a flat monthly fee for unlimited access (much like the telephone company), whereas others charge per hour of use (much like a long-distance telephone call).

Internet Society (ISOC): ISOC is closet the Internet has to an owner. ISOC is an open-membership professional society with more than 175 organizational and 8,000 individual members in over 100 countries and includes corporations, government agencies, and foundations that have created the Internet and its technologies.

internetworking: Connecting several networks together so workstations can address messages to the workstations on each of the other networks.

Internet 2: There are many different organizations currently working on the next generation of the Internet, including the Abilene network, vBNS, and CA*net 3. Although each is working in a slightly different fashion, they join together with each other and parts of the regular Internet at gigapops (gigabit points of presence).

interoperability: The interconnection of dissimilar networks in a manner that allows them to operate as though they were similar.

IntraLATA: Circuits that are totally within one LATA (local access transport area).

intranet: Using Internet protocols on an network internal to an organization so that information is accessible using a browser, for example, but only by employees, not the public at large. Usually done by requiring a password to access a selected set of Web sites and protecting the site by a firewall so no outsiders can access it.

intrusion detection system (IDS): An IDS monitors a network segment, a server, or an application on the server for signs of unauthorized access and issues an alarm when an intrusion is detected. A misuse detection IDS compares monitored activities with signatures of known attacks, whereas an anomaly detection IDS compares monitored activities with the "normal" set of activities.

inverse multiplexer: Hardware that takes one high-speed transmission and divides it among several transmission circuits.

IPX/SPX: Internetwork packet exchange/sequenced packet exchange (IPX/SPX), based on a routing protocol developed by Xerox in the 1970s, is the primary network protocol used by Novell NetWare. About 40 percent of all installed LANs use it.

IRTF: *See* **Internet Research Task Force (IRTF).**

ISDN: Integrated services digital network. A hierarchy of digital switching and transmission systems. The ISDN provides voice, data, and image in a unified manner. It is synchronized so all digital elements speak the same "language" at the same speed. *See also* **basic rate interface (BRI)** and **primary rate interface (PRI).**

ISO: International Organization for Standardization, Geneva, Switzerland. The initials *ISO* stand for its French name. This international standards-making body is best known in data communications for developing the internationally recognized seven-layer network model called the Open Systems Interconnection (OSI) Reference model. *See also* **OSI model.**

ISOC: *See* **Internet Society (ISOC).**

ISP: *See* **Internet Service Provider (ISP).**

ITU-T: *See* **International Telecommunications Union—Telecommunications (ITU-T).**

IXC: *See* **interexchange circuit (IXC).**

J

jack: The physical connecting device at the interface that mates with a compatible receptacle—a plug.

jitter: Type of analog communication line distortion caused by the variation of a signal from its reference timing positions, which can cause data transmission errors, particularly at high speeds. This variation can be in amplitude, time, frequency, or phase.

jumper: 1. A small connector that fits over a set of pins on a microcomputer circuit card. 2. A patch cable or wire used to establish a circuit for testing or diagnostics.

K

K: A standard quantity measurement of computer storage. A K is defined loosely as 1,000 bytes. In fact, it is 1,024 bytes, which is the equivalent of 2^{10}.

Kbps: Kilobits per second. A data rate equal to 10^3 bps (1,000 bps).

Kermit: Kermit is a very popular asynchronous file transfer protocol named after Kermit the Frog. Kermit protocol was developed by Columbia University, which released it as a free software communications package. Various versions of Kermit can be found on public bulletin board systems for downloading to a microcomputer.

key management: The process of controlling the secret keys used in encryption.

KHz: Kilohertz; 1 KHz is equal to 1,000 cycles per second in a frequency.

kilobits per second (Kbps): *See* **Kbps**.

kilometer: A metric measurement equal to 0.621 mile or 3,280.8 feet.

L

LAN: *See* **local area network (LAN)**.

laser: *L*ight *a*mplification by *s*timulated *e*mission of *r*adiation. A device that transmits an extremely narrow and coherent beam of electromagnetic energy in the visible light spectrum. (*Coherent* means that the separate waves are in phase with one another rather than jumbled as in normal light.)

LATA: Local access transport area. One of approximately 200 local telephone service areas in the United States roughly paralleling major metropolitan areas. The LATA subdivisions were established as a result of the AT&T/Bell divestiture to distinguish local from long-distance service. Circuits with both end points within the LATA (intraLATAs) generally are the sole responsibility of the local telephone company. Circuits that cross outside the LATA (interLATAs) are passed on to an interexchange carrier like AT&T, MCI, or US Sprint.

leased circuit: A leased communication circuit that goes from your site to some other location. It is a clear, unbroken communication path that is yours to use 24 hours per day, 7 days per week. *Also called private circuit* or **dedicated circuit**.

line: A circuit, channel, or link. It carries the data communication signals. An early telephone technology term that may imply a physical connection, such as with a copper wire. *Compare with* **channel**, **circuit**, and **link**.

link: An unbroken circuit path between two points. *Sometimes called* a **line**, **channel**, or **circuit**.

Listserv: A listserver (or Listserv) is a mailing list. One part, the Listserv processor, processes commands such as requests to subscribe, unsubscribe, or to provide more information about the Listserv. The second part is the Listserv mailer. Any message send to the Listserv mailer is re-sent to everyone on the mailing list.

LLC: The logical link control, or LLC, sublayer is just an interface between the MAC sublayer and software in layer 3 (the network layer) that enables the software and hardware in the MAC sublayer to be separated from the logical functions in the LLC sublayer. By separating the LLC sublayer from the MAC sublayer, it is simpler to change the MAC hardware and software without affecting the software in layer 3. The most commonly used LLC protocol is IEEE 802.2.

local access transport area (LATA): *See* **LATA**.

local area network (LAN): A network that is located in a small geographic area, such as an office, a building, a complex of buildings, or a campus, and whose communication technology provides a high-bandwidth, low-cost medium to which many nodes can be connected. These networks typically do not use common carrier circuits, and their circuits do not cross public thoroughfares or property owned by others. LANs are not regulated by the FCC or state public utilities commissions.

local exchange carrier: The local telephone company, such as one of the seven regional Bell operating companies (RBOCs).

local loop: The part of a communication circuit between the subscriber's equipment and the equipment in the local central office.

log: 1. A record of everything pertinent to a system function. 2. A collection of messages that provides a history of message traffic.

logical link control (LLC): *See* **LLC**.

longitudinal redundancy check (LRC): A system of error control based on the formation of a block check following preset rules. The check formation rule is applied in the same manner to each character. In a simple case, the LRC is created by forming a parity check on each bit position of all characters in the block. (That is, the first bit of the LRC character creates odd parity among the 1-bit positions of the characters in the block.)

LRC: *See* **longitudinal redundancy check (LRC).**

M

M: Mega. The designation for 1 million, as in 3 megabits per second (3 Mbit/s).

MAC: *See* **media access control (MAC).**

MAN: *See* **metropolitan area network (MAN).**

Manchester encoding: The digital transmission technique used in the physical layer of Ethernet LANs. See Chapter 3.

management information base (MIB): The extent of information that can be retrieved from a user microcomputer when using the Simple Network Management Protocol (SNMP) for network management. MIBs are sets of attributes and definitions that pertain to specific network devices.

Mbps: A data rate equal to 10^6 bps. Sometimes called megabits per second (1,000,000 bps).

mean times: *See* **MTBF, MTTD, MTTF,** and **MTTR.**

media access control (MAC): A data link layer protocol that defines how packets are transmitted on a local area network. *See also* **CSMA/CD, token bus,** and **Token Ring.**

Medium: The matter or substance that carries the voice or data transmission. For example, the medium can be copper (wires), glass (fiber-optic cables), or air (microwave or satellite).

megabit: One million bits.

megabyte: One million bytes.

mesh network: A network topology in which there are direct point-to-point connections among the computers.

message: A communication of information from a source to one or more destinations. A message usually is composed of three parts: (1) a heading, containing a suitable indicator of the beginning of the message together with some of the following information: source, destination, date, time, routing; (2) a body containing the information to be communicated; (3) an ending containing a suitable indicator of the end of the message.

message switching: An operation in which the entire message being transmitted is switched to the other location without regard to whether the circuits actually are interconnected at the time of your call. This usually involves a message store and forward facility.

meter: A metric measurement equal to 39.37 inches.

metropolitan area network (MAN): A network that usually covers a citywide area. Because MANs use LAN and fiber-optic technologies, transmission speeds can vary between 2 million and 100 million bps.

MHz: megahertz; 1 MHz is equal to 1 million cycles per second in a frequency.

MIB: *See* **management information base (MIB).**

MIME: *See* **Multipurpose Internet Mail Extension (MIME).**

MIPS: One million instructions per second. Used to describe a computer's processing power.

mirroring: A process in which the database server automatically backs up the disk during each database transaction. During this process, the computer writes on two different hard disks on the same disk circuit every time the hard disk is updated. This creates two mirror images of the database data. Disk mirroring can be accomplished only when the database server contains two physical disk drives, because the records or data structures are written to both disks simultaneously. Should a problem develop with one disk, the second disk is available instantly with identical information on it. *Compare with* **duplexing.**

mnemonic: A group of characters used to assist the human memory. A mnemonic frequently is an acronym.

modem: A contraction of the words *mo*dulator-**dem**odulator. A modem is a device for performing necessary signal transformation between terminal devices and communication circuits. Modems are used in pairs, one at either end of the communication circuit.

modulation, amplitude: The form of modulation in which the amplitude of the carrier is varied in accordance with the instantaneous value of the modulating signal.

modulation, frequency: A form of modulation in which the frequency of the carrier is varied in accordance with the instantaneous value of the modulating signal.

modulation, phase: A form of modulation in which the phase of the carrier is varied in accordance with the instantaneous value of the modulating signal. Phase modulation has two related techniques. Phase shift keying (PSK) uses a 180° change in phase to indicate a change in the binary value (0 or 1), Differential phase shift keying (DPSK) uses a 180° change in phase every time a 1 bit is transmitted; otherwise, the phase remains the same.

modulation, pulse code: *See* **pulse code modulation (PCM).**

MTBF: mean time between failures. The statistic developed by vendors to show the reliability of their equipment. It can be an actual calculated figure that generally is more accurate, or it can be a practical (theoretical) figure.

MTTD: Mean time to diagnose. The time it takes the network testing and problem management staff to diagnose a network problem.

MTTF: Mean time to fix. The time it takes vendors to remedy a network problem once they arrive on the premises.

MTTR: 1. Mean time to repair—the combination of mean time to diagnose, mean time to respond, and mean time to fix, indicating the entire length of time it takes to fix a fault in equipment. 2. Mean time to respond—the time it takes the vendor to respond when a network problem is reported.

multidrop (multipoint): A line or circuit interconnecting several stations/nodes in a sequential fashion.

multiplexer: A device that combines data traffic from several low-speed communication circuits onto a single high-speed circuit. The two popular types of multiplexing are FDM (frequency division multiplexing) and TDM (time division multiplexing). In FDM, the voice-grade link is divided into subcircuits, each covering a different frequency range in such a manner that each subcircuit can be employed as though it were an individual circuit. In TDM, separate time segments are assigned to each terminal. During these time segments, data may be sent without conflicting with data sent from another terminal.

multiplexing (MUX): The subdivision of a transmission circuit into two or more separate circuits. This can be achieved by splitting the frequency range of the circuit into narrow frequency bands (**frequency division multiplexing**) or by assigning a given circuit successively toseveral different users at different times (**time division multiplexing**).

Multipurpose Internet Mail Extension (MIME): An application-layer standard protocol that enables SMTP mail messages to transfer nontext characters such as graphics and software. The sending e-mail client translates the nontext characters into something that resembles text using MIME codes and attaches it to the message. The receiving e-mail client translates the MIME codes back into the original graphic or software file.

MUX: *See* **multiplexing (MUX).**

N

NAK: *See* **negative acknowledgment (ACK).**

nanosecond: One billionth ($^1/_{1,000,000,000}$) of a second or 10^{-9}.

NAP: *See* **network access point (NAP).**

NAT: *See* **network address translation (NAT).**

National Institute of Standards and Technology (NIST): Formerly the National Bureau of Standards. The agency of the U.S. government responsible for developing information processing standards for the federal government.

NCO: *See* **network cost of ownership (NCO).**

negative acknowledgment (NAK): The return signal that reports an error in the message received. The opposite of **acknowledgment (ACK).**

network: 1. A series of points connected by communication circuits. 2. The switched telephone network is the network of telephone lines normally used for dialed telephone calls. 3. A private network is a network of communication circuits confined to the use of one customer.

network access point (NAP): An "intersection" on the Internet where many national and regional ISPs connect to exchange data.

network address translation (NAT): NAT is the process of translating between one set of private IP addresses inside a network and a set of public IP addresses outside the network for use on the Internet. NAT is transparent in that no computer notices that it is being done.

network cost of ownership (NCO): NCO is a measure of how much it costs per year to keep one computer operating. NCO includes the cost of support staff to attach it to the network, install software, administer the network (e.g., create user IDs, back up user data), provide training and technical support, and upgrade hardware and software. NCO is often $1,500 to $3,500 per computer per year. *Compare with* **total cost of ownership (TCO).**

network interface card (NIC): An NIC allows the computer to be physically connected to the network cable; the NIC provides the physical-layer connection from the computer to the network.

network operating system (NOS): The NOS is the software that controls the network. The NOS provides the data link and the network layers and must interact with the application software and the computer's own operating system. Every NOS provides two sets of software: one that runs on the network server(s) and one that runs on the network client(s).

network operations center (NOC): Any centralized network management control site.

network profile: Every LAN microcomputer has a profile that outlines what resources it has available to other microcomputers in the network and what resources it can use elsewhere in the network.

network service: An application available on a network—for example, file storage.

NIC: *See* **network interface card (NIC).**

NIST: *See* **National Institute of Standards and Technology (NIST).**

NOC: *See* **network operations center (NOC).**

node: In a description of a network, the point at which the links join input–output devices. It could be a computer or a special-purpose device such as a router.

noise: The unwanted change in waveform that occurs between two points in a transmission circuit.

noise, amplitude: A sudden change in the level of power with differing effects, depending on the type of modulation used by the modem.

noise, cross-talk: Noise resulting from the interchange of signals on two adjacent circuits; manifests itself when it is possible to hear other people's telephone conversations.

noise, echo: The "hollow" or echoing characteristic that is heard on voice-grade lines with improper echo suppression.

noise, Gaussian: Noise that is characterized statistically by a Gaussian, or random, distribution.

noise, impulse: Noise caused by individual impulses on the circuit.

noise, intermodulation: Noise that occurs when signals from two independent lines intermodulate. A new signal forms and falls into a frequency band differing from those of both inputs. The new signal may fall into a frequency band reserved for another signal.

NOS: *See* **network operating system (NOS).**

NRZ: Nonreturn to zero. A binary encoding and transmission scheme in which 1's and 0's are represented by opposite and alternating high and low voltages, and in which there is no return to a reference (zero) voltage between encoded bits.

NRZI: Nonreturn to zero inverted. A binary encoding scheme that inverts the signal on a 1 and leaves the signal unchanged for a 0, and in which a change in the voltage state signals a 1-bit value and the absence of a change denotes a 0-bit value.

null character: A control character that can be inserted into or withdrawn from a sequence of characters without altering the message.

null modem cable: A 6- to 8-foot RS232 cable that makes the two microcomputers connected at each end of the cable think they are talking through modems.

O

office, central or end: The common carrier's switching office closest to the subscriber.

Open Shortest Path First (OSPF): A network-layer standard protocol used to exchange route information between routers using dynamic decentralized routing.

Open Systems Interconnection (OSI) Reference model: *See* **OSI model.**

optical fibers: Hair-thin strands of very pure glass (sometimes plastic) over which light waves travel. They are used as a medium over which information is transmitted.

OSI model: The seven-layer Open Systems Interconnection (OSI) Reference model developed by the ISO subcommittee. The OSI model serves as a logical framework of protocols for computer-to-computer communications. Its purpose is to facilitate the interconnection of networks.

OSPF: *See* **Open Shortest Path First (OSPF).**

out-of-band signaling: A method of signaling that uses a frequency that is within the passband of the transmission facility but outside of a carrier circuit normally used for data transmission.

overhead: Computer time used to keep track of or run the system, as compared with computer time used to process data.

P

packet: A group of binary digits, including data and control signals, that is switched as a composite whole. The data, control signals, and error-control information are arranged in a specific format. A packet often is a 128-character block of data.

packet assembly/disassembly (PAD): *See* **PAD.**

Packet Layer Protocol (PLP): *See* **PLP.**

packet switching: Process whereby messages are broken into finite-size packets that always are accepted by the network. The message packets are forwarded to the other party over a multitude of different circuit paths. At the other end of the circuit, the packets are reassembled into the message, which is then passed on to the receiving terminal.

packet switching network (PSN): A network designed to carry data in the form of packets. The packet and its format are internal to that network. The external interfaces may handle data in different formats, and format conversion may be done by the user's computer.

PAD: Packet assembly/disassembly. Equipment providing packet assembly and disassembly between asynchronous transmission and the packet-switching network.

PAM: *See* **pulse amplitude modulation (PAM)**.

parallel: Describes the way the internal transfer of binary data takes place within a computer. It may be transmitted as a parallel word, but it is converted to a serial or bit-by-bit data stream for transmission.

parity bit: A binary bit appended to an array of bits to make the number of 1 bits always be odd or even for an individual character. For example, odd parity may require three 1 bits and even parity may require four 1 bits.

parity check: Addition of noninformation bits to a message to detect any changes in the original bit structure from the time it leaves the sending device to the time it is received.

parity checking: *See* **checking, parity**.

PBX: private branch exchange. Telephone switch located at a customer's site that primarily establishes voice communications over tie lines or circuits as well as between individual users and the switched telephone network. Typically also provides switching within a customer site and usually offers numerous other enhanced features, such as least-cost routing and call detail recording.

PCM: *See* **pulse code modulation (PCM)**.

PDN: *See* **public data network (PDN)**.

Pbps: Petabits per second. A data rate equal to 1 quadrillion bits per second (1,000,000,000,000,000).

peer: A dictionary definition of *peer* is "A person who is equal to another in abilities." A peer-to-peer network, therefore, is one in which each microcomputer node has equal abilities. In communications, a peer is a node or station that is on the same protocol layer as another.

peer-to-peer communications: 1. Communication between two or more processes or programs by which both ends of the session exchange data with equal privilege. 2. Communication between two or more network nodes in which either side can initiate sessions because no primary–secondary relationship exists.

Peer-to-Peer LAN: A network in which a microcomputer can serve as both a server and a user. Every microcomputer has access to all the network's resources on an equal basis.

permanent virtual circuit (PVC): A virtual circuit that resembles a leased line because it can be dedicated to a single user. Its connections are controlled by software.

phase modulation: *See* **modulation, phase**.

pirate: A person who obtains the latest software programs without paying for them. A skilled software pirate is able to break the protection scheme that is designed to prevent copying.

plain old telephone network (POTS): The nickname for the public switched telephone network. Often used when referring to dial-up Internet access using a modem.

PKI: *See* **public key infrastructure (PKI)**.

PLP: Packet Layer Protocol (PLP) is the routing protocol that performs the network layer functions (e.g., routing and addressing) in X.25 networks.

point of presence: (POP) The physical access location of an ISP or voice or data communications carrier.

point-to-point: Denoting a circuit, circuit, or line that has only two terminals. A link. An example is a single microcomputer connected to a mainframe.

polling: Any procedure that sequentially queries several terminals in a network.

polling, hub: A type of sequential polling in which the polling device contacts a terminal, that terminal contacts the next terminal, and so on, until all the terminals have been contacted.

polling, roll call: Polling accomplished from a prespecified list in a fixed sequence, with polling restarted when the list is completed.

polynomial checking: A checking method using polynomial functions to test for errors in data in transmission. Also called **cyclical redundancy check (CRC)**.

POP: 1. *See* **Post Office Protocol (POP)**. See **point-of-presence (POP)**.

port: One of the circuit connection points on a front-end processor or local intelligent controller.

Post Office Protocol (POP): An application-layer standard used to communicate between the client and the e-mail server.

POTS: *See* **plain old telephone network (POTS).**

PPP: PPP (multilink Point-to-Point Protocol) is an inverse multiplexing protocol for combining circuits of different speeds (e.g., a 64,000-bps circuit with a 14,400-bps circuit), with data allocated to each circuit is based on speed and need. PPP enables the user to change the circuits allocated to the PPP multiplexed circuit in mid-transmission so that the PPP circuit can increase or decrease the capacity. PPP is the successor to SLIP.

Primary Rate Interface In ISDN, twenty-three 64,000 bits per second D circuits for data and one 64,000 bits per second B circuit for signaling (23 B+D). See also **Basic Rate Interface.**

private branch exchange (PBX): *See* **PBX.**

propagation delay: The time necessary for a signal to travel from one point on the circuit to another, such as from a satellite dish up to a satellite or from Los Angeles to New York.

protocol: A formal set of conventions governing the format and control of inputs and outputs between two communicating devices. This includes the rules by which these two devices communicate as well as handshaking and line discipline.

protocol stack: The set of software required to process a set of protocols.

PSK: Phase shift keying; *see* **modulation, phase.**

PSN: *See* **packet switching network (PSN).**

PTT: Postal, telephone and telegraph. These are the common carriers owned by governments; the government is the sole or monopoly supplier of communication facilities.

public data network (PDN): A network established and operated for the specific purpose of providing data transmission services to the public. It can be a public packet-switched network or a circuit-switched network. Public data networks normally offer value-added services for resource sharing at reduced costs and with high reliability. These time-sharing networks are available to anyone with a modem.

public key encryption: Public key encryption uses two keys. The public key is used to encrypt the message and a second, very different private key is used to decrypt the message. Even though the sender knows both the contents of the outgoing message and the public encryption key, once it is encrypted, the message cannot be decrypted without the private key. Public key encryption is one of the most secure encryption techniques available.

public key infrastructure (PKI): The PKI is the process of using public key encryption on the Internet. PKI begins with a certificate authority (CA), which is a trusted organization that can vouch for the authenticity of the person or organization using authentication (e.g., VeriSign). The CA issues a digital certificate that is the requestor's public key encrypted using the CA's private key as proof of identify. This certificate is then attached to the user's e-mail or Web transactions. The receiver then verifies the certificate by decrypting it with the CA's public key—and must also contact the CA to ensure that the user's certificate has not been revoked by the CA.

pulse amplitude modulation (PAM): Amplitude modulation of a pulse carrier. PAM is used to translate analog voice data into a series of binary digits before they are transmitted.

pulse code modulation (PCM): Representation of a speech signal by sampling at a regular rate and converting each sample to a binary number. In PCM, the information signals are sampled at regular intervals and a series of pulses in coded form are transmitted, representing the amplitude of the information signal at that time.

Q

QAM: Quadrature amplitude modulation. A sophisticated modulation technique that uses variations in signal amplitude, which allows data-encoded symbols to be represented as any of 16 states to send 4 bits on each signal.

Quality of Service (QoS): The ability of devices to give different priorities to different types of messages so that some messages (e.g., voice telephone data) are transmitted faster than other messages (e.g., e-mail).

quantizing error: The difference between the PAM signal and the original voice signal. The original signal has a smooth flow, but the PAM signal has jagged "steps."

R

RBOC: Regional Bell operating company. One of the seven companies created after divestiture of the old

Bell system to provide local communications. Includes Ameritech, Bell Atlantic, BellSouth, NYNEX, Pacific Telesis, Southwestern Bell, and US West.

reclocking time: *See* **turnaround time**.

redundancy: The portion of the total information contained in a message that can be eliminated without loss of essential information.

Regional Bell operating company (RBOC): *See* **RBOC**.

reliability: A characteristic of the equipment, software, or network that relates to the integrity of the system against failure. Reliability usually is measured in terms of mean time between failures (MTBF), the statistical measure of the interval between successive failures of the hardware or software under consideration.

request for comment (RFC): A proposed standard for the Internet on which anyone in the world is invited to comment.

request for proposal (RFP): A request for proposal is used to solicit bids from vendors for new network hardware, software, and services. RFPs specify what equipment, software, and services are desired and ask vendors to provide their best prices.

repeater: A device used to boost the strength of a signal. Repeaters are spaced at intervals throughout the length of a communication circuit.

response time: The time the system takes to react to a given input; the time interval from when the user presses the last key to the terminal's typing the first letter of the reply. Response time includes (1) transmission time to the computer; (2) processing time at the computer, including access time to obtain any file records needed to answer the inquiry; and (3) transmission time back to the terminal.

retrain time: *See* **turnaround time**.

RFC: *See* **request for comment (RFC)**.

RFP: *See* **request for proposal (RFP)**.

ring: 1. The hot wire in a telephone circuit. 2. An audible sound used for signaling the recipient of an incoming telephone call. 3. A LAN topology having a logical geometric arrangement in the shape of a ring.

RIP: *See* **Routing Information Protocol (RIP)**.

risk: The level or amount of exposure to an item when compared with other items. It is a hazard or chance of loss. Risk is the degree of difference, as in, "What level of risk does one threat have when compared to the other threats?"

risk assessment: The process by which one identifies threats, uses a methodology to determine the tangible or intangible exposures, and develops a sequenced list of the threats from the one having the highest risk to the one having the lowest risk. The list may be in a sequence based on tangible dollar losses or on intangible criteria such as public embarrassment, likelihood of occurrence, most dangerous, most critical to the organization, and greatest delay. *Also called risk ranking* or *risk analysis.*

RMON: Remote monitoring. The definitions of what is stored and therefore retrievable from a remote user microcomputer when using the Simple Network Management Protocol (SNMP). It is referred to as the RMON MIB (management information base). *See also* **management information base (MIB)** and **Simple Network Management Protocol (SNMP)**.

router: A device that connects two similar networks having the same network protocol. It also chooses the best route between two networks when there are multiple paths between them. *Compare with* **bridge**, **brouter**, and **gateway**.

Routing Information Protocol (RIP): A network-layer standard protocol used to exchange route information between routers using dynamic decentralized routing.

RS232: A technical specification published by the Electronic Industries Association that specifies the mechanical and electrical characteristics of the interface for connecting data terminal equipment (DTE) and data circuit terminating equipment (DCE). It defines interface circuit functions and their corresponding connector pin assignments.

RS449: An Electronic Industries Association standard for data terminal equipment (DTE) and data circuit terminating equipment (DCE) connection that specifies interface requirements for expanded transmission speeds (up to 2 million bps), longer cable lengths, and 10 additional functions.

S

SDLC: *See* **synchronous data link control (SDLC)**.

serial: 1. Transmitting bits one at a time and in sequence. 2. The sequential or consecutive occurrence of two or more related activities in a single device or circuit.

Server: A computer that provides a particular service to the client computers on the network. In larger LANs, the server is dedicated to being a server. In a peer-to-peer LAN, the server may be both a server and a client computer. There may be file, database, network, access, modem, facsimile, printer, and gateway servers.

service-level agreement (SLA): An SLA specifies the exact type of performance and fault conditions that the organization will accept and what compensation the service provider must provide if it fails to meet the SLA. For example, the SLA might state that network availability must be 99 percent or higher and that the MTBF for T1 circuits must be 120 days or more.

session: A logical connection between two terminals. This is the part of the message transmission when the two parties are exchanging messages. It takes place after the communication circuit has been set up and is functioning.

signal: A signal is something that is sent over a communication circuit. It might be a control signal used by the network to control itself.

signal-to-noise ratio: The ratio, expressed in dB, of the usable signal to the noise signal present.

Simple Network Management Protocol (SNMP): An application-layer protocol standard used in network management for monitoring and configuring network devices. *See also* **management information base (MIB)** and **RMON**.

Simple Mail Transfer Protocol (SMTP): An application-layer protocol standard used to transfer e-mail messages across the Internet.

simplex: A circuit capable of transmission in one direction only. *Contrast with* **full duplex** and **half Duplex**.

single cable: A one-cable system in broadband LANs in which a portion of the bandwidth is allocated for "send" signals and a portion for "receive" signals, with a guardband in between to provide isolation from interference.

SLIP: Serial Line Internet Protocol (SLIP) is a proposed standard for inverse multiplexing. It has been surpassed by PPP.

SMDS: Switched multimegabit data service.

SMTP: *See* **Simple Mail Transfer Protocol (SMTP)**.

SNA: *See* **systems network architecture (SNA)**.

SNMP: *See* **Simple Network Management Protocol (SNMP)**.

SONET: *See* **synchronous optical network (SONET)**.

spike: A sudden increase of electrical power on a communication circuit. *Spike* is a term used in the communication industry. *Contrast with* **surge**.

spread spectrum: The U.S. military developed spread spectrum through-the-air radio transmission technology primarily to overcome the problem of intentional interference by hostile jamming and secondarily for security. A spread spectrum signal is created by modulating the original transmitted radio frequency (RF) signal with a spreading code that causes "hopping" of the frequency from one frequency to another. By contrast, conventional AM and FM radio uses only one frequency to transmit its signal.

start bit: A bit that precedes the group of bits representing a character. Used to signal the arrival of the character in asynchronous transmission.

static routing: *See* **decentralized routing**.

statistical multiplexer: Stat mux or STDM. A time division multiplexer (TDM) that dynamically allocates communication circuit time to each of the various attached terminals, according to whether a terminal is active or inactive at a particular moment. Buffering and queuing functions also are included. *See also* **concentrator**.

stop bit: A bit that follows the group of bits representing a character. Used to signal the end of a character in asynchronous transmission.

store and forward: A data communications technique that accepts messages or transactions, stores them, and then forwards them to the next location or person as addressed in the message header.

STX: A control character used in ASCII and EBCDIC data communications to mean start of text.

surge: A sudden increase in voltage on a 120-volt electrical power line. A term used in the electric utilities industry. *Contrast with* **spike**.

switch: Switches connect more than two LAN segments that use the same data link and network protocol. They may connect the same or different types of cable. Switches typically provide ports for 4, 8, 16, or 32 separate LAN segments, and most enable all ports to be in use simultaneously, so they are faster than bridges.

switched circuit: A dial-up circuit in which the communication path is established by dialing. If the entire circuit path is unavailable, there is a busy signal, which prevents completion of the circuit connection.

Switched Multimegabit Data Service (SMDS): *See* **SMDS**.

switched network: Any network that has switches used for directing messages from the sender to the ultimate recipient.

switched network, circuit switched: A switched network in which switching is accomplished by disconnecting and reconnecting lines in different configurations to set up a continuous pathway between the sender and the recipient. *See also* **circuit switching**.

switched network, store and forward: A switched network in which the store-and-forward principle is used to handle transmission between senders and recipients. *See also* **store and forward**.

switching: Identifying and connecting independent transmission links to form a continuous path from one location to another.

symbol rate: The speed in baud is the number of symbols per second. If each signal represents only one bit, *symbol rate* is the same as *bits per second*. When each signal contains more than one bit, *symbol rate* does not equal *bits per second.*

Synchronization character (SYN): An 8-bit control character that is sent at the beginning of a message block to establish synchronization (timing) between the sender and the receiver. Term used for the characters preceding an Ethernet packet. Term used for a TCP open connection request.

synchronous data link control (SDLC): A protocol for managing synchronous, code-transparent, serial bit-by-bit information transfer over a link connection. Transmission exchanges may be full duplex or half duplex and over switched or nonswitched links. The configurations of the link connection may be point to point, multipoint, or loop. SDLC is the protocol used in IBM's systems network architecture.

synchronous optical network (SONET): The National Exchange Carriers Association standard for optical transmission at gigabits-per-second speeds. For example, digital signals transmit on T1 circuits at 1,544,000 bps and on T3 circuits at 44,376,000 bps. The slowest SONET OC-1 optical transmission rate of 51,840,000 bps is slightly faster than the T3 rate.

synchronous transmission: Form of transmission in which data is sent as a fixed-length block or frame. *Compare with* **asynchonous transmission**.

systems network architecture (SNA): The name of IBM's conceptual framework that defines the data communication interaction between computer systems or terminals.

T

T carrier: A hierarchy of digital circuits designed to carry speech and other signals in digital form. Designated T1 (1.544 Mbps), T2 (6.313 Mbps), T3 (44.736 Mbps), and T4 (274.176 Mbps).

tariff: The formal schedule of rates and regulations pertaining to the communication services, equipment, and facilities that constitute the contract between the user and the common carrier. Tariffs are filed with the appropriate regulatory agency (FCC or state public utilities commission) for approval and published when approved.

TASI: Time assisted speech interpolation. The process of interleaving two or more voice calls on the same telephone circuit simultaneously.

Tbps: Terabits per second. A data rate equal to 1 trillion bits per second (1,000,000,000,000).

TCM: Trellis-coded modulation (TCM) is a modulation technique related to QAM that combines phase modulation and amplitude modulation. There are several different forms of TCM that transmit 5, 6, 7, or 8 bits per signal, respectively.

TCP/IP: Transmission Control Protocol/Internet Protocol is probably the oldest networking standard, developed for ARPANET, and now used on the Internet. One of the most commonly used network protocols.

TDM: *See* **multiplexer**.

telecommunications: A term encompassing voice, data, and image transmissions that are sent over some medium in the form of coded signals.

telecommuting: Telecommuting employees perform some or all of their work at home instead of going to the office each day.

teleconferencing: With teleconferencing, people from diverse geographic locations can "attend" a business meeting in both voice and picture format. In fact, even documents can be shown and copied at any of the remote locations.

telephony: A generic term to describe voice communications. Pronounced "tel-ef-on-e," not "tel-e-fon-e."

Telnet: Telnet enables users on one computer to log in to other computers on the Internet.

10Base-T: An Ethernet LAN standard (IEEE 802.3) that runs at 10 million bps and uses unshielded twisted-pair wires.

10Base2: An Ethernet LAN standard that runs at 10 million bps, uses baseband transmission techniques, and allows 200 meters maximum cable length.

10Base5: An Ethernet LAN standard that runs at 10 million bps, uses baseband transmission techniques, and allows 500 meters maximum cable length.

10Broad36: An Ethernet LAN standard that runs at 10 million bps, uses broadband transmission techniques, and allows 3,600 meters maximum cable length.

100Base-T: An Ethernet LAN standard that runs at 100 million bps and uses unshielded twisted-pair wires.

1000Base-T: An Ethernet LAN standard the runs at 1 billion bps and uses unshielded twisted-pair wires.

thick Ethernet: Refers to the original Ethernet specification that uses thick coaxial cable that is both grounded and shielded. The many layers of shielding are of polyvinyl and aluminum, which make the cable wider in diameter than other Ethernet cables. The heavy shielding also makes the cable more expensive and less flexible; therefore, it is impractical for many installations.

thin Ethernet: Refers to the 10Base2 baseband Ethernet, meaning the version that transmits at 10 million bps in baseband at 200 meters maximum. It uses thin coaxial cable. *Also called* **cheapnet**.

threat: A potentially adverse occurrence or unwanted event that could be injurious to the network, the computing environment, the organization, or a business application. Threats are acts or events the organization wants to prevent from taking place, such as lost data, theft, disasters, virus infections, errors, illegal access, and unauthorized disclosure. In other words, threats are events no one wants to occur.

3DES: *See* **triple DES (3DES)**.

throughput: The total amount of useful information that is processed or communicated during a specific time period.

Time assisted speech interpolation (TASI): *See* **TASI**.

Time division multiplexing (TDM): *See* **multiplexer**.

token: The special sequence of characters used to gain access to a Token Ring or token-bus network to transmit a packet.

token bus: A LAN with a bus topology that uses a token-passing approach to network access. In a token-bus LAN, the next logical node or station is not necessarily the next physical node because it uses preassigned priority algorithms. Message requests are not handled in consecutive order by stations. *Contrast with* **Token Ring**.

token passing: A method of allocating network access wherein a terminal can send a message only after it has acquired the network's electronic token.

Token Ring: A LAN with a ring topology that uses a token-passing approach to network access. In a Token Ring LAN, the next logical station also is the next physical station because the token passes from node to node. *Contrast with* **token bus**.

topology: The basic physical or geometric arrangement of the network—for example, a ring, star, or bus layout. The topology is the network's logical arrangement, but it is influenced by the physical connections of its links and nodes. This is in contrast to its configuration, which is the actual or practical layout, including software and hardware constraints. Topologies are the building blocks of a network configuration. *Compare with* **configuration**.

total cost of ownership (TCO): TCO is a measure of how much it costs per year to keep one computer operating. TCO includes the cost of support staff to attach it to the network, install software, administer the network (e.g., create user IDs, back up user data), provide training and technical support, and upgrade hardware and software, along with the cost of "wasted time" when the network is down. TCO is often $10,000 per computer per year. *Compare to* **network cost of ownership (NCO)**.

transceiver: A device that transmits and/or receives data to or from computers on an Ethernet LAN. Also a hub.

transmission rate of information bits (TRIB): *See* **TRIB**.

tree: A network arrangement in which the stations hang off a common "branch," or data bus, like leaves on the branch of a tree.

TRIB: Transmission rate of information bits. A TRIB is the network's throughput. It is the effective rate of data transfer over a communication circuit per unit of time. Usually expressed in bits per second.

triple DES (3DES): 3DES is a symmetric encryption technique that involves using DES three times, usually with three different keys, to produce the encrypted text, which produces a stronger level of security than DES, because it has a total of 168 bits as the key (i.e., 3×56 bits).

trunk: A voice communication circuit between switching devices or end offices.

turnaround time: The time required to reverse the direction of transmission from send to receive or vice versa on a half-duplex circuit.

twisted pair: A pair of wires used in standard telephone wiring. They are twisted to reduce interference caused by the other twisted pairs in the same cable bundle. Twisted-pair wires go from homes and offices to the telephone company end office.

U

UDP: *See* **User Datagram Protocol (UDP)**.

uninterruptible power supply (UPS): Provides backup electrical power if the normal electrical power fails or if the voltage drops to unacceptably low levels.

unipolar transmission: A form of digital transmission in which the voltage changes between 0 volts to represent a binary 0 and some positive value (e.g., +15 volts) to represent a binary 1. *See also* **bipolar transmission**.

uniform resource locator (URL): *See* **URL**.

unshielded twisted-pair (UTP) wires: The type of wiring used in 10Base-T Ethernet networks. Same as **twisted pair**.

upload: The process of loading software and data from the nodes of a network (terminals or microcomputers), over the network media, and to the host mainframe computer.

UPS: *See* **uninterruptible power supply (UPS)**.

URL: To use a browser to access a Web server, you must enter the server's addresses or URL (uniform resource locator). All Web addresses begin with seven characters: http://.

USASCII: *See* **ASCII**.

User Datagram Protocol (UDP): A connectionless transport layer protocol standard used by TCP to send short messages such as DNS requests.

user profile: The user profile specifies what data and network resources a user can access, and the type of access (read-only, write, create, delete, etc.).

UTP: *See* **unshielded twisted-pair (UTP) wires**.

V

V.*nn*: The V.*nn* series of ITU-T standards relating to the connection of digital equipment to the analog telephone network. Primarily concerned with the modem interface. See Chapter 3 for definitions.

value-added network (VAN): A corporation that sells services of a value-added network. Such a network is built using the communication offerings of traditional common carriers, connected to computers that permit new types of telecommunication tariffs to be offered. The network may be a packet switching or message switching network.

VBNS: *See* **very-high-performance backbone network service (vBNS)**.

VDSL: *See* **very-high-data-rate digital subscriber line (VDSL)**.

VDT: Video display terminal.

vertical redundancy check (VRC): *See* **parity check**.

very-high-data-rate digital subscriber line (VDSL): A form of DSL that provides very high speed transmission (e.g., up to 51 Mbps) over traditional telephone lines for very short distances.

very-high-performance backbone network service (vBNS): One part of Internet 2 run by MCI World-Com.

video teleconferencing: Video teleconferencing provides real-time transmission of video and audio signals to enable people in two or more locations to have a meeting.

virtual: Conceptual or appearing to be, rather than actually being.

virtual circuit: A temporary transmission circuit in which sequential data packets are routed between two points. It is created by the software in such a way that users think they have a dedicated point-to-point leased circuit.

virtual private network (VPN): A hybrid network that includes both public and private facilities. The user leases a bundle of circuits and configures the VPN on an as-needed basis so that some traffic travels on the private leased network and some travels on the common carrier's public network.

virus: Viruses are executable programs that copy themselves onto other computers. Most viruses attach themselves to other programs or to special parts on disks, and as those files execute or are accessed, the virus spreads. Viruses cause unwanted events—some are harmless (such as nuisance messages) and others are serious (such as the destruction of data). Some viruses change their appearances as they spread, making detection more difficult.

voice-grade circuit: A term that applies to circuits suitable for transmission of speech, digital or analog data, or facsimile, generally with a frequency range of about 300 to 3300 Hz contained within a 4,000-Hz circuit.

VPN: *See* **virtual private network (VPN).**

VRC: Vertical redundancy check. Same as **parity check.**

W

WAN: *See* **wide area network (WAN).**

WAP: *See* **Wireless Application Protocol (WAP).**

Web: *See* **World Wide Web.**

Web browser: A software package on the client computer that enables a user to access a Web server.

Web crawler: A Web crawler searches through all the Web servers it knows to find information about a particular topic.

Web server: A Web server stores information in a series of text files called pages. These text files or pages use a structured language called HTML (Hypertext Markup Language) to store their information.

Wide Area Network (WAN): A network spanning a large geographical area. Its nodes can span city, state, or national boundaries. WANs typically use circuits provided by common carriers. *Contrast with* **backbone network (BN), local area network (LAN),** and **metropolitan area network (MAN).**

Wireless Application Protocol (WAP): A de facto standard set of protocols for connecting wireless devices to the Web. WAP provides a variety of protocols at the application, transport, and network layers to enable devices with very small display screen to display standard Web information.

wiring closet: A central point at which all the circuits in a system begin or end, to allow cross-connection.

World Wide Web: The Web provides a graphical user interface and enables the display of rich graphical images, pictures, full-motion video, and sound clips.

X

X.nn: The X.nn series of ITU-T standards relating to transmission over public data networks.

X.400: An OSI standard that defines how messages are to be encoded for the transmission of e-mail and graphics between dissimilar computers and terminals. X.400 defines what is in an electronic address and what the electronic envelope should look like. Approved by the CCITT.

X.500: An OSI standard that defines where to find the address to put on the electronic envelope of a X.400 transmission. X.500 is the directory of names and addresses similar to the yellow pages of a telephone directory.

Xmodem: Xmodem is an asynchronous file transmission protocol that takes the data being transmitted and divides it into blocks. Each block has a start of header (SOH) character, a 1-byte block number, 128 bytes of data, and a 1-byte checksum for error checking.

Y

Ymodem: Ymodem is an asynchronous file transmission protocol. The primary benefit of the Ymodem protocol is CRC-16 error checking.

Z

Zmodem: Zmodem is a newer asynchronous file transmission protocol written to overcome some of the problems in older protocols. It uses CRC-32 with continuous ARQ and dynamically adjusts its packet size according to communication circuit conditions to increase efficiency. It usually is the preferred protocol of most bulletin board systems.

INDEX

447